Macintosh®
Revealed

Volume Three: **Mastering the Toolbox**

Macintosh Library

Related Titles

Macintosh® Revealed

> **Volume One: Unlocking the Toolbox, Second Edition**
> Stephen Chernicoff

> **Volume Two: Programming with the Toolbox, Second Edition**
> Stephen Chernicoff

> **Volume Three: Mastering the Toolbox**
> Stephen Chernicoff

> **Volume Four: Expanding the Toolbox**
> Stephen Chernicoff

How to Write Macintosh® Software, Second Edition
Scott Knaster

Object-Oriented Programming for the Macintosh®, Second Edition *(forthcoming)*
Kurt J. Schmucker and Carl Nelson

HyperTalk™ Programming (Version 1.2), Revised Edition
Dan Shafer

The Waite Group's HyperTalk™ 2.0 Bible
The Waite Group

Macintosh® Hard Disk Management
Charles Rubin and Bencion J. Calica

Using ORACLE® with HyperCard®
Dan Shafer

For the retailer nearest you, or to order directly from the publisher, call 800-257-5755. International orders telephone 609-461-6500.

Macintosh® Revealed

Volume Three: Mastering the Toolbox

Stephen Chernicoff

HAYDEN BOOKS

A Division of Howard W. Sams & Company
11711 North College, Suite 141, Carmel, IN 46032 USA

For

David,

who is mastering his first language.

© 1989 by Stephen Chernicoff

FIRST EDITION
SECOND PRINTING—1990

International Standard Book Number: 0-672-48402-1
Library of Congress Catalog Card Number: 85-8611

Acquisitions Editor: *Greg Michael*
Development Editor: *C. Herbert Feltner*
Technical Review: *Scott Knaster*
Editor: *Albright Communications, Inc.*
Cover Design: *Celeste Design*
Indexer: *Ted Laux*
Composition: *Hartman Publishing*

Printed in the United States of America

Trademark Acknowledgments

Contents

Preface

When I wrote the original *Macintosh Revealed* back in 1984, perhaps the hardest part of the job was knowing where to stop. There are so many features in the Macintosh Toolbox, so many ways to use it, so many options and capabilities it places at your disposal, that the two volumes and 1100-odd pages of that first edition could easily have run twice as long and still not exhausted the subject. (If you don't believe this, just look at Apple's own official handbook, *Inside Macintosh*, now in its fifth volume and counting.)

But as always, stubborn realities intervened. Apple had a whole team of highly talented writers to produce its technical documentation; I had only one keyboard and one badly worn set of fingers. Besides, I could only stuff so many pages into each volume without breaking the binding machine, and the publisher was hoping to have the book in the stores sometime before the turn of the millennium. Much as I would have liked to cover everything, I had to make some hard choices about which topics to include and which to leave out.

This book gives me a chance to fill in some of those omissions. Here you'll learn how to print documents on paper from a Macintosh program, generate sounds through the built-in speaker, write a working desk accessory, design your own windows and menus, and more. Volume One unlocked the Toolbox and Volume Two showed you how to structure your application programs around it. Volume Three will take you the next step on the road to mastering its secrets and subtleties. As a Macintosh philosopher once said, the journey is the reward.

Acknowledgments

Every author dreams of the day when true "desktop publishing" will become a reality: when we can sit down at our computers, strap on our 256-gigabaud, thought-activated brainwave decoder helmets and think creative thoughts, and out will pop finished books, bound and crated and ready to ship. Until that day arrives, we will have to go on producing books the old-fashioned way, by writing them. Here are some of the people who helped me write this one:

My tireless wife and partner, **Helen,** has remained constant through all my many moods and meanderings, and has been an unfailing source of sympathy, encouragement, and back rubs; and my ubiquitous children, **Ann** and **David,** have kept me supplied with hugs and kisses and giggles and perspective and made sure I didn't take anything (least of all myself) too seriously. My love and gratitude to them are more than they can know.

The many-talented **Scott Knaster,** a man for all seasons, gave the manuscript his usual thorough and thoughtful review. Scott is a terrific writer and an all-around good guy, even if he does root for the wrong baseball team.

David Cásseres and **Jay Patel,** of Apple's Macintosh Print Shop, and **Scott "ZZ" Zimmerman,** of Macintosh Technical Support, were patient and helpful with even my dumbest questions. Special thanks to the "other" Scottie Zimmerman, who graciously forgave my mistaking her gender and forwarded my cryptic messages to their proper destination.

Sam Roberts, Fred Huxham, and **Brian Hamlin,** all of Farallon Computing, Inc., helped me rid my code of six-legged intruders.

Nancy Albright edited the manuscript with sensitivity and tact, and let me put most of the commas where I wanted them.

Greg Michael, Scott Arant, Wendy Ford, Don Herrington, and the rest of the team at Howard W. Sams & Company miraculously transformed my scribbles and doodles into a real, live book.

Bill Gladstone of Waterside Productions, Inc., took care of business so I could take care of the writing.

With help and support from friends like these, who needs a thought-activated brainwave decoder?

CHAPTER

1

Mastering the Tools

This is the third volume in the *Macintosh Revealed* series on the Apple Macintosh computer and its built-in User Interface Toolbox. *Mastering the Toolbox* continues the discussion begun in the two earlier volumes, *Unlocking the Toolbox* and *Programming with the Toolbox*, and assumes you're already acquainted with the material they contain. If you've read those first two volumes, you'll find this book's overall format and approach familiar; if you haven't read them, go out and buy them right now! You'll need to understand the basics of Toolbox programming in order to get the most out of this book.

Although, strictly speaking, the term *Toolbox* refers to only a part of the built-in code that the Macintosh carries in its read-only memory, we will use it loosely throughout this book to refer to the total body of standard support code released by Apple for use by Macintosh application programs. In this broader sense, the Toolbox includes not only the User Interface Toolbox proper, but also the Macintosh Operating System, the QuickDraw graphics routines, and a variety of standard packages, definition functions, and other pieces of code available in the form of resources, either in the system resource file or elsewhere.

This book focuses on a number of topics that had to be left out of the first two volumes because of time and space limitations:

- Chapter 2, "Rolling Your Own," describes some of the many ways in which you can customize the operations of the Toolbox to your own special needs.
- Chapter 3, "In the Driver's Seat," discusses device drivers, the low-level programs through which the Macintosh communicates with the outside world. The basic concepts introduced here lay the foundation for the livelier topics that follow.
- Chapter 4, "Looking Good on Paper," covers the very important subject of printing, and how to ensure that "what you get is what you see."
- Chapter 5, "Sound and Fury," is about the Macintosh's sound-generating capabilities.
- Chapter 6, "Playing with a Full Desk," explains how desk accessories work and how to write them.

As in Volumes One and Two, each chapter is divided into two distinct parts. The text of the chapter itself emphasizes conceptual continuity and high-level understanding, and is intended to be read sequentially. Section numbers enclosed in square brackets, such as [2.1.1], lead to the reference sections following the chapter, where the various Toolbox routines and data structures are covered in complete detail; these are designed for quick lookup and compact expression. (Occasionally, minor or supplementary topics may appear in the reference sections only, with no supporting discussion in the main text.) Cross-references preceded by a roman numeral and a colon refer to other volumes in the series: for example, [II:2.1.1] refers to Volume Two, section 2.1.1.

Elements of the Toolbox, such as procedures, functions, and data types, are defined in the reference sections in the form of Pascal declarations. Since you're assumed to have read Volumes One and Two, you should find these declarations no mystery; if you need a refresher, refer back to the first chapter of either of those volumes for further elaboration. The declarations are followed by a series of numbered notes giving concise information on the Toolbox entities being discussed. Finally, many reference sections end with a box containing information of interest to assembly-language programmers only.

Once again, for the sake of clarity, some liberties have been taken with the names of procedure and function parameters as they appear in Apple's official *Inside Macintosh* manual. Such changes have no effect on the code you write, since you never use the parameter names when you call a Toolbox routine from your own program. Names that *do* appear in the calling program, such as Toolbox constants and variables or the fields in a record, are given correctly, of course (though perhaps with minor variations in capitalization style).

Most of the topics discussed in the text chapters are illustrated with detailed Pascal programming examples. Even if you aren't a Pascal programmer, you're expected to have a good enough working knowledge of the language (or enough general programming sophistication) to follow the logic of the examples and apply them in your own language of choice. All programs are fully commented in the body of the code and extensively analyzed in the accompanying text, but in some cases there hasn't been room for the kind of exhaustive discussion of every routine that was done for the `MiniEdit` program of Volume Two. You will, however, find complete source listings of all the example programs in Appendix H.

Some of the programs (specifically those dealing with printing in Chapter 4) consist of extensions or enhancements to the original `MiniEdit`. Others are entirely new and self-contained (the window and control definition functions of Chapter 2 and the `StopWatch` desk accessory of Chapter 6); like `MiniEdit` itself, these are intended to serve as a framework or shell, within which to develop your own definition functions and desk accessories. To save you the trouble of typing the programs yourself, a software disk containing the complete source code is available by mail directly from the author, using the order form on the last page of the book.

Needless to say, all the example programs come with the usual spineless disclaimer. Although they have been tried and appear to work as intended, they have not been subjected to rigorous insecticide treatment and cannot be certified to comply with all applicable Federal health, safety, and pest control regulations.

In the event of bugs, bombs, crashes, or similar unforeseen mishaps, the author and publisher will disavow all knowledge of their existence. Under no circumstances will the author or publisher be held accountable for any damage to life, limb, person, or property arising from the use of these programs or of software based upon them, including but not limited to plague, pestilence, bankruptcy, gambling losses, crop failure, alien invasion, or thermonuclear meltdown. Please report any arthropod sightings and suggested extermination measures to the author at the address given on the mail-order form at the back of the book, or in care of

Howard W. Sams & Company
P.O. Box 775
Carmel, IN 46032

Finally, a few words about typographical conventions. As in the first two volumes, an alternate `computer-voice` typeface is used for the names of Toolbox entities, fragments of program code, and characters typed on the keyboard or displayed on the screen. This serves as a kind of implicit quotation mark to set off such formal, computer-related material from ordinary body text. All numerals in the text, whether set in computer voice or in plain type, are understood to be decimal unless preceded by a dollar sign ($), which identifies them as hexadecimal (base-16). In keeping with the usual convention, the letters A to F denote hexadecimal digits with numerical values from 10 to 15: for example, the hexadecimal constant $BD stands for 11 sixteens plus 13, or decimal 189.

Shaded "by-the-way" boxes like this one enclose side comments, helpful hints, exceptional cases, and other material subordinate to the main discussion.

That covers the preliminaries, so let's get on to the good stuff. The road to Toolbox mastery begins on the next page. The journey begins with a single step.

CHAPTER

2

Rolling Your Own

The more you learn about the Macintosh Toolbox, the more you come to appreciate the remarkable degree of flexibility that's been designed into it. On the one hand, by giving you a ready-made set of tools for manipulating windows, menus, and the like, it helps you write programs that behave in the standard, predictable, "Macintosh way." On the other hand, if you need to depart from the standard behavior in some way, you can tailor, or *customize*, various aspects of the Toolbox to meet your program's own special needs.

We've already learned about some of these customizing provisions in Volume Two, such as dialog filter functions [II:7.4.5] and TextEdit's click-loop [II:5.6.1] and word-break [II:5.6.2] routines. Now we're ready to go into the subject more deeply. In this chapter, we'll learn how to customize the operations of the QuickDraw graphics routines and how to define your own nonstandard types of windows, controls, and menus

Customizing QuickDraw

Let's begin with QuickDraw. All of QuickDraw's great diversity of drawing operations [I:5, I:8.3.3, I:8.3.4] are based on a small number of low-level drawing routines. When you call a QuickDraw routine like LineTo [I:5.2.4] or PaintOval [I:5.3.4] to draw something into a graphics port, QuickDraw in turn calls one of the low-level routines

5

to do the actual drawing. By replacing or modifying these low-level routines, you can redefine QuickDraw's drawing operations to suit yourself.

Each graphics port has its own set of low-level routines, allowing QuickDraw to vary its behavior from one port to another. A field in the GrafPort record named grafProcs [I:4.2.2] points to a record of type QDProcs [2.1.1] (commonly pronounced "cutie-prox"). This record in turn holds pointers to the low-level drawing routines for that port. If there is no QDProcs record (that is, if grafProcs = NIL), the port simply uses the standard QuickDraw definitions for all its drawing operations.

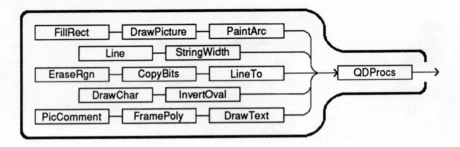

Figure 2-1 The QuickDraw bottleneck

Because all of QuickDraw's forty-odd drawing operations must pass through the narrow confines of the QDProcs record (Figure 2–1), it is often called a *bottleneck record* and the low-level drawing routines it points to are called *bottleneck routines*. There are bottleneck routines for each of the following operations:

- transferring bit images from one bit map to another [2.1.2]
- drawing lines with the graphics pen [2.1.3]
- drawing each of the standard shapes (rectangles, rounded rectangles, ovals, arcs and wedges, polygons, and regions) [2.1.4]
- drawing and measuring text [2.1.5]
- saving and retrieving picture definitions [2.1.6]
- processing picture comments [2.1.7]

The standard routines for all these operations are built into ROM and available through the normal trap mechanism. The Toolbox routine

SetStdProcs [2.1.1] initializes a QDProcs record to point to the standard bottleneck routines; you can then change any of the record's pointers to point to your own routines instead. You can replace the standard routine wholesale with a substitute routine of your own, but usually you'll just want to modify its operation with some additional processing before or after calling the standard routine. You should never call any of the bottleneck routines directly from the program level, however: always use the high-level Quick-Draw routines instead.

The new color version of QuickDraw used on the Macintosh II defines a new type of graphics port, CGrafPort ("color graphics port"), and an extended bottleneck record, CQDProcs, to go with it. To set up the bottlenecks in a color graphics port, you must use the new initialization routine SetStdCProcs instead of the old SetStdCProcs described here. Color QuickDraw, color graphics ports, and related arcana are covered at length in Volume Four. If you're content to do your drawing in glorious, living black-and-white, you can still use a plain old-fashioned GrafPort, even on a Macintosh II, and everything you read here will remain correct.

In general, redefining bottleneck routines is an unusual thing to do. About the only common use for this capability is drawing to graphics devices other than the Macintosh screen. For instance, hardcopy printing on the Macintosh is done by drawing into a special graphics port, called a *printing port*, whose bottleneck routines have been modified to send their output to the printer instead of the screen. We'll have more to say on this subject when we talk about printing in Chapter 4.

Picture Comments

One other thing bottleneck routines *are* good for is handling picture comments. Recall from Volume One that a *picture* [I:5.4] is like a tape recording of a sequence of QuickDraw commands, which can be "played back" to reconstruct the image the commands represent. The commands are recorded in the picture definition in a compact, encoded form that's entirely private to QuickDraw itself. The details of the encoding are of no concern to either the program recording the picture or the one playing it back (which may or may not be the same program).

However, the encoding format for pictures also includes a special command type called a *picture comment* [2.1.7]. Application programs can use this to embed extra information of their own within a picture definition. The body of a picture comment consists of an integer *comment type* identifying the kind of information the comment represents, along with any additional *comment data* that a particular comment type may require. The structure and meaning of the comment data vary from one comment type to another.

Any program can define its own comment types and write them into a picture definition with the QuickDraw routine `PicComment` [2.1.7]. For instance, the MacDraw graphics editor uses them (among other things) to group drawing commands into smaller subpictures to be treated as distinct units, to break up large bit maps and text strings into smaller, more manageable pieces, and to draw arrow heads at either or both ends of a line segment. Similarly, the LaserWriter printer driver uses picture comments to control various special capabilities of the printer, such as curve smoothing and text rotation, and to incorporate drawing commands expressed directly in the LaserWriter's PostScript command language.

Because picture comments are meaningful only to the program that created them (and possibly other programs specifically designed to work with it), QuickDraw itself doesn't know what they mean or how to handle them. When it encounters them in the course of a picture definition, it simply passes them along to the bottleneck routine designated in the `commentProc` field of the `QDProcs` record [2.1.1]. The standard version of this routine, `StdComment` [2.1.7], just ignores all picture comments, regardless of type. By replacing this with a routine of its own, a program can "listen in" on the stream of picture comments as they go by, pick out those it recognizes, and deal with them as it pleases.

Naturally, if every program can define its own comment types and the integer codes that denote them, the possibility of conflict arises. Apple's original policy was that all comment types had to be registered for uniqueness with the Macintosh Technical Support group, in the same way as creator signatures and file types [I:7.3.1]. More recently, a new convention has been adopted in which each program "earmarks" its own comments by including its creator signature within the data of the comments themselves. Thus, as long as the program's signature is officially registered, its comment types need not be. Details on the new identification scheme are given in Apple's Macintosh Technical Note #181.

If you really want to master the Toolbox, by the way, you should certainly know about Macintosh Technical Notes. They're published several times a year and provide a wealth of programming hints, tips, techniques, and up-to-the-minute technical information. You can obtain them either directly from Apple or through a variety of other channels, including user groups, bulletin boards, and the Apple Programmer's and Developer's Association (APDA). Other topics pertaining to the present discussion that you'll find covered in Tech Notes are QuickDraw's internal picture format (Tech Note #21), MacDraw picture comments (#27), and LaserWriter picture comments (#91).

Customizing Windows

In Volume Two, Chapter 3, we learned how to use the Toolbox to create and manipulate windows. While the Toolbox routines we discussed there define the standard behavior shared by all windows, they don't determine what the windows actually look like on the screen. That job is left to a *window definition function*, separate from the Toolbox itself, that's associated with each window via a handle in the windowDefProc field of the window record [II:3.1.1]. If you don't like the normal Macintosh-style document windows, you can change their appearance by substituting your own definition function in place of the standard one.

Window definition functions are stored as resources of type 'WDEF' [2.5.1]. When you create a new window, you identify the definition function by giving a *window definition ID*. (If you're building the window "from scratch" with the Toolbox routine NewWindow [II:3.2.2], you simply supply the definition ID as an argument; if you're using the corresponding resource-based routine, GetNewWindow, to create the window from a template [II:3.7.1], the definition ID is included as part of the template.) The definition ID is a 16-bit integer, whose first 12 bits give the resource ID of the definition function for drawing this window (see Figure 2–2).

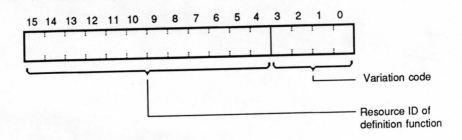

Figure 2–2 Window definition ID

The same definition function can implement several related types of window, distinguished by means of a *variation code* in the last 4 bits of the definition ID. For example, all the standard document windows, dialog boxes, and alert boxes are drawn by a single definition function, which is stored in ROM (or in the system resource file on older models) as 'WDEF' resource number 0. Thus, they're all represented by definition IDs between 0 and 15—that is, with 0 in the first 12 bits. The last 4 bits distinguish the various types of window: DocumentProc, DBoxProc, PlainDBoxProc, and so on [II:3.2.2]. The one standard type of window that isn't handled by this definition function is the rounded-corner style (RDocProc) used for desk accessories like the Calculator and Puzzle. It has a separate definition function of its own with a resource ID of 1, corresponding to window definition IDs from 16 to 31. In this case, the variation code in the last 4 bits specifies the radius of the rounded corners (see [II:3.2.2, note 14]).

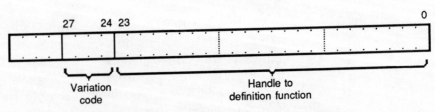

Figure 2–3 Format of windowDefProc field

When you create a window, the Toolbox takes the definition ID you specify, splits it into its component parts (the definition function's resource ID and the variation code), and reads the definition function into memory if it isn't there already. Then it stores a handle to the definition function in the last 3 bytes of the new window record's `windowDefProc` field [II:3.1.1], with the variation code in the first byte (see Figure 2–3). Later, when it needs to perform some type-related action such as drawing the window on the screen, it uses this handle to locate the definition function and passes it the variation code as a parameter.

As the Macintosh evolves toward full 32-bit addresses, the whole of the `windowDefProc` field will eventually be needed just to hold the definition function handle, and the variation code will have to be moved elsewhere—most likely to the `awFlags` field of the new *auxiliary window record*, which we'll be learning about in Volume Four. The scheme we've just described applies only to the original, 24-bit system. No program should ever assume it knows what the `windowDefProc` field actually contains or where to find the window's variation code.

Structure of Window Definition Functions

In some ways, a window definition function is similar to the Quick-Draw bottleneck record. That is, it is a collection of low-level operations that are "factored out" of the Toolbox itself and defined elsewhere so they can be changed easily. Instead of just a collection of pointers to the relevant routines, however, the definition function is a piece of executable code [2.2.1] that actually performs the various operations on demand.

To tell the definition function which specific operation to perform, the Toolbox passes it an integer *message code* [2.2.1] as a parameter. It also receives a pointer to the window it is to operate on, along with the value of the variation code taken from the first byte of the window's `windowDefProc` field, as described above. Finally, there's an additional long-integer *message parameter*, whose meaning depends on the particular operation requested. For some operations, the definition function is expected to return a long-integer function result; for others, the function result is meaningless and should simply be set to 0.

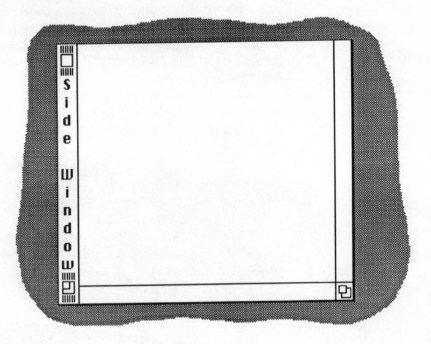

Figure 2–4 A side window

To illustrate how window definition functions work, let's look at an example. We'll invent a new type of window, which we'll call a "side window." It resembles the standard Macintosh document window, but has its title bar running vertically down the left side rather than horizontally across the top (Figure 2–4). To use this type of window in a program, we would include its definition function as a 'WDEF' resource [2.5.1] in the program's resource file, using any resource ID we choose. Then we would modify all the program's window templates [II:3.7.1] to use the corresponding definition ID, as shown in Figure 2–2. For example, if we give the definition function a resource ID of 100, the window templates should specify a definition ID of 1600.

Our definition function for side windows will ignore the standard variation codes for alert and dialog windows, but will honor those that refer to a window's size and zoom boxes. That is, just as for standard document windows, we will recognize bits 2 and 3 of the variation code (counting the rightmost bit as number 0) as the "no-grow" and "zoom" bits, respectively. If the definition function's resource ID is 100, a window definition ID of 1600 (16*100 + 0) will denote a side window with a size box but no zoom box; 1604, one with neither a size nor a zoom box; 1608, one with both; and 1612, one with a zoom box but no size box.

Program 2–1 (SideWindow) shows the overall structure of our definition function for side windows. Subsidiary routines, included within the main function definition, handle each of the possible message codes that the function may receive from the Toolbox. (For example, the message code WDraw [2.2.3] is handled by a subsidiary routine named DoDraw.) We'll discuss each of these subsidiary routines in general terms, and a few of them in greater detail; the complete listing of the definition function is given in Appendix H.

The main body of the definition function is essentially just a case statement that dispatches on the message code to the applicable subsidiary routine. Before doing so, it converts the window pointer passed in by the Toolbox into an equivalent pointer of type WindowPeek [II:3.1.1], which it keeps in a global variable where the subsidiary routines can use it to access the internal fields of the window record. It also initializes the global variable Result to 0; the subsidiary routines can change this to a different value if appropriate. On return from the subsidiary routine, the main function returns the value of this variable as its function result.

These "global" variables, Peek and Result, are not really global in the usual sense of the word: that is, they don't reside in the program's application global space, located via processor register A5. Because a window definition function is not part of the running application program, it can't always assume that A5 is properly set up at the time it is called. This means it cannot safely refer to any of the global variables that reside in the "A5 world."

In fact, if you look closely at Program 2–1, you'll see that it's just a function definition, with no main program and no true global declarations of its own. The variables Peek and Result are actually declared locally within the definition function SideWindow, but are then shared globally by all of the other, subsidiary routines nested within it (DoNew, DoCalcRgns, and so on). The lifetime of these variables is thus limited to each single activation of the definition function: they don't retain their values from one call to the next, the way true globals would.

Program 2-1 Skeleton of a window definition function

```
function SideWindow (VarCode : INTEGER; TheWindow : WindowPtr;
                     MsgCode : INTEGER; MsgParam  : LONGINT)
                     : LONGINT;
```

{ Skeleton program to illustrate the structure of a window definition function. }

```
uses
    MemTypes, QuickDraw, OSIntf, ToolIntf, PackIntf;
```

{ "Global" Declarations }

```
    var
        Peek   : WindowPeek;            {Pointer for "peeking" into window's fields [II:3.1.1]}
        Result : LONGINT;              {Function result}
```

{ Forward Declarations }

```
procedure DoNew; forward;
        { Initialize window. }
procedure DoCalcRgns; forward;
        { Calculate window's regions. }
procedure DoDraw; forward;
        { Draw window on screen. }
procedure DoDrawGIcon; forward;
        { Draw grow icon. }
procedure DoGrow; forward;
        { Draw outline for sizing window. }
procedure DoHit; forward;
        { Locate mouse click. }
procedure DoDispose; forward;
        { Prepare to dispose of window. }
```

{ Additional forward declarations for remaining program routines }

```
procedure DoNew;

  { Initialize window. }

  begin {DoNew}
    . . .
  end; {DoNew}
```

Program 2-1 Skeleton of a window definition function *(continued)*

```
procedure DoCalcRgns;

    { Calculate window's regions. }

    begin {DoCalcRgns}
        . . .
    end; {DoCalcRgns}


procedure DoDraw;

    { Draw window on screen. }

    begin {DoDraw}
        . . .
    end; {DoDraw}


procedure DoDrawGIcon;

    { Draw grow icon. }

    begin {DoDrawGIcon}
        . . .
    end; {DoDrawGIcon}


procedure DoGrow;

    { Draw outline for sizing window. }

    begin {DoGrow}
        . . .
    end; {DoGrow}


procedure DoHit;

    { Find part of window where mouse was pressed. }

    begin {DoHit}
        . . .
    end; {DoHit}
```

Program 2–1 Skeleton of a window definition function *(continued)*

```
procedure DoDispose:

    { Prepare to dispose of window. }

    begin {DoDispose}
        . . .
    end:   {DoDispose}

{ Main routine. }

    begin {SideWindow}

        Peek    := WindowPeek(TheWindow):      {Convert to a "peek" pointer [II:3.1.1]}
        Result := 0:                           {Initialize function result}

        case MsgCode of

            WNew:
                DoNew:                         {Initialize window}

            WCalcRgns:
                DoCalcRgns:                    {Calculate window's regions}

            WDraw:
                DoDraw:                        {Draw window on screen}

            WDrawGIcon:
                DoDrawGIcon:                   {Draw grow icon}

            WGrow:
                DoGrow:                        {Draw outline for sizing window}

            WHit:
                DoHit:                         {Find part of window where mouse was pressed}

            WDispose:
                DoDispose                      {Prepare to dispose of window}

            end: {case MsgCode}

        SideWindow := Result                   {Return function result}

    end:   {SideWindow}
```

In case the definition function needs to maintain additional information about a window, a 4-byte field is set aside in the window record [II:3.1.1] for its convenience. Just as the window's `refCon` field is reserved for the private use of the application program, the `dataHandle` field belongs to the definition function. As the name implies, this field is typically used to hold a handle to an auxiliary data record, in which the definition function can keep whatever extra information it needs to do its job. Our `SideWindow` function uses such a record to hold up-to-date positions for the various parts of a window (its title bar, close box, and so on) as the window is moved around on the screen. Program 2–2 shows the type definition.

Program 2–2 `SideWindow`'s auxiliary data record

```
type

    DRHandle   = ^DRPtr;
    DRPtr      = ^DataRecord;
    DataRecord = record

                UserState  : Rect;      {Zoomed-in position in global coordinates [II:3.3.2]}
                StdState   : Rect;      {Zoomed-out position in global  coordinates [II:3.3.2]}

                TitleBar   : Rect;      {Title bar in global coordinates}
                CloseBox   : Rect;      {Close box in global coordinates}
                ZoomBox    : Rect;      {Outer zoom box in global coordinates}
                SmallZoom  : Rect;      {Inner zoom box in global coordinates}
                SizeBox    : Rect;      {Size box in global coordinates}

                HOffset    : INTEGER;   {Horizontal offset to close and zoom boxes, in pixels}
                VOffset    : INTEGER;   {Vertical offset to close and zoom boxes, in pixels}
                TitleRect  : Rect       {Rectangle enclosing title, in global coordinates}

        end; {DataRecord}
```

When the window zooming feature was introduced in the Macintosh Plus version of the Toolbox (ROM version $75), room had to be found in the window record to keep track of each window's "zoomed-in" and "zoomed-out" positions on the screen. Since the standard window definition functions weren't using the dataHandle field for anything, it was appropriated for this new purpose instead. The Toolbox routine `ZoomWindow` [II:3.3.2] now expects to find a handle in this field to a record of type `WStateData` [II:3.3.2], which in turn holds a pair of rectangles, `userState` and `stdState`, representing the window's two zoom positions.

Consequently, any definition function that supports zooming and wishes to use the `dataHandle` field for its own purposes *must* now use it for a handle to an auxiliary data record. The first two fields of the record *must* designate the window's zoomed-in and zoomed-out positions, respectively, as in `SideWindow`'s data record (Program 2–2). These may be followed by any further fields the definition function cares to add for its own use. Furthermore, it's up to the definition function itself to keep the rectangles up to date when the user moves or resizes the window on the screen.

Creating and Destroying Windows

Each time the Toolbox creates a new window record, it calls the window's definition function with the message code `WNew` [2.2.2], giving the definition function a chance to do any special initialization of its own that it may require. In particular, if the definition function uses an auxiliary data record, the `WNew` message provides an opportunity to allocate the record, initialize its fields, and store its handle in the window's `dataHandle` field. In `SideWindow`'s case (Program 2–3), we also take this occasion to check the window's variation code and the version of the ROM we're running under, to see if the window will need a zoom box. If it does, we set the window's `spareFlag` field [II:3.1.1] accordingly and call the `SideWindow` routine `SetUpZoomRects` to initialize the zoom-in and zoom-out rectangles in the data record.

Program 2–3 Initialize window

```
{ Global declarations }

const
    ZoomMask = $0008;                        {Mask for extracting zoom bit from variation code}

var
    Peek : WindowPeek;                       {Pointer for "peeking" into window's fields [II:3.1.1]}


procedure DoNew;

    { Initialize window. }

    var
        theData      : DRHandle;             {Handle to definition function's  data record}
        zoomBit      : INTEGER;              {Zoom bit from window variation code}
        machineType  : INTEGER;              {Type of machine we're running on  [I:3.1.3]}
        romVersion   : INTEGER;              {Version number of machine's ROM [I:3.1.3]}

    begin {DoNew}

        with Peek^ do
            begin

                dataHandle := NewHandle (SIZEOF(DataRecord)); {Allocate data record [I:3.2.1,  II:3.1.1]}

                MoveHHi (dataHandle);        {Move data record to end of heap [I:3.2.5]}
                HLock   (dataHandle);        {Lock data record [I:3.2.4]}

                theData := DRHandle(dataHandle);    {Convert to typed handle}

                zoomBit := BitAnd (VarCode, ZoomMask); {Extract zoom bit from variation code [I:2.2.2]}
                Environs (romVersion, machineType);    {Find out machine configuration [I:3.1.3]}
                spareFlag := (zoomBit <> 0) and (romVersion >= MacPlusROM);  {Set zoom flag [II:3.1.1]}

                if spareFlag then            {Zoom box requested and available? [I:3.1.3]}
                    SetUpZoomRects (theData);    {Initialize zoom rectangles}

                HUnlock (dataHandle)         {Unlock data record [I:3.2.4]}
            end {with Peek^}

    end; {DoNew}
```

The `SetUpZoomRects` routine is shown in Program 2–4. Two points need to be noted. First, the window's zoomed-in position (`UserState`) is taken from its port rectangle [I:4.2.2], which gives its current position on the screen. Notice, though, that the port rectangle is expressed in the window's own local coordinate system, whereas the Toolbox expects `UserState` to be given in global (screen-relative) coordinates. So our `SetUpZoomRects` routine must save the current graphics port, make the window itself the current port, use `LocalToGlobal` [I:4.4.2] to convert the rectangle's top-left and bottom-right corners, and then restore the current port to its previous value.

Second, the window's zoomed-out position is derived from the rectangle representing the entire screen, suitably inset to leave room for the menu bar and title bar, as well as the window's frame and the drop shadow along its right and bottom edges. Ordinarily, we would get the screen rectangle from the `bounds` rectangle [I:4.2.1] of QuickDraw's global screen map, `ScreenBits` [I:4.3.1]. Recall from Volume One, however, that QuickDraw globals such as `ScreenBits` reside in the program's application global space, or "A5 world." As we've already seen, the contents of this area are off limits to the definition function. So instead of referring directly to the variable `ScreenBits`, we have to access the screen map indirectly: first we call `GetWMgrPort` [II:3.6.1] for a pointer to the Window Manager port, then we get the screen map from its `portBits` field [I:4.2.2].

Notice that our `SetUpZoomRects` routine assumes a constant value of 20 pixels for the height of the menu bar. In today's evolving Macintosh environment, this is no longer a valid assumption. Not only do many of the new large-screen displays maintain a larger menu bar, but a new feature of the Toolbox, the Script Manager, may also adjust the height of the menu bar to accommodate foreign writing systems such as Japanese or Arabic. The latest versions of the system software (ROM $76 and $78 and `System` file 4.1) include a utility routine named `GetMBarHeight` for finding the current height of the menu bar. We'll be covering this routine in Volume Four; for now, we'll just assume a 20-pixel menu bar for the sake of simplicity.

Program 2–4 Initialize zoom rectangles

{ Global declarations }

```
const
    MenuBarHeight = 20;              {Height of menu bar in pixels}
    ScreenMargin  =  2;             {Margin around zoomed-out windows, in pixels}
    TitleBarWidth = 19;             {Width of title bar in pixels}
    FrameWidth    =  1;             {Thickness of window frame in pixels}
    ShadowExtra   =  1;             {Extra thickness for window's drop shadow}


procedure SetUpZoomRects (theData : DRHandle);

    { Initialize zoom rectangles. }

    var
        savePort : GrafPtr;         {Pointer to previous current port  [I:4.2.2]}
        wmPort   : GrafPtr;         {Pointer to Window Manager port  [II:3.6.1]}

    begin  {SetUpZoomRects}

        with theData^^ do
            begin

                UserState := TheWindow^.portRect;   {Use current size for zoom-in  [I:4.2.2, II:3.3.2]}

                GetPort (savePort);         {Save previous port [I:4.3.3]}
                    SetPort (TheWindow);    {Get into the window's port [I:4.3.3]}
                    with UserState do
                        begin
                            LocalToGlobal (topLeft);    {Convert rectangle to global coordinates [I:4.4.2]}
                            LocalToGlobal (botRight)
                        end; {with UserState}
                SetPort (savePort);         {Restore previous port [I:4.3.3]}

                GetWMgrPort (wmPort);       {Get Window Manager port [II:3.6.1]}
                StdState := wmPort^.portBits.bounds;   {Use full screen for zoom-out [I:4.2.2, II:3.3.2]}
                InsetRect (StdState, ScreenMargin + FrameWidth,  {Inset by screen margin and      }
                                     ScreenMargin + FrameWidth);{   width of window frame [I:4.4.4]}
```

Program 2-4 Initialize zoom rectangles *(continued)*

```
with StdState do
    begin
        top     := top     + MenuBarHeight;           {Leave room for menu bar at top}
        left    := left    + (TitleBarWidth - 1);     {Leave room for title bar at left}
        bottom  := bottom  - ShadowExtra;             {Leave room for drop shadow}
        right   := right   - ShadowExtra              {   at bottom and right       }
    end  {with StdState}

end  {with theData^^}

end;    {SetUpZoomRects}
```

Just before destroying a window record, the Toolbox calls the window's definition function with the message WDispose [2.2.2], allowing the definition function to do any last-minute housekeeping that may be needed. Our SideWindow function responds to this message with a routine named DoDispose (Program 2-5), which simply disposes of the auxiliary data record that was allocated earlier by DoNew (Program 2-3).

Program 2-5 Prepare to dispose of window

```
{ Global declaration }

var
    Peek : WindowPeek;                    {Pointer for "peeking" into window's fields [II:3.1.1]}


procedure DoDispose;

    { Prepare to dispose of window. }

    begin  {DoDispose}

        with Peek^ do
            DisposHandle (dataHandle)     {Dispose of data record [I:3.2.2]}

    end;    {DoDispose}
```

Calculating Window Regions

In creating a new window, the Toolbox also creates a pair of `Region`
data structures [I:4.1.5] to hold the window's content and structure
regions, and stores handles to them in the `contRgn` and `strucRgn`
fields of the new window record [II:3.1.1]. However, the Toolbox itself
doesn't determine the actual values of these regions. Instead, it asks
the window's definition function to do the job, by sending it the
message `WCalcRgns` [2.2.2]. The definition function is expected to
set the location and shape of the two regions, using the window's
`portRect` field [I:4.2.2] to tell it where the window is located on the
screen.

Program 2–6 Calculate window's regions

```
{ Global declaration }

var
    Peek : WindowPeek;                              {Pointer for "peeking" into window's fields [II:3.1.1]}

procedure DoCalcRgns;

    { Calculate window's regions. }

    var
        theData : DRHandle;                         {Handle to definition function's data record}

    begin {DoCalcRgns}

        with Peek^ do
            begin
                MoveHHi (dataHandle);               {Move data record to end of heap [I:3.2.5]}
                HLock    (dataHandle);              {Lock data record [I:3.2.4]}

                    theData := DRHandle(dataHandle); {Convert to typed handle}
                    CalcContRgn (theData);          {Calculate content region}
                    CalcStrucRgn;                   {Calculate structure region}
                    CalcBoxes (theData);            {Calculate title bar, close, zoom, and size boxes}

                HUnlock (dataHandle)                {Unlock data record [I:3.2.4]}
            end {with Peek^}

    end;    {DoCalcRgns}
```

Thereafter, whenever the size of the window is changed (for instance, by the Toolbox routines `SizeWindow` or `ZoomWindow` [II:3.3.2]), the `WCalcRgns` message is sent again, asking the definition function to update the content and structure regions to the new size. This message is *not* sent, however, when the window is merely moved to a new position on the screen with no change in its dimensions. In that case, the Toolbox can adjust the window's regions for itself, without any help from the definition function: it simply uses `OffsetRgn` [I:4.4.7] to move the regions through a horizontal and vertical displacement without changing their size or shape.

Our `SideWindow` function's `DoCalcRgns` routine (Program 2–6) just "passes the buck" to the more specialized routines `CalcContRgn` and `CalcStrucRgn`, which do the actual work. These calculations are relatively straightforward, and we need not discuss them in detail here; see Appendix H for the code. The one point of interest is that, besides adjusting the window's content and structure regions, we also have to update its zoom-in rectangle so that `ZoomWindow` [II:3.3.2] will use the new size when zooming the window in. (Remember, maintaining the zoom rectangles is the definition function's responsibility!)

We have to be a little bit careful, though. After all, zooming the window out to full-screen dimensions is also a size change and causes a `WCalcRgns` call to the definition function. We want to avoid disturbing the zoom-in rectangle in that case, or we'll forget where to zoom back in to. So `SideWindow` defines a utility function, named `ZoomedOut`, to decide whether the window is currently in its zoomed-out state. It does this by comparing the current port rectangle with the zoom-out rectangle, `StdState`, defined in the auxiliary data record (Program 2–2). To allow a little margin of error, the two rectangles don't have to match exactly: they're considered to coincide if they're within 7 pixels of each other in each coordinate. You'll find the code for the `ZoomedOut` function and its helper, `NearPoint`, near the end of the `SideWindow` listing in Appendix H. The `CalcContRgn` routine (also in Appendix H) then uses the statement

```
if not ZoomedOut then
   UserState := globalRect
```

to update the zoom-in rectangle, where `globalRect` is the window's port rectangle converted to global coordinates.

Program 2-7 Calculate size box

{ Global declarations }

```
const
    NoGrowMask  = $0004;              {Mask for extracting no-grow bit from variation code}
    SizeBoxSize = 16;                {Size of size box in pixels}
    FrameWidth  =  1;                {Thickness of window frame in pixels}

var
    Peek : WindowPeek;               {Pointer for "peeking" into window's fields [II:3.1.1]}



procedure CalcSizeBox (theData : DRHandle);

    { Calculate size box. }

    var
        noGrowBit : INTEGER;         {No-grow bit from window variation code}

    begin {CalcSizeBox}

        noGrowBit := BitAnd (VarCode, NoGrowMask);{Extract no-grow bit [I:2.2.2]}

        with Peek^, theData^^ do
            with contRgn^^.rgnBBox do        {Use content region as basis [II:3.1.1, I:4.1.5]}
                if noGrowBit = 0 then         {Is there a size box?}

                    SetRect (SizeBox, right  - (SizeBoxSize - FrameWidth), {Inset from right [I:4.1.2]}
                                      bottom - (SizeBoxSize - FrameWidth), {Inset from bottom}
                                      right,                {Set flush with window at right}
                                      bottom)               {Set flush with window at bottom}

                else
                    SetRect (SizeBox, 0, 0, 0, 0)   {Set to empty rectangle [I:4.1.2]}

    end;    {CalcSizeBox}
```

In addition to updating the content region, structure region, and zoom-in box when a window is resized, our `SideWindow` function also has to update the contents of its own auxiliary data record, where it keeps track of the window's title bar, close box, and so forth. `DoCalcRgns` does this by calling another `SideWindow` routine, `CalcBoxes`, which in turn calls a series of specialized routines named `CalcTitleBar`, `CalcCloseBox`, `CalcZoomBox`, and `CalcSizeBox`. Again, the calculations are fairly straightforward and needn't concern us here. Just by way of example, one of the routines, `CalcSizeBox`, is shown in Program 2–7; you can read the rest in Appendix H.

Drawing the Window

The main business of a window definition function, of course, is drawing windows on the screen. (Actually, it only draws the window's frame; what's inside the content region is the application program's responsibility.) The message `WDraw` [2.2.3] is the signal to draw all or part of a window; the parameter `msgParam` [2.2.1] tells how much to draw. The normal value for this parameter is 0; this means to draw the entire window frame, including the title bar, size box, and anything else that's part of the window's fixed structure, as opposed to its contents. (There are other possible values for `msgParam`, which we'll talk about in a minute.)

Before sending the message `WDraw`, the Toolbox sets the current graphics port to the Window Manager port [II:3.6.1], whose bit map is the entire screen. It also sets the port's clipping boundaries to include only those portions of the window that are exposed to view on the screen. Thus the definition function can simply draw the entire window in global coordinates; the Toolbox sees to it that only the parts that should appear on the screen are actually drawn. In drawing the window, the definition function should take into account the values of various flags in the window record [II:3.1.1]: the `hilited` flag tells whether the window should be highlighted as the currently active window, `goAwayFlag` tells whether it has a close box, and `spareFlag` tells whether it has a zoom box. If the `visible` flag is FALSE, the window should not be drawn at all.

> The definition function must not permanently alter any of the port's pen or text characteristics: if it needs to change any of them for its own purposes, it must be careful to restore them to their original values before returning.

Program 2–8 Draw window on screen

```
{ Global declaration }

var
    Peek : WindowPeek;                              {Pointer for "peeking" into window's fields [II:3.1.1]}


procedure DoDraw;

    { Draw window on screen. }

    var
        theData : DRHandle;                         {Handle to definition function's data record}

    begin {DoDraw}

        with Peek^ do
            if visible then                         {Is window visible? [II:3.1.1]}
                begin
                    MoveHHi (dataHandle);           {Move data record to end of heap [I:3.2.5]}
                    HLock   (dataHandle);           {Lock data record [I:3.2.4]}

                    theData := DRHandle(dataHandle);   {Convert to typed handle}

                    CalcBoxes (theData);            {Recalculate title bar, close, zoom, and size boxes}

                    case LoWord(MsgParam) of        {Extract low word of message parameter [I:2.2.3]}

                    WInGoAway:
                        ToggleCloseBox (theData);   {Toggle close box}

                    WInZoomIn, WInZoomOut:
                        ToggleZoomBox (theData);    {Toggle zoom box}

                    otherwise
                        DrawWindow (theData)        {Draw window}

                    end; {case MsgParam}

                    HUnlock (dataHandle)            {Unlock data record [I:3.2.4]}
                end {if visible}

    end; {DoDraw}
```

The message WDraw is also sent by the Toolbox routines TrackGoAway and TrackBox [II:3.5.4], while tracking the mouse after a press in the window's close or zoom box. In this case, the message asks the definition function to reverse the state of the box, from unhighlighted to highlighted or vice versa, as the mouse moves in and out of it. To identify which of the two boxes to toggle, the Toolbox passes a nonzero value for msgParam. The values used are the same as the *hit codes* [2.2.5] that the definition function uses to report mouse clicks in the close or zoom boxes; we'll be discussing them more fully in a later section. The hit code WInGoAway means to toggle the state of the close box; WInZoomIn or WInZoomOut means to toggle the zoom box.

Program 2–8 shows SideWindow's drawing routine, DoDraw. Before drawing the window, it calls another SideWindow routine, CalcBoxes, to recalculate the positions of the window's title bar, close, zoom, and size boxes and store them in the auxiliary data record. You can find CalcBoxes and its subsidiary routines listed in Appendix H. We've already seen this routine called earlier by our DoCalcRgns routine (Program 2–6); we have to call it again here in case the window has been moved in the meantime. (Recall that no WCalcRgns message is sent when a window is merely moved without being resized.)

Once the boxes have been recalculated, we can go ahead and do our drawing. The value of msgParam tells whether to draw the whole window or just toggle the close or zoom box. (We have to extract the relevant value with LoWord [I:2.2.3] because of an apparent bug in the Toolbox that fails to clear the first word of the long-integer parameter.) Drawing the whole window, though somewhat complicated in detail, involves no conceptual issues we need to discuss here; see the code in Appendix H, routines DrawWindow, DrawFrame, DrawTitleBar, DrawCloseBox, DrawZoomBox, and DrawTitle. The technique used for toggling the close and zoom boxes, however, is worth examining in detail.

Program 2-9 Toggle close or zoom box

{ Global declaration }

```
const
    BoxSize = 11;                                    {Size of close and zoom boxes in pixels}


procedure ToggleBox (theBox : Rect; maskString : Str255);

    { Toggle close or zoom box. }

    var
        theMask   : BitMap;                          {Bit map for transferring bits [I:4.2.1]}
        theBits   : array [1..BoxSize] of INTEGER;   {Array for holding bit image}
        wmPort    : GrafPtr;                         {Pointer to Window Manager port [II:3.6.1]}

    begin {ToggleBox}

        with theMask do
            begin

                StuffHex (@theBits, maskString);     {Stuff the bit image [I:2.2.4]}

                baseAddr := @theBits;                {Point to the bit image [I:4.2.1]}
                rowBytes := 2;                       {Set row width [I:4.2.1]}
                SetRect (bounds, 0, 0, BoxSize, BoxSize);  {Set boundary rectangle [I:4.1.2, I:4.2.1]}

                GetWMgrPort (wmPort);                {Get Window Manager port [II:3.6.1]}
                CopyBits (theMask,                   {Copy from mask bit map [I:5.1.4]}
                        wmPort^.portBits,            {    to the screen [I:4.2.2]        }
                        bounds,                      {From mask's full boundary rectangle [I:4.2.1]}
                        theBox,                      {    to the close or zoom box          }
                        SrcXOr,                      {Invert pixels under the mask [I:5.1.3]}
                        NIL)                         {No additional clipping region}

            end {with theMask}

    end;   {ToggleBox}
```

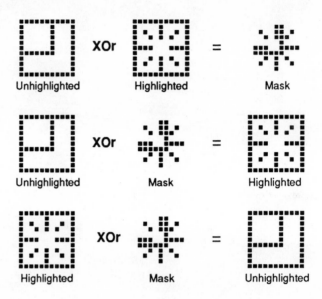

Figure 2-5 Toggling the zoom box

The WDraw message doesn't tell the definition function explicitly whether to highlight or unhighlight the box; it just says to toggle it from one state to the other. The definition function itself could presumably keep track of which state the box is in, but there's a neat little trick it can use instead. The idea is to construct a mask representing the "exclusive or" of the box's highlighted and unhighlighted images. That is, the mask has a 1 bit in every position where the corresponding bits in the two images are different, and a 0 wherever they're the same (see Figure 2–5). Such a mask has an interesting property: combining it with either of the two original images, again using the "exclusive or" operation, converts it into the opposite image. Thus it isn't necessary to remember which state the box is in: the toggling operation is exactly the same in either case.

Our SideWindow function uses a single routine named Toggle-Box (Program 2–9) to toggle both the window's close and zoom boxes. This routine accepts two parameters: a rectangle giving the location of the box in global coordinates, and a string of hexadecimal digits representing the mask to toggle it with. It constructs a bit map to hold the mask, sets its contents with StuffHex [I:2.2.4], and transfers it to the screen with CopyBits [I:5.1.4], using a transfer mode of SrcXOr [I:5.1.3]. The specialized routines ToggleCloseBox and ToggleZoomBox simply set up the appropriate hex string to define the mask and pass it on for ToggleBox to use. One of these routines,

`ToggleZoomBox`, is shown in Program 2–10; the other works exactly the same way, but with a different mask and box location.

Program 2–10 Toggle zoom box

```
procedure ToggleZoomBox (theData : DRHandle);

  { Toggle zoom box. }

  var
     maskString : Str255;                          {Hexadecimal string defining mask [I:2.1.1]}

  begin {ToggleZoomBox}

     maskString := CONCAT ('0000',                 {Set up mask string}
                           '0600',
                           '2680',
                           '1700',
                           '0200',
                           '73C0',
                           '7E00',
                           '1500',
                           '2480',
                           '0400',
                           '0000');

     with theData^^do
        ToggleBox (ZoomBox, maskString)            {Copy the bits}

  end;  {ToggleZoomBox}
```

Grow Icons and Grow Images

Recall from Volume Two, Chapter 3, that a window's *size region*, the area that the user drags with the mouse to make the window larger or smaller, may belong either to the window's frame (the part drawn automatically by the Toolbox) or to its content region (the part drawn by the application program). In our nifty new side windows, as in the standard type of document window, the size region lies within the content region. This means that it doesn't get drawn by the `WDraw` message, which draws only the window's frame. Instead, the Toolbox provides a separate routine, `DrawGrowIcon` [II:3.3.4], for drawing a window's "grow icon," the visible representation of its size region on the screen. The application program calls `DrawGrowIcon` as part of its task of drawing the window's contents; `DrawGrowIcon` in turn calls the window definition function with the message `WDrawGIcon` [2.2.4].

> For windows whose size region is part of the frame, the definition function should draw it (along with the rest of the frame) in response to the message `WDraw`. On receiving the `WDrawGIcon` message, the definition function should simply return without doing anything.

Program 2–11 (`DoDrawGIcon`) shows how our `SideWindow` function responds to the `WDrawGIcon` message. The first thing we do is check the window's variation code to see if it has a size box; if not (or if the window is invisible), there's nothing to draw. Assuming there is a size box, we save the current graphics port for later restoration, make the window the current port, save its pen characteristics, and set the pen to its normal, default state. After calculating the top-left coordinates of the size box, we draw the horizontal

Program 2–11 Draw grow icon

```
{ Global declarations }

const
   NoGrowMask  = $0004;          {Mask for extracting no-grow bit from variation code}
   SizeBoxSize = 16;             {Size of size box in pixels}
   FrameWidth  = 1;              {Thickness of window frame in pixels}

var
   Peek : WindowPeek;            {Pointer for "peeking" into window's fields [II:3.1.1]}

procedure DoDrawGIcon;

   { Draw grow icon. }

   var
      noGrowBit : INTEGER;       {No-grow bit from window variation code}
      savePort  : GrafPtr;       {Pointer to previous current port [I:4.2.2]}
      savePen   : PenState;      {Saved state of graphics pen [I:5.2.1]}
      boxTop    : INTEGER;       {Top edge of size box in local coordinates}
      boxLeft   : INTEGER;       {Left edge of size box in local coordinates}
```

Program 2-11 Draw grow icon *(continued)*

```
begin {DoDrawGIcon}

    with TheWindow^, Peek^ do
        begin

            noGrowBit := BitAnd (VarCode, NoGrowMask);  {Extract no-grow bit [I:2.2.2]}

            if visible and (noGrowBit = 0) then  {Window visible and has a size box? [II:3.1.1]}

                begin
                    GetPort (savePort);              {Save previous port [I:4.3.3]}

                    SetPort (TheWindow);             {Get into the window's port [I:4.3.3]}
                    GetPenState (savePen);           {Save previous pen state [I:5.2.1]}

                        PenNormal;                   {Set standard pen characteristics [I:5.2.2]}

                        with portRect do             {Find top-left corner in local coordinates}
                            begin
                                boxTop  := bottom - (SizeBoxSize - FrameWidth);
                                boxLeft := right  - (SizeBoxSize - FrameWidth)
                            end; {with portRect}

                        MoveTo (boxLeft, portRect.top);     {Move to top of window [I:5.2.4]}
                        LineTo (boxLeft, portRect.bottom);  {Draw line to bottom [I:5.2.4]}

                        MoveTo (portRect.left,  boxTop);    {Move to left of window [I:5.2.4]}
                        LineTo (portRect.right, boxTop);    {Draw line to right [I:5.2.4]}

                        DrawSizeBox (boxTop, boxLeft);      {Draw size box}

                    SetPenState (savePen);           {Restore previous pen state [I:5.2.1]}

                    SetPort (savePort);              {Restore previous port [I:4.3.3]}
                end {if}

        end {with TheWindow^, Peek^}

end; {DoDrawGIcon}
```

and vertical lines at those positions marking the edges of the scroll bars (see Figure 2–5, earlier in this chapter). Next we call another `SideWindow` routine, `DrawSizeBox`, to draw the grow icon itself, restore the previous pen characteristics and graphics port, and return.

In `DrawSizeBox` (Program 2–12), we begin by calculating the rectangle enclosing the size box and clearing it to white. Then we check the `hilited` flag in the window record [II:3.1.1] to see if the window is currently active or inactive. If it's inactive, there's nothing more to do. If it's active, we go ahead and draw the familiar pair of overlapping rectangles that form the grow icon, as in Figure 2–5.

Program 2–12 Draw size box

```
{ Global declarations }

const
    FrameWidth      = 1;        {Thickness of window frame in pixels}
    GIconSmallOffset = 3;       {Offset to origin of small square in grow icon}
    GIconSmallSize  = 7;        {Size of small square in grow icon}
    GIconBigOffset  = 5;        {Offset to origin of large square in grow icon}
    GIconBigSize    = 9;        {Size of large square in grow icon}

var
    Peek : WindowPeek;          {Pointer for "peeking" into window's fields [II:3.1.1]}

procedure DrawSizeBox (boxTop : INTEGER; boxLeft : INTEGER);

    { Draw size box. }

    var
        theBox : Rect;          {Utility rectangle for drawing boxes [I:4.1.2]}

    begin {DrawSizeBox}

        with TheWindow^, Peek^, theBox do
            begin

                SetPt (topLeft, boxLeft, boxTop);        {Set top-left corner [I:4.1.1]}
                botRight := portRect.botRight;           {Set bottom-right corner [I:4.2.2]}
                InsetRect (theBox, FrameWidth, FrameWidth); {Inset by frame width [I:4.4.4]}
                EraseRect (theBox);                      {Clear interior to white [I:5.3.2]}
```

Program 2–12 Draw size box *(continued)*

```
if hilited then                              {Is window highlighted? [II:3.1.1]}
    begin

        SetRect      (theBox, boxLeft,       {Set up bigger box [I:4.1.2]}
                              boxTop,
                              boxLeft + GIconBigSize,
                              boxTop  + GIconBigSize);
        OffsetRect (theBox, GIconBigOffset,  {Move into position [I:4.4.4]}
                              GIconBigOffset);
        FrameRect  (theBox);                 {Draw outline [I:5.3.2]}


        SetRect      (theBox, boxLeft,       {Set up smaller box [I:4.1.2]}
                              boxTop,
                              boxLeft + GIconSmallSize,
                              boxTop  + GIconSmallSize);
        OffsetRect (theBox, GIconSmallOffset,{Move into position [I:4.4.4]}
                              GIconSmallOffset);
        EraseRect  (theBox);                 {Clear interior [I:5.3.2]}
        FrameRect  (theBox)                  {Draw outline [I:5.3.2]}

    end {if hilited}

end {with TheWindow^, Peek^, theBox}

end;   {DrawSizeBox}
```

When the user presses the mouse inside a window's size region, the application program is expected to call the Toolbox routine `GrowWindow` [II:3.5.4] to track the mouse for as long as the button remains down. As visual feedback for the user, `GrowWindow` displays a *grow image* on the screen, showing how the window's size will change when the button is released. The actual appearance of the grow image is determined by the window's definition function, which draws it in response to the message `WGrow` [2.2.4]. For side windows—just as for standard document windows—the grow image consists of a dotted outline of the window, including its title bar, scroll bars, and size box (Figure 2–6).

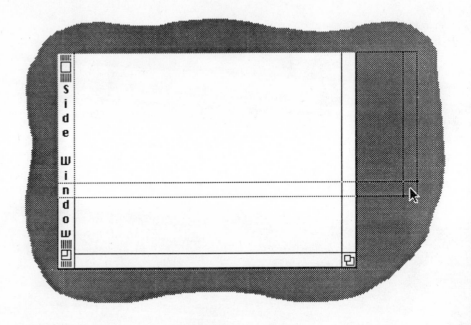

Figure 2–6 Grow image

Program 2–13 Draw outline for sizing window

{ Global declarations }

```
const
    FrameWidth    = 1;                    {Thickness of window frame in pixels}
    TitleBarWidth = 19;                   {Width of title bar in pixels}
    SizeBoxSize   = 16;                   {Size of size box in pixels}


procedure DoGrow;

    { Draw outline for sizing window. }

    type
        RectPtr = ^Rect;                  {Pointer type for converting message parameter}

    var
        thePtr  : RectPtr;                {Pointer for converting message parameter}
        theRect : Rect;                   {Rectangle to be drawn [I:4.1.2]}
        linePos : INTEGER;                {Horizontal or vertical position for drawing line}
```

Program 2-13 Draw outline for sizing window *(continued)*

```
begin {DoGrow}

        thePtr   := RectPtr(MsgParam);          {Convert message parameter}
        theRect := thePtr^;                      {Get the rectangle}

    with theRect do
        begin

            InsetRect (theRect, -FrameWidth, -FrameWidth);{Enlarge by width of window frame [I:4.4.4]}
            linePos := left;                              {Save edge for later drawing}
            left    := left - (TitleBarWidth - FrameWidth);{Make room for title bar [I:4.1.2]}

            FrameRect (theRect);                     {Draw window outline [I:5.3.2]}

            MoveTo (linePos, top);                   {Move to top-right of title bar [I:5.2.4]}
            LineTo (linePos, bottom);                {Draw to bottom-right of title bar [I:5.2.4]}

            linePos := right - SizeBoxSize;          {Find left edge of size box [I:4.1.2]}
            MoveTo (linePos, top);                   {Move to top of window [I:5.2.4]}
            LineTo (linePos, bottom);                {Draw line to bottom [I:5.2.4]}

            linePos := bottom - SizeBoxSize;         {Find top edge of size box [I:4.1.2]}
            MoveTo (left, linePos);                  {Move to left of window [I:5.2.4]}
            LineTo (right, linePos)                  {Draw line to right [I:5.2.4]}

        end {with theRect}

end; {DoGrow}
```

> Don't confuse the similar terms *grow icon* and *grow image*. A window's grow icon is the graphical representation of its size region on the screen; its grow image is the visual feedback displayed while tracking a mouse press in the size region.

Our `SideWindow` routine responds to the `WGrow` message by executing the routine `DoGrow`, shown in Program 2-13. The parameter `msgParam` [2.2.1] is a pointer to a rectangle giving the location and dimensions of the grow image to be drawn, in global coordinates. `DoGrow` has to do a bit of pointer prestidigitation to outmaneuver Pascal's type restrictions and get its hands on the rectangle. Then it simply draws the outlines of the window, title bar, scroll bars, and size box.

Before sending the message WGrow, the Toolbox sets the current graphics port to the Window Manager port [II:3.6.1], so that the grow image can be drawn directly in global coordinates. It also sets the port's pen pattern to Gray [I:5.1.2], producing dotted lines instead of solid ones, and its pen mode to NotPatXOr [I:5.1.3]. The latter serves two purposes. The "NotPat" part inverts the gray pattern before drawing with it, so it will show up even against the screen's usual gray background. The "XOr" causes the pattern to erase itself when it's drawn a second time in the same place. Each time the user moves the mouse while dragging the window's size region, the Toolbox sends two WGrow calls to the definition function: one with the old bounding rectangle to erase the previous grow image, then another with the new rectangle to draw a fresh image. As long as the definition function uses the pen pattern and mode provided by the Toolbox, it can just draw its grow image in a straightforward way, without worrying about the details of erasing and repositioning the image as it follows the mouse.

Locating Mouse Clicks

The final responsibility of the window definition function is finding the part of the window that was "hit" by a mouse click. The Toolbox routine FindWindow [II:3.5.1] calls the definition function with the message WHit [2.2.5]. It passes the point to be located, in global coordinates, as the value of msgParam [2.2.1], with the vertical coordinate in the first word of the long-integer parameter and the horizontal coordinate in the second word. The definition function returns a *hit code* [2.2.5] as its function result, identifying the part of the window that contains the given point.

> Notice that the hit codes used by the definition function don't have the same values as the corresponding part codes returned by FindWindow itself. For example, the hit code representing the window's content region, WInContent [2.2.5], has an integer value of 1, while the value of the equivalent FindWindow part code, InContent [II:3.5.1], is 3.

SideWindow's response to the message WHit is shown in Program 2-14 (DoHit). By the time this routine is called, SideWindow's main routine will already have initialized the global variable `Result` to 0, corresponding to the hit code `WNoHit` [2.2.5]. If the window is invisible, we simply skip all the hit tests and return that as the final result. Otherwise, we recalculate the locations of all the window's parts, in case the window has moved since the last time they were calculated; then we convert the parameter `msgParam` to a point and begin testing the parts one by one to see which one contains that point. Notice that we carefully avoid returning the codes `WInGoAway`, `WInZoomIn`, `WInZoomOut`, or `WInGrow` unless the window is in its active (highlighted) state. If it's inactive, we report the close and zoom boxes as part of the title bar (`WInDrag`) and the size box as part of the content region (`WInContent`). If the given point isn't in any identifiable part of the window, we report the result as `WNoHit`.

Program 2–14 Locate mouse click

```
{ Global declarations }

var
   Peek    : WindowPeek;              {Pointer for "peeking" into window's fields [II:3.1.1]}
   Result  : LONGINT;                 {Function result [II:3.1.1]}


procedure DoHit;

   { Locate mouse click. }

   var
      theData    : DRHandle;          {Handle to definition function's data record}
      mousePoint : Point;             {Point where mouse was pressed, in global coordinates}

   begin {DoHit}

      with Peek^ do
         if visible then               {Is window visible? [II:3.1.1]}
            begin
               MoveHHi (dataHandle);   {Move data record to end of heap [I:3.2.5]}
               HLock   (dataHandle);   {Lock data record [I:3.2.4]}
                  theData := DRHandle(dataHandle); {Convert to typed handle}
                  with theData^^ do
                     begin

                        CalcBoxes (theData);    {Recalculate title bar, close, zoom, and size boxes}

                        mousePoint := Point(MsgParam);  {Get mouse point from message parameter}
```

Program 2-14 Locate mouse click *(continued)*

```
        if hilited then                        {Is window active? [II:3.1.1]}
          begin

            if PtInRect (mousePoint, CloseBox) then    {In close box? [I:4.4.3]}
                Result := WInGoAway          {Report close box [III:2.2.5]}

            else if PtInRect (mousePoint, ZoomBox) then {In zoom box? [I:4.4.3]}
                begin
                  if ZoomedOut then                {Which state is window in?}
                      Result := WInZoomIn          {Report zoom-in box [III:2.2.5]}
                  else
                      Result := WInZoomOut         {Report zoom-out box [III:2.2.5]}
                end {if}
            else if PtInRect (mousePoint, SizeBox) then {In size box? [I:4.4.3]}
                Result := WInGrow           {Report size box [III:2.2.5]}

          end; {if hilited}


        if Result = WNoHit then               {Nothing found yet? [III:2.2.5]}
          begin

            if PtInRect (mousePoint, TitleBar) then   {In title bar? [I:4.4.3]}
                Result := WInDrag            {Report drag region [III:2.2.5]}

            else if PtInRgn (mousePoint, contRgn) then
                                             {In content region? [I:4.4.3]}
                Result := WInContent         {Report content region [III:2.2.5]}

            {else
                Result := WNoHit}            {Report no hit [III:2.2.5]}

          end {if Result = WNoHit}


        end; {with theData^^}
      HUnlock (dataHandle)                    {Unlock data record [I:3.2.4]}
    end {if visible}

  end; {DoHit}
```

Customizing Controls

Controls (such as pushbuttons, checkboxes, and scroll bars) are implemented in much the same way as windows. The Toolbox determines the general behavior shared by all controls, but the appearance and properties of each particular type are defined by a *control definition function.* The application program calls the Toolbox when it needs to perform any operation on a control; the Toolbox in turn calls the definition function to draw the control on the screen or regulate its interactions with the mouse.

The resource type for control definition functions is 'CDEF' [2.5.2]. Control types, like window types, are identified by an ID code (in this case, a *control definition ID*) consisting of a 12-bit resource ID for the definition function and a 4-bit variation code (see Figure 2–2). Just as for windows, the Toolbox reads the definition function into memory and stores its handle into a field of the control record, named contrlDefProc [II:6.1.1]. (Actually, on systems with 24-bit addresses, the handle only occupies the last 3 bytes of the field; the variation code is copied into the first byte, as shown earlier for windows in Figure 2–3. On 32-bit systems, the handle takes up the whole field and the variation code is moved to a field of the *auxiliary control record,* which we'll be discussing in Volume Four.)

There are two standard control definition functions, kept in the system resource file on some models of Macintosh and in ROM on others. 'CDEF' resource number 0 (corresponding to definition IDs from 0 to 15) implements all the standard pushbuttons, checkboxes, and radio buttons; 'CDEF' number 1 (definition ID 16) defines the standard vertical and horizontal scroll bars. You can define additional control types for a program to use by writing your own definition functions and storing them in the program's application resource file.

The parameters passed to a control definition function [2.3.1] are exactly analogous to those for a window definition function: the variation code from the control definition ID, a handle to the control itself, a message code identifying the operation to be performed, and an additional long-integer parameter whose meaning depends on the operation. The function returns a long-integer result, which is meaningful for some operations but not for others; in the latter cases, the result is simply set to 0.

Figure 2-7 Three-way controls

Now that we've seen how window definition functions work, we needn't examine those for controls in such great detail. An example control definition function, named ThreeState, is listed in Appendix H, but we won't be dissecting it routine by routine, the way we did with SideWindow in the preceding section. It defines a new type of checkbox and radio button similar to the standard ones, but with a third, neutral state in addition to the usual on and off states. This gives the user the choice of turning a particular property or option on, turning it off, or leaving it unchanged from its previous setting. The neutral state is represented on the screen by filling the box or button with a light gray pattern (see Figure 2–7).

The ThreeState definition function implements the standard variation codes CheckboxProc and RadioButProc [II:6.2.1], but not PushButProc. (Pushbuttons have no use for a neutral state, since they cause an immediate action rather than setting a property or option for later use.) The function also recognizes the modifier UseWFont [II:6.2.1] to display the control's title in the text font of its owning window instead of using the system font. If the function is stored as a 'CDEF' resource with a resource ID of, say, 100, we might define a constant to use in constructing control definition IDs

```
const
   ThreeStateProc = 1600;
```

representing the resource ID shifted left 4 bits. A definition ID of 1601 (ThreeStateProc + CheckboxProc) would then denote a three-way checkbox, and 1610 (ThreeStateProc + RadioButProc + UseWFont) would stand for a three-way radio button with its title in the window's text font.

One of the definition function's responsibilities is to define the number and nature of a control's parts and to assign integer *part codes* to stand for them. (Scroll bars, for instance, have five parts, denoted by the part codes InUpButton, InDownButton, InPageUp, InPageDown, and InThumb [II:6.4.1].) In the case of our three-way checkboxes and radio buttons, as for their standard counterparts, the entire control consists of a single part, denoted (for both checkboxes and radio buttons) by the standard part code InCheckbox [II:6.4.1].

Program 2–15 Mouse-down event in a three-way checkbox

```
procedure DoThreeWayCheckbox (theControl : ControlHandle; startPoint : Point);

   { Handle mouse-down event in a three-way checkbox. }

   var
      thePart  : INTEGER;                              {Part of control where mouse was released}
      oldValue : INTEGER;                              {Previous setting of checkbox}
      newValue : INTEGER;                              {New setting of checkbox}

   begin  {DoThreeWayCheckbox}

      thePart := TrackControl (theControl, startPoint, NIL); {Track mouse with no action procedure [II:6.4.2]}

      if thePart = InCheckbox then                     {Was it released in the checkbox? [II:6.4.1]}

         begin
            oldValue := GetCtlValue (theControl);       {Get previous setting [II:6.2.4]}
            newValue := (oldValue + 1) mod 3;           {Cycle to next value}
            SetCtlValue (theControl, newValue)          {Set new value [II:6.2.4]}
         end  {then}

      {else do nothing}

   end;   {DoThreeWayCheckbox}
```

We'll allow our three-way controls to take on any of three settings in the contrlValue field of the control record [II:6.1.1]: 0 for off, 1 for on, or 2 for neutral. Accordingly, our ThreeState definition function will initialize the minimum and maximum settings (contrlMin and contrlMax [II:6.1.1]) to 0 and 2, respectively. However, it is the application program's responsibility, not that of the definition function, to make sure the actual setting is properly maintained as the user manipulates the control with the mouse.

Program 2–15 (DoThreeWayCheckbox) shows how the application might respond to a click in a three-way checkbox. (This program is analogous to the one in Volume Two, Program 6–3, for standard two-state checkboxes.) Since each checkbox is a separate entity independent of all others, all that's needed is to find the control's previous setting and cycle it among the values 0, 1, and 2. As we'll see later, the Toolbox will automatically call the control's definition function, after changing its setting, to redraw it on the screen in its new state.

Program 2–16 Mouse-down event in a three-way radio button

{ Global declarations }

```
const
    NButtons      = {whatever};      {Number of radio buttons in group}
    OffState      = 0;               {Setting of buttons in "off" state}
    OnState       = 1;               {Setting of buttons in "on" state}
    NeutralState  = 2;               {Setting of buttons in neutral state}


var
    TheButtons : array [1..NButtons] of ControlHandle;   {Group of related radio buttons}

procedure DoThreeWayRadioButton (theControl : ControlHandle; startPoint : Point);

    { Handle mouse-down event in a three-way radio button. }

    var
        thePart     : INTEGER;         {Part of control where mouse was released}
        whichButton : 1..NButtons;     {Index into array of radio buttons}
        thisButton  : ControlHandle;   {Handle to a radio button [II:6.1.1]}
        thisValue   : INTEGER;         {Setting of this button}
        otherValue  : INTEGER;         {New setting for other buttons in group}
```

Program 2-16 Mouse-down event in a three-way radio button *(continued)*

```
begin  {DoThreeWayRadioButton}

    thePart:= TrackControl (theControl, startPoint, NIL);
                                        {Track mouse with no action procedure [II:6.4.2]}
    if thePart = InCheckbox then        {Was it released in the same button? [II:6.4.1]}

        begin

            thisValue := GetCtlValue (theControl);   {Get previous setting [II:6.2.4]}
            case thisValue of                        {What state is button in?}

                OffState, NeutralState:              {Is it off or neutral?}
                    begin
                        thisValue  := OnState;       {Turn this button on }
                        otherValue := OffState       {  and all others off}
                    end; {OffState, NeutralState}

                OnState:                             {Is it on?}
                    begin
                        thisValue  := NeutralState;  {Turn all buttons neutral}
                        otherValue := NeutralState
                    end   {OnState}

            end; {case thisValue}

            for whichButton := 1 to NButtons do      {Iterate through array of radio buttons}
                begin

                    thisButton := TheButtons[whichButton];   {Get button from array}

                    if thisButton = theControl then          {Is this the button that was clicked?}
                        SetCtlValue (thisButton, thisValue)  {Set clicked button to new state [II:6.2.4]}
                    else
                        SetCtlValue (thisButton, otherValue) {Set other buttons to new state [II:6.2.4]}

                end {for whichButton}

        end {then}

    {else do nothing}

end; {DoThreeWayRadioButton}
```

The routine for handling mouse clicks in a three-way radio button (Program 2–16) is a bit more complicated, since changes in the state of one button must be reflected to the others in the same group. We use an array of control handles named TheButtons to represent a group of related radio buttons. The group as a whole can be in one of two conditions: either exactly one button is on and all the rest are off (representing a choice among mutually exclusive options) or all the buttons are in the neutral state (leaving the previously selected option still in effect). Clicking a single button when it's off or neutral turns that button on and all the others off; clicking the button that's already on turns all of them to neutral. The routine first examines the current state of the button that was clicked and decides on the new settings for that button and for all the others. Then it iterates through the entire array of buttons, setting each one to the appropriate value.

Creating and Destroying Controls

The Toolbox calls the definition function with the messages InitCntl and DispCntl [2.3.2] just after creating a new control and just before destroying an old one. Like the window messages WNew and WDispose [2.2.2] that we discussed earlier, they give the definition function a chance to do any needed initialization and finalization of its own.

Just as the window record has both a refCon and a dataHandle field, for use by the application program and the definition function, respectively, the control record [II:6.1.1] has a pair of analogous fields, contrlRfCon and contrlData. The InitCntl message is typically used to initialize the contents of the contrlData field; for example, the standard definition function for scroll bars allocates a new region to hold the location of the control's scroll box and stores the region handle in this field. The DispCntl message then provides the opportunity to dispose of this region before the control itself is destroyed. More generally, a definition function might use the InitCntl and DispCntl messages to create and destroy an auxiliary data record whose handle is kept in the contrlData field.

Our example definition function ThreeState makes no use of the contrlData field. Its routine for responding to the InitCntl message, DoInit, simply initializes the contrlMin and contrlMax fields to the constants OffState and NeutralState (0 and 2), respectively. ThreeState takes no special action on receiving the message DispCntl. Its DoDisp routine does nothing at all, and is included purely as a dummy placeholder for use in developing your own definition functions.

Calculating Regions

When a control is moved or resized within its window, the Toolbox first sets the new enclosing rectangle in the `contrlRect` field of the control record [II:6.1.1]. Then it sends the message `CalcCRgns` [2.3.2] to the control's definition function, asking it to recalculate the exact region the control occupies within that rectangle. The parameter `msgParam` contains a handle to an existing region, which the definition function should set to the new size and shape of the control, in local (window) coordinates. Our `ThreeState` function just sets the region to the entire enclosing rectangle, using the Toolbox routine `RectRgn` [I:4.1.7].

For dial-type controls (those with a moving indicator like the scroll box in a window's scroll bar), the `CalcCRgns` message can also be used to ask for just the region occupied by the indicator. The high-order bit of `msgParam` distinguishes between the two types of request: 0 for the whole control, 1 for just the indicator. The definition function must, of course, remember to mask off this flag before attempting to use the parameter as a region handle. The rest of the parameter's first byte is reserved for future use, so to ensure compatibility, the entire byte should be masked off, not just the first bit.

Mouse Clicks and Part Codes

To find out where in a control the mouse was clicked, the Toolbox routines `FindWindow` and `TestCntl` [II:6.4.1] call the control definition function with the message `TestCntl` [2.3.4]. The point to be tested, in local coordinates, is passed in the `msgParam` parameter, with the vertical coordinate preceding the horizontal as usual. The definition function is expected to return a part code designating the part of the control containing the given point. It should return a zero result if the point is not in the control at all, if it is not in any identifiable part, or if the control is currently inactive. The definition function can tell if a control is inactive by examining its `contrlHilite` field [II:6.1.1] for the special value 255 ($FF) [II:6.3.3].

Unlike the window part codes used by `FindWindow` [II:3.5.1], those for controls have no predefined meanings; they're determined entirely by the definition function for a given type of control. The

Toolbox simply passes them along to the application program, assuming that it will understand them and know what to do with them. The only restriction is that a dial's moving indicator must have a part code of 129 (hexadecimal $81) or greater.

Drawing Controls

The message DrawCntl [2.3.3] asks the definition function to draw all or part of a control. The value of msgParam is a part code specifying which part of the control to draw, or 0 for the whole thing. The control's appearance on the screen should take into account the values of various fields in the control record [II:6.1.1], such as contrlVis, contrlHilite, contrlMin, contrlMax, and contrlValue. In particular, if contrlHilite = 255, the control should be drawn in some distinctive way to show that it is currently inactive.

In drawing a control, the definition function can safely assume that the control's window is the current graphics port, and can simply draw the control (or the specified part) directly in the window's local coordinate system. The Toolbox will also have set the port's clipping boundaries to automatically exclude any portions of the control that are obscured from view by other overlapping objects on the screen. The definition function should not tamper with these clipping boundaries, and should also take care to leave the port's text characteristics and pen properties in the same state in which it finds them.

A special case arises when a dial-type control has its setting or range changed with the Toolbox routines SetCtlValue, SetCtlMin, or SetCtlMax [II:6.2.4]. The dial's indicator must be redrawn to reflect the change, but the Toolbox doesn't know the indicator's part code (which could be anything from 129 to 255). Therefore it uses a special value of 129, which is understood to refer to the control's indicator (or all indicators, if there's more than one). The definition function must recognize this special case and redraw all indicators according to the new setting and range values.

Tracking and Positioning

An important special category of controls are *dials*, which can be adjusted over a continuous range of settings by dragging a moving *indicator* with the mouse. The most familiar example of a dial is a scroll bar, whose indicator (the scroll box) controls the vertical or horizontal positioning of information within a window. As the user manipulates a dial with the mouse, the Toolbox calls upon the dial's definition function for help in repositioning the indicator and adjusting the dial's numerical setting to match.

When the mouse button is pressed in a control, the application program normally calls the Toolbox routine TrackControl [II:6.4.2] to track the mouse and respond as appropriate. If the initial press was in the indicator of a dial, TrackControl ordinarily drags an outline of the indicator to follow the mouse's movements until the button is released, then redraws the indicator at its new position and updates the setting of the dial accordingly. First, however, TrackControl calls the definition function with the message DragCntl [2.3.5], offering it the opportunity to substitute a "custom" tracking method of its own in place of the standard one. (For instance, a dial representing a navigator's compass might want to drag the compass needle to a different angle instead of changing its location on the screen.) If the definition function chooses to do its own tracking, it notifies the Toolbox by returning a nonzero result; if it returns 0, the Toolbox will proceed to track the mouse in the standard way.

The DragCntl message is also sent by the Toolbox routine DragControl [II:6.4.3], which performs the more unusual operation of dragging an entire control rather than just its indicator. The value passed to the definition function for msgParam [2.3.1] tells it which operation to perform: 0 for the entire control, nonzero for just the indicator. The definition function may, of course, choose to do its own tracking in one case and leave the other to the Toolbox by returning a zero result.

Even when the standard tracking method is used, the Toolbox still needs some help from the definition function to do the job. First of all, it needs to know the size and shape of the outline to display as the user drags the indicator. It gets this from the definition function by sending it the message `CalcCRgns` [2.3.2] with the high-order bit of `msgParam` set. As we discussed earlier, this asks for just the region occupied by the indicator, rather than the whole control.

Second, the Toolbox needs to know the limiting rectangles for dragging the indicator on the screen. There are two such rectangles, with the same meanings as those supplied as parameters to `DragControl` [II:6.4.3]. One confines the movements of the indicator itself, the other the area within which the mouse will continue to track. There's also an axis constraint that can be used to limit the tracking to horizontal or vertical motion only; see [II:6.4.3] for details.

The Toolbox requests all this information from the definition function by sending it the message `ThumbCntl` [2.3.5]. `msgParam` holds a pointer to a data record of the form

```
record
    limitRect : Rect;
    trackRect : Rect;
    axis      : INTEGER
end;
```

On entry, the first 4 bytes of this structure (corresponding to the field selector `limitRect.topLeft`) give the point where the mouse was pressed, in window-relative coordinates. The definition function is expected to fill in the record with the limiting rectangles and axis constraint for dragging the indicator.

After the mouse button is released, the change in the indicator's position must be translated into an equivalent adjustment in the numerical setting of the control. Once again, the Toolbox calls upon the definition function for help, this time with the message `PosCntl` [2.3.5]. `msgParam` gives the *relative* vertical and horizontal offset from the point where the mouse was pressed to where it was released. Using this information, the definition function must redraw the dial with its indicator properly repositioned, calculate the corresponding change in its numerical setting, and store the new setting in its `contrlValue` field [II:6.1.1].

Notice that the `PosCntl` message is sent only after the user has dragged a dial's indicator to a new position with the mouse. This message is *not* used when the dial's setting is changed directly, via the Toolbox routine `SetCtlValue` [II:6.2.4], or when its range is changed with `SetCtlMin` or `SetCtlMax`, even though these operations also require the indicator to be visibly repositioned on the screen. Instead, in these cases, the Toolbox sends the message `DrawCntl` with a part code of `129`, as described earlier under "Drawing Controls." The definition function must be prepared to respond to both methods of repositioning the indicator.

Finally, the definition function can be used to define an *action procedure* to be called by `TrackControl` [II:6.4.2] while tracking the mouse. Action procedures provide a way of making something happen repeatedly or continuously for as long as the mouse button is held down inside a control. (In Volume Two, Chapter 6, we saw how to use one to implement continuous scrolling when the mouse is pressed and held in a window's scroll bar.) There are three ways of specifying an action procedure to `TrackControl`:

- Pass a pointer to the desired procedure as the `actionProc` parameter to `TrackControl` [II:6.4.2].

- Pass the value `POINTER(-1)` for the `actionProc` parameter. This tells `TrackControl` to look for the action procedure in the `contrlAction` field of the control record [II:6.1.1] instead. (The Toolbox provides a routine named `SetCtlAction` [II:6.4.2] for setting the contents of this field.)

- Set *both* the `actionProc` parameter and the `contrlAction` field to `POINTER(-1)`. `TrackControl` will then call the definition function with the message `AutoTrack` [2.3.5], asking it to play the role of the action procedure.

This last method allows a given type of control to define its own default action procedure, to be used if the application program doesn't provide one explicitly. The definition function should respond to the message `AutoTrack` by simply performing whatever action is appropriate for the action procedure. See [II:6.4.2] for more information on the form and behavior of action procedures.

Customizing Menus

Menus, too, can be customized, using a *menu definition procedure* [2.4.1] of resource type 'MDEF' [2.5.3]. One such procedure is built into the system, either in ROM or in the system resource file, with a resource ID of 0; it defines the standard type of text menu that we learned about in Volume Two, Chapter 4. Just as for windows and controls, you can place additional definition procedures in a program's application resource file to implement nonstandard menu types of your own.

Menu templates of resource type 'MENU' [II:4.8.1] include the resource ID of the menu's definition procedure. The Toolbox routine GetMenu [II:4.2.2], which builds a new menu from a template, reads the definition procedure into memory (if it isn't already there) and stores a handle to it in the menuProc field of the menu record [II:4.1.1]. The alternate routine NewMenu [II:4.2.2], which creates a new menu "from scratch," always sets up this field with a handle to the standard definition procedure for text menus. If you want to use a different definition procedure, you have to store its handle explicitly in the menu record for yourself, after the menu is created.

> NewMenu also initializes the menuWidth and menuHeight fields [II:4.1.1] under the assumption that the new menu is of the standard text type. After storing a different procedure handle in the menuProc field, always call CalcMenuSize [II:4.7.1] to recalculate the menu's dimensions according to its new type.

Structure of Menu Definition Procedures

The parameters of a menu definition procedure [2.4.1] differ somewhat from those for windows and controls. For one thing, it's a definition *procedure*, not a definition *function*. That is, it doesn't return a function result: when it has to pass information back to the Toolbox, it uses a variable parameter instead. Notice also that it has no varCode parameter, as window and control definition functions do. There's no such thing as a "menu definition ID," analogous to those for windows and controls. This means that each type of menu must be defined independently; a group of related menu types can't share the same definition procedure the way window or control types can.

One way in which menu definition procedures *do* resemble those for windows and controls is that they accept an integer message code (msgCode) telling them what operation to perform. (For ordinary pulldown menus, there are only three such messages: MDrawMsg, MChooseMsg, and MSizeMsg [2.4.1].) The message code is followed by a handle to the menu record itself (theMenu), along with a rectangle (menuFrame) giving its location on the screen in global coordinates. The remaining parameters, mousePoint and theItem, are used only by the message MChooseMsg, which we'll be discussing in the next section.

You may recall from Volume Two that the fixed fields of the menu record [II:4.1.1] are followed by an indefinite amount of "hidden data" that's not directly accessible to an application program written in Pascal. The exact content and format of the hidden data are determined entirely by the definition procedure and may vary from one type of menu to another. Since the definition procedure can store any information there that it wishes, there's no need to reserve a special field in the menu record for its private use, like those in the window record (dataHandle) and control record (contrlData).

Menu Messages

When the Toolbox creates a new menu, it calls the menu's definition procedure with the message MSizeMsg [2.4.2], asking it to calculate the menu's screen dimensions. The same message is also sent when the application program explicitly calls the Toolbox routine CalcMenuSize [II:4.7.1], such as after storing a new procedure handle into the menu's menuProc field. The definition procedure should respond by looking in the menu's hidden data for the current number and contents of its items, calculating its width and height in pixels, and storing them in its menuWidth and menuHeight fields [II:4.1.1].

When the user presses the mouse in the menu bar, the application program calls the Toolbox routine MenuSelect [II:4.5.1] to track the mouse's movements until the button is released. Each time the mouse moves into a menu title, MenuSelect asks the menu's definition procedure to draw the menu on the screen, by sending it the message MDrawMsg [2.4.2]. The definition procedure should draw the menu within the rectangle specified by its menuFrame parameter [2.4.2]. It should take into account the current state of the menu's enableFlags field [II:4.1.1] and "dim" any items that are marked as disabled. In particular, if the low-order bit of enableFlags is 0, the entire menu is disabled and *all* its items should be dimmed, regardless of the state of their individual flags.

> The definition procedure can safely assume that the Window Manager port [II:3.6.1] is the current port, and that its text characteristics have been set to the standard system typeface and size. If the definition procedure wishes to change these settings, it must be sure to restore them to their original values before returning control to the Toolbox.

As the user drags the mouse through a menu's items, MenuSelect repeatedly calls the definition procedure with the message MChooseMsg [2.4.3], asking it to identify and highlight the item containing the mouse. The procedure's mousePoint parameter [2.4.1] gives the location of the mouse in global coordinates; this information, along with the menuFrame rectangle, allows the definition procedure to determine which item the mouse is currently in. The parameter theItem gives the item number of the previously highlighted item, if any. If the mouse is still in the same item, the definition procedure should do nothing; otherwise it should unhighlight the previous item, highlight the new one, and pass back the new item number in theItem. If the mouse is outside the menu's frame (or in a disabled item, according to enableFlags), the definition procedure should simply unhighlight the previous item and set theItem to 0.

Nuts and Bolts

Like any other program, a definition function or procedure may need some auxiliary resources of its own (strings, icons, patterns, or whatever) in order to do its job. Don't forget that the definition routine itself is also a resource, of type 'WDEF', 'CDEF', or 'MDEF'. The auxiliary resources it uses are said to be *owned* by the one containing the routine. When the definition routine is copied from one resource file to another, its owned resources must tag along for the ride, since the routine can't function properly without them.

Ownership of one resource by another isn't limited to definition routines. The owning resource may belong to any of several other resource types that also contain executable machine code. One that we've already encountered in Volume One is 'PACK' [I:7.5.2], the resource type for utility code packages such as the Standard File Package [II:8.3] and the Disk Initialization Package [II:8.4]. Later in this volume, we'll be learning about two more, 'DRVR' [3.3.1] (device drivers and desk accessories) and 'PDEF' [4.6.2] (printing code).

For owned resources to accompany their owner automatically when it's copied to a new resource file, the utility programs that handle resources have to be able to recognize them. This is made possible by a special numbering scheme [2.5.4] that marks them as owned resources and identifies the type and ID number of their owner. If your definition routine (or driver, desk accessory, or whatever) has any resources of its own, you have to be sure to number them in accordance with these conventions.

For every owned resource, the first 2 bits of the 16-bit resource ID must be 11, yielding an ID number in the range -1 to -16384. The next 3 bits identify the type of the owning resource, according to the table in [2.5.4]. (For example, for resources owned by a window definition function, these three bits must be 001, corresponding to resource IDs between -14336 and -12289.) Next comes the 6-bit resource ID of the owning resource, and finally a 5-bit identifying number for the individual owned resource. Notice that these rules restrict the owning resource to an ID number from 0 to 63 and limit it to no more than 32 owned resources of a given type.

Unfortunately, the numbering rules for owned resources conflict with other numbering conventions that apply to certain specific resource types. Earlier in this chapter, for instance, we saw that window and control definition functions must have resource IDs no longer than 12 bits, so that they can be embedded within a properly formed definition ID (see Figure 2–2). This prevents them from following the numbering scheme described above for owned resources, with the result that they cannot be owned by another resource. Similarly, the special numbering rules for fonts and related resources ('FONT', 'NFNT', 'FOND' [I:8.4.5], 'FWID' [I:8.4.6]) prevent them from being owned. Life is hard.

REFERENCE

2.1 Customizing QuickDraw

2.1.1   Bottleneck Record

Definitions

```
type
    QDProcsPtr = ^QDProcs;

    QDProcs  = record
                textProc    : Ptr;      {Draw text [2.1.5]}
                lineProc    : Ptr;      {Draw lines [2.1.3]}
                rectProc    : Ptr;      {Draw rectangles [2.1.4]}
                rRectProc   : Ptr;      {Draw rounded rectangles [2.1.4]}
                ovalProc    : Ptr;      {Draw ovals [2.1.4]}
                arcProc     : Ptr;      {Draw arcs and wedges [2.1.4]}
                polyProc    : Ptr;      {Draw polygons [2.1.4]}
                rgnProc     : Ptr;      {Draw regions [2.1.4]}
                bitsProc    : Ptr;      {Copy bit images [2.1.2]}
                commentProc : Ptr;      {Process picture comments [2.1.7]}
                txMeasProc  : Ptr;      {Measure text [2.1.5]}
                getPicProc  : Ptr;      {Retrieve picture definitions [2.1.6]}
                putPicProc  : Ptr       {Save picture definitions [2.1.6]}
            end;

procedure SetStdProcs
        (var theProcs : QDProcs);       {Bottleneck record to initialize}
```

57

Notes

1. A `QDProcs` record holds pointers to the low-level "bottleneck" routines on which all QuickDraw operations are based.

2. Each graphics port can have its own set of bottleneck routines, identified via the `grafProcs` field of the `GrafPort` record [I:4.2.2].

3. A `NIL` value for `grafProcs` designates the standard, built-in bottleneck routines, described in sections [2.1.2] to [2.1.6].

4. `SetStdProcs` initializes a `QDProcs` record to the standard bottleneck routines. You can then selectively change individual fields to install your own routines in place of the standard ones.

5. Custom bottleneck routines must accept the same parameters as the standard ones, as shown in [2.1.2] to [2.1.6]. They should exhibit the same general behavior as the standard routines, with whatever modifications may be needed for a particular purpose.

6. Custom bottleneck routines may (but are not required to) call the standard routines, modifying the results as needed with pre- or postprocessing. Application programs should never call the bottlenecks directly.

Assembly Language Information

Field offsets in a bottleneck record:

(Pascal) Field name	(Assembly) Offset name	Offset in bytes
textProc	textProc	0
lineProc	lineProc	4
rectProc	rectProc	8
rRectProc	rRectProc	12
ovalProc	ovalProc	16
arcProc	arcProc	20
polyProc	polyProc	24
rgnProc	rgnProc	28
bitsProc	bitsProc	32
commentProc	commentProc	36
txMeasProc	txMeasProc	40
getPicProc	getPicProc	44
putPicProc	putPicProc	48

Notes

1. The bottleneck routines rectProc, rRectProc, ovalProc, arcProc, polyProc, and rgnProc perform shape-drawing operations in the current port's bit map. StdRect, StdRRect, StdOval, StdArc, StdPoly, and StdRgn are the standard versions of these routines.

2. These bottlenecks are called by the high-level QuickDraw shape-drawing routines [I:5.3.2–I:5.3.7].

3. Each routine takes a parameter of type GrafVerb, telling it which of the five basic drawing operations to perform. The remaining parameters define the shape to be drawn; see sections [I:5.3.2] to [I:5.3.7] for their meanings.

4. Drawing always takes place in the current graphics port, and all shapes are defined in that port's local coordinate system.

5. *Framing* a shape draws its outline, using the port's current pen size, pattern, and mode [I:5.2.1]. Pixels in the shape's interior are left unchanged.

6. *Painting* a shape fills it completely with the port's current pen pattern (pnPat [I:5.1.1, I:5.2.1]), using the current pen mode.

7. *Filling* a shape fills it completely with the port's fill pattern (fillPat [I:5.1.1]). The transfer mode is always PatCopy [I:5.1.3].

8. The calling program supplies the fill pattern as a parameter to the high-level QuickDraw routines (FillRect, FillOval, and so on). These routines in turn store the pattern into the port's fillPat field before calling the corresponding bottleneck routine.

9. *Erasing* a shape fills it completely with the port's current background pattern (bkPat [I:5.1.1]). The transfer mode is always PatCopy [I:5.1.3].

10. *Inverting* a shape reverses all pixels it encloses, from white to black and vice versa.

11. The bottleneck routines should do nothing if the graphics pen is hidden: that is, if the port's pen level (pnVis [I:5.2.3]) is negative, or if either dimension of the pen size (pnSize [I:5.2.1]) is zero or negative.

12. Shape-drawing operations should never change the pen location.

13. All drawing operations must be clipped to the intersection of the current port's boundary rectangle, port rectangle, clipping region, and visible region. Only those portions of shapes that fall within all these boundaries should actually be drawn.

14. Drawing operations should never affect pixels outside the boundaries of the shape being drawn. (*Exception:* Framing a polygon may draw outside the polygon's boundary; see [I:5.3.6].)

15. The `arcProc` routine should respond to the `frame` operation by drawing just the specified arc itself. For all other operations, it should draw the wedge bounded by the arc and the two radii joining its endpoints to the center of its oval.

Assembly Language Information

Assembly-language constants:

Name	Value	Meaning
Frame	0	Draw outline
Paint	1	Fill with current pen pattern
Erase	2	Fill with background pattern
Invert	3	Invert pixels
Fill	4	Fill with specified pattern

Trap macros:

(Pascal) Routine name	(Assembly) Trap macro	Trap word
StdRect	_StdRect	$A8A0
StdRRect	_StdRRect	$A8AF
StdOval	_StdOval	$A8B6
StdArc	_StdArc	$A8BD
StdPoly	_StdPoly	$A8C5
StdRgn	_StdRgn	$A8D1

2.1.5   Text Drawing

Definitions

```
type
   QDProcs = record
           textProc   : Ptr;        {Draw text}
           . . . ;
           txMeasProc : Ptr;        {Measure text}
           . . .
       end;
```

```
procedure StdText
          (charCount    : INTEGER;           {Number of characters to be drawn}
           theText      : Ptr;               {Pointer to text to be drawn}
           scaleNumer : Point;               {Numerators of scale factors}
           scaleDenom : Point);              {Denominators of scale factors}
function  StdTxMeas
          (charCount       : INTEGER;        {Number of characters to be drawn}
           theText         : Ptr;            {Pointer to text to be drawn}
           var scaleNumer : Point;           {Numerators of scale factors}
           var scaleDenom : Point;           {Denominators of scale factors}
           var fontProps  : FontInfo)        {Metric information about text font}
                        : INTEGER;           {Width of text in pixels}
```

Notes

1. The bottleneck routines `textProc` and `txMeasProc` draw and measure text. `StdText` and `StdTxMeas` are the standard versions of these routines.

2. These bottlenecks are called by the high-level QuickDraw text routines `DrawChar`, `DrawString`, `DrawText` [I:8.3.3], `CharWidth`, `StringWidth`, and `TextWidth` [I:8.3.4].

3. `theText` points to the first character to be drawn or measured; `charCount` is the number of characters.

4. Text drawing takes place in the current graphics port, beginning at the port's current pen location (`pnLoc` [I:5.2.1]).

5. The `textProc` routine must clip to the intersection of the port's boundary rectangle, port rectangle, clipping region, and visible region. Only those portions of characters that fall within all these boundaries should actually be drawn.

6. The `textProc` routine should leave the pen positioned after the last character of the specified text, even if it lies outside the port's clipping boundaries. `txMeasProc` should leave the original pen location unchanged.

7. Both routines must take into account the current settings of the port's text characteristics (`txFont`, `txFace`, and `txSize` [I:8.3.1]), and should widen all space characters as specified by `spExtra` [I:8.3.1].

8. The parameters `scaleNumer` and `scaleDenom` specify scale factors to be applied to the text. The scale factor in each dimension (horizontal and vertical) is given by the ratio of `scaleNumer` to `scaleDenom` in that

dimension. That is, the width of each character is multiplied by

scaleNumer.h / scaleDenom.h

and the height by

scaleNumer.v / scaleDenom.v

9. The txMeasProc routine takes an additional parameter, a font information record [I:8.2.6] in which it returns the metric characteristics of the port's current font.

Assembly Language Information

Trap macros:

(Pascal) Routine name	(Assembly) Trap macro	Trap word
StdText	_StdText	$A882
StdTxMeas	_StdTxMeas	$A8ED

2.1.6   Picture Processing

Definitions

```
type
   QDProcs = record
           . . . :
             getPicProc : Ptr;          {Retrieve picture definitions}
             putPicProc : Ptr           {Save picture definitions}
           end;
procedure StdGetPic
           (toAddr    : Ptr;           {Address to read to}
           byteCount : INTEGER);       {Number of bytes to read}
procedure StdPutPic
           (fromAddr  : Ptr;           {Address to write from}
           byteCount : INTEGER);       {Number of bytes to write}
```

Notes

1. The bottleneck routines putPicProc and getPicProc store and retrieve information in QuickDraw picture definitions [I:5.4.1]. StdGetPic and StdPutPic are the standard versions of these routines.

2. When a picture definition is open, most high-level QuickDraw routines call the putPicProc bottleneck to record their operations as part of the picture. getPicProc is called by the high-level routine DrawPicture [I:5.4.3] to retrieve the operations and "play back" the picture.

3. Both operations apply to the open picture definition, if any, in the current graphics port.

4. The port's open picture is located via the picSave field in the GrafPort record [I:4.2.2]. This field holds a handle to a private QuickDraw data structure, whose first 4 bytes in turn contain a handle to the picture record [I:5.4.1]. If picSave is NIL, the bottleneck routines should do nothing.

5. fromAddr is a pointer to the first byte of information to be recorded in the picture; toAddr points to the memory location where the first byte of retrieved information is to be stored.

6. byteCount specifies the number of bytes to be transferred.

Assembly Language Information

Trap macros:

(Pascal) Routine name	(Assembly) Trap macro	Trap word
StdGetPic	_StdGetPic	$A8EE
StdPutPic	_StdPutPic	$A8F0

2.1.7   Picture Comments

Definitions

```
type
   QDProcs = record
            . . . :
                commentProc : Ptr:          {Process picture comments}
            . . .
         end;
procedure StdComment
         (commentType : INTEGER;           {Comment type}
          dataSize    : INTEGER;           {Length of comment data in bytes}
          commentData : Handle);           {Handle to comment data}
procedure PicComment
         (commentType : INTEGER;           {Comment type}
          dataSize    : INTEGER;           {Length of comment data in bytes}
          commentData : Handle);           {Handle to comment data}
const
   PicLParen = 0:                          {Begin command grouping}
   PicRParen = 1:                          {End command grouping}
```

Notes

1. The `commentProc` bottleneck routine processes picture comments read from a previously recorded picture definition. `StdComment` is the standard version of this routine.

2. This bottleneck is called by the high-level QuickDraw routine `DrawPicture` [I:5.4.3] when it encounters a comment in the course of "playing back" a picture.

3. Picture comments can be used to embed extra, application-specific information within a QuickDraw picture definition.

4. The high-level QuickDraw routine `PicComment` inserts a comment into the current port's open picture definition, if any.

5. The standard bottleneck routine, `StdComment`, simply ignores all comments. Application programs can replace it with a routine of their own to interpret picture comments in whatever way is appropriate.

6. `commentType` is an integer code identifying the nature of the comment.

7. `commentData` is a handle to the data constituting the comment itself; `dataSize` gives the length of the data in bytes.

8. Serious application programs should register their comment types for uniqueness with Apple's Macintosh Technical Support group, to avoid conflicts with those used by other applications. Macintosh Technical Notes #27 and #91 list the comment types reserved for use by MacDraw and the LaserWriter printer driver, respectively. However, a new convention described in Tech Note #181 allows applications to define their own comment types without having to register them officially with Apple.

9. The special comment types `PicLParen` and `PicRParen` can be used as brackets to group sequences of comments within a picture.

Assembly Language Information

Trap macros:

(Pascal) Routine name	(Assembly) Trap macro	Trap word
PicComment	_PicComment	$A8F2
StdComment	_StdComment	$A8F1

Standard comment types:

Name	Value	Meaning
PicLParen	0	Begin command grouping
PicRParen	1	End command grouping

2.2   Customizing Windows

2.2.1   Window Definition Function

Definitions

```
function  YourWindowDef
          (varCode    : INTEGER;        {Variation code}
           theWindow  : WindowPtr;      {Pointer to the window}
           msgCode    : INTEGER;        {Operation to be performed}
           msgParam   : LONGINT)        {Additional data for performing operation}
               : LONGINT;               {Result returned by operation}
```

```
const
    WDraw       = 0;        {Draw window frame [2.2.3]}
    WHit        = 1;        {Find where mouse was pressed [2.2.5]}
    WCalcRgns   = 2;        {Calculate structure and content regions [2.2.2]}
    WNew        = 3;        {Initialize new window [2.2.2]}
    WDispose    = 4;        {Prepare to dispose of window [2.2.2]}
    WGrow       = 5;        {Draw feedback image for resizing window [2.2.4]}
    WDrawGIcon  = 6;        {Draw size region [2.2.4]}
```

Notes

1. A window definition function defines the appearance and behavior of one or more types of window. The Toolbox calls it whenever it needs to draw all or part of a window on the screen or determine its interactions with the mouse.

2. The function heading shown above is only a model for defining your own window definition functions. There is no Toolbox routine named YourWindowDef.

3. Window definition functions are stored in resource files under resource type 'WDEF' [2.5.1].

4. When a window is created, the resource ID of its definition function is given by the first 12 bits of the window definition ID (the windowType parameter to NewWindow [II:3.2.2] or the corresponding field of the window template [II:3.7.1] supplied to GetNewWindow). The last 4 bits are a *variation code*, allowing the same definition function to implement more than one type of window. Thus the definition ID is determined by the formula

   $$defID = 16*rsrcID + varCode$$

5. The Toolbox reads the definition function into memory from its resource file, if necessary, and places a handle to it in the window record's windowDefProc field [II:3.1.1].

6. On original Macintosh systems using 24-bit addresses, the first byte of the windowDefProc field holds the variation code. It is stripped out and passed as a parameter when the definition function is called, identifying the particular type of window being manipulated. On 32-bit systems,

the handle occupies the entire field and the variation code is stored in the `awFlags` field of the auxiliary window record (see Volume Four).

7. The definition function's `msgCode` parameter designates the operation to be performed, and is always one of the constants shown above (`WDraw` to `WDrawGIcon`). `msgParam` gives further information for some operations; see [2.2.3–2.2.5] for details.

8. The function result is meaningful only in response to the message `WHit` [2.2.5]. In all other cases, the function should simply return 0.

9. The `dataHandle` field of the window record [II:3.1.1] is reserved for the private use of the window definition function, typically to hold a handle to an auxiliary data record.

10. If the definition function supports window zooming (more specifically, if it can ever respond to the message `WHit` [2.2.5] with the hit codes `WInZoomIn` or `WInZoomOut`), its auxiliary data record must begin with a pair of rectangles defining the window's zoomed-in and zoomed-out positions. These rectangles correspond to the `userState` and `stdState` fields of the Toolbox-defined `WStateData` record [II:3.3.2]. It is the definition function's responsibility to maintain these fields correctly. They may be followed by any additional fields the definition function itself may choose to define.

11. The definition function cannot assume that processor register A5 is set up properly at the time it is called, and thus cannot access any of the information stored in the application global space, or "A5 world." In particular, this means it must not refer directly to any of the QuickDraw global variables listed in [I:4.3.1].

Assembly Language Information

Window message codes:

Name	Value	Meaning
WDrawMsg	0	Draw window frame
WHitMsg	1	Find where mouse was pressed
WCalcRgnMsg	2	Calculate structure and content regions
WInitMsg	3	Initialize new window
WDisposeMsg	4	Prepare to dispose of window
WGrowMsg	5	Draw feedback image for resizing window
WGIconMsg	6	Draw size region

2.2.2   Creating and Destroying Windows

Definitions

```
const
    WCalcRgns = 2;                    {Calculate structure and content regions}
    WNew      = 3;                    {Initialize new window}
    WDispose  = 4;                    {Prepare to dispose of window}
```

Notes

1. The message WNew is sent to the window definition function when a new window is created. This allows the definition function to perform any special initialization it may require, such as allocating an auxiliary data record and placing its handle in the dataHandle field of the window record [II:3.1.1].

2. The message WDispose is sent just before a window record is destroyed. The definition function can then perform any final housekeeping chores, such as disposing of its auxiliary data record, if any.

3. The message WCalcRgns is sent whenever a window's size is changed, asking the definition function to recalculate the window's structure and content regions.

4. The new dimensions of the window are given by its port rectangle, found in the portRect field of the window record [I:4.2.2].

5. The Toolbox creates a window's structure and content regions automatically when the window itself is first created, and stores their handles in the strucRgn and contRgn fields of the window record [II:3.1.1]. The definition function should simply update the size and shape of these existing regions.

6. The definition function must not alter the window's visible and clipping regions (visRgn and clipRgn [I:4.2.2]). Only the Toolbox and the application program, respectively, should manipulate these regions.

7. Bear in mind that the port rectangle is expressed in window-relative (local) coordinates, while the structure and content regions must be given in screen-relative (global) coordinates. It is the definition function's responsibility to do the necessary conversion.

8. The WCalcRgns message is not sent when a window is merely moved on the screen, with no change in size. The Toolbox simply offsets the

structure and content regions to their new locations, with no help from the definition function.

9. The WCalcRgns message is never sent if the window is invisible.

2.2.3   Drawing Windows

Definitions

```
const
    WDraw      = 0;                    {Draw window frame}
    WNoHit     = 0;                    {Draw entire window frame}
    WInGoAway  = 4;                    {Toggle close region only}
    WInZoomIn  = 5;                    {Toggle zoom region only}
    WInZoomOut = 6;                    {Toggle zoom region only}
```

Notes

1. The message WDraw instructs the window definition function to draw a window's frame on the screen.

2. The function's msgParam parameter [2.2.1] tells how much of the window to draw. A value of 0 (corresponding to the hit code WNoHit [2.2.5]) specifies the entire window frame.

3. For functions that support more than one variant window type, the varCode parameter [2.2.1] tells which variant to draw.

4. The window should be drawn in its active or inactive state, depending on the current value of the hilited flag in the window record [II:3.1.1]. The definition function itself determines how this affects the window's appearance.

5. The window's goAwayFlag field [II:3.1.1] tells whether to draw a close region. On Macintosh systems that support the zooming feature [II:3.3.2], the spareFlag field [II:3.1.1] tells whether to draw a zoom region.

6. If the window's visible field [II:3.1.1] is FALSE, the definition function should simply return without drawing anything.

7. Before sending the WDraw message, the Toolbox will have set the current graphics port to the Window Manager port [II:3.6.1], whose port rectangle is the entire screen.

8. The port's clipping boundaries will have been set to include only those portions of the window's structure region that are exposed to view on the screen. The definition function should simply draw the entire window frame, letting the Toolbox take care of the clipping.

9. The port's text characteristics [I:8.3.1] are normally set to the standard system typeface and size. If the definition function wishes to use some other text characteristics for the window's title, it must set them for itself, then restore the original values before returning.

10. On receiving the value WInGoAway for msgParam [2.2.1], the definition function should simply toggle the appearance of the window's close region, from unhighlighted to highlighted or vice versa, instead of drawing the entire window frame. Similarly, a msgParam value of WInZoomIn or WInZoomOut means to toggle the window's zoom region.

11. If the window doesn't have the specified (close or zoom) region, the definition function should simply return without doing anything.

2.2.4 Resizing Windows

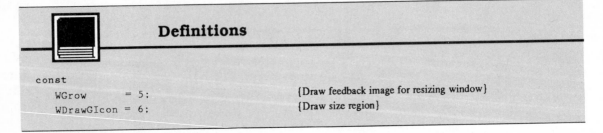

Definitions

```
const
    WGrow      = 5;              {Draw feedback image for resizing window}
    WDrawGIcon = 6;             {Draw size region}
```

Notes

1. The message WDrawGIcon is sent by the Toolbox routine DrawGrowIcon [II:3.3.4], instructing the window definition function to draw a window's size region ("grow icon") on the screen.

2. The size region should be drawn in its active or inactive state, depending on the current value of the hilited flag in the window record [II:3.1.1]. The definition function itself determines how this affects the size region's appearance.

3. If the window's visible field [II:3.1.1] is FALSE, the definition function should simply return without drawing anything.

4. This message is meaningful only for windows (such as standard document windows) whose size region is part of the content region. If the

size region is part of the window's frame, it is drawn by the WDraw message [2.2.3] instead. In this case, the definition function should do nothing in response to the message WDrawGIcon.

5. The message WGrow instructs the window definition function to draw a window's grow image on the screen, providing visual feedback to the user for resizing the window.

6. This message is sent repeatedly by the Toolbox routine GrowWindow [II:3.5.4], while tracking the mouse as the user drags the window's size region.

7. The definition function itself determines the appearance of the window's grow image. For example, the grow image for a standard document window consists of the window's outline along with the outlines of its title bar, scroll bars, and size box.

8. msgParam [2.2.1] is a pointer to a rectangle in global (screen) coordinates, defining the bounding box in which to draw the grow image.

9. Before sending the WGrow message, the Toolbox will have set the current graphics port to the Window Manager port [II:3.6.1], whose port rectangle is the entire screen.

10. The port's pen pattern will have been set to Gray [I:5.1.2] and its pen mode to NotPatXOr [I:5.1.3], producing a dotted outline that erases and redraws itself as it follows the mouse's movements. The definition function should not disturb these settings, but should simply use the pen characteristics provided by the Toolbox.

2.2.5   Locating Mouse Clicks

Definitions

```
const
    WHit        = 1;                    {Find where mouse was pressed}

                                        {Window hit codes: }
    WNoHit      = 0;                        {None of the following}
    WInContent  = 1;                        {In content region}
    WInDrag     = 2;                        {In drag region}
    WInGrow     = 3;                        {In size region}
    WInGoAway   = 4;                        {In close region}
    WInZoomIn   = 5;                        {In zoom region of a "zoomed-out" window}
    WInZoomOut  = 6;                        {In zoom region of a "zoomed-in" window}
```

Notes

1. The message WHit asks the window definition function to find which part of a window, if any, contains a given point (normally the point where the mouse button was pressed).

2. The definition function's msgParam parameter [2.2.1], nominally a long integer, is actually a Point record [I:4.1.1], with its vertical coordinate in the high-order word and horizontal in the low.

3. The point is expressed in *global (screen) coordinates.*

4. The definition function returns a *hit code* as its result, identifying which part of the window, if any, was "hit" by the mouse.

5. If the given point lies outside the window, or is part of the window's frame but not in any other identifiable region, the definition function should return the hit code WNoHit.

6. The definition function should never return the hit code WInGoAway if the goAwayFlag field in the window record [II:3.1.1] is FALSE.

7. The hit codes WInZoomIn and WInZoomOut should never be reported if the window's spareFlag field [II:3.1.1] is FALSE, or when running on an early-model Macintosh that doesn't support the zooming feature (ROM version less than $75 [I:3.1.3]).

8. If the window is currently inactive (hilited = FALSE in the window record [II:3.1.1]), the hit codes WInGrow, WInGoAway, WInZoomIn, and WInZoomOut should not be reported. In a standard document window, for example, the size box is reported as part of the content region when the window is inactive, and the close and zoom boxes are reported as part of the drag region (title bar).

9. Notice that the hit codes reported by the definition function are *not* the same as the corresponding part codes returned by the Toolbox function FindWindow [II:3.5.1].

Assembly Language Information

Window hit codes:

Name	Value	Meaning
WNoHit	0	None of the following
WInContent	1	In content region
WInDrag	2	In drag region
WInGrow	3	In size region

Name	Value	Meaning
WInGoAway	4	In close region
WInZoomIn	5	In zoom region of a "zoomed-out" window
WInZoomOut	6	In zoom region of a "zoomed-in" window

2.3 Customizing Controls

2.3.1   Control Definition Function

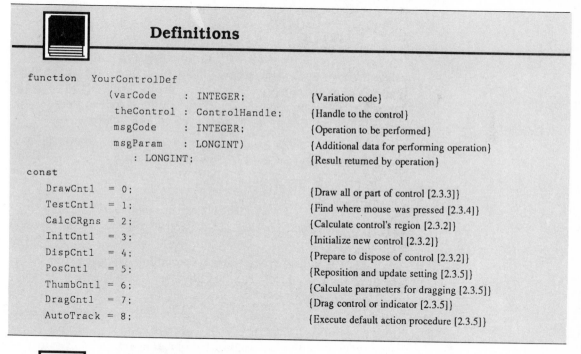

Definitions

```
function   YourControlDef
              (varCode     : INTEGER;          {Variation code}
               theControl  : ControlHandle;    {Handle to the control}
               msgCode     : INTEGER;          {Operation to be performed}
               msgParam    : LONGINT)          {Additional data for performing operation}
                 : LONGINT;                    {Result returned by operation}
const
   DrawCntl  = 0;                              {Draw all or part of control [2.3.3]}
   TestCntl  = 1;                              {Find where mouse was pressed [2.3.4]}
   CalcCRgns = 2;                              {Calculate control's region [2.3.2]}
   InitCntl  = 3;                              {Initialize new control [2.3.2]}
   DispCntl  = 4;                              {Prepare to dispose of control [2.3.2]}
   PosCntl   = 5;                              {Reposition and update setting [2.3.5]}
   ThumbCntl = 6;                              {Calculate parameters for dragging [2.3.5]}
   DragCntl  = 7;                              {Drag control or indicator [2.3.5]}
   AutoTrack = 8;                              {Execute default action procedure [2.3.5]}
```

Notes

1. A control definition function defines the appearance and behavior of one or more types of control. The Toolbox calls it whenever it needs to draw all or part of a control on the screen or determine its interactions with the mouse.

2. The function heading shown above is only a model for defining your own control definition functions. There is no Toolbox routine named `YourControlDef`.

3. Control definition functions are stored in resource files under resource type 'CDEF' [2.5.2].

4. When a control is created, the resource ID of its definition function is given by the first 12 bits of the control definition ID (the controlType parameter to NewControl [II:6.2.1] or the corresponding field of the control template [II:6.5.1] supplied to GetNewControl). The last 4 bits are a *variation code*, allowing the same definition function to implement more than one type of control. Thus the definition ID is determined by the formula

$$defID = 16*rsrcID + varCode$$

5. The Toolbox reads the definition function into memory from its resource file, if necessary, and places a handle to it in the control record's contrlDefProc field [II:6.1.1].

6. On original Macintosh systems using 24-bit addresses, the first byte of the contrlDefProc field holds the variation code. It is stripped out and passed as a parameter when the definition function is called, identifying the particular type of control being manipulated. On 32-bit systems, the handle occupies the entire field and the variation code is stored in the acFlags field of the auxiliary control record (see Volume Four).

7. The definition function's msgCode parameter designates the operation to be performed, and is always one of the constants shown above (DrawCntl to AutoTrack). msgParam gives further information for some operations; see [2.3.2–2.3.5] for details.

8. The function result is meaningful only in response to the messages TestCntl [2.3.4] and DragCntl [2.3.5]. In all other cases, the function should simply return 0.

9. The contrlData field of the control record [II:6.1.1] is reserved for the private use of the control definition function, typically to hold a handle to an auxiliary data record.

10. The definition function cannot assume that processor register A5 is set up properly at the time it is called, and thus cannot access any of the information stored in the application global space, or "A5 world." In particular, this means it must not refer directly to any of the QuickDraw global variables listed in [I:4.3.1].

Assembly Language Information

Control message codes:

Name	Value	Meaning
DrawCtlMsg	0	Draw all or part of control
HitCtlMsg	1	Find where mouse was pressed
CalcCtlMsg	2	Calculate control's region
NewCtlMsg	3	Initialize new control
DispCtlMsg	4	Prepare to dispose of control
PosCtlMsg	5	Reposition and update setting
ThumbCtlMsg	6	Calculate parameters for dragging
DragCtlMsg	7	Drag control or indicator
TrackCtlMsg	8	Execute default action procedure

2.3.2   Creating and Destroying Controls

Definitions

```
const
    CalcCRgns = 2;          {Calculate control's region within its window}
    InitCntl  = 3;          {Initialize new control}
    DispCntl  = 4;          {Prepare to dispose of control}
```

Notes

1. The message InitCntl is sent to the control definition function when a new control is created. This allows the definition function to perform any special initialization it may require, such as allocating an auxiliary data record and placing its handle in the contrlData field of the control record [II:6.1.1].

2. The message DispCntl is sent just before a control record is destroyed. The definition function can then perform any final housekeeping chores, such as disposing of its auxiliary data record, if any.

3. The message CalcCRgns asks the definition function to recalculate the region a control (or its indicator) occupies within its window.

4. The control's current dimensions are given by its enclosing rectangle, found in the `contrlRect` field of the control record [II:6.1.1].

5. A region handle is passed in the last 3 bytes of the definition function's `msgParam` parameter [2.2.1]. This region will already have been created by the Toolbox; the definition function should simply update its size and shape.

6. If the high-order bit of `msgParam` is set, the definition function should calculate the region occupied by the control's moving indicator (such as the scroll box or "thumb" of a scroll bar), rather than that of the entire control. Controls other than dials (that is, those that have no moving indicator) should simply ignore such calls.

7. The remainder of `msgParam`'s first byte is reserved for future use. To ensure future compatibility, this entire byte (not just the first bit) should be stripped out before using the handle.

8. The calculated region must be expressed in window-relative (local) coordinates. This is the same form in which the enclosing rectangle is given in the control record.

2.3.3 Drawing Controls

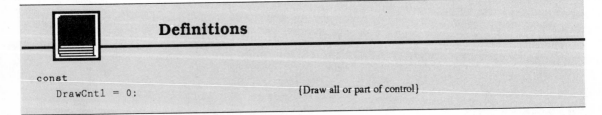

Definitions

```
const
    DrawCntl = 0;                        {Draw all or part of control}
```

Notes

1. The message `DrawCntl` instructs the control definition function to draw all or part of a control on the screen.

2. The function's `msgParam` parameter [2.3.1] is a part code telling how much of the control to draw. A value of 0 specifies the entire control.

3. The definition function itself determines the values and meanings of a control's part codes. Moving indicators, if any, should have part codes of 129 or greater.

4. For functions that support more than one variant control type, the `varCode` parameter [2.3.1] tells which variant to draw.

5. The control or part should be drawn in its normal or highlighted state, depending on the current value of the `contrlHilite` field in the control record [II:6.1.1]. If `contrlHilite = 255`, the control should be drawn in

its inactive state. The definition function itself determines how these conditions affect the control's appearance.

6. The control should be drawn so as to reflect its current setting and range, given by its `contrlValue`, `contrlMin`, and `contrlMax` fields [II:6.1.1].

7. If the control's `contrlVis` field [II:6.1.1] is 0, the definition function should simply return without drawing anything.

8. Before sending the `DrawCntl` message, the Toolbox will have set the current graphics port to the control's owning window.

9. The window's clipping boundaries will have been set to include only those portions of its structure region that are exposed to view on the screen. The definition function should simply draw the entire control or the requested part, letting the Toolbox take care of the clipping.

10. If the definition function wishes to set its own text characteristics for the control's title, it should save the window's previous settings, then restore them before returning.

11. The Toolbox routines `SetCtlValue`, `SetCtlMin`, and `SetCtlMax` [II:6.2.4] send this message, with a special part code of 129, to redraw a control after changing its setting or range. This value is understood to refer to the control's indicator (or all indicators, if there's more than one), regardless of part code. The definition function should respond by redrawing the indicator(s) according to the current values of `contrlValue`, `contrlMin`, and `contrlMax` [II:6.1.1].

2.3.4   **Locating Mouse Clicks**

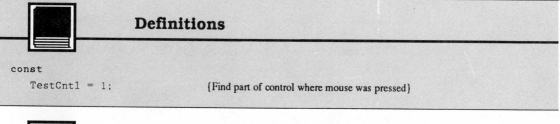

Definitions

```
const
    TestCntl = 1;                {Find part of control where mouse was pressed}
```

Notes

1. The message `TestCntl` asks the control definition function to find which part of a control, if any, contains a given point (normally the point where the mouse button was pressed).

2. The definition function's `msgParam` parameter [2.3.1], nominally a long integer, is actually a `Point` record [I:4.1.1], with its vertical coordinate in the high-order word and horizontal in the low.

3. The point is expressed in the local coordinate system of the control's owning window.

4. The definition function returns a *part code* as its result, identifying which part of the control, if any, was "hit" by the mouse.

5. The definition function itself determines the values and meanings of a control's part codes. Moving indicators, if any, should have part codes of 129 or greater.

6. If the given point lies outside the control, or is not in any identifiable part, the definition function should return a part code of 0.

7. If the control is currently inactive (contrlHilite = 255 in the control record [II:6.1.1, II:6.3.3]), the definition function should return a part code of 0.

2.3.5   Tracking and Positioning

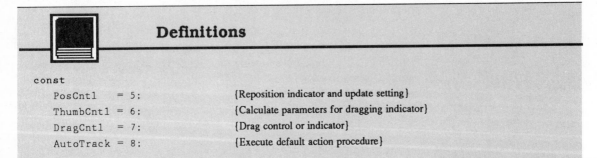

Definitions

```
const
    PosCntl   = 5;          {Reposition indicator and update setting}
    ThumbCntl = 6;          {Calculate parameters for dragging indicator}
    DragCntl  = 7;          {Drag control or indicator}
    AutoTrack = 8;          {Execute default action procedure}
```

Notes

1. The message ThumbCntl is sent by the Toolbox routine TrackControl [II:6.4.2], asking the control definition function to calculate the constraint parameters for dragging a control's indicator with the mouse.

2. msgParam [2.3.1] is a pointer to a data record to be filled in by the definition function, of the form

```
record
    limitRect : Rect;          {Rectangle limiting movement}
    trackRect : Rect;          {Rectangle limiting tracking}
    axis      : INTEGER        {Axis constraint}
end;
```

The fields of this record have the same meanings as the corresponding parameters of the Toolbox routine DragControl [II:6.4.3], but apply just to dragging the control's indicator rather than the whole control. Notice that this is just a hypothetical record structure, and is not actually defined as a Toolbox data type.

3. On entry to the definition function, the first 4 bytes of the parameter record (equivalent to the field selector `limitRect.topLeft`) contain the point where the mouse was pressed, corresponding to the `DragControl` parameter `startPoint` [II:6.4.3].

4. The values of `startPoint`, `limitRect`, and `trackRect` are all expressed in the local coordinate system of the control's owning window.

5. The message `DragCntl` is sent by the Toolbox routines `DragControl` [II:6.4.3] and `TrackControl` [II:6.4.2], allowing the control definition routine to override the standard methods of mouse tracking, if it chooses, with "custom" methods of its own.

6. The function's `msgParam` parameter [2.3.1] tells whether to drag the entire control (`msgParam = 0`) or just its indicator (`msgParam ≠ 0`).

7. If the definition function chooses to do its own mouse tracking, it should keep control for as long as the user holds down the mouse button, reading the mouse's position with `GetMouse` [II:2.4.1] and providing visual feedback on the screen in whatever way it wishes.

8. When the button is released, the definition function should reposition the control or its indicator as needed, by calling either `MoveControl` [II:6.3.2], to move the entire control, or its own `PosCntl` routine (see notes 10–13, below), to reposition the indicator and adjust the control's setting to match.

9. After tracking the mouse, the definition function should notify the Toolbox by returning a nonzero result. If it doesn't do its own mouse tracking, it should return `0` to request the standard tracking methods, as described in [II:6.4.3] for `DragControl` and [II:6.4.2] for `TrackControl`.

10. The message `PosCntl` is sent by the Toolbox routine `TrackControl` [II:6.4.2] when the user releases the mouse button after dragging a control's indicator. It instructs the control definition function to reposition the indicator and adjust the control's setting to match.

11. `msgParam` [2.3.1] is a point telling how far the mouse was moved while dragging the indicator, from the point where the button was pressed to the point where it was released. The high-order word gives the vertical offset, the low-order the horizontal.

12. The definition function should reposition and redraw the control's indicator according to the given offset, calculate the corresponding change in the control's setting, and store the new setting into the `contrlValue` field of the control record [II:6.1.1].

13. This message is *not* used to redraw a control on the screen when its setting or range are changed with the Toolbox routines `SetCtlValue`, `SetCtlMin`, or `SetCtlMax` [II:6.2.4]. This is done with the `DrawCntl`

message instead, using a special part code of 129 for msgParam (see [2.3.3, note 11]).

14. The message AutoTrack is sent by the Toolbox routine TrackControl [II:6.4.2], instructing the control definition function to execute its default action procedure for tracking the mouse in a control.

15. See [II:6.4.2] for the form and behavior of the action procedure.

16. This message is used only when both the actionProc parameter to TrackControl [II:6.4.2] and the contrlAction field in the control record [II:6.1.1] are set to the value ProcPtr(-1). Any other value in either place overrides the default action procedure supplied by the definition function.

2.4 Customizing Menus

2.4.1 Menu Definition Procedure

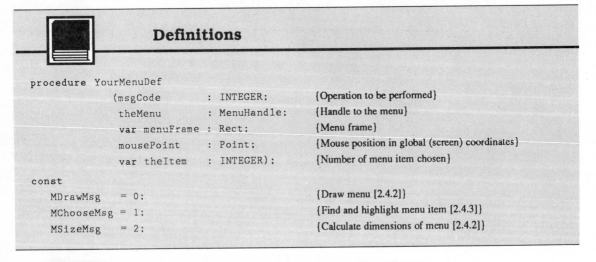

Definitions

```
procedure YourMenuDef
              (msgCode       : INTEGER;      {Operation to be performed}
               theMenu       : MenuHandle;   {Handle to the menu}
           var menuFrame     : Rect;         {Menu frame}
               mousePoint    : Point;        {Mouse position in global (screen) coordinates}
           var theItem       : INTEGER);     {Number of menu item chosen}
const
    MDrawMsg   = 0;                          {Draw menu [2.4.2]}
    MChooseMsg = 1;                          {Find and highlight menu item [2.4.3]}
    MSizeMsg   = 2;                          {Calculate dimensions of menu [2.4.2]}
```

Notes

1. A menu definition procedure defines the appearance and behavior of a particular type of menu. The Toolbox calls it whenever it needs to draw a menu on the screen or determine its interactions with the mouse.

2. The procedure heading shown above is only a model for defining your own menu definition procedures. There is no Toolbox routine named `YourMenuDef`.

3. Menu definition procedures are stored in resource files under resource type `'MDEF'` [2.5.3].

4. When a menu is created from a predefined template, using the Toolbox routine `GetMenu` [II:4.2.2], the template resource [II:4.8.1] includes the resource ID of the menu definition procedure. The Toolbox reads the definition procedure into memory from its resource file, if necessary, and places a handle to it in the menu record's `menuProc` field [II:4.1.1].

5. When a menu is created from scratch, using the Toolbox routine `NewMenu` [II:4.2.2], it is automatically set up as a standard text menu. To use a different type of menu, the application program must explicitly store a handle to the desired definition procedure in the menu's `menuProc` field.

6. After installing a nonstandard definition procedure, the application program must call `CalcMenuSize` [II:4.7.1] to recalculate the menu's dimensions.

7. The definition procedure's `msgCode` parameter designates the operation to be performed, and is always one of the constants shown above (`MDrawMsg` to `MSizeMsg`). The use of the remaining parameters depends on the operation: see [2.4.2, 2.4.3] for details.

8. The definition procedure may define the structure of the "hidden data" in the menu record's `menuData` field [II:4.1.1] in any way it chooses.

9. The definition procedure cannot assume that processor register A5 is set up properly at the time it is called, and thus cannot access any of the information stored in the application global space, or "A5 world." In particular, this means it must not refer directly to any of the QuickDraw global variables listed in [I:4.3.1].

Assembly Language Information

Menu message codes:

Name	Value	Meaning
MDrawMsg	0	Draw menu
MChooseMsg	1	Find and highlight menu item
MSizeMsg	2	Calculate dimensions of menu

2.4.2   Menu Display

Definitions

```
const
    MDrawMsg = 0;               {Draw menu}
    MSizeMsg = 2;               {Calculate dimensions of menu}
```

Notes

1. The message `MSizeMsg` asks the menu definition procedure to calculate a menu's width and height in screen pixels, according to the current contents of the menu's items.

2. The definition procedure should store the calculated dimensions in the `menuWidth` and `menuHeight` fields of the menu record [II:4.1.1].

3. This message is sent by the Toolbox routine `CalcMenuSize` [II:4.7.1], which is called automatically whenever a new menu is created. The application program should also call `CalcMenuSize` explicitly after installing a nonstandard definition procedure in a menu's `menuProc` field [II:4.1.1].

4. The message `MDrawMsg` instructs the menu definition procedure to draw a menu on the screen.

5. The function's `menuFrame` parameter [2.4.1] gives the rectangle within which the menu is to be drawn, in global (screen) coordinates.

6. Any items that are marked as disabled in the menu record's `enableFlags` field [II:4.1.1] should be "dimmed" in some way. The standard way of doing this is to paint over them with a gray pattern, using the `PatBic` transfer mode [I:5.1.3]. Note, however, that the pattern must be built "by hand," since the standard pattern `Gray` [I:5.1.2] is a QuickDraw global variable residing in the application global space, and thus is inaccessible from within the definition procedure (see [2.4.1, note 9]).

7. If the low-order bit of `enableFlags` [II:4.1.1] is 0, the entire menu is disabled and should be dimmed.

8. Before sending the message `MDrawMsg`, the Toolbox will have set the current graphics port to the Window Manager port [II:3.6.1], whose port rectangle is the entire screen.

9. The port's text characteristics [I:8.3.1] are normally set to the standard system typeface and size. If the definition procedure wishes to use some other text characteristics for the menu's items, it must set them for itself, then restore the original values before returning.

2.4.3   Locating Mouse Clicks

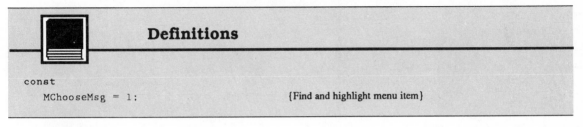

Definitions

```
const
    MChooseMsg = 1;                          {Find and highlight menu item}
```

Notes

1. The message `MChooseMsg` asks the menu definition procedure to find and highlight the menu item, if any, that contains a given point (normally the current mouse position).

2. The definition procedure's `mousePoint` parameter [2.4.1] gives the mouse position; `menuFrame` gives the rectangle enclosing the menu.

3. Both the mouse point and the menu frame are expressed in global (screen) coordinates.

4. The parameter `theItem` gives the number of the item that was previously highlighted, or 0 if none.

5. The definition procedure should unhighlight the previous item, find and highlight the item containing the given mouse point, and return its item number via the variable parameter `theItem`.

6. If the item containing the mouse point is the same one designated by `theItem`, the definition procedure should do nothing.

7. If the mouse point is outside the menu's frame or in a disabled item, or if the entire menu is disabled, the definition procedure should simply unhighlight the previous item, if any, without highlighting a new one. It should then return 0 in `theItem`.

2.5   Customizing-Related Resources

2.5.1   Resource Type 'WDEF'

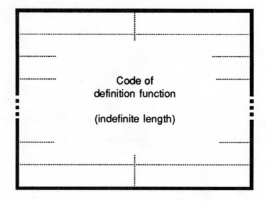

Code of
definition function

(indefinite length)

Structure of a 'WDEF' resource

Notes

1. A resource of type 'WDEF' contains a window definition function [2.2.1].

2. The resource data is simply the machine-language code of the definition function.

3. The function's entry point must be at the beginning.

4. The resource ID of the 'WDEF' resource is the same as the first 12 bits of the window definition ID, as specified by the windowType parameter to NewWindow [II:3.2.2] or by the corresponding field of the window template [II:3.7.1] supplied to GetNewWindow.

5. Two standard 'WDEF' resources are kept in the system resource file, or in ROM on some Macintosh models.   Number 0 draws standard document windows and dialog and alert boxes (window definition IDs 0 to 15 [II:3.2.2], depending on variation code); number 1 draws rounded-corner desk accessory windows (definition ID 16; variation code gives radius of corners [II:3.2.2, note 14]).

2.5.2　　Resource Type 'CDEF'

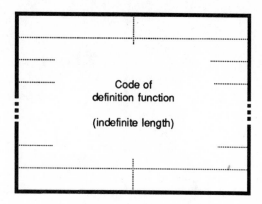

Code of
definition function

(indefinite length)

Structure of a 'CDEF' resource

Notes

1. A resource of type 'CDEF' contains a control definition function [2.3.1].

2. The resource data is simply the machine-language code of the definition function.

3. The function's entry point must be at the beginning.

4. The resource ID of the 'CDEF' resource is the same as the first 12 bits of the control definition ID, as specified by the controlType parameter to NewControl [II:6.2.1], or by the corresponding field of the control template [II:6.5.1] supplied to GetNewControl.

5. Two standard 'CDEF' resources are kept in the system resource file, or in ROM on some Macintosh models. Number 0 draws standard pushbuttons, checkboxes, and radio buttons (control definition IDs 0 to 15 [II:6.2.1], depending on variation code); number 1 draws standard scroll bars (definition ID 16, variation codes ignored).

2.5.3   Resource Type 'MDEF'

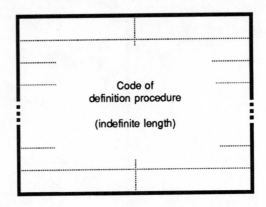

Structure of an 'MDEF' resource

Notes

1. A resource of type 'MDEF' contains a menu definition procedure [2.4.1].
2. The resource data is simply the machine-language code of the definition procedure.
3. The procedure's entry point must be at the very beginning.
4. One standard 'MDEF' resource is kept in the system resource file (or in ROM on some Macintosh models). It has a resource ID of 0, and draws the standard type of text menu.

2.5.4   Owned Resources

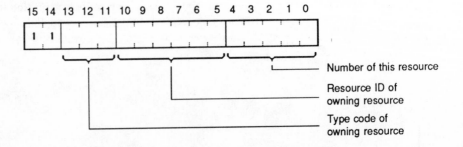

Resource ID of an owned resource

Type codes for owning resources:

Type Code	Resource Type	See Section
0	'DRVR'	[3.3.1]
1	'WDEF'	[2.5.1]
2	'MDEF'	[2.5.3]
3	'CDEF'	[2.5.2]
4	'PDEF'	[4.6.2]
5	'PACK'	[I:7.5.2]
6	Reserved	
7	Reserved	

Notes:

1. Resources that are "owned" by another resource must be numbered in a special way so that they can be recognized and properly handled by resource-handling software.

2. The first 2 bits (bits 15 and 14) must both be 1 to mark this as an owned resource.

3. Bits 13–11 identify the type of the owning resource, as shown in the table.

4. Bits 10–5 give the resource ID of the owning resource within the specified type. Notice that this limits owning resources to IDs in the range 0 to 63.

5. Bits 4–0 identify this individual owned resource. Thus a single owning resource can't own more than 32 other resources of a given type.

6. 'WDEF' [2.5.1] and 'CDEF' [2.5.2] resources cannot be owned by other resources, because their resource IDs must be no longer than 12 bits in order to form part of a window or control definition ID [2.5.1, note 4; 2.5.2, note 4]. Thus they cannot conform to the conventions just described.

7. Font-related resources such as 'FONT' [II:8.4.5], 'NFNT' [II:8.4.5], and 'FWID' [II:8.4.6] also cannot be owned, because they are subject to numbering conventions that conflict with those given above.

CHAPTER

3

In the Driver's Seat

Deep in the subterranean recesses of the Macintosh lurk the *device drivers*. These fugitive creatures are seldom seen outside their shadowy haunts in the depths of the Operating System; and there most Macintosh programmers are content to let them remain, their very existence rarely acknowledged save for the indispensable work they do. Chances are, you'll never have to write a device driver of your own—but a basic acquaintance with their anatomy and habits will help you understand some of the other, livelier topics we'll be discussing in later chapters: printing, sound, and desk accessories. So summon your courage while we drag these elusive beasts into the light for closer examination.

A driver's purpose in life is to control an input/output device, such as a disk drive, printer, or modem. The trouble with devices is that there are so many different kinds, and new ones being invented all the time—each with its own unique properties and idiosyncrasies. The diversity is more than the Macintosh Toolbox can cope with all by itself. So to help it out, each device has its own driver, with the specialized expertise needed to deal with that particular device. The driver shields the device's peculiarities from the rest of the system by hiding them behind a standard, uniform programming interface.

One good reason for learning about drivers is that they form the basis of the desk accessories that all Macintosh users know and adore. A desk accessory is really a "mini-application" pretending to be a peripheral device. By masquerading behind the standard driver interface, it can share the screen amicably with whatever other program happens to be running. In this chapter, we'll consider the general properties shared by all drivers; in Chapter 6, we'll come back and focus on those that are specific to desk accessories alone.

Driver Identification

Macintosh devices fall into two categories: those that are built right into the Mac itself and those that are peripheral and connected to the machine with plug-in cables. The drivers for built-in devices are stored permanently in ROM, where they're always available when needed. These include the *disk driver* for the standard Sony disk drive, the *sound driver* for the built-in audio speaker, and the *serial driver* for communicating through the serial ports on the back of the machine. (Recent models also have a pair of *AppleTalk drivers* in ROM for communicating with other computers and remote devices over the AppleTalk network.)

Drivers for peripheral devices are stored in disk files as resources of resource type 'DRVR' [3.3.1] and loaded into RAM when needed. They're typically "built on top of" the standard serial driver and use it to communicate with the device through the serial port. In Chapter 4, we'll look at one important example of such a driver, the *printer driver*.

> The Macintosh Plus and other recent models include a SCSI (Small Computer Standard Interface) parallel port in addition to the serial ports. Special provisions have been added to the Toolbox to allow SCSI devices to carry their own drivers, which are loaded directly into memory via the SCSI port, rather than from a disk-based resource file. The details of this process needn't concern us here; if you're curious, see the "SCSI Manager" chapter of *Inside Macintosh*, Volume IV.

Every driver has a name and a *unit number*. The unit number is simply its index in the *unit table* [3.1.3], a master list of all drivers currently installed in the system. For each driver, the table holds a handle to a *device control entry* [3.1.4], which in turn contains all the pertinent information about that driver. (We'll examine the structure of the device control entry later in this chapter.) On the original Skinny and Fat Macs, the unit table has room for 32 installed drivers, with unit numbers from 0 to 31. On the Macintosh Plus, it has been expanded to accommodate up to 48 drivers, numbered from 0 to 47; the latest models have a 64-element unit table, indexed from 0 to 63.

Each driver also has a *driver reference number*, which is simply the bitwise binary complement of its unit number. In two's-complement arithmetic, this means that the unit and reference numbers are related arithmetically by the formula

```
refNum = -(unitNum + 1)
```

For example, the printer driver has a unit number of 2 and a reference number of -3. The driver reference number always lies between -1 and -32 (or -48 or -64, depending on the model). Its negative sign serves to distinguish it from a file reference number [I:8.2.2], which is always positive. The names and numbers of the standard drivers and desk accessories are summarized in [3.1.3].

For drivers residing in resource files, the driver name and unit number are the same as the resource name and ID [I:6.4.1]. By convention, the names of true device drivers always begin with a period (.), while those of desk accessories may begin with any character *except* a period. As we learned in Volume Two, this allows you to build a menu of available desk accessories by calling the Toolbox routines `AddResMenu` or `InsertResMenu` [II:4.3.3] with a resource type of `'DRVR'`. You may recall that these routines automatically suppress any resource name that begins with a period. Thus driver names like `.Print` and `.Sound` will be omitted, leaving only the desk accessories to appear on the menu.

Working with Drivers

Just as for files [II:8], the Toolbox includes two separate sets of routines for working with drivers. The *low-level routines* give you complete control over the details of each operation; the *high-level routines* are simpler and easier to use, but give up some of that fine control. As we did when we learned about files in Volume Two, we'll confine ourselves here to the high-level routines, which are perfectly adequate for most straightforward purposes. If you're a glutton for detail, Apple's *Inside Macintosh* manual will tell you more about the low-level system than you probably want to know.

Because the low-level routines are designed to be called from assembly language, they're register- rather than stack-based. All of them accept a pointer in register A0 to a *parameter block*, a long, complicated variant record structure containing all the pertinent information about the operation to be performed. For this reason, most low-level routines have names beginning with the letters PB, for "parameter block."

Only the low-level routines actually reside in ROM; the high-level routines are merely part of the Pascal interface "glue." All they do is set up an appropriate parameter block, place its address in register A0, and call the corresponding low-level routine to do the work. In assembly language, only the low-level, register-based routines are available.

Before attempting to use any driver, you have to *open* it for operation with the Toolbox routine OpenDriver [3.2.1]. You identify the driver by name and get back a driver reference number, which you then use in all further operations. If the requested driver is not yet installed in the unit table, OpenDriver reads it into memory from its resource file, creates a device control entry (commonly called a DCE), stores a handle to the DCE in the appropriate slot in the unit table, and returns a reference number based on its unit number (that is, its position in the table). Subsequent calls to OpenDriver will simply use this existing DCE and unit number.

Once the driver is open, you can use it to transfer data to and from the device with the Toolbox routines FSRead and FSWrite [3.2.2]. If these names have a familiar ring, it's because they're the same routines we used in Volume Two [II:8.2.3] for reading and writing files; the letters FS stand for "file system." These same routines can operate on either drivers or files, depending on the sign of the reference number you supply as a parameter.

Two more routines, Control and Status [3.2.3], are used to control the operation of a device, select option settings, and so forth, and to request information about the current state of the device. The exact nature of the control operation or status information is specified by a *control code* or *status code* that you supply as a parameter. Each driver and device has its own set of control and status operations, and its own codes to denote them. (We'll see some examples when we talk about the printer driver in Chapter 4.) Both the `Control` and `Status` routines also accept a pointer to a parameter area in memory, which is used to supply further data to a control operation or to return the requested information from a status call. Again, the exact contents of the parameter area depend on the driver and the particular operation you specify.

The Toolbox routine `KillIO` [3.2.3] immediately terminates any input/output operation in progress on a given device and cancels any further operations that may be pending. This is actually a special Control call, designated by a control code of 1. That is, the statement

```
result := KillIO (anyDriver)
```

is equivalent to

```
result := Control (anyDriver, 1, NIL)
```

When you're through using a driver, `CloseDriver` [3.2.1] completes any pending input/output operations and frees the memory space the driver occupies. The driver's device control entry remains, however, so it can be used again if the driver is later reopened for further use.

The Device Control Entry

The device control entry, or DCE [3.1.4], is the basic data structure in which the Toolbox keeps all of its information about a driver. The DCE is created the first time the driver is opened for operation, and remains allocated continuously thereafter—even when one application program ends and another is started. Even if you close the driver itself, its DCE remains installed in the system unit table, and will be used again the next time the driver is reopened. The Toolbox routine `DCtlEntry` [3.1.4] returns a handle to it.

In assembly language, you can get a driver's DCE handle directly from the unit table. You'll find the address of the unit table in the assembly-language global variable `UTableBase`; the driver's unit number (not its reference number!) gives the offset of its DCE handle in long words from the beginning of the table.

The first field of the DCE, dCtlDriver, holds a handle to the driver itself in memory. (For drivers that reside in ROM, it's a simple pointer instead of a handle.) This is followed by a word of flags (dCtlFlags) describing the driver's properties and current status. Other fields hold the driver's reference number (dCtlRefNum) and its current byte position for reading and writing (dCtlPosition).

If a driver needs memory space for its own private use, it can allocate a block from the heap and keep a handle to it in the dCtlStorage field of the DCE. Each driver is also allowed to place one window on the screen and one menu in the menu bar; the dCtlWindow and dCtlMenu fields hold the window pointer and the menu ID, respectively. These capabilities are normally used only by desk accessories, so we'll postpone discussing them (as well as the event mask, dCtlEMask) until Chapter 6.

Driver Flags

Let's take a closer look at the driver's flag word, dCtlFlags [3.1.2]. The first byte of the flag word defines general properties of the driver, and is copied from the header of the driver itself [3.1.1] when it is first opened. Four of the flags in this byte tell which of the standard driver operations—Read, Write, Control, and Status—the driver is able to perform. (All drivers are required to respond to Open and Close operations.) You can test or manipulate these flags with the assembly-language constants dReadEnable, dWritEnable, dCtlEnable, and dStatEnable, respectively; no corresponding constants are defined at the Pascal level.

Whenever the Toolbox invokes any driver operation, it first locks the driver and its DCE in place, so they can't float around the heap while the operation is in progress. It unlocks them again on completion, allowing them to be moved between calls, if necessary, to make room for other objects. However, if the dNeedLock flag is set, the driver and DCE will remain locked even between operations, for as long as the driver remains open for business.

Drivers that reside in the application heap also run the risk of being obliterated when the heap is reinitialized (for instance, when a new program is started up). By setting the dNeedGoodBye flag, the driver can ask to be notified when this is about to happen. The "goodbye kiss" takes the form of a special Control call with a control code of -1 (defined as an assembly-language constant named GoodBye). The driver can respond by saving critical data, relocating itself to the system heap, or whatever else it needs to survive the coming cataclysm (or at least to expire gracefully). The Note Pad desk accessory, for instance, uses this opportunity to save the contents of its current page to the disk before its host program terminates.

The last remaining flag in the first byte of the flag word, dNeedTime, is discussed later in this chapter under "Periodic Tasks." The second byte is used by the system to maintain information on the driver's current status: the dRAMBased flag tells whether it resides in ROM or RAM, dOpened tells whether it is currently open for business, and drvrActive tells whether it is actively engaged in an input/ output operation.

The Driver I/O Queue

Many drivers perform their input/output operations *asynchronously*. Instead of immediately carrying out all I/O requests as it receives them from the running program, the driver simply places them in a *driver I/O queue* for later execution. Each time an operation is completed, the device sends an *interrupt* signal to the Macintosh processor, causing it to suspend whatever it's doing and execute an *interrupt handler* routine. The interrupt handler fetches the next request from the queue, begins the requested operation, and then resumes the interrupted program from the point of suspension. When the operation is complete, it will generate another interrupt, the interrupt handler will start the next operation in the queue, and so on.

Each driver has its own I/O queue [3.1.5, 3.1.6]. The head of the queue is kept in the dCtlQHdr field of the device control entry; its elements are parameter blocks representing pending driver requests waiting to be carried out. Like all queue elements, the parameter block begins with a qLink field pointing to the next element in the queue (or NIL for the last element). This is followed by a field named qType that identifies the type of queue. Queue types are nominally denoted by constants of the enumerated type QTypes [3.1.6]: for a driver I/O queue, the type is IOQType. However, the parameter block's qType field is formally defined to be of type INTEGER rather than QTypes, so it actually contains the integer value ORD(IOQType), or 2.

The next two fields of the parameter block identify the particular driver operation that was requested. ioTrap contains a copy of the machine-language trap word that initiated the request; by examining this word, the driver can tell whether it was a Read, Write, Control, or Status call. The next field, `ioCmdAddr`, holds the memory address of the Toolbox routine corresponding to that trap. In the case of Control and Status calls, there are also a `csCode` field, holding the specific control or status code, and a field named `csParam`, corresponding to the `params` parameter of the Toolbox `Control` and `Status` routines. The rest of the parameter block is of no concern to us here; if you care, you'll find it covered in prodigious detail in *Inside Macintosh.*

The calling program may specify that a given driver operation is to be performed *synchronously* rather than asynchronously. A synchronous request is queued in the usual way, but when the time comes to carry it out, the driver executes it in its entirety, instead of just starting it and waiting for a later interrupt to signal completion. The two types of request are distinguished by a flag in bit 10 of the trap word: 0 for synchronous, 1 for asynchronous. The assembly-language trap macros for driver operations accept an optional parameter named `ASYNC` for setting this flag: for example,

```
_Read        ,ASYNC
```

The driver decides whether to perform the operation synchronously or asynchronously by examining the relevant bit of the trap word, which it finds in the `ioTrap` field of the parameter block [3.1.5]. A bit number for testing or manipulating this flag is defined as an assembly-language constant named `AsyncTrpBit`.

Periodic Tasks

Some drivers have a *periodic task* that must be performed at regular intervals to keep the driver working properly. For example, the Alarm Clock desk accessory has to update the time displayed on the screen once each second, or a network or modem driver might need to poll periodically for incoming data. The Toolbox routine `SystemTask`

[6.2.4] keeps track of all the drivers' periodic tasks and executes them when needed. The running application program is expected to call this routine frequently enough for all periodic tasks to be carried out on schedule.

The dNeedTime flag in the DCE's flag word informs the Toolbox that the driver has a periodic task; the dCtlDelay field tells how often the task must be performed. The periodic task itself is actually a Control call with a control code of 65, identified by the assembly-language constant AccRun. (The Acc stands for "accessory": this is one of the special control codes for communicating with desk accessories, which we'll be learning about in Chapter 6 [6.1.2].)

The length of the delay between executions of the periodic task is expressed in *ticks* (sixtieths of a second), the basic unit of time on the Macintosh system clock. A value of 0 tells the SystemTask routine to run the periodic task at every opportunity, without reference to the system clock. Otherwise, SystemTask uses the dCtlCurTicks field of the DCE as a counter to count the ticks between executions of the periodic task, and runs it again when the required number of ticks has elapsed.

Driver Structure

The heart of a driver is the set of machine-language routines that actually do the work. In a full-functioned driver, there are five such routines:

- The Open routine prepares the driver for operation.
- The Prime routine performs all input/output (reading and writing) operations.
- The Control routine handles control requests.
- The Status routine handles status requests.
- The Close routine prepares the driver to terminate operation.

Some of these routines may be omitted if the driver doesn't perform certain operations: for instance, a driver that does no input/output can dispense with the Prime routine, or one that doesn't provide status information can do without the Status routine. At a minimum, the Open and Close routines must always be present.

The actual code of the driver is preceded by a short *driver header* [3.1.1] giving the location of each routine, along with other information about the driver as a whole. The first four words of the header are used to initialize various fields of the device control entry [3.1.4] when the driver is opened: the flag word, the periodic delay (for drivers with a periodic task), the event mask (for desk accessories), and the menu ID (if any). These are followed by the locations of the five driver routines, expressed as offsets in bytes from the beginning of the header. Next comes the name of the driver (in Pascal string form, preceded by a 1-byte character count) and then the code of the driver itself.

The driver routines are intended to be written in assembly language, and use processor registers (rather than the stack) to receive their parameters and return their results. They all receive a pointer to a parameter block representing the requested operation in register A0 and a pointer to the driver's device control entry in A1. All except the Open routine return a result code in register D0; for reasons too obscure to explain, the Open routine must place its result code in the `ioResult` field of the parameter block [3.1.5] instead.

Most Macintosh software development systems provide some sort of special "glue" to convert the register-based calling conventions just described into equivalent stack-based calls, allowing you to write driver routines in a high-level language instead of assembly language. Details vary, so consult your own language documentation. In general, such special arrangements are intended for writing desk accessories; true device drivers are still written in assembly language.

Driver routines that can be called via an interrupt are subject to special restrictions on register usage, memory usage, and return of control. You needn't worry about such things unless you're writing an interrupt-driven device driver—in which case, you don't have to be told to see *Inside Macintosh* for more information.

The driver's Open routine does whatever is necessary to prepare the driver for operation. In particular, it must initialize the fields of the device control entry [3.1.4]. As noted above, some of these fields (dCtlFlags, dCtlDelay, dCtlEMask, dCtlMenu) are automatically initialized from the corresponding fields of the driver header; if any of these values need to be overridden for any reason, the Open routine can store new values directly into the fields of the DCE. It might also want to

- allocate space in the heap for the driver's private storage and store a handle to it in the DCE's dCtlStorage field

- open a window on the screen (normally only desk accessories do this) and store a pointer to it in the dCtlWindow field

- load its own interrupt handlers into memory and set the appropriate system interrupt vectors to point to them

- perform any other special initialization that a particular driver might require

The Prime routine performs all input/output (reading and writing) operations. It can tell them apart by examining the trap word in the ioTrap field of the parameter block [3.1.5], whose low-order byte will be 2 for a Read request, 3 for a Write. Other fields of the parameter block, such as ioBuffer and ioReqCount, give further information about the requested operation.

The Control routine handles all control requests sent to the driver. The csCode field of the parameter block [3.1.5] identifies the specific control operation requested, and the csParam field contains any additional parameter data supplied by the caller. In general, the meanings of these two fields are determined by the Control routine itself. However, certain control codes have special, system-defined meanings that the Control routine must be prepared to handle:

- A control code of 1 (KillCode) designates a KillIO operation. The Control routine must immediately terminate any data transfer currently in progress and cancel any others that may be pending in the I/O queue.

- A control code of -1 (GoodBye) identifies a "good-bye kiss," signaling that the application heap is about to be reinitialized. For drivers with the dNeedGoodBye flag set in the DCE, the Control routine must respond with whatever action is necessary to deal with this situation.

- A control code of 65 (AccRun) instructs the Control routine to execute the driver's periodic task, if any.

In addition, for desk accessories, there are several other standard control codes [6.1.2] that the Control routine must be prepared to handle. We will discuss these in detail in Chapter 6.

The Status routine responds to requests for status information about the driver. The `csCode` field of the parameter block [3.1.5] holds a status code identifying the specific information requested; the information is returned in the `csParam` field. Again, the meaning of the various status codes and the format of the corresponding status information is determined by the Status routine itself, and varies from driver to driver.

Finally, the Close routine must reverse the effects of the Open routine and prepare the driver to close up shop. This might include releasing the driver's private storage from the heap, closing its window on the screen, restoring interrupt vectors to their original state, and generally undoing whatever the Open routine may have done.

This concludes our study of device drivers and their inscrutable ways. We will now allow these bizarre creatures to slither back into their accustomed obscurity. The coast is clear; you can come out from under your desk.

REFERENCE

3.1 Driver-Related Data Structures

3.1.1 Driver Structure

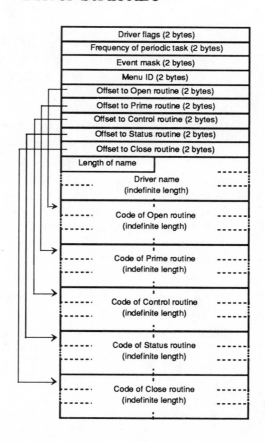

105

Notes

1. The contents of the driver flag word are detailed in [3.1.2].

2. For drivers with a periodic task, the second word of the driver tells how often the task must be performed, in ticks (sixtieths of a second).

3. A value of 0 for the task frequency specifies that the task should be performed at every opportunity (that is, at every call to the Toolbox routine SystemTask [6.2.4]).

4. The event mask is used only by desk accessories; see [6.1.1] for its structure.

5. The menu ID is also used only by desk accessories. It should have an appropriate value for an owned resource [2.5.4], based on the unit number (resource ID) of the 'DRVR' resource itself. See [3.1.4, note 12] for further information.

6. The driver name is given in Pascal string form, preceded by a 1-byte character count.

7. For true input/output device drivers, the driver name should begin with a period (.), to prevent the driver from being listed as a desk accessory on the Apple menu. Names of desk accessories may begin with any character other than a period.

8. The locations of the driver's routines (Open, Prime, Control, Status, Close) are given as offsets in bytes from the beginning of the driver.

9. All driver routines must begin at a word boundary: that is, the routine offset must be an even number.

10. All driver routines are register-based; see register usage information below. Most Macintosh software development systems include special provisions for writing drivers (including desk accessories) in a higher-level language, converting the low-level register-based calls into appropriate stack-based equivalents. See your own language documentation for details.

11. The Open routine prepares the driver for operation.

12. In particular, the Open routine is responsible for properly initializing the fields of the device control entry [3.1.4].

13. When written in assembly language, the Open routine must return its result code in the ioResult field of the parameter block, rather than in register D0.

14. The Prime routine handles all input/output operations initiated via the Toolbox routines FSRead and FSWrite [3.2.2] (or the corresponding low-level routines, PBRead and PBWrite).

15. Read and Write calls can be distinguished by comparing the low-order byte of the trap word, found in the `ioTrap` field of the parameter block [3.1.5], with the assembly-language constants `ARdCmd` and `AWtCmd` (below).

16. The Control and Status routines handle driver control and status requests initiated via the Toolbox routines `Control` and `Status` [3.2.3] (or their low-level counterparts, `PBControl` and `PBStatus`).

17. The specific Control or Status operation requested is identified by a code in the `csCode` field of the parameter block [3.1.5].

18. The Control routine must also handle KillIO requests initiated via `KillIO` [3.2.3] (or `PBKillIO`). A control code of 1 (assembly-language constant `KillCode`) designates a KillIO operation.

19. The Close routine prepares to terminate the driver's operations by reversing the effects of the Open routine.

20. For true input/output drivers, the Prime, Control, and Status routines should be interrupt-driven. See *Inside Macintosh* for further information.

21. In assembly language, synchronous portions of driver routines may use all registers freely; asynchronous portions must preserve all registers except A0–A3 and D0–D3; routines that can be called via an interrupt must preserve all registers except A0–A1 and D0–D2. See *Inside Macintosh* for further restrictions on interrupt-driven driver routines.

Assembly Language Information

Field offsets in a driver header:

(Assembly) Offset name	Offset in bytes	Meaning
drvrFlags	0	Driver flags
drvrDelay	2	Frequency of periodic task, in ticks
drvrEMask	4	Event mask
drvrMenu	6	Menu ID
drvrOpen	8	Offset to Open routine
drvrPrime	10	Offset to Prime routine
drvrCtl	12	Offset to Control routine
drvrStatus	14	Offset to Status routine
drvrClose	16	Offset to Close routine
drvrName	18	Driver name

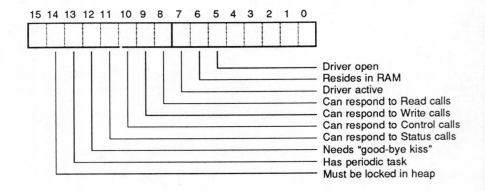

Assembly-language constants:

Name	Value	Meaning
ARdCmd	2	Low-order byte of trap word for a Read operation
AWtCmd	3	Low-order byte of trap word for a Write operation
KillCode	1	Control code for a KillIO operation

Register usage:

Routine	Register	Contents
All driver routines	A0.L (in)	Pointer to parameter block
	A1.L (in)	Pointer to device control entry
	D0.W (out)	Result code

3.1.2   Driver Flags

```
 15 14 13 12 11 10  9  8  7  6  5  4  3  2  1  0
┌──┬──┬──┬──┬──┬──┬──┬──┬──┬──┬──┬──┬──┬──┬──┬──┐
│  │  │  │  │  │  │  │  │  │  │  │  │  │  │  │  │
└──┴──┴──┴──┴──┴──┴──┴──┴──┴──┴──┴──┴──┴──┴──┴──┘
```

- Driver open
- Resides in RAM
- Driver active
- Can respond to Read calls
- Can respond to Write calls
- Can respond to Control calls
- Can respond to Status calls
- Needs "good-bye kiss"
- Has periodic task
- Must be locked in heap

Driver flags

Notes

1. The figure shows the contents of the driver flag word in the first 2 bytes of a driver header [3.1.1].

2. The flags in the first byte give descriptive information about the driver for use by the system; those in the second byte are reserved for the system itself to maintain information on the current state of the driver.

3. A value of 1 in bit 5 (dOpened) means that the driver is currently open; 0 means it is closed.

4. A 1 in bit 6 (dRAMBased) means that the driver resides in RAM; 0 means it resides in ROM.

5. Bit 7 (drvrActive) is set to 1 during the execution of any of the driver's routines, 0 at other times.

6. Bits 8 to 11 (dReadEnable, dWritEnable, dCtlEnable, dStatEnable) tell which specific driver calls the driver can handle. A value of 1 means it can respond to the given call, 0 means it cannot. All drivers must be prepared to respond to Open and Close calls.

7. A 1 in bit 12 (dNeedGoodBye) means that the driver needs to be notified with a "good-bye kiss" whenever the application heap is about to be reinitialized (for instance, when a new application program is started up). This allows the driver to attend to any special housekeeping it may require before being erased from memory.

8. The "good-bye kiss" is given by a special Control call with a control code of -1 in the csCode field of the parameter block [3.1.5]. An assembly-language constant, GoodBye, is defined for this value.

9. A 1 in bit 13 (dNeedTime) means that the driver has a periodic task that must be performed regularly. The second word of the driver header [3.1.1] tells how often the task must be performed, in ticks (sixtieths of a second).

10. The driver is notified to perform its periodic task by a Control call [3.2.3] with a control code of $41 (assembly-language constant AccRun).

11. A 1 in bit 14 (dNeedLock) means that the driver and its device control entry [3.1.4] must be locked in memory continuously for as long as the driver is open for operation. A 0 means they must be locked only during actual execution of driver routines, and may be unlocked between calls. For drivers that reside in ROM, this flag is always set.

12. The assembly-language constants dOpened, dReadEnable, and so on (below) are bit numbers for use with the BTST, BSET, BCLR, and BCHG instructions.

13. Notice that dReadEnable, dWritEnable, and so on, are defined as bit numbers within the *high-order byte* of the flag word, not within the word as a whole.

Assembly Language Information

Bit numbers in the driver flag word:

Name	Value	Meaning
dOpened	5	Driver open
dRAMBased	6	Resides in RAM
drvrActive	7	Driver active
dReadEnable	0	Can respond to Read calls
dWritEnable	1	Can respond to Write calls
dCtlEnable	2	Can respond to Control calls
dStatEnable	3	Can respond to Status calls
dNeedGoodBye	4	Needs "good-bye kiss"
dNeedTime	5	Has periodic task
dNeedLock	6	Must be locked in heap

Assembly-language constants:

Name	Value	Meaning
GoodBye	-1	Control code for "good-bye kiss"
AccRun	65	Control code for periodic task

3.1.3   Unit Table

Bytes	
0-3	Reserved (4 bytes)
4-7	Reserved (4 bytes)
8-11	Handle to .Print DCE (4 bytes)
12-15	Handle to .Sound DCE (4 bytes)
16-19	Handle to .Sony DCE (4 bytes)
20-23	Handle to .AIn DCE (4 bytes)
24-27	Handle to .AOut DCE (4 bytes)
28-31	Handle to .BIn DCE (4 bytes)
32-35	Handle to .BOut DCE (4 bytes)
36-39	Handle to .MPP DCE (4 bytes)
40-43	Handle to .ATP DCE (4 bytes)
44-47	Reserved (4 bytes)
48-51	Handle to Calculator DCE (4 bytes)
52-55	Handle to Alarm Clock DCE (4 bytes)
56-59	Handle to Key Caps DCE (4 bytes)
60-63	Handle to Puzzle DCE (4 bytes)
64-67	Handle to Note Pad DCE (4 bytes)
68-71	Handle to Scrapbook DCE (4 bytes)
72-75	Handle to Control Panel DCE (4 bytes)
76-79	Handle to Chooser DCE (4 bytes)
80-83	Unused (4 bytes)
188-191	Unused (4 bytes)

Standard driver numbers:

Unit Number	Reference Number	Driver Name	Description
2	-3	.Print	Printer driver
3	-4	.Sound	Sound driver
4	-5	.Sony	Sony disk driver
5	-6	.AIn	Serial driver, port A (modem port) in
6	-7	.AOut	Serial driver, port A (modem port) out
7	-8	.BIn	Serial driver, port B (printer port) in
8	-9	.BOut	Serial driver, port B (printer port) out
9	-10	.MPP	Network driver (Macintosh Packet Protocol)
10	-11	.ATP	Network driver (AppleTalk Transaction Protocol)
12	-13	Calculator	Calculator desk accessory
13	-14	Alarm Clock	Alarm Clock desk accessory
14	-15	Key Caps	Key Caps desk accessory
15	-16	Puzzle	Puzzle desk accessory
16	-17	Note Pad	Note Pad desk accessory
17	-18	Scrapbook	Scrapbook desk accessory
18	-19	Control Panel	Control Panel desk accessory
19	-20	Chooser	Chooser desk accessory

Notes

1. The unit table holds handles to the device control entries [3.1.4] for all drivers currently installed in the system.

2. The unit table resides in a nonrelocatable block in the system heap.

3. The assembly-language global variable UTableBase (below) holds the address of the first entry in the table.

4. The unit table has a maximum capacity of 32 entries on early Macintosh models, 48 or 64 on later models. In assembly language, the number of entries currently in the table can be found in the global variable UnitNtryCnt.

5. Each driver's position within the table is called its *unit number*, expressed in long words relative to the start of the table. Thus the unit number is always between 0 and 47 (0 and 31 on early models).

6. The unit number is the same as the driver's resource ID (under resource type 'DRVR' [3.3.1]), normally in the system resource file.

7. The *driver reference number* is the bitwise complement of the unit number. The two numbers are thus related arithmetically by the formula

        refNum = -(unitNum + 1)

   For example, the printer driver has a unit number of 2 and a reference number of -3.

8. The table lists the standard device drivers and desk accessories, with their standard unit and reference numbers.

9. The sound, disk, and serial drivers (as well as the network drivers on the Macintosh Plus) are permanently resident in ROM. The printer driver and desk accessories are resources, normally included in the system resource file.

10. The unit and reference numbers shown in the table may differ in some versions of the System file.

11. Recent versions of the disk driver use unit number 1 (reference number -2) to refer to the hard disk, if any. Unit number 4 (reference number -5) continues to refer to the internal and external $3\frac{1}{2}$-inch disk drives. The name of the disk driver is still .Sony.

12. Unit numbers from 27 to 31 are reserved for desk accessories found in the application resource file rather than in the System file.

13. On the Macintosh Plus, unit numbers 32 to 39 are reserved for drivers loaded from peripheral devices via the SCSI (Small Computer Standard Interface) port. See *Inside Macintosh*, Volume IV, for further information.

Assembly Language Information

Assembly-language global variables:

Name	Address	Meaning
UTableBase	$11C	Pointer to start of unit table
UnitNtryCnt	$1D2	Number of entries in unit table

3.1.4   Device Control Entry

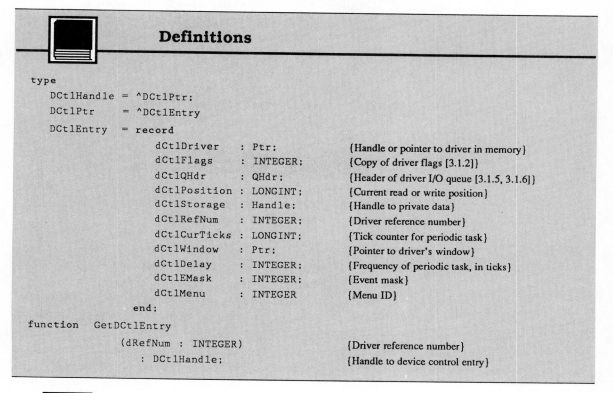

Definitions

```
type
    DCtlHandle = ^DCtlPtr:
    DCtlPtr    = ^DCtlEntry
    DCtlEntry  = record
                    dCtlDriver   : Ptr:          {Handle or pointer to driver in memory}
                    dCtlFlags    : INTEGER;      {Copy of driver flags [3.1.2]}
                    dCtlQHdr     : QHdr;         {Header of driver I/O queue [3.1.5, 3.1.6]}
                    dCtlPosition : LONGINT;      {Current read or write position}
                    dCtlStorage  : Handle;       {Handle to private data}
                    dCtlRefNum   : INTEGER;      {Driver reference number}
                    dCtlCurTicks : LONGINT;      {Tick counter for periodic task}
                    dCtlWindow   : Ptr;          {Pointer to driver's window}
                    dCtlDelay    : INTEGER;      {Frequency of periodic task, in ticks}
                    dCtlEMask    : INTEGER;      {Event mask}
                    dCtlMenu     : INTEGER       {Menu ID}
                 end;
function   GetDCtlEntry
                 (dRefNum : INTEGER)            {Driver reference number}
                    : DCtlHandle;               {Handle to device control entry}
```

Notes

1. The device control entry (DCE) is created when the driver is first opened and remains in existence continuously until the system is restarted.

2. The DCE resides in the system heap and is located via a handle in the unit table [3.1.3].

3. The DCE (as well as the driver itself) is locked in place during execution of any driver routine. If the `dNeedLock` flag [3.1.2] is set in the `dCtlFlags` field, they will remain locked continuously (even between calls) for as long as the driver remains open for operation.

4. Most fields are set automatically by the system. Only `dCtlStorage` and `dCtlWindow` (and sometimes `dCtlMenu`) must be initialized by the driver's own Open routine (see notes 10–13, below).

5. The fields dCtlFlags, dCtlDelay, dCtlEMask, and dCtlMenu are copied from the header of the driver itself [3.1.1] when the driver is opened. The driver's Open routine may change these values if, for some reason, it needs to override the values given in the driver header.

6. For RAM-based drivers, dCtlDriver holds a handle to the driver in memory; for drivers that reside in ROM, it holds a simple pointer.

7. dCtlQHdr is the actual header of the driver I/O queue (not just a pointer), embedded within the device control entry. See [3.1.6] for the structure of a queue header and [3.1.5] for further information on the driver I/O queue.

8. The low-order byte of the queue header's qFlags field [3.1.6] holds the version number of the driver to which the queue belongs.

9. dCtlRefNum is the driver's reference number, which is the bitwise complement of its unit number (resource ID). The two numbers are thus related arithmetically by the formula

    refNum = -(unitNum + 1)

   For example, the printer driver has a resource ID of 2 and a reference number of -3.

10. dCtlWindow holds a pointer to the driver's window record, if any. The driver's Open routine creates the window and stores its pointer here. This field is normally used only by desk accessories.

11. *Inside Macintosh* gives the type of dCtlWindow as WindowPtr, but in fact, Apple's Toolbox interface files declare it as an untyped Ptr. To access the driver's window, you must explicitly typecast it to a WindowPtr.

12. dCtlMenu holds the resource ID of the driver's menu, also normally used only by desk accessories. As stated above (note 5), this field is automatically initialized from the driver header [3.1.1] when the desk accessory is opened. However, since the menu is an owned resource [2.5.4], its resource ID may have been changed by the Font/DA Mover when the desk accessory was installed in the System file. The value of the menu ID in the driver header is *not* automatically adjusted to match. To make sure the DCE is set properly, the desk accessory's own Open routine should calculate the correct menu ID (based on the reference number found in the dCtlRefNum field) and explicitly store the resulting value into dCtlMenu.

13. dCtlStorage holds a handle to an optional private data record. The driver's Open routine allocates the record and stores its handle in this field.

14. dCtlPosition may be used by the driver's Prime routine to maintain its current byte position during Read and Write operations.

15. dCtlCurTicks is used by the system to time the interval between executions of the driver's periodic task. The frequency with which the task is to be performed is given by dCtlDelay.

16. The function GetDCtlEntry returns the device control entry for a given driver, identified by its reference number.

17. GetDCtlEntry is part of the Pascal Toolbox interface, not part of the Toolbox itself. It doesn't reside in ROM and can't be called from assembly language via the trap mechanism. Instead, the driver's device control entry is accessible directly from the unit table [3.1.3].

Assembly Language Information

Field offsets in a device control entry:

(Pascal) Field name	(Assembly) Offset name	Offset in bytes
dCtlDriver	dCtlDriver	0
dCtlFlags	dCtlFlags	4
dCtlQHdr	dCtlQueue	6
dCtlQHdr.qHead	dCtlQHead	8
dCtlQHdr.qTail	dCtlQTail	12
dCtlPosition	dCtlPosition	16
dCtlStorage	dCtlStorage	20
dCtlRefNum	dCtlRefNum	24
dCtlCurTicks	dCtlCurTicks	26
dCtlWindow	dCtlWindow	30
dCtlDelay	dCtlDelay	34
dCtlEMask	dCtlEMask	36
dCtlMenu	dCtlMenu	38

Assembly-language constant:

Name	Value	Meaning
DCtlEntrySize	40	Size of device control entry, in bytes

3.1.5   Driver I/O Queue

Definitions

```
type
    ParamBlkType = (IOParam,                        {Input/output operation}
                    FileParam,                      {File operation}
                    VolumeParam,                    {Volume operation}
                    CntrlParam);                    {Control or status operation}

    ParmBlkPtr   = ^ParamBlockRec;
    ParamBlockRec = record
                    qLink        : QElemPtr;        {Pointer to next queue element}
                    qType        : INTEGER;         {Queue type}
                    ioTrap       : INTEGER;         {Copy of trap word}
                    ioCmdAddr    : Ptr;             {Pointer to Toolbox routine}
                    ioCompletion : ProcPtr;         {Pointer to completion routine}
                    ioResult     : OSErr;           {Result code}
                    ioNamePtr    : StringPtr;       {Driver name}
                    ioVRefNum    : INTEGER;         {Volume or drive reference number}
                    case ParamBlkType of
                        IOParam :
                        (ioRefNum    : INTEGER;     {Driver reference number}
                         ioVersNum   : SignedByte;  {Version number (unused)}
                         ioPermssn   : SignedByte;  {Read/write permission}
                         ioMisc      : Ptr;         {Unused}
                         ioBuffer    : Ptr;         {Address to transfer to/from}
                         ioReqCount  : LONGINT;     {Number of bytes requested}
                         ioActCount  : LONGINT;     {Actual number of bytes transferred}
                         ioPosMode   : INTEGER;     {Positioning mode}
                         ioPosOffset : LONGINT);    {Positioning offset}
                        FileParam :
                        ( . . . );
                        VolumeParam :
                        ( . . . );
                        CntrlParam :
                        (ioCRefNum : INTEGER;       {Driver reference number}
                         csCode    : INTEGER;       {Control or status code}
                         csParam   : array [0..10] of INTEGER)
                                                    {Parameters for operation}
            end;
```

Notes

1. Each device driver has its own I/O queue, which holds pending requests for operations by that driver.

2. The driver I/O queue is a standard Operating System queue [3.1.6], whose header is embedded in the driver's device control entry [3.1.4].

3. Each element of the queue is a parameter block record representing a pending driver operation.

4. Like all queue elements [3.1.6], the parameter block is preceded by 4 bytes of flags (inaccessible from Pascal), followed by a 4-byte pointer (qLink) to the next element in the queue and a 2-byte integer (qType) designating the type of queue.

5. For a driver I/O queue, qType always equals 2, the value of ORD(IOQType) [3.1.6].

6. ioTrap holds a copy of the trap word for the Toolbox call that invoked this driver operation; ioCmdAddr holds the address of the corresponding Toolbox routine in memory (usually in ROM).

7. Bit 10 of the trap word specifies whether the operation is asynchronous (1) or synchronous (0). The assembly-language trap macros for input/output operations accept an optional parameter named ASYNC for setting this flag. For example, the instruction might read

   ```
   _Read       ,ASYNC
   ```

8. The assembly-language constant AsyncTrpBit (below) is a bit number for testing or manipulating the ASYNC flag with the BTST, BSET, BCLR, and BCHG instructions.

9. For Control and Status calls, csCode holds an integer code designating the specific operation requested. Values and meanings vary from driver to driver; see [4.4.3] for control codes used by the printer driver and [6.1.2] for those used by desk accessories.

10. For Control calls, csParam contains up to 11 words (22 bytes) of additional parameter data; for Status calls, the requested status information is returned in this field. Exact contents and format differ for each specific driver and operation; see [4.4.3] and [6.1.2] for those pertaining to the printer driver and to desk accessories.

11. The remaining fields of the parameter block are needed only if you are making low-level input/output calls at the file, volume, or device level, or writing a true device driver (as distinct from a desk accessory). In those cases, see *Inside Macintosh* for complete information.

Assembly Language Information

Field offsets in a parameter block:

(Pascal) Field name	(Assembly) Offset name	Offset in bytes
qLink	ioLink	0
qType	ioType	4
ioTrap	ioTrap	6
ioCmdAddr	ioCmdAddr	8
. . .	. . .	. . .
ioCRefNum	ioRefNum	24
csCode	csCode	26
csParam	csParam	28

Assembly-language constant:

Name	Value	Meaning
AsyncTrpBit	10	Bit number for ASYNC flag

3.1.6   Operating System Queues

Definitions

```
type
   QHdrPtr  = ^QHdr;
   QHdr     = record
                 qFlags : INTEGER;          {Flags}
                 qHead  : QElemPtr;         {First entry in queue}
                 qTail  : QElemPtr          {Last entry in queue}
              end;
   QElemPtr = ^QElm;
   QElem    = record
                 case QTypes of
                 VType    : (vblQElem : VBLTask);
                 IOQType  : (ioQElem  : ParamBlockRec);
                 DrvQType : (drvQElem : DrvQEl);
                 EvType   : (evQElem  : EvQEl);
                 FSQType  : {vcbQElem : VCB)
              end;
```

```
QTypes = (DummyType,        {Unused}
          VType,            {Vertical retrace queue}
          IOQType,          {Driver or file I/O queue}
          DrvQType,         {Disk drive queue}
          EvType,           {Event queue}
          FSQType);         {File system (volume) queue}
```

Notes

1. QHdr and QElem represent general-purpose queue headers and queue elements. They are used for a variety of purposes in the Macintosh Operating System, as enumerated in the definition of QTypes.

2. Driver I/O queues are discussed in [3.1.4]. See *Inside Macintosh* for information on other types of queue.

3. The contents of qFlags are specific to each type of queue, and vary from one queue type to another.

4. The structure of individual queue elements also differs for each type of queue; to accommodate the various possibilities, QElem is defined as a variant record structure. See [3.1.4] for details on the elements of a driver I/O queue, and *Inside Macintosh* for the others.

5. Queue elements are nonrelocatable objects, referred to by pointers rather than handles. They are normally created and destroyed by the system, not by the application program, and reside either in fixed memory locations or in the system heap.

6. All queue elements, regardless of type, begin with 4 bytes of flags, followed by a 4-byte pointer (qLink) to the next element and a 2-byte integer (qType) designating the type of queue. (Compare the definition of a parameter block in [3.1.4].)

7. The integer type code in a queue element's qType field corresponds to a value of the enumerated type QTypes. For the vertical retrace queue, for example, it will equal 1, the value of ORD (VType).

8. The Pascal pointer type QElemPtr points directly to the qLink field of the next element. It thus bypasses the element's flags, making them inaccessible from Pascal. The flags are used exclusively by the system, and are of no interest to the application program.

Assembly Language Information

Field offsets in a queue header:

(Pascal) Field name	(Assembly) Offset name	Offset in bytes
qFlags	qFlags	0
qHead	qHead	2
qTail	qTail	6

Assembly-language constant:

Name	Value	Meaning
QHeadSize	10	Size of queue header in bytes

Field offsets from a queue element pointer:

(Pascal) Field name	(Assembly) Offset name	Offset in bytes
qLink	qLink	0
qType	qType	4

Queue types:

Name	Value	Meaning
VType	1	Vertical retrace queue
IOQType	2	Driver or file I/O queue
DrvQType	3	Disk drive queue
EvType	4	Event queue
FSQType	5	File system (volume) queue

3.1.7   Manipulating Queues

Definitions

```
procedure Enqueue
        (newElement : QElemPtr;        {Element to be inserted}
         theQueue   : QHdrPtr);        {Queue to insert it in}
```

```
function  Dequeue
             (oldElement  :  QElemPtr;        {Element to be removed}
              theQueue    :  QHdrPtr)         {Queue to remove it from}
                 :  OSErr;                    {Result code}
const
   QErr  =  -1;                               {Element not found in queue}
```

Notes

1. These routines insert and remove elements in Operating System queues. See [3.1.6] for the structure of such queues.

2. Elements added with `Enqueue` are placed at the end of the queue.

3. `Dequeue` doesn't deallocate the dequeued element from memory.

4. If the specified element is not found in the queue, `Dequeue` returns the error code `QErr`.

5. A quick way to remove all elements from a queue is simply to set the `qHead` and `qTail` fields in its queue header to `NIL`.

6. Both operations temporarily disable interrupts while the queue is being manipulated.

7. When called from assembly language, these routines are register-based; see register usage information below.

8. All queue manipulation is normally done by the Operating System; you will rarely need to call these routines for yourself.

Assembly Language Information

Trap macros:

(Pascal) Routine name	(Assembly) Trap macro	Trap word
Enqueue	_Enqueue	$A96F
Dequeue	_Dequeue	$A96E

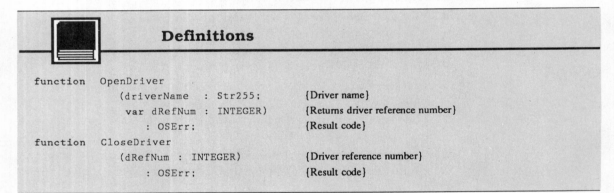

Register usage:

Routine	Register	Contents
Enqueue	A0.L (in)	newElement
	A1.L (in)	theQueue
Dequeue	A0.L (in)	oldElement
	A1.L (in)	theQueue
	D0.W (out)	result code

3.2 Driver Operations

3.2.1 Opening and Closing Drivers

Definitions

```
function   OpenDriver
           (driverName   : Str255;          {Driver name}
            var dRefNum : INTEGER)           {Returns driver reference number}
                : OSErr;                     {Result code}
function   CloseDriver
           (dRefNum : INTEGER)               {Driver reference number}
                : OSErr;                     {Result code}
```

Notes

1. OpenDriver opens a driver for operation; CloseDriver closes it.

2. The driver is identified to OpenDriver by name; the corresponding driver reference number is returned via the variable parameter dRefNum. You then use this number to identify the driver for all further operations.

3. If the driver is not already in memory, it is read in from a resource file (normally the System file). A device control entry [3.1.4] is created and initialized, and its handle is installed in the unit table [3.1.3].

4. If the driver is a true device driver, its Open routine [3.1.1] is executed only when it is read into memory for the first time. For desk accessories, the Open routine is executed at every call to `OpenDriver`.

5. Closing a driver removes it from memory and releases the space it occupies. The driver is unavailable for further operations until it is reopened.

6. Any pending input/output operations are completed and the driver's Close routine is executed.

7. The driver's device control entry [3.1.4] remains allocated, but is marked as closed via a flag bit in its `dCtlFlags` field [3.1.2].

8. These routines are part of the high-level input/output system and are not directly available from assembly language. The trap macros call the low-level routines `PBOpen` and `PBClose`; see *Inside Macintosh* for details.

Assembly Language Information

Trap macros:

(Pascal) Routine name	(Assembly) Trap macro	Trap word
PBOpen	_Open	$A000
PBClose	_Close	$A001

3.2.2   Reading and Writing

Definitions

```
function  FSRead
          (dRefNum       : INTEGER;      {Driver reference number}
       var byteCount : LONGINT;      {Number of bytes to read}
          toAddr        : Ptr)         {Address to read to}
             : OSErr;                   {Result code}
function  FSWrite
          (dRefNum       : INTEGER;      {Driver reference number}
       var byteCount : LONGINT;      {Number of bytes to write}
          fromAddr      : Ptr)         {Address to write from}
             : OSErr;                   {Result code}
```

Notes

1. These routines transfer information to or from a driver via the driver's Prime routine [3.1.1].

2. The number of bytes specified by `byteCount` are read to or written from consecutive locations in memory, beginning at the address designated by the pointer `toAddr` or `fromAddr`.

3. On a positionable device such as a disk, the transfer begins at the driver's current byte position, as indicated in the `dCtlPosition` field of the device control entry [3.1.4]. This byte position advances as bytes are transferred to or from the device.

4. On completion of either a read or a write, the `byteCount` parameter returns the number of bytes actually transferred.

5. These are the same routines used to read from or write to a file [II:8.2.3]. The value of the reference number supplied determines whether the call applies to a file or a driver.

6. These routines are part of the high-level input/output system and are not directly available from assembly language. The trap macros call the low-level routines `PBRead` and `PBWrite`; see *Inside Macintosh* for details.

Assembly Language Information

Trap macros:

(Pascal) Routine name	(Assembly) Trap macro	Trap word
PBRead	_Read	$A002
PBWrite	_Write	$A003

3.2.3   Device Control

Definitions

```
function  Control
              (dRefNum      : INTEGER;        {Driver reference number}
               controlCode  : INTEGER;        {Control code}
               params       : Ptr)            {Pointer to parameters}
                  : OSErr;                     {Result code}
```

```
function  Status
              (dRefNum     : INTEGER;        {Driver reference number}
               statusCode  : INTEGER;        {Status code}
               params      : Ptr)            {Pointer to parameters}
                     : OSErr;                {Result code}
function  KillIO
              (dRefNum     : INTEGER)        {Driver reference number}
                     : OSErr;                {Result code}
```

Notes

1. Control instructs a driver to perform some special action, typically to control the operation of a device; Status requests information about the current status of the device or its driver.

2. controlCode identifies the specific control operation to be performed; params points to a data structure of up to 11 words (22 bytes) of parameter data for the operation. Control copies these values to the csCode and csParam fields of the parameter block [3.1.5], then calls the driver's Control routine to carry out the operation.

3. statusCode identifies the nature of the status information desired. Status copies this value to the csCode field of the parameter block [3.1.5] and calls the driver's Status routine, which will return the requested information in the parameter block's csParam field. The information is then copied to the location designated by params.

4. The values and meanings of the control and status codes vary from driver to driver, and in turn determine the exact nature of the information passed via params. See [4.4.3] for control codes used by the printer driver and [6.1.2] for those used by desk accessories.

5. KillIO immediately halts any input/output activity in progress on the specified driver and cancels any pending operations.

6. The KillIO operation is actually performed by the driver's Control routine in response to a control code of 1. Calling KillIO is equivalent to calling Control with this value for controlCode.

7. These routines are part of the high-level input/output system and are not directly available from assembly language. The trap macros call the low-level routines PBControl, PBStatus, and PBKillIO; see *Inside Macintosh* for details.

Assembly Language Information

Trap macros:

(Pascal) Routine name	(Assembly) Trap macro	Trap word
PBControl	_Control	$A004
PBStatus	_Status	$A005
PBKillIO	_KillIO	$A006

Assembly-language constant:

Name	Value	Meaning
KillCode	1	Control code for a KillIO operation

3.3 Driver-Related Resources

3.3.1 Resource Type 'DRVR'

Notes

1. A resource of type 'DRVR' contains the code of an input/output device driver or a desk accessory.

2. See [3.1.1] for the internal structure of the resource.

3. The resource ID is the same as the driver's unit number [3.1.3], and must be between 0 and 47 (0 and 31 on early models of Macintosh).

4. Every driver resource must have a resource name as well as a resource ID. For true device drivers, the name begins with a period (.); for desk accessories, it must not.

5. The sound, disk, and serial drivers (as well as the network drivers on the Macintosh Plus) are ROM-based resources [I:6.6.3]. All other drivers and desk accessories reside in resource files, normally the System file.

CHAPTER

4

Looking Good on Paper

For some years now, pundits and prognosticators have been touting the arrival of the "paperless society." The combination of advanced computers and high-speed data communications, so the argument goes, will eliminate the need for old-fashioned printed material entirely. With the advent of sophisticated hardware and software technologies like CD–ROM, electronic mail, and hypertext, we will all soon be plugged into a universal, worldwide information network and will never have to look at a sheet of paper again.

While all this may sound good in theory, the reality has been slower in arriving. Most of us aren't yet ready to bring our computers to the breakfast table just to read the sports page over our morning coffee. As pretty as a document may look on the screen, we still prefer the comfort and familiarity of a physical, printed copy that we can stick in a briefcase, take on an airplane, or curl up with in bed at two in the morning. Our appetite for paper is undiminished, and will probably always be with us.

Recognizing this reality, the Macintosh Toolbox gives you all the tools you need to print hardcopy documents from an application program. In this chapter, we'll learn about these facilities and use them to add a printing capability to our example program, `MiniEdit`. By applying the same techniques in your own programs, you can make your documents look as good on paper as they do on the screen.

Macintosh Printers

In the beginning was the ImageWriter. Right from the start, it was clear that the Macintosh (and its precursor, the Lisa) would need a dot-oriented printer that could faithfully reproduce what users saw on the screen. For a computer that boasted "What You See Is What You Get," the printer had to keep its end of the bargain: what you get is what you see. After an extensive survey of the available candidates, Apple settled on a compact but versatile dot-matrix impact printer from C. Itoh & Company. An "Apple-ized" version, suitably modified for the Macintosh and marketed under Apple's own label, became the original ImageWriter. When the Macintosh was first released in January 1984, this was the standard printer that went with it.

A year later, Apple announced the LaserWriter, a "personal" xerographic printer based on the same laser-beam technology as units literally a hundred times its price. With a resolution of 300 dots per inch, the LaserWriter produces output of near-typeset quality— so close that it takes a magnifying glass to tell the difference. The printer is actually a powerful computer in its own right, featuring a Motorola 68000 microprocessor (the same one used in the Macintosh itself), half a megabyte of ROM holding a useful selection of professional-grade typographic fonts, and 1.5 megabytes of RAM into which additional fonts can be loaded as needed. Also in ROM is an interpreter for PostScript, a page description language developed by Adobe Systems Incorporated. This is a full-featured programming language, complete with variables, assignments, conditionals, loops, procedures, and everything else you would expect, as well as a full range of powerful graphics capabilities. Documents to be printed are transmitted to the LaserWriter in the form of PostScript programs for the interpreter to execute.

The PostScript language includes a number of special features, like text rotation and continuous gray scale, that aren't available through the normal Toolbox printing methods we'll be learning in this chapter. To take full advantage of these capabilities, it's possible to bypass the Toolbox printing routines and program the LaserWriter directly in PostScript via the Quick-Draw picture comment mechanism [2.1.7]. This technique is device-dependent, however, and will work only on a LaserWriter or other PostScript-based printer; on non-PostScript printers (in particular, the ImageWriter), such PostScript picture comments will simply be ignored.

Unfortunately, a complete discussion of PostScript syntax and semantics is beyond the scope of this book. If you're hungry for details, you can find them in Adobe's excellent *PostScript Language Reference Manual* and *PostScript Language Tutorial and Cookbook*, both from Addison-Wesley Publishing Company, Inc. The technique of embedding PostScript commands in picture comments is covered in Macintosh Technical Note #91, and is discussed at some length in Scott Knaster's book, *Macintosh Programming Secrets*, also published by Addison-Wesley.

These two devices—the dot-matrix ImageWriter and the xerographic LaserWriter—remain the standard printers for use with the Macintosh, though both have been replaced over time with newer and better models. The ImageWriter II, introduced in 1985, featured faster operation (up to 250 characters per second, compared to 120 for the original ImageWriter), finer and more precise dot placement for better print quality, improved paper handling (including an optional automatic sheet feeder for non-continuous, separately cut sheets), a limited color capability using a special four-color ribbon, and an optional AppleTalk network connection for sharing the printer among two or more users. More recently, Apple introduced the ImageWriter LQ (for "letter quality"), with 50% higher dot resolution (216 dots per inch, up from 144) and even nicer paper handling capabilities.

The LaserWriter, too, has undergone significant enhancement since the original model. First came the LaserWriter Plus, with more ROM capacity and a wider selection of built-in fonts, 35 instead of the original 11. Then, in 1988, the LaserWriter II line was announced, with three different models in a range of prices and performance characteristics. The second of the three, the LaserWriter II–NT, is roughly comparable to the earlier LaserWriter Plus, but with an updated, faster version of the PostScript interpreter and an expanded RAM capacity of 2 megabytes (increased from 1.5) for page imaging and font storage. At the high end of the line is the LaserWriter II–NTX, with a speedier 68020 processor (along with a separate 68881 math coprocessor for floating-point computations), an expandable RAM capacity of up to 12 megabytes, and an optional hard-disk connection for even more font storage. Finally, at the bottom of the line, there is the LaserWriter II–SC, a hybrid machine that offers the same xerographic laser technology but without a PostScript interpreter. This makes the SC more like a high-resolution, high-quality ImageWriter than a low-end LaserWriter, without PostScript's font scaling and other powerful features.

Lately a number of competing laser printers have begun coming on the market from other manufacturers. Since they all use PostScript as their page description language, everything we say in this chapter about the LaserWriter applies to these other models as well. In general, we will use the name LaserWriter throughout the chapter to refer generically to all PostScript-based printers, and ImageWriter to refer to those that don't use PostScript (including the low-end LaserWriter II–SC).

The Printer Resource File

The Toolbox printing facilities are cleverly designed to shield your program from the details of any particular printer. You can be running a $500 ImageWriter, a $5000 LaserWriter, or a $50,000 phototypesetter. It can be a vintage original, one of the newer models, or any other type of printer that may come along in the future, either from Apple or from another supplier. It may accept page images expressed in control characters and escape sequences that no other device understands, or in a device-independent page-description language like PostScript, or in some other form yet to be invented. It can be plugged directly into the Macintosh or connected remotely over a network. The user can even change printers "behind your back," in the middle of your program, with the Chooser desk accessory. None of these factors make any difference from your program's point of view. You always perform your printing operations in exactly the same standard way, letting the Toolbox make the necessary adjustments for whatever printer you happen to be talking to.

How does the Toolbox manage this remarkable feat of versatility? You can probably guess the answer by now: by factoring out the specialized code for each printer and storing it separately as a resource. The secret truth about the Toolbox printing routines is that there aren't any: there's no "there" there. The code for all the standard printing operations is kept in a *printer resource file*, different for each printer, that resides in the system folder on the user's startup disk. The Toolbox printing routines that you call from your program are just empty shells that load and execute the actual code from the current printer resource file (see Figure 4–1).

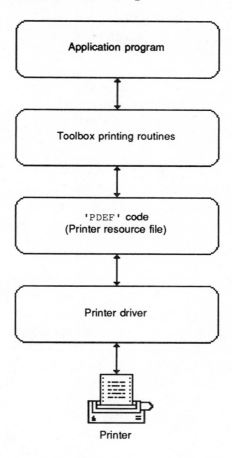

Figure 4–1 Printing code hierarchy

The printer resource file [4.6.3] normally has the same name as the type of printer it supports, such as ImageWriter or Laser-Writer or AppleTalk ImageWriter. Its file type [I:7.3.1] is either 'PRES' ("printer resource"), for printers connected directly to the Macintosh, or 'PRER' ("printer resource, remote"), for those that are accessed over a network. To distinguish among resource files belonging to different types of printer, each one carries a unique creator signature [I:7.3.1], such as 'IWRT' for ImageWriter or 'LWRT' for LaserWriter.

A printer resource file typically includes the following resources:

- a low-level device driver for communicating with this printer (resource type 'DRVR' [3.3.1])

- the executable code for the high-level printing routines, contained in a series of 'PDEF' ("printer definition") resources [4.6.2]

- a *print record* (resource type 'PREC' [4.6.1]) giving the standard settings and characteristics for this type of printer—we'll be learning about print records later in this chapter

- another print record containing the specific settings used in the last printing operation

- dialog templates ('DLOG' [II:7.6.2]) and their associated item lists ('DITL' [II:7.6.3]) for use with the Page Setup... and Print... commands

- a string resource ('STR ' [I:8.4.2]) giving the name of the temporary *spool file* in which output is to be saved before being sent to the printer—again, we'll learn more about spool files later

- any additional resources (dialogs, alerts, strings, icons, and so forth) that the printing routines need in order to operate

There's also usually a set of Finder resources (autograph, bundle, file references, icon lists) just like those we learned about for executable application files in Volume One, Chapter 7. The Finder uses these to install the printer resource file in its disk's desktop file and to display it with a distinctive icon on the screen.

Before attempting any printing-related operation, you must open the printer resource file by calling the initialization routine PrOpen [4.2.1]. (This also reads in the printer driver from the file and opens it for use.) The call to PrOpen must be preceded by the usual litany of other initialization calls: InitGraf [I:4.3.1], InitFonts [I:8.2.4], InitWindows [II:3.2.1], InitMenus [II:4.2.1], TEInit [II:5.2.1], and InitDialogs [II:7.2.1], in precisely that order. When you're all through printing, PrClose [4.2.1] closes the printer resource file and releases its resource map from memory.

Installing a Printer

The user configures the system for a particular printer by selecting its resource file with the Chooser desk accessory. The Chooser looks in the system folder for all files of type 'PRES' or 'PRER' and displays their icons on the screen, allowing the user to select one with the mouse. Then it stores the name of the selected file into the System file as an 'STR ' resource (see Figure 4–2) with an ID number of $E000, or decimal -8192. (Under the conventions we learned earlier [2.5.4], this identifies it as an owned resource belonging to 'PDEF' number 0.) Thereafter, when any of the standard printing routines is called, the Toolbox will locate the 'PDEF' resource containing that routine in the printer resource file, load it in from the disk, and jump to the routine via a jump table at the beginning of the resource body. If the user later changes printers with the Chooser, a different printer resource file will be installed and that printer's 'PDEF' code will be executed instead.

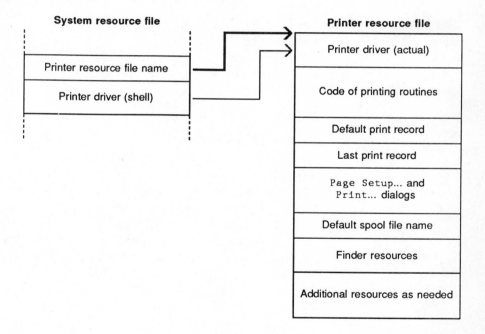

Figure 4–2 Printer resource file

All the Toolbox itself provides is the "glue" code to intercept your printing calls and direct them to the appropriate 'PDEF' resources in the printer resource file. In early versions of the Toolbox, this printing glue was supplied as a separate interface unit, PrLink, which had to be linked into your program after compilation. In more recent systems, the task is handled instead by a new Toolbox trap named _PrGlue, which either resides directly in ROM (version $76 or higher) or is loaded from the System file (version 4.1 or higher) at startup time. The routine definitions in the Pascal Toolbox interface (or the corresponding macros in the assembly-language interface) now generate in-line instructions to push a 4-byte *routine selector* onto the stack, then execute the _PrGlue trap. You'll find the selectors for the various printing routines listed in the "Assembly Language Information" boxes in the reference section; for information on their internal format, see the "Nuts and Bolts" section at the end of this chapter.

> References in this chapter to the "Toolbox printing routines" generally refer to the specialized code taken from the 'PDEF' resources in the printer resource file, rather than to the intermediate glue routines that load and execute them.

The Printer Driver

In addition to the high-level printing routines, the printer resource file also includes a low-level driver for communicating directly with the printer. This specialized driver is normally named .XPrint and has resource ID $E000 (decimal -8192). The main .Print driver in the system resource file (resource ID 2, reference number -3) is only a shell: it simply passes all requests through to the current .XPrint driver, which does the actual work. Changing printers with the Chooser replaces the real driver (.XPrint), while the "pass-along" driver (.Print) remains unaffected.

The Toolbox routines PrDrvrOpen and PrDrvrClose [4.4.1] open and close the printer driver, respectively. The main printing initialization routine, PrOpen [4.2.1], opens the driver for you automatically, so you needn't ordinarily call PrDrvrOpen yourself. However, the finalization routine PrClose [4.2.1] *doesn't* automatically close the driver: it remains open until your program terminates, ready to use again if needed. If for some reason you need to close the driver while your program is still running, you must do it yourself with an explicit call to PrDrvrClose.

Once the driver is open, you can communicate with it directly via the standard driver operations we learned about in the last chapter [3.2]. The Toolbox printing interface also includes a set of low-level routines [4.4] for working specifically with the printer driver. These include a variety of specialized operations implemented via driver Control calls, such as bit-map printing [4.4.4], direct streaming of "raw" text characters [4.4.5], and screen-dump printing, either of single windows or of the entire display screen [4.4.6]. However, not all of these operations are available on all printers, and in general they're no longer necessary or useful. Apple still supports the low-level printing routines for compatibility, but now officially discourages their continued use: newly developed application programs are advised to stick to the high-level printing interface, which we'll be discussing in the rest of this chapter. Since the `'PDEF'` resources containing the high-level printing code get changed at the same time a new driver is installed, programs that use only the high-level interface need never even be aware of what driver they're talking to.

Imaging and Printing

In principle, putting marks on paper is no different from putting them on the screen. You simply draw whatever you want printed, using the old familiar QuickDraw graphics routines that we learned about in Volume One. This is called *imaging* your document. The difference between drawing a document on the screen and imaging it for printing lies in the graphics port that you do your drawing in.

Printing Ports

When you open a document for printing, the Toolbox gives you back a special-purpose graphics port called a *printing port* [4.1.1]. In place of the standard bottleneck routines for screen drawing, the printing port has a set of customized bottlenecks that convert your Quick-Draw calls into the equivalent operations on the printer. The same drawing operations produce the same results on the screen or on paper, depending on which type of port is current at the time. What you draw is what you get.

You obtain a printing port to work with by calling the Toolbox routine `PrOpenDoc` [4.3.1]. Just as when you open a window with `OpenWindow` [II:3.2.2], you have the option of supplying your own storage for the new port (from the stack, for example) via the routine's `printPort` parameter. If you pass `NIL` for this parameter, the Toolbox will allocate the storage for you automatically from the heap. (Like all other data structures based on graphics ports, the printing port is a nonrelocatable object and is referenced by a simple pointer instead of a handle.) Similarly, you can supply your own 522-byte output buffer or have the Toolbox allocate it automatically.

You'll notice in the reference sections that the names the Toolbox uses for printing-related objects have a characteristic flavor all their own: for instance, the record type representing a printing port [4.1.1] is named `TPrPort`, and a pointer to it is a `TPPrPort`. The Apple programmer who first designed the printing code was a devotee of a particular naming style, sometimes called "Hungarian notation" for the nationality of the software engineer who popularized it.

This system uses standard prefixes to indicate the nature of the object being named. In the name `TPPrPort`, for example, the `T` stands for "type," the `P` for "pointer," and the `Pr` for "printing." (The names of most of the Toolbox printing routines begin with this same `Pr` prefix.) Other such prefixes that you'll encounter in the printing definitions include `B` for "byte," `W` for "word," `I` for "integer," `L` for "long integer," `H` for "handle," `F` for "flag" (denoting a Boolean value), and `R` for "rectangle." (Under the capitalization conventions we're using in this book, these will sometimes appear in lower- rather than uppercase.) Although the Hungarian names may look a bit peculiar at first, you'll find they do make sense once you get the hang of them.

The printing port's bottleneck routines can be customized for either of two different printing methods:

- In *draft printing*, imaging and printing take place at the same time. The results of your drawing operations are sent directly to the printer and printed immediately.

- In *spool printing*, imaging and printing are two distinct stages. The page images you draw are saved in a temporary, intermediate form and later sent to the printer in a separate operation.

Not all printers offer both options. Where both are available, the user generally chooses between them by clicking a checkbox or radio button in a dialog box. A well-written application program should be prepared to handle either method.

To accommodate the special needs or properties of a particular type of printer, the Toolbox provides for two extra, printer-dependent printing methods in addition to the standard draft and spool. The code needed to implement such device-specific methods resides in the printer resource file in 'PDEF' resources number 2 and 3, respectively. No existing printer uses this capability at present, but the option is there in case it's ever needed.

Draft Printing

As the name suggests, draft printing was originally intended for producing quick, rough copies of text documents, without much concern for detailed formatting or accurate visual representation. On the ImageWriter, it simply transmits a stream of "raw" text and control characters. The results are fast (up to 250 characters per minute on some models), but not terribly elegant. The ImageWriter printing routines attempt to render the document as faithfully as possible, using the printer's own built-in character fonts and formatting capabilities; but the result is still only a crude approximation to what the user sees on the screen.

At one time, draft printing on the ImageWriter was limited to text only; if you wanted to include bit-map graphics, you had to use the spool printing method instead. More recently, a capability has been added for printing bit maps in draft mode. It uses a new printing routine named PrGeneral, which covers a variety of miscellaneous, advanced printing operations. If you're interested in using this technique, you can find the details in *Inside Macintosh*, Volume V, or in Macintosh Technical Note #128. In any case, because draft printing is done "on the fly," in a single pass down the page, no backing up or reverse paper motion is allowed. That is, the elements of the page image must be drawn strictly in order, from left to right and from top to bottom.

On the LaserWriter, *all* printing takes place in draft mode; there's no such thing as spooling. The bottleneck routines in the LaserWriter's printing port convert your drawing operations into the equivalent PostScript commands and send them directly to the printer. This means there are no restrictions on mixing text and graphics freely within the same page. However, certain QuickDraw operations are not available on the LaserWriter. These include all shape-drawing operations that invert pixels (`InvertRect` [I:5.3.2], `InvertOval` [I:5.3.4], and so forth); the inverting transfer modes `SrcXOr`, `NotSrcXOr`, `PatXOr`, and `NotPatXOr` [I:5.1.3]; and all drawing operations involving regions [I:5.3.7]. All clipping regions are restricted to rectangles only. On the other hand, the LaserWriter offers a number of extra features beyond those ordinarily available in QuickDraw, such as rotated text, dashed lines, and curve smoothing. See Tech Notes #72 and #91 for more information on LaserWriter limitations and techniques.

Spool Printing

The spool method of printing takes place in two stages. In the *spooling* phase, you image your document with QuickDraw operations, just as in draft printing. But instead of being printed immediately, the results are simply stored away (spooled) in some temporary, encoded form. Later, in the *spool printing* phase, this intermediate representation is read back in and sent to the printer.

Notice that the term *spooling* refers specifically to the first stage, in which the document is imaged and saved for later printing. *Spool printing*, however, is used both in a broad sense, to refer to the entire two-stage process, and also more narrowly, to refer to the second stage only. Any confusion you may experience as a result of this dual terminology is perfectly natural, and no cause for undue alarm.

Typically a document's intermediate representation is saved in a *spool file* on the disk, although it could conceivably be held in memory instead. On the ImageWriter, the spool file simply contains a QuickDraw picture [I:5.4.1] for each page of the document. (As we mentioned in the preceding section, spool printing is not defined on the LaserWriter.) During the imaging phase, the printing port's bottleneck routines capture your QuickDraw calls and record them in the picture. In the printing phase, the picture is "played back" and the results are sent to the printer; then the spool file is deleted from the disk.

The spool file's file type is 'PFIL' ("printing file") and its creator is 'PSYS' ("printing system"). Although other printers may choose to implement spooling in some other way, the idea of a spool file containing a picture is so central to the Toolbox printing model that the routine for performing the second stage of spool printing is named PrPicFile [4.3.3]. After you finish imaging a document, you should check to see what printing method is in use and call this routine, if necessary, to complete the spool printing process. Later on, we'll see how our MiniEdit program handles this chore.

In the standard ImageWriter printing dialog (Figure 4–6), both the Best and Faster options specify spool printing. The difference between the two lies in the choice of resolutions and fonts for printing text. The Faster option uses the ImageWriter in its low-resolution mode, 72 dots per inch. Since this just matches the screen's own resolution, the same fonts in which text is displayed on the screen can be used on the printer as well.

The Best option, on the other hand, makes full use of the printer's highest available resolution. On the ImageWriter I and II, this means 144 dots per inch, or double the screen resolution; so the Toolbox looks for a font with twice the point size of the text being printed (18 points for 9-point text, 24 for 12-point text, and so on). Using such a font at double resolution effectively scales it back down to the required size, but yields a higher print quality, with less noticeable "jaggies." The ImageWriter LQ, with its 216-dot-per-inch resolution, uses the same technique with a font triple the nominal text size; and the non-PostScript LaserWriter II–SC, at 300 dots per inch, looks for a quadruple-size font. In any case, if the needed multiple-size font is not available, the ordinary screen font is simply scaled up to two, three, or four times its normal size; this produces the same results as printing at low resolution with the Faster option.

Print Records

Most of the Toolbox printing routines accept a *print record* as a parameter. This is the basic data structure that summarizes all the characteristics of a particular printing job. It includes such things as the type of printer being used, its horizontal and vertical resolution in dots per inch, the dimensions of the paper, the printing method chosen, the name of the spool file (if any), the range of pages and number of copies to be printed, and much more. As a rule, all of this information is filled in for you, either by the Toolbox itself or by the user via on-screen dialogs; with few exceptions, you don't normally store into the fields of the print record yourself.

A print record is a relocatable object of type TPrint [4.1.2], referred to by a handle of type THPrint. It has a standard size of 120 bytes, although at present only 82 of those are actually used; the remaining 38 bytes are reserved for future expansion. To keep the record's type definition down to readable proportions, its contents are broken up into a series of separately defined subrecords [4.1.3–4.1.6]. This is purely a notational convenience, however, since the subrecords are directly embedded within the main print record rather than referenced indirectly with pointers or handles. At the underlying machine level, it's just a single, 120-byte object.

The Printer Information Subrecord

The *printer information subrecord* [4.1.3] holds information on the characteristics of the printer itself. There are actually two subrecords of this same type in each print record. The public one, prInfo, is the one you should use to find the properties of the currently installed printer. The other, prInfoPT, is a private *print-time information subrecord*, used internally by the Toolbox itself.

The first field of the subrecord, iDev, is a QuickDraw device code [I:8.3.1] that the Toolbox uses in selecting fonts for printing text. Officially, the first byte of the device code is supposed to give the driver reference number (normally $FD, or -3, for the standard .Print driver), while the second byte contains modifying information whose meaning varies from one printer to another. In reality, however, some printers play sneaky tricks with this field, such as setting it to 0 to make QuickDraw think they're really the screen instead of a peripheral device. Such shenanigans are strictly between the printer and the Toolbox; never assume you know what the contents of iDev really mean.

The dimensions of the page you're printing on are defined by a pair of related rectangles, the *paper rectangle* and the *page rectangle* (Figure 4–3). Both are expressed in device-dependent printer dots; the fields iVRes and iHRes give the number of dots per inch in the vertical and horizontal directions, respectively. The paper rectangle represents the overall, physical sheet of paper, while the page rectangle defines the printable area only, excluding any margin around the edges that the print head can't reach because of physical or mechanical limitations. Just to keep things entertaining, the page rectangle (rPage) is included in the printer information subrecord, while the paper rectangle (rPaper) is a separate field of the top-level print record [4.1.2]. Presumably there is a reason for this.

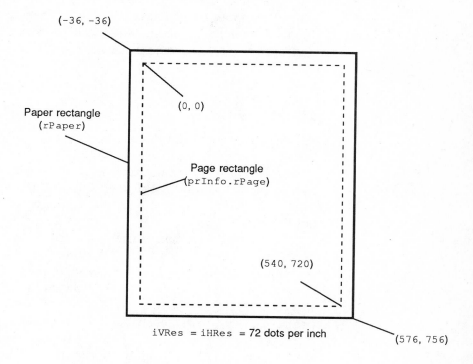

Figure 4–3 Paper and page rectangles

When you open a printing port, the page rectangle taken from the print record also becomes the port's port rectangle and clipping region. The top-left corner of this rectangle always has coordinates (0, 0), and establishes a coordinate system for the printed page. The paper rectangle is also expressed in this same coordinate system, but since it includes the unreachable areas around the edges of the paper, it is normally larger than the page rectangle in all dimensions. In particular, its top-left corner ordinarily has negative coordinates. The coordinates shown in the figure represent the paper and page rectangles for a standard sheet of 8½-by-11-inch letter paper, with a ½-inch margin at all four edges, on a printer with a resolution of 72 dots per inch both horizontally and vertically. (Note that these are just fictitious measurements, and don't correspond to those actually used on the ImageWriter, LaserWriter, or any other known printer.)

> The paper rectangle is intended only as a general guide to the approximate position of the printed page relative to the physical sheet of paper. On most printers, the physical alignment of the paper is inexact and can vary to some extent.

The Style Subrecord

The *style subrecord* [4.1.4] describes the way the printer is to be used for a particular printing job, as distinct from its inherent characteristics. The contents of this subrecord are normally set by the Toolbox as a result of dialogs with the user. In general, they're intended for the private use of the Toolbox itself, and are of no interest to the application program.

The main exception is the wDev field, which identifies the type of printer you're working with. The first byte of this field is an integer code denoting the specific printer type; the second byte holds device-dependent modifiers and flags. The contents of this second byte are shown in [4.1.4] for the ImageWriter I and II only. (For all other Apple printers, they are a closely guarded industrial secret and are not disclosed to the Rest Of Us.) There are bits to select the ImageWriter's dot resolution (72 or 144 dots per inch), the page orientation (tall, also known as *portrait* orientation, or wide, also called *landscape*), and the magnification factor (normal or reduced 50%).

The remaining flag bit controls the shape of the dots making up the printed image. In normal operation, the ImageWriter spaces the dots closer together horizontally than vertically: 80 or 160 per inch instead of 72 or 144. This produces rectangular dots, taller than they are wide, instead of square ones like those on the Macintosh screen. As a result, everything you print comes out looking taller and skinnier on paper than on the screen. (The effect is especially noticeable with graphics, but text characters are also affected in the same way.) Bit 2 of the ImageWriter's wDev field alters the speed of the print head so that the dot resolution is the same horizontally and vertically, yielding square dots that more closely match what appears on the screen. Some programs—particularly graphics editors like

MacPaint—set this flag automatically; others give the user a choice via the `Tall Adjusted` option in the `Page Setup...` dialog box (see Figure 4–5).

> Don't confuse the `wDev` field of the style subrecord with the `iDev` field of the printer information subrecord, described in the preceding section. `iDev` is a QuickDraw device code, used in font selection; `wDev` is a more general code identifying the type of printer and the way it's being used. If you need to know what kind of printer you're talking to, the high-order byte of `wDev` is the place to look.

The fields `iPageV` and `iPageH` give the height and width of the paper you're printing on, in fixed units of $1/120$ of an inch. (Notice that these are the dimensions of the physical paper rectangle, not just the printable page rectangle; they really should be named `iPaperV` and `iPaperH` instead of `iPageV` and `iPageH`.) These measurements are the same as in the print record's `rPaper` field, but expressed in device-independent units that don't vary with the printer's resolution. The number of units per inch (`120`) is defined in the Pascal interface as a constant named `IPrPgFract`.

The remaining fields of the style subrecord are claimed by the Toolbox as private property—trespassers not welcome. These fields are not officially documented or supported, and Apple reserves the right to change them without notice. The information given in our reference section [4.1.4] is strictly unofficial and extracurricular, and you should never ever write code that relies on it. You have been warned.

The Job Subrecord

The *job subrecord* [4.1.5] contains information that applies to this particular printing job only. It includes the printing method to be used (draft or spool), the range of pages to be printed, the number of copies, and the name of the spool file, if any. Most of this information is supplied by the user via a dialog box.

The printing method is specified by a 1-byte code in the `bJDocLoop` field. A value of 0 (`BDraftLoop`) stands for draft printing, 1 (`BSpoolLoop`) for spool printing. (Two additional codes,

`BUser1Loop` and `BUser2Loop`, are reserved for the optional, printer-specific printing methods.) Your program can examine this field to find out which method the user has chosen and respond accordingly.

The fields `iFstPage` and `iLstPage` designate the first and last pages to be printed. As you image your document, the Toolbox counts the pages and doesn't actually begin printing until it reaches the number specified by `iFstPage`; after it finishes `iLstPage`, it stops printing and suppresses the rest. The first page you image is always considered to be number 1, regardless of any other numbering scheme your program itself may be using. For instance, suppose you're printing a file representing a chapter of a book, and the chapter begins on page 137. Even though the first page of the chapter may carry a visible page number (a *folio*, as typographers call it) of 137, the Toolbox will still count it as page 1 of your document. If the user asks to print pages 142 through 151, you'll have to adjust those values to 6 through 15 for the Toolbox's benefit.

Notice also that for the pages to be counted correctly, you must go through the motions of imaging every page in the document, letting the Toolbox decide which ones to print and which to suppress. If you know where to find your own page breaks, you can save some time by imaging only the pages the user has actually requested. For example, if the user specifies pages 4 to 9, you can skip straight to the top of page 4 and not bother imaging the first three pages. Remember, though, that the Toolbox counts only those pages that you actually image. In this case, the first page you image (which is really the fourth page of your document) will look to the Toolbox like page 1. So to make sure the right pages get printed, you'll have to adjust the page range in the print record to run from 1 to 6 instead of 4 to 9.

Similar considerations apply to the `iCopies` field, which tells how many copies to print. In spool printing, you simply image your document once, no matter how many copies the user may have asked for. When you later send the resulting spool file to the printer, the Toolbox looks in the print record's `iCopies` field and automatically prints the requested number of hard copies. In draft mode, however, the situation is different. Since imaging and printing are inseparable, it's up to you to check the value of `iCopies` and explicitly image your document that many times. Thus your imaging code might look something like this:

```
with ThePrintRec.prJob do
   if bJDocLoop = BDraftLoop then
      numCopies := iCopies
   else
      numCopies := 1;

for copyCount := 1 to numCopies do
   {Image the document}
```

> The foregoing remarks don't apply to the LaserWriter or other PostScript-based printers. Even though such printers always operate in draft mode, you only need to image your document once. Your drawing operations will be converted into equivalent PostScript commands and sent to the printer, along with additional instructions telling it how many copies to print. Multiple imaging in draft mode is necessary only on non-PostScript printers like the ImageWriter.

If `bJDocLoop` specifies spool printing, the fields `iFileVol` and `pFileName` give the spool file's volume (or directory) reference number and its file name. Ordinarily these fields are set to `0` and `NIL`, respectively, designating the current volume or folder and the standard file name, `Print File`. There's also a field named `bFileVers` for the spool file's version number, but this is no longer used and should always be `0`.

One last important field in the job subrecord is `pIdleProc`, which holds a pointer to an optional *background procedure*. If a background procedure is present, the Toolbox will call it repeatedly to fill the idle time while waiting for the printer to complete a printing operation. Background procedures are useful for a variety of purposes, such as displaying progress reports on the screen or allowing the user to continue working while concurrently printing a document. We'll be talking about them in more detail later in this chapter under "Printing the Spool File."

The Auxiliary Information Subrecord

The *auxiliary information subrecord* [4.1.6] is used entirely by the Toolbox for its own private purposes. Once again, its exact contents and use may vary from one printer to another, and are subject to change without notice. The information given here is purely for your background understanding, and applies to non-PostScript printers only. It is not guaranteed to remain correct in the future; it may even be wrong by the time you read it!

To save space when printing a spool file, the Toolbox divides the page up into *bands* of a more manageable size. Then it repeatedly redraws the entire page, using the printing port's clipping region to confine the actual drawing to one band at a time. (Without this technique, a single 8½-by-11-inch page image at the ImageWriter's maximum resolution would take up more than a quarter of a megabyte, or twice the total memory capacity of the original Skinny Mac. The ImageWriter LQ, with its 216-dot resolution, would need more than twice again as much space, or over half a megabyte; and at the 300-dot resolution of a LaserWriter II–SC, the page image would weigh in at more than a megabyte!)

The auxiliary information subrecord has fields [4.1.6] giving the number of bands per page, the height and width of each band in dots, the number of bytes of memory needed to hold the band image, and the row width of its bit map [I:4.2.1]. Other fields contain information needed for specific text and graphical operations, such as underlining and pattern scaling. Finally, there's a field that specifies the *scan direction* for breaking the page up into bands.

There are four possible scan directions, depending on which way the page image is oriented relative to the physical sheet of paper (see Figure 4–4). In *portrait orientation*, the image is positioned upright, with the long dimension of the paper running vertically. It's normally scanned from top to bottom, so that it comes out of the printer right-side-up, but it can also be done from bottom to top and come out upside-down. In *landscape orientation*, the long dimension of the paper runs horizontally; the image can be scanned from left to right or from right to left.

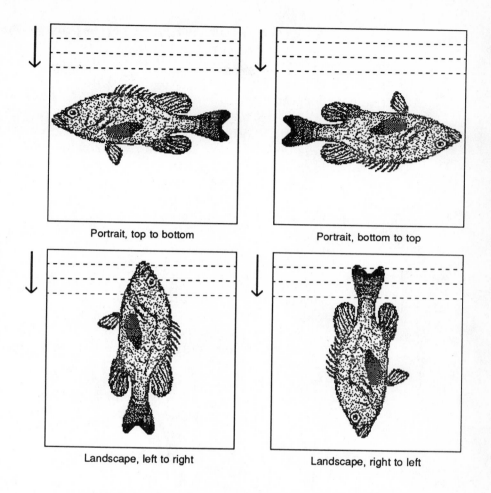

Figure 4–4 Page orientations and scan directions

Initializing Print Records

Surprisingly, there isn't any Toolbox routine for creating a new print record. You simply call NewHandle [I:3.2.1] to allocate a block of the appropriate size, then pass it to the printing routine PrintDefault [4.2.2] to be initialized:

```
rawHandle    := NewHandle (SIZEOF(TPrint));
printHandle := THPrint(rawHandle);
PrintDefault (printHandle)
```

`PrintDefault` fills in the fields of the print record with the standard values for the current printer, which it gets from a template resource (`'PREC'` number 0 [4.6.1]) in the printer resource file.

In our `MiniEdit` program, we'll maintain a separate print record for each window on the screen. We'll have to add a new field, `printRec`, to the window data record (Program II:5–1) where we keep our auxiliary data for each window. Whenever we open a new window, our `DoNew` routine (Program II:5–2) will create and initialize a new print record, using statements similar to those shown above, and store its handle into this field. (You can find the updated version of `DoNew` in the complete `MiniEdit` listing in Appendix H.) We also have to add a couple of lines to our `CloseAppWindow` routine (Program II:7–2) to dispose of the print record when we close a window.

To hold a handle to the active window's print record, we'll define a new global variable, `ThePrintRec`; this is analogous to the existing variables `TheWindow`, `TheScrollBar`, and `TheText`, which keep track of the active window record, scroll bar, and edit record. Our one-time `Initialize` routine (Program II:2–6) will set `ThePrintRec` to `NIL`. (We also have to remember to call `PrOpen` [4.2.1] at initialization time and `PrClose` at the very end, before returning to the Finder.) Then, each time the active window changes, we'll add an appropriate statement to update `ThePrintRec` along with the other global pointers and handles. You'll find such statements in Appendix H in the routines `DoNew`, `ActWindow`, and `DeactWindow`.

Saving Print Records

Whenever a program writes out a document file to the disk, it's recommended practice to include a print record in the document's resource fork. This allows the settings the user specified in the last printing dialog to "stick to the document," so that the same settings can be used again the next time the document is read in and printed. Problems can arise, however, if a different printer is current when the document is read back in, or if the printer resource file has been updated to a newer version in the meantime. The contents of the old print record may no longer be valid in the new printing environment.

To avoid this problem, the Toolbox function `PrValidate` [4.2.2] checks a print record for compatibility with the currently installed printer and its resource file. Every print record begins with a field named `iPrVersion` [4.1.2], which identifies the version number of the printing software that initialized the record. (In each release of the

Toolbox printing interface, the constant `IPrRelease` [4.1.2] gives the current version number; at the time of writing, its value is 3.) `PrValidate` examines this version number, as well as the printer type code in field `wDev` of the style subrecord [4.1.4]. If they don't match the current printer and software, `PrValidate` reinitializes the print record and notifies you by returning a Boolean result of TRUE; if the record is already valid, `PrValidate` just leaves it alone and returns FALSE. (`PrValidate` may also make minor adjustments in the record's contents for internal self-consistency, but it doesn't bother to inform you of these.)

Since `MiniEdit` operates entirely on plain text files and doesn't create any document files of its own, it doesn't save a copy of a document's print record when writing the document out to a file. Ordinarily, though, we would want to include something like the following in our `WriteFile` routine (Program II:8–3) to save the print record in the file's resource fork:

```
GetWTitle (TheWindow, docName);
rsrcHandle := Handle(ThePrintRec);

saveRsrcFile := CurResFile;
   docRsrcFile := OpenResFile (docName);
      AddResource (rsrcHandle, 'PREC', 100, '');
   CloseResFile (docRsrcFile);
UseResFile (saveRsrcFile)
```

Then in `DoRevert` (Program II:8–4), the routine that reads a file back in from the disk, we could retrieve the saved print record with something like

```
saveRsrcFile := CurResFile;
   docRsrcFile := OpenResFile (docName);
      rsrcHandle := Get1Resource ('PREC', 100);
   CloseResFile (docRsrcFile);
UseResFile (saveRsrcFile);

printRec     := THPrint(rsrcHandle);
ThePrintRec := printRec;
PrValidate (ThePrintRec)
```

Printing-Related Dialogs

The Macintosh User Interface Guidelines call for two standard printing-related commands to be included on a program's `File` menu. The `Page Setup...` command presents the user with a dialog box in which to specify various characteristics of the document to be printed, such as the paper size and orientation. The `Print...` command actually initiates the printing process, after requesting information via a dialog about what printing method to use, which pages to print, how many copies, and so forth.

Originally, the dialogs presented by these two commands were intended to gather information for the print record's style [4.1.4] and job [4.1.5] subrecords, respectively. In practice the correspondence is not quite so neat, but the two dialogs are still referred to as the *style dialog* and the *job dialog*. Their exact content and appearance vary from one printer to another, and are defined by template resources in the printer resource file. Figures 4–5 and 4–6 show the standard dialogs for the ImageWriter, and Figures 4–7 and 4–8 for the Laser-Writer.

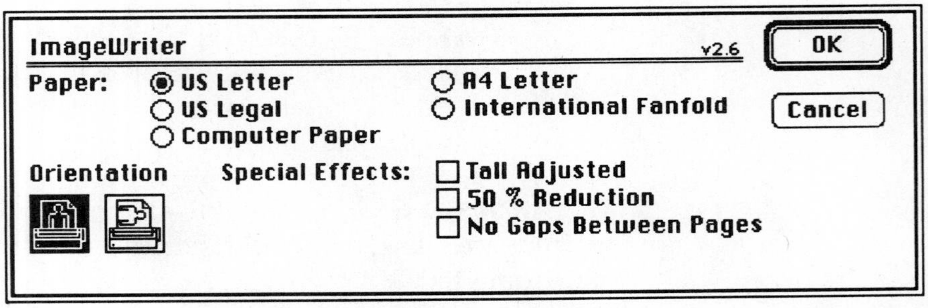

Figure 4–5 ImageWriter style dialog

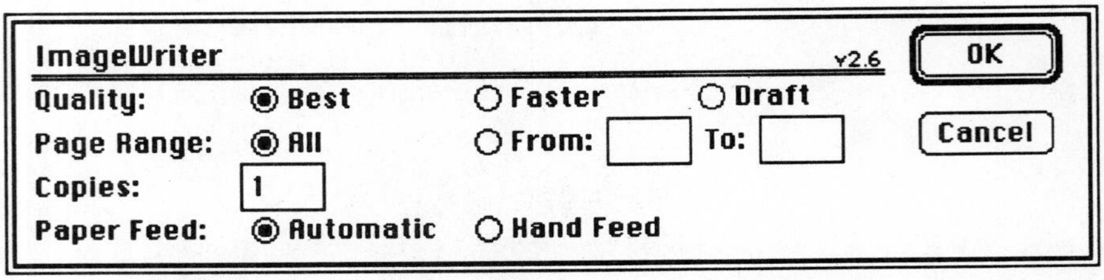

Figure 4–6 ImageWriter job dialog

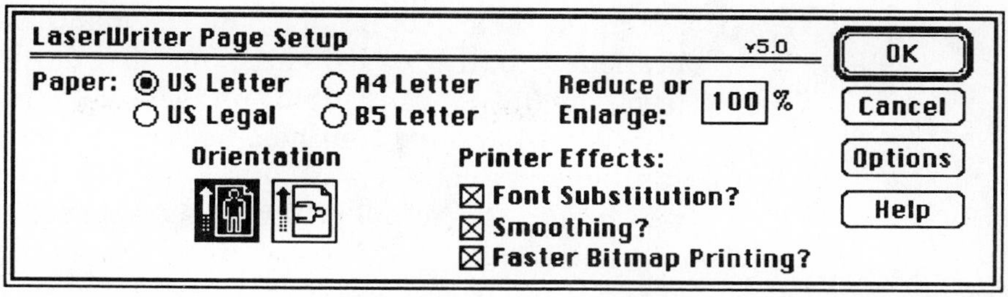

Figure 4–7 LaserWriter style dialog

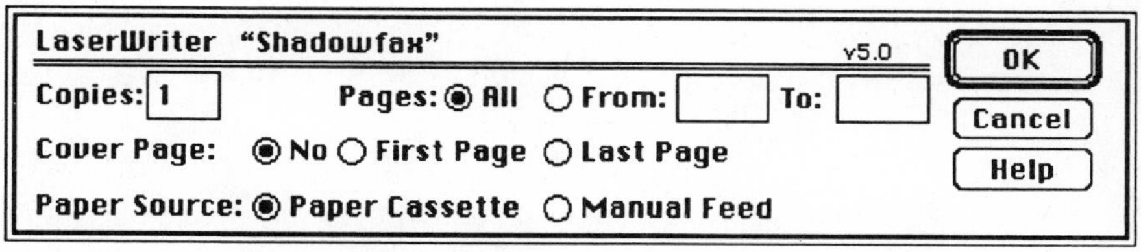

Figure 4–8 LaserWriter job dialog

If you don't like the standard style and job dialogs, you can customize them to suit yourself. The techniques for doing this are discussed at the end of the chapter, in our "Nuts and Bolts" section.

The routines `PrStlDialog` and `PrJobDialog` [4.2.3] display the current printer's standard dialogs on the screen and handle all interactions with the user. If the user confirms the dialog—by clicking the `OK` button—pressing Return or Enter, or some similar action, both routines update the contents of the print record and return `TRUE` as their function result. (They also automatically call `PrValidate` [4.2.2] to check the record for validity with the current printer and printing software.) If the user cancels the dialog, they leave the print record unchanged and return `FALSE`.

To add the `Page Setup...` and `Print...` commands to `MiniEdit`, we begin by modifying our `File` menu (using a resource editor such as `ResEdit`) to include the new commands. After defining a pair of new global constants, `SetupItem` and `PrintItem`, to represent their item numbers on the menu, we add the appropriate branches to the `case` statement in our `DoFileChoice` routine (Program II:4–8), dispatching on these item numbers to a pair of new command-handling routines, `DoSetup` and `DoPrint`. The `DoSetup` routine is straightforward, and is shown in Program 4–1; `DoPrint`, which does the actual printing, is discussed in the next section.

Program 4–1 Handle `Page Setup...` command

```
{ Global variable }

var
    ThePrintRec : THPrint;                         {Handle to active window's print record [4.1.2]}


procedure DoSetup;

    { Handle Page Setup... command. }

    var
        confirmed : BOOLEAN;                       {Did user click OK button?}

    begin {DoSetup}

        InitCursor;                                {Set arrow cursor [II:2.5.2]}
        confirmed := PrStlDialog (ThePrintRec)     {Present style dialog [4.2.3]}

    end;  {DoSetup}
```

There really isn't much for our `DoSetup` routine to do. After making sure the cursor is set to the standard arrow shape, we simply call the Toolbox printing routine `PrStlDialog` [4.2.3] to conduct a style dialog with the user and update the active window's print record as needed. It makes no difference whether the user confirms or cancels the dialog, since `PrStlDialog` will do the right thing in either case; so we just ignore the Boolean result it returns.

Document Printing

When the user chooses the `Print...` menu command, your program should call `PrJobDialog` [4.2.3] to present the standard job dialog on the screen. If the dialog is confirmed (that is, if `PrJobDialog` returns TRUE), you should then proceed to print the document displayed in the currently active window. Document printing consists of the following steps:

1. Open the document with `PrOpenDoc` [4.3.1], obtaining a printing port [4.1.1] to draw in. The new printing port automatically becomes the current port, and will receive all further drawing operations.

2. For each page of the document
   a. Open the page with `PrOpenPage` [4.3.2].
   b. Draw the contents of the page with QuickDraw operations.
   c. Close the page with `PrClosePage` [4.3.2].

3. Close the document with `PrCloseDoc` [4.3.1].

4. If the chosen printing method is spool printing, call `PrPicFile` [4.3.3] to read back the spooled document and send it to the printer.

Program 4–2 (`DoPrint`) shows a simplified version of `MiniEdit`'s routine for responding to the `Print...` command. The actual code is a bit more complicated, but in principle it's no different from the version shown here. The main reason for the added complexity is that we also want to display a dialog box on the screen while printing, to report on the status of the printing operation and give the user a chance to suspend or cancel it in progress. So we'll come back to the final version of `DoPrint` later, in our section on "Displaying a Status Dialog."

Program 4–2 Handle `Print...` command

```
{ Global variables }

var
    TheWindow    : WindowPtr;          {Pointer to currently active window [II:3.1.1]}
    ThePrintRec  : THPrint;            {Handle to active window's print record [4.1.2]}
    ThePrintPort : TPPrPort;           {Pointer to printing port [4.1.1]}

procedure DoPrint;

    { Handle Print... command. }

    var
        confirmed  : BOOLEAN;          {Did user click OK button?}
        numCopies  : INTEGER;          {Number of times to image document}
        copyCount  : INTEGER;          {Counter for imaging document}
```

Program 4–2 Handle `Print... command` *(continued)*

```
begin {DoPrint}

    confirmed := PrJobDialog (ThePrintRec);          {Present job dialog [4.2.3]}
    if not confirmed then EXIT (DoPrint);            {If not confirmed, just exit to main event loop}

    with ThePrintRec^^.prJob do                      {Look in job subrecord [4.1.2]}
        if bJDocLoop = BDraftLoop then               {Draft printing requested? [4.1.5]}
            numCopies := iCopies                     {Image each copy separately [4.1.5]}
        else
            numCopies := 1;                          {Image just once}

    for copyCount := 1 to numCopies do               {Loop on number of copies}
        if PrError = NoErr then                      {Check for errors [4.2.4]}
            begin

                ThePrintPort := PrOpenDoc (ThePrintRec, NIL, NIL); {Open printing port [4.3.1]}
                    for {each page of the document} do           {Loop on pages}
                        if PrError = NoErr then                   {Check for errors [4.2.4]}
                            begin
                                PrOpenPage (ThePrintPort, NIL); {Open the page [4.3.2]}

                                if PrError = NoErr then         {Check for errors [4.2.4]}
                                    {Draw the page};

                                PrClosePage (ThePrintPort)      {Close the page [4.3.2]}
                            end; {if PrError = NoErr}
                    PrCloseDoc (ThePrintPort)                   {Close printing port [4.3.1]}

            end; {if PrError = NoErr}

    SetPort (TheWindow);                             {Restore window as current port [I:4.3.3]}

    with ThePrintRec^^.prJob do                      {Look in job subrecord [4.1.2]}
        if (bJDocLoop = BSpoolLoop) and              {Spool printing? [4.1.5]}
            (PrError = NoErr) then                   {Check for errors [4.2.4]}
            PrPicFile (ThePrintRec, NIL, NIL, NIL, NIL); {Print spool file [4.3.3]}

    IOCheck (PrError);                               {Post error alert, if any [4.2.4, Prog. II:8-1]}
    PrSetError (NoErr)                               {Clear error for next time [4.2.4]}

end; {DoPrint}
```

We begin by presenting the job dialog on the screen with `PrJobDialog` [4.2.3]. If the user dismisses the dialog by canceling rather than confirming it, there's nothing more to do; so we simply skip the rest of the routine and exit back to our main event loop. Assuming the dialog was confirmed, we next look in the print record for the printing method and copy count, to see how many times we have to image the document (as discussed above under "The Job Subrecord"). Then we use a `for` loop to do the imaging the required number of times. After the loop terminates, we must remember to set QuickDraw's current port back to the active window. Finally, if the printing method was spool printing, we call `PrPicFile` [4.3.3] to ship the spool file off to the printer.

One very important point to notice in Program 4–2 is the error handling. After each step of our imaging loop, we carefully check for errors with the Toolbox routine `PrError` [4.2.4]. If all is well, we can proceed normally to the next step; but if we do detect an error, we can't just drop everything and scramble out of the loop. First we have to make sure all of our calls to `PrOpenDoc` and `PrOpenPage` are balanced by the corresponding `PrCloseDoc` and `PrClosePage` calls. Once we've tied up those loose ends, we can safely exit from the imaging loop and pass the error code to our `IOCheck` routine (Program II:8–1), which will post an appropriate message on the screen. Finally, we clear the error with `PrSetError` [4.2.4] so it won't interfere with the next printing operation.

Just to complicate matters further, some error signals are raised by the printing routines as internal signals among themselves, and are cleared automatically when you close the page or document. So you can't assume, just because an error was there a millisecond ago, that it will still be present by the time you get around to dealing with it. Instead of just saving the error code for later processing, you must explicitly call `PrError` again after exiting from your imaging loop, in case the error has evaporated in the meantime.

Imaging the Document

For the sake of readability, `MiniEdit`'s imaging code is divided into two separate routines: `ImagePrep`, which handles the preliminaries, and `ImageDoc`, which does the actual imaging. Instead of calling QuickDraw directly to draw the contents of each page, our strategy is to do it indirectly, via the Toolbox's built-in TextEdit routines. This frees us from all sorts of messy details, such as measuring out text to find the line breaks and repositioning the graphics pen at the start of each new line: TextEdit has already invented all those wheels. All we need to do is create an edit record [II:5.1.1] based on our document's printing port, and TextEdit will draw the text into the printing port for us exactly as if it were being displayed in a window on the screen.

The main responsibility of our `ImagePrep` routine (Program 4–3) is to initialize the printing port and set up the edit record we'll be using to draw text into it. We begin by getting the name of the document we're printing (which is also the title of the active window) and saving it in a global variable, `DocName`; we'll need it later to merge into the text of our status dialog on the screen. Next we copy the window's text characteristics into the printing port, so that the printed document will match the way it appears on the user's screen. (Recall that the QuickDraw routines `TextFont`, `TextSize`, and `TextFace` [I:8.3.2] all implicitly operate on the current port; the printing port became current when our `DoPrint` routine called `PrOpenDoc` [4.3.1].)

Program 4–3 Prepare document for imaging

```
{ Global constants and variables }

const
    PrintMargin = 0.5;                          {Margin around printed page, in inches}

var
    TheWindow     : WindowPtr;                  {Pointer to currently active window [II:3.1.1]}
    ThePrintRec   : THPrint;                    {Handle to active window's print record [4.1.2]}
    TheText       : TEHandle;                   {Handle to active window's edit record [II:5.1.1]}
    TEPrint       : TEHandle;                   {Handle to edit record for printing [II:5.1.1]}
    DocName       : Str255;                     {Name of document being printed [I:8.1.2]}
    PageHeight    : INTEGER;                    {Height of printed page}
    LinesPerPage  : INTEGER;                    {Number of text lines per printed page}
    ThisPage      : INTEGER;                    {Page number of page being printed}
    NextLine      : INTEGER;                    {Line number of next line to be printed}
    Watch         : CursHandle;                 {Handle to wristwatch cursor [II:2.5.1]}
```

Program 4–3 Prepare document for imaging *(continued)*

```
procedure ImagePrep;

   { Prepare document for imaging. }

   var
       hMargin     : INTEGER;                              {Horizontal page margin in printer dots}
       vMargin     : INTEGER;                              {Vertical page margin in printer dots}
       textRect    : Rect;                                 {Boundary of printed page [I:4.1.2]}

   begin {ImagePrep}

       GetWTitle (TheWindow, DocName);                     {Get document name from active window [II:3.2.4]}
       with TheWindow^ do
           begin
               TextFont (txFont);                          {Copy window's text  characteristics to   }
               TextSize (txSize);                          {  current (printing) port [I:8.3.1, I:8.3.2]}
               TextFace (txFace)
           end; {with TheWindow^}

       with ThePrintRec^^.prInfo do                        {Use info subrecord [4.1.2]}
           begin
               hMargin  := ROUND(PrintMargin * iHRes); {Scale page margin by printer's horizontal}
               vMargin  := ROUND(PrintMargin * iVRes); {  and vertical resolution [4.1.3]          }
               textRect := rPage;                          {Start with printer's page rectangle [4.1.3]}
               InsetRect (textRect, hMargin, vMargin)      {Inset by page margins [I:4.4.4]}
           end; {with ThePrintRec^^.prInfo}

       TEPrint := TENew (textRect, textRect);              {Open an edit record [II:5.2.2, 4.1.3]}

       with TEPrint^^, viewRect do                         {Use view rectangle [II:5.1.1]}
           begin

               PageHeight   := bottom - top;               {Find height of text page [I:4.1.2]}
               LinesPerPage := PageHeight div lineHeight; {Find lines per page [II:5.1.1]}
               PageHeight   := LinesPerPage * lineHeight; {Truncate to whole number of lines [II:5.1.1]}
               bottom       := top + PageHeight;           {Get rid of partial line [I:4.1.2]}

               destRect := viewRect;                       {Adjust destination rectangle [II:5.1.1]}

               DisposHandle (hText);                       {Dispose of empty text handle [I:3.2.2]}
               hText    := TheText^^.hText;                {Install text from main edit record [II:5.1.1]}
               teLength := TheText^^.teLength              {Set text length [II:5.1.1]}

           end; {with TEPrint^^, viewRect}
```

Program 4–3 Prepare document for imaging *(continued)*

```
SetCursor (Watch^^);                    {Indicate delay [II:2.5.2]}
    TECalText (TEPrint);                {Wrap text to page [II:5.3.1]}
InitCursor;                             {Restore normal cursor [II:2.5.2]}

ThisPage := 0;                          {Initialize page number}
NextLine := 1                           {Initialize line count}

end;    {ImagePrep}
```

Before creating our edit record for printing, we have to calculate the boundary rectangle it will use for wrapping text. We start with the print record's page rectangle and inset it by a small extra margin, which we've arbitrarily set at half an inch in from each edge. (We define this margin as a global program constant, PrintMargin, so that it can be changed easily.) Since the margin is expressed in inches, we have to scale it by the printer's horizontal and vertical resolution to convert it to device-dependent printer dots. Once we've calculated the text rectangle, we can create the edit record with TENew [II:5.2.2] and store it in the global variable TEPrint. Again, since the printing port is current at this point, the new edit record will automatically be set up to draw into it rather than on the screen.

Next we calculate the height of the page, both in dots and in text lines, and shorten the edit record's clipping (view) rectangle to avoid printing an ugly partial line at the bottom of the page. Then we copy the text handle and text length from the active window's main edit record, TheText, into the new one, TEPrint, that we'll be using for our printing. (Notice that the new edit record will have been given an empty text block to work with at the time it was created. We carefully dispose of this empty block before installing the real one, to avoid cluttering our heap with unrecoverable objects.)

Now we can call the TextEdit routine TECalText [II:5.3.1] to wrap the text to the destination rectangle and calculate the line breaks. Since this can take a while for long documents, we signal the delay by displaying the wristwatch cursor during the operation, then restore the standard arrow shape when it's finished. Finally, we initialize a couple of global variables, ThisPage and NextLine, that we'll be using later in our imaging routine.

The heart of MiniEdit's imaging code is the ImagePage routine (Program 4–4), which images one page of a document. As we'll see later, this routine actually gets called in rather a roundabout way by the code that runs our status dialog. (Figures 4–9 and 4–10 show what the dialog box looks like for draft and spool printing, respectively.) For now we can ignore the details; all we need to know is that `ImagePage` returns a Boolean result telling whether to dismiss the dialog (TRUE) or leave it visible on the screen (FALSE). If the result is TRUE, `ImagePage` also returns an item number via a variable parameter, which will be reported back by the Toolbox as the reason for dismissing the dialog.

Program 4–4 Image one page

```
{ Global constants and variables }

const
    FinishPrint = 3;                                {Item number for document completion}

var
    PrintSuspended : BOOLEAN;                        {Printing temporarily suspended?}
    ThePrintPort   : TPPrPort;                       {Pointer to printing port [4.1.1]}
    TEPrint        : TEHandle;                       {Handle to edit record for printing [II:5.1.1]}
    TheDialog      : DialogPtr;                      {Pointer to printing status dialog [II:7.1.1]}
    DocName        : Str255;                         {Name of document being printed [I:8.1.2]}
    ThisCopy       : INTEGER;                        {Number of copy being printed}
    ThisPage       : INTEGER;                        {Page number of page being printed}
    NextLine       : INTEGER;                        {Line number of next line to be printed}
    LinesPerPage   : INTEGER;                        {Number of text lines per printed page}
    PageHeight     : INTEGER;                        {Height of printed page}


function ImagePage (var itemNumber : INTEGER) : BOOLEAN;

    { Image one page. }

    var
        copyString : Str255;                         {Copy number in string form [I:2.1.1]}
        pageString : Str255;                         {Page number in string form [I:2.1.1]}
        editHandle : Handle;                         {Untyped handle for locking edit record [I:3.1.1]}

    begin {ImagePage}

        if PrintSuspended then                       {Imaging temporarily suspended?}
            begin
                ImagePage := FALSE;                  {Just continue dialog}
                EXIT (ImagePage)                     {Skip page imaging}
            end; {if PrintSuspended}
```

Program 4–4 Image one page *(continued)*

```
ThisPage := ThisPage + 1;                        {Advance page number}
NumToString (ThisPage, pageString);              {Convert numbers to  }
NumToString (ThisCopy, copyString);              {  string form [I:2.3.7]}

ParamText  (copyString, pageString, DocName, ''); {Substitute into dialog text [II:7.4.6]}
DrawDialog (TheDialog);                           {Update text on screen [II:7.4.1]}

editHandle := Handle(TEPrint);                   {Convert to untyped handle [I:3.1.1]}
MoveHHi (editHandle);                            {Move edit record to top of heap [I:3.2.5]}
HLock   (editHandle);                            {Lock edit record [I:3.2.4]}
    with TEPrint^^ do
        begin

            PrOpenPage (ThePrintPort, NIL);      {Open the page [4.3.2]}

                if PrError = NoErr then          {Check for errors [4.2.4]}
                    begin
                        TEUpdate  (viewRect, TEPrint);       {Draw text [II:5.3.2]}
                        OffsetRect (destRect, 0, -PageHeight); {Scroll to next page [I:4.4.4]}
                        NextLine := NextLine + LinesPerPage   {Advance line count}
                    end; {if PrError = NoErr}

            PrClosePage (ThePrintPort);          {Close the page [4.3.2]}

            if PrError <> NoErr then             {Any errors? [4.2.4]}
                begin
                    itemNumber := 0;             {Use dummy item number}
                    ImagePage  := TRUE           {Force exit from dialog}
                end {if PrError <> NoErr}

            else if NextLine > nLines then       {Last line printed? [II:5.1.1]}
                begin
                    itemNumber := FinishPrint;   {Signal completion}
                    ImagePage  := TRUE           {Force exit from dialog}
                end {if NextLine > nLines}

            else
                ImagePage := FALSE               {Continue dialog}

        end; {with TEPrint^^}
    HUnlock (editHandle)                         {Unlock edit record [I:3.2.4]}

end;   {ImagePage}
```

ImagePage begins by checking the value of a global flag named PrintSuspended, to see if the user has temporarily suspended printing operations. This flag is initially set to FALSE, but becomes TRUE when the user clicks the mouse in the dialog's Pause button. In this case, ImagePage simply exits without doing anything, returning a FALSE result to leave the dialog up on the screen. Thus no page imaging can take place while the PrintSuspended flag is TRUE. When the user clicks the button again (its title will have been changed to Resume), the flag will be set back to FALSE and page imaging will proceed normally.

Assuming that printing is not suspended, we must next update the contents of the status dialog on the screen to show the number of the page we're about to image. By the time ImagePage gets called, the dialog will already have been opened on the screen and the global variable TheDialog will contain a pointer to it. After advancing the page number, we convert both the copy and page numbers to string form, merge them (along with the document name) into the text of the dialog with ParamText [II:7.4.6], and redraw the dialog box on the screen with DrawDialog [II:7.4.1].

Now we're ready to draw the contents of the page, sandwiched between calls to PrOpenPage and PrClosePage [4.3.2]. Instead of drawing the text directly with QuickDraw calls, we use the TextEdit routine TEUpdate [II:5.3.2], which in turn will call QuickDraw for us. Ordinarily TEUpdate is used to redraw (update) the contents of a window on the screen; but in this case, since our edit record TEPrint is based on the printing port instead of a window, the text will be sent to the printer instead of the screen.

After drawing the page, we have to scroll the next page into view within the edit record's view rectangle, to prepare for the next ImagePage call. To reposition the document relative to the view rectangle, we offset the destination (wrapping) rectangle upward by the page height, which we calculated earlier in our ImagePrep routine (Program 4–3). We also advance the line number, NextLine, by the number of lines on each page. This variable always contains the number of the first line on the next page about to be printed; it's initialized to 1 by ImagePrep and advanced by each call to ImagePage.

When NextLine exceeds the total number of lines in the document (given by the nLines field of the edit record TEPrint), ImagePage returns TRUE to dismiss the dialog from the screen, along with the item number FinishPrint to signal that the imaging of the document is complete. (This is just a dummy value that we use for internal communication within our program; it doesn't correspond to any actual item in the dialog box.) Otherwise, assuming no printing errors have been detected, we just exit with a FALSE result, telling the Toolbox to leave the dialog visible on the screen.

Displaying a Status Dialog

Since printing is a time-consuming operation, it's a good idea to keep your user informed by displaying a running progress report in a dialog box on the screen. MiniEdit actually uses three different status dialogs, depending on the method and stage of printing. Figure 4–9 shows the one for draft printing, Figures 4–10 and 4–11 those for the imaging and printing phases of spool printing, respectively. (As usual, we've used a resource editor to define the dialogs separately from the program itself and store them into its resource fork as template resources [II:7.6.2].)

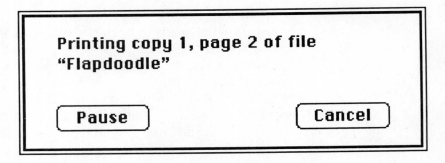

Figure 4–9 MiniEdit Draft Printing dialog

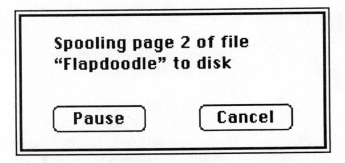

Figure 4–10 MiniEdit Spooling dialog

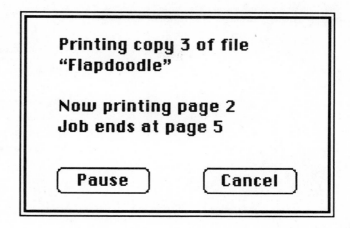

Figure 4–11 `MiniEdit` Spool Printing dialog

`MiniEdit`'s actual `DoPrint` routine (Program 4–5) differs from the simplified version we looked at earlier (Program 4–2) in several respects. First of all, the imaging and printing code has been separated out into a series of subsidiary routines for the sake of readability. (We've already discussed `ImagePrep`, and we'll be coming to `ImageDoc` in just a minute and `SpoolPrint` later in the chapter.) Second, we've added a few extra lines to support the status dialogs: after looking up the printing method in the print record, we set the global variable `DialogID` to the resource ID of the corresponding status dialog; and as we iterate through our imaging loop, we save the running copy count in another global, `ThisCopy`, so we can display it later in the dialog box. Finally, we're a little more meticulous about cursor management, taking care to display the normal arrow cursor while the job dialog is on the screen and the wristwatch while we're busy opening the printing port (which usually entails a perceptible delay).

Program 4–5 Handle `Print...` command

```
{ Global constants and variables }

const
    DraftID = 2000;                    {Resource ID for Draft Printing dialog}
    SpoolID = 2001;                    {Resource ID for Spooling dialog}
```

Program 4–5 Handle Print... command *(continued)*

```
var
   TheWindow     : WindowPtr;            {Pointer to currently active window [II:3.1.1]}
   ThePrintRec   : THPrint;              {Handle to active window's print record [4.1.2]}
   ThePrintPort  : TPPrPort;             {Pointer to printing port [4.1.1]}
   DialogID      : INTEGER;              {Resource ID of printing status dialog}
   ThisCopy      : INTEGER;              {Sequential number of copy being printed}
   Watch         : CursHandle;           {Handle to wristwatch cursor [II:2.5.1]}


procedure DoPrint;

   { Handle Print... command. }

   var
      confirmed  : BOOLEAN;              {Did user click OK button?}
      numCopies  : INTEGER;              {Number of times to image document}
      copyCount  : INTEGER;              {Counter for imaging document}

   begin {DoPrint}

      InitCursor;                        {Set arrow cursor [II:2.5.2]}
      confirmed := PrJobDialog (ThePrintRec);   {Present job dialog [4.2.3]}
      if not confirmed then EXIT (DoPrint);     {If not confirmed, just exit to main event loop}

      with ThePrintRec^^.prJob do        {Look in job subrecord [4.1.2]}
         if bJDocLoop = BDraftLoop then  {Draft printing requested? [4.1.5]}
            begin
               numCopies := iCopies;     {Image each copy separately [4.1.5]}
               DialogID  := DraftID      {Use Draft Printing dialog}
            end {then}
         else
            begin
               numCopies := 1;           {Image just once}
               DialogID  := SpoolID      {Use Spooling dialog}
            end; {else}
```

Program 4–5 Handle Print... command *(continued)*

```
    for copyCount := 1 to numCopies do        {Loop on number of copies}
      if PrError = NoErr then                  {Check for errors [4.2.4]}
        begin

            ThisCopy := copyCount;             {Save in a global for filter function}

            SetCursor (Watch^^);               {Indicate delay [II:2.5.2]}
            ThePrintPort := PrOpenDoc (ThePrintRec, NIL, NIL); {Open printing port [4.3.1]}
            InitCursor;                        {Restore normal cursor [II:2.5.2]}

              if PrError = NoErr then           {Check for errors [4.2.4]}
                begin
                    ImagePrep;                 {Prepare for imaging}
                    ImageDoc                   {Image the document}
                end; {if PrError = NoErr}

            PrCloseDoc (ThePrintPort)          {Close printing port [4.3.1]}

        end; {if PrError = NoErr}

    SetPort (TheWindow);                       {Restore window as current port [I:4.3.3]}

    if PrError = NoErr then                     {Check for errors [4.2.4]}
       SpoolPrint;                             {Print spool file, if any}

    IOCheck (PrError);                         {Post error alert, if any [4.2.4, Prog. II:8-1]}
    PrSetError (NoErr)                         {Clear error for next time [4.2.4]}

  end; {DoPrint}
```

When it comes to actually imaging our document, the status dialogs introduce an extra level of complexity. Instead of doing the imaging itself, our ImageDoc routine (Program 4–6) merely displays and runs the status dialog on the screen. The actual imaging is performed indirectly, via the *filter function* mechanism that we learned about in Volume Two [II:7.4.5]. Recall that the Toolbox routine ModalDialog [II:7.4.2] allows us the option of supplying such a function as a parameter; all events occurring while the dialog is on the screen will then be passed to the filter function for preprocessing before being acted upon by ModalDialog itself.

Program 4–6 Image document

```
{ Global constants and variables }

const
    PausePrint  = 1;                {Item number for Pause/ Resume button}
    CancelPrint = 2;                {Item number for Cancel button}
    FinishPrint = 3;                {Item number for document completion}


var
    TEPrint         : TEHandle;     {Handle to edit record for printing [4.1.1]}
    DialogID        : INTEGER;      {Resource ID of printing status dialog}
    TheDialog       : DialogPtr;    {Pointer to printing status dialog [II:7.1.1]}
    PrintSuspended  : BOOLEAN;      {Printing temporarily suspended?}


procedure ImageDoc;

    { Image document. }

    var
        dlgStorage    : DialogRecord;    {Storage for dialog [II:7.1.1]}
        theItem       : INTEGER;         {Item number returned by dialog}
        printFinished : BOOLEAN;         {Imaging complete?}

    begin {ImageDoc}

        PrintSuspended := FALSE;         {Clear pause flag}
        printFinished  := FALSE;         {Clear completion flag}

        ParamText ('', '', '', '');      {Clear previous dialog text, if any [II:7.4.6]}
        TheDialog := GetNewDialog (DialogID, @dlgStorage, WindowPtr(-1));
                                         {Make dialog from template [II:7.2.2]}

            while (not printFinished) and    {Stop on completion }
                  (PrError = NoErr) do       {  or on error [4.2.4]}
                begin

                    ModalDialog (@ImageFilter, theItem); {Run the dialog [II:7.4.3]}

                    case theItem of
                        PausePrint:
                            DoPause;         {Toggle Pause/Resume button}
                        CancelPrint:
                            PrSetError (IPrAbort);   {Cancel further printing [4.2.4]}
```

Program 4–6 Image document *(continued)*

```
    FinishPrint:
        printFinished := TRUE              {Terminate loop}
    end  {case theItem}

  end; {while}

CloseDialog (TheDialog);                   {Close dialog [II:7.2.3]}
TEPrint^^.hText := NIL;                     {Avoid deallocating text [II:5.1.1]}
TEDispose (TEPrint)                         {Dispose of edit record [II:5.2.2]}

end;   {ImageDoc}
```

In the present case, we pass a pointer to a function named ImageFilter, which we'll be examining in detail a little later (Program 4–8). As we'll see, this function simply passes the user's mouse clicks through unchanged, for the Toolbox to handle in the normal way; but on receiving a null event (meaning that nothing else of significance is going on), the filter function takes the opportunity to image one page of the document. Thus the imaging takes place almost incidentally, as a side effect of running the status dialog.

The first thing ImageDoc does is initialize a pair of Boolean flags, PrintSuspended and printFinished, which will be used to control our imaging loop. Both flags are initially set to FALSE. PrintSuspended becomes TRUE when the user clicks the Pause button in the dialog box; we've already seen how this causes our ImagePage routine (Program 4–4) to skip all further imaging until the flag becomes FALSE again. The other flag, printFinished, will be set to TRUE when we finish imaging our entire document, causing ImageDoc to close its dialog box and exit.

Earlier, our DoPrint routine (Program 4–5) set the global variable DialogID to the resource ID of the status dialog we'll be using, depending on the printing method the user has chosen. Now we pass this value to the Toolbox routine GetNewDialog [II:7.2.2] to read in the template resource and create the dialog. Just for variety, this time we supply our own stack space (dlgStorage) for the dialog record instead of having the Toolbox allocate it for us from the heap. Also, before displaying the dialog on the screen, we call ParamText [II:7.4.6] to clear out the four variable substitution strings, removing any leftover text that may be lurking there from previous dialogs.

Now we're ready to run the status dialog, using a while loop that repeatedly calls ModalDialog [II:7.4.3]. As we learned in Volume

Two, this Toolbox routine processes all events directed to a dialog box, keeping control until the mouse is clicked in an item that's been designated as *enabled;* then it returns the corresponding item number via a variable parameter. (This is, in fact, the very definition of an enabled dialog item: one that causes `ModalDialog` to return, giving the calling program a chance to respond to the mouse click.)

`MiniEdit`'s printing status dialogs each contain two enabled items, the `Pause` and `Cancel` buttons; their item numbers are declared as program constants named `PausePrint` and `CancelPrint`. Also, as we saw earlier, our `ImagePage` routine (Program 4–4) uses the dummy item number `FinishPrint` to signal completion after imaging the last page of a document. Each of these item numbers will be passed back via our filter function to `ModalDialog`, which in turn will report it as the value of the variable parameter `theItem`. `ImageDoc` then uses a `case` statement to examine the item number and decide how to respond. In particular, on receiving the item number `FinishPrint`, it sets the `printFinished` flag to TRUE, causing the `while` loop running the dialog to terminate. Then all that's left is to close the dialog box, dispose of the edit record `TEPrint`, and exit.

Notice that before disposing of the edit record, we're careful to clear its text handle to NIL. Otherwise, `TEDispose` [II:5.2.2] would automatically deallocate the text along with the record itself. Since the identical copy of the text is also shared by the active window's main edit record, `TheText`, we have to make sure it isn't destroyed while the window still needs it.

Instead of waiting for `printFinished` to become TRUE, our `while` loop may be terminated prematurely by a printing-related error. In fact, this is the mechanism we use to cancel further imaging when the user clicks the dialog's `Cancel` button. On receiving the item number `CancelPrint` from `ModalDialog`, we call the Toolbox routine `PrSetError` [4.2.4] to post a special error code, `IPrAbort`. (This is normally the only time an application program will ever need to post a printing error of its own.) The Toolbox printing routines recognize this code as a signal to cancel all printing operations immediately. We will then detect the error with `PrError`, exit from our `while` loop, and close the dialog box, just as if imaging had completed normally.

When the user clicks the dialog's `Pause` button, `ImageDoc` responds by calling the `MiniEdit` routine `DoPause`, shown in Program 4–7. This simple routine toggles the state of the `PrintSuspended` flag, fetches a handle to the `Pause` button, and changes the button's title from `Pause` to `Resume` or back again, according to the new state of the flag. As we know, our `ImagePage` routine (Program 4–4) will refuse to do any page imaging while this flag is `TRUE`.

Program 4–7 Toggle `Pause/Resume` button

```
{ Global constants and variables }

const
    PausePrint = 1;                               {Item number for Pause/ Resume button}

var
    TheDialog       : DialogPtr;                  {Pointer to printing status dialog [II:7.1.1]}
    PrintSuspended  : BOOLEAN;                    {Printing temporarily suspended?}


procedure DoPause;

    { Toggle Pause/Resume button. }

    var
        itemType    : INTEGER;                    {Item type for Pause/Resume button}
        itemRect    : Rect;                       {Display rectangle for Pause/Resume button}
        itemHandle  : Handle;                     {Item handle for Pause/Resume button}
        theButton   : ControlHandle;              {Control handle to Pause/Resume button [II:6.1.1]}

    begin {DoPause}

        PrintSuspended := not PrintSuspended;     {Toggle pause flag}

        GetDItem (TheDialog, PausePrint,          {Get item handle [II:7.3.1]}
                  itemType, itemHandle, itemRect);
        theButton := ControlHandle(itemHandle);   {Convert to typed handle [II:6.1.1]}

        if PrintSuspended then                     {Printing now suspended?}
            SetCTitle (theButton, 'Resume')       {Change button to Resume [II:6.2.3]}
        else
            SetCTitle (theButton, 'Pause')        {Change back to Pause [II:6.2.3]}

    end;  {DoPause}
```

Program 4–8 (`ImageFilter`) shows the filter function we use for handling events in our status dialog. Our `ImageDoc` routine (Program 4–6) passes a pointer to this function when it calls the Toolbox routine `ModalDialog` [II:7.4.3]. As long as the dialog remains on the screen, `ModalDialog` will pass each event it receives to the filter function for preprocessing. As we learned in Volume Two [II:7.4.5], the filter function can handle the event in any of the following ways:

- respond to the event itself
- convert it to the equivalent of a mouse click in a specified dialog item
- modify the contents of the event record and pass it on to the Toolbox for processing
- leave it unchanged for the Toolbox to handle in the normal way

A function result of FALSE tells `ModalDialog` to handle the event in its own standard way, as described in [II:7.4.3]. A TRUE result instructs it to return immediately with the item number given by the variable parameter `itemNumber`; this makes the event appear to the calling program (in this case, `ImageDoc`) as a mouse click in the corresponding dialog item.

Program 4–8 Process event while imaging document

```
{ Global variables }

var
   TheEvent   : EventRecord;                          {Current event [II:2.1.1]}



function ImageFilter (thisDialog      : DialogPtr;
                      var thisEvent   : EventRecord;
                      var itemNumber  : INTEGER)
                         : BOOLEAN;

   { Process event while imaging document. }

   var
      dummyDialog : DialogPtr;                         {Dialog pointer from DialogSelect [II:7.4.4]}
      dummyItem   : INTEGER;                           {Item number from DialogSelect [II:7.4.4]}
```

Program 4–8 Process event while imaging document *(continued)*

```
begin {ImageFilter}

    SystemTask;                                      {Do system idle processing [II:2.7.2]}

    case thisEvent.what of                           {Dispatch on event type [II:2.1.1]}

        NullEvent:
            ImageFilter := ImagePage (itemNumber);   {Image one page}

        KeyDown:
            ImageFilter := FilterKey (thisEvent. itemNumber);   {Process keystroke}

        UpdateEvt:
            if SystemEvent (thisEvent) then          {System window? [6.2.2]}
                ImageFilter := FALSE                 {SystemEvent does the updating}

            else if IsDialogEvent (thisEvent) then   {Dialog window? [II:7.4.4]}
                ImageFilter := DialogSelect (thisEvent. dummyDialog. dummyItem)
                                                     {Update dialog window [II:7.4.4]}
            else
                begin
                    TheEvent := thisEvent;           {Copy to global variable for DoUpdate}
                    DoUpdate;                        {Update application window [Prog. II:5-3]}
                    ImageFilter := FALSE             {Continue dialog}
                end; {else}

        otherwise
            ImageFilter := FALSE                     {Handle as normal event}

    end {case thisEvent.what}

end;  {ImageFilter}
```

The first thing our filter function does is call the Toolbox routine SystemTask [II:2.7.2]. If there are any desk accessories active on the screen, this gives them a chance to perform their periodic tasks so that they can continue to operate properly during the imaging process. Then we examine the what field of the event record [II:2.1.1] to see what type of event it is, and use a case statement to decide what to do in response.

As we explained earlier, the most important case the filter function needs to handle is that of a null event. As long as nothing else of interest is happening, we can take the opportunity to call `ImagePage` (Program 4–4) to image the next page of the document. Usually `ImagePage` will return the value `FALSE`, which the filter function will in turn pass back as its own result; this tells the Toolbox to process the null event in the normal way (that is, to do nothing) and continue the dialog. However, after imaging the last page of the document, `ImagePage` will return `TRUE` along with the dummy item number `FinishPrint`. On receiving these values back from the filter function, `ModalDialog` will dutifully return the item number to *its* calling program, `ImageDoc` (Program 4–6), which will respond by setting the `printFinished` flag, exiting from its `while` loop, and dismissing the dialog from the screen.

One common use for filter functions is to convert certain keystrokes typed by the user into equivalent commands and dialog items. Our `ImageFilter` routine passes all key-down events along to another `MiniEdit` routine, `FilterKey`, which recognizes such keyboard equivalents and responds to them as needed. We'll come back and examine this routine more closely in a minute (Program 4–9).

Another detail the filter function has to take care of is the proper handling of update events. In the course of their normal operations, the Toolbox printing routines sometimes post alert or dialog boxes of their own on the screen. As these dialog windows appear and disappear, they generate update events both for themselves and for other windows already on the screen. Because of the special way in which update events are detected, they must be handled immediately and then cleared via the Toolbox calls `BeginUpdate` and `EndUpdate` [II:3.4.1]. Otherwise, the Toolbox will keep reporting the same event over and over again, preventing any null events from getting through. Without the null events, we will never image the next page of our document and our imaging loop will "hang" forever.

How we handle the update event depends on the type of window. First we call the Toolbox routine `SystemEvent` [6.2.2] to see if it's a system window (containing a desk accessory). If so, `SystemEvent` will automatically relay the event to the accessory for processing before returning; thus by the time we receive a `TRUE` result, the window will already have been updated and the event cleared. If the result from `SystemEvent` is `FALSE`, we next call `IsDialogEvent` [II:7.4.4] to see if the event pertains to a dialog window; if so, we pass it on to `DialogSelect` [II:7.4.4] to handle. Finally, if the window to be updated is neither a system window nor a dialog window, then it must be one of our own document windows, so we call our own `DoUpdate` routine (Program II:5–3) to do the updating. (Notice that we must first copy the event record into our program's global variable TheEvent, where DoUpdate expects to find it.) In any case, we return a function result of FALSE, telling the filter function's calling program, ModalDialog [II:7.4.3], not to return immediately but to continue processing events within the status dialog.

Program 4–9 (FilterKey) shows the MiniEdit routine that checks for keyboard aliases in the printing status dialog. The dialog filter function ImageFilter (Program 4–8) calls this routine whenever it receives a key-down event. After extracting from the event record the character code and the modifier bit representing the Command key, we check for the specific keystrokes Command-period and Command-comma, which we will recognize as equivalent to the dialog's Cancel and Pause buttons, respectively. On receiving either of these keystrokes, we return TRUE for our function result, along with the corresponding item number (CancelPrint or PausePrint) in the variable parameter itemNumber. The filter function will pass these values back to ModalDialog [II:7.4.3], which in turn will return the given item number to our ImageDoc routine (Program 4–6) to respond to as appropriate. On any other keystroke, we return FALSE, telling ModalDialog to leave the dialog up on the screen and continue with its normal event processing.

Program 4–9 Process keystroke in printing dialog

```
{ Global constants }

const
    PausePrint  = 1;                    {Item number for Pause/Resume button}
    CancelPrint = 2;                    {Item number for Cancel button}



function FilterKey (var thisEvent  : EventRecord;
                    var itemNumber : INTEGER)
                       : BOOLEAN;

    { Process keystroke in printing dialog. }

    var
        chCode  : INTEGER;             {Character code from keyboard event}
        ch      : CHAR;                {Character that was typed}
        cmdDown : BOOLEAN;             {Command key down?}
```

Program 4–9 Process keystroke in printing dialog *(continued)*

```
begin {FilterKey}

   with thisEvent do
      begin
         cmdDown := (BitAnd (modifiers, CmdKey) <> 0);
                                        {Test Command key [I:2.2.2, II:2.1.1, II:2.1.5]}
         chCode  :=  BitAnd (message, CharCodeMask);
                                        {Get character code [I:2.2.2, II:2.1.1, II:2.1.4]}
         ch      :=  CHR(chCode)        {Convert to a character}
      end; {with thisEvent}

   FilterKey  := FALSE;                 {Assume normal event processing}
   itemNumber := 0;                     {Initialize to no item}

   if cmdDown then                      {Command key down?}
      begin

         FilterKey := TRUE;             {Masquerade as a pushbutton}

         case ch of

            '.': itemNumber := CancelPrint;   {Command-period means Cancel}

            ',': itemNumber := PausePrint;    {Command-comma means Pause/Resume}

            otherwise
               FilterKey := FALSE       {Report as normal event}

         end {case ch}

      end {then}

end; {FilterKey}
```

Printing the Spool File

In the draft method of printing, everything you draw into the printing port goes directly to the printer. By the time you finish imaging your document, it's already on paper and there's nothing more to do. In spool printing, on the other hand, the results of your drawing operations are not printed immediately, but merely saved in some intermediate form—typically in a spool file on the disk. You must then explicitly read back this intermediate representation from the spool file and send it to the printer to be converted into inkware.

The Toolbox routine that handles this chore for you is PrPicFile [4.3.3]. The first parameter you give it is a print record defining the characteristics of the printing job. PrPicFile gets the spool file's name and volume (or directory) number from the job subrecord [4.1.5], reads back the page images stored in that file, and ships them off to the printer. Then it automatically deletes the spool file from the disk.

PrPicFile uses a printing port to do its job, but not the same one you used earlier for imaging the document. Instead of recording your drawing operations in a spool file, this time the port's bottleneck routines are set up to convert them into the printer's native control codes (or whatever other magical incantations it understands). Since the printing port is a nonrelocatable object, you are given the usual option of providing your own storage for it to avoid fragmenting the heap. You do this by passing as the printPort parameter a pointer to a memory block of length SIZEOF(TPrPort) bytes, which may reside in either the heap or the stack. (If it's a relocatable heap block, don't forget to lock it first and then unlock it again afterwards.) A NIL value for this parameter asks the Toolbox to do the allocation for you.

Recall that PrOpenDoc [4.3.1] gave you the same option for the port you did your original imaging in. If you chose to supply your own storage the first time, there's nothing to stop you from reusing the same block now (provided it's still allocated, of course). But if you earlier let PrOpenDoc allocate a port for you, don't make the mistake of passing that same port to PrPicFile to be used again. The port will have been destroyed by PrCloseDoc [4.3.1] at the end of the imaging phase, leaving you with a nice pointer to nothing at all. (See the signpost up ahead? Next stop . . . the Twilight Zone!) So instead of trying to reuse the old pointer, be sure to set the printPort parameter to NIL, asking the Toolbox to allocate a fresh port for you from the heap.

PrPicFile also uses a pair of buffers (storage areas) in memory, a *spool buffer* to hold input from the spool file and a *print buffer* for output on its way to the printer. Once again, you can either supply your own storage for the buffers or let the Toolbox allocate them for you. The spool buffer is always 522 bytes long, while the size required for the print buffer is given by field `prXInfo.iDevBytes` of the print record. `PrPicFile`'s last parameter, `printStatus`, is an optional *printing status record,* which we'll be discussing shortly.

MiniEdit's routine for the second stage of a spool printing operation is `SpoolPrint`, shown in Program 4–10. As long as no printing errors have occurred during the imaging stage, our main `DoPrint` routine (Program 4–5) always calls this routine next, no matter what printing method is in effect. The first thing `SpoolPrint` does is check the printing method in the print record and exit immediately if it's anything other than spool printing.

Program 4–10 Print spooled document

```
{ Global constants and variables }

const
   SpoolPrintID = 2002;                        {Resource ID for Spool Printing dialog}

var
   ThePrintRec  : THPrint;                     {Handle to active window's print record [4.1.2]}
   PrintStatus  : TPrStatus;                   {Status record for spool printing [4.1.7]}
   TheDialog    : DialogPtr;                   {Pointer to printing status dialog [II:7.1.1]}
   ThisCopy     : INTEGER;                     {Number of copy being printed}
   ThisPage     : INTEGER;                     {Page number of page being printed}


procedure SpoolPrint;

   { Print spooled document. }

   var
      dlgStorage : DialogRecord;               {Storage for dialog [II:7.1.1]}
      theItem    : INTEGER;                    {Item number returned by dialog}

   begin {SpoolPrint}

      with ThePrintRec^^.prJob do             {Look in job subrecord [4.1.2]}
         if (bJDocLoop <> BSpoolLoop) then     {Is there a spool file? [4.1.5]}
            EXIT (SpoolPrint)                   {If not, just exit}
         else
            pIdleProc := @SpoolBackground;     {Install background procedure [4.1.5, Prog. 4-11]}
```

Program 4–10 Print spooled document *(continued)*

```
ThisCopy := 0;                                        {Initialize copy and}
ThisPage := 0;                                        {  page counts  }

TheDialog := GetNewDialog (SpoolPrintID, @dlgStorage, WindowPtr(-1)); {Open dialog [II:7.2.2]}

   PrPicFile (ThePrintRec, NIL, NIL, NIL, PrintStatus);   {Print spool file [4.3.3]}

CloseDialog (TheDialog)                                {Close dialog [II:7.2.3]}

end;   {SpoolPrint}
```

Assuming the print record calls for spool printing, we'll need to call `PrPicFile` to do the job. First, though, there are a few preliminaries to take care of. As we'll see in the next section, we'll be using a *background procedure* to handle some needed chores while spool printing is in progress. Before calling `PrPicFile`, we have to install a pointer to the background procedure in the appropriate field of the print record; we also need to initialize a couple of global variables that the background procedure will be using. Then, while the document is being printed, we'll be maintaining a status dialog on the screen (Figure 4–11), similar to the ones we displayed earlier during the imaging phase (Figures 4–9, 4–10). So we call `GetNewDialog` [II:7.2.2] before `PrPicFile`, to open the dialog on the screen, and `CloseDialog` [II:7.2.3] to close it again afterward.

Background Procedures

Just as you can supply a filter function for `ModalDialog` to execute while running a dialog, you can also provide a *background procedure* to `PrPicFile`. Unlike the dialog filter function, however, this printing background procedure is not event-driven, accepts no parameters, and returns no result. `PrPicFile` simply calls the procedure repeatedly whenever it has nothing else to do, such as while waiting for a completion signal from the printer after beginning a printing operation.

Background procedures give you a general mechanism for gaining control during the spool printing process, and can be used for a variety of purposes. We'll see in a minute how `MiniEdit` uses one to run its status dialog on the screen. Another idea is to have the background procedure run one cycle of the program's main event loop (in `MiniEdit`'s case, by calling the `MainLoop` routine, Program II:2–2). This allows the user to continue running the program normally, with the illusion of printing the document concurrently "in the background." (The reality, of course, is just the reverse: the printing takes place in the foreground, with the program running behind it.)

> If you want to implement this kind of concurrent printing, there are some unexpected pitfalls you should be aware of. For one thing, the Toolbox will get hopelessly confused if you try to start a second printing operation while the first is still in progress. The cleanest way to avoid this is to disable all menu commands pertaining to printing (such as `Page Setup...` and `Print...`) when executing your main loop from within the background procedure. Also, it's crucially important for the background procedure not to alter any properties of the global environment that the printing routines may be depending on, such as the current port or the current resource file. If you must change any of these global settings, be sure to save their previous values and restore them before exiting from the background procedure.

You specify a background procedure by storing a procedure pointer in the print record you supply to `PrPicFile`, in the `pIdleProc` field of the job subrecord [4.1.5]. If this field is `NIL`, the Toolbox will use its own built-in background procedure, which simply polls the keyboard and cancels the printing operation if the user types Command-period. As a courtesy to the user, it's a nice idea to announce the availability of this option with an alert box containing a message such as

```
Printing document; type Command-period to cancel.
```

Program 4–11 Background procedure for spool printing

```
procedure SpoolBackground;

   { Background procedure for spool printing. }

   begin  {SpoolBackground}

      ShowSpoolStatus;                        {Display status on screen}
      DoSpoolEvent                            {Handle mouse and keyboard}

   end;   {SpoolBackground}
```

If you provide your own background procedure, be sure to check for Command-period cancellation requests in addition to any other special processing you may be doing. MiniEdit's background procedure, SpoolBackground (Program 4–11), in turn calls two subsidiary routines. The first, ShowSpoolStatus, updates the contents of the dialog box on the screen to reflect the current state of the printing operation. Not surprisingly, it gets this information from a printing status record—so we'll save it until we discuss such records in the next section. The second subsidiary routine, DoSpoolEvent, handles events involving the status dialog and is shown in Program 4–12.

Program 4–12 Process event during spool printing

```
{ Global constants and variables }

const
   PausePrint  = 1;                           {Item number for Pause/Resume button}
   CancelPrint = 2;                           {Item number for Cancel button}

var
   TheEvent        : EventRecord;             {Current event [II:2.1.1]}
   TheDialog       : DialogPtr;               {Pointer to printing status dialog [II:7.1.1]}
   PrintSuspended  : BOOLEAN;                 {Printing temporarily suspended?}
```

Program 4–12 Process event during spool printing *(continued)*

```
procedure DoSpoolEvent;

    { Process event during spool printing. }

    var
        click   : BOOLEAN;                                    {Mouse clicked in a pushbutton?}
        theItem : INTEGER;                                    {Item number of pushbutton}

    begin {DoSpoolEvent}

        repeat

            SystemTask;                                       {Do system idle processing [II:2.7.2]}

            click := FALSE;                                   {Assume no reportable event}
            if GetNextEvent (EveryEvent, TheEvent) then       {Any events? [II:2.2.1, 2.1.3]}
                case TheEvent.what of                         {Dispatch on event type [II:2.1.1]}

                    MouseDown:
                        click := DialogSelect (TheEvent, TheDialog, theItem);
                                                              {Relay mouse click to dialog [II:7.4.4]}

                    KeyDown:
                        click := FilterKey (TheEvent, theItem);  {Convert keystroke to pushbutton}

                    UpdateEvt:
                        if not SystemEvent (TheEvent) then    {One of our windows? [6.2.2]}
                            begin
                                if IsDialogEvent (TheEvent) then  {Dialog window? [II:7.4.4]}
                                    click := DialogSelect (TheEvent, TheDialog, theItem)
                                                              {Update dialog window [II:7.4.4]}

                                else
                                    DoUpdate                  {Update document window}
                            end {if not SystemEvent (TheEvent)}

                end; {case TheEvent.what}

            if click then                                     {Pushbutton clicked?}
                case theItem of                               {Dispatch on item number}
                    PausePrint: DoPause;                      {Toggle Pause/Resume button}
                    CancelPrint: PrSetError (IPrAbort)        {Cancel further printing [4.2.4]}
                end {case theItem}
```

Program 4–12 Process event during spool printing *(continued)*

```
until (not PrintSuspended)            {Keep control if suspended }
      or (PrError <> NoErr)           {   or until canceled [4.2.4]}

end;   {DoSpoolEvent}
```

Since spool printing is a time-consuming operation that will keep us away from our main event loop for long periods, we start out by calling `SystemTask` [II:2.7.2] to give any open desk accessories the time they need for their periodic tasks. Then we initialize the Boolean variable `click` to `FALSE`, meaning that nothing significant has happened involving any of the dialog's pushbuttons. If it turns out that the user has clicked the mouse in one of them or typed its keyboard equivalent, we will change this flag to `TRUE`.

Now we call `GetNextEvent` [II:2.2.1] to retrieve the next event from the Toolbox event queue, and use a `case` statement to dispatch on the event type and respond to it as appropriate. If it's a mouse-down event, we pass it along to the Toolbox routine `DialogSelect` [II:7.4.4], which will track the mouse for as long as the user holds down the button, then return a Boolean result telling whether it was pressed and released inside an enabled dialog item. For a key-down event, we call our own `FilterKey` routine (Program 4–9) to convert it into the equivalent pushbutton click, if any.

On receiving an update event, we have to process it the same way we did earlier in our `ImageFilter` routine (Program 4–8); otherwise, the event will never be cleared and will hang up our printing loop forever. First we call `SystemEvent` [6.2.2] to see if the window to be updated is a system (desk accessory) window; if so, the Toolbox will automatically update it for us before returning `TRUE`. If it isn't a system window, we try `IsDialogEvent` [II:7.4.4] next, to see if it's a dialog window; in that case, we call `DialogSelect` [II:7.4.4] to do the updating. If both `SystemEvent` and `IsDialogEvent` return `FALSE`, it must be one of our own document windows that needs updating—so our `DoUpdate` routine (Program II:5–3) will do the job.

Once we've handled the event itself, we go back and check the `click` flag to see if it was a pushbutton click (or its keyboard equivalent). If so, we dispatch on the item number to decide how to respond. For the `Pause` button, we call the same `DoPause` routine (Program 4–7) that we used earlier in the imaging phase. For the

`Cancel` button, we post the printing error `IPrAbort` [4.2.4], just as before.

Finally, notice that the entire body of our `DoSpoolEvent` routine is enclosed within a great big `repeat` loop. Ordinarily, the global flag `PrintSuspended` will be FALSE, causing the loop (and the routine itself) to terminate after just one pass; but if the user clicks the dialog's `Pause` button (or types the equivalent keystroke, Command-comma), our `DoPause` routine will set `PrintSuspended` to TRUE. The `repeat` loop will then retain control, effectively suspending printing operations, for as long as this flag remains TRUE. When the user clicks the button (now labeled `Resume`) again, `DoPause` will set the flag back to FALSE, the loop will terminate, `DoSpoolEvent` will return, and printing will proceed normally. (Notice that the loop is also terminated by any printing error, including the `IPrAbort` error that we post in response to the `Cancel` button; so `Cancel` will override `Pause` and cause an immediate exit, killing the printing operation in progress.)

The Printing Status Record

As we've already mentioned, `PrPicFile` accepts a *printing status record* [4.1.7] as a parameter. The fields of this record hold information on the progress of the spool printing operation, such as the total number of copies and pages to be printed, the current copy and page number, and so forth. The Toolbox keeps this information continually updated as it prints the document; your printing background procedure can then use it to track what's going on and keep the user informed with status messages on the screen. The status record also includes a handle to the print record for the current printing job and a pointer to the printing port, in case the background procedure has no other way of getting its hands on these vital data structures.

Program 4–13 (`ShowSpoolStatus`) shows how `MiniEdit` uses the printing status record. Our background procedure (Program 4–11) calls this routine to update the contents of the status dialog. `ShowSpoolStatus` begins with a couple of preliminary tests to avoid annoying visual glitches on the screen. The first time the Toolbox calls the background procedure, the fields of the status record are not yet initialized. To avoid displaying spurious copy and page numbers in the dialog box, we first check to make sure both numbers are within the proper range, and simply exit from the routine immediately if they aren't. Secondly, in actual operation, the background procedure gets called far more often than the copy and page numbers change; redisplaying the same numbers over and over again in the dialog box causes a flickering effect that's annoying and distracting to the user. So we save the copy and page numbers from one call to the next in a pair of global variables, `ThisCopy` and `ThisPage`, and exit without doing anything if these values haven't changed since last time.

Program 4–13 Display status during spool printing

```
{ Global variables }

var
    ThePrintRec  : THPrint;          {Handle to active window's print record [4.1.2]}
    PrintStatus  : TPrStatus;        {Status record for spool printing [4.1.7]}
    TheDialog    : DialogPtr;        {Pointer to printing status dialog [II:7.1.1]}
    DocName      : Str255;           {Name of document being printed [I:8.1.2]}
    ThisCopy     : INTEGER;          {Number of copy being printed}
    ThisPage     : INTEGER;          {Page number of page being printed}


procedure ShowSpoolStatus;

    { Display status during spool printing. }

    var
        curPage    : INTEGER;        {Current page number}
        lastPage   : INTEGER;        {Last page to be printed}
        copyString : Str255;         {Current copy number in string form [I:2.1.1]}
        pageString : Str255;         {Current page number in string form [I:2.1.1]}
        lastString : Str255;         {Last page number in string form [I:2.1.1]}

    begin {ShowSpoolStatus}

        with PrintStatus. ThePrintRec^^.prJob do
            begin

                if not (iCurCopy in [1..iTotCopies]) or    {Copy or page count}
                   not (iCurPage in [1..iTotPages]) then    {out of range? [4.1.7]}
                        EXIT (ShowSpoolStatus);             {Suppress spurious numbers}
                if (iCurCopy = ThisCopy) and                {Copy and page counts unchanged}
                   (iCurPage = ThisPage) then               {since last time? [4.1.7]}
                        EXIT (ShowSpoolStatus);             {Avoid screen flicker}
```

Program 4–13 Display status during spool printing *(continued)*

```
curPage  := (iFstPage - 1) + iCurPage;   {Convert to document-relative}
lastPage := (iFstPage - 1) + iTotPages;  {page numbers [4.1.5, 4.1.7]}

NumToString (iCurCopy, copyString);      {Convert numbers}
NumToString (curPage,  pageString);      {to string form}
NumToString (lastPage, lastString);      {[I:2.3.7, 4.1.7]}

ParamText (copyString, DocName, pageString, lastString);
                                         {Substitute into dialog text [II:7.4.6]}
ShowWindow (TheDialog);                  {Display dialog window [II:3.3.1]}
DrawDialog (TheDialog);                  {Update text on screen [II:7.4.1]}

ThisCopy := iCurCopy;                    {Save "raw" copy and page counts}
ThisPage := iCurPage                     {for comparison next time}

    end {with PrintStatus, ThePrintRec^^.prJob}

end;   {ShowSpoolStatus}
```

Assuming the copy and page numbers are valid and need to be updated, we must next convert the current and final page numbers to document-relative form. The page numbers reported in the printing status record include only those pages that are included in the document's spool file. If the spool file doesn't begin with the first page of the document, these numbers won't match the numbering of pages within the document as a whole. So we have to adjust them by the number of the first page actually spooled, which we obtain from the iFstPage field in the print record's job subrecord [4.1.5].

Once we've adjusted the page numbers, we can convert them to string form with the utility procedure NumToString [I:2.3.7]. Then we merge the resulting strings (as well as the name of the document) into the text of the status dialog with ParamText [II:7.4.6] and redisplay the dialog's contents on the screen. Finally, before returning, we have to remember to save the copy and page numbers so they'll be available for comparison the next time this routine is called.

Printing from the Finder

Instead of using a program's own Print... command, the user can also print from the Finder level, by selecting one or more of the program's document files and choosing the Print command from the

Finder's `File` menu. The creator signature [I:7.3.1] associated with each file tells the Finder what program it belongs to. The Finder automatically starts up the program, identifying the selected file(s) by means of the *Finder startup handle* that we learned about in Volume One [I:7.3.4]. An integer *startup message* in the first field of the startup information notifies the program that the files are to be printed (`AppPrint`) rather than simply opened for work (`AppOpen`). To support Finder printing, each application program must check for this message at startup time and respond to it by printing the requested files.

A program can retrieve and manipulate the startup information provided by the Finder by using the Toolbox routines `CountAppFiles`, `GetAppFiles`, and `ClrAppFiles` [I:7.3.4]. In the case of printing, it's often possible to skip or shorten some of the program's standard initialization sequence: for instance, there's generally no need to open a window for displaying each file's contents on the screen. On the other hand, it *is* necessary to present the usual style and job dialogs before printing each document, allowing the user to specify the characteristics and options to be used for this printing job. After printing all the requested files, the program should simply close up shop and exit back to the Finder.

`MiniEdit`'s routine for processing the Finder startup information is shown in Program 4–14. This is an expanded version of the routine `DoStartup`, which we originally examined in Volume Two (Program II:8–7). At that time, if the user attempted to print a file from the Finder, all we could do was post an alert on the screen reading

```
Sorry, MiniEdit can't print a file.
```

Now that we've added a printing capability to our program, we're prepared to deal with Finder printing in a more meaningful way.

Program 4–14 Process Finder startup information

```
{ Global constants and variables }

const
    FndrPrintID = 1003;                    {Resource ID for Finder Print alert [II:7.6.1]}
    WrongTypeID = 1004;                    {Resource ID for Wrong Type alert [II:7.6.1]}

var
    FinderPrint : BOOLEAN;                 {Printing from Finder?}
    ErrorFlag   : BOOLEAN;                 {I/O error flag}
```

Program 4–14 Process Finder startup information *(continued)*

```
procedure DoStartup;

    { Process Finder startup information [Prog. II:8-7]. }

    var
        theMessage : INTEGER;          {Open or print? [I:7.3.4]}
        nDocs      : INTEGER;          {Number of documents selected in Finder}
        thisDoc    : INTEGER;          {Index number of document}
        docInfo    : AppFile;          {Startup information for one document [I:7.3.4]}
        ignore     : INTEGER;          {Item code returned by alert}

    begin {DoStartup}

        CountAppFiles (theMessage, nDocs);      {Get no. of docs and startup message [I:7.3.4]}
        FinderPrint := (theMessage = AppPrint);  {Printing requested? [I:7.3.4]}

        if nDocs = 0 then              {If no documents selected, }
            DoNew                      {just open an empty  window}

        else
            for thisDoc := 1 to nDocs do    {Otherwise loop through documents}
                begin

                    GetAppFiles (thisDoc, docInfo);    {Get startup information [I:7.3.4]}
                    with docInfo do

                        if fType = 'TEXT' then         {Is it a text file? [I:7.3.4]}
                            begin
                                ErrorFlag := FALSE;            {Clear I/O error flag}
                                OpenFile (fName, vRefNum);     {Read file into a window}

                                if FinderPrint and not ErrorFlag then    {Printing requested?}
                                    begin

                                        ParamText (fName, '', '', '');   {Merge in file  name [II:7.4.6]}
                                        InitCursor;                      {Set arrow cursor [II:2.5.2]}

                                        ignore := NoteAlert (FndrPrintID, NIL); {Post alert [II:7.4.2]}
                                        DoSetup;                         {Get page setup information}
                                        DoPrint;                         {Print the file}

                                        CloseAppWindow                   {Dispose of data structures}

                                    end; {if FinderPrint and not ErrorFlag}
```

Program 4–14 Process Finder startup information *(continued)*

```
            if not ErrorFlag then              {No errors detected?}
                ClrAppFiles (thisDoc)          {Mark file as processed [I:7.3.4]}
        end {then}

    else
        begin
            ParamText (fName, '', '', '');      {Merge in file name [II:7.4.6]}
            InitCursor;                         {Set arrow cursor [II:2.5.2]}
            ignore := StopAlert (WrongTypeID, NIL)  {Post alert [II:7.4.2]}
        end {else}

    end; {for thisDoc}

if FinderPrint then                             {Printing from Finder?}
    begin
        Finalize; {Close up shop}
        ExitToShell                             {Return to Finder [I:7.1.3]}
    end {if FinderPrint}

end; {DoStartup}
```

As before, we begin by calling CountAppFiles [I:7.3.4] to find out how many files the user selected in the Finder and what operation (Open or Print) was applied to them. We set a global flag named FinderPrint to show which operation was chosen; we'll be using this flag (both here and in other routines as well) to control the course of the program's startup sequence. If the number of files reported by CountAppFiles is zero, then we simply call our DoNew routine (Program II:5–2) to start us off with an empty window on the screen. Otherwise we loop through the designated files with GetAppFiles [I:7.3.4], checking each one's file type [I:7.3.1] and posting an error alert if it isn't a plain ASCII text file.

Assuming the file is of the right type, we next call the MiniEdit routine OpenFile (Program II:8–6) to read it into memory. OpenFile in turn calls DoNew (Program II:5–2) to create a window for the file and DoRevert (Program II:8–4) to read its contents in from the disk. If you compare the versions of these routines in Appendix H with the originals from Volume Two, you'll find that we've added a few extra lines to skip certain steps when the FinderPrint flag is TRUE. For example, if we're only printing a file, DoNew doesn't need to display the file's window on the screen or create a scroll bar for it, and DoRevert needn't calculate the line breaks in the file's text or initialize the location of its insertion point. (Even though the window is invisible, however, we can't dispense with it entirely: some of our printing routines rely on information taken from the window record, such as its title and text characteristics.)

If `FinderPrint` is TRUE, we can proceed to call our `DoSetup` and `DoPrint` routines (Programs 4–1 and 4–5) to conduct the style and job dialogs and print the file; then we call `CloseAppWindow` (Program II:7–6) to dispose of the window record and its associated data structures. (If `FinderPrint` is FALSE, we simply skip all these steps and leave the file displayed in a window on the screen for the user to edit.) One small problem that arises is that if the user has selected more than one file for printing from the Finder, the printing dialogs will be displayed separately for each, with no indication as to which occurrence of the dialogs applies to which file. So before calling `DoSetup` and `DoPrint`, we first display an alert box (Figure 4–12) with the name of the file about to be printed.

Figure 4–12 `MiniEdit` Finder Print alert

After we've finished processing all of the files selected from the Finder, we check the `FinderPrint` flag one last time. If it's TRUE, we call our `Finalize` routine to take care of any last-minute housekeeping chores, then exit back to the Finder with `ExitToShell` [I:7.1.3]. (The `Finalize` routine is a new addition in this version of `MiniEdit`; see Appendix H for details. In the original `MiniEdit` in Volume Two, the one-time finalization consisted of a single call to the routine `WriteDeskScrap`, and was performed directly by the main program proper.) If `FinderPrint` is FALSE, we simply return from `DoStartup` to the point of call and continue with the normal operation of the program.

Nuts and Bolts

Now that we've learned how to use the Toolbox for straightforward printing operations, let's look at some of its more exotic features and capabilities. Chances are you'll never use most of these techniques, but who knows? Some day, one of them may be just what you need to handle an unusual programming problem.

Format of Routine Selectors

As we mentioned earlier, recent versions of the Toolbox include a machine-level trap named _PrGlue, which resides either in ROM or in the system resource file. This single trap implements all of the standard printing routines that we've discussed in this chapter. Before executing the trap, your program pushes a 4-byte *routine selector* onto the stack to identify the specific printing operation to be performed. (Needless to say, the machine instructions to handle this chore are generated automatically by the Toolbox interface files, so you never have to think about it at the source-language level.)

The exact values of the selectors for the various printing routines are listed in the "Assembly Language Information" boxes in the reference sections following this chapter. At first glance, they look rather puzzling. Why, for instance, is the routine PrValidate [4.2.2] represented by the selector $52040498? What in the world could that mean? As you might suspect, this bizarre-looking number actually contains several different items of information packed together sardine-style.

The internal format of these selectors is not documented in *Inside Macintosh*, Macintosh Technical Notes, or any other Apple publication known to man or sardine. Nevertheless, your intrepid author has managed, by means too devious to reveal and at severe peril to life and limb, to learn the details of the encoding. They are publicly disclosed for the first time in Figure 4–13. (Now you know why this book is called *Macintosh Revealed*.) Beware, however: this information is not officially supported by Apple, and is subject to abrupt, unannounced, and cataclysmic change. It is presented here solely for the edification and amusement of the reading public, and carries no warranties, express or implied, as to its accuracy, merchantability, or fitness for any purpose but wrapping sardines. Persons attempting to write working code based upon it will receive no sympathy when their programs collapse in a heap of smoldering debris. Have a nice day.

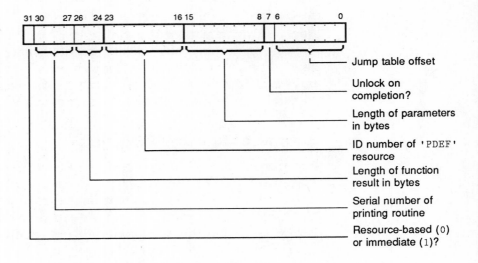

Figure 4–13 Printing routine selector format

The first 5 bits of the selector are simply a serial code number identifying the desired printing routine: 0 for PrOpenDoc, 1 for PrCloseDoc, and so on. Numbers from 0 to 15 (that is, those with 0 in the high-order bit) designate routines contained in a 'PDEF' resource loaded from the printer resource file. Those from 16 to 31 (high-order bit equal to 1) are performed directly by the Toolbox itself, without recourse to any 'PDEF'.

The next 3 bits give the length in bytes of the function result, if any, returned on the stack. If this value is 0, the routine is a simple procedure that returns no result. Similarly, the third byte of the selector gives the number of bytes of parameters that the routine expects to find on the stack on entry.

For routines that reside in the printer resource file, the second byte of the selector holds the resource ID of the relevant 'PDEF' resource. You'll find these 'PDEF' numbers for the standard printing routines summarized in a table in section [4.6.2]. Notice that the document printing routines PrOpenDoc, PrCloseDoc, PrOpenPage, and PrClosePage are listed under four different 'PDEF' resources, numbers 0 to 3. This is because the printer resource file can contain different versions of these routines corresponding to different printing methods that the user can select. The selectors for these routines all specify a 'PDEF' number of 0; the actual resource number (from 0 to 3) is taken from the bJDocLoop field of the print record [4.1.5].

To locate the various routines within the body of the resource, each 'PDEF' begins with a jump table consisting of executable jump (JMP) instructions to the entry points of the routines. The last 7 bits of the routine selector give the offset of the routine's jump table entry in bytes relative to the beginning of the resource. The Toolbox uses this offset to find and execute the jump instruction in the table, which in turn directs control to the beginning of the routine itself.

The remaining (high-order) bit in the last byte of the routine selector is a flag, telling the Toolbox whether to unlock the 'PDEF' resource in the heap after completing the printing operation. This bit is set to 1 for one-time, stand-alone operations like PrintDefault [4.2.2], PrStlDialog [4.2.3], or PrValidate [4.2.2], and to 0 for those that are just part of a continuing sequence of calls, like the document printing operations PrOpenDoc [4.3.1], PrOpenPage, and PrClosePage [4.3.2]. This tells the Toolbox to leave the 'PDEF' containing the routine's code locked in place in the heap, where it will still be available for the next operation in the sequence. Only when you finally terminate the document printing sequence, by calling PrClosePage [4.3.2], is the unlock bit set to 1; this allows the 'PDEF' to be unlocked and eventually purged from the heap to make room for something else.

Customizing the Printing Dialogs

If the standard style and job dialogs provided by the Toolbox don't meet your needs, you can customize them to suit yourself—either by appending additional dialog items of your own or by modifying the appearance or arrangement of the standard items. The technique for doing all this is a bit tricky. It depends on a little-known, low-level Toolbox routine, undocumented in *Inside Macintosh*, called PrDlgMain [4.5.1]. Ordinarily, you call the standard routines PrStlDialog and PrJobDialog [4.2.3] to present the printing dialogs, and they in turn call PrDlgMain for you. To customize the dialogs, you bypass the standard routines and call PrDlgMain directly.

Although you can alter the visual layout of the standard dialogs on the screen, it's important not to delete any of the standard items or change their logical positions in the item list (such as by inserting items of your own in the middle of the list). The only safe way to modify the item list is by appending items at the end. Also, bear in mind that even though *you* can't delete or reorder the standard items, Apple itself may do so at any time: never write code that depends on any item having a specific item number.

Apple also reserves the right in the future to expand the standard printing dialogs up to half the physical height of the screen, leaving your own items limited to the other half. If this isn't a big enough playpen for you, you should probably move your toys to a separate dialog box, activated by its own distinct menu command (perhaps named Print Options... or something similar).

PrDlgMain accepts two parameters: a handle to a print record and a pointer to a *dialog initialization routine.* The job of the initialization routine is to create and initialize a *printing dialog record* of type TPrDlg [4.5.1]. This is an extended form of dialog record [II:7.1.1] with several additional fields tacked onto the end. The most important of these are a pair of procedure pointers, to a *filter function* [II:7.4.5] for processing events in the dialog and a *response procedure* for responding to mouse clicks in its items. We've already discussed filter functions earlier in this chapter and looked at an example of their use. The response procedure takes two parameters, a dialog pointer and an item number, and defines the action to be taken when the mouse is clicked in the specified item. Another field holds a handle to the print record the dialog is to fill in; there are also a number of private fields for the Toolbox's own use.

PrDlgMain begins by calling the initialization routine designated by its initProc parameter. The initialization routine returns a pointer to a printing dialog record, which includes both the dialog definition itself and the filter function and response procedure that determine its behavior. PrDlgMain then displays the dialog on the screen and calls ModalDialog [II:7.4.3] to handle its interactions with the user, passing the filter function pointer from the printing dialog record. Each time `ModalDialog` returns an item number, `PrDlgMain` relays it to the record's response procedure for action. When the user clicks the `OK` button, `PrDlgMain` dismisses the dialog from the screen, updates and validates the print record, and returns `TRUE`; if the `Cancel` button is clicked instead, it leaves the print record unchanged and returns `FALSE`.

To use the standard style and job dialogs, you simply call the Toolbox routines `PrStlDialog` and `PrJobDialog` [4.2.3], as we learned earlier. These in turn call the general-purpose routine `PrDlgMain`, passing it a pointer to one of the built-in initialization routines `PrStlInit` and `PrJobInit` [4.5.1]. To customize one of the dialogs, you call `PrDlgMain` directly, passing a pointer to an initialization routine of your own instead of the standard one.

Program 4–15 illustrates in schematic form the technique for customizing the style dialog. (The equivalent method would of course apply to the job dialog as well.) Our custom initialization routine, `InitStyleDialog`, begins by calling the corresponding built-in routine, `PrStlInit`; this returns a pointer to a `TPrDlg` record describing the standard style dialog. We then use this record to find the dialog's item list and append our own extra items at the end.

Program 4–15 Customizing a printing dialog

```
{ Global variables }

var
    StdStlFilter    : ProcPtr;              {Filter function for standard style dialog}
    StdStlResponse  : ProcPtr;              {Response procedure for standard style dialog}

{ Forward declarations }

function StyleFilter (thisDialog     : DialogPtr;
                      var thisEvent  : EventRecord;
                      var itemNumber : INTEGER) : BOOLEAN; forward;
    { Filter function for customized style dialog. }


function StyleResponse (thisDialog : DialogPtr; itemNumber : INTEGER); forward;
    { Response procedure for customized style dialog. }
```

Program 4-15 Customizing a printing dialog *(continued)*

```
function InitStyleDialog (printRec : THPrint) : TPPrDlg;

    { Initialize customized style dialog. }

    var
        stdStlDlg : TPPrDlg;                              {Record defining standard style dialog [4.5.1]}

    begin  {InitStyleDialog}

        stdStlDlg := PrStlInit (printRec);               {Get standard style dialog [4.5.1]}
        with stdStlDlg^ do
            begin

                {Append extra items to end of dlg's item list}

                StdStlFilter    := pFltrProc;            {Save standard filter function [4.5.1]}
                pFltrProc       := @StyleFilter;         {Install custom filter function [4.5.1]}

                StdStlResponse := pItemProc;             {Save standard response procedure [4.5.1]}
                pItemProc      := @StyleResponse         {Install custom response procedure [4.5.1]}

            end;  {with stdStlDlg^}

        InitStyleDialog := stdStlDlg                     {Return pointer to record [4.5.1]}

    end;    {InitStyleDialog}


function StyleFilter {(thisDialog     : DialogPtr;        }
                     { var thisEvent  : EventRecord;      }
                     { var itemNumber : INTEGER) : BOOLEAN};

    { Filter function for customized style dialog. }

    var
        . . . ;

    begin  {StyleFilter}

        {Do customized event filtering, calling StdStlFilter if necessary}

    end;    {StyleFilter}
```

Program 4–15 Customizing a printing dialog *(continued)*

```
function StyleResponse {(thisDialog : DialogPtr; itemNumber : INTEGER)};

    { Response procedure for customized style dialog. }

    var
       . . . ;

    begin {StyleResponse}

       if {itemNumber is one of our items} then
          {Take appropriate action to respond to this item}
       else
          {Call StdStlResponse for standard processing of thisDialog and itemNumber}

    end;   {StyleResponse}
```

The printing dialog record also includes pointers to the Toolbox's standard filter function and response procedure for the style dialog. After saving these pointers in a pair of global variables, `StdStlFilter` and `StdStlResponse`, we replace them in the record with pointers to our own substitute routines, `StyleFilter` and `StyleResponse`. These routines can use the globals to locate and call the original routines when needed; in particular, the custom response procedure *must* call the original one to respond to any mouse clicks it receives for the standard items of the original dialog.

> For a more fully developed example of customizing the printing dialogs, see Macintosh Technical Note #95.

Customizing Paper Sizes

It's also possible to customize the list of paper sizes offered to the user in the style dialog (see Figure 4–5). The contents of this list are defined by a *paper size table* [4.5.2], which gives the names to be displayed in the dialog box (US Letter, International Fanfold, and so forth) along with the corresponding paper dimensions in 120ths of an inch. 'PREC' resource number 3 in the printer resource file contains a table of standard paper sizes for this printer. If you wish, you can override this table with one of your own, stored in your application resource file as 'PREC' number 4. If no such resource is present, the Toolbox will use the list in the printer resource file instead.

> Notice that the paper size table must always include exactly six pairs of paper dimensions and six title strings, even if there aren't that many actual paper sizes to define. The first word of the table tells how many of the entries are significant. Also notice that the title strings are packed together as closely as possible, without any padding bytes—even if this means that some of them don't begin on even word boundaries. Use one-character dummy strings for any unused titles at the end of the list.

Advanced Operations

Recent versions of the Toolbox printing code (beginning with version 2.5 of the ImageWriter resource file and LaserWriter 4.0) include a generic routine named PrGeneral, which provides a variety of advanced printing operations for specialized needs. We've already mentioned this feature earlier in connection with draft printing of bit maps on the ImageWriter. Other capabilities include determining the range of dot resolutions available on a given printer and finding the page orientation (portrait or landscape) currently in effect; more may be added in the future. The desired operation and its parameters are specified in a complex data block, whose exact form and contents vary from one operation to another. For information on the available operations and on the PrGeneral mechanism itself, see *Inside Macintosh*, Volume V, or Macintosh Technical Note #128.

REFERENCE

4.1 Printing-Related Data Structures

4.1.1   Printing Port

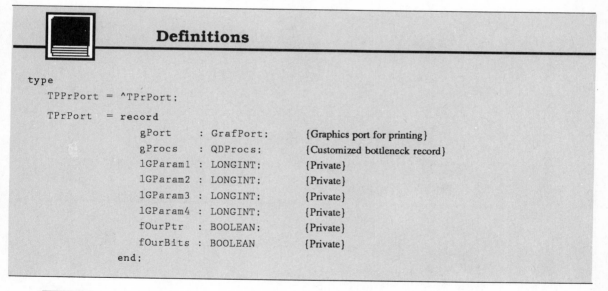

Definitions

```
type
    TPPrPort = ^TPrPort;

    TPrPort  = record
                gPort    : GrafPort;     {Graphics port for printing}
                gProcs   : QDProcs;      {Customized bottleneck record}
                lGParam1 : LONGINT;      {Private}
                lGParam2 : LONGINT;      {Private}
                lGParam3 : LONGINT;      {Private}
                lGParam4 : LONGINT;      {Private}
                fOurPtr  : BOOLEAN;      {Private}
                fOurBits : BOOLEAN       {Private}
            end;
```

Notes

1. A printing port is a special QuickDraw graphics port [I:4.2.2], extended and customized for hardcopy printing instead of drawing on the screen.

2. Printing ports are created and destroyed by the Toolbox routines `PrOpenDoc` and `PrCloseDoc` [4.3.1].

3. `gPort` is a complete graphics port record [I:4.2.2] (not just a pointer) embedded within the printing port record.

4. `gProcs` is a bottleneck record [2.1.1] containing customized drawing routines for hardcopy printing. The port's bottleneck pointer (`gPort.grafProcs`) is set to point to this record.

5. The remaining fields of the printing port are reserved for the private use of the Toolbox, and are of no concern to the application program.

Assembly Language Information

Field offsets in a printing port:

(Pascal) Field name	(Assembly) Offset name	Offset in bytes
gPort	gPort	0
gProcs	gProcs	108

Assembly-language constant:

Name	Value	Meaning
IPrPortSize	178	Size of printing port record in bytes

4.1.2 Print Record

Definitions

```
type
   THPrint = ^TPPrint;
   TPPrint = ^TPrint;
   TPrint  = record
               iPrVersion : INTEGER;      {Version stamp}
               prInfo     : TPrInfo;      {Printer information subrecord [4.1.3]}
               rPaper     : Rect;         {Paper rectangle}
               prStl      : TPrStl;       {Style subrecord [4.1.4]}
               prInfoPT   : TPrInfo;      {Print-time information subrecord [4.1.3]}
               prXInfo    : TPrXInfo;     {Auxiliary information subrecord [4.1.6]}
               prJob      : TPrJob;       {Job subrecord [4.1.5]}
```

```
            printX      : array [1..19] of INTEGER
                                     {Padding to fill to 120 bytes}
       end;

const
   IPrRelease = 3;                   {Current version number of printing routines}
```

Notes

1. A print record summarizes all the information needed to carry out a single printing job.

2. The contents of the print record are set automatically by the Toolbox routines `PrintDefault` **[4.2.2]**, `PrStlDialog` **[4.2.3]**, and `PrJobDialog` **[4.2.3]**. In general, your program should just leave them alone; exceptions are noted where applicable in later sections.

3. It is recommended practice to save a copy of the print record in a document's resource fork when writing the document out to a disk file. The document will thus "remember" its own printing settings from one session to the next.

4. `iPrVersion` identifies the version of the Toolbox printing routines that initialized this print record. The constant `IPrRelease` gives the current version number (version 3 at the time this book went to print).

5. `rPaper` is the *paper rectangle*, which defines the overall dimensions of the physical sheet of paper. Don't confuse this with the page rectangle [4.1.3], which represents the printable area only.

6. The paper rectangle's coordinate system is defined by the page rectangle. That is, the top-left corner of the printable page (the page rectangle) has coordinates (0, 0); that of the physical sheet (the paper rectangle) typically has negative coordinates relative to that point.

7. The coordinates of the paper rectangle are expressed in printer dots. The number of dots per inch is given by the `iVRes` and `iHRes` fields of the printer information subrecord [4.1.3].

8. The coordinates of the paper rectangle are only approximate, since the physical alignment of paper in some printers is inexact and is not subject to program testing or control.

9. The remaining fields of the print record are specialized subrecords, and are discussed in sections [4.1.3] to [4.1.6]. Notice that the subrecords are not referred to by pointers or handles, but are embedded directly within the print record itself.

10. printX is a dummy array, included to fill out the print record to a standard size of 120 bytes. However, the Toolbox reserves the right to use this space for its own private purposes, now or in the future. Never store anything into it yourself.

Assembly Language Information

Field offsets in a print record:

(Pascal) Field name	(Assembly) Offset name	Offset in bytes
iPrVersion	iPrVersion	0
prInfo	prInfo	2
rPaper	rPaper	16
prStl	prStl	24
prInfoPT	prInfoPT	32
prXInfo	prXInfo	46
prJob	prJob	62

Assembly-language constants:

Name	Value	Meaning
IPrintSize	120	Size of print record in bytes
IPrRelease	3	Current version number of printing routines

4.1.3   Printer Information Subrecord

Definitions

```
type
   TPPrInfo = ^TPrInfo;

   TPrInfo  = record
                 iDev  : INTEGER;        {Printer's device code}
                 iVRes : INTEGER;        {Vertical resolution in dots per inch}
                 iHRes : INTEGER;        {Horizontal resolution in dots per inch}
                 rPage : Rect            {Page rectangle}
              end;
```

Notes

1. The printer information subrecord is the part of the print record [4.1.2] that summarizes the characteristics of a particular printer.

2. The print record actually contains two subrecords of this type, `prInfo` and `prInfoPT`. The second is used privately by the Toolbox and is of no interest to the application program. (PT stands for "print time.")

3. `iDev` is the printer's device code [I:8.3.1], used by the Toolbox for selecting appropriate text fonts.

4. The first byte of `iDev` is the reference number of the printer driver, normally `-3` (`$FD`); the contents of the second byte are private to the Toolbox.

5. Some printers use `iDev` in unusual and devious ways, such as setting it to 0 to fool QuickDraw into thinking they are really the Macintosh screen. Your program should never assume it knows what this field actually means.

6. `iVRes` and `iHRes` are the vertical and horizontal resolution of the printer, in dots per inch.

7. `rPage` is the *page rectangle*, which defines the printable area of the page. Don't confuse this with the paper rectangle [4.1.2], which represents the overall dimensions of the physical sheet of paper.

8. The top-left corner of the page rectangle always has coordinates (0, 0); its bottom-right corner defines the extent (height and width) of the printable page.

9. The coordinates of the page rectangle are expressed in printer dots, at the resolution given by `iVRes` and `iHRes`.

Assembly Language Information

Field offsets in a printer information subrecord:

(Pascal) Field name	(Assembly) Offset name	Offset in bytes
iDev	iDev	0
iVRes	iVRes	2
iHRes	iHRes	4
rPage	rPage	6

4.1.4 Style Subrecord

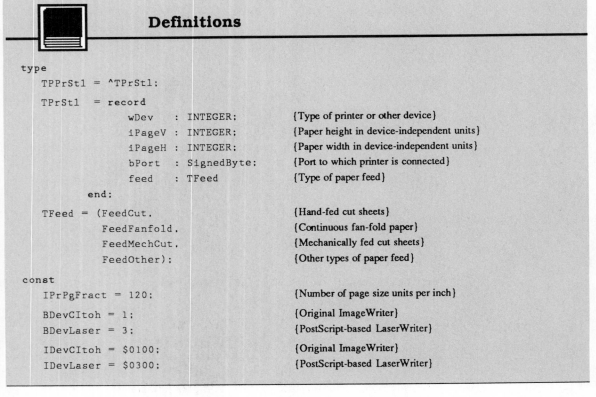

Definitions

```
type
    TPPrStl = ^TPrStl;

    TPrStl  = record
                  wDev    : INTEGER;        {Type of printer or other device}
                  iPageV  : INTEGER;        {Paper height in device-independent units}
                  iPageH  : INTEGER;        {Paper width in device-independent units}
                  bPort   : SignedByte;     {Port to which printer is connected}
                  feed    : TFeed           {Type of paper feed}
              end;

    TFeed = (FeedCut,                       {Hand-fed cut sheets}
             FeedFanfold,                   {Continuous fan-fold paper}
             FeedMechCut,                   {Mechanically fed cut sheets}
             FeedOther);                    {Other types of paper feed}
const
    IPrPgFract = 120;                       {Number of page size units per inch}

    BDevCItoh = 1;                          {Original ImageWriter}
    BDevLaser = 3;                          {PostScript-based LaserWriter}

    IDevCItoh = $0100;                      {Original ImageWriter}
    IDevLaser = $0300;                      {PostScript-based LaserWriter}
```

Device type codes:

Value	Meaning
0	Macintosh screen
1	Original ImageWriter
3	PostScript-based LaserWriter
4	LaserWriter II–SC
5	ImageWriter LQ

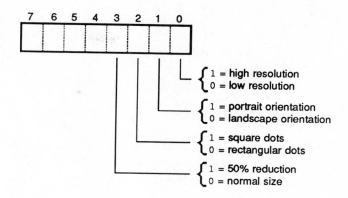

ImageWriter style flags

Notes

1. The style subrecord is the part of the print record [4.1.2] that specifies the way the printer is to be used for a particular job (as distinct from the printer's inherent characteristics).

2. This subrecord was originally intended to hold the information obtained via the style dialog [4.2.3], while the job subrecord [4.1.5] would correspond to the job dialog [4.2.3]. In practice the correspondence has become somewhat blurred, and the style subrecord actually includes information from both dialogs.

3. All fields except the first byte of wDev are considered private to the Toolbox, and their contents and usage are subject to change without notice. The information given here is for your background understanding only; your program should never assume it knows what these fields actually mean.

4. The first byte of wDev identifies the type of printer or other device to which output is directed (see table). The second byte contains modifying information on the way the printer is currently being used; its exact contents and format vary from one printer to another and should never be altered except by the Toolbox itself.

5. For the original ImageWriter (including the ImageWriter II), the modifying information has the format shown in the figure. Apple does

not guarantee the continued accuracy of this information, and it is liable to change in future versions of the printing software; never write code that relies on it. For all other printers (including later-model ImageWriters such as the LQ), the contents of this byte are not revealed to mere mortals.

6. The constants `BDevCItoh` and `BDevLaser` represent the "raw" type codes for the original ImageWriter and PostScript-based LaserWriter, respectively. `IDevCItoh` and `IDevLaser` are corresponding word-length constants with the type code correctly positioned in the high-order byte. Apple's official interface files do not yet include named constants for the more recent ImageWriter LQ and LaserWriter II–SC.

7. `iPageV` and `iPageH` give the dimensions of the physical sheet of paper, according to the paper size chosen by the user in the style dialog (US Letter, International Fanfold, and so forth). Notice that this corresponds to the *paper* rectangle [4.1.2], not the *page* rectangle [4.1.3]; the names should really be `iPaperV` and `iPaperH`.

8. `iPageV` and `iPageH` are expressed in device-independent units of $\frac{1}{120}$ of an inch. (The constant `IPrPageFract` gives the number of units per inch.) This differs from the print record's `rPaper` field [4.1.2], which is measured in dots at printer-dependent resolution.

9. `bPort` identifies the serial or SCSI port to which the printer is connected: 1 for the normal printer port (port B), 0 for the modem port (port A). The user designates one port or the other with the Chooser desk accessory at the time the printer is installed.

10. `feed` identifies the method of paper feed being used, as a value of the enumerated type `TFeed`:

    - `FeedCut` stands for hand-fed, individually cut sheets; when this method is used, printing will pause at the end of each page and the user will be prompted with an alert to insert the next sheet.
    - `FeedFanfold` stands for continuous-feed "accordion" paper.
    - `FeedMechCut` stands for mechanically fed cut sheets (for example, on an ImageWriter II with the optional sheet feeder).
    - `FeedOther` stands for any other method of paper feed.

Assembly Language Information

Field offsets in a style subrecord:

(Pascal) Field name	(Assembly) Offset name	Offset in bytes
wDev	wDev	0
iPageV	iPageV	2
iPageH	iPageH	4
bPort	bPort	6
feed	feed	7

Assembly-language constants:

Name	Value	Meaning
IPrSt1Size	8	Size of a style subrecord in bytes
IPrPgFract	120	Number of page size units per inch

4.1.5   Job Subrecord

Definitions

```
type
   TPPrJob = ^TPrJob:

   TPrJob  = record
                iFstPage   : INTEGER;      {First page to be printed}
                iLstPage   : INTEGER;      {Last page to be printed}
                iCopies    : INTEGER;      {Number of copies to be printed}
                bJDocLoop  : SignedByte:   {Printing method (draft or spool)}
                fFromUsr   : BOOLEAN;      {Private}
                pIdleProc  : ProcPtr;      {Pointer to background procedure}
                pFileName  : StringPtr;    {Name of spool file}
                iFileVol   : INTEGER;      {Reference number of spool file's volume}
                bFileVers  : SignedByte:   {Version number of spool file}
                bJobX      : SignedByte    {Padding}
             end;
```

```
const
    IPrPgFst  =     1;          {Minimum page number to be printed}
    IPrPgMax  =  9999;          {Maximum page number to be printed}
    BDraftLoop = 0;             {Draft printing}
    BSpoolLoop = 1;             {Spooling}
    BUser1Loop = 2;             {Printer-specific method number 1}
    BUser2Loop = 3;             {Printer-specific method number 2}
```

Notes

1. The job subrecord is the part of the print record [4.1.2] that specifies how a document is to be printed on a particular occasion.

2. This subrecord was originally intended to hold the information obtained via the job dialog [4.2.3], while the style subrecord [4.1.4] would correspond to the style dialog [4.2.3]. In practice the correspondence has become somewhat blurred, and the job dialog actually contributes to the contents of both subrecords.

3. `iFstPage` and `iLstPage` specify the range of pages to be printed. The minimum and maximum values allowed for these fields are given by the constants `IPrPgFst` and `IPrPgMax`.

4. The page range is defined with reference to the printing routine `PrOpenPage` [4.3.2]. The first call to `PrOpenPage` is always considered to begin page 1, independent of any other numbering scheme the application program itself may use.

5. To print the range of pages requested by the user, you should either
   - image the entire document, leaving it to the Toolbox to suppress those pages that fall outside the requested range, or
   - set `iFstPage` to 1 and `iLstPage` to the number of pages in the range, then image only the pages actually requested

6. `iCopies` is the number of copies to be printed. In draft printing, the application program must look at this field and explicitly image the document the specified number of times. In spooling, the program need only image the document once; when the spool file is later printed, the Toolbox will automatically print the requested number of copies.

7. `bJDocLoop` specifies the printing method to be used, and should normally be one of the constants `BDraftLoop` or `BSpoolLoop`. (The other two values, `BUser1Loop` and `BUser2Loop`, denote alternative, device-specific printing methods; they have no meaning on any currently supported printer.)

8. `pIdleProc` is a pointer to a background procedure to be run repeatedly while awaiting completion of output operations on the printer.

9. The background procedure takes no parameters and returns no result.

10. Background procedures must not attempt to do any printing of their own, and must be careful not to change the current port or other properties of the global environment that the printing routines may rely on.

11. A NIL value for pIdleProc designates the standard background procedure, which simply checks for the keystroke Command-period and responds to it by canceling the printing operation.

12. If you use the standard background procedure, you should display an alert box with a suitable message, such as Printing document; type Command-period to cancel.

13. The printing routines PrOpenDoc [4.3.1], PrintDefault [4.2.2], PrValidate [4.2.2], PrStlDialog [4.2.3], and PrJobDialog [4.2.3] all reset pIdleProc to NIL. You must wait until after completing all of these operations before installing your own background procedure in place of the standard one.

14. To achieve the effect of concurrent printing, use a background procedure that performs one pass of your program's main event loop. Such a procedure should disable the menu items Page Setup and Print, as well as any other operations related to printing. (Alternatively, you might wish to change the Print command to something like Cancel Printing.)

15. The background procedure can use a printing status record [4.1.7] to monitor the progress of the printing operation and post a running status message on the screen.

16. To cancel printing from within a background procedure, issue the call PrSetError(IPrAbort) [4.2.4].

17. pFileName, iFileVol, and bFileVers give the name, volume (or directory) reference number, and version number of the spool file. These fields are meaningful only for spooling operations; in draft printing, they are ignored.

18. pFileName is initialized to NIL, representing the standard spool file name taken from the printer resource file [4.6.3] for the current printer. The name normally used is Print File.

19. iFileVol is initialized to 0, denoting the current volume or directory [II:8.1.2].

20. File version numbers are handled inconsistently by different parts of the Toolbox. To avoid problems, bFileVers should always be left at its initial value of 0.

21. bJobX is an extra byte of padding, included to fill out the job subrecord to an even number of bytes. However, the Toolbox reserves the right to use this field for its own private purposes, now or in the future. Never store anything into it yourself.

Assembly Language Information

Field offsets in a job subrecord:

(Pascal) Field name	(Assembly) Offset name	Offset in bytes
iFstPage	iFstPage	0
iLstPage	iLstPage	2
iCopies	iCopies	4
bJDocLoop	bJDocLoop	6
fFromUsr	fFromApp	7
pIdleProc	pIdleProc	8
pFileName	pFileName	12
iFileVol	iFileVol	16
bFileVers	bFileVers	18
bJobX	bJobX	19

Assembly-language constant:

Name	Value	Meaning
IPrJobSize	20	Size of a job subrecord in bytes

Page range limits:

Name	Value	Meaning
IPrPgFst	1	Minimum page number to be printed
IPrPgMax	9999	Maximum page number to be printed

Printing methods:

Name	Value	Meaning
BDraftLoop	0	Draft printing
BSpoolLoop	1	Spooling
BUser1Loop	2	Printer-specific method number 1
BUser2Loop	3	Printer-specific method number 2

4.1.6 Auxiliary Information Subrecord

Definitions

```
type
    TPPrXInfo = ^TPrXInfo;

    TPrXInfo  = record
                    iRowBytes  :  INTEGER;      {Row width of each band in bytes}
                    iBandV     :  INTEGER;      {Height of each band in dots}
                    iBandH     :  INTEGER;      {Width of each band in dots}
                    iDevBytes  :  INTEGER;      {Size of band image in bytes}
                    iBands     :  INTEGER;      {Number of bands per page}
                    bPatScale  :  SignedByte;   {Used in scaling patterns}
                    bULThick   :  SignedByte;   {Thickness of underline, in dots}
                    bULOffset  :  SignedByte;   {Offset below baseline, in dots}
                    bULShadow  :  SignedByte;   {Width of break around descenders, in dots}
                    scan       :  TScan;        {Scan direction}
                    bXInfoX    :  SignedByte    {Padding}
                end;

    TScan = (ScanTB,                            {Scan from top to bottom}
             ScanBT,                            {Scan from bottom to top}
             ScanLR,                            {Scan from left to right}
             ScanRL);                           {Scan from right to left}
```

Notes

1. The auxiliary information subrecord is a part of the print record [4.1.2] containing private information on how to match the page image to the characteristics of a particular printer.

2. All fields except `iDevBytes` are considered private to the Toolbox, and their contents and usage are subject to change without notice. The information given below is for your background understanding only; your program should never assume it knows what these fields actually mean.

3. `iBands` is the number of bands into which the page is to be broken for output to the printer.

4. `iBandV` and `iBandH` are the height and width of each band in dots, at the resolution given by the `iVRes` and `iHRes` fields of the printer information subrecord [4.1.3].

5. iRowBytes is the row width of the bit map [I:4.2.1] representing each band.

6. iDevBytes is the number of bytes needed to hold the bit image for each band. If you supply your own buffer storage for the defBuf parameter to PrPicFile [4.3.3], this is the size of the buffer you should allocate.

7. bPatScale is used by QuickDraw when scaling patterns to the resolution of the printer.

8. bULThick, bULOffset, and bULShadow are the characteristics for underlined text at the printer's resolution. bULThick gives the thickness of the underline, bULOffset its offset below the baseline, and bULShadow the width of the break around descenders, all in printer dots.

9. scan specifies the scan direction for breaking the page into bands, as a value of the enumerated type TScan.

10. bXInfoX is an extra byte of padding, included to fill out the subrecord to an even number of bytes. However, the Toolbox reserves the right to use this field for its own private purposes, now or in the future. Never store anything into it yourself.

Assembly Language Information

Field offsets in an auxiliary information subrecord:

(Pascal) Field name	(Assembly) Offset name	Offset in bytes
iRowBytes	iRowBytes	0
iBandV	iBandV	2
iBandH	iBandH	4
iDevBytes	iDevBytes	6
iBands	iBands	8
bPatScale	bPatScale	10
bULThick	bULThick	11
bULOffset	bULOffset	12
bULShadow	bULShadow	13
scan	scan	14
bXInfoX	bXInfoX	15

Assembly-language constant:

Name	Value	Meaning
lPrXInfoSize	16	Size of an auxiliary information subrecord, in bytes

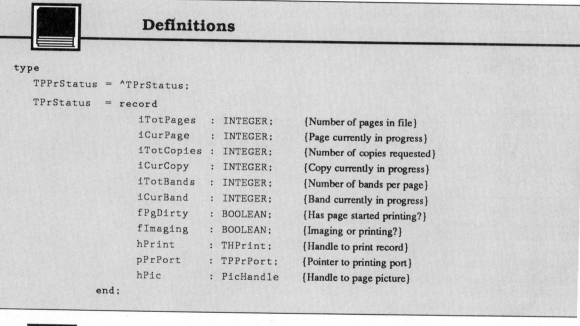

Scan directions:

Name	Value	Meaning
ScanTB	0	Scan top to bottom
ScanBT	1	Scan bottom to top
ScanLR	2	Scan left to right
ScanRL	3	Scan right to left

4.1.7 Printing Status Record

Definitions

```
type
   TPPrStatus = ^TPrStatus;

   TPrStatus  = record
                iTotPages  : INTEGER;     {Number of pages in file}
                iCurPage   : INTEGER;     {Page currently in progress}
                iTotCopies : INTEGER;     {Number of copies requested}
                iCurCopy   : INTEGER;     {Copy currently in progress}
                iTotBands  : INTEGER;     {Number of bands per page}
                iCurBand   : INTEGER;     {Band currently in progress}
                fPgDirty   : BOOLEAN;     {Has page started printing?}
                fImaging   : BOOLEAN;     {Imaging or printing?}
                hPrint     : THPrint;     {Handle to print record}
                pPrPort    : TPPrPort;    {Pointer to printing port}
                hPic       : PicHandle    {Handle to page picture}
              end;
```

Notes

1. A printing status record reports on the status of a spool printing operation.

2. The application program supplies a record of this type to the printing routine PrPicFile [4.3.3]. A background procedure [4.1.5] can then use this record to monitor the progress of the printing operation and post a running status message on the screen.

3. iTotCopies, iTotPages, and iTotBands give the total number of copies to be printed (as requested by the user), the number of pages in the spool file, and the number of bands making up each page. The

corresponding fields `iCurCopy`, `iCurPage`, and `iCurBand` report which copy, page, and band are currently being printed.

4. `fPgDirty` tells whether anything has yet been printed on the page designated by `iCurPage`.

5. `fImaging` is `TRUE` while a band is being imaged, `FALSE` while the image is being sent to the printer.

6. `hPrint` and `pPrPort` hold, respectively, a handle to the print record and a pointer to the printing port for this operation.

7. For printers that spool their pages in the form of QuickDraw pictures [I:5.4.1], `hPic` is a handle to the picture for the current page.

8. The fields `iTotBands`, `iCurBand`, `fImaging`, and `hPic` are considered private to the Toolbox, and their contents and usage are subject to change without notice. The information given above is for your background understanding only; your program should never assume it knows what these fields actually mean.

Assembly Language Information

Field offsets in a printing status record:

(Pascal) Field name	(Assembly) Offset name	Offset in bytes
iTotPages	iTotPages	0
iCurPage	iCurPage	2
iTotCopies	iTotCopies	4
iCurCopy	iCurCopy	6
iTotBands	iTotBands	8
iCurBand	iCurBand	10
fPgDirty	fPgDirty	12
fImaging	fImaging	13
hPrint	hPrint	14
pPrPort	pPrPort	18
hPic	hPic	22

Assembly-language constant:

Name	Value	Meaning
lPrStatSize	26	Size of a printing status record in bytes

4.2 Preliminary Operations

4.2.1 Initializing the Toolbox for Printing

Definitions

```
procedure PrOpen;
procedure PrClose;
```

Notes

1. `PrOpen` prepares for printing by opening the printer resource file and the printer driver.

2. Before calling `PrOpen`, you must first call `InitGraf` [I:4.3.1], `InitFonts` [I:8.2.4], `InitWindows` [II:3.2.1], `InitMenus` [II:4.2.1], `TEInit` [II:5.2.1], and `InitDialogs` [II:7.2.1].

3. `PrClose` closes the printer resource file and releases the memory occupied by its resource map.

4. `PrClose` does *not* close the printer driver. The driver normally remains open continuously for as long as your program runs, but if necessary you can close it explicitly with `PrDrvrClose` [4.4.1].

5. The trap macros for these routines expand to call the universal printing trap `_PrGlue` with the routine selectors given below.

Assembly Language Information

Trap macros and routine selectors:

(Pascal) Routine name	(Assembly) Trap macro	Trap word	Routine selector
PrOpen	_PrOpen	$A8FD	$C8000000
PrClose	_PrClose	$A8FD	$D0000000

4.2.2   Initializing Print Records

Definitions

```
procedure  PrintDefault
              (printRec : THPrint);          {Print record to initialize}
function   PrValidate
              (printRec : THPrint)           {Print record to validate}
                : BOOLEAN;                    {Was record altered?}
```

Notes

1. `PrintDefault` initializes a print record to the standard default values for the current printer.

2. The default values are taken from `'PREC'` resource number 0 [4.6.1] in the current printer resource file [4.6.3].

3. `PrValidate` verifies the validity of a print record for the currently installed printer and printing routines.

4. If the print record is not valid for the current printer, or if its `iPrVersion` field [4.1.2] refers to an obsolete version of the printing routines, it is reinitialized to the current standard values.

5. A function result of `TRUE` means that the print record was invalid and had to be reinitialized; `FALSE` means that it was valid as it was.

6. If necessary, the contents of the print record may also be adjusted for internal self-consistency. Such changes are not reflected in the function result.

7. The trap macros for these routines expand to call the universal printing trap `_PrGlue` with the routine selectors given below.

Assembly Language Information

Trap macros and routine selectors:

(Pascal) Routine name	(Assembly) Trap macro	Trap word	Routine selector
PrintDefault	_PrintDefault	$A8FD	$20040480
PrValidate	_PrValidate	$A8FD	$52040498

4.2.3   **Printing-Related Dialogs**

Definitions

```
function   PrStlDialog
              (printRec : THPrint)        {Handle to print record}
                  : BOOLEAN;              {Was dialog confirmed?}
function   PrJobDialog
              (printRec : THPrint)        {Handle to print record}
                  : BOOLEAN;              {Was dialog confirmed?}
procedure  PrJobMerge
              (sourceRec : THPrint;       {Print record to copy from}
               destRec   : THPrint);      {Print record to copy to}
```

Notes

1. `PrStlDialog` conducts a style dialog with the user; `PrJobDialog` conducts a job dialog.

2. The style dialog is meant to be presented in response to the `Page Setup` menu command. It defines a document's overall printing-related properties, such as the paper size and orientation.

3. The job dialog is meant to be presented in response to the `Print` menu command. It includes information pertaining to a single printing job, such as the print quality, page range, and number of copies.

4. Both dialogs are taken from the current printer resource file [4.6.3].

5. Both routines return a function result of `TRUE` if the user confirmed the dialog (by clicking the `OK` button or its equivalent), `FALSE` if the dialog was canceled.

6. If the dialog was confirmed, both routines update the print record accordingly, then validate its contents with `PrValidate` [4.2.2]. If the dialog was canceled, the print record is left unchanged.

7. After updating the print record, `PrJobDialog` copies it into the printer resource file to be used again next time. This makes the results of the job dialog "stick to the printer."

8. If `PrStlDialog` returns `TRUE`, the application program should save the updated print record in the document's resource file, allowing the results of the style dialog to "stick to the document."

9. On receiving a TRUE result from PrJobDialog, the application program should proceed with the requested printing operation.

10. PrJobMerge copies the results of a job dialog from one print record (sourceRec) to another (destRec).

11. Both records are validated for consistency with PrValidate [4.2.2].

12. This routine is useful for applying the results of one job dialog to several documents, such as when printing from the Finder.

13. The trap macros for these routines expand to call the universal printing trap _PrGlue with the routine selectors given below.

Assembly Language Information

Trap macros and routine selectors:

(Pascal) Routine name	(Assembly) Trap macro	Trap word	Routine selector
PrStlDialog	_PrStlDialog	$A8FD	$2A040484
PrJobDialog	_PrJobDialog	$A8FD	$32040488
PrJobMerge	_PrJobMerge	$A8FD	$5804089C

4.2.4   Error Reporting

Definitions

```
function  PrError
            : INTEGER;                        {Result code from last printing operation}
procedure PrSetError
          (errCode : INTEGER);               {Result code to post}
const
   NoErr      =    0;                         {No error; all is well}
   IPrSavPFil =   -1;                         {Error saving print file}
   IIOAbort   =  -27;                         {I/O error}

   IPrAbort   =  128;                         {Cancel printing}
```

Notes

1. `PrError` returns the result code from the last printing operation.

2. The result code returned in the normal case is `0` (`NoErr`). Any nonzero result code denotes an error.

3. Error codes listed here are only those directly related to printing. Errors from other parts of the Toolbox can also occur in the course of printing operations, and will be reported by `PrError`. See Appendix E for a complete list of Toolbox error codes.

4. In assembly language, the result code is also available in the global variable `PrintErr`.

5. `PrSetError` posts a printing-related result code by storing it into the global variable `PrintErr`.

6. The main use for this routine by an application program is to cancel a printing operation in progress by posting the code `IPrAbort`.

7. Don't store into `PrintErr`—either directly or via `PrSetError`—if it already contains a nonzero value.

8. The trap macros for these routines expand to call the universal printing trap `_PrGlue` with the routine selectors given below.

Assembly Language Information

Trap macros and routine selectors:

(Pascal) Routine name	(Assembly) Trap macro	Trap word	Routine selector
PrError	_PrError	$A8FD	$BA000000
PrSetError	_PrSetError	$A8FD	$C0000200

Assembly-language global variable:

Name	Address	Meaning
PrintErr	$944	Result code from last printing operation

Assembly-language constant:

Name	Value	Meaning
IPrAbort	128	Cancel printing

4.3 Document Printing

4.3.1 Opening and Closing a Document

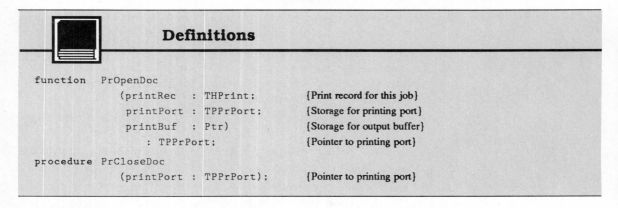

Definitions

```
function  PrOpenDoc
            (printRec  : THPrint;          {Print record for this job}
             printPort : TPPrPort;         {Storage for printing port}
             printBuf  : Ptr)              {Storage for output buffer}
                : TPPrPort;                {Pointer to printing port}
procedure PrCloseDoc
            (printPort : TPPrPort);        {Pointer to printing port}
```

Notes

1. PrOpenDoc initializes a printing port for printing a document; PrCloseDoc closes and destroys an existing printing port.

2. printRec is a handle to a print record defining the properties and parameters of the printing job. Always validate the record with PrValidate [4.2.2] before using it to open a printing port.

3. The new printing port is automatically made the current port. You can then proceed to draw directly into it with QuickDraw operations.

4. The port is customized for spooling or draft printing, as specified in the print record (field prJob.bJDocLoop [4.1.5]).

5. The port rectangle, boundary rectangle, and clipping region are all set equal to the page rectangle (prInfo.rPage [4.1.3]) taken from the print record.

6. The optional parameters printPort and printBuf allow you to supply your own storage for the new printing port and its output buffer.

7. If these parameters are NIL (the usual case), PrOpenDoc will allocate the port for you from the heap, and will direct its output to the volume buffer for the spool file's volume (field prJob.iFileVol of the print record [4.1.5]).

8. If you choose to provide your own storage for the printing port, the size of the required block is given by the Pascal expression SIZEOF(TPrPort), or in assembly language by the constant

IPrPortSize [4.1.1]. The size needed for the output buffer is 522 bytes. Notice that both are nonrelocatable objects and are identified by pointers rather than handles.

9. Every call to PrOpenDoc must be balanced by a corresponding call to PrCloseDoc on completion of the job.

10. PrCloseDoc closes the printing port and (if it was allocated automatically from the heap) releases the space it occupies.

11. In spool printing, PrCloseDoc must be followed by PrPicFile [4.3.3] to print the contents of the spool file.

12. The trap macros for these routines expand to call the universal printing trap _PrGlue with the routine selectors given below.

13. The trap macro for PrCloseDoc is spelled _PrClosDoc.

Assembly Language Information

Trap macros and routine selectors:

(Pascal) Routine name	(Assembly) Trap macro	Trap word	Routine selector
PrOpenDoc	_PrOpenDoc	$A8FD	$04000C00
PrCloseDoc	_PrClosDoc	$A8FD	$08000484

4.3.2   Page Imaging

Definitions

```
procedure PrOpenPage
            (printPort : TPPrPort;        {Pointer to the printing port}
             pageFrame : TPRect);         {Frame rectangle for scaling}
procedure PrClosePage
            (printPort : TPPrPort);       {Pointer to the printing port}
type
    TPRect = ^Rect;                       {Pointer to a rectangle}
const
    IPFMaxPgs = 128;                      {Maximum number of pages in a spool file}
```

Notes

1. `PrOpenPage` begins printing a page of a document; `PrClosePage` finishes it.

2. While a page is open, you can proceed to draw into it with QuickDraw operations.

3. `printPort` is the printing port in which the document is being printed.

4. Every call to `PrOpenPage` reinitializes the printing port. If you are using nonstandard text characteristics [I:8.3.1] or pen characteristics [I:5.2.1], you must explicitly reset them at the beginning of every page.

5. Pages are suppressed if they fall outside the range defined by `iFstPage` and `iLstPage` in the job subrecord [4.1.5]. For this purpose, the first call to `PrOpenPage` within a document is always considered to begin page 1, independent of any other numbering scheme the application program itself may use.

6. To print the range of pages requested by the user, you should either
   - image the entire document, leaving it to the Toolbox to suppress those pages that fall outside the requested range, or
   - set `iFstPage` to 1 and `iLstPage` to the number of pages in the range, then image only the pages actually requested

7. QuickDraw pictures [I:5.4.1] are commonly used to spool page images for later printing. Never call `OpenPicture` [I:5.4.2] yourself while a page is open.

8. The `pageFrame` parameter specifies a rectangle in page-relative coordinates, which will be recorded as the picture frame [I:5.4.1] and later scaled to the page rectangle when the spool file is printed. In draft printing, this parameter is ignored.

9. `pageFrame` is normally set to `NIL`, causing the page to be printed without scaling.

10. Every call to `PrOpenPage` must be balanced by a corresponding call to `PrClosePage`.

11. `PrClosePage` takes whatever actions are appropriate at the end of a page, such as (in draft printing) ejecting the paper and prompting the user, if necessary, to insert another sheet, or (in spooling) closing the picture representing the page and updating the spool file's page directory.

12. The maximum number of pages that can be spooled to a single file is `IPFMaxPgs`. To print more than this number, you must break the document into pieces and spool and print each piece separately.

13. The trap macros for these routines expand to call the universal printing trap _PrGlue with the routine selectors given below.

14. The trap macro for PrClosePage is spelled _PrClosPage.

Assembly Language Information

Trap macros and routine selectors:

(Pascal) Routine name	(Assembly) Trap macro	Trap word	Routine selector
PrOpenPage	_PrOpenPage	$A8FD	$10000808
PrClosePage	_PrClosPage	$A8FD	$1800040C

4.3.3   Spool Printing

Definitions

```
procedure PrPicFile
          (printRec        : THPrint;        {Print record for this job}
           printPort       : TPPrPort;       {Storage for printing port}
           spoolBuf        : Ptr;            {Input buffer for reading spool file}
           printBuf        : Ptr;            {Output buffer for writing to printer}
           var printStatus : TPrStatus);     {Record for reporting status}
```

Notes

1. PrPicFile prints a spool file containing a previously spooled document.

2. This routine constitutes the second phase of the spool printing process. It is normally called immediately after PrCloseDoc [4.3.1], which completes the first (spooling) phase. In draft printing, PrPicFile is not used.

3. printRec is a handle to a print record defining the properties and parameters of the printing job.

4. The spool file's name and volume are given by the pFileName and iFileVol fields of the print record's job subrecord [4.1.5].

5. The spool file is deleted from the disk on successful completion.

6. If the `pIdleProc` field of the job subrecord [4.1.5] contains a pointer to a background procedure, the procedure will be called repeatedly at every opportunity during the spool printing process (such as while waiting for a completion signal from the printer after beginning a printing operation).

7. A `NIL` value for `pIdleProc` designates the standard background procedure, which simply checks for the keystroke Command-period and responds to it by canceling the printing operation.

8. `printStatus` is a status record [4.1.7] in which to report on the progress of the printing operation.

9. The optional parameters `printPort`, `spoolBuf`, and `printBuf` allow you to supply your own storage for the printing port and input/output buffers.

10. If these parameters are `NIL` (the usual case), `PrPicFile` will allocate the port and print buffer for you from the heap, and will use the spool file's volume buffer for reading the file.

11. If you choose to provide your own storage for the printing port, the size of the required block is given by the Pascal expression `SIZEOF(TPrPort)`, or in assembly language by the constant `IPrPortSize` [4.1.1]. The size needed for the spool buffer is 522 bytes; for the print buffer, it is given by the `iDevBytes` field of the auxiliary information subrecord [4.1.6]. Notice that these are all nonrelocatable objects, and are identified by pointers rather than handles.

12. `PrPicFile` uses a brand-new printing port of its own, *not* the same port that was used earlier in the spooling phase. Unless you originally allocated your own port for spooling and passed it to `PrOpenDoc` [4.3.1], the spooling port will have been closed and destroyed by `PrCloseDoc` [4.3.1] and can't be used again for the printing phase.

13. The trap macro for this routine expands to call the universal printing trap `_PrGlue` with the routine selector given below.

Assembly Language Information

Trap macro and routine selector:

(Pascal) Routine name	(Assembly) Trap macro	Trap word	Routine selector
PrPicFile	_PrPicFile	$A8FD	$60051480

4.4 Low-Level Printing

4.4.1   Opening and Closing the Printer Driver

Definitions

```
procedure  PrDrvrOpen;
procedure  PrDrvrClose;
```

Notes

1. These two routines open and close the printer driver, respectively.

2. If the printer driver is not already in memory, PrDrvrOpen reads it into the heap from the system resource file.

3. The initialization routine PrOpen [4.2.1] automatically opens the printer driver for you, but PrClose doesn't close it. If you wish to close the driver, you must do it explicitly with PrDrvrClose.

4. The trap macros for these routines expand to call the universal printing trap _PrGlue with the routine selectors given below.

Assembly Language Information

Trap macros and routine selectors:

(Pascal) Routine name	(Assembly) Trap macro	Trap word	Routine selector
PrDrvrOpen	_PrDrvrOpen	$A8FD	$80000000
PrDrvrClose	_PrDrvrClose	$A8FD	$88000000

4.4.2   Printer Driver Attributes

Definitions

```
function  PrDrvrVers
             : INTEGER;                    {Version number of printer driver}
function  PrDrvrDCE
             : Handle;                     {Handle to driver's device control entry}
procedure PrPurge;
procedure PrNoPurge;
```

Notes

1. PrDrvrVers returns the version number of the currently installed printer driver; PrDrvrDCE returns a handle to its device control entry [3.1.4].

2. The printer driver's name is .Print. Its unit number is 2, and its driver reference number is therefore -3.

3. If the printer driver is up-to-date, its version number should match that of the printing routines themselves, as given by the constant IPrRelease [4.1.2].

4. PrNoPurge marks the printer driver unpurgeable, so that it cannot be removed from the heap; PrPurge makes it purgeable again.

5. The trap macros for these routines expand to call the universal printing trap _PrGlue with the routine selectors given below.

Assembly Language Information

Trap macros and routine selectors:

(Pascal) Routine name	(Assembly) Trap macro	Trap word	Routine selector
PrDrvrVers	_PrDrvrVers	$A8FD	$9A000000
PrDrvrDCE	_PrDrvrDCE	$A8FD	$94000000
PrPurge	_PrPurge	$A8FD	$A8000000
PrNoPurge	_PrNoPurge	$A8FD	$B0000000

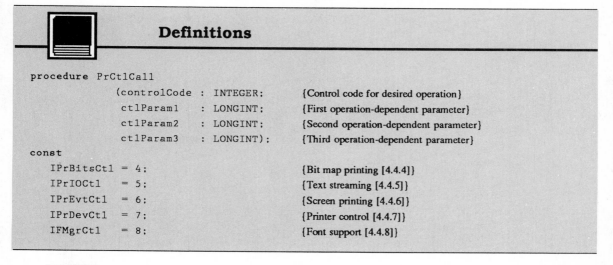

Assembly-language constants:

Name	Value	Meaning
IPrDrvrID	2	Unit number (resource ID) of printer driver
IPrDrvrRef	-3	Reference number of printer driver
IPrDrvrDev	$FD00	Device code [I:8.3.1] of printer driver

4.4.3   Low-Level Operations

Definitions

```
procedure PrCtlCall
            (controlCode : INTEGER;     {Control code for desired operation}
            ctlParam1    : LONGINT;     {First operation-dependent parameter}
            ctlParam2    : LONGINT;     {Second operation-dependent parameter}
            ctlParam3    : LONGINT);    {Third operation-dependent parameter}
const
   IPrBitsCtl = 4;                      {Bit map printing [4.4.4]}
   IPrIOCtl   = 5;                      {Text streaming [4.4.5]}
   IPrEvtCtl  = 6;                      {Screen printing [4.4.6]}
   IPrDevCtl  = 7;                      {Printer control [4.4.7]}
   IFMgrCtl   = 8;                      {Font support [4.4.8]}
```

Notes

1. PrCtlCall issues a low-level Control call [3.2.3] directly to the printer driver.

2. controlCode identifies the control operation to be performed.

3. Depending on the operation, it may require as many as three additional parameters (ctlParam1, ctlParam2, ctlParam3). The values supplied for these parameters will be copied into the first 6 words (12 bytes) of the parameter block's csParam field [3.1.5].

4. See [4.4.4] to [4.4.8] for details on specific control operations and their parameters.

5. The trap macro for this routine expands to call the universal printing trap _PrGlue with the routine selector given below.

6. There is currently no advantage to using the low-level driver operations in place of the high-level ones covered in [4.2] and [4.3]. Apple continues to support the low-level interface for backward compatibility, but recommends that all new programs use the high-level interface instead.

Assembly Language Information

Trap macro and routine selector:

(Pascal) Routine name	(Assembly) Trap macro	Trap word	Routine selector
PrCtlCall	_PrCtlCall	$A8FD	$A0000E00

Printer driver control codes:

Name	Value	Meaning
IPrBitsCtl	4	Bit map printing
IPrIOCtl	5	Text streaming
IPrEvtCtl	6	Screen printing
IPrDevCtl	7	Printer control
IFMgrCtl	8	Font support

4.4.4   Bit Map Printing

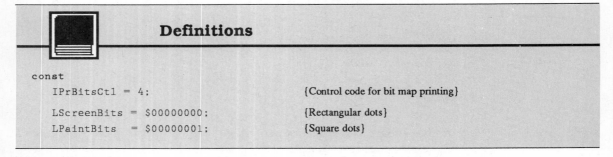

Definitions

```
const
  IPrBitsCtl = 4;                    {Control code for bit map printing}

  LScreenBits = $00000000;           {Rectangular dots}
  LPaintBits  = $00000001;           {Square dots}
```

Notes

1. The control code IPrBitsCtl is used with PrCtlCall [4.4.3] to transmit bit maps directly to the printer.

2. ctlParam1 [4.4.3] is a pointer to a standard QuickDraw bit map [I:4.2.1].

3. ctlParam2 [4.4.3] is a pointer to a rectangle defining the portion of the bit map to be printed.

4. The rectangle is expressed in the local coordinate system defined by the bit map's boundary rectangle.

5. ctlParam3 [4.4.3] must be one of the constants LScreenBits or LPaintBits. This parameter controls the horizontal resolution at which the bit map is to be printed, which determines the shape of the resulting dots.

6. On the ImageWriter printer, LScreenBits specifies the printer's standard horizontal resolution of 80 dots per inch. Since the vertical resolution is only 72 dots per inch, the resulting images appear "squashed," with rectangular dots narrower than they are high.

7. LPaintBits slows down the ImageWriter's print head to a horizontal resolution of 72 dots per inch, producing true square dots like those on the Macintosh screen. Printing is slower, but more faithfully reproduces the image as it appears on the screen.

8. LPaintBits corresponds to the Tall Adjusted option in the ImageWriter style dialog [4.2.3].

9. Only the ImageWriter driver honors the parameter LScreenBits; on the LaserWriter, always use LPaintBits.

Assembly Language Information

Control parameters for bit map printing:

Name	Value	Meaning
LScreenBits	$00000000	Rectangular dots
LPaintBits	$00000001	Square dots

4.4.5   Text Streaming

Definitions

```
const
    lPrIOCtl = 5;                        {Control code for text streaming}
```

Notes

1. The control code IPrIOCtl is used with PrCtlCall [4.4.3] to transmit text directly to the printer.

2. The text will be printed in the printer's own native character font, bypassing the usual Toolbox font selection and formatting capabilities. This type of printing is considerably faster than imaging with QuickDraw, but the results will not match what the user sees on the screen.

3. ctlParam1 [4.4.3] is a pointer to the first text character to be transmitted.

4. ctlParam2 [4.4.3] gives the length of the text in bytes, which must not exceed 32767.

5. ctlParam3 [4.4.3] must be 0.

6. Streamed text can include embedded control characters or escape sequences understood directly by the printer itself; see your printer manual for further information. It's generally best to avoid relying on such features, however, since they make your program printer-dependent.

4.4.6   Screen Printing

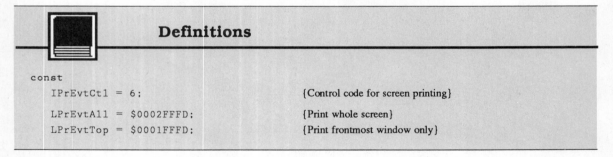

Definitions

```
const
    IPrEvtCtl = 6;                      {Control code for screen printing}

    LPrEvtAll = $0002FFFD;              {Print whole screen}
    LPrEvtTop = $0001FFFD;              {Print frontmost window only}
```

Notes

1. The control code IPrEvtCtl is used with PrCtlCall [4.4.3] to dump all or part of the screen directly to the printer.

2. ctlParam1 [4.4.3] must be one of the constants LPrEvtAll or LPrEvtTop. This parameter controls whether the entire screen is to be printed or just the frontmost window.

3. `ctlParam2` and `ctlParam3` [4.4.3] are meaningless and should be set to 0.

4. This control call is used by the standard `'FKEY'` number 4 [II:2.9.2] to dump the the frontmost window to the printer (or the whole screen, if the Caps Lock key is down) when the user types Command-Shift-4.

5. The constants `LPrEvtAll` and `LPrEvtTop` are defined incorrectly in some versions of the Pascal interface files. The values shown above are the correct ones.

6. Screen printing is implemented only on the ImageWriter printer.

Assembly Language Information

Control parameters for screen printing:

Name	Value	Meaning
LPrEvtAll	$0002FFFD	Print whole screen
LPrEvtTop	$0001FFFD	Print frontmost window only

4.4.7   Printer Control

Definitions

```
const
    IPrDevCtl = 7;                              {Control code for printer control}

    LPrReset      = $00010000;                  {Begin new document}
    LPrDocOpen    = $00010000;                  {Begin new document}
    LPrDocClose   = $00050000;                  {End document}

    LPrPageOpen   = $00040000;                  {Begin new page}
    LPrPageClose  = $00020000;                  {End page}
    LPrPageEnd    = $00020000;                  {End page}

    LPrLineFeed   = $00030000;                  {Start new line}
    LPrLFStd      = $0003FFFF;                  {Start new line with standard paper advance}
    LPrLFSixth    = $0003FFFF;                  {Start new line with 1/6-inch paper advance}
    LPrLFEighth   = $0003FFFE;                  {Start new line with 1/8-inch paper advance}
```

Notes

1. The control code `IPrDevCtl` is used with `PrCtlCall` [4.4.3] to perform various printer control operations in a device-independent way.

2. Always include these calls to structure your printing job when using low-level operations such as bit map printing [4.4.4], text streaming [4.4.5], and screen printing [4.4.6]. Do not attempt to mix such operations with high-level printing routines such as `PrOpenDoc`, `PrCloseDoc` [4.3.1], `PrOpenPage`, and `PrClosePage` [4.3.2].

3. `ctlParam1` [4.4.3] must be one of the constants shown; `ctlParam2` and `ctlParam3` are meaningless and should be set to 0.

4. `LPrDocOpen` and `LPrDocClose` perform whatever control operations a particular printer may require at the beginning and end of a document, such as opening and closing a network connection, resetting the printer's internal state, and allocating and releasing input/output buffers.

5. On some printers, the low-order byte of the `LPrDocOpen` parameter tells how many copies of the document to print.

6. `LPrPageOpen` and `LPrPageClose` perform the appropriate control operations for starting and ending a page, such as ejecting the paper or advancing past the fold.

7. `LPrReset` and `LPrPageEnd` are older names for the parameters `LPrDocOpen` and `LPrPageClose`, and are still supported for backward compatibility.

8. `LPrLineFeed` returns to the left edge of the page rectangle to begin a new line of printing. The low-order word of the parameter tells how far to advance the paper for the new line.

9. The paper advance is specified in printer dots, at the resolution given by the `iVRes` field in the printer information subrecord [4.1.3]. For example, a parameter value of `LPrLineFeed + 12` advances the paper 12 dots; `LPrLineFeed` alone simply returns to the left margin without advancing the paper.

10. The constants `LPrLFSixth` and `LPrLFEighth` are device-independent parameters that advance the paper one sixth and one eighth of an inch, respectively, regardless of the printer's dot resolution. `LPrLFStd` is a synonym for `LPrLFSixth`, representing a standard paper advance of one sixth of an inch.

11. Notice that the assembly-language constants (below) have different values than their Pascal counterparts. `IPrReset`, `IPrPageEnd`, and `IPrLineFeed` represent only the high-order word of the parameter; `IPrLFStd`, `IPrLFSixth`, and `IPrLFEighth` represent only the low-order word.

12. At the time this book went to press, constant definitions for the new parameters `IPrDocOpen`, `IPrDocClose`, `IPrPageOpen`, and `IPrPageClose` had not yet been added to the assembly-language interface files. By the time you read this, the oversight may have been corrected.

Assembly Language Information

Control parameters for printer control:

Name	Value	Meaning
IPrReset	1	Begin new document
IPrPageEnd	2	End page
IPrLineFeed	3	Start new line
LPrLFStd	-1	Advance paper standard amount
LPrLFSixth	-1	Advance paper ⅙ inch
LPrLFEighth	-2	Advance paper ⅛ inch

4.4.8　　Font Support

Definitions

```
const
    IFMgrCtl = 8;                          {Control/status code for font support}
type
    FMOutPtr = ^FMOutput;
    FMOutput = packed record
                errNum      : INTEGER;      {Reserved}
                fontHandle  : Handle;       {Handle to font record [I:8.2.2]}
                bold        : Byte;         {Extra thickness for boldface}
                italic      : Byte;         {Skew factor for italic}
                ulOffset    : Byte;         {Offset from baseline to underline}
                ulShadow    : Byte;         {Width of break around descenders}
                ulThick     : Byte;         {Thickness of underline}
                shadow      : Byte;         {Thickness of shadow}
                extra       : SignedByte;   {Extra width per character}
                ascent      : Byte;         {Ascent above baseline}
                descent     : Byte;         {Descent below baseline}
                widMax      : Byte;         {Maximum character width}
                leading     : SignedByte;   {Leading between lines}
```

unused	: Byte;	{Reserved}
numer	: Point;	{Numerators of scale factors}
denom	: Point	{Denominators of scale factors}
end;		

Notes

1. The constant `IFMgrCtl` is used both as a status code and as a control code [3.2.3]. The Toolbox uses it to request help from the printer driver in selecting fonts for a particular printer; application programs should never use this code themselves.

2. After reading a font into memory from a resource file, the Toolbox issues a Status call [3.2.3] to the printer driver with a status code of `IFMgrCtl`. This requests a *font characterization table* describing how to modify the basic font for style variations such as bold, italic, and underline.

3. In the parameter block for the Status call, the first 2 words of `csParam` [3.1.5] hold the address in memory at which the font characterization table is to be stored. The third word (`csParam[2]`) contains the printer's device code [I:8.3.1, 4.1.3].

4. See [4.4.9] for the format of the font characterization table.

5. The Toolbox uses the font characterization table to construct a *font output record* summarizing the metric characteristics of the font. It then passes this record to the printer driver in a Control call [3.2.3] with a control code of `IFMgrCtl`, allowing the driver to make any last-minute adjustments it wishes to the record's contents before the record is used for formatting text.

6. In the parameter block for the Control call, the first 2 words of `csParam` [3.1.5] hold a pointer to the font output record. The third word (`csParam[2]`) contains the printer's device code [I:8.3.1, 4.1.3].

7. The `fontHandle` field of the font output record holds a handle to the font itself.

8. For boldface text, the `bold` field gives the number of dots by which each character is to be thickened horizontally.

9. For italic text, the `italic` field gives the number of dots by which character images are to be skewed horizontally.

10. For underlined text, `ulThick` gives the thickness of the underline, `ulOffset` its offset below the baseline, and `ulShadow` the width of the break around descenders, all in dots.

11. For shadowed text, the `shadow` field gives the thickness of the shadow in dots.

12. For any given combination of style variations, the `extra` field gives the total number of dots by which each character's width is increased.

13. `ascent` and `descent` give the font's overall ascent and descent relative to the baseline, `widMax` the width of the widest character in the font, and `leading` the recommended vertical spacing between lines.

14. The `ascent`, `descent`, `widMax`, and `leading` fields correspond to the similarly-named fields of the `FontInfo` and `FMetricRec` records [I:8.2.6]. Notice, however, that they are single, packed bytes rather than 2-byte integers or 4-byte fixed-point values.

15. The fields `numer` and `denom` specify scale factors for scaling characters to the printer's resolution. The scale factor in each dimension (horizontal or vertical) is given by the ratio of `numer` to `denom` in that dimension. That is, the width of each character is multiplied by

```
numer.h / denom.h
```

and the height by

```
numer.v / denom.v
```

Assembly Language Information

Field offsets in a font output record:

(Pascal) Field name	(Assembly) Offset name	Offset in bytes
errNum	fmOutError	0
fontHandle	fmOutfontH	2
bold	fmOutBold	6
italic	fmOutItalic	7
ulOffset	fmOutULOffset	8
ulShadow	fmOutULShadow	9
ulThick	fmOutULThick	10
shadow	fmOutShadow	11
extra	fmOutExtra	12
ascent	fmOutAscent	13
descent	fmOutDescent	14
widMax	fmOutWidMax	15
leading	fmOutLeading	16
numer	fmOutNumer	18
denom	fmOutDenom	22

4.4.9　　**Font Characterization Table**

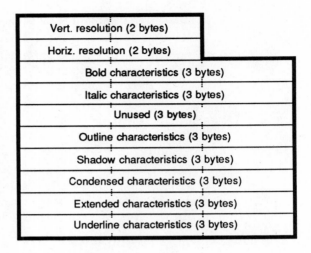

Structure of a font characterization table

Notes

1. A font characterization table contains information needed to apply style variations to fonts for use on a particular printer.

2. The printer driver returns a characterization table in response to the Status call `IFMgrCtl` [4.4.8].

3. The first two words of the table give the vertical and horizontal resolution of the printer, in dots per inch. This information is used for scaling fonts from one printer (or other graphic device) to another.

4. Each of the remaining fields except the last is a 3-byte triple describing the characteristics of a particular style variation.

5. In each triple, the first byte identifies the field of the font output record [4.4.8] to which this style variation applies. The field is designated by a byte offset relative to the record's `bold` field: thus an offset of 0 refers to the `bold` field itself, 1 refers to the `italic` field, 5 to the `shadow` field, and so on.

6. The second byte of each triple gives the value to be stored into the designated field.

7. The third byte of each triple gives the amount to be added to the output record's `extra` field. This represents the number of dots by which each character is widened as a result of this style variation.

8. The last field of the characterization table is a triple defining the font's underline characteristics. The 3 bytes of this triple give the values to be stored into the `ulOffset`, `ulShadow`, and `ulThick` fields of the font output record [4.4.8].

Assembly Language Information

Field offsets in a font characterization table:

Name	Value	Meaning
dpiVert	0	Vertical resolution in dots per inch
dpiHoriz	2	Horizontal resolution in dots per inch
boldChr	4	Boldface characteristics
italChr	7	Italic characteristics
outlineChr	13	Outline characteristics
shadowChr	16	Shadow characteristics
condChr	19	Condensed characteristics
extendChr	22	Extended characteristics
underChr	25	Underline characteristics

4.5 Nuts and Bolts

4.5.1   Customizing the Printing Dialogs

Definitions

```
type
    TPPrDlg = ^TPrDlg;
    TPrDlg  = record
                dlg       : DialogRecord;  {Dialog record [II:7.1.1]}
                pFltrProc : ProcPtr;       {Pointer to filter function [II:7.4.5]}
                pItemProc : ProcPtr;       {Pointer to response procedure}
                hPrintUsr : THPrint;       {Handle to print record [4.1.2]}
                fDoIt     : BOOLEAN;        {Private}
                fDone     : BOOLEAN;        {Private}
```

```
                1User1    : LONGINT;        {Private}
                1User2    : LONGINT;        {Private}
                1User3    : LONGINT;        {Private}
                1User4    : LONGINT;        {Private}
                 . . .
                {Additional fields as needed by the customized dialog}
            end;
function PrDlgMain
            (printRec : THPrint;           {Handle to print record}
             initProc : ProcPtr)           {Pointer to initialization routine}
               : BOOLEAN;                   {Was dialog confirmed?}
function PrStlInit
            (printRec : THPrint)           {Handle to print record}
               : TPPrDlg;                   {Pointer to style dialog}
function PrJobInit
            (printRec : THPrint)           {Handle to print record}
               : TPPrDlg;                   {Pointer to job dialog}
```

Notes

1. `PrDlgMain` conducts a printing-related dialog with the user.

2. This routine is called for you automatically by the standard routines `PrStlDialog` and `PrJobDialog` [4.2.3]. You'll need to call it yourself only if you're using a nonstandard version of one of the printing dialogs.

3. `printRec` is a handle to a print record [4.1.2] for the printing operation to which this dialog pertains.

4. `initProc` is a pointer to an initialization routine, which constructs and returns a *printing dialog record* of type `TPrDlg`. This record contains all the information needed to conduct the requested dialog.

5. After the user dismisses the dialog from the screen, `PrDlgMain` returns a function result of `TRUE` if the dialog was confirmed (by clicking the `OK` button or its equivalent), `FALSE` if it was canceled.

6. If the dialog was confirmed, `PrDlgMain` updates the print record accordingly, then validates its contents with `PrValidate` [4.2.2]. If the dialog was canceled, the print record is left unchanged.

7. dlg is a complete dialog record [II:7.1.1] (not just a pointer) embedded within the printing dialog record. The TPrDlg record is thus ultimately based on a graphics port [I:4.2.2]; this makes it a nonrelocatable object, which must be referred to with a pointer rather than a handle.

8. pFltrProc is a pointer to a filter function [II:7.4.5] for processing events while the dialog is on the screen.

9. pItemProc is a pointer to a *response procedure* of the form

```
procedure Response (theDialog : DialogPtr;
                    itemNumber : INTEGER);
```

which defines the action to be taken when the mouse is clicked in a given dialog item.

10. hPrintUsr is a handle to the print record for this printing operation.

11. The remaining fields of the printing dialog record are reserved for the private use of the Toolbox printing routines.

12. PrStlInit and PrJobInit are the initialization routines passed to PrDlgMain by PrStlDialog and PrJobDialog [4.2.3], to construct the standard style and job dialogs, respectively.

13. To customize the style or job dialog, call PrDlgMain directly (rather than indirectly via PrStlDialog or PrJobDialog), substituting an initialization routine of your own in place of the standard ones. Your initialization routine can in turn call PrStlInit or PrJobInit to obtain the standard dialog, then modify it (or its filter function and response procedure) before passing it back for use by PrDlgMain. See Technical Note #95 for more information and a fully developed example.

14. The trap macros for these routines expand to call the universal printing trap _PrGlue with the routine selectors given below.

Assembly Language Information

Field offset in a printing dialog record:

(Pascal) Field name	(Assembly) Offset name	Offset in bytes
dlg	dlg	0
pFltrProc	pFltrProc	170
pItemProc	pItemProc	174
hPrintUsr	hPrintUsr	178

Assembly-language constant:

Name	Value	Meaning
IPrDlgSz	200	Size of printing dialog record in bytes, excluding custom fields

Trap macros and routine selectors:

(Pascal) Routine name	(Assembly) Trap macro	Trap word	Routine selector
PrDlgMain	_PrDlgMain	$A8FD	$4A040894
PrStlInit	_PrStlInit	$A8FD	$3C04040C
PrJobInit	_PrJobInit	$A8FD	$44040410

4.5.2   Customizing Paper Sizes

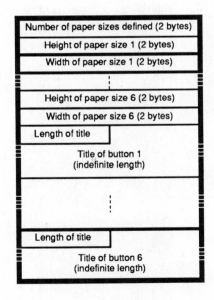

Structure of a paper size table

Notes

1. A paper size table defines the selection of paper sizes to be offered to the user in the printing style dialog [4.2.3].

2. The printer resource file [4.6.3] normally contains a paper size table stored as a resource of type `'PREC'` [4.6.1] with ID number 3. This defines the names and dimensions of the standard paper sizes for use with the given printer.

3. A program can override the standard paper sizes by including a `'PREC'` resource with an ID number of 4 in its own application resource file. If no such resource is present, the dialog will use the standard paper sizes defined in the printer resource file.

4. As many as six paper sizes may be defined. The table must always include exactly six definitions, even if not all are actually meaningful. The first word of the table tells how many of the definitions really count. This value should never be greater than 6; if it is less, some of the definitions at the end of the list will be ignored.

5. All paper dimensions are expressed in device-independent units of 120ths of an inch. (The constant `IPrPageFract` [4.1.4] gives the number of units per inch.)

6. The paper dimensions are followed by six strings giving the titles of the corresponding radio buttons to be displayed in the style dialog. Each string is given in standard Pascal format, preceded by a length byte.

7. Use one-character dummy titles for unused buttons.

8. *WARNING:* The strings representing the button titles must be tightly packed, even if this means they don't begin on even word boundaries. *Do not* add an extra byte at the end of a string to pad it to an even number of bytes.

9. Some standard paper sizes are as follows:

Name	Inches Height	Inches Width	120ths Height	120ths Width
US Letter	11	$8\frac{1}{2}$	1320	1020
US Legal	14	$8\frac{1}{2}$	1680	1020
A4 Letter	$11\frac{2}{3}$	$8\frac{1}{4}$	1400	990
International Fanfold	12	$8\frac{1}{4}$	1440	990
Computer Paper	11	14	1320	1680
Standard Envelope	$4\frac{1}{8}$	$9\frac{1}{4}$	495	1140

4.6 Printing-Related Resources

4.6.1 Resource Type 'PREC'

Version stamp (2 bytes)
Printer information subrecord [4.1.3] (14 bytes)
Paper rectangle (8 bytes)
Style subrecord [4.1.4] (8 bytes)
Print-time information subrecord [4.1.3] (14 bytes)
Auxiliary information subrecord [4.1.6] (16 bytes)
Job subrecord [4.1.5] (20 bytes)
Padding (38 bytes)

Structure of a 'PREC' resource

Notes

1. A resource of type 'PREC' nominally contains a print record [4.1.2].

2. Two print records are normally included in the printer resource file [4.6.3]. Number 0 contains the standard, default settings and characteristics for this printer; number 1 contains those from the last printing operation actually performed, allowing the previous settings to "stick to the printer."

3. A given printer resource file may include any number of additional 'PREC' resources, with arbitrary resource IDs. These are not limited to actual print records; their contents and internal format are determined entirely by the file's own printing routines.

4. In particular, 'PREC' number 3 is used for a paper size table [4.5.2] defining the standard paper sizes to be offered to the user in the style dialog [4.2.3]. An application program can override these with an alternate table of its own, stored as 'PREC' number 4 in the program's application resource file.

Assembly Language Information

Assembly-language constants:

Name	Value	Meaning
LPrintType	$50524543	Resource type for print records ('PREC')
IPrintDef	0	Resource ID of default print record
IPrintLst	1	Resource ID of last-used print record

4.6.2   Resource Type 'PDEF'

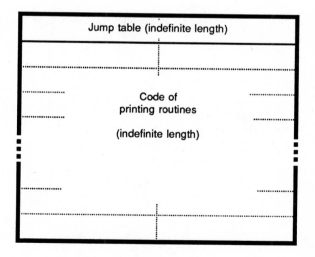

Structure of a 'PDEF' resource

Notes

1. Each printer resource file has its own set of 'PDEF' resources, containing the executable code of the printing routines for one particular type of printer.

2. Each 'PDEF' resource begins with a small jump table giving the locations of the various routines within the body of the resource. For each routine, the table contains an executable jump (JMP) instruction leading to the routine's entry point.

3. 'PDEF' resources 0 to 7 contain the standard printing routines:

Resource ID	Description	Routines
0	Draft printing	PrOpenDoc [4.3.1] PrCloseDoc [4.3.1] PrOpenPage [4.3.2] PrClosePage [4.3.2]
1	Spooling	PrOpenDoc [4.3.1] PrCloseDoc [4.3.1] PrOpenPage [4.3.2] PrClosePage [4.3.2]
2	Printer-specific method #1	PrOpenDoc [4.3.1] PrCloseDoc [4.3.1] PrOpenPage [4.3.2] PrClosePage [4.3.2]
3	Printer-specific method #2	PrOpenDoc [4.3.1] PrCloseDoc [4.3.1] PrOpenPage [4.3.2] PrClosePage [4.3.2]
4	Dialogs/print records	PrintDefault [4.2.2] PrStlDialog [4.2.3] PrJobDialog [4.2.3] PrStlInit [4.5.1] PrJobInit [4.5.1] PrDlgMain [4.5.1] PrValidate [4.2.2] PrJobMerge [4.2.3]
5	Spool printing	PrPicFile [4.3.3]
7	Miscellaneous	PrGeneral [TN #128]

4. Resources 0 to 3 contain different versions of the four standard document printing routines (PrOpenDoc, PrCloseDoc, PrOpenPage, PrClosePage), specialized for different printing methods. The resource ID in each case corresponds to the value of the bJDocLoop field in the print record's job subrecord [4.1.5]: 0 and 1 for draft printing and spooling, 2 and 3 for optional, printer-specific printing methods.

5. Resource number 7 contains a single routine, PrGeneral, which provides a variety of advanced operations for specialized needs. At present these include determining the range of dot resolutions available on a given printer, printing bit maps on the ImageWriter in draft mode, and finding the page orientation (portrait or landscape) currently in effect. For information on these operations and on the PrGeneral mechanism itself, see Macintosh Technical Note #128.

6. A given printer resource file may include any number of additional 'PDEF' resources containing supplementary code needed by the main printing routines. Such extra resources may have any ID numbers other than those shown in the table.

4.6.3   Printer Resource Files

Contents of a printer resource file:

Resource Type	Resource ID	Description
[Signature]	0	Autograph [I:7.5.4, note 6]
'BNDL'	128	Finder bundle [I:7.5.4]
'FREF'	128	File reference ('PRES' or 'PRER') [I:7.5.3]
'ICN#'	128	Icon for printer resource file [I:5.5.4]
'DRVR'	$E000	Printer driver [3.3.1]
'PDEF'	0	Draft printing [4.6.2]
	1	Spooling [4.6.2]
	2	Printer-specific method #1 [4.6.2]
	3	Printer-specific method #2 [4.6.2]
	4	Dialogs/print records [4.6.2]
	5	Spool printing [4.6.2]
	7	Miscellaneous [4.6.2]
'PREC'	0	Default print record [4.6.1]
	1	Last-used print record [4.6.1]
	3	Default paper sizes [4.5.2]

Resource Type	Resource ID	Description
'STR '	$E001	Default spool file name [I:8.4.2]
'DLOG'	$E000	Style dialog [II:7.6.2]
	$E001	Job dialog [II:7.6.2]
'DITL'	$E000	Item list for style dialog [II:7.6.3]
	$E001	Item list for job dialog [II:7.6.3]

Notes

1. Printer resource files have a file type [I:7.3.1] of 'PRES' ("printer resource") or 'PRER' ("printer resource, remote"). The file's creator signature identifies the specific printer to which this resource file belongs (for example, 'IWRT' for ImageWriter or 'LWRT' for LaserWriter).

2. The file always includes a printer driver [3.1.1, 3.3.1] and a series of 'PDEF' resources [4.6.2] containing the code of the standard printing routines for this particular printer.

3. Two print records [4.1.2] are normally included in the file as resources of type 'PREC' [4.6.1]. Number 0 contains the standard, default settings and characteristics for this printer; number 1 contains those from the last printing operation actually performed, allowing the previous settings to "stick to the printer."

4. 'PREC' number 3 contains a paper size table [4.5.2] defining the standard paper sizes to be offered to the user in the style dialog [4.2.3]. A program can override these with an alternate table of its own, stored as 'PREC' number 4 in the program's application resource file.

5. 'STR ' resource number $E001 (-8191) gives the default file name for spooling printed output temporarily to the disk.

6. 'DLOG' resources $E000 and E001 (-8192 and -8191), along with their respective item lists, define the printer's standard style and job dialogs, respectively.

7. The file also includes a set of Finder resources for installing it in the desktop file and displaying its icon on the Finder screen. These include

    - an autograph (or "version data") resource [I:7.5.4, note 6] whose resource type is the same as the file's creator signature

    - a file reference resource ('FREF' [I:7.5.3]) for the file's file type ('PRES' or 'PRER')

- an icon list resource ('ICN#' [I:5.5.4]) containing the icon and mask for displaying the file on the screen
- a bundle resource ('BNDL' [I:7.5.4]) to tie the other Finder resources together

8. Besides the resources shown in the table, the printer resource file may contain any number of additional resources of any types, as needed by the printing code for this specific printer. In particular, it may include any number of additional 'PDEF' [4.6.2] and 'PREC' [4.6.1] resources, holding supplementary code and data, respectively, for use by the file's printing routines.

CHAPTER

5

Sound and Fury

One aspect of the Macintosh that's often overlooked is its sound-generating capability. Used judiciously, sound can be a valuable addition to a program's user interface, offering a variety of useful cues and signals to supplement what the user sees on the screen. With the help of the Toolbox, you can use the Mac's built-in speaker to produce a wide range of sounds, from beeps to jingles to speech to four-part harmony. In this chapter we'll learn how.

> The sound facilities covered here are those of the "classic" Macintosh architecture, and are available on all models. The Macintosh II features more powerful, more flexible sound capabilities, based on a custom-designed stereo sound chip with extended Toolbox support; our discussion of these features will have to wait until Volume Four.

Fundamental Concepts

Before we can discuss how the Macintosh produces sound, let's begin with some basic terms and concepts about sound in general. Figure

247

5–1 shows a graph of a simple sound wave. The horizontal axis represents the passage of time, while the vertical axis measures some continuously varying physical quantity, such as air pressure or voltage. The value of this physical quantity at any given instant (that is, the vertical height of the curve at any point along the horizontal axis) is called the *magnitude* of the sound.

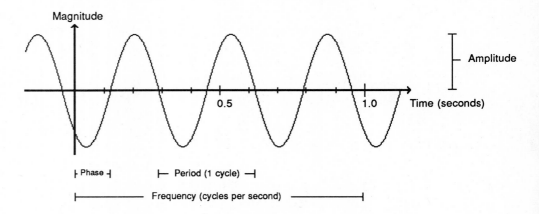

Figure 5–1 Anatomy of a sound wave

The typical sound wave shown in the figure varies in a cyclically recurring way, known as a *sine wave* because it's the graph of the sine function we all remember lovingly from high-school trigonometry. The maximum magnitude that the curve reaches at the peak of each wave is called its *amplitude,* and determines the volume or loudness of the sound. Each repetition of the sine wave, including one complete peak and valley and returning to the original magnitude level, is called a *cycle;* the time needed to complete one cycle, measured along the horizontal (time) axis, is the *period* of the wave.

The spatial distance the wave travels in the course of one cycle is its *wavelength:*

```
wavelength = period × speed
```

Notice that the wavelength depends not only on the period of the wave, but also on the speed of sound, which in turn varies with temperature, pressure, and the physical medium through which it is propagating. In air, at sea level, at 0° C. (32° F.), this comes to approximately 331 meters (1087 feet) per second, or about 741 miles per hour. Thus a wave with a period of 1 millisecond (one thousandth of a second) would have a wavelength of about 331 millimeters, or a bit more than a foot.

The reciprocal of the period is called the *frequency*, and tells the number of times the wave cycle repeats each second:

```
frequency = 1 / period
```

This determines the pitch of the sound as perceived by the ear. Since the period is measured in seconds per cycle, the frequency is expressed in cycles per second, nowadays usually called *hertz* after the nineteenth-century German physicist Heinrich Hertz. The wave in our previous example, with a period of 1 millisecond, would thus have a frequency of 1000 cycles per second, or 1 *kilohertz* (kHz); a period of 1 microsecond (one millionth of a second) would correspond to a frequency of 1,000,000 cycles per second, or 1 *megahertz* (MHz). The wave in Figure 5–1 has a frequency of only 3 hertz, which is really more of a rumble than a sound: for those not born on the planet Krypton, the normal range of audible frequencies runs from about 20 Hz to 20 kHz, or about 20 to 20,000 cycles per second.

One last property of the wave shown in Figure 5–1 is its *phase*, which measures how far its cycle is shifted along the axis relative to some fixed reference point. The reference point in the figure is the vertical axis, which represents an arbitrarily chosen "zero point" in time. More commonly, the phase is measured relative to the beginning of some other wave (often one with a different frequency), and expresses the relationship in time between the peaks and valleys of the two waves. Phase is normally stated as an angle representing a fraction of a complete cycle, either in degrees (one cycle equals 360°) or in radians (one cycle equals 2π radians). In the figure, the vertical axis falls five-eighths of the way through one cycle, or three-eighths in advance of the next; thus the phase would be expressed as 225° or 5π/4 radians (or equivalently, as –135° or –3π/4 radians).

Not all sound waves are pure sine curves. The overall shape of the wave, called the *waveform*, determines the nature or character of the sound as it presents itself to the ear. This subjective quality is called *timbre* (a French word that rhymes more or less with "amber," not "limber"), and is what distinguishes the sound of, say, a clarinet from that of a kazoo. A sine wave corresponds to a pure, undifferentiated musical tone; other waveforms produce other kinds of sound.

In general, the more regular or symmetrical the curve, the more pleasing it will be to the ear.

Figure 5–2 shows examples of some typical types of waveform. The first, a *square wave*, oscillates directly from its maximum positive to its maximum negative amplitude, with no gradual transition in between. This produces a flat, synthetic-sounding timbre like the Macintosh `SysBeep` [II:2.8.1]. The second, a sine wave like the ones we've been discussing, yields a more rounded, musical-sounding tone. Finally, most of the sounds we actually encounter in real life have irregular, complex waveforms like the third one shown in the figure, which might represent a human voice, a doorbell, or a freight train. As we'll see, you can program the Macintosh Toolbox to produce any of these types of sound, as the occasion demands.

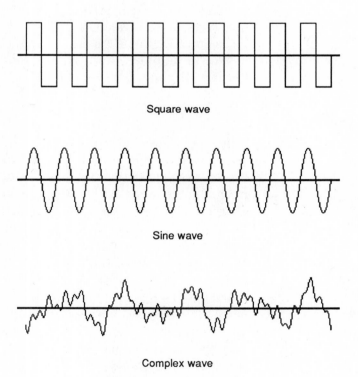

Square wave

Sine wave

Complex wave

Figure 5–2 Typical waveforms

The Sound Generator

Sound production is controlled by a chip called the Synertek SY6522 *Versatile Interface Adapter*, or *VIA*, which also handles a variety of other devices such as the mouse, keyboard, disk motor, and real-time clock. On the "classic" Macintosh, the VIA is assisted in its sound-related activities by a more specialized Sony sound chip that actually drives the speaker. (The Macintosh II has its own custom Apple sound chip instead.) A flag bit in one of the VIA's data registers controls whether the speaker is enabled or disabled; turning this flag off suppresses all sound generation. Although it's possible to communicate directly with the VIA at the assembly-language level, the Toolbox normally handles all such interactions for you, so you needn't concern yourself with the details.

Sound generation by the VIA is synchronized to the video display circuitry, so before we can talk about it we'll have to learn a little about video timing. To create the image you see on the screen, a moving electron beam scans continuously from left to right and top to bottom, "painting" pixels as it goes. On the standard Macintosh display, each horizontal *scan line* contains 512 pixels. On reaching the right edge of the screen, the beam shuts off and returns to the left edge one place farther down, ready to begin the next line. This pause to reposition the electron beam is called the *horizontal retrace* (or *horizontal blanking*) *interval*, and takes as long as painting another 192 pixels on the screen (see Figure 5–3). Thus the total elapsed time from the beginning of one scan line to the beginning of the next is equivalent to 704 pixels altogether.

The standard display is 342 lines high from top to bottom, and is repainted, or *refreshed*, 60 times per second. Like the horizontal retrace at the end of each scan line, there's also a *vertical retrace* or *vertical blanking interval* when the beam reaches the bottom-right corner of the screen and returns to the top-left to start again. (Think of it as "the pause that refreshes.") The vertical retrace takes the equivalent of an extra 28 scan lines, for a total of 370. The time needed to paint one complete screen image, or *frame*, and come back to the beginning is thus equivalent to 370 lines of 704 pixels each, or 260,480 pixels in all. If the refresh rate were exactly 60 Hz (that is, 60 frames per second), then the overall display rate would come to 15,628,800 pixels per second, or 15.6288 MHz. In fact, however, this figure is not quite accurate: the actual pixel rate is 15.6672 MHz, yielding a true screen refresh rate of approximately 60.15 Hz.

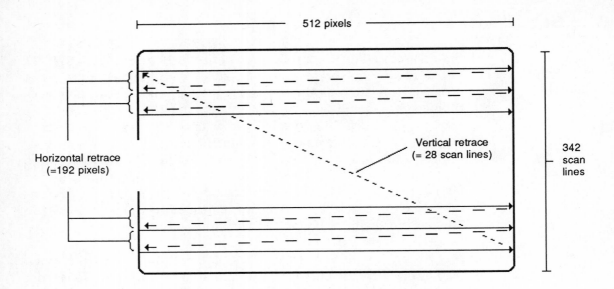

Figure 5–3 Horizontal and vertical retrace

If the sound-enable bit in the VIA's data register is set, a single 8-bit sound magnitude (you might call it a "sound byte") is sent to the built-in speaker at the end of each scan line, when the video circuitry pauses for its horizontal retrace. At 60.15 frames per second and 370 sound samples per frame (counting the extra 28 that occur during the vertical retrace interval), this gives an effective sampling rate of 22,257 samples per second (22.257 kHz), or one approximately every 44.93 microseconds. The magnitude levels for one complete frame are kept in a *sound buffer* in memory and read out one at a time, at the horizontal retrace interval; the buffer is refilled with another 370 values during the vertical retrace interrupt at the end of the frame. You can control the sounds to be emitted by the speaker by storing your own values directly into the buffer, but it's generally more convenient to let the Toolbox do it for you, using the techniques discussed later in this chapter.

The exact location of the sound buffer in memory depends on the model and memory configuration of the Macintosh you're running on, and is kept in the assembly-language global variable

SoundBase [5.1.1]. The same memory buffer is actually shared by both the sound generator and the circuitry that controls the floppy disk drive. The buffer is 370 *words* long instead of 370 bytes; the first (even-addressed) byte of each word holds a sound level, while the second is used to control the speed of the disk motor. Never ever ever (ever!) store into any odd-numbered byte in this buffer.

Magnitude values taken from the sound buffer drive the speaker by a technique known as *pulse-width encoding.* This is the kind of fancy-sounding term that engineers love to toss around to mystify and impress people, but all it really means is that an electrical pulse is sent down a wire to the sound chip, and that the duration (width) of the pulse depends on the specified sound magnitude, from 0 to 255. The sound chip converts the pulse width into a voltage, which is further modified (*attenuated,* the engineers would say) by a 3-bit global volume setting, to arrive at the actual voltage level to be applied to the speaker. As this voltage varies, the speaker converts it into a series of fluctuating pressure waves, which propagate through the air until they are detected by a pair of analog acoustic receivers built into the sides of your head. These, in turn, relay the signal to an ingenious integrated neural decoding device (implemented entirely in meatware), at which point . . . but I digress.

The user normally sets the speaker volume via the Control Panel desk accessory; the setting is kept in battery-powered "parameter RAM" on the clock chip and copied into main RAM each time the system is started up. The Toolbox provides a pair of routines, GetSoundVol and SetSoundVol [5.2.2], for reading and changing the volume setting, but ordinarily you should just leave it alone. If you do have some special reason to set the speaker volume yourself, be sure to save the user's previous setting and change it back again when you're through.

Defining and Playing Sounds

All sound-related operations are handled by the *sound driver*, which resides in ROM and is opened automatically whenever the system is started up. The sound driver is named .Sound and has a driver reference number of -4. As mentioned earlier, you can ask it to generate any of three different kinds of sound, according to your needs:

- *Square-wave* sound consists of a sequence of tones forming a single melodic line. Each tone has a square waveform, producing a flat, synthetic-sounding timbre.

- *Four-tone* sound consists of as many as four separate tones, or "voices," combined harmonically. Each voice is specified independently, with any desired pitch and timbre, and in any phase relationship to the other voices.

- *Free-form* sound consists of a single waveform of arbitrary length and complexity, representing any desired sound (such as speech, electronically sampled music, or sound effects).

Each type of sound has its own *synthesizer*, which is not a piece of fancy electronic hardware, but just a part of the sound driver software itself. You define the sound you want to play by supplying a *synthesizer record* that specifies the desired pitch, timbre, duration, and so forth. There are three types of synthesizer record, one for each type of sound; they're described in detail in the sections that follow. All three begin with an integer-valued type code identifying the type of record and the kind of sound it represents: SWMode, FTMode, or FFMode, for square-wave, four-tone, or free-form sound, respectively [5.1.1].

At the driver level, sound operations are initiated by a Write call [3.2.2] to the sound driver. The ioRefNum field in the parameter block [3.1.5] must contain -4, the reference number of the sound driver. The ioBuffer field points to a synthesizer record defining the sound to be played; ioReqCount gives the size of this record in bytes. In assembly language you have to issue the driver call directly, but in Pascal you usually call the Toolbox routine StartSound [5.2.1] to do it for you.

On receiving a Write request, the sound driver looks at the type code in the first word of the synthesizer record to see which kind of sound to play, and passes control to the corresponding synthesizer. The synthesizer examines the rest of the record for the specific characteristics of the sound, calculates the first frame's worth of magnitude samples, and stores them into the sound buffer in memory. Then it installs a task in the system's vertical retrace queue, which will automatically be called at each vertical retrace interrupt to refill the buffer with the next set of values. Finally, it turns on the sound-enable bit in the VIA data register, causing the sound generator to begin reading values out of the buffer and sending them to the speaker.

Like all input/output operations, sound requests can be issued either *synchronously* or *asynchronously*. Synchronous requests are carried out immediately, with control returning to the calling program only after the operation has been completed. Asynchronous requests, on the other hand, are simply entered in a system queue for eventual execution; control returns immediately to the calling program, which can go about its business while the sound is being played. On asynchronous requests, the program may optionally supply a pointer to a *completion routine,* either in the `ioCompletion` field of the parameter block [3.1.5] or as a parameter to the Toolbox `StartSound` routine [5.2.1]. If such a routine is present, the Toolbox will call it after it finishes playing the requested sound. This can be useful, for instance, for chaining sounds together by having each sound's completion routine issue the request for the next; another approach is for the completion routine to post an application-defined event [II:2.1.2, II:2.3.2], which will trigger the next sound request when it's detected by the program's main event loop.

Completion routines must be written in assembly language, and must preserve the contents of all processor registers except A0–A1 and D0–D2. On entry to the routine, A0 will point to the parameter block for the operation just completed and D0 will contain a result code indicating success or failure. Also, since these routines are executed at the interrupt level, they must not attempt to allocate any new storage from the heap or call any Toolbox routines that may do so.

A NIL value for `StartSound`'s `compRoutine` parameter denotes an asynchronous operation with no completion routine; a value of `POINTER(-1)` calls for synchronous execution. In assembly language, the `ioCompletion` field should be set to NIL in both cases; bit 10 of the trap word issuing the driver request distinguishes between synchronous (0) and asynchronous (1) operations.

Once you've started an asynchronous sound operation, you can cancel it by calling the Toolbox routine StopSound [5.2.1] or by issuing a KillIO call [3.2.3] directly to the sound driver. (There's no way to cancel a synchronous operation, since by definition your program doesn't get control back until after the operation is finished.) Both StopSound and KillIO immediately halt the operation currently in progress and cancel any others that may be pending in the I/O queue. The two differ slightly in their handling of completion routines, however: StopSound executes only the completion routine of the operation in progress, while KillIO executes those of the pending operations as well.

The Toolbox routine SoundDone [5.2.1] tests whether all previously issued sound requests have been completed. It returns TRUE if there are no current or pending sound operations, FALSE if there are any. To obtain this information in assembly language, you can check the value of the ioResult field [3.1.5] in each operation's parameter block: this field is set to 1 when a request is entered in the queue, then replaced with a result code when the operation is completed.

Square-Wave Sound

The synthesizer record defining a square-wave sound [5.1.2] consists of a mode field containing the constant SWMode [5.1.1], followed by an array of single tones to be strung together into a melodic line. Each tone's pitch, amplitude, and duration are defined by a record of type Tone. The array nominally contains 5001 tones, but in fact you can make it any length you need up to this maximum; the end of the array is marked by a dummy Tone record with all its fields set to 0.

The amplitude of each tone is measured on a scale from 0 to 255, and its duration is given in ticks, or sixtieths of a second. (We now know that there are really about 60.15 ticks per second, but never mind.) The pitch is specified by an integer *count*, which gives the period of the square wave—that is, the length of time it takes to oscillate through one full cycle, as we saw earlier in Figure 5–1. This period is expressed in a peculiar unit, equal to the time needed for the video circuitry to paint 20 pixels on the screen. (Why 20? Who knows? Maybe the programmer ran out of toes.) At the standard pixel rate of 15.6672 MHz, there are 783,360 such count units each second (15,667,200 divided by 20). Since the frequency of the wave is the reciprocal of the period, we get the following relationship between the frequency and the count, as given in the synthesizer record:

```
count = 783360 / frequency
```

For example, the standard reference frequency used by piano tuners, 440 Hz for the A above middle C, would be represented by a count value of `1780` (783,360 divided by 440, rounded to the nearest integer).

The figure in section [5.1.2] shows the proper count values for the single octave beginning with middle C. If necessary, you can transpose these values to a different register by halving the count (equivalent to doubling the frequency) for each octave upward, or doubling the count (halving the frequency) for each octave downward. For example, to play an E-flat two octaves above middle C, you would start with the count value shown for E-flat (decimal `2518`, or hexadecimal `$09D6`) and divide by 4 (2 to the second power, for a two-octave transposition), yielding a count of `630`, or `$0276`.

> Musical purists will note that these values are for an equal-tempered scale such as a piano keyboard, in which D-sharp and E-flat, for instance, are the same note. Violinists and other misfits accustomed to just-tempered tuning know that these are really two distinct notes—but to those of us without canine blood, the difference is not readily discernible. If you're a stickler for precision, you can find a table of just-tempered count values in Volume II of Apple's *Inside Macintosh* manual; if you've never heard of the "comma of Didymus," just use the values shown in [5.1.2] and don't give it a second thought.

Program 5–1 (`Enterprise`) shows how to use square-wave sound to play a simple, probably familiar melody. First we define a series of constants representing the count values for the notes of the scale, taken from section [5.1.2]. (We've included a full set of these constants for general use, even though this particular program doesn't actually use all of them.) The duration values for whole-notes, half-notes, dotted quarters, and so on are defined in relative terms, in beats rather than seconds or ticks; we can then scale them to any desired tempo, fast or slow. The tempo itself is expressed as a metronome setting in beats per minute, and can easily be adjusted by changing a single constant definition.

Program 5–1 Define and play a square-wave sound

```
procedure Enterprise;

    { Define and play a square-wave sound. }

const
    CNatural  = 2994;                       {Count value for C-natural [5.1.2]}
       CSharp = 2826;                       {Count value for C-sharp [5.1.2]}
        DFlat = 2826;                       {Count value for D-flat [5.1.2]}
    DNatural  = 2668;                       {Count value for D-natural [5.1.2]}
       DSharp = 2518;                       {Count value for D-sharp [5.1.2]}
        EFlat = 2518;                       {Count value for E-flat [5.1.2]}
    ENatural  = 2377;                       {Count value for E-natural [5.1.2]}
    FNatural  = 2243;                       {Count value for F-natural [5.1.2]}
       FSharp = 2117;                       {Count value for F-sharp [5.1.2]}
        GFlat = 2117;                       {Count value for G-flat [5.1.2]}
    GNatural  = 1998;                       {Count value for G-natural [5.1.2]}
       GSharp = 1886;                       {Count value for G-sharp [5.1.2]}
        AFlat = 1886;                       {Count value for A-flat [5.1.2]}
    ANatural  = 1780;                       {Count value for A-natural [5.1.2]}
       ASharp = 1680;                       {Count value for A-sharp [5.1.2]}
        BFlat = 1680;                       {Count value for B-flat [5.1.2]}
    BNatural  = 1586;                       {Count value for B-natural [5.1.2]}

    WholeNote     = 4;                      {Duration of whole-note in beats}
    DottedHalf    = 3;                      {Duration of dotted half-note in beats}
    HalfNote      = 2;                      {Duration of half-note in beats}
    DottedQuarter = 1.5;                    {Duration of dotted quarter-note in beats}
    QuarterNote   = 1;                      {Duration of quarter-note in beats}
    DottedEighth  = 0.75;                   {Duration of dotted eighth-note in beats}
    EighthNote    = 0.5;                    {Duration of eighth-note in beats}

    FullVolume     = 255;                   {Amplitude setting for full volume}
    TicksPerMinute = 3600;                  {Number of system clock ticks per minute}

    nTones    =   8;                        {Number of tones in melody}
    metronome = 120;                        {Metronome setting (beats per minute)}

var
    theSound  : SWSynthPtr;                 {Pointer to synthesizer record [5.1.2]}
    rawPtr    : Ptr;                        {Untyped pointer for creating record [I:3.1.1]}
    soundSize : INTEGER;                    {Size of synthesizer record in bytes}
    tempo     : REAL;                       {Number of clock ticks per beat}
```

Program 5-1 Define and play a square-wave sound *(continued)*

```
begin {Enterprise}

    soundSize := (nTones+1)*SIZEOF(Tone) + SIZEOF(INTEGER);    {Calculate size of record [5.1.2]}
    rawPtr    := NewPtr (soundSize);                           {Allocate block from heap [I:3.2.1]}
    theSound  := SWSynthPtr(rawPtr);                           {Convert to a typed pointer [5.1.2]}

    with theSound^ do
        begin

            mode  := SWMode;                                  {Specify square-wave sound [5.1.2, 5.1.1]}
            tempo := TicksPerMinute / metronome;              {Find number of ticks per beat}

            with triplets[0] do                               {Define first tone [5.1.2]}
                begin
                    count     := CNatural;                    {Set pitch [5.1.2]}
                    amplitude := FullVolume;                  {Set volume [5.1.2]}
                    duration  := ROUND(DottedQuarter * tempo) {Set duration in ticks [5.1.2]}
                end; {with triplets[0]}

            with triplets[1] do                               {Define next tone [5.1.2]}
                begin
                    count     := FNatural;                    {Set pitch [5.1.2]}
                    amplitude := FullVolume;                  {Set volume [5.1.2]}
                    duration  := ROUND(EighthNote * tempo)    {Set duration in ticks [5.1.2]}
                end; {with triplets[1]}

            with triplets[2] do                               {Define next tone [5.1.2]}
                begin
                    count     := BFlat;                       {Set pitch [5.1.2]}
                    amplitude := FullVolume;                  {Set volume [5.1.2]}
                    duration  := ROUND(DottedHalf * tempo)    {Set duration in ticks [5.1.2]}
                end; {with triplets[2]}

            with triplets[3] do                               {Define next tone [5.1.2]}
                begin
                    count     := ANatural;                    {Set pitch [5.1.2]}
                    amplitude := FullVolume;                  {Set volume [5.1.2]}
                    duration  := ROUND(QuarterNote * tempo)   {Set duration in ticks [5.1.2]}
                end; {with triplets[3]}
```

Program 5–1 Define and play a square-wave sound *(continued)*

```
with triplets[4] do                              {Define next tone [5.1.2]}
   begin
      count      := FNatural;                     {Set pitch [5.1.2]}
      amplitude  := FullVolume;                   {Set volume [5.1.2]}
      duration   := ROUND((HalfNote/3) * tempo)   {Set duration in ticks [5.1.2]}
   end; {with triplets[4]}

with triplets[5] do                              {Define next tone [5.1.2]}
   begin
      count      := DNatural;                     {Set pitch [5.1.2]}
      amplitude  := FullVolume;                   {Set volume [5.1.2]}
      duration   := ROUND((HalfNote/3) * tempo)   {Set duration in ticks [5.1.2]}
   end; {with triplets[5]}

with triplets[6] do                              {Define next tone [5.1.2]}
   begin
      count      := GNatural;                     {Set pitch [5.1.2]}
      amplitude  := FullVolume;                   {Set volume [5.1.2]}
      duration   := ROUND((HalfNote/3) * tempo)   {Set duration in ticks [5.1.2]}
   end; {with triplets[6]}

with triplets[7] do                              {Define next tone [5.1.2]}
   begin
      count      := CNatural div 2;               {Set pitch [5.1.2]}
      amplitude  := FullVolume;                   {Set volume [5.1.2]}
      duration   := ROUND(WholeNote * tempo)      {Set duration in ticks [5.1.2]}
   end; {with triplets[7]}

with triplets[8] do                              {Dummy tone to mark end of sequence [5.1.2]}
   begin
      count      := 0;                            {Set pitch [5.1.2]}
      amplitude  := 0;                            {Set volume [5.1.2]}
      duration   := 0                             {Set duration in ticks [5.1.2]}
   end  {with triplets[8]}

   end; {with theSound^}

StartSound (rawPtr, soundSize, NIL);             {Play the sound [5.2.1]}
DisposPtr  (rawPtr)                              {Dispose of synthesizer record [I:3.2.2]}

end; {Enterprise}
```

The first thing our sound procedure does is calculate the size of the synthesizer record and allocate a block for it from the heap. The record must be big enough to hold a `Tone` record [5.1.2] for each note in the melody, plus one more for the dummy zero entry at the end and an extra 2 bytes for the `mode` field. Since we'll just be playing the sound once and then discarding it, we can afford to allocate it as a nonrelocatable block. The Toolbox allocation routine `NewPtr` [I:3.2.2] returns an untyped pointer to the block, which we immediately convert to type `SWSynthPtr` [5.1.2] so we can access the record's internal fields. (If the record were going to remain allocated for a longer period of time, we would probably want to make it a relocatable block instead, to avoid fragmenting the heap. We would then have to lock the block and dereference its handle each time we played the sound, and of course remember to unlock it again afterward—perhaps by using a completion routine.)

Now that we have a pointer to the synthesizer record, we can proceed to fill in its fields. First we set the `mode` field to indicate square-wave sound, and calculate the scale factor for the specified tempo, in ticks per beat. Then we step through the array of `Tone` records, setting each note's pitch (count), volume (amplitude), and duration. Notice how in note 7 we start with the nominal count constant for C-natural and divide it by 2, to transpose it to the octave above middle C. After setting the last tone to all zeros to mark the end of the sequence, we call `StartSound` [5.2.1] to play the sound and then `DisposPtr` [I:3.2.2] to deallocate the synthesizer record.

Four-Tone Sound

Whereas the synthesizer record for square-wave sound can represent a whole series of tones to be played in sequence, a four-tone synthesizer record [5.1.3] just denotes a single, unchanging sound. The sound may consist of as many as four distinct tones, or "voices," combined harmonically to form a chord; their pitches, timbres, and phase relationships are given by a separate *sound record* [5.1.3], located via a pointer in the `sndRec` field of the main synthesizer record. Although the four voices are defined independently, any change in any one of them requires a whole new sound record and a separate call to `StartSound` [5.2.1].

The sound record begins with a `duration` field that tells how long the sound lasts, in ticks. This is followed by the fields that define the individual characteristics of the four voices. The timbre of each voice is given by a `Wave` array [5.1.3], which holds 256 byte-length magnitude samples representing one or more complete cycles of the voice's waveform. Negative values are not allowed in the `Wave` array, so the magnitude samples must be *normalized:* that is, offset upward by the same fixed amount, so that they all come out positive (see Figure 5–4). The number of samples corresponding to one cycle of the wave is called the *wavelength.* Typically the entire `Wave` array represents a single cycle, so the wavelength is 256; but other values are also possible. For instance, if the waveform were repeated four times in the space of a 256-byte array, the wavelength would be 64.

Recall that the sound generator sends one magnitude value to the speaker each time the video circuitry performs a horizontal retrace, or approximately 22,257 times per second. In the case of four-tone sound, the effective sound magnitude is found by adding together the individual magnitudes for the four independent voices, taken from their respective `Wave` arrays. The sound record gives a *phase offset* for each voice, which is the index within the array from which the first sample is to be taken. This determines where in the waveform the sound begins playing, and thus controls the phase relationship between this voice and the others.

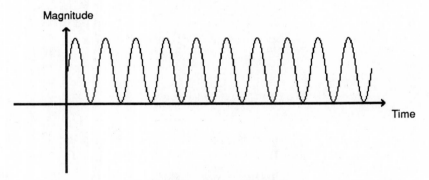

Figure 5–4 Normalized waveform

Each voice also has a *sampling rate,* a fixed-point number that tells how many elements of the `Wave` array to skip between one sound sample and the next: for example, if the sampling rate is 20, every twentieth element of the array will be sampled. Sampling rates of less than 1 cause the same array element to be used several times in succession: a rate of 0.25, for example, repeats each element for four consecutive sound samples. On reaching the end of the array, the sound driver simply cycles back to the beginning and repeats the waveform again, as many times as necessary to make the sound last for the specified duration.

Since the sampling rate controls how long it takes to complete one pass through the Wave array, it effectively determines the pitch of the sound. At 22,257 sound samples per second (each representing rate bytes of the array) and wavelength bytes per wave cycle, the resulting frequency is given by the formula

```
frequency = 22257 * (rate/wavelength)
```

or

```
rate = (frequency*wavelength) / 22257
```

For example, at a wavelength of 256 bytes per cycle, the reference frequency of 440 Hz (A above middle C) corresponds to a sampling rate of approximately 5.0609. Sampling rates for the octave beginning with middle C are shown in the figure in section [5.1.3]. (Once again, the values given are for equal-tempered rather than just-tempered tuning.) To transpose these values to different registers, double the given rate for each octave upward, or halve it for each octave down.

Program 5–2 (PlayChord) uses four-tone sound to play a single four-note chord, a C-major dominant seventh. Once again, we begin by defining pitch constants for the notes of the scale, this time using the sampling rates given in section [5.1.3] instead of the count values from [5.1.2]. We specify these constants in hexadecimal rather than decimal form, to make it easier to typecast them later to type Fixed, as required for the four-tone sound record.

Program 5–2 Define and play a four-tone sound

```
procedure PlayChord;

   { Define and play a four-tone sound. }

   const
      CNatural  = $0003025D;            {Sampling rate for C-natural [5.1.3]}
        CSharp  = $0003302C;            {Sampling rate for C-sharp [5.1.3]}
        DFlat   = $0003302C;            {Sampling rate for D-flat [5.1.3]}
      DNatural   = $000360B5;           {Sampling rate for D-natural [5.1.3]}
```

Program 5–2 Define and play a four-tone sound *(continued)*

```
        DSharp   = $00039420;        {Sampling rate for D-sharp [5.1.3]}
        EFlat    = $00039420;        {Sampling rate for E-flat [5.1.3]}
      ENatural   = $0003CA99;        {Sampling rate for E-natural [5.1.3]}
      FNatural   = $00040450;        {Sampling rate for F-natural [5.1.3]}
        FSharp   = $00044176;        {Sampling rate for F-sharp [5.1.3]}
        GFlat    = $00044176;        {Sampling rate for G-flat [5.1.3]}
      GNatural   = $0004823E;        {Sampling rate for G-natural [5.1.3]}
        GSharp   = $0004C6E1;        {Sampling rate for G-sharp [5.1.3]}
        AFlat    = $0004C6E1;        {Sampling rate for A-flat [5.1.3]}
      ANatural   = $00050F98;        {Sampling rate for A-natural [5.1.3]}
        ASharp   = $00055CA2;        {Sampling rate for A-sharp [5.1.3]}
        BFlat    = $00055CA2;        {Sampling rate for B-flat [5.1.3]}
      BNatural   = $0005AE41;        {Sampling rate for B-natural [5.1.3]}


      chordLength    = 1.0;          {Duration of chord in seconds}
      TicksPerSecond = 60;           {Number of system clock ticks per second}

  var
      theSynth     : FTSynthRec;     {Synthesizer record [5.1.3]}
      theSound     : FTSoundRec;     {Sound record [5.1.3]}
      theWave      : Wave;           {Waveform array [5.1.3]}
      waveIndex    : 0..255;         {Index into wave array}
      rawMagnitude : REAL;           {Unnormalized, unscaled sound magnitude}

  begin {PlayChord}

      for waveIndex := 0 to 255 do         {Index through wave array}
         begin
             rawMagnitude          := SIN ( (2*Pi) * (waveIndex/256) ); {Find raw magnitude}
             theWave[waveIndex] := ROUND( (rawMagnitude + 1.0) * 127) {Normalize and scale}
         end; {for waveIndex}

      with theSound do                      {Fill in sound record}
         begin

             duration := ROUND(chordLength * TicksPerSecond); {Set sound duration [5.1.3]}

             sound1Rate  := Fixed(CNatural);  {Set pitch [5.1.3, I:2.3.1]}
             sound1Phase := 0;                {Set phase [5.1.3]}
             sound1Wave  := @theWave;         {Set waveform [5.1.3]}
```

Program 5–2 Define and play a four-tone sound *(continued)*

```
sound2Rate   := Fixed(ENatural);      {Set pitch [5.1.3, I:2.3.1]}
sound2Phase  := 0;                    {Set phase [5.1.3]}
sound2Wave   := @theWave;             {Set waveform [5.1.3]}


sound3Rate   := Fixed(GNatural);      {Set pitch [5.1.3, I:2.3.1]}
sound3Phase  := 0;                    {Set phase [5.1.3]}
sound3Wave   := @theWave;             {Set waveform [5.1.3]}


sound4Rate   := Fixed(BFlat);         {Set pitch [5.1.3, I:2.3.1]}
sound4Phase  := 0;                    {Set phase [5.1.3]}
sound4Wave   := @theWave              {Set waveform [5.1.3]}

end; {with theSound}

with theSynth do                      {Fill in synthesizer record}
   begin
      mode   := FTMode;               {Set mode to four-tone [5.1.3, 5.1.1]}
      sndRec := @theSound             {Point to sound record [5.1.3]}
   end; {with theSynth}

StartSound (@theSynth, SIZEOF(theSynth), POINTER(-1))  {Play the sound [5.1.2]}

end; {PlayChord}
```

Although each of the four voices in our chord could theoretically have its own waveform, we will in fact use the same waveform for all of them, a pure sine wave like the ones shown earlier in Figures 5–1 and 5–2. The first thing we have to do is fill in the magnitude values in the Wave array. Since Pascal's SIN function expects its argument to be expressed in radians, we convert each of the 256 array indices into an equivalent fraction of a complete cycle (2π radians) and find its sine. Then we normalize it by adding 1.0, to make all the negative values positive, and scale it to the range of values that can be represented in a single byte.

Next it's time to initialize the contents of the sound record. Since this record has a known, fixed size, we can simply declare it on the stack as a local variable instead of allocating it dynamically from the heap. (Notice, however, that this only works because we're playing our sound synchronously. If the sound request were asynchronous, it would still be pending when we exit from the routine and deallocate the local variables, leaving a bomb ticking where our pretty music is supposed to be. If you're using asynchronous sound, make sure all your data structures live in the heap and not on the stack.) After the sound record is filled in, we initialize the synthesizer record to point to it, set the synthesizer's `mode` field to `FTMode` [5.1.1], call `StartSound` [5.2.1] to play the sound synchronously, and we're done. There's no need to deallocate the data structures as we did in our earlier square-wave routine, since they reside on the stack and will be deallocated automatically on exit from the routine.

Free-Form Sound

A free-form synthesizer record [5.1.4] can represent any kind of sound your application requires, such as electronically sampled music, synthesized speech, or exotic sound effects. Like the voices in a four-tone sound record, a free-form sound is defined by an array of magnitude samples—in this case, of type `FreeWave` [5.1.4]. Instead of being located via a pointer, the array is embedded directly within the free-form synthesizer record. It's nominally declared with 30,001 byte-length elements but in fact, you can make it any size you need: the `recordSize` parameter you supply to `StartSound` [5.2.1] will tell the sound driver how big the array really is. Where you get the values to load into the array is up to your own ingenuity.

The contents of a free-form wave array are not repeated cyclically to fill an allotted length of time, like a four-tone wave, but are simply played once through from beginning to end. The synthesizer record's `count` field contains a sampling rate like those used in four-tone sound. This controls the spacing between magnitude samples sent to the speaker and thus the duration and pitch of the resulting sound. Since the sampling interval is approximately 44.93 microseconds (corresponding to a frequency of 22.257 kHz), the length of the sound is given by the formula

```
duration = 0.00004493 * (arrayLength/count)
```

If the waveform contains a pattern that repeats periodically every `wavelength` bytes, it will produce a tone with a frequency of

```
frequency = 22257 * (count/wavelength)
```

REFERENCE

5.1 Defining Sounds

5.1.1   Types of Sound

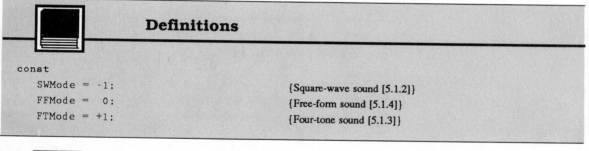

Definitions

```
const
  SWMode = -1;        {Square-wave sound [5.1.2]}
  FFMode =  0;        {Free-form sound [5.1.4]}
  FTMode = +1;        {Four-tone sound [5.1.3]}
```

Notes

1. These constants are used in the `mode` field of a synthesizer record, to identify the type of record and the kind of sound it represents.

2. *Square-wave* sound [5.1.2] consists of a sequence of tones forming a single melodic line. Each tone has a square waveform, producing a flat, synthetic-sounding timbre.

3. *Four-tone* sound [5.1.3] consists of as many as four separate tones, or "voices," combined harmonically. Each voice is specified independently, with any desired pitch and timbre, and in any phase relationship to the other voices.

4. *Free-form* sound [5.1.4] consists of a single waveform of arbitrary length and complexity, representing any desired sound (such as speech, electronically sampled music, or sound effects).

5. In assembly language, the global variable SoundBase holds the base address of the hardware sound buffer in RAM; SoundDCE points to the sound driver's device control entry [3.1.4]; SdEnable and SoundActive are 1-byte flags telling whether the sound generator is currently enabled and whether it is currently producing sound.

Assembly Language Information

Assembly-language global variables:

Name	Address	Meaning
SoundBase	$266	Pointer to start of sound buffer
SoundDCE	$27A	Pointer to sound driver's device control entry [3.1.4]
SdEnable	$261	Sound generator currently enabled? (1 byte)
SoundActive	$27E	Sound generator currently active? (1 byte)

5.1.2   Square-Wave Sound

Definitions

```
type
   SWSynthPtr = ^SWSynthRec;
   SWSynthRec = record
                  mode     : INTEGER;   {Type of sound: must be SWMode [5.1.1]}
                  triplets : Tones      {Tones to be played}
               end;

   Tones = array [0..5000] of Tone;     {Any number of tones}
   Tone  = record
              count     : INTEGER;      {Determines pitch of tone}
              amplitude : INTEGER;      {Volume of tone, 0-255}
              duration  : INTEGER       {Duration of tone in ticks}
           end;
```

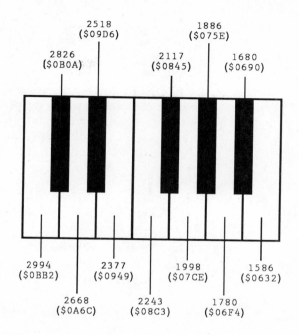

Count values for musical tones

Notes

1. SWSynthRec is a square-wave synthesizer record, representing a sequence of tones forming a single melodic line.

2. The mode field must contain the constant value SWMode [5.1.1], denoting square-wave sound.

3. triplets is an array of type Tones giving the pitch, amplitude, and duration of each tone in the sequence. All tones will have a square waveform, producing a flat, synthetic-sounding timbre.

4. The Tones array nominally contains 5001 entries, but may actually be of any length up to this maximum. Notice that the array itself is embedded within the synthesizer record, not just a pointer or handle.

5. The last meaningful Tone entry is followed by one with all fields equal to 0, to mark the end of the array.

6. Use `NewHandle` or `NewPtr` [I:3.2.1] to allocate a block of exactly the needed size for your synthesizer record, then typecast the resulting pointer to an `SWSynthPtr`. The size required is 6 bytes for each tone, plus an extra 6 bytes for the final zero entry and 2 more for the `mode` field.

7. A tone's `count` field gives the period of its square wave, which determines its pitch. The unit in which the period is expressed is the time required for the Macintosh video circuitry to paint 20 pixels on the screen, at its standard pixel rate of 15.6672 MHz. Thus the count is related to the frequency by the formula

```
count = (15667200/20) / frequency
      = 783360 / frequency
```

For example, a frequency of 440 Hz (A above middle C) corresponds to a count of 1780.

8. Count values for the octave above middle C are shown in the figure. To produce the same notes in a different register, double the count (or shift left one bit) for each octave lower, halve (or shift right one bit) for each octave higher.

9. The values in the figure are based on an equal-tempered scale such as a piano keyboard. Slightly different count values are needed for just-tempered tuning, as on a violin or other continuously tuned instruments; see *Inside Macintosh* for further details.

10. In assembly language, the global variable `CurPitch` holds the count value for the tone currently being generated. The contents of this variable are meaningful only for square-wave sound.

11. The `amplitude` field gives the volume of the tone, on a scale from 0 (silence) to 255 (maximum volume). When played, this value will be scaled to the maximum speaker volume [5.2.2] selected by the user via the Control Panel desk accessory.

12. The `duration` field gives the duration of the tone in ticks (sixtieths of a second).

Assembly Language Information

Assembly-language global variable:

Name	Address	Meaning
CurPitch	$280	Count value for current square-wave tone

5.1.3   Four-Tone Sound

Definitions

```
type
    FTSynthPtr = ^FTSynthRec;
    FTSynthRec = record
                    mode   : INTEGER;        {Type of sound:  must be FTMode [5.1.1]}
                    sndRec : FTSndRecPtr      {Sound to be played}
                 end;

    FTSndRecPtr = ^FTSoundRec;
    FTSoundRec  = record
                    duration    : INTEGER;    {Duration of sound, in ticks}
                    sound1Rate  : Fixed;      {Sampling rate for voice 1}
                    sound1Phase : LONGINT;    {Phase offset for voice 1}
                    sound2Rate  : Fixed;      {Sampling rate for voice 2}
                    sound2Phase : LONGINT;    {Phase offset for voice 2}
                    sound3Rate  : Fixed;      {Sampling rate for voice 3}
                    sound3Phase : LONGINT;    {Phase offset for voice 3}
                    sound4Rate  : Fixed;      {Sampling rate for voice 4}
                    sound4Phase : LONGINT;    {Phase offset for voice 4}
                    sound1Wave  : WavePtr;    {Waveform for voice 1}
                    sound2Wave  : WavePtr;    {Waveform for voice 2}
                    sound3Wave  : WavePtr;    {Waveform for voice 3}
                    sound4Wave  : WavePtr;    {Waveform for voice 4}
                 end;

    WavePtr = ^Wave;
    Wave    = packed array [0..255] of Byte;  {256 magnitude samples}
```

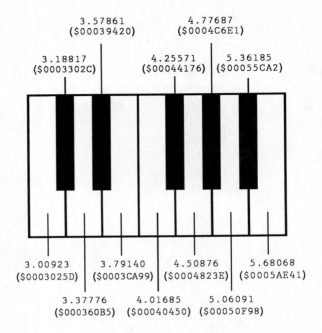

Sampling rates for musical tones

 Notes

1. FTSynthRec is a four-tone synthesizer record, representing as many as four separate tones, or "voices," combined harmonically.

2. Unlike a square-wave synthesizer record [5.1.2], a four-tone record denotes a single, unchanging sound and not a sequence of changing tones or harmonies. Any change in any of the four voices requires a new record and a separate call to StartSound [5.2.1].

3. The mode field must contain the constant value FTMode [5.1.1], denoting four-tone sound.

4. sndRec is a pointer to a *sound record* of type FTSoundRec, giving the pitch, timbre, and phase of each of the four combined voices.

5. The duration field of the sound record gives the duration of the sound in ticks (sixtieths of a second).

6. Each voice's timbre is defined by a `Wave` array of 256 byte-length magnitudes, representing one or more cycles of the desired waveform. The number of bytes in each cycle is called the *wavelength*.

7. Magnitudes in the `Wave` array are normalized by adding the amplitude of the wave to each value, so that all true magnitudes, both positive and negative, are represented by positive values in the array.

8. The pitch for each voice is given by a *sampling rate*, which determines how frequently the corresponding waveform is to be repeated. One magnitude value (sample) is taken from the `Wave` array each time the Macintosh video circuitry performs a horizontal retrace. The sampling rate tells how many elements of the array to advance between samples: for example, a rate of 20 causes every twentieth element to be sampled, while a rate of 0.25 repeats each element for four consecutive samples.

9. The sampling interval is the video circuitry's standard horizontal retrace interval, approximately 44.93 microseconds or 22,257 samples per second. Since each sample represents (rate/wavelength) cycles, the sampling rate is related to the frequency by the formula

   ```
   frequency = 22257 * (rate/wavelength)
   ```

   or

   ```
   rate = (frequency*wavelength) / 22257
   ```

   For example, if the wavelength is 256 bytes (that is, if the entire `Wave` array represents a single cycle of the sound wave), a frequency of 440 Hz (A above middle C) corresponds to a sampling rate of approximately 5.0609.

10. Sampling rates for the octave above middle C are shown in the figure. To produce the same notes in a different register, double the sampling rate for each octave higher, halve for each octave lower.

11. The values in the figure are based on an equal-tempered scale such as a piano keyboard. Slightly different sampling rates are needed for just-tempered tuning, as on a violin or other continuously tuned instruments; see *Inside Macintosh* for further details.

12. The phase value for each voice gives the index in the `Wave` array from which the first sample is to be taken. This determines the relative offset, or phase relationship, between this voice's waveform and those of the other three voices.

13. When played, the combined amplitude of the four voices will be scaled to the maximum speaker volume [5.2.2] selected by the user via the Control Panel desk accessory.

14. In assembly language, the global variable `SoundPtr` holds a pointer to the sound record for the sound currently being generated. The contents of this variable are meaningful only for four-tone sound.

Assembly Language Information

Assembly-language global variable:

Name	Address	Meaning
SoundPtr	$262	Pointer to current four-tone sound record

5.1.4   Free-Form Sound

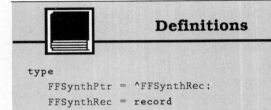

Definitions

```
type
    FFSynthPtr = ^FFSynthRec;
    FFSynthRec = record
                     mode       : INTEGER;     {Type of sound: must be FFMode [5.1.1]}
                     count      : Fixed;       {Sampling rate}
                     waveBytes  : FreeWave     {Waveform}
                 end;
    FreeWave   = packed array [0..30000] of Byte;
```

Notes

1. `FFSynthRec` is a free-form synthesizer record, defining a single waveform of arbitrary length and complexity. It may represent any desired sound, such as speech, electronically sampled music, or sound effects.

2. When played with `StartSound` [5.2.1], the free-form wave is not repeated cyclically like a four-tone wave [5.1.3], but is simply played through once from beginning to end.

3. The `mode` field must contain the constant value `FFMode` [5.1.1], denoting free-form sound.

4. `waveBytes` is an array of type `FreeWave`, containing a series of byte-length magnitudes that define the desired waveform.

5. Magnitudes in the array are normalized by adding the amplitude of the wave to each value, so that all true magnitudes, both positive and negative, are represented by positive values in the array.

6. When played, the amplitude of the wave will be scaled to the maximum speaker volume [5.2.2] selected by the user via the Control Panel desk accessory.

7. The `waveBytes` array nominally contains 30,001 entries, but may actually be of any length up to this maximum. Notice that the array itself is embedded within the synthesizer record, not just a pointer or handle.

8. Use `NewHandle` or `NewPtr` [I:3.2.1] to allocate a block of exactly the needed size for your synthesizer record, then typecast the resulting pointer to an `FFSynthPtr`. The size required is equal to the length of the `waveBytes` array plus an extra 6 bytes for the `mode` and `count` fields.

9. `count` gives the *sampling rate,* which determines the duration and pitch of the sound produced. One magnitude value (sample) is taken from the `waveBytes` array each time the Macintosh video circuitry performs a horizontal retrace. The sampling rate tells how many elements of the array to advance between samples: for example, a rate of 20 causes every twentieth element to be sampled, whereas a rate of 0.25 repeats each element for four consecutive samples.

10. The first sample is always taken from byte 0 of the array.

11. The sampling interval is the video circuitry's standard horizontal retrace interval, approximately 44.93 microseconds or 22,257 samples per second. Thus the overall duration of the sound in seconds is given by the formula

```
duration = 0.00004493 * (arrayLength/count)
```

For example, an array 3000 bytes long, sampled at a rate of 0.1, will produce a sound lasting approximately 1.35 seconds.

12. For waveforms that repeat periodically, such as musical tones, the number of bytes in each cycle is called the *wavelength.* Since each sample represents (count/wavelength) cycles, the sampling rate is related to the frequency by the formula

```
frequency = 22257 * (count/wavelength)
```

or

```
count = (frequency*wavelength) / 22257
```

For example, if the wavelength is 100 bytes, a frequency of 440 Hz (A above middle C) corresponds to a sampling rate of approximately 1.9769.

5.2 Playing Sounds

5.2.1 Starting and Stopping Sounds

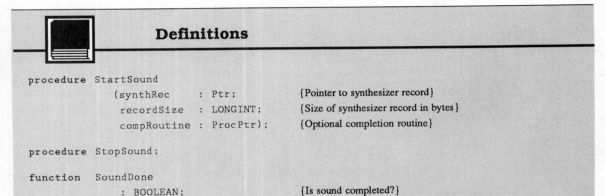

Definitions

```
procedure StartSound
        (synthRec    : Ptr;            {Pointer to synthesizer record}
         recordSize  : LONGINT;        {Size of synthesizer record in bytes}
         compRoutine : ProcPtr);       {Optional completion routine}

procedure StopSound;

function SoundDone
            : BOOLEAN;                 {Is sound completed?}
```

Notes

1. StartSound issues a specified sound from the Macintosh speaker.

2. synthRec is a pointer to a synthesizer record defining the sound to be produced; recordSize gives the size of the record in bytes.

3. The synthesizer record may be of type SWSynthRec [5.1.2] for square-wave sound, FTSynthRec [5.1.3] for four-tone, or FFSynthRec [5.1.4] for free-form. The specific type is identified by the record's mode field, which must contain one of the constants SWMode, FTMode, or FFMode [5.1.1].

4. Sound requests are normally issued asynchronously: the request is simply queued for later execution by the sound driver. Control then returns immediately to the calling program, which can continue to run while the sound is being produced.

5. compRoutine is a pointer to an optional *completion routine*, to be executed on completion of the sound request.

6. The completion routine, if any, must be written in assembly language. On entry, register A0 will point to the parameter block [3.1.5] for the completed operation and D0 will contain its result code. The completion routine must preserve the contents of all registers except A0–A1 and D0–D2, and must not attempt to allocate any new storage from the heap.

7. If compRoutine = NIL, the sound request will be executed asynchronously with no completion routine.

8. If `compRoutine = ProcPtr(-1)`, the sound request will be performed synchronously: control will not return to the calling program until after the request has been completed.

9. `StopSound` immediately cancels all current and pending sound operations.

10. The current operation's completion routine is executed, if any.

11. `SoundDone` tests whether all previously issued sound requests have been completed. It returns `FALSE` if there are any current or pending sound operations, `TRUE` if none.

12. These routines are part of the Pascal interface to the Toolbox, not part of the Toolbox itself. They don't reside in ROM and can't be called from assembly language via the trap mechanism. You can perform the same operations from assembly language by issuing the equivalent low-level device calls directly to the sound driver.

13. In all sound driver calls, the `ioRefNum` field of the parameter block [3.1.5] must be set to `-4`, the driver reference number for the sound driver. See *Inside Macintosh* for more information on low-level driver calls.

14. To play a sound from assembly language, issue a `_Write` call [3.2.2] to the sound driver. The parameter block's `ioBuffer` field [3.1.5] must point to the synthesizer record defining the sound, with `ioReqCount` giving the size of the record in bytes. To specify a completion routine, set the `ioCompletion` field to point to it.

15. To cancel sound from assembly language, issue a `_KillIO` call [3.2.3] to the sound driver. Unlike the high-level `StopSound` routine, this will execute the completion routines of all pending sound requests in addition to the one currently being played. If you're using square-wave sound, you must also set the global variable `CurPitch` [5.1.2] to 0.

16. To check for completion of a sound request from assembly language, look in the parameter block's `ioResult` field [3.1.5]. A value of 1 in this field means that the request is still pending; any other value is a result code posted on completion of the request.

Assembly Language Information

Trap macros:

(Pascal) Routine name	(Assembly) Trap macro	Trap word
PBWrite	_Write	$A003
PBKillIO	_KillIO	$A006

Assembly-language global variable:		
Name	**Address**	**Meaning**
CurPitch	$280	Count value for current square-wave tone

5.2.2 Speaker Volume

Definitions

```
procedure GetSoundVol
          (var newLevel : INTEGER);      {New volume setting}

procedure SetSoundVol
          (curLevel : INTEGER);          {Current volume setting}
```

Notes

1. GetSoundVol returns the current speaker volume setting; SetSoundVol changes it.

2. The speaker volume ranges from 0 (silence) to 7 (loudest). All sounds issued through the speaker are scaled to this maximum volume.

3. The user normally sets the desired speaker volume via the Control Panel desk accessory. This setting is kept in "parameter RAM" on the battery-powered clock chip, and is used to initialize the actual speaker volume each time the Macintosh is started up.

4. SetSoundVol sets the current speaker volume, but not the user-selected value in parameter RAM. Thus the new setting will remain in effect only until the next time the system is restarted.

5. Don't change the speaker volume permanently. Before calling SetSoundVol, obtain the previous value with GetSoundVol and restore it again before exiting from your program.

6. These routines are part of the Pascal interface to the Toolbox, not part of the Toolbox itself. They don't reside in ROM and can't be called from assembly language via the trap mechanism. In assembly language, the current volume setting is kept in the last three bits of the global variable SdVolume (see below).

Assembly Language Information

Assembly-language global variable:

Name	Address	Meaning
SdVolume	$260	Current speaker volume (1 byte)

CHAPTER

6

Playing with a Full Desk

Everyone loves desk accessories—those handy little gadgets that live on your Apple menu and can spring to life at a click of the mouse, alongside whatever else you happen to be doing. In the beginning there were only seven desk accessories, provided by Apple with the first release of the Macintosh system software: the Alarm Clock, Calculator, Control Panel, Key Caps, Note Pad, Puzzle, and Scrapbook. Today, Macintosh users can choose among hundreds of desk accessories, and more keep appearing all the time, both commercially and in the public domain. Some have capabilities rivaling those of full-fledged application programs: there are text-editor desk accessories, graphics-painting desk accessories, terminal-program desk accessories, and spreadsheet desk accessories. The range of possibilities seems endless.

In this chapter, we'll learn all about desk accessories, how they work internally, and how they communicate with the Toolbox and the running program. As usual, we'll approach the subject by studying an example, a simple desk accessory named `StopWatch`. Once you understand how it works, you can use it as a starting point for developing your own desk accessories. You'll find a complete source listing in Appendix H.

Life as a Desk Accessory

The overriding fact of life for a desk accessory is that it doesn't control its own destiny. An accessory is only a guest on another program's screen, and is completely dependent on the hospitality of that program (called, appropriately enough, the *host program*) for all the necessities of its existence. The accessory can display a window on the screen, but when the user presses the mouse in the window's title bar, it's the host program that receives the event; the host program, not the accessory, must then call the Toolbox to track the mouse and drag the window to its new location. The accessory can place a menu in the menu bar, but when the user chooses an item from the menu, it's the host program that receives the choice; it then passes the menu and item number to the Toolbox, which in turn relays them to the desk accessory for action. The accessory can schedule a periodic task to be executed at regular intervals, but it won't get the chance unless the host program voluntarily surrenders control often enough to give it the time it needs. If the host program doesn't cooperate, the desk accessory can't function.

Not that there aren't compensating advantages. As a mere dependent, the desk accessory is also blissfully free of care and responsibility. It needn't bother with an event loop, since the host program will handle all interactions with the user and spoon-feed the accessory only those events that require its attention. This means the accessory can dispense with all the elaborate machinery we learned about in Volume Two for moving and sizing windows, tracking menu choices, and so forth. Instead, it can just concentrate on the things it cares about, such as responding to its own menu items and to mouse clicks in its content region. As long as the host program lives up to its responsibilities, the desk accessory can lead a simple and happy life.

All this is made possible by a cunning deception. To gain entry to the host program's world, the desk accessory craftily disguises itself as a device driver. This allows it to make itself at home in the heap without interfering with the host's normal activities. It receives all its instructions via the standard driver calls Open, Control, and Close, which we learned about in Chapter 3. All an accessory has to do to earn its keep is respond appropriately to these three driver calls.

Theoretically, a desk accessory could also choose to implement the other two standard driver routines, Prime and Status. In ordinary circumstances, these routines will never be called, since the Toolbox communicates with the accessory entirely through Open, Control, and Close calls. Still, the capability is there if you ever think of anything useful to do with it. Desk accessories work a little bit differently under Apple's new multitasking environment, MultiFinder. The user can now keep two or more application programs active in memory at the same time, switching freely from one to another with a click of the mouse. Each program has its own independent stack and heap and has the illusion of having the entire system to itself, though with only a portion of the total available memory.

Instead of residing in any particular program's heap, all desk accessories are now hosted by a special piece of system software called DA Handler, which runs under MultiFinder as a separate application program, side by side with the others. (This has the surprising consequence that clicking the mouse in any accessory's window causes *all* open accessories to come to the front together, as a complete "layer" of windows!) The user can still choose to avoid the DA Handler and run an accessory the old way, from within the active program's heap, by holding down the Option key while opening the accessory from the Apple menu. From the desk accessory's point of view it makes no difference whether it's being hosted by DA Handler or by an ordinary application program, and everything we say in this chapter applies equally well in both environments.

Like all drivers, each desk accessory has a *device control entry*, or *DCE* [3.1.4], holding all the information the Toolbox needs to run the accessory. The Toolbox creates the DCE the first time the accessory is opened, and installs a handle to it in the system unit table [3.1.3]. From then on, the DCE remains in existence until the crack of doom or until the system is shut down, whichever occurs first. Even if the user closes the accessory, terminates the host program, and starts up another program in its place, the DCE lingers in the heap like the Cheshire Cat's grin, ready to be used again the next time the accessory is reopened.

When they're not in use, desk accessories reside in resource files (normally the System file) under resource type 'DRVR' [3.3.1], waiting to be read into memory when needed. An accessory's resource ID is called its *unit number,* and determines its position in the unit table [3.1.3]. Usually, though, the accessory is identified by its *driver reference number,* which is the bitwise binary complement of the unit number and is related to it arithmetically by the now-familiar formula

```
refNum = -(unitNum + 1)
```

Each accessory also has a resource name by which it can be listed on a menu. We learned in Volume Two, Chapter 4, how the host program uses the Toolbox routine AddResMenu or InsertResMenu [II:4.3.3] to build an "Apple menu" of available 'DRVR' resources. As we've also learned, both these routines suppress all resource names that begin with a period (.). Names of this form are reserved for true input/output drivers like .Print and .Sound, to keep them from appearing on the Apple menu; desk accessory names may begin with any character other than a period.

Desk Accessory Structure

Structurally, a desk accessory has the same form as any other device driver [3.1.1]. Its executable code is preceded by a *driver header* containing flags and other global information. The header also includes offsets that locate the various driver routines within the body of the accessory. At the machine-language level, all driver routines receive a pointer to the accessory's DCE in register A1, along with a pointer in A0 to a *parameter block* [3.1.5] describing the requested operation. The Control and Close routines (as well as Prime and Status, if present) are expected to return a result code in register D0; the Open routine returns it in the ioResult field of the parameter block, instead of the register.

Notice that the parameters passed in the A registers are simple pointers, not handles. Before issuing any driver call, the Toolbox locks both the driver (in this case, the accessory) and its DCE into place in the heap. The dereferenced DCE pointer in A1 can thus be relied on to remain valid for the duration of the call. The parameter block is a nonrelocatable object, so the pointer in A0 is reliable too. On completion, the Toolbox unlocks the accessory and DCE again (unless the dNeedLock flag [3.1.2] is set in the DCE's dCtlFlags field [3.1.4], in which case they remain locked continuously, even between driver calls).

When you write a desk accessory in Pascal (or any other high-level language), special provisions are needed to structure the resulting object code as a desk accessory instead of a stand-alone application program. There are as many different ways of doing this as there are software development systems to do it on. One way or another, though, all of them must deal with the same basic issues. We can discuss the possibilities in general terms here, but you'll have to consult your own language documentation for specifics.

First, you need some way of incorporating a driver header at the beginning of your accessory's code. Some systems treat the header as a special resource type that you define and include with a resource compiler like RMaker or Rez; others provide a utility file containing a dummy header, which you link into your code with a linker. Sometimes you tell the compiler to add a desk accessory header by embedding a compile-time directive in your source code; sometimes you use a special menu command like Build Desk Accessory in place of the usual Compile command.

Second, you have to identify which parts of your program are the driver routines, so the offsets in the header can be set to point to them. Again, different development systems have different conventions for doing this. Some only expect you to supply the three "real" desk accessory routines, Open, Control, and Close; others insist that you provide Prime and Status routines as well, even if they're just dummy routines that return immediately without doing anything. In some systems, you have to give your driver routines standard names like Open, Ctl, and Close, or DrvrOpen, DrvrControl, and DrvrClose; some systems don't care what you call them, but insist that they be the first three routines declared in your program. Still other systems direct all incoming driver calls to a central dispatch routine (supplied by you), which in turn calls the appropriate program routine depending on an integer selector code that it receives as an extra parameter.

Finally, no matter what development system you use, the register-based driver calls received from the Toolbox must somehow be converted to stack-based Pascal form. All development systems generate "glue" code to do the conversion, but as usual, conventions vary wildly. The DCE and parameter block pointers that the Toolbox passes in the registers may simply be copied to the stack as a DCtlPtr [3.1.4] and a ParmBlkPtr [3.1.5], or they may be converted at the Pascal level to the underlying records themselves (DCtlEntry and ParamBlockRec). The DCE may be passed as the first parameter and the parameter block as the second, or the other way around. The parameter block may be omitted from Open and Close calls and included only for Control; or the control code and parameter (fields csCode and csParam) may be extracted from the parameter block and passed as parameters in their own right. The driver routines may be treated as functions and expected to return a result code, or they may be procedures, with the system-generated "glue" automatically supplying a result code of NoErr.

What's an author to do? In the face of all this diversity, which system's conventions should we follow in our example desk accessory? Well, since we can't please everybody, we may as well please nobody. Instead of playing favorites, we'll present our example in a generic form that doesn't quite match that of any development system known to human science. No matter what system you're using, you'll have to make a few minor changes in the example program before it will compile and run successfully; consult your own language documentation for specifics.

StopWatch: A Simple Desk Accessory

The example desk accessory is named StopWatch. It isn't intended to do anything particularly useful, just touch all the bases: maintain a window on the screen (Figure 6–1), place a menu in the menu bar (Figure 6–2), respond to the mouse and keyboard, support the standard cut-and-paste editing operations, and perform a periodic task. Like the MiniEdit program of Volume Two, you can use it as a framework on which to build your own, presumably more inspiring programs.

Figure 6–1 StopWatch window

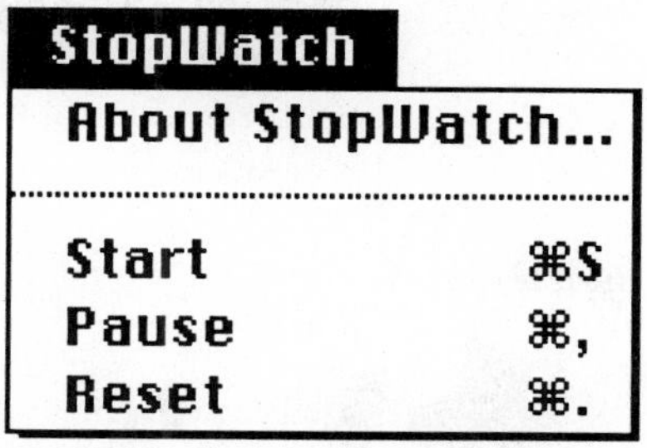

StopWatch

About StopWatch...	
Start	⌘S
Pause	⌘,
Reset	⌘.

Figure 6–2 StopWatch menu

When the user chooses StopWatch from the Apple menu, it comes up on the screen initially displaying the number 0 in its window. Choosing the Start menu command (or typing Command–S on the keyboard) will start the clock running, counting upward by tenths of a second. The Pause command (or Command-comma) temporarily suspends the clock and changes the command name on the menu from Pause to Resume. In this paused state, Resume or Command-comma starts the clock running again from the point of suspension. Reset (or Command-period) stops the clock and sets its value back to 0, ready to start over again. For convenience, Stop-Watch accepts the Return and Enter keys as synonyms for Start, the space bar for Pause/Resume, and the Clear key (on the numeric keypad) for Reset.

Instead of starting the clock from 0, the user may type in a different number of seconds from the keyboard. Only the digits 0-9 are accepted as keyboard input; all other characters are rejected with a beep. StopWatch also supports mouse-based text selection and cut-and-paste editing, allowing numerical values to be pasted in from the host program or from other desk accessories such as the Calculator, Key Caps, or Note Pad. Starting the clock with a value other than 0 causes it to count down instead of up; again it can be suspended and restarted with the Pause/Resume command, the space bar, or Command-comma. When the clock counts down to 0 it sounds the alarm, beeping and flashing the menu bar once per second until it is reset.

Program 6–1 shows StopWatch's top-level structure. The three main driver routines, which we're calling DoOpen, DoControl, and DoClose, do all the work; the main program does nothing, and is included strictly for form. (In fact, some development systems require you to define your desk accessory as a Pascal unit instead of a full-fledged program, with no main program block at all.) The driver routines are declared forward at the beginning of the program, to meet the requirement of some systems that they be the first three routines declared. This arrangement also allows them to refer to one another if necessary.

Program 6–1 Skeleton of a desk accessory

```
program StopWatch:

   { Skeleton program to illustrate desk accessory structure. }

uses
   MemTypes, QuickDraw, OSIntf, ToolIntf, PackIntf:


{ Global Declarations }

   . . . :

{ Forward Declarations }

procedure DoOpen (pbPtr : ParamBlkPtr; dcePtr : DCtlPtr); forward:
procedure DoControl (pbPtr : ParamBlkPtr; dcePtr : DCtlPtr); forward:
procedure DoClose (pbPtr : ParamBlkPtr; dcePtr : DCtlPtr); forward:
   { Additional forward declarations for remaining program routines }


procedure DoOpen {(pbPtr : ParamBlkPtr; dcePtr : DCtlPtr)}:

   { Handle driver Open call [Prog. 6-2]. }

   begin {DoOpen}
      . . .
   end;   {DoOpen}
```

Program 6–1 Skeleton of a desk accessory *(continued)*

```
procedure DoControl ((pbPtr : ParamBlkPtr; dcePtr : DCtlPtr));

   { Handle driver Control call [Prog. 6-8]. }

   begin {DoControl}
      . . .
   .end;  {DoControl}


procedure DoClose ((pbPtr : ParamBlkPtr; dcePtr : DCtlPtr));

   { Handle driver Close call [Prog. 6-17]. }

   begin {DoClose}
      . . .
   end;  {DoClose}


{ Main program. }

   begin {StopWatch}

      {Do nothing}

   end.  {StopWatch}
```

In the rest of this chapter we'll examine the code of the StopWatch program more closely, one routine at a time. Unfortunately, we haven't room to study every line of the program in exhaustive detail, so we'll just focus on those routines that demonstrate important points about desk accessories and how they work. For a complete listing of the program, see Appendix H.

The Open Routine

When the user chooses an item from the Apple menu, the host program first calls the Toolbox routine GetItem [II:4.6.1] to get the name of the chosen desk accessory. Then it passes the name to OpenDeskAcc [6.2.1], which reads the accessory into memory from its resource file and prepares it for operation. If this is the first time the accessory has been opened since system startup, `OpenDeskAcc` also creates a device control entry for it and installs the DCE's handle in the unit table. Then (whether this is the first time or not), it calls the accessory's Open routine to create its data structures and initialize the fields of its DCE.

Program 6–2 (`DoOpen`) is `StopWatch`'s Open routine. For purposes of illustration, we're assuming that this and the other top-level driver routines receive a parameter block pointer and a DCE pointer as parameters, taken straight from registers `A0` and `A1` where the Toolbox left them. On systems with different parameter conventions for these routines, the code of the routine will have to be revised accordingly.

The first thing the Open routine does is dereference the DCE pointer to get the DCE record itself. From this point on, we will pass the record around directly, instead of the pointer, to simplify life for the subsidiary routines. (We can do this safely because we know the DCE is locked for the duration of any driver call.) Next we test whether `StopWatch` is already open, by checking the DCE's `dCtlWindow` field [3.1.4] to see if it already contains a window pointer. If so, we just call `SelectWindow` [II:3.5.2] to bring the existing window to the front of the screen. (Here and elsewhere in the program, we first have to typecast `dCtlWindow` to a window pointer, since the Toolbox interface defines it as a simple `Ptr`.) If `dCtlWindow` is `NIL`, the accessory isn't already open, so we call the `StopWatch` routines `SetUpDCE` and `SetUpData` to initialize the device control entry and set up our internal data structures for operation.

Program 6–2 Handle driver Open call

```
procedure DoOpen (pbPtr : ParamBlkPtr; dcePtr : DCtlPtr);

    { Handle driver Open call. }

    var
        oldWindow : WindowPtr;                          {Pointer to existing StopWatch window [II:3.1.1]}

    begin {DoOpen}

        with dcePtr^ do
```

Program 6–2 Handle driver Open call *(continued)*

```
if dCtlWindow = NIL then                          {Is there a window open already? [3.1.4]}
    begin
        SetUpDCE   (dcePtr^);                      {If not, initialize DCE}
        SetUpData  (dcePtr^)                       {  and data record  }
    end {then}

else
    begin
        oldWindow := WindowPtr(dCtlWindow);       {Otherwise convert to typed pointer [3.1.4]}
        SelectWindow (oldWindow)                    {Just activate existing window [II:3.5.2]}
    end {else}

end;  {DoOpen}
```

Initializing the Device Control Entry

You may recall that the Toolbox automatically initializes some of the
DCE's fields (dCtlFlags, dCtlDelay, dCtlEMask, and dCtlMenu
[3.1.4]) from the driver header [3.1.1] when the DCE is first created.
Most development systems preset these fields of the header to
standard default values, which you can change or override if necessary with resource utilities like ResEdit, RMaker, or Rez. To be on the
safe side, though, it's probably best for the accessory to reinitialize
these fields directly in the DCE, to make sure they have the right
values for proper operation. In our StopWatch program, this task is
handled by the routine SetUpDCE (Program 6–3).

Program 6–3 Initialize device control entry

```
{ Global constants }

const                                       {Bit masks for DCE flags:  }
    dReadEnable   = $0100;                   {Can respond to Read calls [3.1.2]}
    dWritEnable   = $0200;                   {Can respond to Write calls [3.1.2]}
    dCtlEnable    = $0400;                   {Can respond to Control calls [3.1.2]}
    dStatEnable   = $0800;                   {Can respond to Status calls [3.1.2]}
    dNeedGoodBye  = $1000;                   {Needs "good-bye kiss" [3.1.2]}
    dNeedTime     = $2000;                   {Has periodic task [3.1.2]}
    dNeedLock     = $4000;                   {Must be locked in heap [3.1.2]}
```

Program 6–3 Initialize device control entry *(continued)*

```
procedure SetUpDCE (var dce : DCtlEntry);

   { Initialize device control entry. }

   var
      flagBits : INTEGER;                              {Flag bits for DCE flag word [3.1.2, 3.1.4]}

   begin {SetUpDCE}

      with dce do
         begin

            flagBits  := dCtlEnable + dNeedTime;       {Set up flags [3.1.2]}
            dCtlFlags := BitAnd (dCtlFlags, $FF);      {Extract low byte [I:2.2.2]}
            dCtlFlags := BitOr  (dCtlFlags, flagBits); {Merge in high byte [I:2.2.2]}

            dCtlDelay := 6;                            {Execute task ten times per second [3.1.4]}
            dCtlEMask := MDownMask + KeyDownMask + AutoKeyMask + UpdateMask + ActivMask;
                                                       {Initialize event mask [3.1.4, 6.1.1]}

            dCtlStorage := NewHandle (SIZEOF(DataRecord)) {Allocate private data record [I:3.2.1]}

         end  {with dce}

   end;    {SetUpDCE}
```

The first DCE field to be initialized is dCtlFlags [3.1.2]. Unfortunately, the Pascal-level Toolbox interface doesn't define mask constants for manipulating these flag bits. (They are included as bit-number constants at the assembly level.) So the program has to declare these constants explicitly for itself. For convenience, our StopWatch program includes a full set of these mask constants, even though it actually uses only two of them.

The two flags we need to set are dCtlEnable, signifying that this desk accessory can respond to driver Control calls, and dNeedTime, to schedule a periodic task for execution. The remaining flag bits (dReadEnable, dWriteEnable, dStatEnable, dNeedGoodBye, dNeedLock) are all cleared to 0. In setting the flags, it's important not to disturb the low-order byte of the flag word, where the Toolbox keeps its own private flag bits. So SetUpDCE carefully extracts the existing value from the low byte with BitAnd [I:2.2.2], then merges the new settings into the high byte with BitOr.

Next the `dCtlDelay` field must be set to tell the Toolbox how often to run our periodic task. Since we'll be updating the clock on the screen ten times a second, we set the task frequency to 6 ticks, or one tenth of a second. Then we initialize `dCtlEMask`, a standard Toolbox event mask [6.1.1, II:2.1.3] telling which types of event this accessory is prepared to handle. A typical desk accessory will accept activate/deactivate and update events for its own window, along with mouse-down, key-down, and auto-key events when the window is active. Other event types are of no interest, and must be handled by the Toolbox or the host program instead.

> Apple's *Inside Macintosh* manual warns pointedly that a desk accessory *must not* accept mouse-up events, but doesn't deign to say why, or what dire consequences will befall those foolish enough to disobey. The reasons of the gods must remain forever beyond the ken of mere mortals.

Global Storage

Because it isn't a full-fledged application program, a desk accessory has no access to the application global space, or "A5 world" (discussed in Volume One, Chapter 3). Among other things, this is where programs normally keep their global variables—so an accessory isn't allowed to have any. Instead, it has to keep its global data in a relocatable block in the heap, located via a handle in the `dCtlStorage` field of its device control entry [3.1.4]. This block must be allocated when the desk accessory is opened and deallocated again when it is closed.

> The lack of an A5 world also means that an accessory can't refer to any of QuickDraw's global variables, such as `ThePort`, `ScreenBits`, or the standard fill patterns `Black`, `White`, `Gray`, and so on [I:4.3.1]. You can, of course, still use `GetPort` [I:4.3.3] to get a pointer to the current graphics port; the fill patterns are available from the standard system pattern list [I:5.1.2], or you

can build your own copies with StuffHex [I:2.2.4]. If you're really desperate, you can pry your way into the A5 world by doing pointer arithmetic from the system global CurrentA5 [I:3.1.3], located at hexadecimal address $904. Be aware, however, that this sort of breaking and entering is tricky, hazardous, and illegal in many states. Neither Apple nor the author or publisher of this book will pay your bail.

Program 6–4 shows the type definition for the data record in which StopWatch keeps its global data. Bear in mind that this is not a Toolbox data structure, but a private record type defined by StopWatch for its own internal use, analogous to the window data record used by MiniEdit (Program II:5–1). The last line of our SetUpDCE procedure (Program 6–3) allocates a data record from the heap and stores its handle into the dCtlStorage field of the DCE. This handle will be passed to all other StopWatch routines that need access to the global data. Next, the StopWatch routine SetUpData (Appendix H) is called to initialize the contents of the data record. It in turn calls a series of subsidiary routines named SetUpResources, SetUpMenu, SetUpWindow, SetUpText, and InitFlags, all of which we'll be looking at in a minute.

Program 6–4   StopWatch data record

```
type
    DRHandle   = ^DRPtr;
    DRPtr      = ^DataRecord;
    DataRecord = record

                    RefNum      : INTEGER;      {Driver reference number}
                    RsrcBase    : INTEGER;      {Base ID for owned resources}
                    IBeam       : CursHandle;   {Handle to I-beam cursor [II:2.5.1]}

                    TheMenu     : MenuHandle;   {Handle to StopWatch menu [II:4.1.1]}
                    TheWindow   : WindowPtr;    {Pointer to StopWatch window [II:3.1.1]}
                    TheText     : TEHandle;     {Handle to edit record [II:5.1.1]}

                    TargetTime  : LONGINT;      {Starting or stopping time on system clock [II:2.7.1]}
                    PauseTime   : LONGINT;      {Time of pause on systemclock}
```

Program 6–4 StopWatch **data record** *(continued)*

```
CountDown    : BOOLEAN;        {Counting down (toward zero)?}
ClockRunning : BOOLEAN;        {Is stopwatch running?}
ClockPaused  : BOOLEAN;        {Is stopwatch paused?}
ClockBeeping : BOOLEAN         {Is stopwatch beeping?}

end;    {DataRecord}
```

Owned Resources

Before a desk accessory can be used, it must be installed as a 'DRVR' resource in the system resource file. The usual way of doing this is with Apple's Font/DA Mover utility program. Most development systems, when compiling or building a desk accessory, will stamp the resulting object file with the Mover's creator signature [I:7.3.1], 'DMOV'. Opening the file from the Finder will then automatically cause the Mover to be started up. The file type for such files is 'DFIL'; they appear in the Finder as a little suitcase icon marked with a rectangular grid resembling the familiar Calculator desk accessory (Figure 6–3).

StopWatch

Figure 6–3 Desk accessory file icon

When an accessory is installed in the System file, any resources it uses (other than the 'DRVR' resource itself) must be copied along with it. For the Font/DA Mover to recognize the resources as belonging to the desk accessory, they must be numbered according to the standard rules for owned resources [2.5.4], as shown in Figure 6–4. That is, bits 15 and 14, the two high-order bits of the resource ID, must both be 1; bits 13–11 must be 000, denoting an owning resource of type 'DRVR'; and bits 10–5 must correspond to the accessory's unit number (the resource ID of its 'DRVR' resource). Bits 4–0 may contain any value at all, and are used to identify each individual owned resource within its resource type. (Notice that this limits the accessory to no more than 32 resources of any given type.)

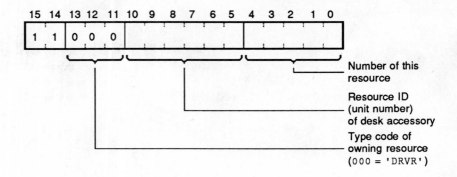

Figure 6–4 Resource ID of desk accessory resources

Expressed arithmetically, the ID of an owned resource belonging to a desk accessory has the form

```
$C000 + (32 * unitNum) + rsrcNum
```

where `unitNum` is the unit number of the accessory and `rsrcNum` is the individual ID number of this particular resource, from 0 to 31. The Font/DA Mover will recognize this pattern as designating an owned resource, and will automatically copy the resource into the `System` file along with the desk accessory itself. If the `System` file already contains an accessory with the same unit number (resource ID) as the one being installed, the Mover will look for an unused unit number and use that one instead. To maintain the connection between the accessory and its owned resources, the Mover will automatically adjust all their ID numbers by changing bits 10–5 to match the new unit number.

One consequence of this arrangement is that you can't know in advance, when you write a desk accessory, what its unit number will be when it is finally installed in the `System` file. And since the unit number determines the resource IDs of the accessory's owned resources, they aren't known in advance either. So you have to arrange for the accessory to calculate the IDs for itself at run time, using the reference number it finds in the `dCtlRefNum` field of its DCE [3.1.4]. (The resources themselves must of course be created separately, with something like `ResEdit` or `RMaker` or `Rez`, and placed in the accessory's resource file for the Mover to copy into the `System` file at installation time.)

Program 6–5 (`SetUpResources`) shows the routine that handles this chore for our `StopWatch` desk accessory. First it gets the accessory's reference number from the DCE and saves it in the global data record for convenience. Then it complements the reference number with `BitNot` [I:2.2.2], to convert it into a unit number, and uses the result to calculate the base value for all owned resource IDs. This base value is also stored away in the data record under the name `RsrcBase`. Finally the routine reads in the standard I-beam cursor [II:2.5.2] from the system resource file and saves it in the data record for later use.

Program 6–5 Initialize `StopWatch` resources

```
procedure SetUpResources (dce : DCtlEntry; dataHandle : DRHandle);

   { Initialize StopWatch resources. }

   const
       flagBits = $C000;                              {Flag bits for owned resources [2.5.4]}

   var
       unitNum : INTEGER;                             {StopWatch's unit number [3.1.3]}

   begin {SetUpResources}

       with dce, dataHandle^^ do
          begin

              RefNum     := dCtlRefNum;               {Save reference number in data record [3.1.4]}

              unitNum    := BitNot    (RefNum);       {Convert to unit number [I:2.2.2]}
              unitNum    := BitShift  (unitNum, 5);   {Shift into position [I:2.2.2]}
              RsrcBase   := BitOr     (flagBits, unitNum); {Merge in flag bits [I:2.2.2]}

              IBeam      := GetCursor (IBeamCursor)   {Get cursor from system file [II:2.5.2]}

          end {with}

   end; {SetUpResources}
```

The Mover's automatic renumbering of resources can cause problems when one resource refers to another by ID number. If resource A contains the ID of resource B and the unit number of their owning desk accessory is changed on installation, the Mover will change the IDs of both resources, but will not adjust A's copy of B's ID to match. If your accessory's resources contain any such embedded IDs, it's up to you to update them to the correct values at run time.

One special case that the Mover is smart enough to handle is the resource ID of a dialog's item list (resource type 'DITL' [II:7.6.3]), embedded within the corresponding alert or dialog template ('ALRT' [II:7.6.1] or 'DLOG' [II:7.6.2]). It will also correctly adjust the IDs of any 'ICON' [I:5.5.3], 'PICT' [I:5.5.5], and 'CNTL' [II:6.5.1] resources included in the item list. So you needn't worry about fixing these specific cases yourself; all other embedded resource IDs are your responsibility.

Desk Accessory Menu

Each open desk accessory is entitled to place one menu in the menu bar. The menu ID (which for resource-based menus is the same as the resource ID) must be negative. This allows the Toolbox to distinguish menus belonging to desk accessories from those belonging to the host program, which will always have positive IDs. The menu ID should also follow the conventions stated above for owned resources, to make sure it doesn't conflict with those of any other accessories that may happen to be open at the same time.

Program 6–6 Initialize StopWatch menu

```
procedure SetUpMenu (var dce : DCtlEntry; dataHandle : DRHandle);

   { Initialize StopWatch menu. }

   begin {SetUpMenu}

      with dce, dataHandle^^ do
```

Program 6–6 Initialize `StopWatch` menu *(continued)*

```
begin

    dCtlMenu := RsrcBase;                    {Store menu ID in DCE [3.1.4]}
    TheMenu  := GetMenu (dCtlMenu);          {Get menu from resource file [II:4.2.2]}
    TheMenu^^.menuID := dCtlMenu;            {Set correct menu ID in menu record [II:4.1.1]}

    InsertMenu (TheMenu, 0);                 {Install at end of menu bar [II:4.4.1]}
    DrawMenuBar                              {Show menu title on screen [II:4.4.3]}

  end {with}

end;    {SetUpMenu}
```

Although the device control entry [3.1.4] includes a field for the menu ID, `dCtlMenu`, the Toolbox offers no help in automatically creating the menu. The accessory's Open routine must build the menu for itself (or read it in from a resource file) and explicitly insert it in the menu bar. Program 6–6 (`SetUpMenu`) shows how `StopWatch` handles this task.

Since there's only one menu, we can just use the value we calculated earlier for `RsrcBase` (Program 6–5) as its menu ID. Notice that we explicitly store the menu ID into the field reserved for it in the DCE, instead of relying on the value already copied there by the Toolbox from the header of our `'DRVR'` resource. This way we can be sure we're using the correct ID, even if the Font/DA Mover may have changed it from its original value when installing it in the system resource file. Similarly, we have to store the same value into the `menuID` field of the menu record [II:4.1.1], to make sure the menu knows its own ID. (This is one of those cases where the Mover doesn't update an embedded resource ID for us. Someday there may be a version of the Mover smart enough to handle this case correctly, but for now we have to take care of it ourselves.)

Besides storing the menu ID into the appropriate fields of the DCE and the menu record, we also save a handle to the menu record itself in our global data record under the name `TheMenu`, to make it available to other parts of the `StopWatch` program. Then we insert the menu at the end of the menu bar and redraw the menu bar, making the menu's title visible to the user on the screen.

For desk accessories that need more than just a single menu, it's possible to take over the entire menu bar and put up as many menus as you wish. The Toolbox global variable `MBarEnable`, at low-memory address $A20, is normally set to 0, signifying that the menu bar is under the control of the host program. A negative value in this location means that the menu bar belongs to a desk accessory instead; the value must be the same as the menu ID found in the `dCtlMenu` field of the accessory's DCE.

An accessory wishing to make use of this feature must, of course, take over the menu bar only when it's actually active on the screen, and give it back to the host program on becoming inactive. On receiving an activate event, the accessory should do the following:

1. Copy its nominal menu ID from its DCE into `MBarEnable`.
2. Call `GetMenuBar` [II:4.4.4] to save the existing menu bar for later restoration.
3. Empty the menu bar with `ClearMenuBar` [II:4.4.1].
4. Insert whatever menus it needs with `InsertMenu` [II:4.4.1], or substitute a preconstructed menu bar of its own with `SetMenuBar` [II:4.4.4].
5. Display the new menu bar on the screen with `DrawMenuBar` [II:4.4.3].

(Instead of building a new menu bar from scratch, the accessory might choose instead to read it in as a resource with `Get-NewMBar` [II:4.4.2].) On receiving a deactivate event, the accessory should

1. Restore the previous menu bar with `SetMenuBar` [II:4.4.4].
2. Redisplay the menu bar with `DrawMenuBar` [II:4.4.3].
3. Clear the value of `MBarEnable` to 0, to restore control of the menu bar to the host program.

Notice that there is no middle ground: you either get one single menu (the normal case) or the whole menu bar.

Desk Accessory Window

If a desk accessory wishes to maintain a window on the screen, its Open routine must create the window record and place a pointer to it in the `dCtlWindow` field of the DCE [3.1.4]. Program 6–7 (`SetUp-Window`) shows how our `StopWatch` program does it. After receiving the window pointer from the Toolbox, we have to typecast it to an untyped `Ptr`, since that's the way it's declared in the DCE. For convenience, we also save it in our global data record as `TheWindow`.

Program 6–7 Initialize `StopWatch` window

```
procedure SetUpWindow (var dce : DCtlEntry; dataHandle : DRHandle);

  { Initialize StopWatch window. }

  var
     peek : WindowPeek;                        {Pointer for "peeking" into window's fields [II:3.1.1]}

  begin {SetUpWindow}

    with dce, dataHandle^^ do
      begin

        TheWindow   := GetNewWindow (RsrcBase, NIL, WindowPtr(-1));
                                                {Make new window from template [II:3.2.2]}
        dCtlWindow := Ptr(TheWindow);          {Store window pointer in DCE [3.1.4]}

        peek := WindowPeek(TheWindow);         {Convert to a "peek" pointer [II:3.1.1]}
        peek^.windowKind := dCtlRefNum         {Set window class to ref. number [II:3.1.1]}

      end {with dce, dataHandle^^}

  end;    {SetUpWindow}
```

Notice that there's no need for the accessory to display the window on the screen: the Toolbox will do that automatically if it finds a window pointer in the DCE on return from the accessory's Open routine. One important bit of housekeeping that must be taken care of, however, is to store the accessory's reference number (not its unit number!) into the `windowKind` field of the window record [II:3.1.1]. This is essential to allow the Toolbox to tell which accessory the window belongs to, so it can relay events affecting the window to the proper destination. Why the Toolbox doesn't set this field for you is another of those unanswered mysteries that make Macintosh programming so endlessly entertaining and delightful.

Since `StopWatch` displays text in its window, its Open routine must also create a TextEdit record [II:5.1.1] and initialize its text characteristics. The routine that does this, `SetUpText`, really doesn't contribute anything new to our understanding of desk accessory programming, so we won't examine it in too much detail here; see Appendix H for the code. There are just a couple of points worth mentioning.

One is that `SetUpText` calls another `StopWatch` routine, `Read-DeskScrap` (also listed in Appendix H), to copy the global desk scrap [I:7.4] into the internal TextEdit scrap. This allows the user to cut or copy text from the host program (or another desk accessory) and paste it into the `StopWatch` window. Notice, though, that the host program must do its part by writing the text *to* the desk scrap before transferring control to the accessory. Without the host's cooperation, the accessory is powerless.

The other important point is that before making the `StopWatch` window the current port (in order to initialize its text characteristics), we must be careful to save the previous port and restore it again before returning control. A desk accessory must always remember that it is a guest in someone else's home, and conduct itself accordingly. This means preserving the host program's current port, current resource file, and all other properties of the global environment exactly the way it finds them, as befits a well-bred houseguest.

The Control Routine

A desk accessory's Control routine is where the action is. Once the accessory is open for business, it receives a stream of Control calls from the Toolbox notifying it of events and circumstances it needs to respond to. These include keystrokes typed when the accessory is active, mouse clicks in its window, items chosen by the user from its menu, standard cut-and-paste editing operations, and executions of its periodic task. All these different types of Control call are identified by standard *control codes* [6.1.2] passed in the `csCode` field of the parameter block [3.1.5]. Responding to Control calls is what desk accessories do for a living.

Program 6–8 (`DoControl`) shows our `StopWatch` accessory's Control routine. It's really just a glorified `case` statement, which dispatches on the control code to the specialized subsidiary routines that do the actual work. Unfortunately, the constant definitions for the desk accessory control codes are not included in the standard Pascal interface files, so StopWatch must declare them for itself.

Program 6–8 Handle driver Control call

```
{ Global constants }

const
    KillCode   =   1;                        {Standard control codes: }
    GoodBye    =  -1;                         {KillIO operation [3.2.3]}
                                             {"Good-bye kiss" [3.1.2]}

    AccEvent   =  64;                         {User event [6.1.3]}
    AccRun     =  65;                         {Periodic task [6.1.3]}
    AccCursor  =  66;                         {Adjust cursor [6.1.3]}
    AccMenu    =  67;                         {Menu item [6.1.3]}
    AccUndo    =  68;                         {Undo command [6.1.3]}
    AccCut     =  70;                         {Cut command [6.1.3]}
    AccCopy    =  71;                         {Copy command [6.1.3]}
    AccPaste   =  72;                         {Paste command [6.1.3]}
    AccClear   =  73;                         {Clear command [6.1.3]}


procedure DoControl (pbPtr : ParamBlkPtr; dcePtr : DCtlPtr);

    { Handle driver Control call. }

    var
        dataHandle : DRHandle;               {Handle to StopWatch data record}
        paramPtr   : ^LONGINT;               {Pointer for converting parameter field}

    begin {DoControl}

        with pbPtr^, dcePtr^ do
            begin

                MoveHHi (dCtlStorage);       {Move data record to end of heap [I:3.2.5]}
                HLock   (dCtlStorage);       {Lock data record [I:3.2.4]}

                    dataHandle := DRHandle(dCtlStorage);   {Convert to typed handle [3.1.4]}
                    paramPtr   := @csParam;                {Convert to long integer [3.1.5]}
```

Program 6–8 Handle driver Control call *(continued)*

```
case csCode of

    AccEvent:
        DoEvent (dataHandle, paramPtr^);        {Handle user event}

    AccRun:
        PeriodicTask (dataHandle);              {Perform periodic task}

    AccCursor:
        FixCursor (dataHandle);                 {Adjust cursor for region ofscreen}

    AccMenu:
        DoMenuChoice (dataHandle, paramPtr^);   {Handle user's menu choice}

    AccUndo:
        DoUndo (dataHandle);                    {Handle Undo command}

    AccCut:
        DoCut (dataHandle);                     {Handle Cut command}

    AccCopy:
        DoCopy (dataHandle);                    {Handle Copy command}

    AccPaste:
        DoPaste (dataHandle);                   {Handle Paste command}

    AccClear:
        DoClear (dataHandle);                   {Handle Clear command}

    GoodBye:
        DoGoodBye (pbPtr, dcePtr);              {Handle "good-bye kiss"}

    KillCode:
        DoKillIO (dataHandle)                   {Perform KillIO operation}

    end; {case ctlCode}

    HUnlock (dCtlStorage)                        {Unlock data record [I:3.2.4]}

end {with pbPtr^, dcePtr^}

end; {DoControl}
```

Once again, as in the Open routine, the Toolbox locks the accessory and its device control entry in place before issuing a Control call, and the parameter block is a nonrelocatable object in the first place—so we can safely dereference the DCE and parameter block pointers that we receive as arguments. The first thing our `DoControl` routine does is lock the `StopWatch` data record (via the `dCtlStorage` handle in the DCE), so all the subsidiary routines can safely access the accessory's global data as well.

Some of the Control calls accept additional data in the first 4 bytes of the parameter block's `csParam` field [6.1.2, 3.1.5]. `DoControl` uses a utility variable, `paramPtr`, to convert these 4 bytes to a long integer that it can pass to the appropriate subsidiary routines as a parameter. On return from the subsidiary routines, `DoControl` unlocks the data record again before exiting back to the Toolbox and the host program.

Two of the control codes shown here, `KillCode` and `GoodBye`, are included for completeness even though `StopWatch` should never actually receive either of them. Since it has no need for a special "good-bye kiss," its Open routine disables them by clearing the `dNeedGoodBye` flag in the DCE (see Program 6–3, `SetUpDCE`, above). As for the standard driver operation KillIO [3.2.3], the Toolbox will never issue such a call to a desk accessory. Theoretically, the host program might issue it directly, but that would assume a degree of specialized knowledge of a particular accessory's properties that the host program ordinarily doesn't have. (The host program typically doesn't even know in advance what accessories will be available in the system at run time!)

Nevertheless, if a desk accessory did choose to respond to good-bye kisses or KillIO calls, it would receive them in the form of special control codes and handle them as shown here. For lack of anything more meaningful to do with them, `StopWatch` treats a good-bye kiss as equivalent to a driver Close call, and KillIO as equivalent to its menu command `Reset`.

Event Processing

Like any other Macintosh program, a desk accessory is *event-driven.* That is to say, its actions are determined by the sequence of *events* reported to it by the Toolbox. Unlike a full-fledged application program, however, an accessory doesn't have an event loop of its own. Instead, it has to hitch a ride on the event loop of its host program.

The host program requests events by repeatedly calling the Toolbox routine `GetNextEvent` [II:2.2.1]. Before reporting an event to the host program, `GetNextEvent` first passes it to another Toolbox routine, `SystemEvent` [6.2.2], to see whether it pertains to a desk accessory. If so, `SystemEvent` intercepts the event and relays it to the accessory in the form of a Control call, with a control code of `AccEvent` [6.1.2] and a pointer to the event record [II:2.1.1] in the first 4 bytes of the parameter block's `csParam` field [3.1.5]. `SystemEvent` then returns a Boolean result telling whether the event was intercepted and relayed to an accessory, or whether it must be processed by the host program instead. Notice that `SystemEvent` is always called internally by the Toolbox itself: it is not intended for public use by any application program or desk accessory.

The events relayed to a desk accessory ordinarily include all window events (activate, deactivate, update) affecting the accessory's window, as well as all keyboard events (key-down, key-up, auto-key) when the accessory is active. However, the accessory can refuse any of these event types, if it chooses, by excluding them from its event mask [6.1.1]. Instead of relaying such events to the accessory, `SystemEvent` will leave them for the host program to handle in its own way.

> Besides window and keyboard events, `SystemEvent` will also relay mouse-up events to an active accessory if permitted by the accessory's event mask. Recall, however, that desk accessories are not *supposed* to accept mouse-up events, for unexplained but presumably weighty reasons. Whom the gods would destroy, they first confuse.

Mouse-down events are singled out for special treatment. In order to intercept such events, `SystemEvent` would first have to call `FindWindow` [II:3.5.1] to determine whether the mouse was pressed in a desk accessory's window. Then, depending on the answer, it could either relay the event to the accessory or leave it alone for the host program to handle. But in the latter case, the host program would immediately have to call `FindWindow` again, to find out which of its own windows the event occurred in, so it could respond accordingly.

To avoid this duplication of effort, `SystemEvent` makes no attempt to intercept mouse-down events, but just passes them through to the host program untouched. On learning from `FindWindow` that the mouse press occurred in a system window (one belonging to a desk accessory), the host program is expected to call yet another Toolbox routine, `SystemClick` [6.2.2], to handle it. `SystemClick` will then determine where in the window the mouse was pressed and respond accordingly:

- If the click was in the window's title bar, it calls `DragWindow` [II:3.5.4] to follow the mouse with an outline of the window until the button is released, then move the window to the new location.

- If the click was in the window's close box, it calls `TrackGoAway` [II:3.5.4] to track the mouse until the button is released. If it's released inside the close box, `SystemClick` then calls `CloseDeskAcc` [6.2.1] to close the accessory.

- If the click was in the window's content region, it relays the mouse-down event as an `AccEvent` Control call for the accessory to deal with in whatever way is appropriate.

An unusual wrinkle arises when the mouse is clicked in a modeless dialog box belonging to a desk accessory. The Toolbox routine `IsDialogEvent` [II:7.4.4] identifies dialog windows by checking their `windowKind` field [II:3.1.1] for the value `DialogKind`; but in order for the window to be recognized as a system window in the first place, its `windowKind` field must hold the accessory's (negative) reference number instead. So the accessory must explicitly set the `windowKind` field to `DialogKind` before calling `IsDialogEvent`, then set it back to the window's own reference number afterward, so that the window will again be recognized as a system window on the next call to `SystemEvent`.

Program 6–9 Handle user event

```
procedure DoEvent (dataHandle : DRHandle; ctlParam : LONGINT);

   { Handle user event. }

   type
      EventPtr = ^EventRecord;                        {Pointer to an event record [II:2.1.1]}

   var
      evtPtr    : EventPtr;                           {Typed pointer for converting control parameter}
      theEvent  : EventRecord;                        {Event record for this event [II:2.1.1]}
      activate  : BOOLEAN;                            {Activate or deactivate window?}

   begin {DoEvent}

      evtPtr    := EventPtr(ctlParam);                {Convert control parameter to typed pointer}
      theEvent := evtPtr^;                            {Get event record}
      with theEvent do

         case what of                                {Dispatch on event type [II:2.1.1, II:2.1.2]}

            MouseDown:
               DoMouseDown (theEvent, dataHandle);    {Handle mouse-down event}

            KeyDown, AutoKey:
               DoKeystroke (theEvent, dataHandle);    {Handle keyboard event}

            UpdateEvt:
               DoUpdate (dataHandle);                 {Handle update event}

            ActivateEvt:
               DoActivate (theEvent, dataHandle)      {Handle activate (or deactivate) event}

         end {case what}

   end;    {DoEvent}
```

Program 6–9 (DoEvent) shows StopWatch's routine for responding to relayed events. All it does is retrieve the event record and dispatch on the event type to some other StopWatch routine that handles that type of event. These other routines (DoMouseDown,

DoKeystroke, DoUpdate, and DoActivate) are all pretty straightforward, and we needn't bother with them here: see Appendix H for the code. One point worth noting is that DoActivate must remember to enable the accessory's menu in the menu bar when its window becomes active, and disable it again when the window becomes inactive. It also performs the needed transfers between the TextEdit scrap and the external desk scrap, allowing text to be cut and pasted between the accessory and the outside world.

Menu Choices

When the user presses the mouse in the menu bar, the host program is expected to call the Toolbox routine MenuSelect [II:4.5.1] to track the mouse and determine which menu item is chosen. If the menu containing the chosen item has a negative menu ID, MenuSelect knows that the menu belongs to a desk accessory. It then calls another Toolbox routine, SystemMenu [6.2.3], to relay the menu choice to the desk accessory for action.

Like SystemEvent, which we discussed earlier, SystemMenu is intended strictly for the private use of the Toolbox itself. It examines the device control entries of all known accessories until it finds one whose dCtlMenu field matches the chosen menu ID. Then it relays the choice to the accessory as a Control call with a control code of AccMenu [6.1.2]. The specific item chosen is identified by passing its menu ID and item number in the first 2 words (4 bytes) of the parameter block's csParam field [3.1.5]. After the accessory has processed the item, MenuSelect reports a menu ID of 0 to the host program, to tell it there's nothing for it to do.

Program 6–10 (DoMenuChoice) shows how StopWatch responds to choices from its menu. It extracts the menu ID and item number, verifies that the menu ID matches its own, and dispatches on the item number to the routine that handles the indicated menu command. These routines (DoAbout, DoStart, DoPause, DoReset) contain much of the programming logic that makes StopWatch behave like a stopwatch. But they have nothing to teach us about how desk accessories work in general, so we won't go into them here; if you're curious, you can read the code for yourself in Appendix H. After one of these routines has executed the chosen menu command, DoMenuChoice must call HiliteMenu(0) [II:4.5.4] to unhighlight the menu title, which will have been left highlighted by MenuSelect.

Program 6–10 Handle user's menu choice

```
{ Global constants }

const                                            {Item numbers for menu commands: }
    AboutItem = 1;                                   {About StopWatch... command}
    StartItem = 3;                                   {Start command}
    PauseItem = 4;                                   {Pause command}
    ResetItem = 5;                                   {Reset command}

procedure DoMenuChoice (dataHandle : DRHandle; menuChoice : LONGINT);

    { Handle user's menu choice. }

    var
        whichMenu : INTEGER;                     {Menu ID of selected menu}
        whichItem : INTEGER;                     {Item number of selected item}

    begin {DoMenuChoice}

        whichMenu := HiWord(menuChoice);         {Get menu ID [I:2.2.3]}
        whichItem := LoWord(menuChoice);         {Get item number [I:2.2.3]}

        if whichMenu <> dataHandle^^.RsrcBase then   {Is it the StopWatch menu? [3.1.4]}
            SysBeep(1)                               {Complain if not [II:2.8.1]}
        else
            begin
                case whichItem of

                    AboutItem:
                        DoAbout (dataHandle);    {Handle About StopWatch... command}

                    StartItem:
                        DoStart (dataHandle);    {Handle Start command}

                    PauseItem:
                        DoPause (dataHandle);    {Handle Pause command}

                    ResetItem:
                        DoReset (dataHandle)     {Handle Reset command}

                    end; {case whichItem}

                HiliteMenu(0)                    {Unhighlight menu title [II:4.5.4]}

            end {else}

    end;  {DoMenuChoice}
```

Cut-and-Paste Editing

StopWatch also responds to the standard editing commands Undo, Cut, Copy, Paste, and Clear. These have to be handled differently, however, because the menu they're on (usually titled Edit) belongs to the host program, rather than to StopWatch itself. It's the host program's responsibility to make sure these commands are available and enabled whenever a desk accessory is active on the screen. Because the Edit menu belongs to the host program (and thus has a positive menu ID), MenuSelect will not intercept the user's choices from this menu and pass them directly to the active desk accessory. Instead, it will simply report them back to the host program like any other item chosen from one of its menus.

But the cut-and-paste editing commands are *not* just like any other menu item. On learning from MenuSelect that the user has chosen one of them, the host program must call the Toolbox routine SystemEdit [6.2.3] to see if the command is directed to a desk accessory instead of itself. SystemEdit checks whether the active window on the screen belongs to a desk accessory. If so, it relays the specified editing command to the accessory and returns TRUE, meaning that the command was intercepted; otherwise it simply returns FALSE, telling the host program to handle the command itself.

As usual, the command is relayed to the accessory in the form of a Control call. But instead of AccMenu, the control code used for choices from the accessory's own menu, each of the standard editing commands has its own special control code: AccUndo, AccCut, AccCopy, AccPaste, and AccClear [6.1.2]. StopWatch's Control routine (DoControl, Program 6–8) refers each of these cases to the appropriate StopWatch routine for that command (DoUndo, DoCut, DoCopy, DoPaste, DoClear). These very simple routines, shown in Appendix H, just call the corresponding TextEdit routines (TECut, TECopy, TEPaste [II:5.5.2], TEDelete [II:5.5.3]) to perform the requested editing operations.

Keyboard Aliases

The fact that the Edit menu belongs to the host program rather than the desk accessory makes it difficult for accessories to handle Command-key combinations in the usual way. Ordinarily, when the user types such a combination on the keyboard, the host program calls the Toolbox routine MenuKey [II:4.5.1] to convert the combination into the equivalent menu ID and item number. This isn't possible for a desk accessory, however, because it doesn't know the item numbers for the editing commands on the host program's Edit menu. So if the accessory wishes to use the standard Command-key aliases for these commands, it has to recognize them for itself, without help from the Toolbox.

Program 6–11 Handle keyboard event

```
procedure DoKeystroke (theEvent : EventRecord; dataHandle : DRHandle);

   { Handle keyboard event. }

   var
      chCode : INTEGER;                              {Character code from event message [8.1.1]}
      ch     : CHAR;                                 {Character that was typed}

   begin {DoKeystroke}

      with theEvent do
         begin

            chCode := BitAnd (message, CharCodeMask);   {Extract character code [I:2.2.2, II:2.1.4]}
            ch     := CHR(chCode);                       {Convert to a character}

            if (BitAnd (modifiers, CmdKey) <> 0)         {Command key down? [I:2.2.2, II:2.1.5]}
                   and (what <> AutoKey) then            {Ignore repeats [II:2.1.1, II:2.1.2]}
               DoAlias   (dataHandle, ch)                {Handle as command alias}
            else
               DoTyping (dataHandle, ch)                 {Handle as ordinary keystroke}

         end  {with theEvent}

   end;  {DoKeystroke}
```

Program 6–11 (DoKeystroke) is StopWatch's routine for handling keyboard input, called by DoEvent (Program 6–9) when it receives a key-down or auto-key event. After extracting the character code from the message field of the event record [II:2.1.4], DoKeystroke examines the modifiers field [II:2.1.5] to see if the Command key was down when the character was typed. If so, it calls the StopWatch routine DoAlias to process the keystroke as a command alias; otherwise, it calls DoTyping to process it as an ordinary keystroke.

DoAlias (Program 6–12) interprets the character typed on the keyboard as a menu equivalent (Command–Z for Undo, Command–X for Cut, and so on) and calls the corresponding StopWatch routine to handle the command. In addition to the standard editing commands, we also recognize keyboard aliases for the commands on StopWatch's own menu: Command–S for Start, Command-comma for Pause/Resume, and Command-period for Reset. Notice that for the latter commands, we highlight the title of the StopWatch menu, but we can't do the same for the editing commands because we don't know the menu ID of the host program's Edit menu.

Program 6–12 Handle keyboard command alias

```
procedure DoAlias (dataHandle : DRHandle; ch : CHAR);

   { Handle keyboard command alias. }

   var
      menuChoice : LONGINT;                               {Menu ID and item number}

   begin {DoAlias}

      if ch in ['S', 's', ',', '.'] then                 {Is it a StopWatch menu command?}
         HiliteMenu (dataHandle^^.RsrcBase);             {Highlight menu title [II:4.5.4]}

      case ch of

         'Z', 'z':
            DoUndo  (dataHandle);                        {Command-Z means Undo}

         'X', 'x':
            DoCut   (dataHandle);                        {Command-X means Cut}

         'C', 'c':
            DoCopy  (dataHandle);                        {Command-C means Copy}

         'V', 'v':
            DoPaste (dataHandle);                        {Command-V means Paste}

         'B', 'b':
            DoClear (dataHandle);                        {Command-B means Clear}

         'S', 's':
            DoStart (dataHandle);                        {Command-S means Start}
```

Program 6–12 Handle keyboard command alias *(continued)*

```
',':
    DoPause (dataHandle);          {Command-comma means Pause or Resume}

'.':
    DoReset (dataHandle);          {Command-period means Reset}

otherwise
    SysBeep(1)                     {Unknown command code [II:2.8.1]}

end;  {case ch}

    HiliteMenu (0)                 {Unhighlight menu title [II:4.5.4]}

end;  {DoAlias}
```

DoTyping (Program 6–13) handles ordinary keystrokes, typed without the Command key. The only printable characters it accepts are the digits 0 to 9, which it passes to the Toolbox routine TEKey [II:5.5.1] to insert in the StopWatch window. It does the same with the backspace character, to delete the current selection or the character immediately preceding the insertion point. In addition, it recognizes those keyboard equivalents that don't require the Command key: Return or Enter for the Start command, the space bar for Pause or Resume, and the keypad Clear key for Reset. For all other characters, it just beeps and does nothing.

Program 6–13 Handle character typed from keyboard

```
{ Global constants }

const                              {Character codes [I:8.1.1]: }
    Enter  = $03;                  {Enter character}
    BS     = $08;                  {Backspace character}
    CR     = $0D;                  {Carriage return}
    Clear  = $1B;                  {Clear character}
    Space  = $20;                  {Space character}

    Digit0 = $30;                  {Digit '0'}
    Digit9 = $39;                  {Digit '9'}
```

Program 6–13 Handle character typed from keyboard *(continued)*

```
procedure DoTyping (dataHandle : DRHandle; ch : CHAR);

   { Handle character typed from keyboard. }

   var
      chCode    : INTEGER;                      {Character code [I:8.1.1]}
      menuChoice : LONGINT;                     {Menu ID and item number}

   begin {DoTyping}

      chCode := ORD(ch);                        {Convert to character code}

      if chCode in [CR, Enter, Space, Clear] then {Is it a StopWatch menu command?}
         HiliteMenu (dataHandle^^.RsrcBase);    {Highlight menu title [II:4.5.4]}

      with dataHandle^^ do
         case chCode of                         {Dispatch on character code}

            Digit0..Digit9, BS:
               if ClockRunning then             {Stopwatch already in use?}
                  SysBeep (1)                   {No typing allowed [II:2.8.1]}
               else
                  TEKey (ch, TheText);          {Insert digit or backspace in window [II:5.5.1]}

            CR, Enter:
               DoStart (dataHandle);            {Return or Enter means Start}

            Space:
               DoPause (dataHandle);            {Space means Pause or Resume}

            Clear:
               DoReset (dataHandle);            {Clear means Reset}

            otherwise
               SysBeep (1)                      {Invalid character [II:2.8.1]}

            end; {case chCode}

      HiliteMenu (0)                            {Unhighlight menu title [II:4.5.4]}

   end; {DoTyping}
```

Periodic Task

At least once per tick (sixtieth of a second)—typically on each pass of its main event loop—the host program is expected to call the Toolbox routine SystemTask [6.2.4]. This gives the Toolbox a chance to perform certain routine chores associated with the care and feeding of drivers and desk accessories. The most important of these chores is running their periodic tasks whenever necessary.

An accessory (or other driver) signals that it has a periodic task by setting the dNeedTime flag [3.1.2] in the dCtlFlags field of its device control entry [3.1.4]. The dCtlDelay field tells how often, in ticks, the task is to be performed. Each time SystemTask is called, it scans the unit table [3.1.3] for drivers or accessories whose tasks are due to be run, using the dCtlCurTicks field of the DCE as a counter to time the interval since the last execution. When the required interval has elapsed, SystemTask issues a Control call with the control code AccRun [6.1.2], instructing the accessory to run its periodic task again.

Program 6–14 Perform periodic task

```
procedure PeriodicTask (dataHandle : DRHandle);

   { Perform periodic task. }

   begin  {PeriodicTask}

      with dataHandle^^ do

         if ClockBeeping then                           {Is the clock beeping?}
            DoBeep                                       {Beep it again}

         else if ClockRunning and not ClockPaused then  {Is the clock ticking?}
            AdvanceClock (dataHandle)                    {Advance time on clock}

         else if not ClockPaused then                   {Is the clock idle?}
            TEIdle (TheText)                             {Blink insertion point [II:5.4.3]}

   end;   {PeriodicTask}
```

Program 6–14 (PeriodicTask) is the routine that performs StopWatch's periodic task. You might say this is the routine that makes StopWatch tick. (Then again, you might not. . . .) What it does depends on what state StopWatch is currently in, as indicated by the

Boolean flags ClockRunning, ClockPaused, and ClockBeeping in the global data record. (These flags are set to reflect the current state of the accessory by the command routines DoStart, DoPause, and DoReset.)

- If the clock has run down to zero and is sounding its alarm, the periodic task calls the StopWatch routine DoBeep (Appendix H) to sound it again. This routine simply beeps once and flashes the menu bar.
- If the clock is running, the periodic task calls the StopWatch routine AdvanceClock to update the time displayed in the StopWatch window. This is the interesting case, which we'll get to in a minute.
- If the clock is neither running nor beeping, the periodic task calls the Toolbox routine TEIdle [II:5.4.3] to blink the insertion point on the screen. This indicates to the user that StopWatch is ready to accept keyboard input or editing commands.
- If the clock is running but has been suspended with the Pause command, the periodic task does nothing.

The AdvanceClock routine (Program 6–15) is the real heart of StopWatch's periodic task. The most straightforward approach would be just to find the time currently displayed in the StopWatch window and add or subtract one tenth of a second, depending on whether the clock is counting upward or downward. Unfortunately, we can't always rely on the host program to call SystemTask as often as it should, particularly during time-consuming operations such as mouse tracking, printing, or disk input/output. The elapsed time between executions of our periodic task may sometimes be considerably more than a tenth of a second.

Program 6–15 Advance time on clock

```
procedure AdvanceClock (dataHandle : DRHandle);

   { Advance time on clock. }

   var
      timeNow    : LONGINT;              {Current time on system clock}
      clockTime  : LONGINT;              {Number of seconds showing on stopwatch}
      timeString : Str255;               {String representation of clock time [I:2.1.1]}
```

Program 6–15 Advance time on clock *(continued)*

```
begin {AdvanceClock}

   with dataHandle^^ do
      begin

         timeNow := TickCount;                         {Get current time [II:2.7.1]}

         if CountDown then                             {Counting up or down?}
            clockTime := TargetTime - timeNow          {Ticks till stopping time}
         else
            clockTime := timeNow - TargetTime;         {Ticks since starting time}

         clockTime := (clockTime + 3) div 6;           {Round to nearest tenth of a second}

         if CountDown and (clockTime <= 0) then        {Has time run out?}
            begin
               timeString := '0.0';                    {Avoid negative value}
               StartBeep (dataHandle)                  {Start beep sequence}
            end {then}
         else
            begin
               NumToString (clockTime, timeString);           {Convert to string [I:2.3.7]}
               INSERT ('.', timeString, LENGTH(timeString))   {Insert decimal point}
            end; {else}

         TESetText (@timeString[1], LENGTH(timeString), TheText); {Set window's text [II:5.2.3]}
         TEUpdate  (TheText^^.viewRect, TheText)       {Redisplay text on screen [II:5.3.2]}

      end {with dataHandle^^}

end; {AdvanceClock}
```

So, to keep the clock running smoothly and accurately, we maintain a field named `TargetTime` in our global data record (Program 6–4). Whenever the user starts the clock, our `DoStart` routine records in this field either the system time when the clock was started (if it's counting up from zero) or the time when it is due to run out (if it's counting down from some positive number of seconds). Then, when the periodic task is run, the `AdvanceClock` routine compares the current time on the system clock with the target time, rounds the difference to the nearest tenth of a second, and displays the result in the `StopWatch` window. This ensures that the time shown in the window is correct, even if more than a tenth of a second has gone by since we last executed our periodic task.

Program 6–16 Start beep sequence

```
procedure StartBeep (dataHandle : DRHandle);

   { Start beep sequence. }

   var
      dceHandle : DCtlHandle;                    {Handle to DCE [3.1.4]}

   begin {StartBeep}

      with dataHandle^^ do
         begin

            DoBeep;                              {Sound first beep}

            dceHandle := GetDCtlEntry (RefNum);  {Get DCE handle [3.1.4]}
            dceHandle^^.dCtlDelay := 60;         {Change task interval to once per second [3.1.4]}

            ClockBeeping := TRUE                 {Start periodic beeping}

         end {with dataHandle^^}

   end;   {StartBeep}
```

When the clock counts down to zero, AdvanceClock calls a routine named StartBeep (Program 6–16) to begin sounding the alarm. After sounding the first beep in the sequence, StartBeep changes the task interval in the device control entry from 6 ticks to 60, causing our periodic task to be run once per second instead of ten times a second. Then it sets the ClockBeeping flag in the global data record, telling the periodic task routine (Program 6–14) to sound another beep each time it's called. When the user turns off the alarm with the Reset command, our DoReset routine (see Appendix H) will call the initialization routine InitFlags (also in Appendix H), which will set the task interval back to 6 ticks.

The Close Routine

When a desk accessory's services are no longer required, the Toolbox notifies it to close up shop by sending it a driver Close call. This call is issued by the Toolbox routine CloseDeskAcc [6.2.1], which in turn may be called in any of several ways:

- The user clicks the mouse in the accessory window's close box. As we saw earlier, the host program is expected to pass all mouse clicks in the accessory's window to the Toolbox routine SystemClick [6.2.2] for processing. On learning that the click was in the window's close box, SystemClick will respond by calling CloseDeskAcc. This takes place automatically, with no further action required on the part of the host program.

- The user chooses the menu command Close and the desk accessory's window is frontmost on the screen. In this situation, the host program must explicitly call CloseDeskAcc to dismiss the accessory.

- The host program terminates. As part of the termination sequence, the Toolbox will automatically call CloseDeskAcc for all open desk accessories.

On receiving a Close call, the accessory is expected to dispose of its internal data structures, remove its window and menu from the screen, and generally tidy up after itself. The goal is to leave the host program's environment exactly as we found it. Like a hiker on a wilderness trail, a desk accessory should "take nothing but pictures, leave nothing but footprints."

Program 6–17 Handle driver Close call

```
procedure DoClose (pbPtr : ParamBlkPtr; dcePtr : DCtlPtr);

   { Handle driver Close call. }

   var
      theData    : DRHandle;                {Handle to StopWatch data record}
      rsrcHandle : Handle;                  {Untyped handle for disposing of menu [I:3.1.1]}
```

Program 6–17 Handle driver Close call *(continued)*

```
begin {DoClose}

    with dcePtr^ do
        begin

                MoveHHi (dCtlStorage);              {Move data record to end of heap [I:3.2.5]}
                HLock    (dCtlStorage);             {Lock data handle [I:3.2.4]}
                    theData := DRHandle(dCtlStorage);   {Convert to typed handle [3.1.4]}
                    with theData^^ do
                        begin

                                DeleteMenu (dCtlMenu);              {Remove menu from menu bar [II:4.4.1]}
                                DrawMenuBar;                        {Redraw menu bar [II:4.4.3]}
                                rsrcHandle := Handle(TheMenu);      {Convert to untyped handle [I:3.1.1]}
                                ReleaseResource (rsrcHandle);       {Dispose of menu [I:6.3.2]}

                                DisposeWindow (TheWindow);          {Dispose of window [II:3.2.3]}
                                dCtlWindow := NIL;                  {Clear window pointer from DCE [3.1.4]}

                                TEDispose (TheText)                 {Dispose of edit record [II:5.2.2]}

                        end; {with theData^^}
                HUnlock (dCtlStorage);              {Unlock data handle [I:3.2.4]}

                DisposHandle (dCtlStorage);         {Dispose of data record [I:3.2.2]}
                dCtlStorage := NIL                  {Clear storage handle from DCE [3.1.4]}

        end {with dcePtr^}

end;   {DoClose}
```

Program 6–17 (DoClose) is StopWatch's Close routine. Notice that it isn't enough just to dispose of structures like the window record and global data record. An accessory's DCE, remember, remains behind even after the accessory itself has been purged from the heap, ready to be used again if the accessory is ever reopened. So besides destroying the accessory's data structures, it's also important to clear the fields in the DCE that refer to them (dCtlWindow, `dCtlStorage`), just to make sure no one (the Toolbox or anyone else) is ever tempted to follow these defunct pointers off into the ozone.

The same isn't necessary with `dCtlMenu`, since it's only a resource ID instead of a pointer or handle, and remains valid even after the menu itself is gone. We do have to remember, though, to delete the menu from the menu bar before disposing of it, and then redraw the menu bar without it. If we neglect this bit of housekeeping and the user ever tries to pull down the departed menu, it will instantly demolish the system. That's *one* way to get rid of the ol' DCE!

REFERENCE

6.1 Desk Accessory Structure

6.1.1   Event Mask

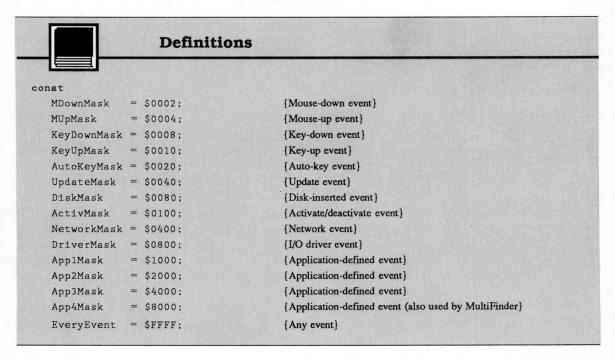

Definitions

```
const
    MDownMask     = $0002;          {Mouse-down event}
    MUpMask       = $0004;          {Mouse-up event}
    KeyDownMask   = $0008;          {Key-down event}
    KeyUpMask     = $0010;          {Key-up event}
    AutoKeyMask   = $0020;          {Auto-key event}
    UpdateMask    = $0040;          {Update event}
    DiskMask      = $0080;          {Disk-inserted event}
    ActivMask     = $0100;          {Activate/deactivate event}
    NetworkMask   = $0400;          {Network event}
    DriverMask    = $0800;          {I/O driver event}
    App1Mask      = $1000;          {Application-defined event}
    App2Mask      = $2000;          {Application-defined event}
    App3Mask      = $4000;          {Application-defined event}
    App4Mask      = $8000;          {Application-defined event (also used by MultiFinder)}
    EveryEvent    = $FFFF;          {Any event}
```

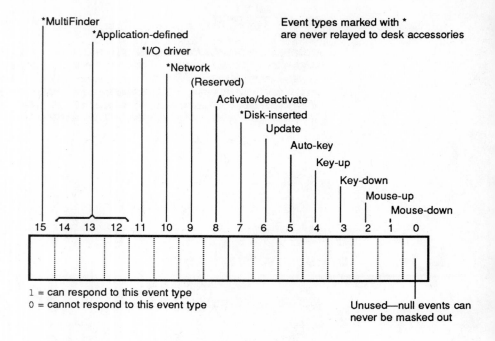

*MultiFinder
*Application-defined
*I/O driver
*Network
(Reserved)
Activate/deactivate
*Disk-inserted
Update
Auto-key
Key-up
Key-down
Mouse-up
Mouse-down

Event types marked with *
are never relayed to desk accessories

15 14 13 12 11 10 9 8 7 6 5 4 3 2 1 0

1 = can respond to this event type
0 = cannot respond to this event type

Unused—null events can
never be masked out

Desk accessory event mask

Notes

1. The `dCtlEMask` field of the device control entry [3.1.4] defines which types of event a desk accessory can respond to.

2. The event mask in the device control entry is automatically initialized from the `drvrEMask` field of the driver header [3.1.1] when the accessory is opened for operation. The accessory's Open routine may then change the mask in the DCE if for some reason it needs to override the value taken from the driver header. The mask in the DCE is the one that actually controls which events the desk accessory will receive.

3. The Toolbox routines `SystemEvent` and `SystemClick` [6.2.2] intercept the specified events pertaining to the desk accessory and relay them to the accessory for action.

4. The event mask has a separate bit for each possible event type [II:2.1.2]. A 1 bit in any position means that the desk accessory is prepared to respond to that type of event; a 0 bit means it is not.

5. The mask constants shown can be combined with `BitAnd`, `BitOr`, `BitXOr`, and `BitNot` [I:2.2.2] to form any combination of event types you need.

6. A typical event mask for a desk accessory would be `$016A`, to accept activate/deactivate, update, mouse-down, key-down, and auto-key events.

7. In general, desk accessories should respond to key-down and auto-key events in some way, even if only with a beep to acknowledge receipt of the keystroke.

8. Desk accessories must not accept mouse-up events.

9. Disk-inserted events are never relayed to a desk accessory, regardless of the setting of the event mask's `DiskMask`.

10. The mask `EveryEvent` includes all possible event types. Desk accessories should never use this value directly (see note 8, above), but may use it as a basis for constructing other event masks, such as

```
BitXOr (EveryEvent, MUpMask)
```

11. The assembly-language constants `MButDwnEvt`, `MButUpEvt`, etc. (below) are bit numbers for use with the `BTST`, `BSET`, `BCLR`, and `BCHG` instructions.

Assembly Language Information

Event types:

Name	Value	Meaning
MButDwnEvt	1	Mouse-down event
MButUpEvt	2	Mouse-up event
KeyDwnEvt	3	Key-down event
KeyUpEvt	4	Key-up event
AutoKeyEvt	5	Auto-key event
UpdatEvt	6	Update event
DiskInsertEvt	7	Disk-inserted event
ActivateEvt	8	Activate/deactivate event
NetworkEvt	10	Network event
IODrvrEvt	11	I/O driver event
App1Evt	12	Application-defined event
App2Evt	13	Application-defined event
App3Evt	14	Application-defined event
App4Evt	15	Application-defined event (also used by MultiFinder)

6.1.2 Control Codes

Desk accessory control codes:

Name	Value	Meaning
KillCode	1	Handle KillIO call [3.2.3]
GoodBye	-1	Handle "good-bye kiss" [3.1.2]
AccEvent	64	Respond to user event
AccRun	65	Perform periodic task
AccCursor	66	Adjust cursor
AccMenu	67	Respond to user's menu choice
AccUndo	68	Execute Undo command
AccCut	70	Execute Cut command
AccCopy	71	Execute Copy command
AccPaste	72	Execute Paste command
AccClear	73	Execute Clear command

Notes

1. When a Control call [3.2.3] is issued to a desk accessory, a control code in the csCode field of the parameter block [3.1.5] identifies the particular Control operation to be performed.

2. The csParam field of the parameter block [3.1.5] may contain further parameters, depending on the specific Control operation.

3. Some software development systems provide "glue" routines to retrieve the values of csCode and csParam from the parameter block and pass them directly as parameters to the desk accessory's Control routine. Consult your own language documentation for details.

4. The names shown for the control codes in the table are defined as assembly-language constants, but are not included in the standard Pascal interface to the Toolbox. To use them at the Pascal level, you must declare them for yourself.

5. KillCode designates a KillIO call [3.2.3]. Since most desk accessories don't do any input/output, they normally need not respond to KillIO.

6. GoodBye identifies a "good-bye kiss," notifying the desk accessory that the application heap is about to be reinitialized (typically because the host program has been terminated and a new one is about to start up).

7. The desk accessory will always receive an ordinary Close call when the host program is terminated. The good-bye kiss is needed only if some

other, special action is needed to allow the accessory to maintain its state through a heap reinitialization. Most accessories can simply dispense with it by clearing the dNeedGoodBye flag in the dCtlFlags field of the device control entry [3.1.2, 3.1.4].

8. AccEvent marks a Toolbox event to which the desk accessory must respond. The first 2 words of csParam hold a pointer (not a handle!) to an event record [II:2.1.1] describing the event.

9. Most events are relayed to the desk accessory by the Toolbox routine SystemEvent [6.2.2], which is called indirectly when the host program calls GetNextEvent [II:2.2.1].

10. Mouse-down events are relayed instead by the Toolbox routine SystemClick [6.2.2]. (The host program is expected to call SystemClick when FindWindow [II:3.5.1] reports that the mouse was clicked in a window belonging to a desk accessory.)

11. AccRun instructs the desk accessory to perform its periodic task. This call is sent only if the dNeedTime flag is set in the dCtlFlags field of the device control entry [3.1.2, 3.1.4], when the required number of ticks (dCtlDelay) has elapsed since the periodic task was last performed.

12. AccCursor tells the desk accessory to adjust the appearance of the cursor on the screen in whatever way it wishes, depending on the cursor's position and the current state of the accessory.

13. This call is sent by the Toolbox routine SystemTask [6.2.4] whenever an accessory's window is active (frontmost on the screen). The host program is expected to call SystemTask on every pass through its main event loop, or at least once per tick.

14. AccMenu reports that the user has chosen an item from the desk accessory's menu. csParam[0] contains the menu ID and csParam[1] gives the item number within the menu.

15. This call is sent by the Toolbox routine SystemMenu [6.2.3], which is called indirectly when the host program calls MenuSelect or MenuKey [II:4.5.1]. These routines recognize a desk accessory menu by its negative menu ID and call SystemMenu to relay the choice to the desk accessory for action.

16. AccUndo, AccCut, AccCopy, AccPaste, and AccClear report that the user has invoked one of the standard editing commands while the desk accessory was active.

17. These calls are sent by the Toolbox routine SystemEdit [6.2.3] whenever an accessory's window is active (frontmost) on the screen. The host program is expected to call SystemEdit whenever the user chooses any of the standard editing commands, to see whether a desk accessory is active and relay the command to the accessory if appropriate.

Assembly Language Information

Assembly-language constants:

Name	Value	Meaning
KillCode	1	Handle KillIO call [3.2.3]
GoodBye	-1	Handle "good-bye kiss" [3.1.2]
AccEvent	64	Respond to user event
AccRun	65	Perform periodic task
AccCursor	66	Adjust cursor
AccMenu	67	Respond to user's menu choice
AccUndo	68	Execute Undo command
AccCut	70	Execute Cut command
AccCopy	71	Execute Copy command
AccPaste	72	Execute Paste command
AccClear	73	Execute Clear command

6.2 Desk Accessory Operations

6.2.1   Opening and Closing Desk Accessories

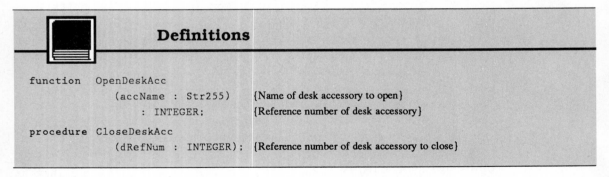

Definitions

```
function  OpenDeskAcc
        (accName : Str255)      {Name of desk accessory to open}
            : INTEGER;          {Reference number of desk accessory}
procedure CloseDeskAcc
        (dRefNum : INTEGER);    {Reference number of desk accessory to close}
```

Notes

1. `OpenDeskAcc` opens a desk accessory and displays it on the screen.

2. The desk accessory is identified by name; `OpenDeskAcc` returns its reference number to be used for further identification.

3. The host program is expected to call `OpenDeskAcc` when the user chooses a desk accessory from the Apple menu.

4. If the designated desk accessory is not already in memory, it is read in from its resource file. The accessory's resource type is 'DRVR' [3.3.1]; its resource name is given by the `accName` parameter.

5. The first time a desk accessory is opened, `OpenDeskAcc` creates a device control entry [3.1.4] and places a handle to it in the system unit table [3.1.3]. The accessory's resource ID (its unit number) determines its position within the unit table.

6. `OpenDeskAcc` calls the desk accessory's Open routine, to initialize its data structures and prepare for operation.

7. On return from the Open routine, if the desk accessory's device control entry [3.1.4] contains a window pointer in its `dCtlWindow` field, `OpenDeskAcc` automatically displays and selects the window, making it the active window. The Open routine should create the window in an invisible state and store its pointer in the DCE, allowing `OpenDeskAcc` to display it on the screen.

8. `OpenDeskAcc` automatically stores the desk accessory's reference number into the the `dCtlRefNum` field of the DCE [3.1.4], but *not* into the window's `windowKind` field [II:3.1.1]. The accessory's Open routine must explicitly copy the reference number from the DCE to the window record.

9. The desk accessory's Open routine must create the accessory's menu, if any, insert it in the menu bar, and redraw the menu bar to display the new menu's title on the screen. `OpenDeskAcc` does not provide these services automatically.

10. `CloseDeskAcc` closes a desk accessory and removes it from the screen.

11. The desk accessory is identified by reference number.

12. The host program is expected to call `SystemClick` [6.2.2] when `FindWindow` [II:3.5.1] reports that the mouse was clicked in a desk accessory's window. If the click was in the window's close box, `SystemClick` will then automatically call `CloseDeskAcc` to close the desk accessory. `CloseDeskAcc` is also called automatically for all open desk accessories when the host program terminates.

13. The host program should call `CloseDeskAcc` explicitly when the user chooses the Close command while a desk accessory is active.

14. `CloseDeskAcc` calls the desk accessory's Close routine, to dispose of its data structures and prepare to terminate operation.

15. If the desk accessory has a window, its Close routine should dispose of the window and clear the window pointer in the `dCtlWindow` field of the device control entry [3.1.4] to `NIL`. If it has a menu, the Close routine should delete the menu from the menu bar, dispose of it, and redraw the menu bar to remove the menu's title from the screen. `CloseDeskAcc` does not provide any of these services automatically.

16. `CloseDeskAcc` does not destroy the desk accessory's device control entry. The DCE remains in existence and will be reused the next time the accessory is opened.

Assembly Language Information

Trap macros:

(Pascal) Routine name	(Assembly) Trap macro	Trap word
OpenDeskAcc	_OpenDeskAcc	$A9B6
CloseDeskAcc	_CloseDeskAcc	$A9B7

6.2.2 Responding to Events

Definitions

```
function  SystemEvent
              (theEvent : EventRecord)        {Event to be processed}
                : BOOLEAN;                    {Was it intercepted as a system event?}

procedure SystemClick
              (theEvent  : EventRecord)       {Event to be processed}
              theWindow  : WindowPtr);        {System window where mouse was pressed}
```

Notes

1. `SystemEvent` determines whether a given event pertains to a desk accessory and, if so, relays it to the accessory for action.

2. This routine is called only by the Toolbox routine `GetNextEvent` [II:2.2.1], to intercept events directed to desk accessories. It should never be called directly by the host program.

3. The function result tells whether the event was intercepted and relayed to a desk accessory (`TRUE`) or must be handled by the host program itself (`FALSE`).

4. Events are relayed to the desk accessory by calling its Control routine with the control code `AccEvent` [6.1.2]. A pointer to the event record is placed in the first 2 words of the parameter block's `csParam` field [3.1.5].

5. Events relayed to the desk accessory include all window events (activate, deactivate, update) affecting the accessory's window, as well as all mouse-up and keyboard (key-down, key-up, auto-key) events when the accessory is active.

6. For mouse-down events, `SystemEvent` does not attempt to determine whether the event occurred in a system window or to relay it to a desk accessory. Instead, the host program is expected to call `FindWindow` [3.5.1] to determine the window affected, and if it is a system window, to pass the event to `SystemClick` (see below) to be processed.

7. For disk-inserted events, `SystemEvent` mounts the new volume and returns `FALSE`, allowing the host program to take further action if appropriate. Such events are never relayed to a desk accessory.

8. Network, I/O driver, and application events are never relayed.

9. Relaying of each event type is further subject to the setting of the corresponding bit in the accessory's event mask [6.1.1], found in the `dCtlEMask` field of its device control entry [3.1.4].

10. `SystemClick` processes a mouse-down event in a system window. The host program is expected to call it when `FindWindow` [3.5.1] returns a part code of `InSysWindow`.

11. `SystemClick` does all the necessary processing to respond to the event, such as activating the window if it's inactive, tracking the mouse in its drag or close region, and moving or closing it if appropriate.

12. If the window belongs to an active desk accessory, mouse clicks in its content region are relayed to the accessory for processing.

13. In assembly language, the interception and relaying of system events is controlled by the 1-byte global flag `SEvtEnb` (see below). This flag is normally set to `TRUE` ($FF); setting it to `FALSE` ($00) disables the relaying of events. `SystemEvent` will then always return `FALSE`, instructing the host program to handle all events for itself.

Assembly Language Information

Trap macros:

(Pascal) Routine name	(Assembly) Trap macro	Trap word
SystemEvent	_SystemEvent	$A9B2
SystemClick	_SystemClick	$A9B3

Assembly-language global variable:

Name	Address	Meaning
SEvtEnb	$15C	Intercept system events? (1 byte)

6.2.3 Handling Menu Commands

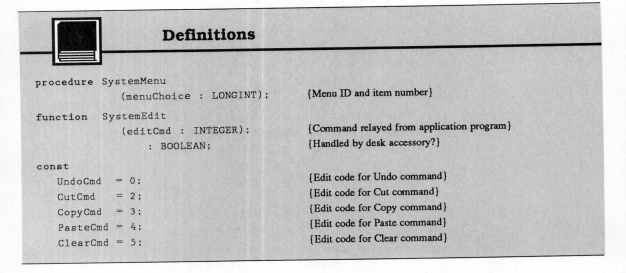

Definitions

```
procedure SystemMenu
          (menuChoice : LONGINT);        {Menu ID and item number}

function SystemEdit
          (editCmd : INTEGER)            {Command relayed from application program}
          : BOOLEAN;                     {Handled by desk accessory?}

const
   UndoCmd  = 0;                         {Edit code for Undo command}
   CutCmd   = 2;                         {Edit code for Cut command}
   CopyCmd  = 3;                         {Edit code for Copy command}
   PasteCmd = 4;                         {Edit code for Paste command}
   ClearCmd = 5;                         {Edit code for Clear command}
```

Menu ID (16 bits)	Item number (16 bits)

Format of menuChoice parameter

Notes

1. SystemMenu accepts a choice by the user from a desk accessory's menu and relays it to the desk accessory for action.

2. This routine is called only by the Toolbox routines `MenuSelect` and `MenuKey` [II:4.5.1], when an item is chosen from a desk accessory's menu. It should never be called directly by the host program.

3. The Toolbox recognizes desk accessory menus by their negative menu IDs. Each accessory's menu ID is kept in the `dCtlMenu` field of its device control entry [3.1.4].

4. The `menuChoice` parameter is a long integer in the same form as the result returned by `MenuSelect` and `MenuKey` [II:4.5.1], with the menu ID in the high-order word and the item number in the low-order word.

5. Menu choices are relayed to the desk accessory by calling its Control routine with the control code `AccMenu` [6.1.2]. The menu ID and item number are placed in the first 2 words of the parameter block's `csParam` field [3.1.5].

6. `SystemEdit` determines whether a desk accessory is currently active (that is, frontmost on the screen), and if so, relays a specified editing command to the accessory for action.

7. The host program is expected to call this routine whenever the user chooses any of the five standard editing commands. It is also the host program's responsibility to make sure these commands are available and enabled whenever a desk accessory is active.

8. The parameter `editCmd` must be one of the constants shown.

9. These constants have inexplicably been removed from Apple's official Toolbox interface. To use them, the host program must now either define them for itself as program constants or arrange its `Edit` menu so that the standard commands have item numbers one greater than the corresponding constant values as shown above. (Notice the gap between the values of `UndoCmd` and `CutCmd`, representing a dividing line on the menu between the `Undo` and `Cut` commands.) If it uses this method, the host program must remember to subtract 1 back from the chosen item number before passing it on to `SystemEdit`.

10. Editing commands are relayed to the desk accessory by calling its Control routine with one of the control codes `AccUndo`, `AccCut`, `AccCopy`, `AccPaste`, or `AccClear` [6.1.2].

11. The Boolean result returned by `SystemEdit` is TRUE if the command was successfully relayed to a desk accessory, FALSE if it must be handled by the host program (for instance, if the active window doesn't contain a desk accessory).

12. The trap macro for `SystemEdit` is spelled `_SysEdit`.

Assembly Language Information

Trap macro:

(Pascal) Routine name	(Assembly) Trap macro	Trap word
SystemMenu	_SystemMenu	$A9B5
SystemEdit	_SysEdit	$A9C2

6.2.4 Performing Periodic Tasks

Definitions

```
procedure SystemTask;
```

Notes

1. SystemTask performs any periodic tasks associated with open desk accessories (or other drivers), under the control of the system clock.

2. The host program is expected to call SystemTask at least once per tick (60 times per second) to ensure that all desk accessories and drivers receive the processor time they need. This is normally done by calling it once on every pass of the program's main event loop; it may have to be called more often during time-consuming operations.

3. An accessory's or driver's periodic task is executed only if the dNeedTime flag is set in the dCtlFlags field of its device control entry [3.1.2, 3.1.4], and only if the required number of ticks (dCtlDelay) has elapsed since the periodic task was last performed.

4. The dCtlCurTicks field of the DCE [3.1.4] is used as a counter to time the interval between executions of the periodic task.

5. The desk accessory or driver is instructed to perform its periodic task by a Control call with the control code AccRun [6.1.2].

6. If a desk accessory is active (frontmost on the screen), SystemTask also sends it the control code AccCursor [6.1.2]. This allows it to adjust the appearance of the cursor according to the cursor's position on the screen and the accessory's own current state.

Assembly Language Information

Trap macro:

(Pascal) Routine name	(Assembly) Trap macro	Trap word
SystemTask	_SystemTask	$A9B4

6.3 Keyboard Routines

6.3.1   Resource Type 'FKEY'

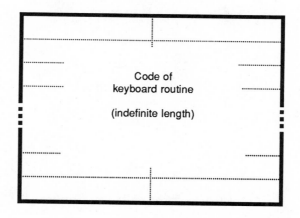

Structure of an 'FKEY' resource

Notes

1. A resource of type 'FKEY' contains a low-level keyboard routine.

2. Keyboard routines are executed automatically when the user types a numeric key (0–9) while holding down both the Command and Shift keys. These keystrokes are intercepted by the low-level keyboard driver and are not reported to the running program via the event mechanism.

3. The resource ID of the 'FKEY' resource designates the key that invokes the routine, and must be between 0 and 9.

4. The resource data is simply the machine-language code of the keyboard routine.

5. The routine's entry point must be at the very beginning.

6. The routine must leave all processor registers unchanged.

7. The User Interface Guidelines define the following standard Command-Shift keystrokes, which should not be overridden by 'FKEY' resources of your own:

Keystroke	Meaning
Command-Shift-1	Eject disk in internal drive
Command-Shift-2	Eject disk in external drive
Command-Shift-3	Dump screen to a MacPaint file
Command-Shift-4	Dump screen to printer

('FKEY' resources 3 and 4 are included in the standard system resource file. There are no actual resources numbered 1 and 2; these operations are implemented internally by the keyboard driver.)

8. The keyboard driver intercepts Command-Shift keystrokes only if the 1-byte global flag ScrDmpEnb is TRUE ($FF). If this flag is FALSE ($00), they're just reported as ordinary keyboard events.

Assembly Language Information

Assembly-language global variable:

Name	Address	Meaning
ScrDmpEnb	$2F8	Intercept Command-Shift keystrokes? (1 byte)

APPENDIX

A

Toolbox Summary

Chapter 2 Customizing

2.1 Customizing QuickDraw

2.1.1 Bottleneck Record

```
type
    QDProcsPtr = ^QDProcs;

    QDProcs     = record
                    textProc    : Ptr;      {Draw text [2.1.5]}
                    lineProc    : Ptr;      {Draw lines [2.1.3]}
                    rectProc    : Ptr;      {Draw rectangles [2.1.4]}
                    rRectProc   : Ptr;      {Draw rounded rectangles [2.1.4]}
                    ovalProc    : Ptr;      {Draw ovals [2.1.4]}
                    arcProc     : Ptr;      {Draw arcs and wedges [2.1.4]}
                    polyProc    : Ptr;      {Draw polygons [2.1.4]}
                    rgnProc     : Ptr;      {Draw regions [2.1.4]}
                    bitsProc    : Ptr;      {Copy bit images [2.1.2]}
                    commentProc : Ptr;      {Process picture comments [2.1.7]}
                    txMeasProc  : Ptr;      {Measure text [2.1.5]}
                    getPicProc  : Ptr;      {Retrieve picture definitions [2.1.6]}
                    putPicProc  : Ptr       {Save picture definitions [2.1.6]}
                 end;

procedure SetStdProcs
            (var theProcs : QDProcs);       {Bottleneck record to initialize}
```

337

2.1.2 Low-Level Bit Transfer

```
type
   QDProcs = record
                 . . . ;
                 bitsProc : Ptr;              {Copy bit images}
                 . . .
             end;
procedure StdBits
             (var fromBitMap : BitMap;        {Bit map to copy from}
              fromRect       : Rect;          {Rectangle to copy from}
              toRect         : Rect;          {Rectangle to copy to}
              mode           : INTEGER;       {Transfer mode}
              clipTo         : RgnHandle);    {Region to clip to}
```

2.1.3 Line Drawing

```
type
   QDProcs = record
                 . . . ;
                 lineProc : Ptr;              {Draw lines}
                 . . .
             end;
procedure StdLine
             (drawTo : Point);               {Point to draw to, in local coordinates}
```

2.1.4 Shape Drawing

```
type
   QDProcs = record
                 . . . ;
                 rectProc  : Ptr;            {Draw rectangles}
                 rRectProc : Ptr;            {Draw rounded rectangles}
                 ovalProc  : Ptr;            {Draw ovals}
                 arcProc   : Ptr;            {Draw arcs and wedges}
                 polyProc  : Ptr;            {Draw polygons}
                 rgnProc   : Ptr;            {Draw regions}
                 . . .
             end;
```

```
GrafVerb = (Frame,                              {Draw outline}
            Paint,                              {Fill with current pen pattern}
            Erase,                              {Fill with background pattern}
            Invert,                            {Invert pixels}
            Fill);                             {Fill with specified pattern}
procedure StdRect
        (whichOp : GrafVerb;                    {Drawing operation to perform}
         theRect : Rect);                       {Rectangle to be drawn}
procedure StdRRect
        (whichOp      : GrafVerb;               {Drawing operation to perform}
         theRect      : Rect;                   {Body of rectangle}
         cornerWidth  : INTEGER;                {Width of corner oval}
         cornerHeight : INTEGER);               {Height of corner oval}
procedure StdOval
        (whichOp : GrafVerb;                    {Drawing operation to perform}
         inRect  : Rect);                       {Rectangle defining oval}
procedure StdArc
        (whichOp    : GrafVerb;                 {Drawing operation to perform}
         inRect     : Rect;                     {Rectangle defining oval}
         startAngle : INTEGER;                  {Starting angle}
         arcAngle   : INTEGER);                 {Extent of arc}
procedure StdPoly
        (whichOp    : GrafVerb;                 {Drawing operation to perform}
         thePolygon : PolyHandle);              {Handle to polygon to be drawn}
procedure StdRgn
        (whichOp   : GrafVerb;                  {Drawing operation to perform}
         theRegion : RgnHandle);                {Handle to region to be drawn}
```

2.1.5 Text Drawing

```
type
   QDProcs = record
           textProc   : Ptr;                    {Draw text}
           . . . ;
           txMeasProc : Ptr;                    {Measure text}
           . . .
        end;
procedure StdText
        (charCount  : INTEGER;                  {Number of characters to be drawn}
         theText    : Ptr;                      {Pointer to text to be drawn}
         scaleNumer : Point;                    {Numerators of scale factors}
         scaleDenom : Point);                   {Denominators of scale factors}
```

```
function   StdTxMeas
              (charCount      :  INTEGER;         {Number of characters to be drawn}
               theText        :  Ptr;             {Pointer to text to be drawn}
               var scaleNumer :  Point;           {Numerators of scale factors}
               var scaleDenom :  Point;           {Denominators of scale factors}
               var fontProps  :  FontInfo)        {Metric information about text font}
                              :  INTEGER;         {Width of text in pixels}
```

2.1.6 Picture Processing

```
type
   QDProcs = record
                 . . . ;
                 getPicProc : Ptr;               {Retrieve picture definitions}
                 putPicProc : Ptr                {Save picture definitions}
             end;

procedure  StdGetPic
              (toAddr     :  Ptr;                 {Address to read to}
               byteCount  :  INTEGER);            {Number of bytes to read}

procedure  StdPutPic
              (fromAddr   :  Ptr;                 {Address to write from}
               byteCount  :  INTEGER);            {Number of bytes to write}
```

2.1.7 Picture Comments

```
type
   QDProcs = record
                 . . . ;
                 commentProc : Ptr;              {Process picture comments}
                 . . .
             end;

procedure  StdComment
              (commentType :  INTEGER;            {Comment type}
               dataSize    :  INTEGER;            {Length of comment data in bytes}
               commentData :  Handle);            {Handle to comment data}

procedure  PicComment
              (commentType :  INTEGER;            {Comment type}
               dataSize    :  INTEGER;            {Length of comment data in bytes}
               commentData :  Handle);            {Handle to comment data}

const
   PicLParen = 0;                                 {Begin command grouping}
   PicRParen = 1;                                 {End command grouping}
```

2.2 Customizing Windows

2.2.1 Window Definition Function

```
function   YourWindowDef
               (varCode    : INTEGER;          {Variation code}
                theWindow  : WindowPtr;         {Pointer to the window}
                msgCode    : INTEGER;           {Operation to be performed}
                msgParam   : LONGINT)           {Additional data for performing operation}
                     : LONGINT;                 {Result returned by operation}
const
   WDraw       = 0;                             {Draw window frame [2.2.3]}
   WHit        = 1;                             {Find where mouse was pressed [2.2.5]}
   WCalcRgns   = 2;                             {Calculate structure and content regions [2.2.2]}
   WNew        = 3;                             {Initialize new window [2.2.2]}
   WDispose    = 4;                             {Prepare to dispose of window [2.2.2]}
   WGrow       = 5;                             {Draw feedback image for resizing window [2.2.4]}
   WDrawGIcon  = 6;                             {Draw size region [2.2.4]}
```

2.2.2 Creating and Destroying Windows

```
const
   WCalcRgns = 2;                               {Calculate structure and content regions}
   WNew      = 3;                               {Initialize new window}
   WDispose  = 4;                               {Prepare to dispose of window}
```

2.2.3 Drawing Windows

```
const
   WDraw       = 0;                             {Draw window frame}

   WNoHit      = 0;                             {Draw entire window frame}
   WInGoAway   = 4;                             {Toggle close region only}
   WInZoomIn   = 5;                             {Toggle zoom region only}
   WInZoomOut  = 6;                             {Toggle zoom region only}
```

2.2.4 Resizing Windows

```
const
    WGrow      = 5;                        {Draw feedback image for resizing window}
    WDrawGIcon = 6;                        {Draw size region}
```

2.2.5 Locating Mouse Clicks

```
const
    WHit       = 1;                        {Find where mouse was pressed}

                                           {Window hit codes:  }
    WNoHit     = 0;                            {None of the following}
    WInContent = 1;                            {In content region}
    WInDrag    = 2;                            {In drag region}
    WInGrow    = 3;                            {In size region}
    WInGoAway  = 4;                            {In close region}
    WInZoomIn  = 5;                            {In zoom region of a "zoomed-out" window}
    WInZoomOut = 6;                            {In zoom region of a "zoomed-in" window}
```

2.3   Customizing Controls

2.3.1 Control Definition Function

```
function   YourControlDef
               (varCode     : INTEGER;     {Variation code}
                theControl  : ControlHandle;  {Handle to the control}
                msgCode     : INTEGER;     {Operation to be performed}
                msgParam    : LONGINT)     {Additional data for performing operation}
                            : LONGINT;     {Result returned by operation}

const
    DrawCntl   = 0;                        {Draw all or part of control [2.3.3]}
    TestCntl   = 1;                        {Find where mouse was pressed [2.3.4]}
    CalcCRgns  = 2;                        {Calculate control's region [2.3.2]}
    InitCntl   = 3;                        {Initialize new control [2.3.2]}
    DispCntl   = 4;                        {Prepare to dispose of control [2.3.2]}
    PosCntl    = 5;                        {Reposition and update setting [2.3.5]}
    ThumbCntl  = 6;                        {Calculate parameters for dragging [2.3.5]}
    DragCntl   = 7;                        {Drag control or indicator [2.3.5]}
    AutoTrack  = 8;                        {Execute default action procedure [2.3.5]}
```

2.3.2 Creating and Destroying Controls

```
const
    CalcCRgns = 2;                    {Calculate control's region within its window}
    InitCntl  = 3;                    {Initialize new control}
    DispCntl  = 4;                    {Prepare to dispose of control}
```

2.3.3 Drawing Controls

```
const
    DrawCntl = 0;                     {Draw all or part of control}
```

2.3.4 Locating Mouse Clicks

```
const
    TestCntl = 1;                     {Find part of control where mouse was pressed}
```

2.3.5 Tracking and Positioning

```
const
    PosCntl   = 5;                    {Reposition indicator and update setting}
    ThumbCntl = 6;                    {Calculate parameters for dragging indicator}
    DragCntl  = 7;                    {Drag control or indicator}
    AutoTrack = 8;                    {Execute default action procedure}
```

2.4   Customizing Menus

2.4.1 Menu Definition Procedure

```
procedure YourMenuDef
            (msgCode      : INTEGER;      {Operation to be performed}
             theMenu      : MenuHandle;   {Handle to the menu}
             var menuFrame : Rect;        {Menu frame}
             mousePoint   : Point;        {Mouse position in global (screen) coordinates}
             var theItem  : INTEGER);     {Number of menu item chosen}
const
    MDrawMsg   = 0;                       {Draw menu [2.4.2]}
    MChooseMsg = 1;                       {Find and highlight menu item [2.4.3]}
    MSizeMsg   = 2;                       {Calculate dimensions of menu [2.4.2]}
```

2.4.2 Menu Display

```
const
   MDrawMsg = 0;                        {Draw menu}
   MSizeMsg = 2;                        {Calculate dimensions of menu}
```

2.4.3 Locating Mouse Clicks

```
const
   MChooseMsg = 1;                      {Find and highlight menu item}
```

Chapter 3 Drivers

3.1 Driver-Related Data Structures

3.1.4 Device Control Entry

```
type
   DCtlHandle = ^DCtlPtr;
   DCtlPtr    = ^DCtlEntry

   DCtlEntry  = record
                   dCtlDriver   : Ptr;        {Handle or pointer to driver in memory}
                   dCtlFlags    : INTEGER;    {Copy of driver flags [3.1.2]}
                   dCtlQHdr     : QHdr;       {Header of driver I/O queue [3.1.5, 3.1.6]}
                   dCtlPosition : LONGINT;    {Current read or write position}
                   dCtlStorage  : Handle;     {Handle to private data}
                   dCtlRefNum   : INTEGER;    {Driver reference number}
                   dCtlCurTicks : LONGINT;    {Tick counter for periodic task}
                   dCtlWindow   : Ptr;        {Pointer to driver's window}
                   dCtlDelay    : INTEGER;    {Frequency of periodic task, in ticks}
                   dCtlEMask    : INTEGER;    {Event mask}
                   dCtlMenu     : INTEGER     {Menu ID}
                end;

function  GetDCtlEntry
             (dRefNum : INTEGER)              {Driver reference number}
                : DCtlHandle;                 {Handle to device control entry}
```

3.1.5 Driver I/O Queue

```
type
   ParamBlkType = (IOParam,                            {Input/output operation}
                   FileParam,                          {File operation}
                   VolumeParam,                        {Volume operation}
                   CntrlParam);                        {Control or status operation}

   ParmBlkPtr   = ^ParamBlockRec;
   ParamBlockRec = record
                   qLink       : QElemPtr;             {Pointer to next queue element}
                   qType       : INTEGER;              {Queue type}
                   ioTrap      : INTEGER;              {Copy of trap word}
                   ioCmdAddr   : Ptr;                  {Pointer to Toolbox routine}
                   ioCompletion : ProcPtr;             {Pointer to completion routine}
                   ioResult    : OSErr;                {Result code}
                   ioNamePtr   : StringPtr;            {Driver name}
                   ioVRefNum   : INTEGER;              {Volume or drive reference number}
                   case ParamBlkType of
                      IOParam :
                        (ioRefNum    : INTEGER;        {Driver reference number}
                         ioVersNum   : SignedByte;     {Version number (unused)}
                         ioPermssn   : SignedByte;     {Read/write permission}
                         ioMisc      : Ptr;            {Unused}
                         ioBuffer    : Ptr;            {Address to transfer to/from}
                         ioReqCount  : LONGINT;        {Number of bytes requested}
                         ioActCount  : LONGINT;        {Actual number of bytes transferred}
                         ioPosMode   : INTEGER;        {Positioning mode}
                         ioPosOffset : LONGINT);       {Positioning offset}
                      FileParam :
                        ( . . . );
                      VolumeParam :
                        ( . . . );
                      CntrlParam :
                        (ioCRefNum : INTEGER;          {Driver reference number}
                         csCode    : INTEGER;          {Control or status code}
                         csParam   : array [0..10] of INTEGER)
                                                       {Parameters for operation}
                   end;
```

3.1.6 Operating System Queues

```
type
   QHdrPtr = ^QHdr:
   QHdr    = record
                qFlags : INTEGER:              {Flags}
                qHead  : QElemPtr:             {First entry in queue}
                qTail  : QElemPtr              {Last entry in queue}
            end:

   QElemPtr = ^QElem
   QElem     = record
                 case QTypes of
                   VType    : (vblQElem : VBLTask):
                   IOQType  : (ioQElem  : ParamBlockRec):
                   DrvQType : (drvQElem : DrvQEl):
                   EvType   : (evQElem  : EvQEl):
                   FSQType  : (vcbQElem : VCB)
               end:

   QTypes = (DummyType,                        {Unused}
             VType,                            {Vertical retrace queue}
             IOQType,                          {Driver or file I/O queue}
             DrvQType,                         {Disk drive queue}
             EvType,                           {Event queue}
             FSQType):                         {File system (volume) queue}
```

3.1.7 Manipulating Queues

```
procedure Enqueue
             (newElement : QElemPtr:           {Element to be inserted}
              theQueue   : QHdrPtr):            {Queue to insert it in}

function  Dequeue
             (oldElement : QElemPtr:           {Element to be removed}
              theQueue   : QHdrPtr)            {Queue to remove it from}
                 : OSErr:                      {Result code}

const
   QErr = -1:                                  {Element not found in queue}
```

3.2 Driver Operations

3.2.1 Opening and Closing Drivers

```
function  OpenDriver
              (driverName  : Str255;           {Driver name}
           var dRefNum : INTEGER)              {Returns driver reference number}
                : OSErr;                        {Result code}

function  CloseDriver
              (dRefNum : INTEGER)               {Driver reference number}
                : OSErr;                        {Result code}
```

3.2.2 Reading and Writing

```
function  FSRead
              (dRefNum        : INTEGER;        {Driver reference number}
           var byteCount : LONGINT;             {Number of bytes to read}
               toAddr          : Ptr)           {Address to read to}
                : OSErr;                        {Result code}

function  FSWrite
              (dRefNum        : INTEGER;        {Driver reference number}
           var byteCount : LONGINT;             {Number of bytes to write}
               fromAddr        : Ptr)           {Address to write from}
                : OSErr;                        {Result code}
```

3.2.3 Device Control

```
function  Control
              (dRefNum        : INTEGER;        {Driver reference number}
               controlCode : INTEGER;           {Control code}
               params          : Ptr)           {Pointer to parameters}
                : OSErr;                        {Result code}

function  Status
              (dRefNum    : INTEGER;            {Driver reference number}
               statusCode : INTEGER;            {Status code}
               params     : Ptr)                {Pointer to parameters}
                : OSErr;                        {Result code}

function  KillIO
              (dRefNum    : INTEGER)            {Driver reference number}
                : OSErr;                        {Result code}
```

Chapter 4 Printing

4.1 Printing-Related Data Structures

4.1.1 Printing Port

```
type
   TPPrPort = ^TPrPort;

   TPrPort  = record
                  gPort    : GrafPort;        {Graphics port for printing}
                  gProcs   : QDProcs;         {Customized bottleneck record}
                  lGParam1 : LONGINT;         {Private}
                  lGParam2 : LONGINT;         {Private}
                  lGParam3 : LONGINT;         {Private}
                  lGParam4 : LONGINT;         {Private}
                  fOurPtr  : BOOLEAN;         {Private}
                  fOurBits : BOOLEAN          {Private}
               end;
```

4.1.2 Print Record

```
type
   THPrint = ^TPPrint;
   TPPrint = ^TPrint;

   TPrint  = record
                  iPrVersion : INTEGER;       {Version stamp}
                  prInfo     : TPrInfo;       {Printer information subrecord [4.1.3]}
                  rPaper     : Rect;          {Paper rectangle}
                  prStl      : TPrStl;        {Style subrecord [4.1.4]}
                  prInfoPT   : TPrInfo;       {Print-time information subrecord [4.1.3]}
                  prXInfo    : TPrXInfo;      {Auxiliary information subrecord [4.1.6]}
                  prJob      : TPrJob;        {Job subrecord [4.1.5]}
                  printX     : array [1..19] of INTEGER
                                              {Padding to fill to 120 bytes}
               end;
const
   IPrRelease = 3;                            {Current version number of printing routines}
```

4.1.3 Printer Information Subrecord

```
type
   TPPrInfo = ^TPrInfo;

   TPrInfo  = record
                  iDev  : INTEGER;        {Printer's device code}
                  iVRes : INTEGER;        {Vertical resolution in dots per inch}
                  iHRes : INTEGER;        {Horizontal resolution in dots per inch}
                  rPage : Rect            {Page rectangle}
              end;
```

4.1.4 Style Subrecord

```
type
   TPPrStl = ^TPrStl;

   TPrStl  = record
                  wDev   : INTEGER;       {Type of printer or other device}
                  iPageV : INTEGER;       {Paper height in device-independent units}
                  iPageH : INTEGER;       {Paper width in device-independent units}
                  bPort  : SignedByte;    {Port to which printer is connected}
                  feed   : TFeed          {Type of paper feed}
              end;

   TFeed = (FeedCut,                      {Hand-fed cut sheets}
            FeedFanfold,                  {Continuous fan-fold paper}
            FeedMechCut,                  {Mechanically fed cut sheets}
            FeedOther);                   {Other types of paper feed}
const
   IPrPgFract = 120;                      {Number of page size units per inch}

   BDevCItoh = 1;                         {Original ImageWriter}
   BDevLaser = 3;                         {PostScript-based LaserWriter}

   IDevCItoh = $0100;                     {Original ImageWriter}
   IDevLaser = $0300;                     {PostScript-based LaserWriter}
```

4.1.5 Job Subrecord

```
type
   TPPrJob = ^TPrJob;

   TPrJob  = record
                iFstPage  : INTEGER;          {First page to be printed}
                iLstPage  : INTEGER;          {Last page to be printed}
                iCopies   : INTEGER;          {Number of copies to be printed}
                bJDocLoop : SignedByte;       {Printing method (draft or spool)}
                fFromUsr  : BOOLEAN;          {Private}
                pIdleProc : ProcPtr;          {Pointer to background procedure}
                pFileName : StringPtr;        {Name of spool file}
                iFileVol  : INTEGER;          {Reference number of spool file's volume}
                bFileVers : SignedByte;       {Version number of spool file}
                bJobX     : SignedByte        {Padding}
             end;

const
   IPrPgFst =    1;                           {Minimum page number to be printed}
   IPrPgMax = 9999;                           {Maximum page number to be printed}

   BDraftLoop = 0;                            {Draft printing}
   BSpoolLoop = 1;                            {Spooling}
   BUser1Loop = 2;                            {Printer-specific method number 1}
   BUser2Loop = 3;                            {Printer-specific method number 2}
```

4.1.6 Auxiliary Information Subrecord

```
type
   TPPrXInfo = ^TPrXInfo;

   TPrXInfo  = record
                 iRowBytes : INTEGER;         {Row width of each band in bytes}
                 iBandV    : INTEGER;         {Height of each band in dots}
                 iBandH    : INTEGER;         {Width of each band in dots}
                 iDevBytes : INTEGER;         {Size of band image in bytes}
                 iBands    : INTEGER;         {Number of bands per page}
                 bPatScale : SignedByte;      {Used in scaling patterns}
                 bULThick  : SignedByte;      {Thickness of underline, in dots}
                 bULOffset : SignedByte;      {Offset below baseline, in dots}
                 bULShadow : SignedByte;      {Width of break around descenders, in dots}
                 scan      : TScan;           {Scan direction}
                 bXInfoX   : SignedByte       {Padding}
              end;

   TScan = (ScanTB,                           {Scan from top to bottom}
            ScanBT,                           {Scan from bottom to top}
            ScanLR,                           {Scan from left to right}
            ScanRL);                          {Scan from right to left}
```

4.1.7 Printing Status Record

```
type
    TPPrStatus = ^TPrStatus;

    TPrStatus  = record
                    iTotPages  : INTEGER;      {Number of pages in file}
                    iCurPage   : INTEGER;      {Page currently in progress}
                    iTotCopies : INTEGER;      {Number of copies requested}
                    iCurCopy   : INTEGER;      {Copy currently in progress}
                    iTotBands  : INTEGER;      {Number of bands per page}
                    iCurBand   : INTEGER;      {Band currently in progress}
                    fPgDirty   : BOOLEAN;      {Has page started printing?}
                    fImaging   : BOOLEAN;      {Imaging or printing?}
                    hPrint     : THPrint;      {Handle to print record}
                    pPrPort    : TPPrPort;     {Pointer to printing port}
                    hPic       : PicHandle     {Handle to page picture}
                 end;
```

4.2 Preliminary Operations

4.2.1 Initializing the Toolbox for Printing

```
procedure PrOpen;
procedure PrClose;
```

4.2.2 Initializing Print Records

```
procedure PrintDefault
            (printRec : THPrint);          {Print record to initialize}

function  PrValidate
            (printRec : THPrint)           {Print record to validate}
                : BOOLEAN;                 {Was record altered?}
```

4.2.3 Printing-Related Dialogs

```
function   PrStlDialog
           (printRec : THPrint)          {Handle to print record}
               : BOOLEAN;                {Was dialog confirmed?}

function   PrJobDialog
           (printRec : THPrint)          {Handle to print record}
               : BOOLEAN;                {Was dialog confirmed?}

procedure  PrJobMerge
           (sourceRec : THPrint;         {Print record to copy from}
            destRec   : THPrint);        {Print record to copy to}
```

4.2.4 Error Reporting

```
function   PrError
               : INTEGER;                {Result code from last printing operation}

procedure  PrSetError
           (errCode : INTEGER);          {Result code to post}

const
   NoErr      =    0;                    {No error; all is well}
   IPrSavPFil =   -1;                    {Error saving print file}
   IIOAbort   =  -27;                    {I/O error}
   IPrAbort   =  128;                    {Cancel printing}
```

4.3 Document Printing

4.3.1 Opening and Closing a Document

```
function   PrOpenDoc
           (printRec  : THPrint;         {Print record for this job}
            printPort : TPPrPort;        {Storage for printing port}
            printBuf  : Ptr)             {Storage for output buffer}
               : TPPrPort;               {Pointer to printing port}

procedure  PrCloseDoc
           (printPort : TPPrPort);       {Pointer to printing port}
```

4.3.2 Page Imaging

```
procedure  PrOpenPage
            (printPort  :  TPPrPort;          {Pointer to the printing port}
             pageFrame  :  TPRect);           {Frame rectangle for scaling}
procedure  PrClosePage
            (printPort  :  TPPrPort);         {Pointer to the printing port}
type
   TPRect = ^Rect;                            {Pointer to a rectangle}
const
   IPFMaxPgs = 128;                           {Maximum number of pages in a spool file}
```

4.3.3 Spool Printing

```
procedure  PrPicFile
            (printRec       :  THPrint;       {Print record for this job}
             printPort      :  TPPrPort;      {Storage for printing port}
             spoolBuf       :  Ptr;           {Input buffer for reading spool file}
             printBuf       :  Ptr;           {Output buffer for writing to printer}
             var printStatus : TPrStatus);    {Record for reporting status}
```

4.4   Low-Level Printing

4.4.1 Opening and Closing the Printer Driver

```
procedure  PrDrvrOpen;

procedure  PrDrvrClose;
```

4.4.2 Printer Driver Attributes

```
function   PrDrvrVers
               : INTEGER;                     {Version number of printer driver}
function   PrDrvrDCE
               : Handle;                      {Handle to driver's device control entry}
procedure  PrPurge;

procedure  PrNoPurge;
```

4.4.3 Low-Level Operations

```
procedure PrCtlCall
              (controlCode : INTEGER;        {Control code for desired operation}
               ctlParam1   : LONGINT;        {First operation-dependent parameter}
               ctlParam2   : LONGINT;        {Second operation-dependent parameter}
               ctlParam3   : LONGINT);       {Third operation-dependent parameter}
const
    IPrBitsCtl = 4;                          {Bit map printing [4.4.4]}
    IPrIOCtl   = 5;                          {Text streaming [4.4.5]}
    IPrEvtCtl  = 6;                          {Screen printing [4.4.6]}
    IPrDevCtl  = 7;                          {Printer control [4.4.7]}
    IFMgrCtl   = 8;                          {Font support [4.4.8]}
```

4.4.4 Bit Map Printing

```
const
    IPrBitsCtl = 4;                          {Control code for bit map printing}

    LScreenBits = $00000000;                 {Rectangular dots}
    LPaintBits  = $00000001;                 {Square dots}
```

4.4.5 Text Streaming

```
const
    IPrIOCtl = 5;                            {Control code for text streaming}
```

4.4.6 Screen Printing

```
const
    IPrEvtCtl = 6;                           {Control code for screen printing}

    LPrEvtAll = $0002FFFD;                   {Print whole screen}
    LPrEvtTop = $0001FFFD;                   {Print frontmost window only}
```

4.4.7 Printer Control

```
const
    IPrDevCtl = 7;                              {Control code for printer control}

    LPrReset      = $00010000;                  {Begin new document}
    LPrDocOpen    = $00010000;                  {Begin new document}
    LPrDocClose   = $00050000;                  {End document}

    LPrPageOpen   = $00040000;                  {Begin new page}
    LPrPageClose  = $00020000;                  {End page}
    LPrPageEnd    = $00020000;                  {End page}

    LPrLineFeed   = $00030000;                  {Start new line}
    LPrLFStd      = $0003FFFF;                  {Start new line with standard paper advance}
    LPrLFSixth    = $0003FFFF;                  {Start new line with 1/6-inch paper advance}
    LPrLFEighth   = $0003FFFE;                  {Start new line with 1/8-inch paper advance}
```

4.4.8 Font Support

```
const
    IFMgrCtl = 8;                               {Control/status code for font support}

type
    FMOutPtr = ^FMOutput;
    FMOutput = packed record
                errNum     : INTEGER;           {Reserved}
                fontHandle : Handle;            {Handle to font record [I:8.2.2]}
                bold       : Byte;              {Extra thickness for boldface}
                italic     : Byte;              {Skew factor for italic}
                ulOffset   : Byte;              {Offset from baseline to underline}
                ulShadow   : Byte;              {Width of break around descenders}
                ulThick    : Byte;              {Thickness of underline}
                shadow     : Byte;              {Thickness of shadow}
                extra      : SignedByte;        {Extra width per character}
                ascent     : Byte;              {Ascent above baseline}
                descent    : Byte;              {Descent below baseline}
                widMax     : Byte;              {Maximum character width}
                leading    : SignedByte;        {Leading between lines}
                unused     : Byte;              {Reserved}
                numer      : Point;             {Numerators of scale factors}
                denom      : Point              {Denominators of scale factors}
            end;
```

4.5 Nuts and Bolts

4.5.1 Customizing the Printing Dialogs

```
type
   TPPrDlg = ^TPrDlg;

   TPrDlg  = record
                dlg       : DialogRecord;     {Dialog record [II:7.1.1]}
                pFltrProc : ProcPtr;          {Pointer to filter function [II:7.4.5]}
                pItemProc : ProcPtr;          {Pointer to response procedure}
                hPrintUsr : THPrint;          {Handle to print record [4.1.2]}
                fDoIt     : BOOLEAN;          {Private}
                fDone     : BOOLEAN;          {Private}
                lUser1    : LONGINT;          {Private}
                lUser2    : LONGINT;          {Private}
                lUser3    : LONGINT;          {Private}
                lUser4    : LONGINT;          {Private}
                iNumFst   : INTEGER;          {Private}
                iNumLst   : INTEGER;          {Private}

                . . .

                {Additional fields as needed by the customized dialog}
             end;

function PrDlgMain
             (printRec : THPrint;            {Handle to print record}
              initProc : ProcPtr)            {Pointer to initialization routine}
                : BOOLEAN;                    {Was dialog confirmed?}

function PrStlInit
             (printRec : THPrint)            {Handle to print record}
                : TPPrDlg;                    {Pointer to style dialog}

function PrJobInit
             (printRec : THPrint)            {Handle to print record}
                : TPPrDlg;                    {Pointer to job dialog}
```

Chapter 5 Sound

5.1 Defining Sounds

5.1.1 Types of Sound

```
const
    SWMode = -1;                          {Square-wave sound [5.1.2]}
    FFMode =  0;                          {Free-form sound [5.1.4]}
    FTMode = +1;                          {Four-tone sound [5.1.3]}
```

5.1.2 Square-Wave Sound

```
type
    SWSynthPtr = ^SWSynthRec;

    SWSynthRec = record
                 mode     : INTEGER;      {Type of sound: must be SWMode [5.1.1]}
                 triplets : Tones         {Tones to be played}
              end;

    Tones = array [0..5000] of Tone;      {Any number of tones}
    Tone  = record
                 count     : INTEGER;     {Determines pitch of tone}
                 amplitude : INTEGER;     {Volume of tone, 0-255}
                 duration  : INTEGER      {Duration of tone in ticks}
              end;
```

5.1.3 Four-Tone Sound

```
type
    FTSynthPtr = ^FTSynthRec;
    FTSynthRec = record
                 mode   : INTEGER;        {Type of sound: must be FTMode [5.1.1]}
                 sndRec : FTSndRecPtr      {Sound to be played}
              end;
```

```
FTSndRecPtr = ^FTSoundRec;

FTSoundRec = record
                 duration    : INTEGER;    {Duration of sound, in ticks}
                 sound1Rate  : Fixed;      {Sampling rate for voice 1}
                 sound1Phase : LONGINT;    {Phase offset for voice 1}
                 sound2Rate  : Fixed;      {Sampling rate for voice 2}
                 sound2Phase : LONGINT;    {Phase offset for voice 2}
                 sound3Rate  : Fixed;      {Sampling rate for voice 3}
                 sound3Phase : LONGINT;    {Phase offset for voice 3}
                 sound4Rate  : Fixed;      {Sampling rate for voice 4}
                 sound4Phase : LONGINT;    {Phase offset for voice 4}
                 sound1Wave  : WavePtr;    {Waveform for voice 1}
                 sound2Wave  : WavePtr;    {Waveform for voice 2}
                 sound3Wave  : WavePtr;    {Waveform for voice 3}
                 sound4Wave  : WavePtr     {Waveform for voice 4}
              end;

WavePtr = ^Wave;
Wave    = packed array [0..255] of Byte; {256 magnitude samples}
```

5.1.4 Free-Form Sound

```
type
   FFSynthPtr = ^FFSynthRec;

   FFSynthRec = record
                   mode      : INTEGER;   {Type of sound: must be FFMode [5.1.1]}
                   count     : Fixed;     {Sampling rate}
                   waveBytes : FreeWave   {Waveform}
                end;

   FreeWave   = packed array [0..30000] of Byte;
```

5.2 Playing Sounds

5.2.1 Starting and Stopping Sounds

```
procedure StartSound
             (synthRec    : Ptr;          {Pointer to synthesizer record}
              recordSize  : LONGINT;      {Size of synthesizer record in bytes}
              compRoutine : ProcPtr);     {Optional completion routine}

procedure StopSound;

function SoundDone
              : BOOLEAN;                  {Is sound completed?}
```

5.2.2 Speaker Volume

```
procedure GetSoundVol
        (var newLevel : INTEGER);        {New volume setting}

procedure SetSoundVol
        (curLevel : INTEGER);            {Current volume setting}
```

Chapter 6 Desk Accessories

6.1 Desk Accessory Structure

6.1.1 Event Mask

```
const
    MDownMask   = $0002;                 {Mouse-down event}
    MUpMask     = $0004;                 {Mouse-up event}
    KeyDownMask = $0008;                 {Key-down event}
    KeyUpMask   = $0010;                 {Key-up event}
    AutoKeyMask = $0020;                 {Auto-key event}
    UpdateMask  = $0040;                 {Update event}
    DiskMask    = $0080;                 {Disk-inserted event}
    ActivMask   = $0100;                 {Activate/deactivate event}
    NetworkMask = $0400;                 {Network event}
    DriverMask  = $0800;                 {I/O driver event}
    App1Mask    = $1000;                 {Application-defined event}
    App2Mask    = $2000;                 {Application-defined event}
    App3Mask    = $4000;                 {Application-defined event}
    App4Mask    = $8000;                 {Application-defined event (also used by MultiFinder)}
    EveryEvent  = $FFFF;                 {Any event}
```

6.2 Desk Accessory Operations

6.2.1 Opening and Closing Desk Accessories

```
function OpenDeskAcc
        (accName : Str255)               {Name of desk accessory to open}
            : INTEGER;                   {Reference number of desk accessory}

procedure CloseDeskAcc
        (dRefNum : INTEGER);             {Reference number of desk accessory to close}
```

6.2.2 Responding to Events

```
function  SystemEvent
             (theEvent : EventRecord)        {Event to be processed}
                 : BOOLEAN;                  {Was it intercepted as a system event?}

procedure SystemClick
             (theEvent  : EventRecord)       {Event to be processed}
              theWindow : WindowPtr);        {System window where mouse was pressed}
```

6.2.3 Handling Menu Commands

```
procedure SystemMenu
             (menuChoice : LONGINT);         {Menu ID and item number}

function  SystemEdit
             (editCmd : INTEGER);            {Command relayed from application program}
                 : BOOLEAN;                  {Handled by desk accessory?}
const
   UndoCmd  = 0;                             {Edit code for Undo command}
   CutCmd   = 2;                             {Edit code for Cut command}
   CopyCmd  = 3;                             {Edit code for Copy command}
   PasteCmd = 4;                             {Edit code for Paste command}
   ClearCmd = 5;                             {Edit code for Clear command}
```

6.2.4 Performing Periodic Tasks

```
procedure SystemTask;
```

APPENDIX B

Resource Formats

Resource Type `'CDEF'` [2.5.2]

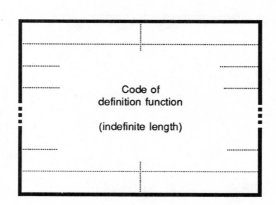

Code of
definition function

(indefinite length)

Resource Type 'DRVR' [3.3.1, 3.1.1]

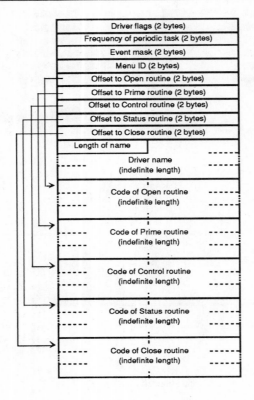

Driver flags (2 bytes)
Frequency of periodic task (2 bytes)
Event mask (2 bytes)
Menu ID (2 bytes)
Offset to Open routine (2 bytes)
Offset to Prime routine (2 bytes)
Offset to Control routine (2 bytes)
Offset to Status routine (2 bytes)
Offset to Close routine (2 bytes)
Length of name
Driver name (indefinite length)
Code of Open routine (indefinite length)
Code of Prime routine (indefinite length)
Code of Control routine (indefinite length)
Code of Status routine (indefinite length)
Code of Close routine (indefinite length)

Resource Type 'FKEY' [6.3.1]

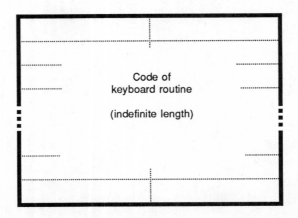

Code of
keyboard routine

(indefinite length)

Resource Type 'MDEF' [2.5.3]

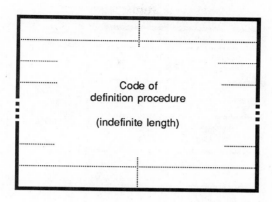

Resource Type 'PDEF' [4.6.2]

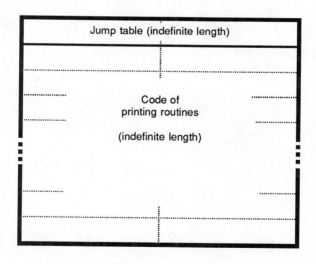

Resource Type 'PREC' [4.6.1]

```
Version stamp (2 bytes)

Printer information
subrecord [4.1.3] (14 bytes)

Paper rectangle (8 bytes)

Style subrecord [4.1.4] (8 bytes)

Print-time information
subrecord [4.1.3] (14 bytes)

Auxiliary information
subrecord [4.1.6] (16 bytes)

Job subrecord [4.1.5] (20 bytes)

Padding
(38 bytes)
```

Paper Size Table (Resource Type 'PREC') [4.5.2]

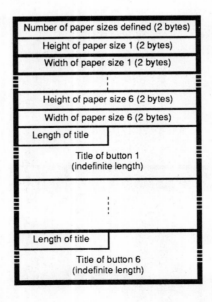

```
Number of paper sizes defined (2 bytes)
Height of paper size 1 (2 bytes)
Width of paper size 1 (2 bytes)

Height of paper size 6 (2 bytes)
Width of paper size 6 (2 bytes)
Length of title
Title of button 1
(indefinite length)

Length of title
Title of button 6
(indefinite length)
```

Resource Type 'WDEF' [2.5.1]

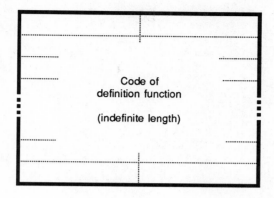

Code of
definition function

(indefinite length)

Reference Figures

Resource ID of an Owned Resource [2.5.4]

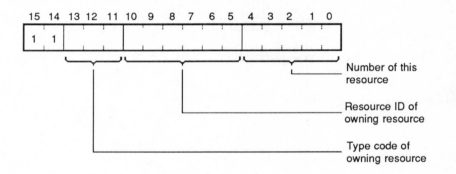

Driver Flags [3.1.2]

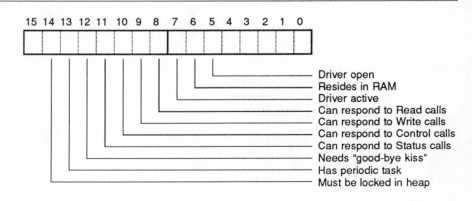

Unit Table [3.1.3]

Bytes	
0-3	Reserved (4 bytes)
4-7	Reserved (4 bytes)
8-11	Handle to .Print DCE (4 bytes)
12-15	Handle to .Sound DCE (4 bytes)
16-19	Handle to .Sony DCE (4 bytes)
20-23	Handle to .Aln DCE (4 bytes)
24-27	Handle to .AOut DCE (4 bytes)
28-31	Handle to .Bin DCE (4 bytes)
32-35	Handle to .BOut DCE (4 bytes)
36-39	Handle to .MPP DCE (4 bytes)
40-43	Handle to .ATP DCE (4 bytes)
44-47	Reserved (4 bytes)
48-51	Handle to Calculator DCE (4 bytes)
52-55	Handle to Alarm Clock DCE (4 bytes)
56-59	Handle to Key Caps DCE (4 bytes)
60-63	Handle to Puzzle DCE (4 bytes)
64-67	Handle to Note Pad DCE (4 bytes)
68-71	Handle to Scrapbook DCE (4 bytes)
72-75	Handle to Control Panel DCE (4 bytes)
76-79	Handle to Chooser DCE (4 bytes)
80-83	Unused (4 bytes)
188-191	Unused (4 bytes)

ImageWriter Style Flags [4.1.4]

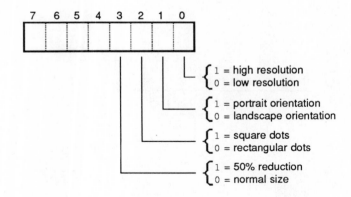

Font Characterization Table [4.4.9]

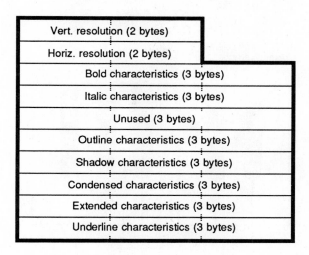

Vert. resolution (2 bytes)
Horiz. resolution (2 bytes)
Bold characteristics (3 bytes)
Italic characteristics (3 bytes)
Unused (3 bytes)
Outline characteristics (3 bytes)
Shadow characteristics (3 bytes)
Condensed characteristics (3 bytes)
Extended characteristics (3 bytes)
Underline characteristics (3 bytes)

Count Values for Musical Tones [5.1.2]

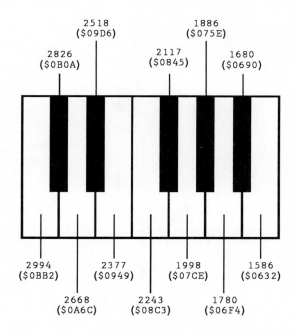

2518 ($09D6)
1886 ($075E)
2826 ($0B0A)
2117 ($0845)
1680 ($0690)

2994 ($0BB2)
2377 ($0949)
1998 ($07CE)
1586 ($0632)

2668 ($0A6C)
2243 ($08C3)
1780 ($06F4)

Sampling Rates for Musical Tones [5.1.3]

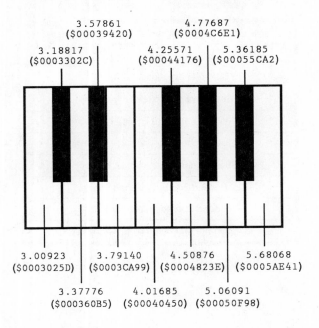

```
                3.57861              4.77687
               ($00039420)         ($0004C6E1)
3.18817                      4.25571       5.36185
($0003302C)                 ($00044176)   ($00055CA2)
```

```
3.00923         3.79140        4.50876          5.68068
($0003025D)    ($0003CA99)    ($0004823E)      ($0005AE41)
```

```
   3.37776       4.01685       5.06091
  ($000360B5)   ($00040450)   ($00050F98)
```

Desk Accessory Event Mask [6.1.1]

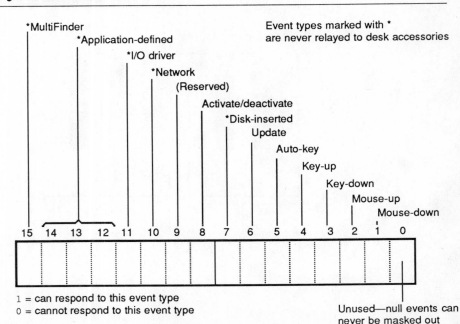

Event types marked with * are never relayed to desk accessories

*MultiFinder
*Application-defined
*I/O driver
*Network
(Reserved)
Activate/deactivate
*Disk-inserted
Update
Auto-key
Key-up
Key-down
Mouse-up
Mouse-down

15 14 13 12 11 10 9 8 7 6 5 4 3 2 1 0

1 = can respond to this event type
0 = cannot respond to this event type

Unused—null events can never be masked out

APPENDIX

D

Reference Tables

Codes for Owning Resources [2.5.4]

Type Code	Resource Type	See Section
0	'DRVR'	[3.3.1]
1	'WDEF'	[2.5.1]
2	'MDEF'	[2.5.3]
3	'CDEF'	[2.5.2]
4	'PDEF'	[4.6.2]
5	'PACK'	[I:7.5.2]
6	Reserved	
7	Reserved	

Standard Driver Numbers [3.1.3]

Unit Number	Reference Number	Driver Name	Description
2	-3	.Print	Printer driver
3	-4	.Sound	Sound driver
4	-5	.Sony	Sony disk driver
5	-6	.AIn	Serial driver, port A (modem port) in
6	-7	.AOut	Serial driver, port A (modem port) out
7	-8	.BIn	Serial driver, port B (printer port) in
8	-9	.BOut	Serial driver, port B (printer port) out
9	-10	.MPP	Network driver (Macintosh Packet Protocol)
10	-11	.ATP	Network driver (AppleTalk Transaction Protocol)
12	-13	Calculator	Calculator desk accessory
13	-14	Alarm Clock	Alarm Clock desk accessory
14	-15	Key Caps	Key Caps desk accessory
15	-16	Puzzle	Puzzle desk accessory
16	-17	Note Pad	Note Pad desk accessory
17	-18	Scrapbook	Scrapbook desk accessory
18	-19	Control Panel	Control Panel desk accessory
19	-20	Chooser	Chooser desk accessory

Device Type Codes for Standard Printers [4.1.4]

Value	Meaning
0	Macintosh screen
1	Original ImageWriter
3	PostScript-based LaserWriter
4	LaserWriter II–SC
5	ImageWriter LQ

Standard Paper Sizes [4.5.2]

| Name | Inches | | 120ths | |
	Height	Width	Height	Width
US Letter	11	$8\frac{1}{2}$	1320	1020
US Legal	14	$8\frac{1}{2}$	1680	1020
A4 Letter	$11\frac{2}{3}$	$8\frac{1}{4}$	1400	990
International Fanfold	12	$8\frac{1}{4}$	1440	990
Computer Paper	11	14	1320	1680
Standard Envelope	$4\frac{1}{8}$	$9\frac{1}{2}$	495	1140

tents of 'PDEF' Resources [4.6.2]

Resource ID	Description	Routines
0	Draft printing	PrOpenDoc [4.3.1]
		PrCloseDoc [4.3.1]
		PrOpenPage [4.3.2]
		PrClosePage [4.3.2]
1	Spooling	PrOpenDoc [4.3.1]
		PrCloseDoc [4.3.1]
		PrOpenPage [4.3.2]
		PrClosePage [4.3.2]
2	Printer-specific method #1	PrOpenDoc [4.3.1]
		PrCloseDoc [4.3.1]
		PrOpenPage [4.3.2]
		PrClosePage [4.3.2]
3	Printer-specific method #2	PrOpenDoc [4.3.1]
		PrCloseDoc [4.3.1]
		PrOpenPage [4.3.2]
		PrClosePage [4.3.2]
4	Dialogs/print records	PrintDefault [4.2.2]
		PrStlDialog [4.2.3]
		PrJobDialog [4.2.3]
		PrStlInit [4.5.1]
		PrJobInit [4.5.1]
		PrDlgMain [4.5.1]
		PrValidate [4.2.2]
		PrJobMerge [4.2.3]
5	Spool printing	PrPicFile [4.3.3]
7	Miscellaneous	PrGeneral [TN #128]

Contents of a Printer Resource File [4.6.3]

Resource Type	Resource ID	Description
[Signature]	0	Autograph [I:7.5.4, note 6]
'BNDL'	128	Finder bundle [I:7.5.4]
'FREF'	128	File reference ('PRES' or 'PRER') [I:7.5.3]
'ICN#'	128	Icon for printer resource file [I:5.5.4]
'DRVR'	$E000	Printer driver [3.3.1]
'PDEF'	0	Draft printing [4.6.2]
	1	Spooling [4.6.2]
	2	Printer-specific method #1 [4.6.2]
	3	Printer-specific method #2 [4.6.2]
	4	Dialogs/print records [4.6.2]
	5	Spool printing [4.6.2]
	7	Miscellaneous [4.6.2]
'PREC'	0	Default print record [4.6.1]
	1	Last-used print record [4.6.1]
	3	Default paper sizes [4.5.2]
'STR '	$E001	Default spool file name [I:8.4.2]
'DLOG'	$E000	Style dialog [II:7.6.2]
	$E001	Job dialog [II:7.6.2]
'DITL'	$E000	Item list for style dialog [II:7.6.3]
	$E001	Item list for job dialog [II:7.6.3]

Desk Accessory Control Codes [6.1.2]

Name	Value	Meaning
KillCode	1	Handle KillIO call [3.2.3]
GoodBye	-1	Handle "good-bye kiss" [3.1.2]
AccEvent	64	Respond to user event
AccRun	65	Perform periodic task
AccCursor	66	Adjust cursor
AccMenu	67	Respond to user's menu choice
AccUndo	68	Execute Undo command
AccCut	70	Execute Cut command
AccCopy	71	Execute Copy command
AccPaste	72	Execute Paste command
AccClear	73	Execute Clear command

Standard 'FKEY' Operations [6.3.1]

Keystroke	Meaning
Command-Shift-1	Eject disk in internal drive
Command-Shift-2	Eject disk in external drive
Command-Shift-3	Dump screen to a MacPaint file
Command-Shift-4	Dump screen to printer

Error Codes

Operating System Errors

The following is a complete list of Operating System error codes. Not all are covered in these books, and some of the meanings may be obscure. (I don't know what a bit-slip nybble is either.) For the errors you're most likely to encounter, see reference sections [I:3.1.2, I:6.6.1, II:8.2.8, III:4.2.4].

Number	Name	Meaning
0	NoErr	No error; all is well
-1	IPrSavPFil	Error saving print file
-1	QErr	Queue element not found during deletion
-2	VTypErr	Invalid queue element
-3	CorErr	Trap ("core routine") number out of range
-4	UnimpErr	Unimplemented trap
-8	SENoDB	No debugger installed
-17	ControlErr	Driver error during Control operation
-18	StatusErr	Driver error during Status operation

Number	Name	Meaning
-19	ReadErr	Driver error during Read operation
-20	WritErr	Driver error during Write operation
-21	BadUnitErr	Bad unit number
-22	UnitEmptyErr	No such entry in unit table
-23	OpenErr	Driver error during Open operation
-24	CloseErr	Driver error during Close operation
-25	DRemovErr	Attempt to remove an open driver
-26	DInstErr	Attempt to install nonexistent driver
-27	AbortErr	Driver operation canceled
-28	NotOpenErr	Driver not open
-33	DirFulErr	Directory full
-34	DskFulErr	Disk full
-35	NSVErr	No such volume
-36	IOErr	Disk I/O error
-37	BdNamErr	Bad name
-38	FNOpenErr	File not open
-39	EOFErr	Attempt to read past end-of-file
-40	PosErr	Attempt to position before start of file
-41	MFulErr	Memory (system heap) full
-42	TMFOErr	Too many files open (more than 12)
-43	FNFErr	File not found
-44	WPrErr	Disk is write-protected
-45	FLckdErr	File locked
-46	VLckdErr	Volume locked
-47	FBsyErr	File busy
-48	DupFNErr	Duplicate file name
-49	OpWrErr	File already open for writing
-50	ParamErr	Invalid parameter list
-51	RfNumErr	Invalid reference number
-52	GFPErr	Error during GetFPos
-53	VolOffLinErr	Volume off-line
-54	PermErr	Permission violation
-55	VolOnLinErr	Volume already on-line
-56	NSDrvErr	No such drive
-57	NoMacDskErr	Non-Macintosh disk
-58	ExtFSErr	External file system
-59	FSRnErr	Unable to rename file
-60	BadMDBErr	Bad master directory block
-61	WrPermErr	No write permission

Number	Name	Meaning
-64	NoDriveErr	No such drive
-65	OffLinErr	Drive off-line
-66	NoNybErr	Can't find 5 nybbles
-67	NoAdrMkErr	No address mark
-68	DataVerErr	Data read doesn't verify
-69	BadCksmErr	Bad checksum (address mark)
-70	BadBtSlpErr	Bad bit-slip nybbles (address mark)
-71	NoDtaMkErr	No data mark
-72	BadDCksum	Bad checksum (data mark)
-73	BadDBtSlp	Bad bit-slip nybbles (data mark)
-74	WrUnderrun	Write underrun
-75	CantStepErr	Can't step disk drive
-76	Tk0BadErr	Track 0 bad
-77	InitIWMErr	Can't initialize disk chip ("Integrated Wozniak Machine")
-78	TwoSideErr	Two-sided operation on one-sided drive
-79	SpdAdjErr	Can't adjust disk speed
-80	SeekErr	Seek to wrong track
-81	SectNFErr	Sector not found
-85	ClkRdErr	Error reading clock
-86	ClkWrErr	Error writing clock
-87	PRWrErr	Error writing parameter RAM
-88	PRInitErr	Parameter RAM uninitialized
-89	RcvrErr	Receiver error (serial communications)
-90	BreakRecd	Break received (serial communications)
-91	DDPSktErr	Socket error (AppleTalk, Datagram Delivery Protocol)
-92	DDPLenErr	Packet too long (AppleTalk, Datagram Delivery Protocol)
-93	NoBridgeErr	No bridge found (AppleTalk)
-94	LAPProtErr	Protocol error (AppleTalk, Link Access Protocol)
-95	ExcessCollsns	Excessive collisions (AppleTalk)
-97	PortInUse	Port already in use (AppleTalk)
-98	PortNotCf	Port not configured for this connection (AppleTalk)
-99	MemROZError	Error in read-only zone

Number	Name	Meaning
-100	NoScrapErr	No desk scrap
-102	NoTypeErr	No item in scrap of requested type
-108	MemFullErr	No room; heap is full
-109	NilHandleErr	Illegal operation on empty handle
-110	MemAdrErr	Bad memory address
-111	MemWZErr	Illegal operation on free block
-112	MemPurErr	Illegal operation on locked block
-113	MemAZErr	Address not in heap zone
-114	MemPCErr	Pointer check failed
-115	MemBCErr	Block check failed
-116	MemSCErr	Size check failed
-117	MemLockedErr	Attempt to move a locked block
-120	DirNFErr	Directory not found
-121	TMWDOErr	Too many working directories open
-122	BadMovErr	Invalid move operation
-123	WrgVolTypErr	Wrong volume type (not HFS)
-127	FSDSIntErr	Internal file system error
-192	ResNotFound	Resource not found
-193	ResFNotFound	Resource file not found
-194	AddResFailed	AddResource failed
-196	RmvResFailed	RmveResource failed
-198	ResErrAttr	Operation prohibited by resource attribute
-199	MapReadErr	Error reading resource map
-1024	NBPBuffOvr	Buffer overflow (AppleTalk, Name Binding Protocol)
-1025	NBPNoConfirm	Name not confirmed (AppleTalk, Name Binding Protocol)
-1026	NBPConfDiff	Name confirmed for different socket (AppleTalk, Name Binding Protocol)
-1027	NBPDuplicate	Name already exists (AppleTalk, Name Binding Protocol)
-1028	NBPNotFound	Name not found (AppleTalk, Name Binding Protocol)
-1029	NBPNISErr	Names information socket error (AppleTalk, Name Binding Protocol)
-1066	ASPBadVersNum	Unsupported version (AppleTalk Session Protocol)

Number	Name	Meaning
-1067	ASPBufTooSmall	Buffer too small (AppleTalk Session Protocol)
-1068	ASPNoMoreSess	No more sessions on server (AppleTalk Session Protocol)
-1069	ASPNoServers	No servers at this address (AppleTalk Session Protocol)
-1070	ASPParamErr	Parameter error (AppleTalk Session Protocol)
-1071	ASPServerBusy	Server busy (AppleTalk Session Protocol)
-1072	ASPSessClosed	Session closed (AppleTalk Session Protocol)
-1073	ASPSizeErr	Command block too big (AppleTalk Session Protocol)
-1074	ASPTooMany	Too many clients (AppleTalk Session Protocol)
-1075	ASPNoAck	No acknowledgment on attention request (AppleTalk Session Protocol)
-1096	ReqFailed	Request failed (AppleTalk)
-1097	TooManyReqs	Too many concurrent requests (AppleTalk)
-1098	TooManySkts	Too many responding sockets (AppleTalk)
-1099	BadATPSkt	Bad responding socket (AppleTalk Transaction Protocol)
-1100	BadBuffNum	Bad buffer number (AppleTalk)
-1101	NoRelErr	No release received (AppleTalk)
-1102	CBNotFound	Control block not found (AppleTalk)
-1103	NoSendResp	AddResponse before SendResponse (AppleTalk)
-1104	NoDataArea	Too many outstanding calls (AppleTalk)
-1105	ReqAborted	Request canceled (AppleTalk)
-3101	Buf2SmallErr	Buffer too small (AppleTalk)
-3102	NoMPPError	Driver not installed (AppleTalk, Macintosh Packet Protocol)
-3103	CkSumErr	Bad checksum (AppleTalk)
-3104	ExtractErr	No tuple in buffer (AppleTalk)
-3105	ReadQErr	Invalid socket or protocol type (AppleTalk)
-3106	ATPLenErr	Packet too long (AppleTalk Transaction Protocol)
-3107	ATPBadRsp	Bad response (AppleTalk Transaction Protocol)
-3108	RecNotFnd	No AppleBus record (AppleTalk)
-3109	SktClosedErr	Socket closed (AppleTalk)
-4096		No free Connect Control Blocks available (LaserWriter)
-4097		Bad connection reference number (LaserWriter)
-4098		Request already active (LaserWriter)

Number	Name	Meaning
-4099		Write request too big (LaserWriter)
-4100		Connection just closed (LaserWriter)
-4101		Printer closed or not found (LaserWriter)
128	IPrAbort	Printing canceled in progress

"Dire Straits" Errors

The following errors are reported directly to the user—not to the running program—by the "Dire Straits" Manager (officially called the System Error Handler). Errors in this category are considered so serious that recovery is impossible: the Toolbox simply displays a "dire straits" alert box (the one with the bomb icon) on the screen, forcing the user to restart the system. Some people insist that DS really stands for "deep spaghetti," but most Macintosh programmers prefer a more colorful term.

Number	Name	Meaning
1	DSBusErr	Bus error
2	DSAddressErr	Address error
3	DSIllInstErr	Illegal instruction
4	DSZeroDivErr	Attempt to divide by zero
5	DSChkErr	Check trap
6	DSOvflowErr	Overflow trap
7	DSPrivErr	Privilege violation
8	DSTraceErr	Trace trap
9	DSLineAErr	"A emulator" trap
10	DSLineFErr	"F emulator" trap
11	DSMiscErr	Miscellaneous hardware exception
12	DSCoreErr	Unimplemented core routine
13	DSIRQErr	Uninstalled interrupt
14	DSIOCoreErr	I/O core error
15	DSLoadErr	Segment Loader error
16	DSFPErr	Floating-point error
17	DSNoPackErr	Package 0 not present
18	DSNoPk1	Package 1 not present
19	DSNoPk2	Package 2 not present
20	DSNoPk3	Package 3 not present

Number	Name	Meaning
21	DSNoPk4	Package 4 not present
22	DSNoPk5	Package 5 not present
23	DSNoPk6	Package 6 not present
24	DSNoPk7	Package 7 not present
25	DSMemFullErr	Out of memory
26	DSBadLaunch	Can't launch program
27	DSFSErr	File system error
28	DSStkNHeap	Stack/heap collision
30	DSReinsert	Ask user to reinsert disk
31	DSNotTheOne	Wrong disk inserted
33	NegZCBFreeErr	Negative number of free bytes in heap zone
84	MenuPrgErr	Menu purged from heap

Summary of Trap Macros and Trap Words

Trap Macros

The following is an alphabetical list of assembly-language trap macros covered in the three volumes of this book, with their corresponding trap words. For routines belonging to the standard packages, the trap word shown is one of the eight package traps (_Pack0 to _Pack7) and is followed by a routine selector in parentheses; similarly, printing routines list the trap word for the universal printing trap _PrGlue along with a specific routine selector. Routines marked with an asterisk (*) are not included in the original 64K ROM.

Trap Macro Name	Trap Word	Reference Section
_AddPt	$A87E	[I:4.4.1]
_AddResMenu	$A94D	[II:4.3.3]
_AddResource	$A9AB	[I:6.5.3]
_Alert	$A985	[II:7.4.2]
_Allocate	$A010	[II:8.2.5]
_AppendMenu	$A933	[II:4.3.1]
_BackPat	$A87C	[I:5.1.1]
_BeginUpdate	$A922	[II:3.4.1]
_BitAnd	$A858	[I:2.2.2]

Trap Macro Name	Trap Word	Reference Section
_BitClr	$A85F	[I:2.2.1]
_BitNot	$A85A	[I:2.2.2]
_BitOr	$A85B	[I:2.2.2]
_BitSet	$A85E	[I:2.2.1]
_BitShift	$A85C	[I:2.2.2]
_BitTst	$A85D	[I:2.2.1]
_BitXOr	$A859	[I:2.2.2]
_BlockMove	$A02E	[I:3.2.5]
_BringToFront	$A920	[II:3.3.3]
_Button	$A974	[II:2.4.2]
*_CalcMask	$A838	[I:5.1.6]
_CalcMenuSize	$A948	[II:4.7.1]
_CautionAlert	$A988	[II:7.4.2]
_Chain	$A9F3	[I:7.1.1]
_ChangedResource	$A9AA	[I:6.5.2]
_CharWidth	$A88D	[I:8.3.4]
_CheckItem	$A945	[II:4.6.4]
_ClearMenuBar	$A934	[II:4.4.1]
_ClipRect	$A87B	[I:4.3.6]
_Close	$A001	[II:8.2.2, III:3.2.1]
_CloseDeskAcc	$A9B7	[II:4.5.2, III:6.2.1]
_CloseDialog	$A982	[II:7.2.3]
_ClosePgon	$A8CC	[I:4.1.4]
_ClosePicture	$A8F4	[I:5.4.2]
_ClosePort	$A87D	[I:4.3.2]
_CloseResFile	$A99A	[I:6.2.1]
_CloseRgn	$A8DB	[I:4.1.6]
_CloseWindow	$A92D	[II:3.2.3]
_CmpString	$A03C	[I:2.1.2]
_CompactMem	$A04C	[I:3.3.2]
_Control	$A004	[III:3.2.3]
_CopyBits	$A8EC	[I:5.1.2]
*_CopyMask	$A817	[I:5.1.4]
_CopyRgn	$A8DC	[I:4.1.7]
_CouldAlert	$A989	[II:7.5.3]
_CouldDialog	$A979	[II:7.5.3]
_CountMItems	$A950	[II:4.3.4]
_CountResources	$A99C	[I:6.3.3]
_CountTypes	$A99E	[I:6.3.3]
*_Count1Resources	$A80D	[I:6.3.3]

Trap Macro Name	Trap Word	Reference Section
*_Count1Types	$A81C	[I:6.3.3]
_Create	$A008	[II:8.2.1]
_CreateResFile	$A9B1	[I:6.5.1]
_CurResFile	$A994	[I:6.2.2]
_Date2Secs	$A9C7	[I:2.4.3]
_Delay	$A03B	[II:2.7.1]
_Delete	$A009	[II:8.2.7]
_DeleteMenu	$A936	[II:4.4.1]
*_DelMenuItem	$A952	[II:4.3.4]
_DeltaPoint	$A94F	[I:4.4.1]
_Dequeue	$A96E	[III:3.1.7]
_DetachResource	$A992	[I:6.3.2]
_DialogSelect	$A980	[II:7.4.4]
_DIBadMount	$A9E9 (0)	[II:8.4.1]
_DiffRgn	$A8E6	[I:4.4.8]
_DIFormat	$A9E9 (6)	[II:8.4.2]
_DILoad	$A9E9 (2)	[II:8.4.3]
_DisableItem	$A93A	[II:4.6.2]
_DisposControl	$A955	[II:6.2.2]
_DisposDialog	$A983	[II:7.2.3]
_DisposHandle	$A023	[I:3.2.2]
_DisposMenu	$A932	[II:4.2.3]
_DisposPtr	$A01F	[I:3.2.2]
_DisposRgn	$A8D9	[I:4.1.6]
_DisposWindow	$A914	[II:3.2.3]
_DIUnload	$A9E9 (4)	[II:8.4.3]
_DIVerify	$A9E9 (8)	[II:8.4.2]
_DIZero	$A9E9 (10)	[II:8.4.2]
_DragControl	$A967	[II:6.4.3]
_DragWindow	$A925	[II:3.5.4]
_DrawChar	$A883	[I:8.3.3]
_DrawControls	$A969	[II:6.3.1]
_DrawDialog	$A981	[II:7.4.1]
_DrawGrowIcon	$A904	[II:3.3.4]
_DrawMenuBar	$A937	[II:4.4.3]
_DrawPicture	$A8F6	[I:5.4.3]
_DrawString	$A884	[I:8.3.3]
_DrawText	$A885	[I:8.3.3]
_Eject	$A017	[II:8.1.3]

Trap Macro Name	Trap Word	Reference Section
_EmptyHandle	$A02B	[I:3.3.3]
_EmptyRect	$A8AE	[I:4.4.4]
_EmptyRgn	$A8E2	[I:4.4.7]
_EnableItem	$A939	[II:4.6.2]
_EndUpdate	$A923	[II:3.4.1]
_Enqueue	$A96F	[III:3.1.7]
_EqualPt	$A881	[I:4.4.1]
_EqualRect	$A8A6	[I:4.4.5]
_EqualRgn	$A8E3	[I:4.4.8]
_EraseArc	$A8C0	[I:5.3.5]
_EraseOval	$A8B9	[I:5.3.4]
_ErasePoly	$A8C8	[I:5.3.6]
_EraseRect	$A8A3	[I:5.3.2]
_EraseRgn	$A8D4	[I:5.3.7]
_EraseRoundRect	$A8B2	[I:5.3.3]
_ErrorSound	$A98C	[II:7.5.1]
_EventAvail	$A971	[II:2.2.1]
_ExitToShell	$A9F4	[I:7.1.3]
_FillArc	$A8C2	[I:5.3.5]
_FillOval	$A8BB	[I:5.3.4]
_FillPoly	$A8CA	[I:5.3.6]
_FillRect	$A8A5	[I:5.3.2]
_FillRgn	$A8D6	[I:5.3.7]
_FillRoundRect	$A8B4	[I:5.3.3]
_FindControl	$A96C	[II:6.4.1]
*_FindDItem	$A984	[II:7.3.4]
_FindWindow	$A92C	[II:3.5.1]
*_FixATan2	$A818	[I:2.3.6]
*_FixDiv	$A84D	[I:2.3.2]
_FixMul	$A868	[I:2.3.2]
_FixRatio	$A869	[I:2.3.2]
_FixRound	$A86C	[I:2.3.1]
*_Fix2Frac	$A841	[I:2.3.3]
*_Fix2Long	$A840	[I:2.3.1]
_FlashMenuBar	$A94C	[II:4.7.2]
_FlushEvents	$A032	[II:2.3.1]
_FlushVol	$A013	[II:8.1.3]
*_FontMetrics	$A835	[I:8.2.6]
*_FracCos	$A847	[I:2.3.6]
*_FracDiv	$A84B	[I:2.3.4]

Trap Macro Name	Trap Word	Reference Section
*_FracMul	$A84A	[I:2.3.4]
*_FracSin	$A848	[I:2.3.6]
*_FracSqrt	$A849	[I:2.3.4]
*_Frac2Fix	$A842	[I:2.3.3]
_FrameArc	$A8BE	[I:5.3.5]
_FrameOval	$A8B7	[I:5.3.4]
_FramePoly	$A8C6	[I:5.3.6]
_FrameRect	$A8A1	[I:5.3.2]
_FrameRgn	$A8D2	[I:5.3.7]
_FrameRoundRect	$A8B0	[I:5.3.3]
_FreeAlert	$A98A	[II:7.5.3]
_FreeDialog	$A97A	[II:7.5.3]
_FreeMem	$A01C	[I:3.3.1]
_FrontWindow	$A924	[II:3.3.3]
_GetAppParms	$A9F5	[I:7.3.4]
_GetClip	$A87A	[I:4.3.6]
_GetCRefCon	$A95A	[II:6.2.3]
_GetCTitle	$A95E	[II:6.2.3]
_GetCtlAction	$A96A	[II:6.4.2]
_GetCtlValue	$A960	[II:6.2.4]
_GetCursor	$A9B9	[II:2.5.2]
_GetDItem	$A98D	[II:7.3.1]
_GetEOF	$A011	[II:8.2.5]
_GetFileInfo	$A00C	[I:7.3.3]
_GetFName	$A8FF	[I:8.2.5]
_GetFNum	$A900	[I:8.2.5]
_GetFontInfo	$A88B	[I:8.2.6]
_GetFPos	$A018	[II:8.2.4]
_GetHandleSize	$A025	[I:3.2.3]
_GetIndResource	$A99D	[I:6.3.3]
_GetIndType	$A99F	[I:6.3.3]
_GetItem	$A946	[II:4.6.1]
_GetIText	$A990	[II:7.3.2]
_GetItmIcon	$A93F	[II:4.6.5]
_GetItmMark	$A943	[II:4.6.4]
_GetItmStyle	$A941	[II:4.6.3]
_GetKeys	$A976	[II:2.6.1]
_GetMaxCtl	$A962	[II:6.2.4]
_GetMenuBar	$A93B	[II:4.4.4]

Trap Macro Name	Trap Word	Reference Section
_GetMHandle	$A949	[II:4.4.5]
_GetMinCtl	$A961	[II:6.2.4]
_GetMouse	$A972	[II:2.4.1]
_GetNamedResource	$A9A1	[I:6.3.1]
_GetNewControl	$A9BE	[II:6.2.1]
_GetNewDialog	$A97C	[II:7.2.2]
_GetNewMBar	$A9C0	[II:4.4.2]
_GetNewWindow	$A9BD	[II:3.2.2]
_GetNextEvent	$A970	[II:2.2.1]
_GetPattern	$A9B8	[I:5.1.1]
_GetPen	$A89A	[I:5.2.4]
_GetPenState	$A898	[I:5.2.1]
_GetPicture	$A9BC	[I:5.4.2]
_GetPixel	$A865	[I:4.2.3]
_GetPort	$A874	[I:4.3.3]
_GetPtrSize	$A021	[I:3.2.3]
_GetResAttrs	$A9A6	[I:6.4.2]
_GetResFileAttrs	$A9F6	[I:6.6.2]
_GetResInfo	$A9A8	[I:6.4.1]
_GetResource	$A9A0	[I:6.3.1]
_GetRMenu	$A9BF	[II:4.2.2]
_GetScrap	$A9FD	[I:7.4.3]
_GetString	$A9BA	[I:8.1.2]
_GetVol	$A014	[II:8.1.2]
_GetVolInfo	$A007	[II:8.1.1]
_GetWindowPic	$A92F	[II:3.4.3]
_GetWMgrPort	$A910	[II:3.6.1]
_GetWRefCon	$A917	[II:3.2.4]
_GetWTitle	$A919	[II:3.2.4]
*_Get1IxResource	$A80E	[I:6.3.3]
*_Get1IxType	$A80F	[I:6.3.3]
*_Get1NamedResource	$A820	[I:6.3.1]
*_Get1Resource	$A81F	[I:6.3.1]
_GlobalToLocal	$A871	[I:4.4.2]
_GrafDevice	$A872	[I:8.3.2]
_GrowWindow	$A92B	[II:3.5.4]
_HandAndHand	$A9E4	[I:3.2.6]
_HandToHand	$A9E1	[I:3.2.5]
*_HClrRBit	$A068	[I:3.2.4]
*_HGetState	$A069	[I:3.2.4]

Trap Macro Name	Trap Word	Reference Section
_HideControl	$A958	[II:6.3.1]
_HideCursor	$A852	[II:2.5.3]
*_HideDItem	$A827	[II:7.3.3]
_HidePen	$A896	[I:5.2.3]
_HideWindow	$A916	[II:3.3.1]
_HiliteControl	$A95D	[II:6.3.3]
_HiliteMenu	$A938	[II:4.5.4]
_HiliteWindow	$A91C	[II:3.3.4]
_HiWord	$A86A	[I:2.2.3]
_HLock	$A029	[I:3.2.4]
_HNoPurge	$A04A	[I:3.2.4]
_HomeResFile	$A9A4	[I:6.4.3]
_HPurge	$A049	[I:3.2.4]
*_HSetRBit	$A067	[I:3.2.4]
*_HSetState	$A06A	[I:3.2.4]
_HUnlock	$A02A	[I:3.2.4]
_InfoScrap	$A9F9	[I:7.4.2]
_InitAllPacks	$A9E6	[I:7.2.2]
_InitCursor	$A850	[II:2.5.2]
_InitDialogs	$A97B	[II:7.2.1]
_InitFonts	$A8FE	[I:8.2.4]
_InitGraf	$A86E	[I:4.3.1]
_InitMenus	$A930	[II:4.2.1]
_InitPack	$A9E5	[I:7.2.2]
_InitPort	$A86D	[I:4.3.2]
_InitWindows	$A912	[II:3.2.1]
_InsertMenu	$A935	[II:4.4.1]
_InsertResMenu	$A951	[II:4.3.3]
_InsetRect	$A8A9	[I:4.4.4]
_InsetRgn	$A8E1	[I:4.4.7]
*_InsMenuItem	$A826	[II:4.3.1]
_InvalRect	$A928	[II:3.4.2]
_InvalRgn	$A927	[II:3.4.2]
_InverRect	$A8A4	[I:5.3.2]
_InverRgn	$A8D5	[I:5.3.7]
_InverRoundRect	$A8B3	[I:5.3.3]
_InvertArc	$A8C1	[I:5.3.5]
_InvertOval	$A8BA	[I:5.3.4]
_InvertPoly	$A8C9	[I:5.3.6]
_IsDialogEvent	$A97F	[II:7.4.4]

Trap Macro Name	Trap Word	Reference Section
_IUDateString	$A9ED (0)	[I:2.4.4]
_IUTimeString	$A9ED (2)	[I:2.4.4]
_KillControls	$A956	[II:6.2.2]
_KillIO	$A006	[III:3.2.3]
_KillPicture	$A8F5	[I:5.4.2]
_KillPoly	$A8CD	[I:4.1.4]
_Launch	$A9F2	[I:7.1.1]
_Line	$A892	[I:5.2.4]
_LineTo	$A891	[I:5.2.4]
_LoadSeg	$A9F0	[I:7.1.2]
_LocalToGlobal	$A870	[I:4.4.2]
_LodeScrap	$A9FB	[I:7.4.4]
_LongMul	$A867	[I:2.3.3]
*_Long2Fix	$A83F	[I:2.3.1]
_LoWord	$A86B	[I:2.2.3]
_MapPoly	$A8FC	[I:4.4.9]
_MapPt	$A8F9	[I:4.4.9]
_MapRect	$A8FA	[I:4.4.9]
_MapRgn	$A8FB	[I:4.4.9]
*_MaxApplZone	$A063	[I:3.3.4]
*_MaxBlock	$A061	[I:3.3.1]
_MaxMem	$A11D	[I:3.3.1]
*_MaxSizeRsrc	$A821	[I:6.4.3]
*_MeasureText	$A837	[I:8.3.4]
_MenuKey	$A93E	[II:4.5.1]
_MenuSelect	$A93D	[II:4.5.1]
_ModalDialog	$A991	[II:7.4.3]
_MoreMasters	$A036	[I:3.2.5]
_MountVol	$A00F	[II:8.1.3]
_Move	$A894	[I:5.2.4]
_MoveControl	$A959	[II:6.3.2]
*_MoveHHi	$A064	[I:3.2.5]
_MovePortTo	$A877	[I:4.3.5]
_MoveTo	$A893	[I:5.2.4]
_MoveWindow	$A91B	[II:3.3.2]
_Munger	$A9E0	[II:5.5.6]
_NewControl	$A954	[II:6.2.1]
_NewDialog	$A97D	[II:7.2.2]
*_NewEmptyHandle	$A166	[I:3.2.1]

Trap Macro Name	Trap Word	Reference Section
_NewHandle	$A122	[I:3.2.1]
_NewMenu	$A931	[II:4.2.2]
_NewPtr	$A11E	[I:3.2.1]
_NewRgn	$A8D8	[I:4.1.6]
_NewString	$A906	[I:8.1.2]
_NewWindow	$A913	[II:3.2.2]
_NoteAlert	$A987	[II:7.4.2]
_NumToString	$A9EE (0)	[I:2.3.4]
_ObscureCursor	$A856	[II:2.5.4]
_OffLine	$A035	[II:8.1.3]
_OffsetPoly	$A8CE	[I:4.4.6]
_OffsetRect	$A8A8	[I:4.4.4]
_OfsetRgn	$A8E0	[I:4.4.7]
_Open	$A000	[II:8.2.2, III:3.2.1]
_OpenDeskAcc	$A9B6	[II:4.5.2, III:6.2.1]
_OpenPicture	$A8F3	[I:5.4.2]
_OpenPoly	$A8CB	[I:4.1.4]
_OpenPort	$A86F	[I:4.3.2]
_OpenResFile	$A997	[I:6.2.1]
_OpenRF	$A00A	[II:8.2.2]
_OpenRgn	$A8DA	[I:4.1.6]
_Pack0	$A9E7	[I:7.2.1]
_Pack1	$A9E8	[I:7.2.1]
_Pack2	$A9E9	[I:7.2.1]
_Pack3	$A9EA	[I:7.2.1]
_Pack4	$A9EB	[I:7.2.1]
_Pack5	$A9EC	[I:7.2.1]
_Pack6	$A9ED	[I:7.2.1]
_Pack7	$A9EE	[I:7.2.1]
*_Pack8	$A816	[I:7.2.1]
*_Pack9	$A82B	[I:7.2.1]
*_Pack10	$A82C	[I:7.2.1]
*_Pack11	$A82D	[I:7.2.1]
*_Pack12	$A82E	[I:7.2.1]
*_Pack13	$A82F	[I:7.2.1]
*_Pack14	$A830	[I:7.2.1]
*_Pack15	$A831	[I:7.2.1]
_PaintArc	$A8BF	[I:5.3.5]
_PaintOval	$A8B8	[I:5.3.4]

Trap Macro Name	Trap Word	Reference Section
_PaintPoly	$A8C7	[I:5.3.6]
_PaintRect	$A8A2	[I:5.3.2]
_PaintRgn	$A8D3	[I:5.3.7]
_PaintRoundRect	$A8B1	[I:5.3.3]
_ParamText	$A98B	[II:7.4.6]
_PenMode	$A89C	[I:5.2.2]
_PenNormal	$A89E	[I:5.2.2]
_PenPat	$A89D	[I:5.2.2]
_PenSize	$A89B	[I:5.2.2]
_PicComment	$A8F2	[III:2.1.7]
_PinRect	$A94E	[I:4.4.3]
_PortSize	$A876	[I:4.3.5]
_PostEvent	$A02F	[II:2.3.2]
*_PrClosDoc	$A8FD ($08000484)	[III:4.3.1]
*_PrClose	$A8FD ($D0000000)	[III:4.2.1]
*_PrClosPage	$A8FD ($1800040C)	[III:4.3.2]
*_PrCtlCall	$A8FD ($A0000E00)	[III:4.4.3]
*_PrDlgMain	$A8FD ($4A040894)	[III:4.5.1]
*_PrDrvrClose	$A8FD ($88000000)	[III:4.4.1]
*_PrDrvrDCE	$A8FD ($94000000)	[III:4.4.2]
*_PrDrvrOpen	$A8FD ($80000000)	[III:4.4.1]
*_PrDrvrVers	$A8FD ($9A000000)	[III:4.4.2]
*_PrError	$A8FD ($BA000000)	[III:4.2.4]
*_PrGlue	$A8FD	[III:4.2–4.5]
*_PrintDefault	$A8FD ($20040480)	[III:4.2.2]
*_PrJobDialog	$A8FD ($32040488)	[III:4.2.3]
*_PrJobInit	$A8FD ($44040410)	[III:4.5.1]
*_PrJobMerge	$A8FD ($5804089C)	[III:4.2.3]
*_PrNoPurge	$A8FD ($B0000000)	[III:4.4.2]
*_PrOpen	$A8FD ($C8000000)	[III:4.2.1]
*_PrOpenDoc	$A8FD ($04000C00)	[III:4.3.1]
*_PrOpenPage	$A8FD ($10000808)	[III:4.3.2]
*_PrPicFile	$A8FD ($60051480)	[III:4.3.3]
*_PrPurge	$A8FD ($A8000000)	[III:4.4.2]
*_PrSetError	$A8FD ($C0000200)	[III:4.2.4]
*_PrStlDialog	$A8FD ($2A040484)	[III:4.2.3]
*_PrStlInit	$A8FD ($3C04040C)	[III:4.5.1]
*_PrValidate	$A8FD ($52040498)	[III:4.2.2]
_PtInRect	$A8AD	[I:4.4.3]
_PtInRgn	$A8E8	[I:4.4.3]

Trap Macro Name	Trap Word	Reference Section
_PtrAndHand	$A9EF	[I:3.2.6]
_PtrToHand	$A9E3	[I:3.2.5]
_PtrToXHand	$A9E2	[I:3.2.5]
_Pt2Rect	$A8AC	[I:4.1.2]
_PtToAngle	$A8C3	[I:5.3.5]
_PurgeMem	$A04D	[I:3.3.3]
*_PurgeSpace	$A162	[I:3.3.1]
_PutScrap	$A9FE	[I:7.4.3]
_Random	$A861	[I:2.3.5]
_Read	$A002	[II:8.2.3, III:3.2.2]
_RealFont	$A902	[I:8.2.5]
_ReallocHandle	$A027	[I:3.3.3]
_RecoverHandle	$A128	[I:3.2.1]
_RectInRgn	$A8E9	[I:4.4.3]
_RectRgn	$A8DF	[I:4.1.7]
_ReleaseResource	$A9A3	[I:6.3.2]
*_RelString	$A050	[I:2.1.2]
_Rename	$A00B	[II:8.2.7]
_ResError	$A9AF	[I:6.6.1]
_ResrvMem	$A040	[I:3.2.1]
_RmveResource	$A9AD	[I:6.5.3]
_RstFilLock	$A042	[II:8.2.6]
_ScalePt	$A8F8	[I:4.4.9]
_ScrollRect	$A8EF	[I:5.1.5]
_Secs2Date	$A9C6	[I:2.4.3]
_SectRect	$A8AA	[I:4.4.5]
_SectRgn	$A8E4	[I:4.4.8]
*_SeedFill	$A839	[I:5.1.6]
_SelectWindow	$A91F	[II:3.5.2]
_SelIText	$A97E	[II:7.3.2]
_SendBehind	$A921	[II:3.3.3]
_SetApplLimit	$A02D	[I:3.3.4]
_SetClip	$A879	[I:4.3.6]
_SetCRefCon	$A95B	[II:6.2.3]
_SetCTitle	$A95F	[II:6.2.3]
_SetCtlAction	$A96B	[II:6.4.2]
_SetCtlValue	$A963	[II:6.2.4]
_SetCursor	$A851	[II:2.5.2]
_SetDateTime	$A03A	[I:2.4.1]

Trap Macro Name	Trap Word	Reference Section
_SetDItem	$A98E	[II:7.3.1]
_SetEmptyRgn	$A8DD	[I:4.1.7]
_SetEOF	$A012	[II:8.2.5]
_SetFileInfo	$A00D	[I:7.3.3]
_SetFilLock	$A041	[II:8.2.6]
_SetFontLock	$A903	[I:8.2.7]
_SetFPos	$A044	[II:8.2.4]
*_SetFScaleDisable	$A834	[I:8.2.8]
_SetHandleSize	$A024	[I:3.2.3]
_SetItem	$A947	[II:4.6.1]
_SetIText	$A98F	[II:7.3.2]
_SetItmIcon	$A940	[II:4.6.5]
_SetItmMark	$A944	[II:4.6.4]
_SetItmStyle	$A942	[II:4.6.3]
_SetMaxCtl	$A965	[II:6.2.4]
_SetMenuBar	$A93C	[II:4.4.4]
_SetMFlash	$A94A	[II:4.7.2]
_SetMinCtl	$A964	[II:6.2.4]
_SetOrigin	$A878	[I:4.3.4]
_SetPBits	$A875	[I:4.3.4]
_SetPenState	$A899	[I:5.2.1]
_SetPort	$A873	[I:4.3.3]
_SetPt	$A880	[I:4.1.1]
_SetPtrSize	$A020	[I:3.2.3]
_SetRecRgn	$A8DE	[I:4.1.7]
_SetRect	$A8A7	[I:4.1.2]
_SetResAttrs	$A9A7	[I:6.4.2]
_SetResFileAttrs	$A9F7	[I:6.6.2]
_SetResInfo	$A9A9	[I:6.4.1]
_SetResPurge	$A993	[I:6.5.5]
_SetStdProcs	$A8EA	[III:2.1.1]
_SetString	$A907	[I:8.1.2]
_SetVol	$A015	[II:8.1.2]
_SetWindowPic	$A92E	[II:3.4.3]
_SetWRefCon	$A918	[II:3.2.4]
_SetWTitle	$A91A	[II:3.2.4]
_SFGetFile	$A9EA (2)	[II:8.3.2]
_SFPutFile	$A9EA (1)	[II:8.3.3]
_ShieldCursor	$A855	[II:2.5.4]
_ShowControl	$A957	[II:6.3.1]

Trap Macro Name	Trap Word	Reference Section
_ShowCursor	$A853	[II:2.5.3]
*_ShowDItem	$A828	[II:7.3.3]
_ShowHide	$A908	[II:3.3.1]
_ShowPen	$A897	[I:5.2.3]
_ShowWindow	$A915	[II:3.3.1]
_SizeControl	$A95C	[II:6.3.2]
_SizeRsrc	$A9A5	[I:6.4.3]
_SizeWindow	$A91D	[II:3.3.2]
_SpaceExtra	$A88E	[I:8.3.2]
*_StackSpace	$A065	[I:3.3.4]
_Status	$A005	[III:3.2.3]
_StdArc	$A8BD	[III:2.1.4]
_StdBits	$A8EB	[III:2.1.2]
_StdComment	$A8F1	[III:2.1.7]
_StdGetPic	$A8EE	[III:2.1.6]
_StdLine	$A890	[III:2.1.3]
_StdOval	$A8B6	[III:2.1.4]
_StdPoly	$A8C5	[III:2.1.4]
_StdPutPic	$A8F0	[III:2.1.6]
_StdRect	$A8A0	[III:2.1.4]
_StdRgn	$A8D1	[III:2.1.4]
_StdRRect	$A8AF	[III:2.1.4]
_StdText	$A882	[III:2.1.5]
_StdTxMeas	$A8ED	[III:2.1.5]
_StillDown	$A973	[II:2.4.2]
_StopAlert	$A986	[II:7.4.2]
_StringToNum	$A9EE (1)	[I:2.3.4]
_StringWidth	$A88C	[I:8.3.4]
_StuffHex	$A866	[I:2.2.4]
_SubPt	$A87F	[I:4.4.1]
_SysBeep	$A9C8	[II:2.8.1]
_SysEdit	$A9C2	[II:4.5.3, III:6.2.3]
_SystemClick	$A9B3	[II:3.5.3, III:6.2.2]
_SystemEvent	$A9B2	[III:6.2.2]
_SystemMenu	$A9B5	[III:6.2.3]
_SystemTask	$A9B4	[II:2.7.2, III:6.2.4]
_TEActivate	$A9D8	[II:5.4.3]
*_TEAutoView	$A813	[II:5.3.3]
_TECalText	$A9D0	[II:5.3.1]
_TEClick	$A9D4	[II:5.4.1]

Trap Macro Name	Trap Word	Reference Section
_TECopy	$A9D5	[II:5.5.2]
_TECut	$A9D6	[II:5.5.2]
_TEDeactivate	$A9D9	[II:5.4.3]
_TEDelete	$A9D7	[II:5.5.3]
_TEDispose	$A9CD	[II:5.2.2]
_TEGetText	$A9CB	[II:5.2.3]
_TEIdle	$A9DA	[II:5.4.3]
_TEInit	$A9CC	[II:5.2.1]
_TEInsert	$A9DE	[II:5.5.3]
_TEKey	$A9DC	[II:5.5.1]
_TENew	$A9D2	[II:5.2.2]
_TEPaste	$A9DB	[II:5.5.2]
*_TEPinScroll	$A812	[II:5.3.3]
_TEScroll	$A9DD	[II:5.3.3]
*_TESelView	$A811	[II:5.3.3]
_TESetJust	$A9DF	[II:5.3.1]
_TESetSelect	$A9D1	[II:5.4.2]
_TESetText	$A9CF	[II:5.2.3]
_TestControl	$A966	[II:6.4.1]
_TEUpdate	$A9D3	[II:5.3.2]
_TextBox	$A9CE	[II:5.3.2]
_TextFace	$A888	[I:8.3.2]
_TextFont	$A887	[I:8.3.2]
_TextMode	$A889	[I:8.3.2]
_TextSize	$A88A	[I:8.3.2]
_TextWidth	$A886	[I:8.3.4]
_TickCount	$A975	[II:2.7.1]
*_TrackBox	$A83B	[II:3.5.4]
_TrackControl	$A968	[II:6.4.2]
_TrackGoAway	$A91E	[II:3.5.4]
_UnionRect	$A8AB	[I:4.4.5]
_UnionRgn	$A8E5	[I:4.4.8]
_UniqueID	$A9C1	[I:6.5.3]
*_Unique1ID	$A810	[I:6.5.3]
_UnloadSeg	$A9F1	[I:7.1.2]
_UnlodeScrap	$A9FA	[I:7.4.4]
_UnmountVol	$A00E	[II:8.1.3]
_UpdateResFile	$A999	[I:6.5.4]
*_UpdtControls	$A953	[II:6.3.1]

Trap Macro Name	Trap Word	Reference Section
*_UpdtDialog	$A978	[II:7.4.1]
_UprString	$A854	[I:2.1.2]
_UseResFile	$A998	[I:6.2.2]
_ValidRect	$A92A	[II:3.4.2]
_ValidRgn	$A929	[II:3.4.2]
_WaitMouseUp	$A977	[II:2.4.2]
_Write	$A003	[II:8.2.3, III:3.2.2]
_WriteResource	$A9B0	[I:6.5.4]
_XOrRgn	$A8E7	[I:4.4.8]
_ZeroScrap	$A9FC	[I:7.4.3]
*_ZoomWindow	$A83A	[II:3.3.2]

Trap Words

Here is the same list sorted numerically by trap word. Again, routine selectors are given in parentheses following the trap word for printing routines and those belonging to the standard packages, and routines marked with an asterisk (*) are not included in the original 64K ROM.

Trap Word	Trap Macro Name	Reference Section
$A000	_Open	[II:8.2.2, III:3.2.1]
$A001	_Close	[II:8.2.2, III:3.2.1]
$A002	_Read	[II:8.2.3, III:3.2.2]
$A003	_Write	[II:8.2.3, III:3.2.2]
$A004	_Control	[III:3.2.3]
$A005	_Status	[III:3.2.3]
$A006	_KillIO	[III:3.2.3]
$A007	_GetVolInfo	[II:8.1.1]
$A008	_Create	[II:8.2.1]
$A009	_Delete	[II:8.2.7]
$A00A	_OpenRF	[II:8.2.2]
$A00B	_Rename	[II:8.2.7]
$A00C	_GetFileInfo	[I:7.3.3]
$A00D	_SetFileInfo	[I:7.3.3]
$A00E	_UnmountVol	[II:8.1.3]

Trap Word	Trap Macro Name	Reference Section
$A00F	_MountVol	[II:8.1.3]
$A010	_Allocate	[II:8.2.5]
$A011	_GetEOF	[II:8.2.5]
$A012	_SetEOF	[II:8.2.5]
$A013	_FlushVol	[II:8.1.3]
$A014	_GetVol	[II:8.1.2]
$A015	_SetVol	[II:8.1.2]
$A017	_Eject	[II:8.1.3]
$A018	_GetFPos	[II:8.2.4]
$A01C	_FreeMem	[I:3.3.1]
$A11D	_MaxMem	[I:3.3.1]
$A11E	_NewPtr	[I:3.2.1]
$A01F	_DisposPtr	[I:3.2.2]
$A020	_SetPtrSize	[I:3.2.3]
$A021	_GetPtrSize	[I:3.2.3]
$A122	_NewHandle	[I:3.2.1]
$A023	_DisposHandle	[I:3.2.2]
$A024	_SetHandleSize	[I:3.2.3]
$A025	_GetHandleSize	[I:3.2.3]
$A027	_ReallocHandle	[I:3.3.3]
$A128	_RecoverHandle	[I:3.2.1]
$A029	_HLock	[I:3.2.4]
$A02A	_HUnlock	[I:3.2.4]
$A02B	_EmptyHandle	[I:3.3.3]
$A02D	_SetApplLimit	[I:3.3.4]
$A02E	_BlockMove	[I:3.2.5]
$A02F	_PostEvent	[II:2.3.2]
$A032	_FlushEvents	[II:2.3.1]
$A035	_OffLine	[II:8.1.3]
$A036	_MoreMasters	[I:3.2.5]
$A03A	_SetDateTime	[I:2.4.1]
$A03B	_Delay	[II:2.7.1]
$A03C	_CmpString	[I:2.1.2]
$A040	_ResrvMem	[I:3.2.1]
$A041	_SetFilLock	[II:8.2.6]
$A042	_RstFilLock	[II:8.2.6]
$A044	_SetFPos	[II:8.2.4]
$A049	_HPurge	[I:3.2.4]

Trap Word	Trap Macro Name	Reference Section
$A04A	_HNoPurge	[I:3.2.4]
$A04C	_CompactMem	[I:3.3.2]
$A04D	_PurgeMem	[I:3.3.3]
*$A050	_RelString	[I:2.1.2]
*$A054	_UprString	[I:2.1.2]
*$A061	_MaxBlock	[I:3.3.1]
*$A162	_PurgeSpace	[I:3.3.1]
*$A063	_MaxApplZone	[I:3.3.4]
*$A064	_MoveHHi	[I:3.2.5]
*$A065	_StackSpace	[I:3.3.4]
*$A166	_NewEmptyHandle	[I:3.2.1]
*$A067	_HSetRBit	[I:3.2.4]
*$A068	_HClrRBit	[I:3.2.4]
*$A069	_HGetState	[I:3.2.4]
*$A06A	_HSetState	[I:3.2.4]
*$A80D	_Count1Resources	[I:6.3.3]
*$A80E	_Get1IxResource	[I:6.3.3]
*$A80F	_Get1IxType	[I:6.3.3]
*$A810	_Unique1ID	[I:6.5.3]
*$A811	_TESelView	[II:5.3.3]
*$A812	_TEPinScroll	[II:5.3.3]
*$A813	_TEAutoView	[II:5.3.3]
*$A816	_Pack8	[I:7.2.1]
*$A817	_CopyMask	[I:5.1.4]
*$A818	_FixATan2	[I:2.3.6]
*$A81C	_Count1Types	[I:6.3.3]
*$A81F	_Get1Resource	[I:6.3.1]
*$A820	_Get1NamedResource	[I:6.3.1]
*$A821	_MaxSizeRsrc	[I:6.4.3]
*$A826	_InsMenuItem	[II:4.3.1]
*$A827	_HideDItem	[II:7.3.3]
*$A828	_ShowDItem	[II:7.3.3]
*$A82B	_Pack9	[I:7.2.1]
*$A82C	_Pack10	[I:7.2.1]
*$A82D	_Pack11	[I:7.2.1]
*$A82E	_Pack12	[I:7.2.1]
*$A82F	_Pack13	[I:7.2.1]
*$A830	_Pack14	[I:7.2.1]

Trap Word	Trap Macro Name	Reference Section
·*$A831	_Pack15	[I:7.2.1]
*$A834	_SetFScaleDisable	[I:8.2.8]
*$A835	_FontMetrics	[I:8.2.6]
*$A837	_MeasureText	[I:8.3.4]
*$A838	_CalcMask	[I:5.1.6]
*$A839	_SeedFill	[I:5.1.6]
*$A83A	_ZoomWindow	[II:3.3.2]
*$A83B	_TrackBox	[II:3.5.4]
*$A83F	_Long2Fix	[I:2.3.1]
*$A840	_Fix2Long	[I:2.3.1]
*$A841	_Fix2Frac	[I:2.3.3]
*$A842	_Frac2Fix	[I:2.3.3]
*$A847	_FracCos	[I:2.3.6]
*$A848	_FracSin	[I:2.3.6]
*$A849	_FracSqrt	[I:2.3.4]
*$A84A	_FracMul	[I:2.3.4]
*$A84B	_FracDiv	[I:2.3.4]
*$A84D	_FixDiv	[I:2.3.2]
$A850	_InitCursor	[II:2.5.2]
$A851	_SetCursor	[II:2.5.2]
$A852	_HideCursor	[II:2.5.3]
$A853	_ShowCursor	[II:2.5.3]
$A854	_UprString	[I:2.1.2]
$A855	_ShieldCursor	[II:2.5.4]
$A856	_ObscureCursor	[II:2.5.4]
$A858	_BitAnd	[I:2.2.2]
$A859	_BitXOr	[I:2.2.2]
$A85A	_BitNot	[I:2.2.2]
$A85B	_BitOr	[I:2.2.2]
$A85C	_BitShift	[I:2.2.2]
$A85D	_BitTst	[I:2.2.1]
$A85E	_BitSet	[I:2.2.1]
$A85F	_BitClr	[I:2.2.1]
$A861	_Random	[I:2.3.5]
$A865	_GetPixel	[I:4.2.3]
$A866	_StuffHex	[I:2.2.4]
$A867	_LongMul	[I:2.3.3]
$A868	_FixMul	[I:2.3.2]
$A869	_FixRatio	[I:2.3.2]

Trap Word	Trap Macro Name	Reference Section
$A86A	_HiWord	[I:2.2.3]
$A86B	_LoWord	[I:2.2.3]
$A86C	_FixRound	[I:2.3.1]
$A86D	_InitPort	[I:4.3.2]
$A86E	_InitGraf	[I:4.3.1]
$A86F	_OpenPort	[I:4.3.2]
$A870	_LocalToGlobal	[I:4.4.2]
$A871	_GlobalToLocal	[I:4.4.2]
$A872	_GrafDevice	[I:8.3.2]
$A873	_SetPort	[I:4.3.3]
$A874	_GetPort	[I:4.3.3]
$A875	_SetPBits	[I:4.3.4]
$A876	_PortSize	[I:4.3.5]
$A877	_MovePortTo	[I:4.3.5]
$A878	_SetOrigin	[I:4.3.4]
$A879	_SetClip	[I:4.3.6]
$A87A	_GetClip	[I:4.3.6]
$A87B	_ClipRect	[I:4.3.6]
$A87C	_BackPat	[I:5.1.1]
$A87D	_ClosePort	[I:4.3.2]
$A87E	_AddPt	[I:4.4.1]
$A87F	_SubPt	[I:4.4.1]
$A880	_SetPt	[I:4.1.1]
$A881	_EqualPt	[I:4.4.1]
$A882	_StdText	[III:2.1.5]
$A883	_DrawChar	[I:8.3.3]
$A884	_DrawString	[I:8.3.3]
$A885	_DrawText	[I:8.3.3]
$A886	_TextWidth	[I:8.3.4]
$A887	_TextFont	[I:8.3.2]
$A888	_TextFace	[I:8.3.2]
$A889	_TextMode	[I:8.3.2]
$A88A	_TextSize	[I:8.3.2]
$A88B	_GetFontInfo	[I:8.2.6]
$A88C	_StringWidth	[I:8.3.4]
$A88D	_CharWidth	[I:8.3.4]
$A88E	_SpaceExtra	[I:8.3.2]
$A890	_StdLine	[III:2.1.3]
$A891	_LineTo	[I:5.2.4]

Trap Word	Trap Macro Name	Reference Section
$A892	_Line	[I:5.2.4]
$A893	_MoveTo	[I:5.2.4]
$A894	_Move	[I:5.2.4]
$A896	_HidePen	[I:5.2.3]
$A897	_ShowPen	[I:5.2.3]
$A898	_GetPenState	[I:5.2.1]
$A899	_SetPenState	[I:5.2.1]
$A89A	_GetPen	[I:5.2.4]
$A89B	_PenSize	[I:5.2.2]
$A89C	_PenMode	[I:5.2.2]
$A89D	_PenPat	[I:5.2.2]
$A89E	_PenNormal	[I:5.2.2]
$A8A0	_StdRect	[III:2.1.4]
$A8A1	_FrameRect	[I:5.3.2]
$A8A2	_PaintRect	[I:5.3.2]
$A8A3	_EraseRect	[I:5.3.2]
$A8A4	_InverRect	[I:5.3.2]
$A8A5	_FillRect	[I:5.3.2]
$A8A6	_EqualRect	[I:4.4.5]
$A8A7	_SetRect	[I:4.1.2]
$A8A8	_OffsetRect	[I:4.4.4]
$A8A9	_InsetRect	[I:4.4.4]
$A8AA	_SectRect	[I:4.4.5]
$A8AB	_UnionRect	[I:4.4.5]
$A8AC	_Pt2Rect	[I:4.1.2]
$A8AD	_PtInRect	[I:4.4.3]
$A8AE	_EmptyRect	[I:4.4.4]
$A8AF	_StdRRect	[III:2.1.4]
$A8B0	_FrameRoundRect	[I:5.3.3]
$A8B1	_PaintRoundRect	[I:5.3.3]
$A8B2	_EraseRoundRect	[I:5.3.3]
$A8B3	_InverRoundRect	[I:5.3.3]
$A8B4	_FillRoundRect	[I:5.3.3]
$A8B6	_StdOval	[III:2.1.4]
$A8B7	_FrameOval	[I:5.3.4]
$A8B8	_PaintOval	[I:5.3.4]
$A8B9	_EraseOval	[I:5.3.4]
$A8BA	_InvertOval	[I:5.3.4]
$A8BB	_FillOval	[I:5.3.4]

Trap Word	Trap Macro Name	Reference Section
$A8BD	_StdArc	[III:2.1.4]
$A8BE	_FrameArc	[I:5.3.5]
$A8BF	_PaintArc	[I:5.3.5]
$A8C0	_EraseArc	[I:5.3.5]
$A8C1	_InvertArc	[I:5.3.5]
$A8C2	_FillArc	[I:5.3.5]
$A8C3	_PtToAngle	[I:5.3.5]
$A8C5	_StdPoly	[III:2.1.4]
$A8C6	_FramePoly	[I:5.3.6]
$A8C7	_PaintPoly	[I:5.3.6]
$A8C8	_ErasePoly	[I:5.3.6]
$A8C9	_InvertPoly	[I:5.3.6]
$A8CA	_FillPoly	[I:5.3.6]
$A8CB	_OpenPoly	[I:4.1.4]
$A8CC	_ClosePgon	[I:4.1.4]
$A8CD	_KillPoly	[I:4.1.4]
$A8CE	_OffsetPoly	[I:4.4.6]
$A8D1	_StdRgn	[III:2.1.4]
$A8D2	_FrameRgn	[I:5.3.7]
$A8D3	_PaintRgn	[I:5.3.7]
$A8D4	_EraseRgn	[I:5.3.7]
$A8D5	_InverRgn	[I:5.3.7]
$A8D6	_FillRgn	[I:5.3.7]
$A8D8	_NewRgn	[I:4.1.6]
$A8D9	_DisposRgn	[I:4.1.6]
$A8DA	_OpenRgn	[I:4.1.6]
$A8DB	_CloseRgn	[I:4.1.6]
$A8DC	_CopyRgn	[I:4.1.7]
$A8DD	_SetEmptyRgn	[I:4.1.7]
$A8DE	_SetRecRgn	[I:4.1.7]
$A8DF	_RectRgn	[I:4.1.7]
$A8E0	_OfsetRgn	[I:4.4.7]
$A8E1	_InsetRgn	[I:4.4.7]
$A8E2	_EmptyRgn	[I:4.4.7]
$A8E3	_EqualRgn	[I:4.4.8]
$A8E4	_SectRgn	[I:4.4.8]
$A8E5	_UnionRgn	[I:4.4.8]
$A8E6	_DiffRgn	[I:4.4.8]

Trap Word		Trap Macro Name	Reference Section
$A8E7		_XOrRgn	[I:4.4.8]
$A8E8		_PtInRgn	[I:4.4.3]
$A8E9		_RectInRgn	[I:4.4.3]
$A8EA		_SetStdProcs	[III:2.1.1]
$A8EB		_StdBits	[III:2.1.2]
$A8EC		_CopyBits	[I:5.1.2]
$A8ED		_StdTxMeas	[III:2.1.5]
$A8EE		_StdGetPic	[III:2.1.6]
$A8EF		_ScrollRect	[I:5.1.5]
$A8F0		_StdPutPic	[III:2.1.6]
$A8F1		_StdComment	[III:2.1.7]
$A8F2		_PicComment	[III:2.1.7]
$A8F3		_OpenPicture	[I:5.4.2]
$A8F4		_ClosePicture	[I:5.4.2]
$A8F5		_KillPicture	[I:5.4.2]
$A8F6		_DrawPicture	[I:5.4.3]
$A8F8		_ScalePt	[I:4.4.9]
$A8F9		_MapPt	[I:4.4.9]
$A8FA		_MapRect	[I:4.4.9]
$A8FB		_MapRgn	[I:4.4.9]
$A8FC		_MapPoly	[I:4.4.9]
*$A8FD		_PrGlue	[III:4.2–4.5]
*$A8FD	($04000C00)	_PrOpenDoc	[III:4.3.1]
*$A8FD	($08000484)	_PrClosDoc	[III:4.3.1]
*$A8FD	($10000808)	_PrOpenPage	[III:4.3.2]
*$A8FD	($1800040C)	_PrClosPage	[III:4.3.2]
*$A8FD	($20040480)	_PrintDefault	[III:4.2.2]
*$A8FD	($2A040484)	_PrStlDialog	[III:4.2.3]
*$A8FD	($32040488)	_PrJobDialog	[III:4.2.3]
*$A8FD	($3C04040C)	_PrStlInit	[III:4.5.1]
*$A8FD	($44040410)	_PrJobInit	[III:4.5.1]
*$A8FD	($4A040894)	_PrDlgMain	[III:4.5.1]
*$A8FD	($52040498)	_PrValidate	[III:4.2.2]
*$A8FD	($5804089C)	_PrJobMerge	[III:4.2.3]
*$A8FD	($60051480)	_PrPicFile	[III:4.3.3]
*$A8FD	($80000000)	_PrDrvrOpen	[III:4.4.1]
*$A8FD	($88000000)	_PrDrvrClose	[III:4.4.1]
*$A8FD	($94000000)	_PrDrvrDCE	[III:4.4.2]
*$A8FD	($9A000000)	_PrDrvrVers	[III:4.4.2]
*$A8FD	($A0000E00)	_PrCtlCall	[III:4.4.3]

Trap Word	Trap Macro Name	Reference Section
*$A8FD ($A8000000)	_PrPurge	[III:4.4.2]
*$A8FD ($B0000000)	_PrNoPurge	[III:4.4.2]
*$A8FD ($BA000000)	_PrError	[III:4.2.4]
*$A8FD ($C0000200)	_PrSetError	[III:4.2.4]
*$A8FD ($C8000000)	_PrOpen	[III:4.2.1]
*$A8FD ($D0000000)	_PrClose	[III:4.2.1]
$A8FE	_InitFonts	[I:8.2.4]
$A8FF	_GetFName	[I:8.2.5]
$A900	_GetFNum	[I:8.2.5]
$A902	_RealFont	[I:8.2.5]
$A903	_SetFontLock	[I:8.2.7]
$A904	_DrawGrowIcon	[II:3.3.4]
$A906	_NewString	[I:8.1.2]
$A907	_SetString	[I:8.1.2]
$A908	_ShowHide	[II:3.3.1]
$A910	_GetWMgrPort	[II:3.6.1]
$A912	_InitWindows	[II:3.2.1]
$A913	_NewWindow	[II:3.2.2]
$A914	_DisposWindow	[II:3.2.3]
$A915	_ShowWindow	[II:3.3.1]
$A916	_HideWindow	[II:3.3.1]
$A917	_GetWRefCon	[II:3.2.4]
$A918	_SetWRefCon	[II:3.2.4]
$A919	_GetWTitle	[II:3.2.4]
$A91A	_SetWTitle	[II:3.2.4]
$A91B	_MoveWindow	[II:3.3.2]
$A91C	_HiliteWindow	[II:3.3.4]
$A91D	_SizeWindow	[II:3.3.2]
$A91E	_TrackGoAway	[II:3.5.4]
$A91F	_SelectWindow	[II:3.5.2]
$A920	_BringToFront	[II:3.3.3]
$A921	_SendBehind	[II:3.3.3]
$A922	_BeginUpdate	[II:3.4.1]
$A923	_EndUpdate	[II:3.4.1]
$A924	_FrontWindow	[II:3.3.3]
$A925	_DragWindow	[II:3.5.4]
$A927	_InvalRgn	[II:3.4.2]
$A928	_InvalRect	[II:3.4.2]
$A929	_ValidRgn	[II:3.4.2]

Trap Word	Trap Macro Name	Reference Section
$A92A	_ValidRect	[II:3.4.2]
$A92B	_GrowWindow	[II:3.5.4]
$A92C	_FindWindow	[II:3.5.1]
$A92D	_CloseWindow	[II:3.2.3]
$A92E	_SetWindowPic	[II:3.4.3]
$A92F	_GetWindowPic	[II:3.4.3]
$A930	_InitMenus	[II:4.2.1]
$A931	_NewMenu	[II:4.2.2]
$A932	_DisposMenu	[II:4.2.3]
$A933	_AppendMenu	[II:4.3.1]
$A934	_ClearMenuBar	[II:4.4.1]
$A935	_InsertMenu	[II:4.4.1]
$A936	_DeleteMenu	[II:4.4.1]
$A937	_DrawMenuBar	[II:4.4.3]
$A938	_HiliteMenu	[II:4.5.4]
$A939	_EnableItem	[II:4.6.2]
$A93A	_DisableItem	[II:4.6.2]
$A93B	_GetMenuBar	[II:4.4.4]
$A93C	_SetMenuBar	[II:4.4.4]
$A93D	_MenuSelect	[II:4.5.1]
$A93E	_MenuKey	[II:4.5.1]
$A93F	_GetItmIcon	[II:4.6.5]
$A940	_SetItmIcon	[II:4.6.5]
$A941	_GetItmStyle	[II:4.6.3]
$A942	_SetItmStyle	[II:4.6.3]
$A943	_GetItmMark	[II:4.6.4]
$A944	_SetItmMark	[II:4.6.4]
$A945	_CheckItem	[II:4.6.4]
$A946	_GetItem	[II:4.6.1]
$A947	_SetItem	[II:4.6.1]
$A948	_CalcMenuSize	[II:4.7.1]
$A949	_GetMHandle	[II:4.4.5]
$A94A	_SetMFlash	[II:4.7.2]
$A94C	_FlashMenuBar	[II:4.7.2]
$A94D	_AddResMenu	[II:4.3.3]
$A94E	_PinRect	[I:4.4.3]
$A94F	_DeltaPoint	[I:4.4.1]
$A950	_CountMItems	[II:4.3.4]
$A951	_InsertResMenu	[II:4.3.3]

Trap Word	Trap Macro Name	Reference Section
*$A952	_DelMenuItem	[II:4.3.4]
*$A953	_UpdtControls	[II:6.3.1]
$A954	_NewControl	[II:6.2.1]
$A955	_DisposControl	[II:6.2.2]
$A956	_KillControls	[II:6.2.2]
$A957	_ShowControl	[II:6.3.1]
$A958	_HideControl	[II:6.3.1]
$A959	_MoveControl	[II:6.3.2]
$A95A	_GetCRefCon	[II:6.2.3]
$A95B	_SetCRefCon	[II:6.2.3]
$A95C	_SizeControl	[II:6.3.2]
$A95D	_HiliteControl	[II:6.3.3]
$A95E	_GetCTitle	[II:6.2.3]
$A95F	_SetCTitle	[II:6.2.3]
$A960	_GetCtlValue	[II:6.2.4]
$A961	_GetMinCtl	[II:6.2.4]
$A962	_GetMaxCtl	[II:6.2.4]
$A963	_SetCtlValue	[II:6.2.4]
$A964	_SetMinCtl	[II:6.2.4]
$A965	_SetMaxCtl	[II:6.2.4]
$A966	_TestControl	[II:6.4.1]
$A967	_DragControl	[II:6.4.3]
$A968	_TrackControl	[II:6.4.2]
$A969	_DrawControls	[II:6.3.1]
$A96A	_GetCtlAction	[II:6.4.2]
$A96B	_SetCtlAction	[II:6.4.2]
$A96C	_FindControl	[II:6.4.1]
$A96E	_Dequeue	[III:3.1.7]
$A96F	_Enqueue	[III:3.1.7]
$A970	_GetNextEvent	[II:2.2.1]
$A971	_EventAvail	[II:2.2.1]
$A972	_GetMouse	[II:2.4.1]
$A973	_StillDown	[II:2.4.2]
$A974	_Button	[II:2.4.2]
$A975	_TickCount	[II:2.7.1]
$A976	_GetKeys	[II:2.6.1]
$A977	_WaitMouseUp	[II:2.4.2]
*$A978	_UpdtDialog	[II:7.4.1]
$A979	_CouldDialog	[II:7.5.3]

Trap Word	Trap Macro Name	Reference Section
$A97A	_FreeDialog	[II:7.5.3]
$A97B	_InitDialogs	[II:7.2.1]
$A97C	_GetNewDialog	[II:7.2.2]
$A97D	_NewDialog	[II:7.2.2]
$A97E	_SelIText	[II:7.3.2]
$A97F	_IsDialogEvent	[II:7.4.4]
$A980	_DialogSelect	[II:7.4.4]
$A981	_DrawDialog	[II:7.4.1]
$A982	_CloseDialog	[II:7.2.3]
$A983	_DisposDialog	[II:7.2.3]
*$A984	_FindDItem	[II:7.3.4]
$A985	_Alert	[II:7.4.2]
$A986	_StopAlert	[II:7.4.2]
$A987	_NoteAlert	[II:7.4.2]
$A988	_CautionAlert	[II:7.4.2]
$A989	_CouldAlert	[II:7.5.3]
$A98A	_FreeAlert	[II:7.5.3]
$A98B	_ParamText	[II:7.4.6]
$A98C	_ErrorSound	[II:7.5.1]
$A98D	_GetDItem	[II:7.3.1]
$A98E	_SetDItem	[II:7.3.1]
$A98F	_SetIText	[II:7.3.2]
$A990	_GetIText	[II:7.3.2]
$A991	_ModalDialog	[II:7.4.3]
$A992	_DetachResource	[I:6.3.2]
$A993	_SetResPurge	[I:6.5.5]
$A994	_CurResFile	[I:6.2.2]
$A997	_OpenResFile	[I:6.2.1]
$A998	_UseResFile	[I:6.2.2]
$A999	_UpdateResFile	[I:6.5.4]
$A99A	_CloseResFile	[I:6.2.1]
$A99C	_CountResources	[I:6.3.3]
$A99D	_GetIndResource	[I:6.3.3]
$A99E	_CountTypes	[I:6.3.3]
$A99F	_GetIndType	[I:6.3.3]
$A9A0	_GetResource	[I:6.3.1]
$A9A1	_GetNamedResource	[I:6.3.1]
$A9A3	_ReleaseResource	[I:6.3.2]
$A9A4	_HomeResFile	[I:6.4.3]

Trap Word	Trap Macro Name	Reference Section
$A9A5	_SizeRsrc	[I:6.4.3]
$A9A6	_GetResAttrs	[I:6.4.2]
$A9A7	_SetResAttrs	[I:6.4.2]
$A9A8	_GetResInfo	[I:6.4.1]
$A9A9	_SetResInfo	[I:6.4.1]
$A9AA	_ChangedResource	[I:6.5.2]
$A9AB	_AddResource	[I:6.5.3]
$A9AD	_RmveResource	[I:6.5.3]
$A9AF	_ResError	[I:6.6.1]
$A9B0	_WriteResource	[I:6.5.4]
$A9B1	_CreateResFile	[I:6.5.1]
$A9B2	_SystemEvent	[III:6.2.2]
$A9B3	_SystemClick	[II:3.5.3, III:6.2.2]
$A9B4	_SystemTask	[II:2.7.2, III:6.2.4]
$A9B5	_SystemMenu	[III:6.2.3]
$A9B6	_OpenDeskAcc	[II:4.5.2, III:6.2.1]
$A9B7	_CloseDeskAcc	[II:4.5.2, III:6.2.1]
$A9B8	_GetPattern	[I:5.1.1]
$A9B9	_GetCursor	[II:2.5.2]
$A9BA	_GetString	[I:8.1.2]
$A9BC	_GetPicture	[I:5.4.2]
$A9BD	_GetNewWindow	[II:3.2.2]
$A9BE	_GetNewControl	[II:6.2.1]
$A9BF	_GetRMenu	[II:4.2.2]
$A9C0	_GetNewMBar	[II:4.4.2]
$A9C1	_UniqueID	[I:6.5.3]
$A9C2	_SysEdit	[II:4.5.3, III:6.2.3]
$A9C6	_Secs2Date	[I:2.4.3]
$A9C7	_Date2Secs	[I:2.4.3]
$A9C8	_SysBeep	[II:2.8.1]
$A9CB	_TEGetText	[II:5.2.3]
$A9CC	_TEInit	[II:5.2.1]
$A9CD	_TEDispose	[II:5.2.2]
$A9CE	_TextBox	[II:5.3.2]
$A9CF	_TESetText	[II:5.2.3]
$A9D0	_TECalText	[II:5.3.1]
$A9D1	_TESetSelect	[II:5.4.2]
$A9D2	_TENew	[II:5.2.2]
$A9D3	_TEUpdate	[II:5.3.2]

Trap Word		Trap Macro Name	Reference Section
$A9D4		_TEClick	[II:5.4.1]
$A9D5		_TECopy	[II:5.5.2]
$A9D6		_TECut	[II:5.5.2]
$A9D7		_TEDelete	[II:5.5.3]
$A9D8		_TEActivate	[II:5.4.3]
$A9D9		_TEDeactivate	[II:5.4.3]
$A9DA		_TEIdle	[II:5.4.3]
$A9DB		_TEPaste	[II:5.5.2]
$A9DC		_TEKey	[II:5.5.1]
$A9DD		_TEScroll	[II:5.3.3]
$A9DE		_TEInsert	[II:5.5.3]
$A9DF		_TESetJust	[II:5.3.1]
$A9E0		_Munger	[II:5.5.6]
$A9E1		_HandToHand	[I:3.2.5]
$A9E2		_PtrToXHand	[I:3.2.5]
$A9E3		_PtrToHand	[I:3.2.5]
$A9E4		_HandAndHand	[I:3.2.6]
$A9E5		_InitPack	[I:7.2.2]
$A9E6		_InitAllPacks	[I:7.2.2]
$A9E7		_Pack0	[I:7.2.1]
$A9E8		_Pack1	[I:7.2.1]
$A9E9		_Pack2	[I:7.2.1]
$A9E9	(0)	_DIBadMount	[II:8.4.1]
$A9E9	(2)	_DILoad	[II:8.4.3]
$A9E9	(4)	_DIUnload	[II:8.4.3]
$A9E9	(6)	_DIFormat	[II:8.4.2]
$A9E9	(8)	_DIVerify	[II:8.4.2]
$A9E9	(10)	_DIZero	[II:8.4.2]
$A9EA		_Pack3	[I:7.2.1]
$A9EA	(1)	_SFPutFile	[II:8.3.3]
$A9EA	(2)	_SFGetFile	[II:8.3.2]
$A9EB		_Pack4	[I:7.2.1]
$A9EC		_Pack5	[I:7.2.1]
$A9ED		_Pack6	[I:7.2.1]
$A9ED	(0)	_IUDateString	[I:2.4.4]
$A9ED	(2)	_IUTimeString	[I:2.4.4]
$A9EE		_Pack7	[I:7.2.1]
$A9EE	(0)	_NumToString	[I:2.3.4]
$A9EE	(1)	_StringToNum	[I:2.3.4]

Trap Word	Trap Macro Name	Reference Section
$A9EF	_PtrAndHand	[I:3.2.6]
$A9F0	_LoadSeg	[I:7.1.2]
$A9F1	_UnloadSeg	[I:7.1.2]
$A9F2	_Launch	[I:7.1.1]
$A9F3	_Chain	[I:7.1.1]
$A9F4	_ExitToShell	[I:7.1.3]
$A9F5	_GetAppParms	[I:7.3.4]
$A9F6	_GetResFileAttrs	[I:6.6.2]
$A9F7	_SetResFileAttrs	[I:6.6.2]
$A9F9	_InfoScrap	[I:7.4.2]
$A9FA	_UnlodeScrap	[I:7.4.4]
$A9FB	_LodeScrap	[I:7.4.4]
$A9FC	_ZeroScrap	[I:7.4.3]
$A9FD	_GetScrap	[I:7.4.3]
$A9FE	_PutScrap	[I:7.4.3]

Summary of Assembly-Language Variables

System Globals

Listed below are all assembly-language global variables covered in the three volumes of this book, together with their hexadecimal addresses. *Warning:* The addresses given may be subject to change in future versions of the Toolbox; always refer to these variables by name instead of using the addresses directly. Variables marked with an asterisk (*) are not available under the original 64K ROM.

Variable Name	Address	Reference Section	Meaning
ACount	$A9A	[II:7.5.2]	Stage of last alert minus 1
ANumber	$A98	[II:7.5.2]	Resource ID of last alert
ApFontID	$984	[I:8.2.1]	True font number of current application font
ApplLimit	$130	[I:3.3.4]	Application heap limit
ApplZone	$2AA	[I:3.1.3]	Pointer to start of application heap
AppParmHandle	$AEC	[I:7.3.4]	Handle to Finder startup information
BufPtr	$10C	[I:3.1.3]	Pointer to end of application global space

Variable Name	Address	Reference Section	Meaning
CaretTime	$2F4	[II:5.4.3]	Current blink interval in ticks
CurActivate	$A64	[II:3.4.3]	Pointer to window awaiting activate event
CurApName	$910	[I:7.3.4]	Name of current application (maximum 31 characters)
CurApRefNum	$900	[I:6.2.2, I:7.3.4]	Reference number of application resource file
CurDeactivate	$A68	[II:3.4.3]	Pointer to window awaiting deactivate event
CurMap	$A5A	[I:6.2.2]	Reference number of current resource file
CurPageOption	$936	[I:7.1.1]	Integer specifying screen and sound buffers
CurPitch	$280	[III:5.1.2]	Count value for current square-wave tone
CurrentA5	$904	[I:3.1.3]	Base pointer for application globals
CurStackBase	$908	[I:3.1.3]	Pointer to base of stack
DABeeper	$A9C	[II:7.5.1]	Pointer to current sound procedure
DAStrings	$AA0	[II:7.4.6]	Handles to four text substitution strings
DeskPattern	$A3C	[I:5.1.2]	Screen background pattern
DlgFont	$AFA	[II:7.5.1]	Current font number for dialogs and alerts
DoubleTime	$2F0	[II:5.4.1]	Current double-click interval in ticks
FinderName	$2E0	[I:7.1.3]	Name of program to exit to (maximum 15 characters)
*FractEnable	$BF4	[I:8.2.8]	Use fractional character widths? (1 byte)
FScaleDisable	$A63	[I:8.2.8]	Turn off font scaling? (1 byte)
GrayRgn	$9EE	[II:3.6.1]	Handle to region defining gray desktop
HeapEnd	$114	[I:3.1.3]	Pointer to end of application heap
Key1Trans	$29E	[I:8.4.4]	Pointer to keyboard configuration routine
Key2Trans	$2A2	[I:8.4.4]	Pointer to keypad configuration routine
KeyMap	$174	[II:2.6.1]	System keyboard map

Variable Name	Address	Reference Section	Meaning
KeypadMap	$17C	[II:2.6.1]	System keypad map
Lo3Bytes	$31A	[I:3.2.4]	Mask for extracting address from a master pointer
*MBarHeight	$BAA	[II:4.4.3]	Height of menu bar in pixels
MBState	$172	[II:2.4.2]	State of mouse button
MemTop	$108	[I:3.1.3]	Pointer to end of physical memory
MenuFlash	$A24	[II:4.7.2]	Current flash count for menu items
MenuList	$A1C	[II:4.4.4]	Handle to current menu bar
PrintErr	$944	[III:4.2.4]	Result code from last printing operation
ResErr	$A60	[I:6.6.1]	Result code from last resource-related call
ResLoad	$A5E	[I:6.3.4]	Load resources automatically?
ResumeProc	$A8C	[II:7.2.1]	Pointer to restart procedure
ROMBase	$2AE	[I:3.1.3]	Pointer to start of ROM
ROMFont0	$980	[I:8.2.1]	Handle to system font
*ROMMapInsert	$B9E	[I:6.6.3]	Include ROM-based resources in search? (1 byte)
ScrapCount	$968	[I:7.4.2]	Current scrap count
ScrapHandle	$964	[I:7.4.2]	Handle to contents of desk scrap
ScrapName	$96C	[I:7.4.2]	Pointer to scrap file name
ScrapSize	$960	[I:7.4.2]	Current size of desk scrap
ScrapState	$96A	[I:7.4.2]	Current state of desk scrap
ScrDmpEnb	$2F8	[III:6.3.1]	Intercept Command-Shift keystrokes? (1 byte)
ScrnBase	$824	[I:3.1.3]	Pointer to start of screen buffer
SdEnable	$261	[III:5.1.1]	Sound generator currently enabled? (1 byte)
SdVolume	$260	[III:5.2.2]	Current speaker volume (1 byte)
SEvtEnb	$15C	[III:6.2.2]	Intercept system events? (1 byte)
SoundActive	$27E	[III:5.1.1]	Sound generator currently active? (1 byte)
SoundBase	$266	[I:3.1.3, III:5.1.1]	Pointer to start of sound buffer
SoundDCE	$27A	[III:5.1.1]	Pointer to sound driver's device control entry [3.1.4]
SoundPtr	$262	[III:5.1.3]	Pointer to current four-tone sound record

Variable Name	Address	Reference Section	Meaning
SPFont	$204	[I:8.2.1]	True font number of default application font
SysEvtMask	$144	[II:2.3.2]	System event mask
SysMap	$A58	[I:6.2.2]	True reference number (not 0) of system resource file
SysMapHndl	$A54	[I:6.2.2]	Handle to resource map of system resource file
SysResName	$AD8	[I:6.2.2]	Name of system resource file (string, maximum 19 characters)
SysZone	$2A6	[I:3.1.3]	Pointer to start of system heap
TEScrpHandle	$AB4	[II:5.5.4]	Handle to text scrap
TEScrpLength	$AB0	[II:5.5.4]	Length of text scrap in characters
TEWdBreak	$AF6	[II:5.6.2]	Pointer to built-in word-break routine
TheCrsr	$844	[II:2.5.2]	Current cursor record
TheMenu	$A26	[II:4.5.4]	Menu ID of currently highlighted menu
Ticks	$16A	[II:2.7.1]	System clock
Time	$20C	[I:2.4.1]	Current date and time in "raw" seconds
*TmpResLoad	$B9F	[I:6.6.3]	Load resources automatically just this once? (1 byte)
TopMapHndl	$A50	[I:6.2.2]	Handle to resource map of most recently opened (not necessarily current) resource file
UnitNtryCnt	$1D2	[III:3.1.3]	Number of entries in unit table
UTableBase	$11C	[III:3.1.3]	Pointer to start of unit table
*WidthTabHandle	$B2A	[I:8.2.6]	Handle to global width table for current font
WindowList	$9D6	[II:3.1.1]	Pointer to first window in window list
WMgrPort	$9DE	[II:3.6.1]	Pointer to Window Manager port

QuickDraw Globals

The QuickDraw global variables listed below are located at the given offsets relative to the QuickDraw globals pointer, which in turn is pointed to by address register A5.

Variable Name	Offset Bytes	Reference Section	Meaning
ThePort	0	[I:4.3.3]	Current graphics port
White	-8	[I:5.1.2]	Standard white pattern
Black	-16	[I:5.1.2]	Standard black pattern
Gray	-24	[I:5.1.2]	Standard gray pattern
LtGray	-32	[I:5.1.2]	Standard light gray pattern
DkGray	-40	[I:5.1.2]	Standard dark gray pattern
Arrow	-108	[II:2.5.2]	Standard arrow cursor
ScreenBits	-122	[I:4.2.1]	Screen bit map
RandSeed	-126	[I:2.3.8]	"Seed" for random number generation

Example Program Source Listings

Following are complete listings of the source code for the example programs developed in this volume. All of the programs listed here are available on a mail-order disk directly from the author; see the order form on the last page of this volume.

SideWindow **Window Definition Function**

SideWindow is a window definition function for a window with its title bar at the left side instead of the top. See Chapter 2 for a complete discussion.

```
function SideWindow (VarCode : INTEGER; TheWindow : WindowPtr;
                MsgCode : INTEGER; MsgParam  : LONGINT)
                    : LONGINT;

{ Window definition function for a window with its title bar at the  left side instead of the top [Prog. III:2-1].  }

uses
   MemTypes,                            {Elementary data types}
   QuickDraw,                           {QuickDraw graphics routines}
   OSIntf,                              {Macintosh Operating System}
   ToolIntf,                            {User Interface Toolbox}
   PackIntf;                            {Standard packages}
```

421

```
{ - - - - - - - - - - - - - - - - - - - - - - - - - - - - - - - - - - - - - - - - - - - - - - - - - - - - }

{ Global Declarations }

  const

    MacPlusRom  = $75;                          {ROM version number for Macintosh Plus}

    ZoomMask    = $0008;                        {Mask for extracting zoom bit from variation code}
    NoGrowMask  = $0004;                        {Mask for extracting no-grow bit from variation code}

    MenuBarHeight = 20;                          {Height of menu bar in pixels}
    ScreenMargin  = 2;                           {Margin around zoomed-out windows, in pixels}

    FrameWidth  = 1;                             {Thickness of window frame in pixels}
    ShadowExtra = 1;                             {Extra thickness for window's drop shadow}

    TitleBarWidth = 19;                          {Width of title bar in pixels}
    HighlightGap  = 1;                           {Width of gap surrounding highlight lines, in pixels}
    MinHighlight  = 6;                           {Minimum height of highlight lines, in pixels}

    BoxSize       = 11;                          {Size of close and zoom boxes in pixels}
    SmallZoomSize = 7;                           {Size of inner zoom box in pixels}

    SizeBoxSize      = 16;                       {Size of size box in pixels}
    GIconSmallOffset = 3;                        {Offset to origin of small square in grow icon}
    GIconSmallSize   = 7;                        {Size of small square in grow icon}
    GIconBigOffset   = 5;                        {Offset to origin of large square in grow icon}
    GIconBigSize     = 9;                        {Size of large square in grow icon}

  type

    DRHandle    = ^DRPtr;
    DRPtr       = ^DataRecord;
    DataRecord  = record

                    UserState : Rect;           {Zoomed-in position in global coordinates [II:3.3.2]}
                    StdState  : Rect;           {Zoomed-out position in global coordinates [II:3.3.2]}

                    TitleBar  : Rect;           {Title bar in global coordinates}
                    CloseBox  : Rect;           {Close box in global coordinates}
                    ZoomBox   : Rect;           {Outer zoom box in global coordinates}
```

```
            SmallZoom : Rect;              {Inner zoom box in global coordinates}
            SizeBox   : Rect;              {Size box in global coordinates}

            HOffset    : INTEGER;          {Horizontal offset to close and zoom boxes, in pixels}
            VOffset    : INTEGER;          {Vertical offset to close and zoom boxes, in pixels}
            TitleRect  : Rect             {Rectangle enclosing title, in global coordinates}


      end; {DataRecord}


  var


     Peek   : WindowPeek;                  {Pointer for "peeking" into window's fields [II:3.1.1]}
     Result : LONGINT;                     {Function result}
```

{- -}

{ Forward Declarations }

```
procedure DoNew; forward;
     { Initialize window. }
   procedure SetUpZoomRects (theData : DRHandle); forward;
        { Initialize zoom rectangles. }
procedure DoCalcRgns; forward;
     { Calculate window's regions. }
   procedure CalcContRgn (theData : DRHandle); forward;
        { Calculate content region. }
   procedure CalcStrucRgn; forward;
        { Calculate structure region. }
   procedure CalcBoxes (theData : DRHandle); forward;
        { Calculate title bar, close, zoom, and size boxes. }
      procedure CalcTitleBar (theData : DRHandle); forward;
           { Calculate title bar. }
      procedure CalcCloseBox (theData : DRHandle); forward;
           { Calculate close box. }
      procedure CalcZoomBox (theData : DRHandle); forward;
           { Calculate zoom box. }
      procedure CalcSizeBox (theData : DRHandle); forward;
           { Calculate size box. }
procedure DoDraw; forward;
     { Draw window on screen. }
   procedure DrawWindow (theData : DRHandle); forward;
        { Draw window on screen. }
```

```
    procedure DrawFrame; forward;
        { Draw window's frame. }
    procedure DrawTitleBar (theData: DRHandle); forward;
        { Draw title bar. }
      procedure DrawCloseBox (theData: DRHandle); forward;
          { Draw close box. }
      procedure DrawZoomBox (theData: DRHandle); forward;
          { Draw zoom box. }
      procedure DrawTitle (theData: DRHandle); forward;
          { Draw window's title. }
  procedure ToggleCloseBox (theData : DRHandle); forward;
      { Toggle close box. }
  procedure ToggleZoomBox (theData : DRHandle); forward;
      { Toggle zoom box. }
    procedure ToggleBox (theBox : Rect; maskString : Str255); forward;
        { Toggle close or zoom box. }
procedure DoDrawGIcon; forward;
    { Draw grow icon. }
  procedure DrawSizeBox (boxTop : INTEGER; boxLeft : INTEGER); forward;
      { Draw size box. }
procedure DoGrow; forward;
    { Draw outline for sizing window. }
procedure DoHit; forward;
    { Locate mouse click. }
procedure DoDispose; forward;
    { Prepare to dispose of window. }
function ZoomedOut : BOOLEAN; forward;
    { Is window in zoomed-out state? }
  function NearPoint (point1 : Point; point2 : Point) : BOOLEAN; forward;
      { Are two points "near" each other? }


{ - - - - - - - - - - - - - - - - - - - - - - - - - - - - - - - - - - - - - - - - - - - - - - - - - - - - - - - - - - - - - - - }


procedure DoNew;

  { Initialize window [Prog. III:2-3]. }


  var
    theData    : DRHandle;        {Handle to definition function's data record}
    zoomBit    : INTEGER;         {Zoom bit from window variation code}
    machineType : INTEGER;        {Type of machine we're running on [I:3.1.3]}
    romVersion : INTEGER;         {Version number of machine's ROM [I:3.1.3]}
```

```
begin {DoNew}

   with Peek^ do
     begin

         dataHandle := NewHandle (SIZEOF(DataRecord));      {Allocate data record [I:3.2.1, II:3.1.1]}

         MoveHHi (dataHandle);                              {Move data record to end of heap [I:3.2.5]}
         HLock   (dataHandle);                              {Lock data record [I:3.2.4]}

           theData := DRHandle(dataHandle);                 {Convert to typed handle}

           zoomBit := BitAnd (VarCode, ZoomMask);           {Extract zoom bit from variation code [I:2.2.2]}
           Environs (romVersion, machineType);              {Find out machine configuration [I:3.1.3]}
           spareFlag := (zoomBit <> 0) and (romVersion >= MacPlusROM);  {Set zoom flag [II:3.1.1]}

           if spareFlag then                                {Zoom box requested and available? [I:3.1.3]}
              SetUpZoomRects (theData);                     {Initialize zoom rectangles}

         HUnlock (dataHandle)                               {Unlock data record [I:3.2.4]}
       end {with Peek^}

   end;  {DoNew}
```

```
{- - - - - - - - - - - - - - - - - - - - - - - - - - - - - - - - - - - - - - - - - - - - - - - - - - - - - - - - - - - - - - - - - - - - - - - - - - -}
```

```
procedure SetUpZoomRects ((theData : DRHandle));

   { Initialize zoom rectangles [Prog. III:2-4]. }

   var
      savePort : GrafPtr;                                   {Pointer to previous current port [I:4.2.2]}
      wmPort   : GrafPtr;                                   {Pointer to Window Manager port [II:3.6.1]}

   begin {SetUpZoomRects}

      with theData^^ do
        begin

            UserState := TheWindow^.portRect;               {Use current size for zoom-in [I:4.2.2, II:3.3.2]}

            GetPort (savePort);                             {Save previous port [I:4.3.3]}
              SetPort (TheWindow);                          {Get into the window's port [I:4.3.3]}
```

```
            with UserState do
               begin
                  LocalToGlobal (topLeft);          {Convert rectangle to global coordinates [I:4.4.2]}
                  LocalToGlobal (botRight)
               end; {with UserState}
            SetPort (savePort);                       {Restore previous port [I:4.3.3]}

            GetWMgrPort (wmPort);                      {Get Window Manager port [II:3.6.1]}
            StdState := wmPort^.portBits.bounds;       {Use full screen for zoom-out [I:4.2.2, II:3.3.2]}
            InsetRect (StdState, ScreenMargin + FrameWidth,  {Inset by screen margin and        }
                                 ScreenMargin + FrameWidth); {  width of window frame [I:4.4.4]  }
            with StdState do
               begin
                  top    := top    + MenuBarHeight;        {Leave room for menu bar at top}
                  left   := left   + (TitleBarWidth - 1);  {Leave room for title bar at left}
                  bottom := bottom - ShadowExtra;          {Leave room for drop shadow}
                  right  := right  - ShadowExtra           {    at bottom and right      }
               end {with StdState}

         end {with theData^^}

   end; {SetUpZoomRects}


{- - - - - - - - - - - - - - - - - - - - - - - - - - - - - - - - - - - - - - - - - - - - - - - - - - - - - - - - - -}


procedure DoCalcRgns;

   { Calculate window's regions [Prog. III:2-6]. }

   var
      theData : DRHandle;                       {Handle to definition function's data record}

   begin {DoCalcRgns}

      with Peek^ do
         begin
            MoveHHi (dataHandle);               {Move data record to end of heap [I:3.2.5]}
            HLock   (dataHandle);               {Lock data record [I:3.2.4]}

            theData := DRHandle(dataHandle);    {Convert to typed handle}

            CalcContRgn (theData);              {Calculate content region}
            CalcStrucRgn;                       {Calculate structure region}
```

```
        CalcBoxes (theData);                    {Calculate title bar, close, zoom, and size boxes}

      HUnlock (dataHandle)                       {Unlock data record [I:3.2.4]}
    end {with Peek^}

  end;  {DoCalcRgns}
```

```
{ - - - - - - - - - - - - - - - - - - - - - - - - - - - - - - - - - - - - - - - - - - - - - - - - - - - - - - - - }
```

```
procedure CalcContRgn {(theData : DRHandle)};

  { Calculate content region. }

  var
    savePort   : GrafPtr;                        {Pointer to previous current port [I:4.2.2]}
    globalRect : Rect;                           {Port rectangle in global coordinates [I:4.1.2]}

  begin {CalcContRgn}

    with TheWindow^, Peek^, theData^^, globalRect do
      begin

        globalRect := portRect;                  {Start with local port rectangle [I:4.2.2]}

        GetPort (savePort);                      {Save previous port [I:4.3.3]}
          SetPort (TheWindow);                   {Get into the window's port [I:4.3.3]}
          LocalToGlobal (topLeft);               {Convert rectangle to global coordinates [I:4.4.2]}
          LocalToGlobal (botRight);
        SetPort (savePort);                      {Restore previous port [I:4.3.3]}

        RectRgn (contRgn, globalRect);           {Set content region [I:4.1.7, II:3.1.1]}

        if not ZoomedOut then                    {Are we in zoomed-out state?}
          UserState := globalRect                {If not, save as zoomed-in state [II:3.3.2]}

      end {with TheWindow^, Peek^, theData^^, globalRect}

  end;  {CalcContRgn}
```

```
{ - - - - - - - - - - - - - - - - - - - - - - - - - - - - - - - - - - - - - - - - - - - - - - - - - - - - - - - - }
```

```
procedure CalcStrucRgn;

  { Calculate structure region. }

  var
    tempRect : Rect;                              {Utility rectangle for building region [I:4.1.2]}
    tempRgn  : RgnHandle;                         {Utility region for adding drop shadow [I:4.1.5]}

  begin {CalcStrucRgn}

    with Peek^, tempRect do
      begin

        tempRect := contRgn^^.rgnBBox;            {Start with content region [II:3.1.1, I:4.1.5]}

        InsetRect (tempRect, -FrameWidth, -FrameWidth);   {Enlarge by width of window frame [I:4.4.4]}
        left := left - (TitleBarWidth - FrameWidth);      {Make room for title bar [I:4.1.2]}
        RectRgn (strucRgn, tempRect);             {Set structure region [I:4.1.7, II:3.1.1]}

        tempRgn := NewRgn;                        {Create utility region [I:4.1.6]}
        OffsetRect (tempRect, ShadowExtra, ShadowExtra);  {Add shadow at right and bottom [I:4.4.4]}
        RectRgn    (tempRgn, tempRect);           {Set it to the rectangle [I:4.1.7]}
        UnionRgn   (strucRgn, tempRgn, strucRgn); {Merge into structure region [I:4.4.8, II:3.1.1]}
        DisposeRgn (tempRgn)                      {Dispose of utility region [I:4.1.6]}

      end  {with Peek^, tempRect}

  end;    {CalcStrucRgn}
```

```
{ - - - - - - - - - - - - - - - - - - - - - - - - - - - - - - - - - - - - - - - - - - - - - - - - - - - - - - - - - - }
```

```
procedure CalcBoxes {(theData : DRHandle)};

  { Calculate title bar, close, zoom, and size boxes. }

  begin {CalcBoxes}

    CalcTitleBar (theData);                       {Calculate title bar}
    CalcCloseBox (theData);                       {Calculate close box}
    CalcZoomBox  (theData);                       {Calculate zoom box}
    CalcSizeBox  (theData)                        {Calculate size box}

  end;    {CalcBoxes}
```

```
{ - - - - - - - - - - - - - - - - - - - - - - - - - - - - - - - - - - - - - - - - - - - - - - - - - - - - - - - - - - }
```

```
procedure CalcTitleBar {(theData : DRHandle)};

  var
    hInset : INTEGER;                              {Horizontal inset for title rectangle}
    vInset : INTEGER;                              {Vertical inset for title rectangle}

  { Calculate title bar. }

  begin {CalcTitleBar}

    with Peek^. theData^^ do
      begin

        with contRgn^^.rgnBBox do                  {Use content region as basis [II:3.1.1, I:4.1.5]}
          SetRect (TitleBar, left - TitleBarWidth,  {Move left by width of title bar [I:4.1.2]}
                             top - FrameWidth,       {Allow for frame at top}
                             left,                   {Title bar's right = content region's left}
                             bottom + FrameWidth);   {Allow for frame at bottom}

        TitleRect := TitleBar;                      {Start with full title bar}
        hInset    := FrameWidth + HighlightGap;     {Leave room for frame and gap}
        vInset    := hInset + MinHighlight;         {Add minimum highlight}
        InsetRect (TitleRect, hInset, vInset);      {Inset the rectangle [I:4.4.4]}

        HOffset := (TitleBarWidth - BoxSize) div 2; {Center boxes horizontally in title bar}
        VOffset := FrameWidth + MinHighlight + (2 * HighlightGap) {Leave room at top and bottom}

      end {with Peek^, theData^^}

  end;  {CalcTitleBar}
{ - - - - - - - - - - - - - - - - - - - - - - - - - - - - - - - - - - - - - - - - - - - - - - - - - - - - - - }

procedure CalcCloseBox {(theData : DRHandle)};

  { Calculate close box. }

  begin {CalcCloseBox}

    with Peek^. theData^^ do
      if goAwayFlag then                            {Is there a close box? [II:3.1.1]}
        begin
          with TitleBar do
            SetRect (CloseBox, left + HOffset,      {Inset from left of title bar [I:4.1.2]}
                              top + VOffset,         {Inset from top of title bar}
```

```
                                        left + (HOffset + BoxSize),        {Add in size of close box}
                                        top  + (VOffset + BoxSize));        {Add in size of close box}
                with TitleRect do
                    top := top + (BoxSize + MinHighlight + 2 * HighlightGap)  {Make room for close box}
                end {then}
            else
                SetRect (CloseBox, 0, 0, 0, 0)                             {Set to empty rectangle [I:4.1.2]}

    end;    {CalcCloseBox}

{ - - - - - - - - - - - - - - - - - - - - - - - - - - - - - - - - - - - - - - - - - - - - - - - - - - - - - - - - - - - - - - - - - }

procedure CalcZoomBox ({(theData : DRHandle)};

    { Calculate zoom box. }

    begin {CalcZoomBox}

        with Peek^, theData^^ do

            if spareFlag then                                             {Is there a zoom box? [II:3.1.1]}
                begin
                    with TitleBar do
                        SetRect (ZoomBox, left    + HOffset,              {Inset from left of title bar [I:4.1.2]}
                                          bottom - (VOffset + BoxSize),   {Allow for size of zoom box}
                                          left    + (HOffset + BoxSize),  {Allow for size of zoom box}
                                          bottom - VOffset);              {Inset from bottom of title bar}
                    with ZoomBox do
                        SetRect (SmallZoom, left,                         {Set up inner box [I:4.1.2]}
                                            top,
                                            left + SmallZoomSize,
                                            top  + SmallZoomSize);
                    with TitleRect do
                        bottom := bottom - (BoxSize + MinHighlight + 2 * HighlightGap)
                                                                          {Make room for zoom box}

                end {then}

            else
                SetRect (ZoomBox, 0, 0, 0, 0)                             {Set to empty rectangle [I:4.1.2]}

    end;    {CalcZoomBox}

{ - - - - - - - - - - - - - - - - - - - - - - - - - - - - - - - - - - - - - - - - - - - - - - - - - - - - - - - - - - - - - - - - - }
```

```
procedure CalcSizeBox {(theData : DRHandle)};

   { Calculate size box [Prog. III:2-7]. }

   var
      noGrowBit : INTEGER;                      {No-grow bit from window variation code}

   begin {CalcSizeBox}

      noGrowBit := BitAnd (VarCode, NoGrowMask);   {Extract no-grow bit [I:2.2.2]}

      with Peek^, theData^^ do
         with contRgn^^.rgnBBox do             {Use content region as basis [II:3.1.1, I:4.1.5]}
            if noGrowBit = 0 then               {Is there a size box?}

               SetRect (SizeBox, right  - (SizeBoxSize - FrameWidth), {Inset from right [I:4.1.2]}
                                 bottom - (SizeBoxSize - FrameWidth), {Inset from bottom}
                                 right,          {Set flush with window at right}
                                 bottom)         {Set flush with window at bottom}

            else
               SetRect (SizeBox, 0, 0, 0, 0)    {Set to empty rectangle [I:4.1.2]}

   end;   {CalcSizeBox}
```

{- -}

```
procedure DoDraw;

   { Draw window on screen [Prog. III:2-8]. }

   var
      theData : DRHandle;                       {Handle to definition function's data record}

   begin {DoDraw}

      with Peek^ do
         if visible then                        {Is window visible? [II:3.1.1]}
            begin
               MoveHHi (dataHandle);            {Move data record to end of heap [I:3.2.5]}
               HLock   (dataHandle);            {Lock data record [I:3.2.4]}

               theData := DRHandle(dataHandle); {Convert to typed handle}
```

```
        CalcBoxes (theData);                    {Recalculate title bar, close, zoom, and size boxes}

        case LoWord(MsgParam) of                {Extract low word of message parameter [I:2.2.3]}

          WInGoAway:
            ToggleCloseBox (theData);           {Toggle close box}

          WInZoomIn, WInZoomOut:
            ToggleZoomBox (theData);            {Toggle zoom box}

          otherwise
            DrawWindow (theData)                {Draw window}

          end; {case MsgParam}

        HUnlock (dataHandle)                     {Unlock data record [I:3.2.4]}
      end {if visible}

  end; {DoDraw}
```

```
{ - - - - - - - - - - - - - - - - - - - - - - - - - - - - - - - - - - - - - - - - - - - - - - - - - - - - - - - - - - - - - - - - - - - - - - - }


procedure DrawWindow {(theData : DRHandle)};

  { Draw window on screen. }

  var
    savePen : PenState;                          {Saved state of graphics pen [I:5.2.1]}

  begin {DrawWindow}

    GetPenState (savePen);                       {Save previous pen state [I:5.2.1]}
    PenNormal;                                   {Make sure pen has standard properties [I:5.2.2]}

      DrawFrame;                                 {Draw window's frame}

      DrawTitleBar (theData);                    {Draw title bar}

    SetPenState (savePen)                        {Restore previous pen state [I:5.2.1]}

  end; {DrawWindow}

{ - - - - - - - - - - - - - - - - - - - - - - - - - - - - - - - - - - - - - - - - - - - - - - - - - - - - - - - - - - - - - - - - - - - - - - - }
```

```
procedure DrawFrame;

   {  Draw window's frame.  }

   var
      theFrame  : Rect;                                    {Rectangle for drawing frame [I:4.1.2]}
      theShadow : Rect;                                    {Rectangle for drawing shadow [I:4.1.2]}

   begin {DrawFrame}

      with TheWindow^. Peek^ do
         begin

            theFrame := contRgn^^.rgnBBox;                 {Get bounding box of structure region [II:3.1.1, I:4.1.5]}
            InsetRect (theFrame, -FrameWidth, -FrameWidth);   {Enlarge by width of window frame [I:4.4.4]}

            FrameRect (theFrame);                          {Draw frame [II:5.3.2]}

            theShadow := strucRgn^^.rgnBBox;               {Get bounding box of struct. region [II:3.1.1, I:4.1.5]}
            InsetRect (theShadow, ShadowExtra, ShadowExtra);  {Inset by shadow thickness [I:4.4.4]}

            PenSize (ShadowExtra, ShadowExtra);            {Set pen to shadow thickness [I:5.2.2]}
               with theShadow do
                  begin
                     MoveTo (right, top);                  {Move to top-right corner [I:5.2.4]}
                     LineTo (right, bottom);               {Draw to bottom-right corner [I:5.2.4]}
                     LineTo (left,  bottom)                {Draw to bottom-left corner [I:5.2.4]}
                  end; {with theFrame}
            PenNormal                                      {Restore normal pen [I:5.2.2]}

         end {with TheWindow^, Peek^}

   end; {DrawFrame}

{- - - - - - - - - - - - - - - - - - - - - - - - - - - - - - - - - - - - - - - - - - - - - - - - - - - - - - - - -}

procedure DrawTitleBar {(theData : DRHandle)};

   { Draw title bar. }

   var
      vTop    : INTEGER;                                   {Top of highlight lines, in pixels}
      vBottom : INTEGER;                                   {Bottom of highlight lines, in pixels}
      hRight  : INTEGER;                                   {Horizontal position of last highlight line, in pixels}
      hPos    : INTEGER;                                   {Horizontal position of highlight line, in pixels}
```

```
begin  {DrawTitleBar}

   with TheWindow^, Peek^, theData^^, TitleBar do
     begin

         EraseRect  (TitleBar);                              {Clear interior to white [I:5.3.2]}
         FrameRect  (TitleBar);                              {Draw outline [I:5.3.2]}

         if hilited then                                    {Is window highlighted? [II:3.1.1]}
            begin

               vTop     := top      + (FrameWidth + HighlightGap);   {Leave room for frame and gap}
               vBottom  := bottom   - (FrameWidth + HighlightGap);   {  at top and bottom    }
               vBottom  := vBottom - pnSize.v;                        {Adjust for height of pen}

               hPos    := left  + HOffset;                  {Start at left edge}
               hRight  := right - HOffset;                  {End at right edge}

               while hPos <= hRight do                      {Draw the lines}
                  begin
                     MoveTo (hPos, vTop);                   {Move to top [I:5.2.4]}
                     LineTo (hPos, vBottom);                {Draw to bottom [I:5.2.4]}
                     hPos := hPos + 2                       {Position for next line}
                  end; {while}

               DrawCloseBox (theData);                      {Draw close box}
               DrawZoomBox   (theData)                      {Draw zoom box}

            end; {if visible}

         DrawTitle (theData)                                {Draw title}

     end {with TheWindow^, Peek^, theData^^, TitleBar}

   end;   {DrawTitleBar}

{- - - - - - - - - - - - - - - - - - - - - - - - - - - - - - - - - - - - - - - - - - - - - - - - - - - - - - - - - - - - - - - - - -}


procedure DrawCloseBox {(theData : DRHandle)};

   { Draw close box. }

   var
      clearRect : Rect;                                     {Rectangle for clearing white space around box}
```

```
   begin {DrawCloseBox}

      with Peek^, theData^^ do
         if goAwayFlag then                             {Is there a close box? [II:3.1.1]}
            begin

               clearRect := CloseBox;                   {Start with close box}
               InsetRect (clearRect, -HighlightGap, -HighlightGap);   {Enlarge by size of gap [I:4.4.4]}
               EraseRect (clearRect);                   {Clear to white [I:5.3.2]}

               FrameRect (CloseBox)                     {Draw outline of box  [I:5.3.2]}

            end {if}

   end; {DrawCloseBox}
```

{- -}

```
procedure DrawZoomBox {(theData : DRHandle)};

   { Draw zoom box. }

   var
      clearRect : Rect;                                 {Rectangle for clearing white space around box}
      smallBox  : Rect;                                 {Smaller box inside zoom icon}

   begin {DrawZoomBox}

      with Peek^, theData^^, ZoomBox do
         if spareFlag then                              {Is there a close box? [II:3.1.1]}
            begin

               clearRect := ZoomBox;                    {Start with zoom box}
               InsetRect (clearRect, -HighlightGap, -HighlightGap);   {Enlarge by size of gap [I:4.4.4]}
               EraseRect (clearRect);                   {Clear to white [I:5.3.2]}

               FrameRect (ZoomBox);                     {Draw outer box [I:5.3.2]}
               FrameRect (SmallZoom)                    {Draw inner box [I:5.3.2]}

            end {if}

   end; {DrawZoomBox}
```

{- -}

```
procedure DrawTitle {(theData : DRHandle)};

   { Draw window's title. }

   var
      fontProperties : FontInfo;          {Characteristics of system font [I:8.2.6]}
      rectHeight    : INTEGER;            {Height of title rectangle}
      rectWidth     : INTEGER;            {Width of title rectangle}
      charHeight    : INTEGER;            {Vertical height of each character}
      maxChars      : INTEGER;            {Maximum number of characters displayed}
      textHeight    : INTEGER;            {Total height of displayed characters}
      heightAdjust  : INTEGER;            {Adjustment for excess title height}
      chIndex       : INTEGER;            {Index of character to be drawn}
      theChar       : CHAR;               {Character to be drawn}
      baseLine      : INTEGER;            {Baseline for drawing characters}
      chWidth       : INTEGER;            {Width of character in pixels}
      chOffset      : INTEGER;            {Offset to left edge of character}
      chLeft        : INTEGER;            {Left edge of character}

   begin {DrawTitle}

      with Peek^, theData^^, TitleRect, fontProperties do
         begin

            GetFontInfo (fontProperties);          {Get font characteristics [I:8.2.6]}
            charHeight := ascent + descent;        {Calculate character height [I:8.2.6]}

            rectHeight := bottom - top;            {Find height of title rectangle [I:4.1.2]}
            rectWidth  := right  - left;           {Find width of title rectangle [I:4.1.2]}

            maxChars   := rectHeight div charHeight; {Find maximum number of characters [I:4.1.2]}
            if LENGTH(titleHandle^^) < maxChars then {Is title shorter than the maximum? [II:3.1.1]}
               maxChars := LENGTH(titleHandle^^);  {Reduce to actual title length [II:3.1.1]}

            textHeight   := maxChars * charHeight;  {Find height of characters}
            heightAdjust := (rectHeight - textHeight) div 2; {Calculate excess height}
            InsetRect (TitleRect, 0, heightAdjust); {Adjust height of rectangle [I:4.4.4]}
            EraseRect (TitleRect);                  {Clear to white [I:5.3.2]}

            baseLine := top + ascent;               {Initialize baseline [I:8.2.6]}
            for chIndex := 1 to maxChars do         {Loop through characters}
               begin

                  theChar := titleHandle^^[chIndex]; {Get next character [II:3.1.1]}
```

```
        chWidth   := CharWidth (theChar);          {Get width of character [I:8.3.4]}
        chOffset  := (rectWidth - chWidth) div 2;  {Center character in rectangle}
        chLeft    := left + chOffset;              {Find left edge of character}

        MoveTo    (chLeft, baseLine);              {Position the pen [I:5.2.4]}
        DrawChar  (theChar);                       {Draw the character [I:8.3.3]}

        baseLine := baseLine + charHeight          {Advance to next baseline}

      end {for chIndex}

    end {with Peek^, theData^^, TitleRect, fontProperties}

  end;    {DrawTitle}
```

{- -}

```
procedure ToggleCloseBox {(theData : DRHandle)};

  { Toggle close box. }

  var
    maskString : Str255;                           {Hexadecimal string defining mask [I:2.1.1]}

  begin {ToggleCloseBox}

    maskString := CONCAT ('0000',                  {Set up mask string}
                          '0400',
                          '2480',
                          '1500',
                          '0000',
                          '71C0',
                          '0000',
                          '1500',
                          '2480',
                          '0400',
                          '0000');

    with theData^^ do
      ToggleBox (CloseBox, maskString)             {Copy the bits}

  end;    {ToggleCloseBox}
```

{- -}

```
procedure ToggleZoomBox {(theData : DRHandle)};

   { Toggle zoom box [Prog. III:2-10]. }

   var
      maskString : Str255;                        {Hexadecimal string defining mask [I:2.1.1]}

   begin {ToggleZoomBox}

      maskString := CONCAT ('0000',               {Set up mask string}
                            '0600',
                            '2680',
                            '1700',
                            '0200',
                            '73C0',
                            '7E00',
                            '1500',
                            '2480',
                            '0400',
                            '0000');

         with theData^^ do
            ToggleBox (ZoomBox, maskString)        {Copy the bits}

   end; {ToggleZoomBox}

{---------------------------------------------------------------------------------}

procedure ToggleBox {(theBox : Rect; maskString : Str255)};

   { Toggle close or zoom box [Prog. III:2-9]. }

   var
      theMask : BitMap;                           {Bit map for transferring bits [I:4.2.1]}
      theBits : array [1..BoxSize] of INTEGER;    {Array for holding bit  image}
      wmPort  : GrafPtr;                          {Pointer to Window Manager port [II:3.6.1]}

   begin {ToggleBox}

      with theMask do
         begin

            StuffHex (@theBits, maskString);      {Stuff the bit image [I:2.2.4]}

            baseAddr := @theBits;                 {Point to the bit image [I:4.2.1]}
```

```
        rowBytes := 2;                              {Set row width [I:4.2.1]}
        SetRect (bounds, 0, 0, BoxSize, BoxSize);   {Set boundary rectangle [I:4.1.2, I:4.2.1]}

        GetWMgrPort (wmPort);                        {Get Window Manager port [II:3.6.1]}
        CopyBits (theMask,                           {Copy from mask bit map [I:5.1.4]}
                  wmPort^.portBits,                  { to the screen [I:4.2.2] }
                  bounds,                            {From mask's full boundary  rectangle [I:4.2.1]}
                  theBox,                            { to the close or zoom box }
                  SrcXOr,                            {Invert pixels under the mask [I:5.1.3]}
                  NIL)                               {No additional clipping  region}

    end  {with theMask}

  end;  {ToggleBox}


{ - - - - - - - - - - - - - - - - - - - - - - - - - - - - - - - - - - - - - - - - - - - - - - - - - - - - - - - - }

procedure DoDrawGIcon;

  { Draw grow icon [Prog. III:2-11]. }

  var
    noGrowBit : INTEGER;                             {No-grow bit from window variation code}
    savePort  : GrafPtr;                             {Pointer to previous current port [I:4.2.2]}
    savePen   : PenState;                            {Saved state of graphics pen [I:5.2.1]}
    boxTop    : INTEGER;                             {Top edge of size box in local coordinates}
    boxLeft   : INTEGER;                             {Left edge of size box in local coordinates}

  begin {DoDrawGIcon}

    with TheWindow^, Peek^ do
      begin

        noGrowBit := BitAnd (VarCode, NoGrowMask);   {Extract no-grow bit [I:2.2.2]}

        if visible and (noGrowBit = 0) then          {Window visible and has a size box? [II:3.1.1]}
          begin
            GetPort (savePort);                      {Save previous port [I:4.3.3]}

            SetPort (TheWindow);                     {Get into the window's port [I:4.3.3]}
            GetPenState (savePen);                   {Save previous pen state [I:5.2.1]}

            PenNormal;                               {Set standard pen characteristics [I:5.2.2]}

            with portRect do                         {Find top-left corner in local coordinates}
```

```
          begin
             boxTop  := bottom - (SizeBoxSize - FrameWidth);
             boxLeft := right  - (SizeBoxSize - FrameWidth)
          end; {with portRect}

       MoveTo (boxLeft, portRect.top);      {Move to top of window [I:5.2.4]}
       LineTo (boxLeft, portRect.bottom);   {Draw line to bottom [I:5.2.4]}

       MoveTo (portRect.left,  boxTop);     {Move to left of window [I:5.2.4]}
       LineTo (portRect.right, boxTop);     {Draw line to right [I:5.2.4]}

       DrawSizeBox (boxTop, boxLeft);       {Draw size box}

     SetPenState (savePen);                 {Restore previous pen state [I:5.2.1]}

   SetPort (savePort);                      {Restore previous port [I:4.3.3]}
 end {if}

     end {with TheWindow^, Peek^}

  end;   {DoDrawGIcon}

{- - - - - - - - - - - - - - - - - - - - - - - - - - - - - - - - - - - - - - - - - - - - - - - - - - - - - -}

procedure DrawSizeBox {(boxTop : INTEGER; boxLeft : INTEGER)};

  { Draw size box [Prog. III:2-12]. }

  var
     theBox : Rect;                          {Utility rectangle for drawing boxes [I:4.1.2]}

  begin {DrawSizeBox}

    with TheWindow^, Peek^, theBox do
      begin

        SetPt (topLeft, boxLeft, boxTop);       {Set top-left corner [I:4.1.1]}
        botRight := portRect.botRight;          {Set bottom-right corner [I:4.2.2]}
        InsetRect (theBox, FrameWidth, FrameWidth);  {Inset by frame width [I:4.4.4]}

        EraseRect (theBox);                     {Clear interior to white [I:5.3.2]}

        if hilited then                         {Is window highlighted? [II:3.1.1]}
          begin
```

```
        SetRect     (theBox, boxLeft,                      {Set up bigger box  [I:4.1.2]}
                             boxTop,
                             boxLeft + GIconBigSize,
                             boxTop  + GIconBigSize);
        OffsetRect (theBox, GIconBigOffset,               {Move into position  [I:4.4.4]}
                             GIconBigOffset);
        FrameRect   (theBox);                              {Draw outline [I:5.3.2]}

        SetRect     (theBox, boxLeft,                      {Set up smaller box  [I:4.1.2]}
                             boxTop,
                             boxLeft + GIconSmallSize,
                             boxTop  + GIconSmallSize);
        OffsetRect (theBox, GIconSmallOffset,             {Move into position  [I:4.4.4]}
                             GIconSmallOffset);
        EraseRect   (theBox);                              {Clear interior [I:5.3.2]}
        FrameRect   (theBox)                               {Draw outline [I:5.3.2]}

      end  {if hilited}

   end  {with TheWindow^, Peek^, theBox}

end;  {DrawSizeBox}


{- - - - - - - - - - - - - - - - - - - - - - - - - - - - - - - - - - - - - - - - - - - - - - - - - - - - - - - - - -}


procedure DoGrow;

  { Draw outline for sizing window [Prog. III:2-13]. }

  type
     RectPtr = ^Rect;                                      {Pointer type for converting message parameter}

  var
     thePtr  : RectPtr;                                    {Pointer for converting message parameter}
     theRect : Rect;                                       {Rectangle to be drawn [I:4.1.2]}
     linePos : INTEGER;                                    {Horizontal or vertical position for drawing line}

  begin {DoGrow}

     thePtr  := RectPtr(MsgParam);                         {Convert message parameter}
     theRect := thePtr^;                                   {Get the rectangle}

     with theRect do
       begin
```

```
    InsetRect (theRect, -FrameWidth, -FrameWidth);      {Enlarge by width of window frame [I:4.4.4]}
    linePos := left;                                    {Save edge for later drawing}
    left    := left - (TitleBarWidth - FrameWidth);     {Make room for title bar [I:4.1.2]}


    FrameRect (theRect);                                 {Draw window outline  [I:5.3.2]}


    MoveTo (linePos, top);                               {Move to top-right of title  bar [I:5.2.4]}
    LineTo (linePos, bottom);                            {Draw to bottom-right of  title bar [I:5.2.4]}


    linePos := right - SizeBoxSize;                      {Find left edge of size box  [I:4.1.2]}
    MoveTo (linePos, top);                               {Move to top of window  [I:5.2.4]}
    LineTo (linePos, bottom);                            {Draw line to bottom  [I:5.2.4]}


    linePos := bottom - SizeBoxSize;                     {Find top edge of size box  [I:4.1.2]}
    MoveTo (left, linePos);                              {Move to left of window  [I:5.2.4]}
    LineTo (right, linePos)                              {Draw line to right [I:5.2.4]}


  end  {with theRect}


end;   {DoGrow}


{- - - - - - - - - - - - - - - - - - - - - - - - - - - - - - - - - - - - - - - - - - - - - - - - - - - - - - - - - - - - - - -}


procedure DoHit;

  { Locate mouse click [Prog. III:2-14]. }


  var
    theData    : DRHandle;                               {Handle to definition function's data record}
    mousePoint : Point;                                  {Point where mouse was pressed, in global coordinates}

  begin {DoHit}

    with Peek^ do
      if visible then                                    {Is window visible? [II:3.1.1]}
        begin
          MoveHHi (dataHandle);                          {Move data record to end of  heap [I:3.2.5]}
          HLock   (dataHandle);                          {Lock data record [I:3.2.4]}
            theData := DRHandle(dataHandle);             {Convert to typed handle}
          with theData^^ do
            begin

                CalcBoxes (theData);                     {Recalculate title bar, close, zoom, and size  boxes}

                mousePoint := Point(MsgParam);           {Get mouse point from message parameter}
```

```
          if hilited then                              {Is window active? [II:3.1.1]}
             begin

                 if PtInRect (mousePoint, CloseBox) then    {In close box? [I:4.4.3]}
                    Result := WInGoAway                      {Report close box  [III:2.2.5]}

                 else if PtInRect (mousePoint, ZoomBox) then {In zoom box? [I:4.4.3]}
                    begin
                       if ZoomedOut then                     {Which state is window in?}
                          Result := WInZoomIn                {Report zoom-in box  [III:2.2.5]}
                       else
                          Result := WInZoomOut               {Report zoom-out box [III:2.2.5]}
                    end {if}

                 else if PtInRect (mousePoint, SizeBox) then {In size box? [I:4.4.3]}
                    Result := WInGrow                        {Report size box  [III:2.2.5]}

                end; {if hilited}

           if Result = WNoHit then                           {Nothing found yet?  [III:2.2.5]}
              begin

                 if PtInRect (mousePoint, TitleBar) then     {In title bar? [I:4.4.3]}
                    Result := WInDrag                        {Report drag region  [III:2.2.5]}

                 else if PtInRgn (mousePoint, contRgn) then  {In content region?  [I:4.4.3]}
                    Result := WInContent                     {Report cont. region  [III:2.2.5]}

                 {else
                    Result := WNoHit}                        {Report no hit [III:2.2.5]}

              end {if Result = WNoHit}

          end; {with theData^^}
       HUnlock (dataHandle)                                  {Unlock data record [I:3.2.4]}
      end {if visible}

  end;  {DoHit}

{- - - - - - - - - - - - - - - - - - - - - - - - - - - - - - - - - - - - - - - - - - - - - - - - - - - -}


procedure DoDispose;

  { Prepare to dispose of window [Prog. III:2-5]. }
```

```
   begin {DoDispose}

      with Peek^ do
         DisposHandle (dataHandle)                    {Dispose of data record [I:3.2.2]}

   end;   {DoDispose}
```

{ - }

```
function ZoomedOut { : BOOLEAN};

   { Is window in zoomed-out state? }

   var
      windowRect  : Rect;                              {Rectangle representing window's content region}
      zoomOutRect : Rect;                              {Rectangle representing zoomed-out state}
      theData     : DRHandle;                          {Handle to definition function's data record}

   begin {ZoomedOut}

      with Peek^ do
         begin

            theData     := DRHandle(dataHandle);       {Convert to typed handle [II:3.1.1]}
            windowRect  := contRgn^^.rgnBBox;          {Get content rectangle [II:3.1.1, I:4.1.5]}
            zoomOutRect := theData^^.StdState;         {Get zoomed-out state [II:3.3.2]}

            if not NearPoint (windowRect.topLeft,      {Do top-left corners match?}
                              zoomOutRect.topLeft) then
               ZoomedOut := FALSE                      {If not, answer no}
            else
               ZoomedOut := NearPoint (windowRect.botRight,   {Else test bottom-right}
                                       zoomOutRect.botRight)

         end {with Peek^}

   end;   {ZoomedOut}
```

{ - }

```
function NearPoint {(point1 : Point; point2 : Point) : BOOLEAN};

   { Are two points "near" each other? }
```

```
const
   nearEnough = 7;                                    {Maximum allowable distance between points}

var
   testRect : Rect;                                   {Utility rectangle for testing distance [I:4.1.2]}

begin {NearPoint}

   Pt2Rect    (point1, point1, testRect);            {Start with empty rectangle at first point [I:4.1.2]}
   InsetRect (testRect, -nearEnough, -nearEnough);   {Enlarge by allowable distance [I:4.4.4]}
   NearPoint := PtInRect (point2, testRect)          {Does it enclose second point? [I:4.4.3]}

end;   {NearPoint}
```

{- }

```
{ Main routine. }

begin {SideWindow}

   Peek    := WindowPeek(TheWindow);                 {Convert to a "peek" pointer [II:3.1.1]}
   Result := 0;                                      {Initialize function result}

   case MsgCode of

      WNew:
         DoNew;                                       {Initialize window}

      WCalcRgns:
         DoCalcRgns;                                  {Calculate window's regions}

      WDraw:
         DoDraw;                                       {Draw window on screen}

      WDrawGIcon:
         DoDrawGIcon;                                 {Draw grow icon}

      WGrow:
         DoGrow;                                       {Draw outline for sizing window}

      WHit:
         DoHit;                                        {Locate mouse click}

      WDispose:
         DoDispose                                     {Prepare to dispose of window}
```

```
        end; {case MsgCode}

    SideWindow := Result                              {Return function result}

  end;  {SideWindow}
```

`ThreeState` **Control Definition Function**

`ThreeState` is a control definition function for a three-way checkbox or radio button, with a neutral state in addition to the usual on and off. See Chapter 2 for a complete discussion.

```
function ThreeState (VarCode : INTEGER; TheControl : ControlHandle;
                MsgCode : INTEGER; MsgParam  : LONGINT)
                    : LONGINT;
```

{ Control definition function for a checkbox or radio button with an on, off, and neutral state. }

```
uses
  MemTypes.                              {Elementary data types}
  QuickDraw.                             {QuickDraw graphics routines}
  OSIntf.                                {Macintosh Operating System}
  ToolIntf.                              {User Interface Toolbox}
  PackIntf;                              {Standard packages}
```

{ - }

{ Global Declarations }

```
  const

    MacPlusRom = $75;                    {ROM version number for Macintosh Plus}

    ButtonSize  = 12;                    {Size of checkbox or radio button, in pixels}
    ButtonLeft  =  2;                    {Horizontal offset from edge of enclosing rectangle}
    TitleGap    =  4;                    {Gap from box or button to beginning of title}
    DotInset    =  3;                    {Inset around black dot inside radio buttons}
    ThickBorder =  2;                    {Border thickness for highlighting}

    OffState     = 0;                    {Control is in "off" state}
    OnState      = 1;                    {Control is in "on" state}
    NeutralState = 2;                    {Control is in neutral state}
```

```
      InNone  = 0;                              {Part code representing no part at all}
      DrawAll = 0;                              {Message parameter for drawing entire control}

      BlackString   = 'FFFFFFFFFFFFFFFF';       {Hexadecimal string defining black pattern}
      GrayString    = 'AA55AA55AA55AA55';       {Hexadecimal string defining gray pattern}
      LtGrayString  = '8822882288228822';       {Hexadecimal string defining light gray pattern}

      CR = $0D;                                 {Character code for carriage return [I:8.1.1]}

  var

      Result : LONGINT;                         {Function result}
```

{- -}

```
{ Forward Declarations }

procedure DoInit; forward;
     { Initialize control. }
procedure DoCalc; forward;
     { Calculate region occupied by control. }
procedure DoDraw; forward;
     { Draw control on screen. }
  procedure DrawButton; forward;
       { Draw checkbox or radio button. }
    procedure DrawCheckbox (boxRect : Rect); forward;
         { Draw checkbox. }
    procedure DrawRadioButton (buttonRect : Rect); forward;
         { Draw radio button. }
  procedure DrawTitle; forward;
       { Draw control's title. }
    procedure DrawTitleText; forward;
         { Draw text of control's title. }
      procedure DimTitle (titleLeft : INTEGER); forward;
           { Dim text of control's title. }
procedure DoTest; forward;
     { Find part of control where mouse was pressed. }
procedure DoPos; forward;
     { Reposition indicator and update control's setting. }
procedure DoThumb; forward;
     { Calculate parameters for DragControl. }
procedure DoDrag; forward;
     { Drag control or indicator. }
procedure DoTrack; forward;
     { Default action procedure for TrackControl. }
```

```
procedure DoDisp; forward;
     { Prepare to dispose of control. }
```

{ - }

```
procedure DoInit;

   { Initialize control. }

   begin {DoInit}

      SetCtlMin (TheControl, OffState);        {Set minimum value [II:6.2.4]}
      SetCtlMax (TheControl, NeutralState)     {Set maximum value [II:6.2.4]}

   end;   {DoInit}
```

{ - }

```
procedure DoCalc;

   { Calculate region occupied by control. }

   const
      AddrMask = $00FFFFFF;                     {Flag for extracting address from a pointer or handle}

   var
      theRegion : RgnHandle;                    {Region to be set [I:4.1.5]}

   begin {DoCalc}

      MsgParam   := BitAnd (MsgParam, AddrMask);    {Strip off indicator flag  [I:2.2.2]}
      theRegion := RgnHandle(MsgParam);            {Convert to a region handle [I:4.1.5]}

      with TheControl^^ do
        RectRgn (theRegion, contrlRect)            {Set region to enclosing rectangle [I:4.1.7, II:6.1.1]}

   end;   {DoCalc}
```

{ - }

```
procedure DoDraw;

   { Draw control on screen. }
```

```
    var
       saveClip : RgnHandle;                    {Previous clipping region [I:4.1.5]}
       savePen  : PenState;                     {Previous state of graphics pen [I:5.2.1]}

    begin {DoDraw}

       with TheControl^^, contrlOwner^ do
          if (MsgParam in [DrawAll, InCheckbox, InThumb])  {Is drawing request applicable? [II:6.4.1]}
               and (BitTst (@contrlVis, 7)) then    {Is the control visible? [I:2.2.1, II:6.1.1]}
             begin

                saveClip := NewRgn;              {Allocate temporary region [I:4.1.6]}
                GetClip (saveClip);              {Save previous clipping region [I:4.3.6]}

                   ClipRect (contrlRect);        {Clip to enclosing rectangle [I:4.3.6, II:6.1.1]}
                   SectRgn   (clipRgn, saveClip, clipRgn);  {Intersect with previous region [I:4.4.8, I:4.2.2]}

                   GetPenState (savePen);        {Save previous pen state [I:5.2.1]}

                      DrawButton;                {Draw the checkbox or radio button}
                      DrawTitle;                      {Draw the title}

                   SetPenState (savePen);        {Restore previous pen state [I:5.2.1]}

                SetClip (saveClip);              {Restore previous clipping region [I:4.3.6]}
                DisposeRgn (saveClip)            {Dispose of temporary region [I:4.1.6]}

             end {if}

       end; {DoDraw}

{ - - - - - - - - - - - - - - - - - - - - - - - - - - - - - - - - - - - - - - - - - - - - - - - - - - - - - - - - - - - - - - - - - - - - - - - - - - - - - - - - - - - }

procedure DrawButton;

   { Draw checkbox or radio button. }

   const
      VarMask = $0007;                           {Mask for extracting button type from variation code}

   var
      rectHeight : INTEGER;                      {Height of control's enclosing rectangle}
      buttonTop  : INTEGER;                      {Vertical offset from top of enclosing rectangle}
      buttonRect : Rect;                         {Rectangle defining checkbox or radio button [I:4.1.2]}
      buttonType : INTEGER;                      {Variety of button requested}
```

```
begin {DrawButton}

   with TheControl^^.contrlRect do
      begin

          rectHeight := bottom - top;                  {Find rectangle height [I:4.1.2]}
          buttonTop  := (rectHeight - ButtonSize) div 2;   {Find vertical offset}

          SetRect    (buttonRect, 0, 0, ButtonSize, ButtonSize);  {Set rectangle size [I:4.1.2]}
          OffsetRect (buttonRect, left + ButtonLeft, top + buttonTop);
                                                        {Move into place [I:4.4.4, I:4.1.2]}

          buttonType := BitAnd (VarCode, VarMask);   {Extract button type from variation code [I:2.2.2]}
          case buttonType of

             CheckboxProc:
                DrawCheckbox (buttonRect);            {Draw checkbox}

             RadioButProc:
                DrawRadioButton (buttonRect)          {Draw radio button}

             end {case VarCode}

         end  {with theControl^^.contrlRect}

   end;   {DrawButton}
```

{ - }

```
procedure DrawCheckbox ((boxRect : Rect));

   { Draw checkbox. }

   var
      thePattern : Pattern;                      {Pattern for filling neutral checkboxes [I:5.1.1]}

   begin {DrawCheckbox}

      with TheControl^^, boxRect do
         begin

             EraseRect (boxRect);                 {Clear to white [I:5.3.2]}

             case contrlValue of
```

```
        OffState:
          {Do nothing};                               {Just leave interior of box white}

        OnState:
          begin
            PenNormal;                                {Make sure pen is normal thickness [I:5.2.2]}

            MoveTo (left  + 1, top     + 1);  {Move to top-left [I:5.2.4]}
            LineTo (right - 1, bottom - 1);   {Draw to bottom-right  [I:5.2.4]}
            MoveTo (right - 1, top        );  {Move to top-right [I:5.2.4]}
            LineTo (left,        bottom - 1)  {Draw to bottom-left [I:5.2.4]}
          end; {OnState}

        NeutralState:
          begin
            StuffHex (@thePattern, LtGrayString);     {Define light gray pattern [I:2.2.4]}
            FillRect (boxRect, thePattern)            {Fill interior with light gray  [I:5.3.2]}
          end {NeutralState}

        end; {case contrlValue}

      if contrlHilite = InCheckbox then               {Is checkbox highlighted?  [II:6.3.3, II:6.4.1]}
        PenSize (ThickBorder, ThickBorder);           {Use extra pen thickness  [I:5.2.2]}
      FrameRect (boxRect)                             {Outline the checkbox [I:5.3.2]}

    end {with theControl^^, boxRect}

  end;  {DrawCheckbox}

{- - - - - - - - - - - - - - - - - - - - - - - - - - - - - - - - - - - - - - - - - - - - - - - - - - - - -}


procedure DrawRadioButton {(buttonRect : Rect)};

  { Draw radio button. }

  var
    thePattern : Pattern;                             {Pattern for filling radio buttons [I:5.1.1]}
    dotRect    : Rect;                                {Rectangle enclosing inner black dot [I:4.1.2]}

  begin {DrawRadioButton}

    with TheControl^^, buttonRect do
      begin

        EraseRect (buttonRect);                       {Clear to white [I:5.3.2]}
```

```
        case contrlValue of

            OffState:
                {Do nothing};                          {Just leave interior of button white}

            OnState:
                begin
                    dotRect := buttonRect;             {Start from full button}
                    InsetRect (dotRect, DotInset, DotInset);   {Inset to inner dot [I:4.4.4]}
                    StuffHex   (@thePattern, BlackString);     {Define black pattern [I:2.2.4]}
                    FillOval   (dotRect, thePattern)   {Paint the dot [I:5.3.4]}
                end; {OnState}


            NeutralState:
                begin
                    StuffHex  (@thePattern, LtGrayString);   {Define light gray pattern [I:2.2.4]}
                    FillOval  (buttonRect, thePattern)       {Fill interior with light gray [I:5.3.4]}
                end {NeutralState}

            end; {case contrlValue}


        if contrlHilite = InCheckbox then              {Is button highlighted? [II:6.3.3, II:6.4.1]}
            PenSize (ThickBorder, ThickBorder);        {Use extra pen thickness [I:5.2.2]}
        FrameOval (buttonRect)                         {Outline the button [I:5.3.4]}

    end {with theControl^^, buttonRect}

  end;    {DrawRadioButton}
```

{- -}

```
procedure DrawTitle;

  { Draw control's title. }

  var
     saveFont : INTEGER;                               {Previous font number [I:8.2.1]}
     saveSize : INTEGER;                               {Previous type size in points}
     saveFace : Style;                                 {Previous type style [I:8.3.1]}
     wFontBit : INTEGER;                               {Window font flag from variation code [II:6.2.1]}

  begin {DrawTitle}

    with TheControl^^, contrlOwner^ do
      begin
```

```
        saveFont := txFont;                               {Save previous font number [I:8.3.1]}
        saveSize := txSize;                               {Save previous type size [I:8.3.1]}
        saveFace := txFace;                               {Save previous type style [I:8.3.1]}

      wFontBit := BitAnd (VarCode, UseWFont);  {Extract window font flag  [I:2.2.2, II:6.2.1]}
      if wFontBit = 0 then                                {Window font specified?}
        begin
          TextFont (SystemFont);                          {Use system font [I:8.3.2, I:8.2.1]}
          TextSize (0);                                   {Use standard type size [I:8.3.2]}
          TextFace ([])                                   {Use plain text style [I:8.3.2, I:8.3.1]}
        end; {if}

      DrawTitleText;                                      {Draw the text}

      TextFont (saveFont);                                {Restore previous font number [I:8.3.2]}
      TextSize (saveSize);                                {Restore previous type size [I:8.3.2]}
      TextFace (saveFace)                                 {Restore previous type style [I:8.3.2]}

    end {with theControl^^, contrlOwner^}

  end; {DrawTitle}


{ - - - - - - - - - - - - - - - - - - - - - - - - - - - - - - - - - - - - - - - - - - - - - - - - - - - - }


procedure DrawTitleText;

  { Draw text of control's title. }

  var
    fontProperties : FontInfo;                            {Characteristics of title font [I:8.2.6]}
    lineHeight     : INTEGER;                             {Height per line of text}
    nLines         : INTEGER;                             {Number of lines in title}
    textHeight     : INTEGER;                             {Total height of title in pixels}
    rectHeight     : INTEGER;                             {Height of control's enclosing rectangle}
    titleOffset    : INTEGER;                             {Offset of title from top of rectangle}
    titleLeft      : INTEGER;                             {Left edge of title in local coordinates}
    baseLine       : INTEGER;                             {Baseline for drawing characters}
    firstChar      : INTEGER;                             {Index of first character in line}
    chIndex        : INTEGER;                             {Character index within title}
    lineLength     : INTEGER;                             {Number of characters in line}

  begin {DrawTitleText}

    with TheControl^^, contrlRect, fontProperties do
      begin
```

```
      GetFontInfo (fontProperties);          {Get font characteristics [I:8.2.6]}
      lineHeight := ascent + descent;        {Calculate line height [I:8.2.6]}

      nLines := 1;                           {Assume one line of text}
      for chIndex := 1 to LENGTH(contrlTitle) do   {Loop through characters of title [II:6.1.1]}
         if contrlTitle[chIndex] = CHAR(CR) then    {Carriage return? [II:6.1.1, I:8.1.1]}
            nLines := nLines + 1;            {Increment line count}

      textHeight  := nLines * lineHeight;    {Find total text height}
      rectHeight  := bottom - top;           {Find rectangle height [I:4.1.2]}
      titleOffset := (rectHeight - textHeight) div 2;  {Find title offset}

      baseLine  := top + titleOffset + ascent;   {Find first baseline [I:8.2.6]}
      titleLeft := left + ButtonLeft + ButtonSize + TitleGap;  {Find left edge of text}
      firstChar := 1;                        {Start at beginning of title}

      for chIndex := 1 to LENGTH(contrlTitle) do   {Loop through characters of title [II:6.1.1]}
         if (contrlTitle[chIndex] = CHAR(CR)) or    {Carriage return? [II:6.1.1, I:8.1.1]}
               (chIndex = LENGTH(contrlTitle)) then   {End of title? [II:6.1.1]}
            begin
               lineLength := chIndex - firstChar;   {Find length of line}
               if chIndex = LENGTH(contrlTitle) then  {End of title? [II:6.1.1]}
                  lineLength := lineLength + 1;  {Include last character}

               MoveTo (titleLeft, baseLine);   {Position pen for drawing [I:5.2.4]}
               DrawText (@contrlTitle, firstChar, lineLength);  {Draw the text [I:8.3.3]}

               baseLine  := baseLine + lineHeight;   {Advance to next baseline}
               firstChar := chIndex + 1        {Advance to first character of next line}
            end; {if}

      if contrlHilite = 255 then              {Is control inactive? [II:6.1.1, II:6.3.3]}
         DimTitle (titleLeft)                 {Dim the text}

   end {with theControl^^, contrlRect, fontProperties}

   end;   {DrawTitleText}

{ - - - - - - - - - - - - - - - - - - - - - - - - - - - - - - - - - - - - - - - - - - - - - - - - - - - }


procedure DimTitle {(titleLeft : INTEGER)};

   { Dim text of control's title. }

   var
```

```
        titleRect  : Rect;                              {Rectangle enclosing title [I:4.1.2]}
        thePattern : Pattern;                           {Pattern for dimming text [I:5.1.1]}

    begin {DimTitle}

        with TheControl^^, titleRect do
          begin

            titleRect := contrlRect;                    {Start with control's enclosing rectangle [II:6.1.1]}
            left := titleLeft;                          {Exclude checkbox or radio button}

            StuffHex (@thePattern, GrayString);         {Define gray pattern [I:2.2.4]}
            PenPat    (thePattern);                     {Set gray pattern [I:5.2.2]}
            PenMode   (PatBic);                         {Set "bit clear" mode  [I:5.2.2, I:5.1.3]}

            PaintRect (titleRect)                       {Dim the text [I:5.3.2]}

          end  {with TheControl^^, titleRect}

    end;   {DimTitle}

{ - - - - - - - - - - - - - - - - - - - - - - - - - - - - - - - - - - - - - - - - - - - - - - - - - - - - - - - }

procedure DoTest;

  { Find part of control where mouse was pressed.  }

  const
    inactive = 255;                                     {Highlighting code for inactive control [II:6.3.3]}

  var
    mousePoint : Point;                                 {Point where mouse was pressed, in local coordinates}

  begin {DoTest}

    with TheControl^^ do
      begin

        mousePoint := Point(MsgParam);                  {Convert message parameter [I:4.1.1]}

        if (contrlHilite <> inactive) and               {Is control active? [II:6.1.1, II:6.3.3]}
            (PtInRect (mousePoint, contrlRect))         {Mouse pressed in control? [I:4.4.3, II:6.1.1]}
        then
          Result := InCheckbox                          {Report hit in checkbox [II:6.4.1]}
        else
```

```
        Result := InNone                          {Report no hit}

    end  {with TheControl^^}

  end:  {DoTest}
```
{--}

```
procedure DoPos:
```

  { Reposition indicator and update control's setting. }

```
  begin {DoPos}
```

      {Insert code here to reposition the indicator and update the setting.}
      {In the case of three-state buttons, this operation is not needed.   }

```
  end:  {DoPos}
```
{--}

```
procedure DoThumb:
```

  { Calculate parameters for DragControl. }

```
  begin {DoThumb}
```

      {Insert code here to calculate the DragControl parameters.   }
      {In the case of three-state buttons, this operation is not needed. }

```
  end:  {DoThumb}
```
{--}

```
procedure DoDrag:
```

  { Drag control or indicator. }

```
  begin {DoDrag}
```

      {Insert code here to drag the control or its indicator.   }
      {In the case of three-state buttons, this operation is not needed. }

```
  end:  {DoDrag}
```
{--}

```
procedure DoTrack;

    { Default action procedure for TrackControl. }

    begin {DoTrack}

        {Insert code here to implement the control's default action procedure.  }
        {In the case of three-state buttons, no default action procedure is    }
        {needed.  }

    end;   {DoTrack}
```

{- }

```
procedure DoDisp;

    { Prepare to dispose of control. }

    begin {DoDisp}

        {Insert code here to do any needed cleanup before disposing of the control.}
        {In the case of three-state buttons, no special cleanup is needed.      }

    end;   {DoDisp}
```

{- }

```
    { Main routine. }

    begin {ThreeState}

        Result := 0;                            {Initialize function result}

        HLock (Handle(TheControl));             {Lock control record [I:3.2.4]}

            case MsgCode of

                InitCntl:
                    DoInit;                     {Initialize control}

                CalcCRgns:
                    DoCalc;                     {Calculate region occupied by control}

                DrawCntl:
                    DoDraw;                     {Draw control on screen}
```

```
    TestCntl:
        DoTest;                                          {Find part of control where mouse was pressed}

    PosCntl:
        DoPos;                                           {Reposition indicator and update control's setting}

    ThumbCntl:
        DoThumb;                                         {Calculate parameters for DragControl}

    DragCntl:
        DoDrag;                                          {Drag control or indicator}

    AutoTrack:
        DoTrack;                                         {Default action procedure for TrackControl}

    DispCntl:
        DoDisp                                           {Prepare to dispose of control}

        end;  {case msgCode}

    HUnlock (Handle(TheControl));                        {Unlock control record [I:3.2.4]}

    ThreeState := Result                                 {Return function result}

    end;    {ThreeState}
```

MiniEdit with Printing

MiniEdit is the example application program originally developed in Volume Two. The version shown here includes the printing capability added in Chapter 4 of this volume. Compared with the original in Volume Two, this version also incorporates several bug fixes and some minor restructuring and cleanup for improved readability. A complete description of the changes from the earlier version is included on the MiniEdit 2.0 mail-order disk.

```
program MiniEdit;

{  Example program to illustrate event-driven structure [Prog. II:2-1].  }
```

```
uses
   MemTypes,                                {Elementary data types}
   QuickDraw,                               {QuickDraw graphics routines}
   OSIntf,                                  {Macintosh Operating System}
   ToolIntf,                                {User Interface Toolbox}
   PackIntf,                                {Standard packages}
   MacPrint;                                {Printing routines}
```

{ - }

{Global Declarations}

```
   const

      MacPlusROM = $75;                     {ROM version number for Macintosh Plus}
      ChangeFlag = $0002;                   {Mask for extracting "change bit" from event modifiers}

      MenuBarHeight = 20;                   {Height of menu bar in pixels}
      TitleBarSize  = 18;                   {Size of window title bar in pixels}
      ScreenMargin  = 10;                   {Width of "safety margin" around edge of screen}

      MinWidth  = 80;                       {Minimum width of window in pixels}
      MinHeight = 80;                       {Minimum height of window in pixels}
      SBarWidth = 16;                       {Width of scroll bars in pixels}

      TextMargin  = 4;                      {Inset from window to text rectangle}
      PrintMargin = 0.5;                    {Margin around printed page, in inches}

      DlgTop  = 100;                        {Top edge of dialog box for Get and Put dialogs}
      DlgLeft =  85;                        {Left edge of dialog box for Get and Put dialogs}

      AppleID = 1;                          {Menu ID for Apple menu}
         AboutItem  = 1;                        {Item number for About... command}

      FileID  = 2;                          {Menu ID for File menu}
         NewItem    =  1;                       {Item number for New command}
         OpenItem   =  2;                       {Item number for Open... command}
         CloseItem  =  3;                       {Item number for Close command}
         SaveItem   =  5;                       {Item number for Save command}
         SaveAsItem =  6;                       {Item number for Save As... command}
         RevertItem =  7;                       {Item number for Revert to Saved command}
         SetupItem  =  9;                       {Item number for Page Setup... command}
         PrintItem  = 10;                       {Item number for Print... command}
         QuitItem   = 12;                       {Item number for Quit command}
```

```
EditID   = 3;                          {Menu ID for Edit menu}
   UndoItem   = 1;                        {Item number for Undo command}
   CutItem    = 3;                        {Item number for Cut command}
   CopyItem   = 4;                        {Item number for Copy command}
   PasteItem  = 5;                        {Item number for Paste command}
   ClearItem  = 7;                        {Item number for Clear command}


WindowID  = 1000;                       {Resource ID for window template [II:3.7.1]}
ScrollID  = 1000;                       {Resource ID for scroll bar template [II:6.5.1]}
NoTitleID = 1000;                       {Resource ID of title string for empty window [I:8.4.2]}


AboutID      = 1000;                    {Resource ID for About alert [II:7.6.1]}
SaveID       = 1001;                    {Resource ID for Save alert [II:7.6.1]}
RevertID     = 1002;                    {Resource ID for Revert alert [II:7.6.1]}
FndrPrintID  = 1003;                    {Resource ID for Finder Print alert [II:7.6.1]}
WrongTypeID  = 1004;                    {Resource ID for Wrong Type alert [II:7.6.1]}
TooLongID    = 1005;                    {Resource ID for File Too Long alert [II:7.6.1]}
PrntCnclID   = 1006;                    {Resource ID for Printing Canceled alert [II:7.6.1]}
OpWrID       = 1007;                    {Resource ID for Already Open alert [II:7.6.1]}
IOErrID      = 1008;                    {Resource ID for I/O Error alert [II:7.6.1]}


DraftID      = 2000;                    {Resource ID for Draft Printing dialog [II:7.6.1]}
SpoolID      = 2001;                    {Resource ID for Spooling dialog [II:7.6.1]}
SpoolPrintID = 2002;                    {Resource ID for Spool Printing dialog [II:7.6.1]}
   PausePrint  = 1;                       {Item number for Pause/Resume button}
   CancelPrint = 2;                       {Item number for Cancel button}
   FinishPrint = 3;                       {Item number for document completion}


type


WDHandle    = ^WDPtr;
WDPtr       = ^WindowData;
WindowData  = record

             editRec    : TEHandle;        {Handle to edit record [II:5.1.1]}
             scrollBar  : ControlHandle;   {Handle to scroll bar [II:6.1.1]}
             printRec   : THPrint;         {Handle to print record [III:4.1.2]}

             dirty      : BOOLEAN;         {Document changed since last saved?}
             padding    : Byte;            {Extra byte for padding [I:3.1.1]}

             volNumber  : INTEGER;         {Volume reference number}
             fileNumber : INTEGER          {File reference number}

           end;  {WindowData}
```

```
var

    TheEvent : EventRecord;                      {Current event [II:2.1.1]}

    TheWindow    : WindowPtr;                     {Pointer to currently active window [II:3.1.1]}
    TheScrollBar : ControlHandle;                 {Handle to active window's scroll bar [II:6.1.1]}
    TheText      : TEHandle;                       {Handle to active window's edit record [II:5.1.1]}

    MacPlus : BOOLEAN;                            {Are we running on a Macintosh Plus?}

    ScreenWidth  : INTEGER;                       {Width of screen in pixels}
    ScreenHeight : INTEGER;                       {Height of screen in pixels}

    OldMask : INTEGER;                            {Saved value of system event mask [II:2.1.3, II:2.3.2]}

    AppleMenu : MenuHandle;                       {Handle to Apple menu [II:4.1.1]}
    FileMenu  : MenuHandle;                       {Handle to File menu [II:4.1.1]}
    EditMenu  : MenuHandle;                       {Handle to Edit menu [II:4.1.1]}

    IBeam : CursHandle;                           {Handle to I-beam cursor [II:2.5.1]}
    Watch : CursHandle;                           {Handle to wristwatch cursor [II:2.5.1]}

    OpenCount  : INTEGER;                         {Number of windows opened}
    CloseCount : INTEGER;                         {Number of windows closed}

    ScrapCompare : INTEGER;                       {Previous scrap count for comparison [I:7.4.2]}
    ScrapDirty   : BOOLEAN;                       {Has scrap been changed?}

    ThePrintRec  : THPrint;                       {Handle to active window's print record [III:4.1.2]}
    ThePrintPort : TPPrPort;                      {Pointer to printing port [III:4.1.1]}
    TEPrint      : TEHandle;                       {Handle to edit record for printing [III:4.1.1]}
    PrintStatus  : TPrStatus;                     {Status record for spool printing [III:4.1.7]}

    DocName : Str255;                             {Name of document being printed [I:8.1.2]}

    DialogID  : INTEGER;                          {Resource ID of printing status dialog}
    TheDialog : DialogPtr;                        {Pointer to printing status dialog [II:7.1.1]}

    PageHeight   : INTEGER;                       {Height of printed page}
    LinesPerPage : INTEGER;                       {Number of text lines per printed page}

    ThisCopy : INTEGER;                           {Number of copy being printed}
    ThisPage : INTEGER;                           {Page number of page being printed}
    NextLine : INTEGER;                           {Line number of next line to be printed}

    FinderPrint    : BOOLEAN;                     {Printing from Finder?}
    PrintSuspended : BOOLEAN;                     {Printing temporarily suspended?}
```

```
    Quitting  : BOOLEAN;                          {Closing up shop?}
    Finished  : BOOLEAN;                          {All closed?}
    ErrorFlag : BOOLEAN;                          {I/O error flag}
```

{ - }

{Forward Declarations}

```
procedure Initialize; forward;
      { One-time-only initialization. }
  procedure SetUpMenus; forward;
        { Set up menus. }
  procedure SetUpCursors; forward;
        { Set up cursors. }
  procedure DoStartup; forward;
        { Process Finder startup information. }
procedure MainLoop; forward;
      { Execute one pass of main program loop. }
  procedure FixCursor; forward;
        { Adjust cursor for region of screen. }
  procedure DoEvent; forward;
        { Get and process one event. }
    procedure DoMouseDown; forward;
          { Handle mouse-down event. }
      procedure DoMenuClick; forward;
            { Handle mouse-down event in menu bar. }
        procedure DoMenuChoice (menuChoice : LONGINT); forward;
              { Handle user's menu choice. }
          procedure DoAppleChoice (theItem : INTEGER); forward;
                { Handle choice from Apple menu. }
            procedure DoAbout; forward;
                  { Handle About MiniEdit... command. }
          procedure DoFileChoice (theItem : INTEGER); forward;
                { Handle choice from File menu. }
            procedure DoNew; forward;
                  { Handle New command. }
              procedure OffsetWindow (whichWindow : WindowPtr); forward;
                    { Offset location of new window. }
            procedure DoOpen; forward;
                  { Handle Open... command. }
              procedure OpenFile (fileName : Str255; vNum : INTEGER); forward;
                    { Open document file. }
            procedure DoClose; forward;
                  { Handle Close command. }
              procedure CloseAppWindow; forward;
                    { Close application window. }
```

```
        procedure CloseSysWindow; forward;
            { Close system window. }
    procedure DoSave; forward;
        { Handle Save command. }
    procedure DoSaveAs; forward;
        { Handle Save As... command. }
     procedure WriteFile (theFile : INTEGER; volNum : INTEGER); forward;
            { Write window contents to a file. }
    procedure DoRevert; forward;
        { Handle Revert to Saved command. }
    procedure DoSetup; forward;
        { Handle Page Setup... command. }
    procedure DoPrint; forward;
        { Handle Print... command. }
      procedure ImagePrep; forward;
            { Prepare document for imaging. }
      procedure ImageDoc; forward;
            { Image document. }
        function ImageFilter (thisDialog      : DialogPtr;
                              var thisEvent   : EventRecord;
                              var itemNumber  : INTEGER) : BOOLEAN; forward;
                { Process event while imaging document. }
            function FilterKey (var thisEvent    : EventRecord;
                                var itemNumber   : INTEGER) : BOOLEAN; forward;
                { Process keystroke in printing dialog. }
            function ImagePage (var itemNumber : INTEGER) : BOOLEAN; forward;
                { Image one page. }
        procedure DoPause; forward;
            { Toggle Pause/Resume button. }
      procedure SpoolPrint; forward;
          { Print spooled document. }
      procedure SpoolBackground; forward;
            { Background procedure for spool printing. }
        procedure ShowSpoolStatus; forward;
            { Display status during spool printing. }
        procedure DoSpoolEvent; forward;
            { Process event during spool printing. }
    procedure DoQuit; forward;
        { Handle Quit command. }
procedure DoEditChoice (theItem : INTEGER); forward;
      { Handle choice from Edit menu. }
    procedure DoUndo; forward;
        { Handle Undo command. }
    procedure DoCut; forward;
        { Handle Cut command. }
```

```
        procedure DoCopy; forward;
            { Handle Copy command. }
        procedure DoPaste; forward;
            { Handle Paste command. }
        procedure DoClear; forward;
            { Handle Clear command. }
    procedure DoSysClick (whichWindow : WindowPtr); forward;
        { Handle mouse-down event in system window. }
    procedure DoContent (whichWindow : WindowPtr); forward;
        { Handle mouse-down event in content region of active window. }
        procedure DoScroll (thePart : INTEGER; thePoint : Point); forward;
            { Handle mouse-down event in scroll bar. }
            procedure ScrollText (theControl : ControlHandle; thePart : INTEGER); forward;
                { Scroll text within window. }
            procedure AdjustText; forward;
                { Adjust text within window to match scroll bar setting. }
            function AutoScroll : BOOLEAN; forward;
                { Handle automatic scrolling during text selection. }
        procedure DoSelect (thePoint : Point); forward;
            { Handle mouse-down event in text rectangle. }
            procedure FixEditMenu; forward;
                { Enable/disable editing commands. }
    procedure DoDrag (whichWindow : WindowPtr); forward;
        { Handle mouse-down event in drag region. }
    procedure DoGrow (whichWindow : WindowPtr); forward;
        { Handle mouse-down event in size region. }
        procedure FixScrollBar; forward;
            { Resize window's scroll bar. }
        procedure FixText; forward;
            { Resize window's text rectangle. }
    procedure DoGoAway (whichWindow : WindowPtr); forward;
        { Handle mouse-down event in close region. }
    procedure DoZoom (whichWindow : WindowPtr; inOrOut : INTEGER); forward;
        { Handle mouse-down event in zoom region. }
procedure DoKeystroke; forward;
    { Handle keystroke. }
procedure DoTyping (ch : CHAR); forward;
        { Handle character typed from keyboard. }
procedure DoUpdate; forward;
    { Handle update event. }
procedure DoActivate; forward;
    { Handle activate and deactivate events. }
    procedure ActWindow (whichWindow : WindowPtr); forward;
        { Activate window. }
    procedure DeactWindow (whichWindow : WindowPtr); forward;
        { Deactivate window. }
```

```
procedure Finalize; forward;
    { One-time-only finalization. }
  procedure WindowDirty (isDirty : BOOLEAN); forward;
      { Mark window dirty or clean. }
  procedure AdjustScrollBar; forward;
      { Adjust scroll bar to length of document. }
  procedure ScrollToSelection; forward;
      { Scroll current selection into view. }
  procedure ScrollCharacter (theCharacter : INTEGER; toBottom : BOOLEAN); forward;
      { Scroll character into view. }
  procedure ReadDeskScrap; forward;
      { Copy desk scrap to Toolbox scrap. }
  procedure WriteDeskScrap; forward;
      { Copy Toolbox scrap to desk scrap. }
  procedure IOCheck (resultCode : OSErr); forward;
      { Check for I/O error. }


{ - - - - - - - - - - - - - - - - - - - - - - - - - - - - - - - - - - - - - - - - - - - - - - - - - - - - - - - - - - - }


procedure Initialize;

  { Do one-time-only initialization [Prog. II:2-6]. }

  const
    sysMaskAddr  = $144;              {Address of system event mask [II:2.3.2]}
    masterBlocks = 4;                 {Number of master pointer blocks to preallocate}

  var
    masterCount  : INTEGER;           {Counter for allocating master pointer blocks}
    sysMaskPtr   : ^INTEGER;          {Pointer for finding old event mask}
    newMask      : INTEGER;           {New value for system event mask [II:2.1.3]}
    machineType  : INTEGER;           {Type of machine we're running on [I:3.1.3]}
    romVersion   : INTEGER;           {Version number of machine's ROM [I:3.1.3]}
    scrapInfo    : PScrapStuff;       {Pointer to scrap information record [I:7.4.2]}

  begin {Initialize}

    InitGraf (@ThePort);              {Initialize QuickDraw [I:4.3.1]}
    InitFonts;                        {Initialize fonts [I:8.2.4]}
    InitWindows;                      {Initialize windows [II:3.2.1]}
    InitMenus;                        {Initialize menus [II:4.2.1]}
    TEInit;                           {Initialize text editing [II:5.2.1]}
    InitDialogs (NIL);                {Initialize dialogs [II:7.2.1]}
    PrOpen;                           {Initialize printing [III:4.2.1]}
```

```
MaxApplZone;                               {Expand heap to maximum size [I:3.3.4]}
for masterCount := 1 to masterBlocks do                    {Preallocate master pointers to        }
   MoreMasters;                                            {  minimize heap fragmentation [I:3.2.5]}

Environs (romVersion, machineType);                        {Find out machine configuration [I:3.1.3]}
MacPlus := (romVersion >= MacPlusROM);                     {Macintosh Plus or later? [I:3.1.3]}
with ScreenBits.bounds do                                  {Get boundary rectangle for screen [I:4.2.1]}
   begin
      ScreenWidth  := right  - left;                       {Set screen dimensions [I:4.1.2]}
      ScreenHeight := bottom - top
   end; {with ScreenBits.bounds}

TheWindow     := NIL;                                      {Clear global pointers/handles}
TheScrollBar  := NIL;
TheText       := NIL;
ThePrintRec   := NIL;

sysMaskPtr := POINTER(sysMaskAddr);                        {Point to system event mask [II:2.3.2]}
OldMask    := sysMaskPtr^;                                 {Save old mask value}

newMask := EveryEvent - KeyUpMask - MUpMask;               {Disable key-up and mouse-up events [II:2.1.3]}
SetEventMask (newMask);                                    {Set the mask [II:2.3.2]}
FlushEvents  (EveryEvent, 0);                              {Clear out event queue [II:2.3.1]}

SetUpMenus;                                                {Create program's menus}
SetUpCursors;                                              {Get standard cursors}

OpenCount  := 0;                                           {Initialize window counts}
CloseCount := 0;

ScrapDirty    := FALSE;                                    {Toolbox and desk scraps initially agree}
scrapInfo     := InfoScrap;                                {Get scrap info [I:7.4.2]}
ScrapCompare := scrapInfo^.scrapCount + 1;                 {Force scrap transfer [I:7.4.2]}
ReadDeskScrap;                                             {Read desk scrap into Toolbox scrap}

Quitting  := FALSE;                                        {Initialize global flags}
Finished  := FALSE;
ErrorFlag := FALSE;


DoStartup                                                  {Process Finder startup information}

end;   {Initialize}
```

{- -}

```
procedure SetUpMenus;

   { Set up menus [Prog. II:4-2]. }

   begin {SetUpMenus}

      AppleMenu := GetMenu (AppleID);          {Get Apple menu from resource file [II:4.2.2]}
      AddResMenu (AppleMenu, 'DRVR');          {Add names of available desk accessories [II:4.3.3]}
      InsertMenu (AppleMenu, 0);               {Install at end of menu bar [II:4.4.1]}

      FileMenu := GetMenu (FileID);            {Get File menu from resource file [II:4.2.2]}
      InsertMenu (FileMenu, 0);                {Install at end of menu bar [II:4.4.1]}

      EditMenu := GetMenu (EditID);            {Get Edit menu from resource file [II:4.2.2]}
      InsertMenu (EditMenu, 0);                {Install at end of menu bar [II:4.4.1]}

      DrawMenuBar                              {Show new menu bar on screen [II:4.4.3]}

   end;    {SetUpMenus}
```

{- -}

```
procedure SetUpCursors;

   { Set up cursors [Prog. II:2-7]. }

   begin {SetUpCursors}

      IBeam := GetCursor (IBeamCursor);        {Get cursors from system resource file [II:2.5.2]}
      Watch := GetCursor (WatchCursor);

      InitCursor                               {Set standard arrow cursor [II:2.5.2]}

   end;    {SetUpCursors}
```

{- -}

```
procedure DoStartup;

   { Process Finder startup information [Prog. III:4-14]. }

   var
      theMessage : INTEGER;                    {Open or print? [I:7.3.4]}
      nDocs      : INTEGER;                    {Number of documents selected in Finder}
      thisDoc    : INTEGER;                    {Index number of document}
```

```
    docInfo    : AppFile;                              {Startup information about one document [I:7.3.4]}
    ignore     : INTEGER;                              {Item code returned by alert}

begin {DoStartup}

  CountAppFiles (theMessage, nDocs);                   {Get number of documents and startup message [I:7.3.4]}

  FinderPrint := (theMessage = AppPrint);              {Printing requested? [I:7.3.4]}

  if nDocs = 0 then                                    {If no documents selected,    }
    DoNew                                              {  just open an empty window}

  else
    for thisDoc := 1 to nDocs do                       {Otherwise loop through documents}
      begin

        GetAppFiles (thisDoc, docInfo);                {Get startup information [I:7.3.4]}
        with docInfo do

          if fType = 'TEXT' then                       {Is it a text file? [I:7.3.4]}
            begin
              ErrorFlag := FALSE;                      {Clear I/O error flag}
              OpenFile (fName, vRefNum);               {Read file into a window}

              if FinderPrint and not ErrorFlag then    {Printing requested?}
                begin

                  ParamText (fName, '', '', '');       {Merge in file name [II:7.4.6]}
                  InitCursor;                          {Set arrow cursor [II:2.5.2]}
                  ignore := NoteAlert (FndrPrintID, NIL);   {Post alert [II:7.4.2]}

                  DoSetup;                             {Get page setup information}
                  DoPrint;                             {Print the file}

                  CloseAppWindow                       {Dispose of data structures}

                end; {if FinderPrint and not ErrorFlag}

              if not ErrorFlag then                    {No errors detected?}
                ClrAppFiles (thisDoc)                  {Mark file as processed [I:7.3.4]}
            end {then}

          else
            begin
              ParamText (fName, '', '', '');           {Merge in file name [II:7.4.6]}
```

```
            InitCursor;                              {Set arrow cursor [II:2.5.2]}
            ignore := StopAlert (WrongTypeID, NIL)   {Post alert [II:7.4.2]}
          end {else}

      end; {for thisDoc}

  if FinderPrint then                                {Printing from Finder?}
    begin
      Finalize;                                      {Close up shop}
      ExitToShell                                    {Return to Finder [I:7.1.3]}
    end {if FinderPrint}

  end; {DoStartup}


{- - - - - - - - - - - - - - - - - - - - - - - - - - - - - - - - - - - - - - - - - - - - - - - - -


procedure MainLoop;

  { Execute one pass of main program loop [Prog. II:2-2]. }

  begin {MainLoop}

    if FrontWindow = NIL then                        {Is the desktop empty? [II:3.3.3]}
      begin

        DisableItem (EditMenu, UndoItem);            {Disable inapplicable menu commands [II:4.6.2]}
        DisableItem (EditMenu, CutItem);
        DisableItem (EditMenu, CopyItem);
        DisableItem (EditMenu, PasteItem);
        DisableItem (EditMenu, ClearItem);

        DisableItem (FileMenu, CloseItem);
        DisableItem (FileMenu, SaveItem);
        DisableItem (FileMenu, SaveAsItem);
        DisableItem (FileMenu, RevertItem);
        DisableItem (FileMenu, SetupItem);
        DisableItem (FileMenu, PrintItem)

      end; {if FrontWindow = NIL}

    FixCursor;                                       {Adjust cursor for region of screen}
    SystemTask;                                      {Do system idle processing [II:2.7.2]}

    if TheText <> NIL then
      TEIdle (TheText);                              {Blink cursor [II:5.4.3]}
```

```
    DoEvent                                    {Get and process one event}

  end;   {MainLoop}
```

{ - }

```
procedure FixCursor;

  { Adjust cursor for region of screen [Prog. II:2-8]. }

  var
    mousePoint : Point;                        {Current mouse position in window coordinates  [I:4.1.1]}
    textRect   : Rect;                         {Active window's text rectangle [I:4.1.2]}

  begin {FixCursor}

    if Quitting then                           {Skip cursor adjustment during quit sequence}
      EXIT (FixCursor);

    if FrontWindow = NIL then                  {Screen empty? [II:3.3.3]}
      InitCursor                               {Set arrow cursor [II:2.5.2]}

    else if FrontWindow = TheWindow then       {Is one of our windows active? [II:3.3.3]}
      begin

        GetMouse (mousePoint);                 {Get mouse position [II:2.4.1]}
        textRect := TheText^^.viewRect;        {Get window's text rectangle [II:5.1.1]}

        if PtInRect (mousePoint, textRect) then {Is mouse in text rectangle? [I:4.4.3]}
          SetCursor (IBeam^^)                  {Set I-beam cursor [II:2.5.2]}
        else
          InitCursor                           {Set arrow cursor [II:2.5.2]}

      end {then}

    else                                       {A system window is active:  }
      {Do nothing}                             {  let desk accessory set cursor}

  end; {FixCursor}
```

{ - }

```
procedure DoEvent;

  { Get and process one event [Prog. II:2-5]. }
```

```
begin {DoEvent}

   ErrorFlag := FALSE;                          {Clear I/O error flag}

   if GetNextEvent (EveryEvent, TheEvent) then  {Get next event [II:2.2.1]}

      case TheEvent.what of

         MouseDown:
            if not Quitting then
               DoMouseDown;                      {Handle mouse-down event}

         KeyDown, AutoKey:
            if not Quitting then
               DoKeystroke;                      {Handle keystroke}

         UpdateEvt:
            DoUpdate;                            {Handle update event}

         ActivateEvt:
            DoActivate;                          {Handle activate/deactivate event}

         otherwise
            {Do nothing}

         end {case TheEvent.what}

      else if Quitting and (TheEvent.what = NullEvent) then  {Closing up shop after a Quit command?}
         begin
            if FrontWindow <> NIL then           {Any windows on the screen? [II:3.3.3]}
               DoClose                           {Close the frontmost}
            else
               Finished := TRUE                  {Signal end of program}
         end {if Quitting}

   end;   {DoEvent}

{- - - - - - - - - - - - - - - - - - - - - - - - - - - - - - - - - - - - - - - - - - - - - - - - - - - - - - -}

procedure DoMouseDown;

   { Handle mouse-down event [Prog. II:3-7]. }

   var
      whichWindow : WindowPtr;                   {Window where mouse was pressed [II:3.1.1]}
```

```
    thePart    : INTEGER;                          {Part of screen where mouse was pressed [II:3.5.1]}

begin {DoMouseDown}

    thePart := FindWindow (TheEvent.where, whichWindow); {Where on the screen was mouse pressed? [II:3.5.1]}

    case thePart of

      InDesk:
        {Do nothing};

      InMenuBar:
        DoMenuClick;                               {Handle click in menu bar}

      InSysWindow:
        DoSysClick (whichWindow);                  {Handle click in system window}

      InContent:
        DoContent (whichWindow);                   {Handle click in content region}

      InDrag:
        DoDrag (whichWindow);                      {Handle click in drag region}

      InGrow:
        DoGrow (whichWindow);                      {Handle click in size region}

      InGoAway:
        DoGoAway (whichWindow);                    {Handle click in close region}

      InZoomIn:
        DoZoom (whichWindow, InZoomIn);            {Handle click in zoom region}

      InZoomOut:
        DoZoom (whichWindow, InZoomOut)            {Handle click in zoom region}

      end {case thePart}

  end; {DoMouseDown}

{- - - - - - - - - - - - - - - - - - - - - - - - - - - - - - - - - - - - - - - - - - - - - - - - - - - - - - - -}

procedure DoMenuClick;

  { Handle mouse-down event in menu bar [Prog. II:4-3]. }
```

```
   var
      menuChoice : LONGINT;                    {Menu ID and item number}

   begin {DoMenuClick}

      menuChoice := MenuSelect (TheEvent.where);    {Track mouse [II:4.5.1]}
      DoMenuChoice (menuChoice)                      {Handle user's menu choice}

   end;  {DoMenuClick}
```
{--}
```
procedure DoMenuChoice {(menuChoice : LONGINT)};

   { Handle user's menu choice [Prog. II:4-5]. }

   const
      noMenu = 0;                              {No menu selected}

   var
      theMenu : INTEGER;                       {Menu ID of selected menu}
      theItem : INTEGER;                       {Item number of selected item}

   begin {DoMenuChoice}

      theMenu := HiWord(menuChoice);           {Get menu ID [I:2.2.3]}
      theItem := LoWord(menuChoice);           {Get item number [I:2.2.3]}

      case theMenu of

         noMenu:
            {Do nothing};                      {No menu selected, nothing to do}

         AppleID:
            DoAppleChoice (theItem);           {Handle choice from Apple menu}

         FileID:
            DoFileChoice  (theItem);           {Handle choice from File menu}

         EditID:
            DoEditChoice  (theItem)            {Handle choice from Edit menu}

         end;  {case theMenu}

      HiliteMenu (0)                           {Unhighlight menu title [II:4.5.4]}

   end;  {DoMenuChoice}
```

```
{ -------------------------------------------------------------------------- }

procedure DoAppleChoice {(theItem : INTEGER)};

   { Handle choice from Apple menu [Prog. II:4-6]. }

   var
      accName    : Str255;                       {Name of desk accessory [I:2.1.1]}
      accNumber  : INTEGER;                      {Reference number of desk accessory}

   begin  {DoAppleChoice}

      case theItem of

         AboutItem:
            DoAbout;                             {Handle About MiniEdit...command}

         otherwise
            begin

               if FrontWindow = NIL then         {Is the desktop empty? [II:3.3.3]}
                  begin

                     EnableItem (FileMenu, CloseItem);  {Enable Close command [II:4.6.2]}

                     EnableItem (EditMenu, UndoItem);   {Enable standard editing commands}
                     EnableItem (EditMenu, CutItem);    {  for desk accessory [II:4.6.2]}
                     EnableItem (EditMenu, CopyItem);
                     EnableItem (EditMenu, PasteItem);
                     EnableItem (EditMenu, ClearItem)

                  end;  {if FrontWindow = NIL}

               GetItem (AppleMenu, theItem, accName);  {Get accessory name [II:4.6.1]}
               accNumber := OpenDeskAcc (accName)      {Open desk accessory [II:4.5.2]}

            end  {otherwise}

      end  {case theItem}

   end;  {DoAppleChoice}

{ -------------------------------------------------------------------------- }
```

```
    dataHandle := NewHandle (SIZEOF(WindowData));        {Allocate  window  data  record  [I:3.2.1]}
    SetWRefCon (TheWindow, LONGINT(dataHandle));         {Store as reference constant [II:3.2.4]}

    MoveHHi (dataHandle);                                {Move data record to top of heap [I:3.2.5]}
    HLock   (dataHandle);                                {Lock data record [I:3.2.4]}
       theData := WDHandle(dataHandle);                  {Convert to typed handle}
       with theData^^ do
          begin

             editRec   := TENew (destRect, viewRect);
                                                         {Make edit record [II:5.2.2]}
             if not FinderPrint then                     {Printing from Finder?}
                scrollBar := GetNewControl (ScrollID, TheWindow);    {Make scroll bar [II:6.2.1]}

             printHandle := NewHandle (SIZEOF(TPrint));            {Allocate print record [I:3.2.1]}
             printRec    := THPrint(printHandle);        {Convert to typed handle [III:4.1.2]}
             PrintDefault (printRec);                    {Initialize print record [III:4.2.2]}

             dirty      := FALSE;                         {Document is initially clean}
             fileNumber := 0;                             {Window has no associated file}
             volNumber  := 0;                             {  or volume              }

             if not FinderPrint then                      {Printing from Finder?}
                SetClikLoop (@AutoScroll, editRec);       {Install auto-scroll routine [II:5.6.1]}

             TheScrollBar := scrollBar;                   {Set global handles}
             TheText      := editRec;
             ThePrintRec  := printRec

          end; {with theData^^}

    HUnlock (dataHandle);                                 {Unlock data record [I:3.2.4]}

    EnableItem (FileMenu, CloseItem)                      {Enable Close command on menu [II:4.6.2]}

  end; {DoNew}

{- - - - - - - - - - - - - - - - - - - - - - - - - - - - - - - - - - - - - - - - - - - - - - - - - - - - - - - - - - - - -}

procedure OffsetWindow {(whichWindow : WindowPtr)};

  { Offset location of new window [Prog. II:3-12]. }

  const
     hOffset = 20;                                        {Horizontal offset from previous window, in pixels}
```

```
        vOffset = 20;                                    {Vertical offset from previous window, in pixels}


    var
        windowWidth   : INTEGER;                         {Width of window in pixels}
        windowHeight  : INTEGER;                         {Height of window in pixels}
        hExtra        : INTEGER;                         {Excess screen width in pixels}
        vExtra        : INTEGER;                         {Excess screen height in pixels}
        hMax          : INTEGER;                         {Maximum number of windows horizontally}
        vMax          : INTEGER;                         {Maximum number of windows vertically}
        windowLeft    : INTEGER;                         {Left edge of window in global coordinates}
        windowTop     : INTEGER;                         {Top edge of window in global coordinates}


begin  {OffsetWindow}

    with whichWindow^.portRect do
      begin
        windowWidth  := right  - left;                   {Get window dimensions from }
        windowHeight := bottom - top;                    {  port rectangle [I:4.2.2]}
        windowWidth  := windowWidth + TitleBarSize       {Adjust for title bar}
      end;  {with whichWindow^.portRect}

    hExtra := ScreenWidth  - windowWidth;                {Find excess screen width}
    vExtra := (ScreenHeight - MenuBarHeight) - windowHeight;  {Find excess screen height}

    hMax := (hExtra div hOffset) + 1;                    {Find maximum number of windows horizontally}
    vMax := (vExtra div vOffset) + 1;                    {Find maximum number of windows vertically}

    OpenCount  := OpenCount + 1;                         {Increment open window count}
    windowLeft := (OpenCount mod hMax) * hOffset;        {Calculate horizontal }
    windowTop  := (OpenCount mod vMax) * vOffset;        {  and vertical offset}

    windowLeft := windowLeft + TitleBarSize;             {Adjust for title bar}
    windowTop  := windowTop  + MenuBarHeight;            {  and menu bar   }

    MoveWindow (whichWindow, windowLeft, windowTop, FALSE)  {Move window to new location [II:3.3.2]}

  end;   {OffsetWindow}
```

{- -}


```
procedure DoOpen;

  { Handle Open... command [Prog. II:8-5]. }

  var
    dlgOrigin   : Point;                                 {Top-left corner of dialog box [I:4.1.1]}
```

```
    theTypeList : SFTypeList;              {List of file types to display [II:8.3.2]}
    theReply    : SFReply;                 {Data returned by Get dialog [II:8.3.1]}

 begin {DoOpen}

    SetPt (dlgOrigin, DlgLeft, DlgTop);    {Set up dialog origin [I:4.1.1]}
    theTypeList [0] := 'TEXT';             {Display text files only [II:8.3.2]}

    SFGetFile (dlgOrigin, '', NIL, 1, theTypeList, NIL, theReply);  {Get file name from user [II:8.3.2]}

    with theReply do
       if good then                        {Did user confirm file selection? [II:8.3.1]}
          OpenFile (fName, vRefNum)         {Open file and read into window}

 end;  {DoOpen}
```

```
{- - - - - - - - - - - - - - - - - - - - - - - - - - - - - - - - - - - - - - - - - - - - - - - - - - - - - - - - - - - - - - - -}
```

```
procedure OpenFile {(fileName : Str255; vNum : INTEGER)};

   { Open document file [Prog. II:8-6]. }

   var
      theData    : WDHandle;               {Handle to window's data record}
      dataHandle : Handle;                 {Untyped handle for locking data record [I:3.1.1]}
      theFile    : INTEGER;                {Reference number of file}
      resultCode : OSErr;                  {I/O error code [I:3.1.2]}

 begin {OpenFile}

    resultCode := FSOpen (fileName, vNum, theFile);  {Open the file [II:8.2.2]}
    IOCheck (resultCode);                  {Check for error}
    if ErrorFlag then EXIT (OpenFile);     {On error, exit to main event loop}

    DoNew;                                 {Open a new window}

    dataHandle := Handle(GetWRefCon(TheWindow));  {Get window data [II:3.2.4]}
    MoveHHi (dataHandle);                  {Move data record to top of heap [I:3.2.5]}
    HLock   (dataHandle);                  {Lock data record [I:3.2.4]}

      theData := WDHandle(dataHandle);     {Convert to typed handle}
      with theData^^ do
        begin
           volNumber  := vNum;             {Save volume and file number}
           fileNumber := theFile;          {  in window data record  }
```

```
        SetWTitle (TheWindow, fileName)        {File name becomes window title [II:3.2.4]}
    end;  {with theData^^}


  HUnlock (dataHandle);                        {Unlock data record [I:3.2.4]}


  DoRevert;                                    {Read file into window}


  if ErrorFlag then                            {Error reading file?}
    CloseAppWindow                             {Close and dispose of the window}


end;   {OpenFile}
```

```
{ - - - - - - - - - - - - - - - - - - - - - - - - - - - - - - - - - - - - - - - - - - - - - - - - - - - - - - - - - }


procedure DoClose;

  { Handle Close command [Prog. II:3-3]. }

  begin {DoClose}

    if FrontWindow = TheWindow then            {Is the active window one of ours? [II:3.3.3]}
      CloseAppWindow                           {Close application window}
    else
      CloseSysWindow                           {Close system window}

  end;   {DoClose}


{ - - - - - - - - - - - - - - - - - - - - - - - - - - - - - - - - - - - - - - - - - - - - - - - - - - - - - - - - - }


procedure CloseAppWindow;

  { Close application window [Prog. II:7-2]. }

  const
    saveItem    = 1;                           {Item number for Save button}
    discardItem = 2;                           {Item number for Discard button}
    cancelItem  = 3;                           {Item number for Cancel button}

  var
    theData     : WDHandle;                    {Handle to window's data record}
    dataHandle  : Handle;                      {Untyped handle for destroying data record [I:3.1.1]}
    theTitle    : Str255;                      {Title of window [I:2.1.1]}
    theItem     : INTEGER;                     {Item number for Save alert}
    resultCode  : OSErr;                       {I/O error code [I:3.1.2]}
    thisWindow  : WindowPtr;                   {Pointer to window being closed [II:3.1.1]}
```

```
   thisEditRec : TEHandle;                            {Handle to window's edit record [II:5.1.1]}
   printHandle : Handle;                              {Untyped handle for destroying print record [I:3.1.1]}

begin {CloseAppWindow}

   dataHandle := Handle(GetWRefCon(TheWindow));       {Get window data [II:3.2.4]}
   MoveHHi (dataHandle);                              {Move data record to top of heap [I:3.2.5]}
   HLock   (dataHandle);                              {Lock data record [I:3.2.4]}

      theData := WDHandle(dataHandle);                {Convert to typed handle}
      with theData^^ do
         begin

            if dirty then                             {Have window contents been changed?}
               begin
                  GetWTitle (TheWindow, theTitle);    {Get window title [II:3.2.4]}
                  ParamText (theTitle, '', '', '');   {Substitute into alert text [II:7.4.6]}

                  InitCursor;                         {Set arrow cursor [II:2.5.2]}
                  theItem := CautionAlert (SaveID, NIL);  {Post alert [II:7.4.2]}
                  case theItem of

                     saveItem:
                        begin
                           DoSave;                    {Save window contents to disk}
                           if ErrorFlag then          {Check for I/O error}
                              begin
                                 HUnlock (dataHandle);  {Unlock data record [I:3.2.4]}
                                 EXIT (CloseAppWindow)  {Exit to main event loop}
                              end {if ErrorFlag}
                        end {saveItem};

                     discardItem:
                        {Do nothing};

                     cancelItem:
                        begin
                           Quitting := FALSE;         {Cancel Quit command, if any}
                           HUnlock (dataHandle);      {Unlock data record [I:3.2.4]}
                           EXIT (CloseAppWindow)       {Exit to main event loop}
                        end {cancelItem}

                  end {case theItem}
            end; {if dirty}
```

```
      if fileNumber <> 0 then                    {Is window associated with a file?}
         begin
            resultCode := FSClose (fileNumber);   {Close file [II:8.2.2]}
            IOCheck (resultCode)                  {Post error alert, if any}
         end; {if fileNumber <> 0}

      thisEditRec := editRec;                     {Save handles to edit and print records  }
      printHandle := Handle(printRec)             {   (DoActivate will unlock the data record)}

   end; {with theData^^}

   HUnlock (dataHandle);                          {Unlock data record [I:3.2.4]}

   thisWindow := TheWindow;                       {Save window pointer (DoActivate will change TheWindow)}
   HideWindow (TheWindow);                        {Force deactivate event [II:3.3.1]}

   if GetNextEvent (ActivMask, TheEvent) then     {Get deactivate event [II :2.2.1, II:2.1.2]}
      DoActivate;                                 {   and handle it                    }
   if GetNextEvent (ActivMask, TheEvent) then     {Get activate event [II:2.2.1, II:2.1.2]}
      DoActivate;                                 {   and handle it                    }

   CloseCount := CloseCount + 1;                  {Increment closed window count}
   if CloseCount = OpenCount then                 {Closing last application window on screen?}
      begin
         OpenCount  := 0;                         {Reset window offset to zero}
         CloseCount := 0
      end; {if CloseCount = OpenCount}

   TEDispose       (thisEditRec);                 {Dispose of edit record [II:5.2.2]}
   DisposHandle    (printHandle);                 {Dispose of print record [I:3.2.2]}
   DisposHandle    (dataHandle);                  {Dispose of window data record [I:3.2.2]}
   DisposeWindow (thisWindow)                     {Dispose of window and scroll bar [II:3.2.3]}

end;   {CloseAppWindow}

{- - - - - - - - - - - - - - - - - - - - - - - - - - - - - - - - - - - - - - - - - - - - - - - - - - - - -}


procedure CloseSysWindow;

   { Close system window [Prog. II:4-7]. }

   var
      whichWindow : WindowPeek;                   {Pointer for access to window's fields [II:3.1.1]}
      accNumber   : INTEGER;                      {Reference number of desk accessory [I:7.5.5]}
```

```
   begin {CloseSysWindow}

      whichWindow := WindowPeek(FrontWindow);          {Convert to a WindowPeek [II:3.1.1, II:3.3.3]}

      accNumber := whichWindow^.windowKind;            {Get reference number of desk accessory [II:3.1.1]}
      CloseDeskAcc (accNumber)                          {Close desk accessory [II:4.5.2]}

   end;   {CloseSysWindow}
```

{- -}

```
procedure DoSave;

   { Handle Save command [Prog. II:8-2]. }

   var
      theData    : WDHandle;                            {Handle to window's data record}
      dataHandle : Handle;                              {Untyped handle for locking data record [I:3.1.1]}

   begin {DoSave}

      dataHandle := Handle(GetWRefCon(TheWindow));      {Get window data [II:3.2.4]}
      MoveHHi (dataHandle);                             {Move data record to top of heap [I:3.2.5]}
      HLock   (dataHandle);                             {Lock data record [I:3.2.4]}

         theData := WDHandle(dataHandle);               {Convert to typed handle}
         with theData^^ do
            if fileNumber = 0 then                      {Is window associated with a file?}
               DoSaveAs                                 {Get file name from user}
            else
               WriteFile (fileNumber, volNumber);       {Write to window's file}

      HUnlock (dataHandle)                              {Unlock data record [I:3.2.4]}

   end;   {DoSave}
```

{- -}

```
procedure DoSaveAs;

   { Handle Save As... command [Prog. II:8-8]. }

   var
      dlgOrigin : Point;                                {Top-left corner of dialog box [I:4.1.1]}
      theReply  : SFReply;                              {Data returned by Put dialog [II:8.3.1]}
```

```
  theInfo    : FInfo;                              {File's Finder information [I:7.3.2]}
  theFile    : INTEGER;                            {Reference number of file}
  theData    : WDHandle;                           {Handle to window's data record}
  dataHandle : Handle;                             {Untyped handle for locking data record [I:3.1.1]}
  strHandle  : StringHandle;                       {Handle to title string for empty window [II:8.1.2]}
  untitled   : Str255;                             {Title string for empty window [I:2.1.1]}
  ignore     : INTEGER;                            {Item code returned by alert}
  resultCode : OSErr;                              {I/O error code [I:3.1.2]}

begin {DoSaveAs}

  SetPt      (dlgOrigin, DlgLeft, DlgTop);         {Set up dialog origin [I:4.1.1]}
  SFPutFile (dlgOrigin, 'Save under what file name?', '', NIL, theReply);
                                                   {Get file name from user [II:8.3.3]}

  with theReply do
    begin
      if not good then                             {Did user confirm file selection? [II:8.3.1]}
        begin
          Quitting  := FALSE;                      {Cancel Quit command, if any}
          ErrorFlag := TRUE;                       {Force exit to main event loop}
          EXIT (DoSaveAs)                          {Skip rest of operation}
        end; {if not good}


      resultCode := GetFInfo (fName, vRefNum, theInfo); {Get Finder info [I:7.3.3]}
      case resultCode of

        NoErr:                                     {File already exists [II:8.2.8]}
          if theInfo.fdType <> 'TEXT' then         {Not a text file? [I:7.3.2]}
            begin
              ParamText (fName, '', '', '');       {Substitute file name into  text of alert [II:7.4.6]}
              ignore := StopAlert (wrongTypeID, NIL); {Post alert [II:7.4.2]}

              ErrorFlag := TRUE;                   {Force exit to main event loop}
              EXIT (DoSaveAs)                      {Skip rest of operation}
            end; {if theInfo.fdType <> 'TEXT'}

        FNFErr:                                    {File not found [II:8.2.8]}
          begin
            resultCode := Create (fName, vRefNum, 'MEDT', 'TEXT'); {Create the file [II:8.2.1]}
            IOCheck (resultCode);                  {Check for error}
            if ErrorFlag then EXIT (DoSaveAs)      {On error, exit to main event loop}
          end; {FNFErr}


        otherwise                                  {Unanticipated error}
          begin
```

```
        IOCheck (resultCode);              {Post error alert}
        EXIT (DoSaveAs)                    {Exit to main event loop}
     end {otherwise}

  end; {case resultCode}


dataHandle := Handle(GetWRefCon(TheWindow));  {Get window data [II:3.2.4]}
MoveHHi (dataHandle);                      {Move data record to top of heap [I:3.2.5]}
HLock   (dataHandle);                      {Lock data record [I:3.2.4]}

  theData := WDHandle(dataHandle);         {Convert to typed handle}
  with theData^^ do
     begin

        SetCursor (Watch^^);               {Indicate delay [II:2.5.2]}

        if fileNumber <> 0 then            {Does window already have a file?}
           begin
              resultCode := FSClose (fileNumber); {Close old file [II:8.2.2]}
              IOCheck (resultCode);        {Check for error}
              if ErrorFlag then            {Error detected during close?}
                 begin
                    HUnlock (dataHandle);  {Unlock data record [I:3.2.4]}
                    EXIT (DoSaveAs)        {Exit to main event loop}
                 end {if ErrorFlag}
           end; {if fileNumber <> 0}

        resultCode := FSOpen (fName, vRefNum, theFile); {Open new file [II:8.2.2]}
        IOCheck (resultCode);              {Check for error}
        if ErrorFlag then                  {Error detected during open?}
           begin
              volNumber  := 0;             {Window is left with no file: clear volume}
              fileNumber := 0;             {  and file numbers in window data      }

              strHandle := GetString (noTitleID); {Get string from resource file [I:8.1.2]}
              untitled  := strHandle^^;    {Convert from handle}
              SetWTitle (TheWindow, untitled) {Set new window title [II:3.2.4]}
           end {then}

        else
           begin
              volNumber  := vRefNum;       {Save new volume and file }
              fileNumber := theFile;       {  numbers in window data}
              SetWTitle (TheWindow, fName); {File name becomes new window title [II:3.2.4]}
```

```
                   WriteFile (theFile, vRefNum)  {Write window's contents to file}
              end {else}

         end; {with theData^^}

      HUnlock (dataHandle)                        {Unlock data record [I:3.2.4]}

    end {with theReply}

  end; {DoSaveAs}
```

```
{ - - - - - - - - - - - - - - - - - - - - - - - - - - - - - - - - - - - - - - - - - - - - - - - - - }

procedure WriteFile {(theFile : INTEGER; volNum : INTEGER)};

  { Write window contents to a file [Prog. II:8-3]. }

  var
     textHandle : Handle;                          {Handle to text of file [I:3.1.1]}
     textLength : LONGINT;                         {Length of text in bytes}
     resultCode : OSErr;                           {I/O error code [I:3.1.2]}

  begin {WriteFile}

     SetCursor (Watch^^);                          {Indicate delay [II:2.5.2]}

     with TheText^^ do
       begin
          textHandle := hText;                     {Get text handle and current length}
          textLength := teLength                   { from edit record [II:5.1.1] }
       end; {with TheText^^}

     resultCode := SetFPos (theFile, FSFromStart, 0);  {Reset mark to beginning of file [II:8.2.4]}
     IOCheck (resultCode);                         {Check for error}
     if ErrorFlag then EXIT (WriteFile);           {On error, exit to main event loop}

     MoveHHi (textHandle);                         {Move text to top of heap [I:3.2.5]}
     HLock   (textHandle);                         {Lock text [I:3.2.4]}
       resultCode := FSWrite (theFile, textLength, textHandle^);  {Write text to file [II:8.2.3]}
     HUnlock (textHandle);                         {Unlock text [I:3.2.4]}
     IOCheck (resultCode);                         {Check for error}
     if ErrorFlag then EXIT (WriteFile);           {On error, exit to main event loop}

     resultCode := SetEOF (theFile, textLength);   {Set length of file [II:8.2.5]}
     IOCheck (resultCode);                         {Check for error}
```

```
      if ErrorFlag then EXIT (WriteFile);              {On error, exit to main event loop}

      resultCode := FlushVol (NIL, volNum);            {Flush volume buffer [II:8.1.3]}
      IOCheck (resultCode);                            {Check for error}
      if ErrorFlag then EXIT (WriteFile);              {On error, exit to main event loop}

      WindowDirty (FALSE)                              {Mark window as clean}

  end;  {WriteFile}
```

{ - }

```
procedure DoRevert;

  { Handle Revert to Saved command [Prog. II:8-4]. }

  const
    maxLength = 32767;                                 {Maximum document length in bytes}

  var
    theData     : WDHandle;                            {Handle to window's data record}
    dataHandle  : Handle;                              {Untyped handle for locking data record [I:3.1.1]}
    editHandle  : Handle;                              {Untyped handle for locking edit record [I:3.1.1]}
    fileName    : Str255;                              {Title of window [I:2.1.1]}
    textLength  : LONGINT;                             {Length of file in bytes}
    theItem     : INTEGER;                             {Item number returned by alert}
    resultCode  : OSErr;                               {I/O error code [I:3.1.2]}

  begin {DoRevert}

    dataHandle := Handle(GetWRefCon(TheWindow));       {Get window data [II:3.2.4]}
    MoveHHi (dataHandle);                              {Move data record to top of heap [I:3.2.5]}
    HLock   (dataHandle);                              {Lock data record [I:3.2.4]}

      theData := WDHandle(dataHandle);                 {Convert to typed handle}
      with theData^^ do
        begin

          if dirty then                                {Have window contents been changed?}
            begin
              GetWTitle (TheWindow, fileName);         {Get file name from window title [II:3.2.4]}
              ParamText (fileName, '', '', '');        {Substitute into text of alert [II:7.4.6]}

              InitCursor;                              {Set arrow cursor [II:2.5.2]}
              theItem := CautionAlert (RevertID, NIL); {Post alert [II:7.4.2]}
```

```
    if theItem = Cancel then                    {Did user cancel? [II:7.1.1]}
      begin
        HUnlock (dataHandle);                    {Unlock data record [I:3.2.4]}
        ErrorFlag := TRUE;                       {Force exit to main event loop}
        EXIT (DoRevert)                          {Skip rest of operation}
      end {if theItem = Cancel}
  end; {if dirty}


SetCursor (Watch^^);                             {Indicate delay [II:2.5.2]}


resultCode := GetEOF (fileNumber, textLength);   {Get length of file [II:8.2.5]}
if textLength > maxLength then                   {File too long?}
  begin
    GetWTitle (TheWindow, fileName);             {Get file name from window title [II:3.2.4]}
    ParamText (fileName, '', '', '');            {Substitute into text of alert [II:7.4.6]}

    InitCursor;                                  {Set arrow cursor [II:2.5.2]}
    theItem := StopAlert (TooLongID, NIL);       {Post alert [II:7.4.2]}

    ErrorFlag := TRUE                            {Force exit}
  end {then}
else
  IOCheck (resultCode);                          {Check for I/O error}
if ErrorFlag then                                {Error detected?}
  begin
    HUnlock (dataHandle);                        {Unlock data record [I:3.2.4]}
    EXIT (DoRevert)                              {Exit to main event loop}
  end; {if ErrorFlag}


resultCode := SetFPos (fileNumber, FSFromStart, 0);  {Set mark at beginning of file [II:8.2.4]}
IOCheck (resultCode);                            {Check for error}
if ErrorFlag then                                {Error detected?}
  begin
    HUnlock (dataHandle);                        {Unlock data record [I:3.2.4]}
    EXIT (DoRevert)                              {Exit to main event loop}
  end; {if ErrorFlag}


editHandle := Handle(TheText);                   {Convert to untyped handle [I:3.1.1]}
MoveHHi (editHandle);                            {Move edit record to top of heap [I:3.2.5]}
HLock   (editHandle);                            {Lock edit record [I:3.2.4]}
  with TheText^^ do
    begin

      SetHandleSize (hText, textLength);         {Adjust text to length of file [I:3.2.3, II:5.1.1]}
      teLength := textLength;                    {Set text length [II:5.1.1]}
```

```
            MoveHHi (hText);                          {Move block to top of heap [I:3.2.5]}
            HLock   (hText);                          {Lock text handle [I:3.2.4]}
              resultCode := FSRead (fileNumber, textLength, hText^);
                                                      {Read text of file into block [II:8.2.3]}
              IOCheck (resultCode);                   {Check for error}
            HUnlock (hText)                           {Unlock text handle [I:3.2.4]}


          end; {with theText^^}
        HUnlock (editHandle);                         {Unlock edit record [I:3.2.4]}

        if ErrorFlag then                             {Error detected during read?}
           begin
              HUnlock (dataHandle);                   {Unlock data record [I:3.2.4]}
              EXIT (DoRevert)                         {Exit to main event loop}
           end {if ErrorFlag}


        end; {with theData^^}


     HUnlock (dataHandle);                            {Unlock data record [I:3.2.4]}


     if not FinderPrint then                          {Printing from Finder?}
        begin
           TECalText (TheText);                       {Wrap text to window [II:5.3.1]}
           AdjustScrollBar;                           {Adjust scroll bar to length of text}
           TESetSelect (0, 0, TheText);               {Set insertion point at beginning [II:5.4.2]}

           InvalRect (TheWindow^.portRect);           {Force update to redraw text [II:3.4.2]}
           WindowDirty (FALSE)                        {Mark window as clean}
        end {if not FinderPrint}


  end;  {DoRevert}

{ - - - - - - - - - - - - - - - - - - - - - - - - - - - - - - - - - - - - - - - - - - - - - - - - - - - - - - - }

procedure DoSetup;

  { Handle Page Setup... command [Prog. III:4-1]. }

  var
     confirmed : BOOLEAN;                             {Did user click OK button?}

  begin {DoSetup}

     InitCursor;                                      {Set arrow cursor [II:2.5.2]}
     confirmed := PrStlDialog (ThePrintRec)           {Present style dialog [III:4.2.3]}

  end;  {DoSetup}
```

```
{ - - - - - - - - - - - - - - - - - - - - - - - - - - - - - - - - - - - - - - - - - - - - - - - - - - - - - - - - - - - - - - - - - }


procedure DoPrint;

  {  Handle Print... command [Prog. III:4-5].  }

  var
     confirmed : BOOLEAN;                                  {Did user click OK button?}
     numCopies : INTEGER;                                  {Number of times to image document}
     copyCount : INTEGER;                                  {Counter for imaging document}

  begin {DoPrint}

     InitCursor;                                           {Set arrow cursor [II:2.5.2]}
     confirmed := PrJobDialog (ThePrintRec);               {Present job dialog [III:4.2.3]}
     if not confirmed then EXIT (DoPrint);                 {If not confirmed, just exit to main event loop}

     with ThePrintRec^^.prJob do                           {Look in job subrecord [III:4.1.2]}
        if bJDocLoop = BDraftLoop then                     {Draft printing requested? [III:4.1.5]}
           begin
              numCopies := iCopies;                        {Image each copy separately [III:4.1.5]}
              DialogID  := DraftID                         {Use Draft Printing dialog}
           end {then}
        else
           begin
              numCopies := 1;                              {Image just once}
              DialogID  := SpoolID                         {Use Spooling dialog}
           end; {else}

     for copyCount := 1 to numCopies do                    {Loop on number of copies}
        if PrError = NoErr then                            {Check for errors [III:4.2.4]}
           begin

              ThisCopy := copyCount;                       {Save in a global for filter function}

              SetCursor (Watch^^);                         {Indicate delay [II:2.5.2]}
              ThePrintPort := PrOpenDoc (ThePrintRec, NIL, NIL);    {Open printing port [III:4.3.1]}
              InitCursor;                                  {Restore normal cursor [II:2.5.2]}

                 if PrError = NoErr then                    {Check for errors [III:4.2.4]}
                    begin
                       ImagePrep;                           {Prepare for imaging}
                       ImageDoc                             {Image the document}
                    end; {if PrError = NoErr}
```

```
        PrCloseDoc (ThePrintPort)                  {Close printing port [III:4.3.1]}

      end; {if PrError = NoErr}

   SetPort (TheWindow);                            {Restore window as current port [I:4.3.3]}

   if PrError = NoErr then                         {Check for errors [III:4.2.4]}
      SpoolPrint;                                  {Print spool file, if any}

   IOCheck (PrError);                              {Post error alert, if any [III:4.2.4]}
   PrSetError (NoErr)                              {Clear error for next time [III:4.2.4]}

end; {DoPrint}
```

{- -}

```
procedure ImagePrep;

   { Prepare document for imaging [Prog. III:4-3]. }

   var
      hMargin  : INTEGER;                          {Horizontal page margin in printer dots}
      vMargin  : INTEGER;                          {Vertical page margin in printer dots}
      textRect : Rect;                             {Boundary of printed page [I:4.1.2]}

   begin {ImagePrep}

      GetWTitle (TheWindow, DocName);              {Get document name from active window [II:3.2.4]}
      with TheWindow^ do
         begin
            TextFont (txFont);                     {Copy window's text characteristics to   }
            TextSize (txSize);                     {  current (printing) port [I:8.3.1, I:8.3.2]  }
            TextFace (txFace)
         end; {with TheWindow^}

      with ThePrintRec^^.prInfo do                 {Use info subrecord [III:4.1.2]}
         begin
            hMargin  := ROUND(PrintMargin * iHRes); {Scale page margin by printer's horizontal}
            vMargin  := ROUND(PrintMargin * iVRes); {  and vertical resolution [III:4.1.3]     }
            textRect := rPage;                     {Start with printer's page rectangle [III:4.1.3]}
            InsetRect (textRect, hMargin, vMargin) {Inset by page margins [I:4.4.4]}
         end; {with ThePrintRec^^.prInfo}

      TEPrint := TENew (textRect, textRect);       {Open an edit record [II:5.2.2, III:4.1.3]}
```

```
    with TEPrint^^, viewRect do                    {Use view rectangle [II:5.1.1]}
       begin

          PageHeight    := bottom - top;           {Find height of text page [I:4.1.2]}
          LinesPerPage := PageHeight div lineHeight; {Find lines per page [II:5.1.1]}
          PageHeight    := LinesPerPage * lineHeight; {Truncate to whole number of lines [II:5.1.1]}
          bottom        := top + PageHeight;        {Get rid of partial line [I:4.1.2]}

          destRect := viewRect;                     {Adjust destination rectangle [II:5.1.1]}

          DisposHandle (hText);                     {Dispose of empty text handle [I:3.2.2, II:5.1.1]}
          hText    := TheText^^.hText;              {Install text from main edit record [II:5.1.1]}
          teLength := TheText^^.teLength            {Set text length [II:5.1.1]}

       end; {with TEPrint^^, viewRect}

    SetCursor (Watch^^);                            {Indicate delay [II:2.5.2]}
       TECalText (TEPrint);                         {Wrap text to page [II:5.3.1]}
    InitCursor;                                     {Restore normal cursor [II:2.5.2]}

    ThisPage := 0;                                  {Initialize page number}
    NextLine := 1                                   {Initialize line count}

  end;  {ImagePrep}


{- - - - - - - - - - - - - - - - - - - - - - - - - - - - - - - - - - - - - - - - - - - - - - - - - - - - - -}


procedure ImageDoc;

  { Image document [Prog. III:4-6]. }

  var
     dlgStorage    : DialogRecord;                  {Storage for dialog [II:7.1.1]}
     theItem       : INTEGER;                       {Item number returned by dialog}
     printFinished : BOOLEAN;                       {Imaging complete?}

  begin {ImageDoc}

    PrintSuspended := FALSE;                        {Clear pause flag}
    printFinished  := FALSE;                        {Clear completion flag}

    ParamText ('', '', '', '');                     {Clear previous dialog text, if any [II:7.4.6]}
    TheDialog := GetNewDialog (DialogID, @dlgStorage, WindowPtr(-1));
                                                    {Make dialog from template [II:7.2.2]}
```

```
        while (not printFinished) and        {Stop on completion      }
               (PrError = NoErr) do          {  or on error [III:4.2.4]}
           begin

               ModalDialog (@ImageFilter, theItem);  {Run the dialog [II:7.4.3]}

               case theItem of
                  PausePrint:
                     DoPause;                 {Toggle Pause/Resume button}
                  CancelPrint:
                     PrSetError (IPrAbort);   {Cancel further printing [III:4.2.4]}
                  FinishPrint:
                     printFinished := TRUE    {Terminate loop}
                  end {case theItem}

           end; {while}

        CloseDialog (TheDialog);             {Close dialog [II:7.2.3]}
        TEPrint^^.hText := NIL;              {Avoid deallocating text [II:5.1.1]}
        TEDispose (TEPrint)                  {Dispose of edit record [II:5.2.2]}

   end; {ImageDoc}


{-------------------------------------------------------------------------}


function ImageFilter ({(thisDialog   : DialogPtr;      }
                      { var thisEvent : EventRecord;    }
                      { var itemNumber : INTEGER) : BOOLEAN};

   { Process event while imaging document [Prog. III:4-8]. }

   var
      dummyDialog : DialogPtr;              {Dialog pointer from DialogSelect [II:7.4.4]}
      dummyItem   : INTEGER;                {Item number from DialogSelect [II:7.4.4]}

   begin {ImageFilter}

      SystemTask;                           {Do system idle processing [II:2.7.2]}

      case thisEvent.what of                {Dispatch on event type [II:2.1.1]}

         NullEvent:
            ImageFilter := ImagePage (itemNumber);    {Image one page}

         KeyDown:
            ImageFilter := FilterKey (thisEvent, itemNumber); {Process keystroke}
```

```
      UpdateEvt:
         if SystemEvent (thisEvent) then           {System window? [III:6.2.2]}
            ImageFilter := FALSE                    {SystemEvent does the updating}

         else if IsDialogEvent (thisEvent) then     {Dialog window? [II:7.4.4]}
            ImageFilter := DialogSelect (thisEvent, dummyDialog, dummyItem)
                                                    {Update dialog window [II:7.4.4]}
         else
            begin
               TheEvent := thisEvent:               {Copy to global variable for DoUpdate}
               DoUpdate:                            {Update application window}
               ImageFilter := FALSE                 {Continue dialog}
            end: {else}


      otherwise
         ImageFilter := FALSE                       {Handle as normal event}


      end {case thisEvent.what}


   end:  {ImageFilter}


{ - - - - - - - - - - - - - - - - - - - - - - - - - - - - - - - - - - - - - - - - - - - - - - - - - - - - - - - - - - - - - - - - - }


function FilterKey { (var thisEvent  : EventRecord:      }
                  { var itemNumber : INTEGER) : BOOLEAN};

   { Process keystroke in printing dialog [Prog. III:4-9]. }

   var
      chCode  : INTEGER;                            {Character code from keyboard event}
      ch      : CHAR;                               {Character that was typed}
      cmdDown : BOOLEAN;                            {Command key down?}


   begin {FilterKey}

      with thisEvent do
         begin
            cmdDown := (BitAnd (modifiers, CmdKey) <> 0); {Test Command key [I:2.2.2, II:2.1.1, II:2.1.5]}
            chCode  := BitAnd (message, CharCodeMask);   {Get character code [I:2.2.2, II:2.1.1, II:2.1.4]}
            ch      := CHR(chCode)                        {Convert to a character}
         end: {with thisEvent}


      FilterKey  := FALSE;                          {Assume normal event processing}
      itemNumber := 0:                              {Initialize to no item}
```

```
      if cmdDown then                             {Command key down?}
        begin

          FilterKey := TRUE;                       {Masquerade as a pushbutton}

          case ch of

            '.': itemNumber := CancelPrint;        {Command-period means Cancel}

            ',': itemNumber := PausePrint;         {Command-comma means Pause/Resume}

            otherwise
              FilterKey := FALSE                   {Report as normal event}

            end {case ch}

        end {then}

    end;  {FilterKey}

{ - - - - - - - - - - - - - - - - - - - - - - - - - - - - - - - - - - - - - - - - - - }

function ImagePage {(var itemNumber : INTEGER) : BOOLEAN};

  { Image one page [Prog. III:4-4]. }

  var
    copyString : Str255;                           {Copy number in string form [I:2.1.1]}
    pageString : Str255;                           {Page number in string form [I:2.1.1]}
    editHandle : Handle;                           {Untyped handle for locking edit record [I:3.1.1]}

  begin {ImagePage}

    if PrintSuspended then                         {Imaging temporarily suspended?}
      begin
        ImagePage := FALSE;                        {Just continue dialog}
        EXIT (ImagePage)                           {Skip page imaging}
      end; {if PrintSuspended}

    ThisPage := ThisPage + 1;                      {Advance page number}
    NumToString (ThisPage, pageString);            {Convert numbers to    }
    NumToString (ThisCopy, copyString);            {   string form [I:2.3.7]}

    ParamText  (copyString, pageString, DocName, ''); {Substitute into dialog text [II:7.4.6]}
    DrawDialog (TheDialog);                         {Update text on screen [II:7.4.1]}
```

```
    editHandle := Handle(TEPrint);                      {Convert to untyped handle [I:3.1.1]}
    MoveHHi (editHandle);                               {Move edit record to top of heap [I:3.2.5]}
    HLock   (editHandle);                               {Lock edit record [I:3.2.4]}
      with TEPrint^^ do
        begin

            PrOpenPage (ThePrintPort, NIL);             {Open the page [III:4.3.2]}

              if PrError = NoErr then                   {Check for errors [III:4.2.4]}
                begin
                    TEUpdate   (viewRect, TEPrint);     {Draw text [II:5.3.2]}
                    OffsetRect (destRect, 0, -PageHeight);  {Scroll to next page [I:4.4.4]}
                    NextLine := NextLine + LinesPerPage {Advance line count}
                end; {if PrError = NoErr}

            PrClosePage (ThePrintPort);                 {Close the page [III:4.3.2]}

            if PrError <> NoErr then                    {Any errors? [III:4.2.4]}
              begin
                  itemNumber := 0;                      {Use dummy item number}
                  ImagePage  := TRUE                    {Force exit from dialog}
              end {if PrError <> NoErr}

            else if NextLine > nLines then              {Last line printed? [II:5.1.1]}
              begin
                  itemNumber := FinishPrint;            {Signal completion}
                  ImagePage  := TRUE                    {Force exit from dialog}
              end {if NextLine > nLines}

            else
                ImagePage := FALSE                      {Continue dialog}

          end; {with TEPrint^^}
      HUnlock (editHandle)                              {Unlock edit record [I:3.2.4]}

  end;  {ImagePage}
```

{- -}

```
procedure DoPause;

  { Toggle Pause/Resume button [Prog. III:4-7]. }

  var
     itemType   : INTEGER;                              {Item type for Pause/Resume button}
```

```
     itemRect    : Rect;                           {Display rectangle for Pause/Resume button}
     itemHandle  : Handle;                         {Item handle for Pause/Resume button}
     theButton   : ControlHandle;                  {Control handle to Pause/Resume button [II:6.1.1]}

  begin {DoPause}

     PrintSuspended := not PrintSuspended;          {Toggle pause flag}

     GetDItem (TheDialog, PausePrint,              {Get item handle [II:7.3.1]}
               itemType, itemHandle, itemRect);
     theButton := ControlHandle(itemHandle);       {Convert to typed handle [II:6.1.1]}

     if PrintSuspended then                         {Printing now suspended?}
        SetCTitle (theButton, 'Resume')            {Change button to Resume [II:6.2.3]}
     else
        SetCTitle (theButton, 'Pause')             {Change back to Pause [II:6.2.3]}

  end;   {DoPause}
```

```
{-----------------------------------------------------------------------------------}

procedure SpoolPrint;

  { Print spooled document [Prog. III:4-10]. }

  var
     dlgStorage : DialogRecord;                    {Storage for dialog [II:7.1.1]}
     theItem    : INTEGER;                         {Item number returned by dialog}

  begin {SpoolPrint}

     with ThePrintRec^^.prJob do                   {Look in job subrecord [III:4.1.2]}
        if (bJDocLoop <> BSpoolLoop) then          {Is there a spool file? [III:4.1.5]}
           EXIT (SpoolPrint)                        {If not, just exit}
        else
           pIdleProc := @SpoolBackground;          {Install background procedure [III:4.1.5]}

     ThisCopy := 0;                                 {Initialize copy and}
     ThisPage := 0;                                 {  page counts   }

     TheDialog := GetNewDialog (SpoolPrintID, @dlgStorage, WindowPtr(-1)); {Open dialog [II:7.2.2]}

        PrPicFile (ThePrintRec, NIL, NIL, NIL, PrintStatus);      {Print spool file [III:4.3.3]}

     CloseDialog (TheDialog)                        {Close dialog [II:7.2.3]}

  end;   {SpoolPrint}
```

```
{ - - - - - - - - - - - - - - - - - - - - - - - - - - - - - - - - - - - - - - - - - - - - - - - - - - - - - - - }


procedure SpoolBackground;

   { Background procedure for spool printing [Prog. III:4-11]. }

   begin {SpoolBackground}

      ShowSpoolStatus;                            {Display status on screen}
      DoSpoolEvent                                {Handle mouse and keyboard}

   end; {SpoolBackground}


{ - - - - - - - - - - - - - - - - - - - - - - - - - - - - - - - - - - - - - - - - - - - - - - - - - - - - - - - }


procedure ShowSpoolStatus;

   { Display status during spool printing [Prog. III:4-13]. }

   var
      curPage    : INTEGER;                       {Current page number}
      lastPage   : INTEGER;                       {Last page to be printed}
      copyString : Str255;                        {Current copy number in string form [I:2.1.1]}
      pageString : Str255;                        {Current page number in string form [I:2.1.1]}
      lastString : Str255;                        {Last page number in string form [I:2.1.1]}

   begin {ShowSpoolStatus}

      with PrintStatus. ThePrintRec^^.prJob do
         begin

            if not (iCurCopy in [1..iTotCopies]) or    {Copy or page count  }
               not (iCurPage in [1..iTotPages]) then    {  out of range? [III:4.1.7]}
                  EXIT (ShowSpoolStatus);               {Suppress spurious numbers}
            if (iCurCopy = ThisCopy) and                {Copy and page counts unchanged }
               (iCurPage = ThisPage) then               {  since last time? [III:4.1.7]}
                  EXIT (ShowSpoolStatus);               {Avoid screen flicker}

            curPage  := (iFstPage - 1) + iCurPage;      {Convert to document-relative}
            lastPage := (iFstPage - 1) + iTotPages;     {  page numbers [III:4.1.5, III:4.1.7]}

            NumToString (iCurCopy. copyString);         {Convert numbers to string form}
            NumToString (curPage.  pageString);         {  [I:2.3.7, III:4.1.7]     }
            NumToString (lastPage. lastString);
```

```
        ParamText   (copyString, DocName, pageString, lastString);  {Substitute into dialog text [II:7.4.6]}
        ShowWindow (TheDialog);                          {Display dialog window [II:3.3.1]}
        DrawDialog (TheDialog);                          {Update text on screen [II:7.4.1]}

        ThisCopy := iCurCopy;                            {Save "raw" copy and page counts}
        ThisPage := iCurPage                             {  for comparison next time   }

      end  {with PrintStatus, ThePrintRec^^.prJob}

  end;    {ShowSpoolStatus}
```

{- }

```
procedure DoSpoolEvent;

  { Process event during spool printing [Prog. III:4-12]. }

  var
    click   : BOOLEAN;                                   {Mouse clicked in a pushbutton?}
    theItem : INTEGER;                                   {Item number of pushbutton}

  begin {DoSpoolEvent}

    repeat

      SystemTask;                                        {Do system idle processing [II:2.7.2]}

      click := FALSE;                                    {Assume no reportable event}
      if GetNextEvent (EveryEvent, TheEvent) then        {Any events? [II:2.2.1 II:2.1.3]}
        case TheEvent.what of                            {Dispatch on event type [II:2.1.1]}

          MouseDown:
            click := DialogSelect (TheEvent, TheDialog, theItem);
                                                         {Relay mouse click to dialog [II:7.4.4]}
          KeyDown:
            click := FilterKey (TheEvent, theItem);{Convert keystroke to pushbutton}

          UpdateEvt:
            if not SystemEvent (TheEvent) then     {One of our windows? [III:6.2.2]}
              begin
                if IsDialogEvent (TheEvent) then {Dialog window? [II:7.4.4]}
                  click := DialogSelect (TheEvent, TheDialog, theItem)
                                                         {Update dialog window [II:7.4.4]}
                else
                  DoUpdate                               {Update document window}
              end {if not SystemEvent (TheEvent)}
```

```
            end; {case TheEvent.what}

        if click then                              {Pushbutton clicked?}
          case theItem of                          {Dispatch on item number}
            PausePrint:  DoPause;                   {Toggle Pause/Resume button}
            CancelPrint: PrSetError (IPrAbort)      {Cancel further printing [III:4.2.4]}
          end {case theItem}

      until (not PrintSuspended)                    {Keep control if suspended }
          or (PrError <> NoErr)                     { or until canceled [III:4.2.4]}

  end; {DoSpoolEvent}
```

{- -}

```
procedure DoQuit;

  { Handle Quit command [Prog. II:2-4]. }

  begin {DoQuit}

    Quitting := TRUE                                {Start closing down windows}

  end; {DoQuit}
```

{- -}

```
procedure DoEditChoice {(theItem : INTEGER)};

  { Handle choice from Edit menu [Prog. II:4-9]. }

  const
    undoCmd  = 0;                                   {Constant representing Undo command [II:4.5.3]}
    cutCmd   = 2;                                   {Constant representing Cut command [II:4.5.3]}
    copyCmd  = 3;                                   {Constant representing Copy command [II:4.5.3]}
    pasteCmd = 4;                                   {Constant representing Paste command [II:4.5.3]}
    clearCmd = 5;                                   {Constant representing Clear command [II:4.5.3]}

  begin {DoEditChoice}

    case theItem of

      UndoItem:
        if not SystemEdit (undoCmd) then            {Intercepted by a desk accessory? [II:4.5.3]}
          DoUndo;                                   {Handle Undo command}
```

```
  CutItem:
    if not SystemEdit (cutCmd) then        {Intercepted by a desk accessory? [II:4.5.3]}
      DoCut;                               {Handle Cut command}

  CopyItem:
    if not SystemEdit (copyCmd) then       {Intercepted by a desk accessory? [II:4.5.3]}
      DoCopy;                              {Handle Copy command}

  PasteItem:
    if not SystemEdit (pasteCmd) then      {Intercepted by a desk accessory? [II:4.5.3]}
      DoPaste;                             {Handle Paste command}

  ClearItem:
    if not SystemEdit (clearCmd) then      {Intercepted by a desk accessory? [II:4.5.3]}
      DoClear                              {Handle Clear command}

  end {case theItem}

end;  {DoEditChoice}
```

{- -}

```
procedure DoUndo;

  { Handle Undo command. }

  begin {DoUndo}

    SysBeep(1)                             {Undo command not implemented [II:2.8.1]}

  end;  {DoUndo}
```

{- -}

```
procedure DoCut;

  { Handle Cut command [Prog. II:5-8]. }

  begin {DoCut}

    ScrollToSelection;                     {Make sure selection is visible}

    TECut (TheText);                       {Cut the selection [II:5.5.2]}

    AdjustScrollBar;                       {Adjust scroll bar to length of text}
```

```
      AdjustText;                                {Adjust text to match scroll bar}
      ScrollToSelection;                         {Keep insertion point visible}

      DisableItem (EditMenu, CutItem);           {Disable menu items that operate on}
      DisableItem (EditMenu, CopyItem);          {a nonempty selection [II:4.6.2]}
      DisableItem (EditMenu, ClearItem);

      EnableItem  (EditMenu, PasteItem);         {Enable Paste command [II:4.6.2]}

      ScrapDirty := TRUE;                        {Mark scrap as dirty}
      WindowDirty (TRUE)                         {Mark window as dirty}

   end;   {DoCut}
{------------------------------------------------------------------------------}


procedure DoCopy;

   { Handle Copy command [Prog. II:5-9]. }

   begin {DoCopy}

      ScrollToSelection;                         {Make sure selection is visible}

      TECopy (TheText);                          {Copy the selection [II:5.5.2]}

      EnableItem (EditMenu, PasteItem);          {Enable Paste command [II:4.6.2]}

      ScrapDirty := TRUE                         {Mark scrap as dirty}

   end;   {DoCopy}
{------------------------------------------------------------------------------}


procedure DoPaste;

   { Handle Paste command [Prog. II:5-10]. }

   begin {DoPaste}

      ScrollToSelection;                         {Make sure selection is visible}

      TEPaste (TheText);                         {Paste the scrap [II:5.5.2]}

      AdjustScrollBar;                           {Adjust scroll bar to length of text}
```

```
      AdjustText;                              {Adjust text to match scroll bar}
      ScrollToSelection;                       {Keep selection visible}

      DisableItem (EditMenu, CutItem);         {Disable menu items that operate on}
      DisableItem (EditMenu, CopyItem);        {  a nonempty selection [II:4.6.2]}
      DisableItem (EditMenu, ClearItem);

      WindowDirty (TRUE)                        {Mark window as dirty}

   end; {DoPaste}
```

```
{--------------------------------------------------------------------}
```

```
procedure DoClear;

   { Handle Clear command [Prog. II:5-11]. }

   begin {DoClear}

      ScrollToSelection;                        {Make sure selection is visible}

      TEDelete (TheText);                       {Delete the selection [II:5.5.3]}

      AdjustScrollBar;                          {Adjust scroll bar to length of text}
      AdjustText;                               {Adjust text to match scroll bar}
      ScrollToSelection;                        {Keep insertion point visible}

      DisableItem (EditMenu, CutItem);          {Disable menu items that operate on}
      DisableItem (EditMenu, CopyItem);         {  a nonempty selection [II:4.6.2]}
      DisableItem (EditMenu, ClearItem);

      WindowDirty (TRUE)                        {Mark window as dirty}

   end; {DoClear}
```

```
{--------------------------------------------------------------------}
```

```
procedure DoSysClick {(whichWindow : WindowPtr)};

   { Handle mouse-down event in system window. }

   begin {DoSysClick}

      SystemClick (TheEvent, whichWindow)       {Pass event to Toolbox for handling [II:3.5.3]}

   end; {DoSysClick}
```

```
{-------------------------------------------------------------------------------}

procedure DoContent ((whichWindow : WindowPtr));

   { Handle mouse-down event in content region of active window [Prog. II:6-1]. }

   var                                              {Location of click in window coordinates [I:4.1.1]}
      thePoint   : Point;                           {Handle to control [II:6.1.1]}
      theControl : ControlHandle;                   {Part of control where mouse was pressed [II:6.4.1]}
      thePart    : INTEGER;

   begin {DoContent}

      if whichWindow <> FrontWindow then            {Is it an inactive window? [II:3.3.3]}
         SelectWindow (whichWindow)                 {If so, just activate it [II:3.5.2]}

      else
         begin

            thePoint := TheEvent.where;             {Get point in screen coordinates [II:2.1.1]}
            GlobalToLocal (thePoint);               {Convert to window coordinates [I:4.4.2]}

            thePart := FindControl (thePoint, whichWindow, theControl);
                                                    {Was mouse pressed in a control? [II:6.4.1]}

            if theControl = TheScrollBar then       {Was it in the scroll bar?}
               DoScroll (thePart, thePoint)         {Go scroll the window}

            else if theControl = NIL then           {Not in a control?}

               if PtInRect (thePoint, TheText^^.viewRect) then {Was it in the text rectangle? [I:4.4.3]}
                  DoSelect (thePoint)               {Go handle text selection}

         end {else}

   end;   {DoContent}

{-------------------------------------------------------------------------------}

procedure DoScroll ((thePart : INTEGER; thePoint : Point));

   { Handle mouse-down event in scroll bar [Prog. II:6-6]. }

   begin   {DoScroll}
```

```
        if thePart = InThumb then                          {Dragging the indicator? [II:6.4.1]}

           begin
              thePart := TrackControl (TheScrollBar, thePoint, NIL);
                                                            {Track mouse with no action procedure [II:6.4.2]}
              AdjustText                                    {Adjust text to new setting}
           end {then}

           else

              thePart := TrackControl (TheScrollBar, thePoint, @ScrollText)
                                                            {Track mouse with continuous scroll [II:6.4.2]}

     end;  {DoScroll}
```

```
{ - - - - - - - - - - - - - - - - - - - - - - - - - - - - - - - - - - - - - - - - - - - - - - - - - - - - - - - }
```

```
procedure ScrollText {(theControl : ControlHandle; thePart : INTEGER)};

   {  Scroll text within window [Prog. II:6-8].  }

   var
      delta     : INTEGER;                                 {Amount to scroll by, in lines}
      oldValue  : INTEGER;                                 {Previous setting of scroll bar}

   begin {ScrollText}

      case thePart of

        inUpButton:
           delta := -1;                                    {Scroll up one line at a time}

        inDownButton:
           delta := +1;                                    {Scroll down one line at a time}

        inPageUp:
           with TheText^^, viewRect do
              delta := (top - bottom) div lineHeight + 1;   {Scroll up by height of text rectangle [II:5.1.1]}

        inPageDown:
           with TheText^^, viewRect do
              delta := (bottom - top) div lineHeight - 1;   {Scroll down by height of text rectangle [II:5.1.1]}

        otherwise
           {Do nothing}
```

```
         end;  {case thePart}

     if thePart <> 0 then                          {Is mouse still in the original part?}
       begin
          oldValue := GetCtlValue (theControl);     {Get old setting [II:6.2.4]}
          SetCtlValue (theControl, oldValue + delta); {Adjust by scroll amount [II:6.2.4]}


          AdjustText                                {Scroll text to match new setting}
       end  {if thePart <> 0}

   end;   {ScrollText}
```

{- }


```
procedure AdjustText;

  {  Adjust text within window to match scroll bar setting [Prog. II:6-7].  }


  var
     oldScroll : INTEGER;                           {Old text offset in pixels}
     newScroll : INTEGER;                           {New text offset in pixels}


  begin  {AdjustText}

    with TheText^^ do
      begin

         oldScroll := viewRect.top - destRect.top;          {Get current offset [II:5.1.1]}
         newScroll := GetCtlValue (TheScrollBar) * lineHeight;  {Scroll bar gives new offset [II:6.2.4]}


         if oldScroll <> newScroll then                     {Any difference?}
            TEScroll (0, (oldScroll - newScroll), TheText)   {Scroll by difference [II:5.3.3]}


      end {with TheText^^}

   end;   {AdjustText}
```

{- }


```
function AutoScroll { : BOOLEAN};

  {  Handle automatic scrolling during text selection [Prog. II:6-9].  }


  var
     mousePoint : Point;                             {Mouse location in local (window) coordinates  [I:4.1.1]}
```

```
      textRect    : Rect;                              {Active window's text rectangle [I:4.1.2]}
      saveClip    : RgnHandle;                         {Original clipping region on entry [I:4.1.5]}

  begin {AutoScroll}

      saveClip := NewRgn;                              {Create temporary region [I:4.1.6]}
      GetClip   (saveClip);                            {Set it to existing clipping region [I:4.3.6]}
      ClipRect  (TheWindow^.portRect);                 {Clip to entire port rectangle [I:4.3.6, I:4.2.2]}

        GetMouse (mousePoint);                         {Find mouse location [II:2.4.1]}
        textRect := TheText^^.viewRect;                {Get text rectangle [II:5.1.1]}

        if mousePoint.v < textRect.top then            {Above top of rectangle? [I:4.1.1, I:4.1.2]}
           ScrollText (TheScrollBar, InUpButton)       {Scroll up one line [II:6.4.1]}

        else if mousePoint.v > textRect.bottom then    {Below bottom of rectangle? [I:4.1.1, I:4.1.2]}
           ScrollText (TheScrollBar, InDownButton)     {Scroll down one line [II:6.4.1]}

        {else do nothing};

      SetClip    (saveClip);                           {Restore original clipping region [I:4.3.6]}
      DisposeRgn (saveClip);                           {Dispose of temporary region [I:4.1.6]}

      AutoScroll := TRUE                               {Continue tracking mouse [II:5.6.1]}

  end;   {AutoScroll}

{- - - - - - - - - - - - - - - - - - - - - - - - - - - - - - - - - - - - - - - - - - - - - - - - - - - - - - - - - - - - - -}

procedure DoSelect {(thePoint : Point)};

  { Handle mouse-down event in text rectangle [Prog. II:5-4]. }

  var
     extend : BOOLEAN;                                 {Extend existing selection (Shift-click)?}

  begin {DoSelect}

    with TheEvent do
       extend := (BitAnd(modifiers, ShiftKey) <> 0);   {Shift key down?[I:2.2.2, II:2.1.5]}

    TEClick (thePoint, extend, TheText);               {Do text selection [II:5.4.1]}

    FixEditMenu                                        {Enable/disable menu items}

  end; {DoSelect}
```

```
{ - - - - - - - - - - - - - - - - - - - - - - - - - - - - - - - - - - - - - - - - - - - - - - - - - - - - - - - - - - - - - - - - - - - - - - - - }


procedure FixEditMenu;

   { Enable/disable editing commands [Prog. II:5-5]. }


   var
      editHandle : Handle;                                    {Untyped handle for locking edit record [I:3.1.1]}


   begin {FixEditMenu}

      DisableItem (EditMenu, UndoItem);                       {Disable Undo command [II:4.6.2]}


      editHandle := Handle(TheText);                          {Convert to untyped handle [I:3.1.1]}
      MoveHHi (editHandle);                                   {Move edit record to top of heap [I:3.2.5]}
      HLock   (editHandle);                                   {Lock edit record [I:3.2.4]}
        with TheText^^ do
           if selStart = selEnd then                          {Is selection empty? [II:5.1.1]}
              begin
                 DisableItem (EditMenu, CutItem);             {Disable menu items that operate on}
                 DisableItem (EditMenu, CopyItem);            {  a nonempty selection [II:4.6.2]}
                 DisableItem (EditMenu, ClearItem)
              end {then}
           else
              begin
                 EnableItem (EditMenu, CutItem);              {Enable menu items that operate on }
                 EnableItem (EditMenu, CopyItem);             {  a nonempty selection [II:4.6.2]}
                 EnableItem (EditMenu, ClearItem)
              end; {else}
        HUnlock (editHandle);                                 {Unlock edit record [I:3.2.4]}

        if TEGetScrapLen = 0 then                             {Is scrap empty? [II:5.5.4]}
           DisableItem (EditMenu, PasteItem)                  {Disable Paste command [II:4.6.2]}
        else
           EnableItem  (EditMenu, PasteItem)                  {Enable Paste command [II:4.6.2]}


   end;   {FixEditMenu}

{ - - - - - - - - - - - - - - - - - - - - - - - - - - - - - - - - - - - - - - - - - - - - - - - - - - - - - - - - - - - - - - - - - - - - - - - - }


procedure DoDrag ((whichWindow : WindowPtr));

   { Handle mouse-down event in drag region [Prog. II:3-8]. }


   var
      limitRect : Rect;                                       {Limit rectangle for dragging [I:4.1.2]}
```

```
begin {DoDrag}

   SetRect    (limitRect, 0, MenuBarHeight, ScreenWidth, ScreenHeight); {Set limit rectangle [I:4.1.2]}
   InsetRect (limitRect, ScreenMargin, ScreenMargin);      {Inset by screen margin [I:4.4.4]}

   DragWindow (whichWindow, TheEvent.where, limitRect)    {Let user drag the window [II:3.5.4]}

end;  {DoDrag}
```

{- -}

```
procedure DoGrow ((whichWindow : WindowPtr));

   { Handle mouse-down event in size region [Prog. II:3-9]. }

   var
      sizeRect   : Rect;           {Minimum and maximum dimensions of window [I:4.1.2]}
      newSize    : LONGINT;        {Coded representation of new dimensions}
      newWidth   : INTEGER;        {New width of window}
      newHeight  : INTEGER;        {New height of window}

   begin {DoGrow}

      SetRect (sizeRect,                       {Set size rectangle [I:4.1.2]}
               MinWidth,
               MinHeight,
               ScreenWidth,                    {Maximum width is full screen}
               (ScreenHeight - MenuBarHeight) ); {Maximum height is full screen minus menu bar}

      newSize := GrowWindow (whichWindow, TheEvent.where, sizeRect); {Let user drag size region [II:3.5.4]}

      if newSize <> 0 then                     {Was size changed?}
         begin

            EraseRect (whichWindow^.portRect);   {Clear window to white [I:5.3.2]}

            newWidth  := LoWord(newSize);        {Extract width from low word [I:2.2.3]}
            newHeight := HiWord(newSize);        {Extract height from high word [I:2.2.3]}
            SizeWindow (whichWindow, newWidth, newHeight, TRUE);  {Adjust size of window [II:3.3.2]}

            InvalRect (whichWindow^.portRect);   {Force update of window's contents [II:3.4.2]}

            FixScrollBar;                        {Resize scroll bar}
            FixText                              {Resize text rectangle}

         end {if newSize <> 0}
```

```
   end;   {DoGrow}
```

{- -}

```
procedure FixScrollBar;

   {  Resize window's scroll bar [Prog. II:6-10].  }

   begin {FixScrollBar}

      HideControl (TheScrollBar);                      {Hide scroll bar [II:6.3.1]}

      with TheWindow^.portRect do
        begin

            MoveControl (TheScrollBar.                 {Move top-left corner [II:6.3.2]}
                    right - (SBarWidth - 1),            {Allow for 1-pixel overlap at right}
                    -1);                                {Overlap window top by 1 pixel}

            SizeControl (TheScrollBar.                 {Adjust bottom-right corner [II:6.3.2]}
                    SBarWidth.
                    (bottom + 1) - (top - 1) - (SBarWidth - 1) )   {Allow room for size box}

        end;  {with TheWindow^.portRect}

      ShowControl (TheScrollBar);                      {Redisplay scroll bar [II:6.3.1]}

      ValidRect (TheScrollBar^^.contrlRect)            {Avoid updating again [II:3.4.2]}

   end;   {FixScrollBar}
```

{- -}

```
procedure FixText;

   {  Resize window's text rectangle [Prog. II:6-11].  }

   var
      editHandle : Handle;                    {Untyped handle for locking edit record [I:3.1.1]}
      topLine    : INTEGER;                   {First line visible in window}
      firstChar  : INTEGER;                   {Character position of first character in window}
      maxTop     : INTEGER;                   {Maximum value for top line in window}

   begin {FixText}
```

```
        SetCursor (Watch^^);                              {Indicate delay [II:2.5.2]}

        editHandle := Handle(TheText);                    {Convert to untyped handle [I:3.1.1]}
        MoveHHi (editHandle);                             {Move edit record to top of heap [I:3.2.5]}
        HLock    (editHandle);                            {Lock edit record [I:3.2.4]}
          with TheText^^ do
            begin

                topLine   := GetCtlValue (TheScrollBar);  {Get previous first line [II:6.2.4]}
                firstChar := lineStarts[topLine];         {Find first character previously visible [II:5.1.1]}

                viewRect := TheWindow^.portRect;          {Display text in window's port rectangle [II:3.1.1]}
                with viewRect do
                  begin
                     right  := right  - (SBarWidth - 1);  {Exclude scroll bar, allowing for 1-pixel overlap}
                     bottom := bottom - (SBarWidth - 1);  {Leave space for scroll bar at bottom}
                     bottom := (bottom div lineHeight) * lineHeight    {Get rid of partial line [II:5.1.1]}
                  end; {with viewRect}

                destRect := viewRect;                     {Wrap to same rectangle [II:5.1.1]}
                InsetRect (destRect, TextMargin, TextMargin); {Inset by text margin [I:4.4.4]}

                TECalText (TheText);                      {Recalibrate line starts [II:5.3.1]}
                AdjustScrollBar;                          {Adjust scroll bar to new length}

                ScrollCharacter (firstChar, FALSE)        {Scroll same character to top of window}

            end; {with TheText^^}
        HUnlock (editHandle)                              {Unlock edit record [I:3.2.4]}

   end; {FixText}
```

{ - }

```
procedure DoGoAway ((whichWindow : WindowPtr));

   { Handle mouse-down event in close region [Prog. II:3-10]. }

   begin {DoGoAway}

     if TrackGoAway (whichWindow, TheEvent.where) then    {Track mouse in close region [II:3.5.4]}
        DoClose                                           { and close window if necessary}

   end; {DoGoAway}
```

{ - }

```
procedure DoZoom {(whichWindow : WindowPtr; inOrOut : INTEGER)};

   { Handle mouse-down event in zoom region [Prog. II:3-11]. }

   begin {DoZoom}

      with TheEvent do
         if TrackBox (whichWindow, where, inOrOut) then {Track mouse in zoom region [II:3.5.4]}
            begin

               EraseRect (whichWindow^.portRect);      {Clear window to white [I:5.3.2]}

               ZoomWindow (whichWindow, inOrOut, FALSE); {Zoom the window [II:3.3.2]}

               InvalRect (whichWindow^.portRect);       {Force update of window's contents [II:3.4.2]}

               FixScrollBar;                            {Resize scroll bar}
               FixText                                  {Resize text rectangle}

            end {if TrackBox (whichWindow, where, inOrOut)}

   end;   {DoZoom}
```

{ - }

```
procedure DoKeystroke;

   { Handle keystroke [Prog. II:4-4]. }

   var
      chCode     : INTEGER;        {Character code from event message [I:8.1.1]}
      ch         : CHAR;           {Character that was typed}
      menuChoice : LONGINT;        {Menu ID and item number for keyboard alias}

   begin {DoKeystroke}

      with TheEvent do
         begin

            chCode := BitAnd (message, CharCodeMask); {Extract character code [I:2.2.2, II:2.1.4]}
            ch := CHR(chCode);                        {Convert to a character}

            if BitAnd (modifiers, CmdKey) <> 0 then   {Command key down? [I:2.2.2, II:2.1.5]}
               begin
                  if what <> AutoKey then             {Ignore repeats [II:2.1.1, II:2.1.2]}
```

```
            begin
               menuChoice := MenuKey (ch);         {Get menu equivalent [II:4.5.1]}
               DoMenuChoice (menuChoice)           {Handle as menu choice}
            end {if what <> AutoKey}
        end {then}
      else
        DoTyping (ch)                              {Handle as normal character}

    end {with TheEvent}

  end;   {DoKeystroke}


{- - - - - - - - - - - - - - - - - - - - - - - - - - - - - - - - - - - - - - - - - - - - - - - - - - - - - -}

procedure DoTyping {(ch : CHAR)};

  {  Handle character typed from keyboard [Prog. II:5-6].  }

  begin {DoTyping}

    if TheText = NIL then                          {Is screen empty?}
      begin
        SysBeep(1);                                {Just beep [II:2.8.1]}
        EXIT {DoTyping}                            {  and exit          }
      end; {if TheText = NIL}

    ScrollToSelection;                             {Make sure insertion point is visible}

    TEKey (ch, TheText);                           {Process character [II:5.5.1]}

    AdjustScrollBar;                               {Adjust scroll bar to length of text}
    AdjustText;                                    {Adjust text to match scroll bar}
    ScrollToSelection;                             {Keep insertion point visible}

    DisableItem (EditMenu, CutItem);               {Disable menu items that operate on}
    DisableItem (EditMenu, CopyItem);              {  a nonempty selection [II:4.6.2]}
    DisableItem (EditMenu, ClearItem);

    WindowDirty (TRUE)                             {Mark window as dirty}

  end; {DoTyping}


{- - - - - - - - - - - - - - - - - - - - - - - - - - - - - - - - - - - - - - - - - - - - - - - - - - - - - -}

procedure DoUpdate;
```

```
{  Handle update event [Prog. II:5-3].  }

var
    savePort     : GrafPtr;                {Pointer to previous current port [I:4.2.2]}
    whichWindow  : WindowPtr;              {Pointer to window to be updated [II:3.1.1]}
    theData      : WDHandle;               {Handle to window's data record}
    dataHandle   : Handle;                 {Untyped handle for locking data record [I:3.1.1]}

begin  {DoUpdate}

    GetPort (savePort);                    {Save previous port [I:4.3.3]}

        whichWindow := WindowPtr(TheEvent.message);   {Convert long integer to pointer [II:3.1.1]}
        SetPort (whichWindow);             {Make window the current port [I:4.3.3]}

        BeginUpdate (whichWindow);         {Restrict visible region to update region [II:3.4.1]}

            EraseRect (whichWindow^.portRect);        {Clear update region [I:5.3.2]}

            DrawGrowIcon (whichWindow);    {Redraw size box [II:3.3.4]}
            DrawControls (whichWindow);    {Redraw scroll bar [II:6.3.1]}

            dataHandle := Handle(GetWRefCon(whichWindow));    {Get window data [II:3.2.4]}
            MoveHHi (dataHandle);          {Move data record to top of heap [I:3.2.5]}
            HLock   (dataHandle);          {Lock data record [I:3.2.4]}
                theData := WDHandle(dataHandle);      {Convert to typed handle}
                with theData^^ do
                    TEUpdate (editRec^^.viewRect, editRec);   {Redraw the text [II:5.3.2]}
            HUnlock (dataHandle);          {Unlock data record [I:3.2.4]}

        EndUpdate (whichWindow);           {Restore original visible region [II:3.4.1]}

    SetPort (savePort)                     {Restore original port [I:4.3.3]}

  end:  {DoUpdate}

{------------------------------------------------------------------------------------}


procedure DoActivate;

  {  Handle activate (or deactivate) event [Prog. II:5-14].  }

    var
       whichWindow : WindowPtr;            {Pointer to the window [II:3.1.1]}
```

```
    begin   {DoActivate}

      with TheEvent do
        begin

          whichWindow := WindowPtr(message);        {Convert long integer to pointer [II:3.1.1]}

          if BitAnd(modifiers, ActiveFlag) <> 0 then {Test activate/deactivate bit [I:2.2.2, II:2.1.5]}
            ActWindow   (whichWindow)                {Activate window}
          else
            DeactWindow (whichWindow)                {Deactivate window}

        end {with TheEvent}

    end;   {DoActivate}

{ - - - - - - - - - - - - - - - - - - - - - - - - - - - - - - - - - - - - - - - - - - - - - - - - - - - - - - - - - - }

procedure ActWindow {(whichWindow : WindowPtr)};

  { Activate window. }

  const
    active = 0;                                      {Highlighting code for active scroll bar [II:6.3.3]}

  var
    theData    : WDHandle;                           {Handle to window's data record}
    dataHandle : Handle;                             {Untyped handle for locking data record [I:3.1.1]}

  begin {ActWindow}

    dataHandle := Handle(GetWRefCon(whichWindow)); {Get window data [II:3.2.4]}
    MoveHHi (dataHandle);                            {Move data record to top of heap [I:3.2.5]}
    HLock   (dataHandle);                            {Lock data record [I:3.2.4]}

      theData := WDHandle(dataHandle);               {Convert to typed handle}
    with theData^^ do
      begin

        TheWindow    := whichWindow;                 {Set global pointers/handles}
        TheScrollBar := scrollBar;
        TheText      := editRec;
        ThePrintRec  := printRec;

        SetPort (whichWindow);                       {Make window the current port [I:4.3.3]}
```

```
         DrawGrowIcon  (whichWindow);              {Highlight or unhighlight size box [II:3.3.4]}
         HiliteControl (scrollBar, active);        {Activate scroll bar [II:6.3.3]}
         TEActivate    (editRec);                  {Highlight selection [II:5.4.3]}


         if BitAnd(TheEvent.modifiers, ChangeFlag) <> 0 then
                                                   {Coming from a system window? [I:2.2.2, II:2.1.5]}
            ReadDeskScrap;                         {Copy desk scrap to Toolbox scrap}


         FixEditMenu;                              {Enable/disable editing commands}


         EnableItem (FileMenu, SaveAsItem);        {Enable Save As... command [II:4.6.2]}
         EnableItem (FileMenu, SetupItem);         {Enable Page Setup... command [II:4.6.2]}
         EnableItem (FileMenu, PrintItem);         {Enable Print... command [II:4.6.2]}


         if dirty then                             {Is document dirty?}
            EnableItem (FileMenu, SaveItem);       {Enable Save command [II:4.6.2]}
         if dirty and (fileNumber <> 0) then       {Is there a file to revert to?}
            EnableItem (FileMenu, RevertItem)      {Enable Revert command [II:4.6.2]}


      end; {with theData^^}


   HUnlock (dataHandle)                            {Unlock data record [I:3.2.4]}


end; {ActWindow}

{-------------------------------------------------------------------------------}


procedure DeactWindow {(whichWindow : WindowPtr)};

   { Deactivate window. }

   const
      inactive = 255;                              {Highlighting code for inactive scroll bar [II:6.3.3]}

   var
      theData    : WDHandle;                       {Handle to window's data record}
      dataHandle : Handle;                         {Untyped handle for locking data record [I:3.1.1]}

begin {DeactWindow}

   dataHandle := Handle(GetWRefCon(whichWindow)); {Get window data [II:3.2.4]}
   MoveHHi (dataHandle);                          {Move data record to top of heap [I:3.2.5]}
   HLock   (dataHandle);                          {Lock data record [I:3.2.4]}


      theData := WDHandle(dataHandle);             {Convert to typed handle}
   with theData^^ do
```

```
    begin

        TheWindow     := NIL;                {Clear global pointers/handles}
        TheScrollBar  := NIL;
        TheText       := NIL;
        ThePrintRec   := NIL;

        SetPort (whichWindow);               {Make window the current port [I:4.3.3]}

        DrawGrowIcon  (whichWindow);         {Highlight or unhighlight size box [II:3.3.4]}
        HiliteControl (scrollBar, inactive); {Deactivate scroll bar [II:6.3.3]}
        TEDeactivate  (editRec);             {Unhighlight selection [II:5.4.3]}

        if BitAnd(TheEvent.modifiers, changeFlag) <> 0 then
                                             {Exiting to a system window? [I:2.2.2, II:2.1.5]}
          begin
            WriteDeskScrap;                  {Copy Toolbox scrap to desk scrap}

            EnableItem (EditMenu, UndoItem);  {Enable standard editing commands}
            EnableItem (EditMenu, CutItem);   {  for desk accessory [II:4.6.2]}
            EnableItem (EditMenu, CopyItem);
            EnableItem (EditMenu, PasteItem);
            EnableItem (EditMenu, ClearItem)
          end; {if BitAnd(TheEvent.modifiers, changeFlag) <> 0}

        DisableItem (FileMenu, SaveItem);    {Disable filing commands for desk    }
        DisableItem (FileMenu, SaveAsItem);  {  accessory or empty desk [II:4.6.2]}
        DisableItem (FileMenu, RevertItem);
        DisableItem (FileMenu, SetupItem);
        DisableItem (FileMenu, PrintItem)

      end; {with theData^^}

    HUnlock (dataHandle)                     {Unlock data record [I:3.2.4]}

  end; {DeactWindow}
```

{- -}

```
procedure Finalize;

  { Do one-time-only finalization. }

  begin {Finalize}
```

```
      WriteDeskScrap;                              {Copy Toolbox scrap to desk scrap}

      if PrError = NoErr then                      {Printing still enabled?  [III:4.2.4]}
         PrClose;                                  {Terminate printing [III:4.2.1]}

      SetEventMask (OldMask)                        {Restore original value of system event mask [II:2.3.2]}

   end;  {Finalize}
```

{- }

```
procedure WindowDirty {(isDirty : BOOLEAN)};

   { Mark window dirty or clean [Prog. II:5-7]. }

   var
      theData    : WDHandle;                        {Handle to window's data record}
      dataHandle : Handle;                          {Untyped handle for locking data record [I:3.1.1]}

   begin {WindowDirty}

      dataHandle := Handle(GetWRefCon(TheWindow));  {Get window data [II:3.2.4]}
      MoveHHi (dataHandle);                          {Move data record to top of heap [I:3.2.5]}
      HLock   (dataHandle);                          {Lock data record [I:3.2.4]}

        theData := WDHandle(dataHandle);             {Convert to typed handle}
      with theData^^ do
         begin

            dirty := isDirty;                         {Set flag in data record}

            if isDirty then                           {Is window becoming dirty or clean?}
               begin
                  EnableItem (FileMenu, SaveItem);    {Enable Save command [II:4.6.2]}
                  if fileNumber <> 0 then             {Is window associated with a file?}
                     EnableItem (FileMenu, RevertItem) {Enable Revert command [II:4.6.2]}
               end {then}

            else
               begin
                  DisableItem (FileMenu, SaveItem);   {Disable menu items [II:4.6.2]}
                  DisableItem (FileMenu, RevertItem)
               end {else}

         end; {with theData^^}
```

```
      HUnlock (dataHandle)                          {Unlock data record [I:3.2.4]}

   end;  {WindowDirty}
```

{ - }

```
procedure AdjustScrollBar;

   { Adjust scroll bar to length of document [Prog. II:6-5]. }

   const
     active   =   0;                               {Highlighting code for active scroll bar [II:6.3.3]}
     inactive = 255;                               {Highlighting code for inactive scroll bar [II:6.3.3]}

   var
     windowHeight : INTEGER;                        {Height of text rectangle in lines}
     maxTop       : INTEGER;                        {Maximum value for top line in window}

   begin  {AdjustScrollBar}

     with TheText^^. viewRect do
       begin
         windowHeight := (bottom - top) div lineHeight;   {Get window height [II:5.1.1]}
         maxTop       := nLines - windowHeight      {Avoid white space at bottom [II:5.1.1]}
       end; {with TheText^^, viewRect}

     if maxTop <= 0 then                            {Is text smaller than window?}
       begin
         maxTop := 0;                               {Show all of text}
         HiliteControl (TheScrollBar, inactive)     {Disable scroll bar [II:6.3.3]}
       end {then}
     else
       HiliteControl (TheScrollBar, active);        {Enable scroll bar [II:6.3.3]}

     SetCtlMax (TheScrollBar, maxTop)               {Adjust range of scroll bar [II:6.2.4]}

   end;  {AdjustScrollBar}
```

{ - }

```
procedure ScrollToSelection;

   { Scroll current selection into view [Prog. II:6-13]. }

   var
     editHandle   : Handle;                         {Untyped handle for locking edit record [I:3.1.1]}
```

```
    topLine      : INTEGER;           {First line visible in window}
    bottomLine   : INTEGER;           {First line beyond bottom of window}
    windowHeight : INTEGER;           {Height of text rectangle in lines}


begin {ScrollToSelection}

    editHandle := Handle(TheText);     {Convert to untyped handle [I:3.1.1]}
    MoveHHi (editHandle);              {Move edit record to top of heap [I:3.2.5]}
    HLock   (editHandle);              {Lock edit record [I:3.2.4]}
      with TheText^^. viewRect do
        begin

          topLine      := GetCtlValue (TheScrollBar);    {Get current top line [II:6.2.4]}
          windowHeight := (bottom - top) div lineHeight; {Get window height [II:5.1.1]}
          bottomLine   := topLine + windowHeight;        {Find line beyond bottom}

          if GetCtlMax (TheScrollBar) = 0 then     {Not enough text to fill the window? [II:6.2.4]}
            AdjustText                             {Start of text to top of window}

          else if selEnd < lineStarts[topLine] then    {Whole selection above  window top? [II:5.1.1]}
            ScrollCharacter (selStart, FALSE)          {Start of selection to top of window}

          else if selStart >= lineStarts[bottomLine] then
                                                   {Whole selection below window bottom? [II:5.1.1]}
            ScrollCharacter (selEnd, TRUE)         {End of selection to bottom of window}

        end; {with TheText^^, viewRect}
      HUnlock (editHandle)             {Unlock edit record [I:3.2.4]}

  end;   {ScrollToSelection}
```

{- -}

```
procedure ScrollCharacter {(theCharacter : INTEGER; toBottom : BOOLEAN)};

  { Scroll character into view [Prog. II:6-12]. }

  var
    editHandle   : Handle;             {Untyped handle for locking edit record [I:3.1.1]}
    theLine      : INTEGER;            {Number of line containing character}
    windowHeight : INTEGER;            {Height of text rectangle in lines}

  begin {ScrollCharacter}

    editHandle := Handle(TheText);     {Convert to untyped handle  [I:3.1.1]}
```

```
      MoveHHi  (editHandle);                                 {Move edit record to top of heap [I:3.2.5]}
      HLock    (editHandle);                                 {Lock edit record [I:3.2.4]}
        with TheText^^ do
          begin

            theLine := 0;                                         {Start search at first line}
            while lineStarts[theLine + 1] <= theCharacter do{Find line containing character [II:5.1.1]}
              theLine := theLine + 1;

            if toBottom then                                      {Scrolling to bottom of window?}
              begin
                with viewRect do
                  windowHeight := (bottom - top) div lineHeight; {Get window height}
                theLine := theLine - (windowHeight - 1)     {Offset for window height}
              end; {if toBottom}

            SetCtlValue (TheScrollBar, theLine);              {Adjust setting of scroll bar [II:6.2.4]}
            AdjustText                                        {Scroll text to match new setting}

          end; {with TheText^^}
        HUnlock (editHandle)                                 {Unlock edit record [I:3.2.4]}

    end;    {ScrollCharacter}


{ - - - - - - - - - - - - - - - - - - - - - - - - - - - - - - - - - - - - - - - - - - - - - - - - - - - - - - - - - - - - - - - - - - }


procedure ReadDeskScrap;

   { Read desk scrap into Toolbox scrap [Prog. II:5-12]. }

   var
      scrapLength : LONGINT;                                {Length of desk text scrap in bytes}
      ignore      : LONGINT;                                {Dummy variable for scrap offset}
      result      : OSErr;                                  {Result code from scrap transfer [I:3.1.2]}
      scrapInfo   : PScrapStuff;                            {Pointer to scrap information record}

   begin {ReadDeskScrap}

      scrapInfo := InfoScrap;                               {Get scrap info [I:7.4.2]}
      if ScrapCompare <> scrapInfo^.scrapCount then {Has scrap count changed? [I:7.4.2]}
        begin

            scrapLength := GetScrap (NIL, 'TEXT', ignore);{Check desk scrap for a text item [I:7.4.3]}

            if scrapLength >= 0 then                        {Is there a text item?}
              begin
```

```
            result := TEFromScrap;              {Transfer desk scrap to Toolbox scrap [II:5.5.5]}
          if result <> NoErr then               {Was there an error? [I:3.1.2]}
              scrapLength := result             {Make sure scrap length is negative}
          end; {if scrapLength >= 0}


       if scrapLength > 0 then                  {Was scrap nonempty?}
          EnableItem  (EditMenu, PasteItem)     {Enable Paste command [II:4.6.2]}
       else
          begin
              TESetScrapLen (0);                {Mark Toolbox scrap as empty [II:5.5.4]}
              DisableItem (EditMenu, PasteItem) {Disable Paste command [II:4.6.2]}
          end; {else}


       scrapInfo    := InfoScrap;               {Get scrap info}
       ScrapCompare := scrapInfo^.scrapCount    {Save scrap count for later comparison [I:7.4.2]}


     end {if ScrapCompare <> InfoScrap^.scrapCount}

  end;    {ReadDeskScrap}

{ - - - - - - - - - - - - - - - - - - - - - - - - - - - - - - - - - - - - - - - - - - - - - - - - - - - - - - - - }


procedure WriteDeskScrap;

  { Write Toolbox scrap to desk scrap [Prog. II:5-13]. }

  var
     scrapInfo   : PScrapStuff;                 {Pointer to scrap information record [I:7.4.2]}
     scrapResult : LONGINT;                     {Result code from ZeroScrap [I:7.4.3]}
     teResult    : OSErr;                       {Result code from scrap transfer [I:3.1.2]}


  begin {WriteDeskScrap}

     if ScrapDirty then                         {Has scrap changed since last read?}
       begin

          scrapResult := ZeroScrap;             {Change scrap count [I:7.4.3]}
          if scrapResult = NoErr then           {Was there an error? [I:3.1.2]}
            begin
               scrapInfo    := InfoScrap;        {Get scrap info [I:7.4.2]}
               ScrapCompare := scrapInfo^.scrapCount {Save new scrap count for comparison [I:7.4.2]}
            end; {if scrapResult = NoErr}

          teResult := TEToScrap;                {Transfer Toolbox scrap to desk scrap [II:5.5.5]}
```

```
        ScrapDirty := FALSE                          {Toolbox and desk scraps now agree}

      end {if ScrapDirty}

  end;  {WriteDeskScrap}

{ - - - - - - - - - - - - - - - - - - - - - - - - - - - - - - - - - - - - - - - - - - - - - - - - - - - - - - - - - - - - - - - - - - - - - - }

procedure IOCheck {(resultCode : OSErr)};

  { Check for I/O error [Prog. II:8-1]. }

  var
    alertID     : INTEGER;                           {Resource ID of alert}
    errorString : Str255;                            {Error code in string form [I:2.1.1]}
    ignore      : INTEGER;                           {Item code returned by alert}

  begin {IOCheck}

    if resultCode = NoErr then                       {Just return if no error [I:3.1.2]}
      EXIT (IOCheck);

    case resultCode of

      OpWrErr:                                       {File already open? [II:8.2.8]}
        alertID := OpWrID;                           {Use Already Open alert}

      IPrAbort:                                      {Printing canceled? [III:4.2.4]}
        alertID := PrntCnclID;                       {Use Printing Canceled alert}

      {Insert code here to handle any other specific errors}

      otherwise
        begin
          alertID := IOErrID;                        {Use general I/O Error alert}
          NumToString (resultCode, errorString);     {Convert error code to a string [I:2.3.7]}
          ParamText   (errorString, '', '', '')      {Substitute into text of alert [II:7.4.6]}
        end {otherwise}

      end; {case resultCode}

    InitCursor;                                      {Restore normal cursor  [II:2.5.2]}
    ignore := StopAlert (alertID, NIL);              {Post alert [II:7.4.2]}

    Quitting  := FALSE;                              {Cancel Quit command, if any}
    ErrorFlag := TRUE                                {Force exit to main event loop}
```

```
   end;  {IOCheck}
```

{ - }

```
   { Main program [Prog. II:2-1]. }

   begin {MiniEdit}

      Initialize;                        {Do one-time-only initialization}

      repeat
         MainLoop                        {Execute one pass of main loop}
      until Finished;

      Finalize                           {Do one-time-only finalization}

   end.   {MiniEdit}
```

StopWatch **Desk Accessory**

StopWatch is the example desk accessory developed in Chapter 6. When started from zero, the stopwatch counts upward by tenths of a second; when started from a value greater than zero, it counts downward and beeps when it reaches zero.

```
program StopWatch;

   {Example desk accessory for Macintosh Revealed, Volume Three [Prog. III:6-1].}

uses
   MemTypes,                            {Elementary data types}
   QuickDraw,                           {QuickDraw graphics routines}
   OSIntf,                              {Macintosh Operating System}
   ToolIntf,                            {User Interface Toolbox}
   PackIntf;                            {Standard packages}
```

{ - }

```
{ Global Declarations }

const                                   {Bit masks for DCE flags: }
   dReadEnable  = $0100;                {Can respond to Read calls [III:3.1.2]}
   dWriteEnable = $0200;                {Can respond to Write calls [III:3.1.2]}
```

```
dCtlEnable    = $0400;          {Can respond to Control calls [III:3.1.2]}
dStatEnable   = $0800;          {Can respond to Status calls [III:3.1.2]}
dNeedGoodBye  = $1000;          {Needs "good-bye kiss" [III:3.1.2]}
dNeedTime     = $2000;          {Has periodic task [III:3.1.2]}
dNeedLock     = $4000;          {Must be locked in heap [III:3.1.2]}


                                {Standard control codes: }
KillCode   = 1;                 {KillIO operation [III:3.2.3]}
GoodBye    = -1;                {"Good-bye kiss" [III:3.1.2]}


AccEvent   = 64;                {User event [III:6.1.3]}
AccRun     = 65;                {Periodic task [III:6.1.3]}
AccCursor  = 66;                {Adjust cursor [III:6.1.3]}
AccMenu    = 67;                {Menu item [III:6.1.3]}
AccUndo    = 68;                {Undo command [III:6.1.3]}
AccCut     = 70;                {Cut command [III:6.1.3]}
AccCopy    = 71;                {Copy command [III:6.1.3]}
AccPaste   = 72;                {Paste command [III:6.1.3]}
AccClear   = 73;                {Clear command [III:6.1.3]}


                                {Character codes [III:I:8.1.1]: }
Enter   = $03;                  {Enter character}
BS      = $08;                  {Backspace character}
CR      = $0D;                  {Carriage return}
Clear   = $1B;                  {Clear character}
Space   = $20;                  {Space character}

Digit0 = $30;                   {Character '0'}
Digit9 = $39;                   {Character '9'}


                                {Item numbers for menu commands: }
AboutItem = 1;                  {About StopWatch... command}
StartItem = 3;                  {Start command}
PauseItem = 4;                  {Pause command}
ResetItem = 5;                  {Reset command}


TextMargin = 4;                 {Inset from window to edges of text}


type
   DRHandle   = ^DRPtr;
   DRPtr      = ^DataRecord;
   DataRecord = record
```

```
        RefNum    : INTEGER;                  {Driver reference number}
        RsrcBase  : INTEGER;                  {Base ID for owned resources}
        IBeam     : CursHandle;               {Handle to I-beam cursor [II:2.5.1]}

        TheMenu   : MenuHandle;               {Handle to StopWatch menu [II:4.1.1]}
        TheWindow  : WindowPtr;               {Pointer to StopWatch window [II:3.1.1]}
        TheText    : TEHandle;                {Handle to edit record [II:5.1.1]}

        TargetTime : LONGINT;                 {Starting or stopping time on system  clock [II:2.7.1]}
        PauseTime  : LONGINT;                 {Time of pause on system clock}

        CountDown    : BOOLEAN;               {Counting down (toward zero)?}
        ClockRunning : BOOLEAN;               {Is stopwatch running?}
        ClockPaused  : BOOLEAN;               {Is stopwatch paused?}
        ClockBeeping : BOOLEAN                {Is stopwatch beeping?}

      end; {DataRecord}
```

{ - }

{ Forward Declarations }

```
procedure DoOpen (pbPtr : ParmBlkPtr; dcePtr : DCtlPtr); forward;
     { Handle driver Open call. }
  procedure SetUpDCE (var dce : DCtlEntry); forward;
       { Initialize device control entry. }
  procedure SetUpData (var dce : DCtlEntry); forward;
       { Initialize StopWatch private data. }
    procedure SetUpResources (dce : DCtlEntry; dataHandle : DRHandle); forward;
         { Initialize StopWatch resources. }
    procedure SetUpMenu (var dce : DCtlEntry; dataHandle : DRHandle); forward;
         { Initialize StopWatch menu. }
    procedure SetUpWindow (var dce : DCtlEntry; dataHandle : DRHandle); forward;
         { Initialize StopWatch window. }
    procedure SetUpText (dataHandle : DRHandle); forward;
         { Initialize text editing. }
    procedure InitFlags (var dce : DCtlEntry; dataHandle : DRHandle); forward;
         { Initialize global flags. }
procedure DoControl (pbPtr : ParmBlkPtr; dcePtr : DCtlPtr); forward;
     { Handle driver Control call. }
  procedure DoEvent (dataHandle : DRHandle; ctlParam : LONGINT); forward;
       { Handle user event. }
    procedure DoMouseDown (theEvent : EventRecord; dataHandle : DRHandle); forward;
         { Handle mouse-down event. }
    procedure DoKeystroke (theEvent : EventRecord; dataHandle : DRHandle); forward;
         { Handle keyboard event. }
```

```
        procedure DoTyping (dataHandle : DRHandle; ch : CHAR); forward;
            { Handle character typed from keyboard. }
        procedure DoAlias (dataHandle : DRHandle; ch : CHAR); forward;
            { Handle keyboard command alias. }
    procedure DoUpdate (dataHandle : DRHandle); forward;
        { Handle update event. }
    procedure DoActivate (theEvent : EventRecord; dataHandle : DRHandle); forward;
        { Handle activate (or deactivate) event. }
        procedure ReadDeskScrap; forward;
            { Read desk scrap into Toolbox scrap. }
        procedure WriteDeskScrap; forward;
            { Write Toolbox scrap to desk scrap. }
procedure PeriodicTask (dataHandle : DRHandle); forward;
    { Perform periodic task. }
    procedure AdvanceClock (dataHandle : DRHandle); forward;
        { Advance time on clock. }
    procedure StartBeep (dataHandle : DRHandle); forward;
        { Start beep sequence. }
    procedure DoBeep; forward;
        { Signal that clock has expired. }
procedure FixCursor (dataHandle : DRHandle); forward;
    { Adjust cursor for region of screen. }
procedure DoMenuChoice (dataHandle : DRHandle; menuChoice : LONGINT); forward;
    { Handle user's menu choice. }
    procedure DoAbout (dataHandle : DRHandle); forward;
        { Handle About StopWatch... command. }
    procedure DoStart (dataHandle : DRHandle); forward;
        { Handle Start command. }
        function TextToNum (textHandle : TEHandle) : LONGINT; forward;
            { Convert text to integer. }
    procedure DoPause (dataHandle : DRHandle); forward;
        { Handle Pause command. }
    procedure DoReset (dataHandle : DRHandle); forward;
        { Handle Reset command. }
procedure DoUndo (dataHandle : DRHandle); forward;
    { Handle Undo command. }
procedure DoCut (dataHandle : DRHandle); forward;
    { Handle Cut command. }
procedure DoCopy (dataHandle : DRHandle); forward;
    { Handle Copy command. }
procedure DoPaste (dataHandle : DRHandle); forward;
    { Handle Paste command. }
procedure DoClear (dataHandle : DRHandle); forward;
    { Handle Clear command. }
procedure DoGoodBye (pbPtr : ParmBlkPtr; dcePtr : DCtlPtr); forward;
    { Handle "good-bye kiss." }
```

```
   procedure DoKillIO (dataHandle : DRHandle); forward;
        { Perform KillIO operation. }
procedure DoClose (pbPtr : ParmBlkPtr; dcePtr : DCtlPtr); forward;
      { Handle driver Close call. }

{ - - - - - - - - - - - - - - - - - - - - - - - - - - - - - - - - - - - - - - - - - - - - - - - - - - - - - - - - - - - - - - - - - - - - - - - - - - - - - - - - - - - - - - - - - }


procedure DoOpen {(pbPtr : ParmBlkPtr; dcePtr : DCtlPtr)};

   { Handle driver Open call [Prog. III:6-2]. }

   var
      oldWindow : WindowPtr;                              {Pointer to existing StopWatch window [II:3.1.1]}

   begin  {DoOpen}

      with dcePtr^ do

         if dCtlWindow = NIL then                         {Is there a window open already? [III:3.1.4]}
            begin
               SetUpDCE  (dcePtr^);                        {If not, initialize DCE}
               SetUpData (dcePtr^)                         {  and data record   }
            end {then}

         else
            begin
               oldWindow := WindowPtr(dCtlWindow);         {Otherwise convert to typed pointer [III:3.1.4]}
               SelectWindow (oldWindow)                    {Just activate existing window [II:3.5.2]}
            end {else}

   end;   {DoOpen}

{ - - - - - - - - - - - - - - - - - - - - - - - - - - - - - - - - - - - - - - - - - - - - - - - - - - - - - - - - - - - - - - - - - - - - - - - - - - - - - - - - - - - - - }


procedure SetUpDCE {(var dce : DCtlEntry)};

   { Initialize device control entry [Prog. III:6-3]. }

   var
      flagBits : INTEGER;                                 {Flag bits for DCE flag word [III:3.1.2, III:3.1.4]}

   begin {SetUpDCE}

      with dce do
         begin
```

```
        flagBits  := dCtlEnable + dNeedTime;        {Set up flags [III:3.1.2]}
        dCtlFlags := BitAnd (dCtlFlags, $FF);       {Extract low byte [I:2.2.2]}
        dCtlFlags := BitOr  (dCtlFlags, flagBits);     {Merge in high byte [I:2.2.2]}

        dCtlDelay := 6;                             {Execute task ten times per second [III:3.1.4]}
        dCtlEMask := MDownMask + KeyDownMask + AutoKeyMask + UpdateMask + ActivMask;
                                                    {Initialize event mask [III:3.1.4, II:2.1.3]}

        dCtlStorage := NewHandle (SIZEOF(DataRecord))  {Allocate private data record [I:3.2.1]}

      end  {with dce}

  end;  {SetUpDCE}

{- - - - - - - - - - - - - - - - - - - - - - - - - - - - - - - - - - - - - - - - - - - - - - - - - - - - - - - - - - - - - - - -}

procedure SetUpData {(var dce : DCtlEntry)};

  { Initialize StopWatch private data. }

  var
     dataHandle : DRHandle;                         {Handle to StopWatch data record}

  begin {SetUpData}

    with dce do
      begin
        MoveHHi (dCtlStorage);                      {Move data record to end of heap [I:3.2.5]}
        HLock   (dCtlStorage);                      {Lock data record [I:3.2.4]}

        dataHandle := DRHandle(dCtlStorage);        {Convert to typed handle}

        SetUpResources (dce, dataHandle);           {Initialize StopWatch resources}
        SetUpMenu      (dce, dataHandle);           {Initialize StopWatch menu}
        SetUpWindow    (dce, dataHandle);           {Initialize StopWatch window}
        SetUpText      (dataHandle);                {Initialize text editing}
        InitFlags      (dce, dataHandle);           {Initialize global flags}

        HUnlock (dCtlStorage)                       {Unlock data record [I:3.2.4]}
      end  {with dce}

  end;  {SetUpData}

{- - - - - - - - - - - - - - - - - - - - - - - - - - - - - - - - - - - - - - - - - - - - - - - - - - - - - - - - - - - - - - - -}

procedure SetUpResources {(dce : DCtlEntry; dataHandle : DRHandle)};
```

{ Initialize StopWatch resources [Prog. III:6-5]. }

```
const
   flagBits = $C000;                                 {Flag bits for owned resources [III:2.5.4]}


var
   unitNum : INTEGER;                                {StopWatch's unit number [III:3.1.3]}


begin {SetUpResources}

   with dce, dataHandle^^ do
      begin

          RefNum    := dCtlRefNum;                   {Save reference number in data record [III:3.1.4]}


          unitNum   := BitNot   (RefNum);            {Convert to unit number [I:2.2.2]}
          unitNum   := BitShift (unitNum, 5);        {Shift into position [I:2.2.2]}
          RsrcBase  := BitOr    (flagBits, unitNum); {Merge in flag bits [I:2.2.2]}


          IBeam     := GetCursor (IBeamCursor)       {Get cursor from system file [II:2.5.2]}


      end {with dce, dataHandle^^}

   end; {SetUpResources}

{ - - - - - - - - - - - - - - - - - - - - - - - - - - - - - - - - - - - - - - - - - - - - - - - - - - - - - - - - - - - - - - }


procedure SetUpMenu {(var dce : DCtlEntry; dataHandle : DRHandle)};

   { Initialize StopWatch menu [Prog. III:6-6]. }

   begin {SetUpMenu}

      with dce, dataHandle^^ do
         begin

             dCtlMenu := RsrcBase;                   {Store menu ID in DCE [III:3.1.4]}
             TheMenu   := GetMenu (dCtlMenu);        {Get menu from resource file [II:4.2.2]}
             TheMenu^^.menuID := dCtlMenu;           {Set correct menu ID in menu record [II:4.1.1]}

             InsertMenu (TheMenu, 0);                {Install at end of menu bar [II:4.4.1]}
             DrawMenuBar                             {Show menu title on screen [II:4.4.3]}


         end {with dce, dataHandle^^}

   end; {SetUpMenu}
```

```
{-------------------------------------------------------------------------------}

procedure SetUpWindow {(var dce : DCtlEntry; dataHandle : DRHandle)};

  { Initialize StopWatch window [Prog. III:6-7]. }

  var
     peek : WindowPeek;                         {Pointer for "peeking" into window's fields [II:3.1.1]}

  begin {SetUpWindow}

    with dce, dataHandle^^ do
      begin

         TheWindow := GetNewWindow (RsrcBase, NIL, WindowPtr(-1));
                                                {Make new window from template [II:3.2.2]}
         dCtlWindow := Ptr(TheWindow);          {Store window pointer in DCE [III:3.1.4]}

         peek := WindowPeek(TheWindow);         {Convert to a "peek" pointer [II:3.1.1]}
         peek^.windowKind := dCtlRefNum         {Set window class to reference number [II:3.1.1]}

      end {with dce, dataHandle^^}

  end; {SetUpWindow}

{-------------------------------------------------------------------------------}

procedure SetUpText {(dataHandle : DRHandle)};

  { Initialize text editing. }

  var
     savePort    : GrafPtr;                     {Pointer to previous graphics port [I:4.2.2]}
     textRect    : Rect;                        {Clipping/wrapping rectangle for text display [I:4.1.2]}
     scrapLength : LONGINT;                     {Length of Toolbox scrap in characters}
     scrapHandle : Handle;                      {Handle to contents of Toolbox scrap [I:5.1.2]}
     zeroString  : Str255;                      {Dummy string for initializing text [I:2.1.1]}

  begin {SetUpText}

    with dataHandle^^ do
      begin
         GetPort (savePort);                    {Save previous port [I:4.3.3]}
         SetPort (TheWindow);                   {Get into the window's port [I:4.3.3]}
```

```
        TextFont (Monaco);                        {Set monospace font [I:8.3.2, I:8.2.1]}
        TextSize (12);                            {Set type size [I:8.3.2]}
        TextFace ([Bold]);                        {Use boldface [I:8.3.2, I:8.3.1]}


        textRect := TheWindow^.portRect;          {Set up text rectangle [I:4.2.2]}
        InsetRect (textRect, TextMargin, TextMargin);   {Inset by text margin [I:4.4.4]}
        TheText  := TENew (textRect, textRect); {Make edit record [II:5.2.2]}
        TESetJust (TEJustRight, TheText);         {Justify to right [II:5.3.1, II:5.1.1]}


        ReadDeskScrap;                            {Read desk scrap into Toolbox scrap}
        scrapLength := TEGetScrapLen;             {Get length of Toolbox scrap [II:5.5.4]}
        if scrapLength > 0 then                   {Was there a numeric scrap?}
           begin
              scrapHandle := TEScrapHandle;       {Get scrap handle [II:5.5.4, II:5.1.2]}
              MoveHHi (scrapHandle);              {Move scrap to end of heap [I:3.2.5]}
              HLock   (scrapHandle);              {Lock scrap handle [I:3.2.4]}
                 TESetText (scrapHandle^, scrapLength, TheText);
                                                  {Initialize text from scrap  [II:5.2.3]}
              HUnlock (scrapHandle)               {Unlock scrap handle [I:3.2.4]}
           end {then}
        else
           begin
              zeroString := '0';                  {Make zero string}
              TESetText (@zeroString[1], 1, TheText) {Initialize text to '0' [II:5.2.3]}
           end; {else}


     SetPort (savePort)                           {Restore previous port [I:4.3.3]}
   end {with dataHandle^^}

end;  {SetUpText}
```

{- -}


```
procedure InitFlags ((var dce : DCtlEntry; dataHandle : DRHandle)};

   { Initialize global flags. }

   begin {InitFlags}

      with dataHandle^^ do
         begin

            TargetTime    := 0;                   {Clear start/stop time}

            ClockRunning  := FALSE;               {Clear global flags}
```

```
        ClockPaused  := FALSE;
        ClockBeeping := FALSE;

        dce.dCtlDelay := 6                          {Reset task interval to 1/10 second [III:3.1.4]}

      end {with dataHandle^^}

  end;   {InitFlags}
```

{ - }

```
procedure DoControl {(pbPtr : ParmBlkPtr; dcePtr : DCtlPtr)};

  { Handle driver Control call [Prog. III:6-8]. }

  var
    dataHandle : DRHandle;                          {Handle to StopWatch data record}
    paramPtr   : ^LONGINT;                          {Pointer for converting parameter field}

  begin {DoControl}

    with pbPtr^, dcePtr^ do
      begin

        MoveHHi (dCtlStorage);                      {Move data record to end of heap [I:3.2.5]}
        HLock   (dCtlStorage);                      {Lock data record [I:3.2.4]}

        dataHandle := DRHandle(dCtlStorage);        {Convert to typed handle [III:3.1.4]}
        paramPtr   := @csParam;                     {Convert to long integer [III:3.1.5]}

        case csCode of

          AccEvent:
            DoEvent (dataHandle, paramPtr^);        {Handle user event}

          AccRun:
            PeriodicTask (dataHandle);              {Perform periodic task}

          AccCursor:
            FixCursor (dataHandle);                 {Adjust cursor for region of screen}

          AccMenu:
            DoMenuChoice (dataHandle, paramPtr^);   {Handle user's menu  choice}

          AccUndo:
            DoUndo (dataHandle);                    {Handle Undo command}
```

```
            AccCut:
               DoCut (dataHandle);              {Handle Cut command}

            AccCopy:
               DoCopy (dataHandle);             {Handle Copy command}

            AccPaste:
               DoPaste (dataHandle);            {Handle Paste command}

            AccClear:
               DoClear (dataHandle);            {Handle Clear command}

            GoodBye:
               DoGoodBye (pbPtr, dcePtr);       {Handle "good-bye kiss"}

            KillCode:
               DoKillIO (dataHandle)            {Perform KillIO operation}

            end; {case csCode}

         HUnlock (dCtlStorage)                  {Unlock data record [I:3.2.4]}

      end {with pbPtr^, dcePtr^}

   end; {DoControl}

{ - - - - - - - - - - - - - - - - - - - - - - - - - - - - - - - - - - - - - - - - - - - - - - - - - - - - - - - - - - - - - - - - - - - }

procedure DoEvent {(dataHandle : DRHandle; ctlParam : LONGINT)};

   { Handle user event [Prog. III:6-9]. }

   type
      EventPtr = ^EventRecord;                  {Pointer to an event record [II:2.1.1]}

   var
      evtPtr   : EventPtr;                      {Typed pointer for converting control parameter}
      theEvent : EventRecord;                   {Event record for this event [II:2.1.1]}
      activate : BOOLEAN;                       {Activate or deactivate window?}

   begin {DoEvent}

      evtPtr   := EventPtr(ctlParam);           {Convert control parameter to typed pointer}
      theEvent := evtPtr^;                       {Get event record}
      with theEvent do
```

```
      case what of                                    {Dispatch on event type [II:2.1.1, II:2.1.2]}

        MouseDown:
          DoMouseDown (theEvent, dataHandle);         {Handle mouse-down event}

        KeyDown, AutoKey:
          DoKeystroke (theEvent, dataHandle);         {Handle keyboard event}

        UpdateEvt:
          DoUpdate (dataHandle);                      {Handle update event}

        ActivateEvt:
          DoActivate (theEvent, dataHandle)           {Handle activate (or deactivate) event}

        end  {case what}

  end;   {DoEvent}

{------------------------------------------------------------------------------}

procedure DoMouseDown {(theEvent : EventRecord; dataHandle : DRHandle)};

  { Handle mouse-down event. }

  var
    mousePoint : Point;                               {Point where mouse was pressed [I:4.1.1]}
    extend     : BOOLEAN;                             {Extend existing selection (Shift-click)?}

  begin {DoMouseDown}

    with theEvent, dataHandle^^ do

      if ClockRunning then                            {Stopwatch already in use?}
        SysBeep (1)                                   {No text selection allowed [II:2.8.1]}

      else
        begin

          SetPort (TheWindow);                        {Get into StopWatch window [I:4.3.3]}

          mousePoint := theEvent.where;               {Get mouse point in screen coordinates [II:2.1.1]}
          GlobalToLocal (mousePoint);                 {Convert to window coordinates [I:4.4.2]}

          if PtInRect (mousePoint, TheText^^.viewRect) then   {In text rectangle? [I:4.4.3, II:5.1.1]}
            begin
```

```
                    extend := (BitAnd (modifiers, ShiftKey) <> 0);     {Shift key down? [I:2.2.2, II:2.1.5]}
                    TEClick (mousePoint, extend, TheText)              {Do text selection [II:5.4.1]}
                end {if}

            end {else}

    end;   {DoMouseDown}
```

{---}

```
procedure DoKeystroke ((theEvent : EventRecord; dataHandle : DRHandle));

    { Handle keyboard event [Prog. III:6-11]. }

    var
        chCode : INTEGER;                                   {Character code from event message [I:8.1.1]}
        ch     : CHAR;                                      {Character that was typed}

    begin {DoKeystroke}

        with theEvent do
            begin

                chCode := BitAnd (message, CharCodeMask);   {Extract character code [I:2.2.2, II:2.1.4]}
                ch     := CHR(chCode);                      {Convert to a character}

                if (BitAnd (modifiers, CmdKey) <> 0)        {Command key down? [I:2.2.2, II:2.1.5]}
                        and (what <> AutoKey) then          {Ignore repeats [II:2.1.1, II:2.1.2]}
                    DoAlias  (dataHandle, ch)               {Handle as command alias}
                else
                    DoTyping (dataHandle, ch)               {Handle as ordinary keystroke}

            end {with theEvent}

    end;   {DoKeystroke}
```

{---}

```
procedure DoTyping ((dataHandle : DRHandle; ch : CHAR));

    { Handle character typed from keyboard [Prog. III:6-13]. }

    var
        chCode     : INTEGER;                               {Character code [I:8.1.1]}
        menuChoice : LONGINT;                               {Menu ID and item number}
```

```
    begin {DoTyping}

        chCode := ORD(ch);                               {Convert to character code}

        if chCode in [CR, Enter, Space, Clear] then      {Is it a StopWatch menu command?}
            HiliteMenu (dataHandle^^.RsrcBase);          {Highlight menu title [II:4.5.4]}

        with dataHandle^^ do
            case chCode of                               {Dispatch on character code}

                Digit0..Digit9, BS:
                    if ClockRunning then                 {Stopwatch already in use?}
                        SysBeep (1)                      {No typing allowed [II:2.8.1]}
                    else
                        TEKey (ch, TheText);             {Insert digit or backspace in window [II:5.5.1]}

                CR, Enter:
                    DoStart (dataHandle);                {Return or Enter means Start}

                Space:
                    DoPause (dataHandle);                {Space means Pause or Resume}

                Clear:
                    DoReset (dataHandle);                {Clear means Reset}

                otherwise
                    SysBeep (1)                          {Invalid character [II:2.8.1]}

                end; {case chCode}

        HiliteMenu (0)                                   {Unhighlight menu title [II:4.5.4]}

    end; {DoTyping}

{ - - - - - - - - - - - - - - - - - - - - - - - - - - - - - - - - - - - - - - - - - - - - - - - - - - - - - - - - - - - - - - }

procedure DoAlias {((dataHandle : DRHandle; ch : CHAR)};

    { Handle keyboard command alias [Prog. III:6-12]. }

    var
        menuChoice : LONGINT;                            {Menu ID and item number}

    begin {DoAlias}
```

```
      if ch in ['S', 's', ',', '.'] then              {Is it a StopWatch menu command?}
         HiliteMenu (dataHandle^^.RsrcBase);          {Highlight menu title [II:4.5.4]}

      case ch of

         'Z', 'z':
            DoUndo  (dataHandle);                      {Command-Z means Undo}

         'X', 'x':
            DoCut   (dataHandle);                      {Command-X means Cut}

         'C', 'c':
            DoCopy  (dataHandle);                      {Command-C means Copy}

         'V', 'v':
            DoPaste (dataHandle);                      {Command-V means Paste}

         'B', 'b':
            DoClear (dataHandle);                      {Command-B means Clear}

         'S', 's':
            DoStart (dataHandle);                      {Command-S means Start}

         ',':
            DoPause (dataHandle);                      {Command-comma means Pause or Resume}

         '.':
            DoReset (dataHandle);                      {Command-period means Reset}

         otherwise
            SysBeep(1)                                 {Unknown command code [II:2.8.1]}

         end; {case ch}

      HiliteMenu (0)                                   {Unhighlight menu title [II:4.5.4]}

   end; {DoAlias}

{- - - - - - - - - - - - - - - - - - - - - - - - - - - - - - - - - - - - - - - - - - - - - - - - - - - - - - - - -}


procedure DoUpdate {(dataHandle : DRHandle)};

   { Handle update event. }

   var
      savePort : GrafPtr;                              {Pointer to previous graphics port [I:4.2.2]}
```

```
begin {DoUpdate}

   with dataHandle^^ do
      begin

         GetPort (savePort);                          {Save previous port [I:4.3.3]}
         SetPort (TheWindow);                         {Get into the window's port [I:4.3.3]}

            BeginUpdate (TheWindow);                  {Restrict visible region to update region [II:3.4.1]}

               TEUpdate (TheWindow^.portRect, TheText);  {Redraw text [II:5.3.2]}

            EndUpdate (TheWindow);                    {Restore original visible region [II:3.4.1]}

         SetPort (savePort)                           {Restore previous port [I:4.3.3]}

      end  {with dataHandle^^}

   end;   {DoUpdate}
```

{- -}

```
procedure DoActivate {(theEvent : EventRecord; dataHandle : DRHandle)};

   { Handle activate (or deactivate) event. }


   begin {DoActivate}

      with theEvent, dataHandle^^ do
         begin

            SetPort (theWindow);                      {Make StopWatch window the current port [I:4.3.3]}

            if BitAnd (modifiers, ActiveFlag) <> 0 then   {Activate or deactivate? [I:2.2.2, II:2.1.5]}
               begin
                  TEActivate (TheText);               {Highlight text selection [II:5.4.3]}

                  EnableItem (TheMenu, 0);            {Enable StopWatch menu [II:4.6.2]}
                  DrawMenuBar;                        {Make change visible on screen [II:4.4.3]}

                  ReadDeskScrap                       {Read desk scrap into Toolbox scrap}
               end {then}

            else
```

```
      begin
         TEDeactivate (TheText);            {Unhighlight text selection [II:5.4.3]}

         DisableItem (TheMenu, 0);          {Disable StopWatch menu [II:4.6.2]}
         DrawMenuBar;                       {Make change visible on screen [II:4.4.3]}

         WriteDeskScrap                     {Write Toolbox scrap to desk scrap}
      end {else}

   end {with theEvent, dataHandle^^}

end; {DoActivate}
```

{- }

```
procedure ReadDeskScrap;

   { Read desk scrap into Toolbox scrap. }

   var
      result      : OSErr;         {Result code from scrap transfer [I:3.1.2]}
      scrapLength : LONGINT;       {Length of Toolbox scrap in characters}
      scrapHandle : CharsHandle;   {Handle to contents of Toolbox scrap [I:5.1.2]}
      charIndex   : LONGINT;       {Character index in Toolbox scrap}
      scrapOK     : BOOLEAN;       {Does scrap represent a numerical value?}

   begin {ReadDeskScrap}

      result := TEFromScrap;       {Transfer desk scrap to Toolbox scrap [II:5.5.5]}

      if result < 0 then           {Was there an error? [I:3.1.2]}
         TESetScrapLen (0)         {Mark Toolbox scrap as empty [II:5.5.4]}
      else
         begin
            scrapLength := TEGetScrapLen;            {Get length of Toolbox scrap [II:5.5.4]}
            scrapHandle := CharsHandle(TEScrapHandle); {Get handle to Toolbox scrap [II:5.5.4, II:5.1.2]}

            charIndex := 0;                          {Start at first character}
            scrapOK := TRUE;                         {Presume innocent until proven guilty}
            while (charIndex < scrapLength) and scrapOK do   {Loop until answer is known}
               if scrapHandle^^[charIndex] in ['0'..'9'] then {Is character a digit?}
                  charIndex := charIndex + 1                  {Advance to next character}
               else
                  scrapOK := FALSE;                  {Look no further}
```

```
          if not scrapOK then                    {Any non-digits?}
             TESetScrapLen (0)                    {Mark scrap as empty [II:5.5.4]}
       end {else}

   end; {ReadDeskScrap}
```

{--}

```
procedure WriteDeskScrap;

   { Write Toolbox scrap to desk scrap. }

   var
      ignore : LONGINT;                           {Result code from resetting desk scrap [I:7.4.3]}
      result : OSErr;                             {Result code from scrap transfer [I:3.1.2]}

   begin {WriteDeskScrap}

      ignore := ZeroScrap;                        {Change scrap count [I:7.4.3]}
      result := TEToScrap                         {Transfer Toolbox scrap to desk scrap [II:5.5.5]}

   end; {WriteDeskScrap}
```

{--}

```
procedure PeriodicTask ((dataHandle : DRHandle));

   { Perform periodic task [Prog. III:6-14]. }

   begin {PeriodicTask}

      with dataHandle^^ do

         if ClockBeeping then                     {Is the clock beeping?}
            DoBeep                                {Beep it again}

         else if ClockRunning and not ClockPaused then   {Is the clock ticking?}
            AdvanceClock (dataHandle)             {Advance time on clock}

         else if not ClockPaused then             {Is the clock idle?}
            TEIdle (TheText)                      {Blink insertion point [II:5.4.3]}

   end; {PeriodicTask}
```

{--}

```
procedure AdvanceClock {(dataHandle : DRHandle)};

   { Advance time on clock [Prog. III:6-15]. }

   var
      timeNow    : LONGINT;              {Current time on system clock}
      clockTime  : LONGINT;              {Number of seconds showing on stopwatch}
      timeString : Str255;              {String representation of clock time [I:2.1.1]}

   begin {AdvanceClock}

      with dataHandle^^ do
        begin

           timeNow := TickCount;              {Get current time [II:2.7.1]}

           if CountDown then                  {Counting up or down?}
              clockTime := TargetTime - timeNow    {Ticks till stopping time}
           else
              clockTime := timeNow - TargetTime;   {Ticks since starting time}

           clockTime := (clockTime + 3) div 6;   {Round to nearest tenth of a second}

           if CountDown and (clockTime <= 0) then   {Has time run out?}
              begin
                 timeString := '0.0';              {Avoid negative value}
                 StartBeep (dataHandle)            {Start beep sequence}
              end {then}
           else
              begin
                 NumToString (clockTime, timeString);      {Convert to string [I:2.3.7]}
                 INSERT ('.', timeString, LENGTH(timeString))  {Insert decimal point}
              end; {else}

           TESetText (@timeString[1], LENGTH(timeString), TheText);  {Set window's text [II:5.2.3]}
           TEUpdate  (TheText^^.viewRect, TheText)            {Redisplay text on screen [II:5.3.2]}

        end {with dataHandle^^}

   end; {AdvanceClock}

{-----------------------------------------------------------------------------}

procedure StartBeep {(dataHandle : DRHandle)};
```

```
    { Start beep sequence [Prog. III:6-16]. }

    var
       dceHandle : DCtlHandle;                          {Handle to DCE [III:3.1.4]}

    begin {StartBeep}

       with dataHandle^^ do
          begin

             DoBeep;                                     {Sound first beep}

             dceHandle := GetDCtlEntry (RefNum);         {Get DCE handle [III:3.1.4]}
             dceHandle^^.dCtlDelay := 60;                {Change task interval to once per second [III:3.1.4]}

             ClockBeeping := TRUE                        {Start periodic beeping}

          end {with dataHandle^^}

    end;   {StartBeep}

{- - - - - - - - - - - - - - - - - - - - - - - - - - - - - - - - - - - - - - - - - - - - - - - - - - - - - -}

procedure DoBeep;

    { Signal that clock has expired. }

    begin {DoBeep}

       FlashMenuBar (0);                                 {Invert menu bar [II:4.7.2]}
       SysBeep (1);                                      {Sound a beep [II:2.8.1]}
       FlashMenuBar (0)                                  {Restore menu bar [II:4.7.2]}

    end;   {DoBeep}

{- - - - - - - - - - - - - - - - - - - - - - - - - - - - - - - - - - - - - - - - - - - - - - - - - - - - - -}

procedure FixCursor {(dataHandle : DRHandle)};

    { Adjust cursor for region of screen. }

    var
       mousePoint : Point;                               {Current mouse position in window coordinates [I:4.1.1]}

    begin {FixCursor}
```

```
   with dataHandle^^, TheWindow^ do
      begin

         SetPort (TheWindow);                              {Get into StopWatch window [I:4.3.3]}

         GetMouse (mousePoint);                            {Get mouse position [II:2.4.1]}
         if PtInRect (MousePoint, portRect)               {Is it in the window? [I:4.4.3]}
            and not (ClockRunning or ClockBeeping)        {Can window's contents be edited?}
         then
            SetCursor (IBeam^^)                            {Set I-beam cursor [II:2.5.2]}
         else
            InitCursor                                     {Set arrow cursor [II:2.5.2]}

      end  {with dataHandle^^, TheWindow^}

   end;  {FixCursor}
```

{--}

```
procedure DoMenuChoice ((dataHandle : DRHandle; menuChoice : LONGINT));

   { Handle user's menu choice [Prog. III:6-10]. }

   var
      whichMenu : INTEGER;                                 {Menu ID of selected menu}
      whichItem : INTEGER;                                 {Item number of selected item}

   begin {DoMenuChoice}

      whichMenu := HiWord(menuChoice);                     {Get menu ID [I:2.2.3]}
      whichItem := LoWord(menuChoice);                     {Get item number [I:2.2.3]}

      if whichMenu <> dataHandle^^.RsrcBase then           {Is it the StopWatch menu? [III:3.1.4]}
         SysBeep(1)                                        {Complain if not [II:2.8.1]}
      else
         begin

            case whichItem of

               AboutItem:
                  DoAbout (dataHandle);                    {Handle About StopWatch... command}

               StartItem:
                  DoStart (dataHandle);                    {Handle Start command}

               PauseItem:
                  DoPause (dataHandle);                    {Handle Pause command}
```

```
        ResetItem:
            DoReset (dataHandle)                    {Handle Reset command}

        end; {case whichItem}

        HiliteMenu(0)                               {Unhighlight menu title [II:4.5.4]}

    end {else}

  end; {DoMenuChoice}
```

{- -}

```
procedure DoAbout ((dataHandle : DRHandle)};

  { Handle About StopWatch... command. }

  var
    ignore : INTEGER;                               {Item number for About alert}

  begin {DoAbout}

    with dataHandle^^ do
      ignore := Alert (RsrcBase, NIL)               {Post alert [II:7.4.2]}

  end; {DoAbout}
```

{- -}

```
procedure DoStart ((dataHandle : DRHandle)};

  { Handle Start command. }

  var
    seconds : LONGINT;                              {Number of seconds showing on stopwatch}
    timeNow : LONGINT;                              {Current time on system clock}

  begin {DoStart}

    with dataHandle^^ do

      if ClockRunning then                          {Is stopwatch already running?}
        SysBeep (1)                                 {If so, just beep [II:2.8.1]}

      else
        begin
```

```
      seconds := TextToNum (TheText);        {Get number displayed in window}
      timeNow := TickCount;                   {Get current time [II:2.7.1]}


      if seconds > 0 then                      {Positive number in window?}
        begin
          TargetTime := timeNow + 60*seconds; {Set stopping time in ticks from now}
          CountDown  := TRUE                   {  and count down           }
        end {then}
      else
        begin
          TargetTime := timeNow;              {If zero, start from now}
          CountDown  := FALSE                  {  and count up         }
        end; {else}


      TEDeactivate (TheText);                  {Hide insertion point [II:5.4.3]}

      ClockRunning := TRUE                     {Start clock running}


    end {else}

  end; {DoStart}
```

{ - }


```
function TextToNum {(textHandle : TEHandle) : LONGINT};

  { Convert text to integer. }

  var
    theChars : CharsHandle;              {Handle to characters [II:5.1.2]}
    chIndex  : INTEGER;                  {Index to text character}
    ch       : CHAR;                     {Text character}
    digit    : INTEGER;                  {Digit value of character}
    result   : LONGINT;                  {Function result}


  begin {TextToNum}

    result := 0;                         {Initialize result}

    with textHandle^^ do
      begin
        theChars := CharsHandle(hText);  {Get the characters [II:5.1.1, II:5.1.2]}
        if teLength > 0 then             {Are there any? [II:5.1.1]}
          for chIndex := 0 to (teLength - 1) do {Loop through characters [II:5.1.1]}
            begin
              ch    := theChars^^[chIndex]; {Get next character}
```

```
                digit  := ORD(ch) - ORD('0');        {Convert to digit value}
                result := 10*result + digit          {Shift left and add next digit}
             end {for chIndex}
       end; {with textHandle^^}


     TextToNum := result                              {Return result}


  end; {TextToNum}
```

{- -}

```
procedure DoPause {(dataHandle : DRHandle)};

  { Handle Pause command. }

  var
     timeNow : LONGINT;                               {Current time on system clock}

  begin {DoPause}

    with dataHandle^^ do

      if not ClockRunning then                        {Is the stopwatch idle?}
        SysBeep (1)                                   {Just beep [II:2.8.1]}

      else if not ClockPaused then                    {Is it ticking?}
        begin
          ClockPaused := TRUE;                        {Set pause flag}
          SetItem (TheMenu, PauseItem, 'Resume');     {Change menu item to Resume [II:4.6.1]}

          timeNow := TickCount;                        {Get current time [II:2.7.1]}
          if CountDown then                            {Counting up or down?}
            PauseTime := TargetTime - timeNow          {Save ticks till stopping time}
          else
            PauseTime := timeNow - TargetTime;         {Save ticks since starting time}
        end {then}

      else
        begin
          ClockPaused := FALSE;                        {Clear pause flag}
          SetItem (TheMenu, PauseItem, 'Pause');      {Change menu item back to Pause [II:4.6.1]}

          timeNow := TickCount;                        {Get current time [II:2.7.1]}
          if CountDown then                            {Resuming a countdown?}
            TargetTime := timeNow + PauseTime          {Update stopping time in ticks from now}
          else
```

```
            TargetTime := timeNow - PauseTime        {Update starting time in ticks ago now}
         end {else}

   end;   {DoPause}
```

{ - }

```
procedure DoReset {(dataHandle : DRHandle)};

   { Handle Reset command. }

   var
      timeString : Str255;                            {String for resetting window's text [I:2.1.1]}
      dceHandle  : DCtlHandle;                        {Handle to DCE [III:3.1.4]}

   begin {DoReset}

      with dataHandle^^ do
         begin

            dceHandle := GetDCtlEntry (RefNum);        {Get DCE handle [III:3.1.4]}
            InitFlags (dceHandle^^, dataHandle);       {Reinitialize global flags}

            timeString := '0';  {Reset time to 0}
            TESetText (@timeString[1], 1, TheText);    {Set window's text [II:5.2.3]}
            TEUpdate  (TheText^^.viewRect, TheText);   {Show text on screen [II:5.3.2]}

            TEActivate (TheText)                       {Redisplay insertion point [II:5.4.3]}

         end  {with dataHandle^^}

   end;   {DoReset}
```

{ - }

```
procedure DoUndo {(dataHandle : DRHandle)};

   { Handle Undo command. }

   begin {DoUndo}

      SysBeep (1)                                     {Undo command not implemented [II:2.8.1]}

   end;   {DoUndo}
```

{ - }

```
procedure DoCut {(dataHandle : DRHandle)};

   { Handle Cut command. }

   begin {DoCut}

      with dataHandle^^, TheText^^ do
         if selStart = selEnd then          {Is selection empty? [II:5.1.1]}
            SysBeep (1)                      {Nothing to cut—just beep [II:2.8.1]}
         else
            TECut (TheText)                  {Cut the selection [II:5.5.2]}

   end;   {DoCut}
```

{- -}

```
procedure DoCopy {(dataHandle : DRHandle)};

   { Handle Copy command. }

   begin {DoCopy}

      with dataHandle^^, TheText^^ do
         if selStart = selEnd then          {Is selection empty? [II:5.1.1]}
            SysBeep (1)                      {Nothing to copy—just beep [II:2.8.1]}
         else
            TECopy (TheText)                 {Copy the selection [II:5.5.2]}

   end;   {DoCopy}
```

{- -}

```
procedure DoPaste {(dataHandle : DRHandle)};

   { Handle Paste command. }

   begin {DoPaste}

      with dataHandle^^, TheText^^ do
         if TEGetScrapLen = 0 then          {Is scrap empty? [II:5.5.4]}
            SysBeep (1)                      {Nothing to paste—just beep [II:2.8.1]}
         else
            TEPaste (TheText)                {Paste the selection [II:5.5.2]}

   end;   {DoPaste}
```

```
{------------------------------------------------------------------------}

procedure DoClear {(dataHandle : DRHandle)};

   { Handle Clear command. }

   begin {DoClear}

      with dataHandle^^, TheText^^ do
         if selStart = selEnd then              {Is selection empty? [II:5.1.1]}
            SysBeep (1)                          {Nothing to delete—just beep [II:2.8.1]}
         else
            TEDelete (TheText)                   {Delete the selection [II:5.5.3]}

   end;  {DoClear}

{------------------------------------------------------------------------}

procedure DoGoodBye {(pbPtr : ParmBlkPtr; dcePtr : DCtlPtr)};

   { Handle "good-bye kiss." }

   begin {DoGoodBye}

      DoClose (pbPtr, dcePtr)                    {Treat good-bye as an ordinary Close call}

   end;  {DoGoodBye}

{------------------------------------------------------------------------}

procedure DoKillIO {(dataHandle : DRHandle)};

   { Perform KillIO operation. }

   begin {DoKillIO}

      DoReset (dataHandle)                       {Treat KillIO as a Reset command}

   end;  {DoKillIO}

{------------------------------------------------------------------------}

procedure DoClose {(pbPtr : ParmBlkPtr; dcePtr : DCtlPtr)};

   { Handle driver Close call [Prog. III:6-17]. }
```

```
var
   theData    : DRHandle;                        {Handle to StopWatch data record}
   rsrcHandle : Handle;                          {Untyped handle for disposing of menu [I:3.1.1]}

begin {DoClose}

   with dcePtr^ do
      begin

         MoveHHi (dCtlStorage);                  {Move data record to end of heap [I:3.2.5]}
         HLock   (dCtlStorage);                  {Lock data handle [I:3.2.4]}
            theData := DRHandle(dCtlStorage);     {Convert to typed handle [III:3.1.4]}
            with theData^^ do
               begin

                  DeleteMenu (dCtlMenu);          {Remove menu from menu bar [II:4.4.1]}
                  DrawMenuBar;                    {Redraw menu bar [II:4.4.3]}
                  rsrcHandle := Handle(TheMenu);  {Convert to untyped handle [I:3.1.1]}
                  ReleaseResource (rsrcHandle);   {Dispose of menu [I:6.3.2]}

                  DisposeWindow (TheWindow);      {Dispose of window [II:3.2.3]}
                  dCtlWindow := NIL;              {Clear window pointer from DCE [III:3.1.4]}

                  TEDispose (TheText)             {Dispose of edit record [II:5.2.2]}

               end; {with theData^^}
         HUnlock (dCtlStorage);                  {Unlock data handle [I:3.2.4]}

         DisposHandle (dCtlStorage);             {Dispose of data record [I:3.2.2]}
         dCtlStorage := NIL                      {Clear storage handle from DCE [III:3.1.4]}

      end {with dcePtr^}

end; {DoClose}
```

{ - }

```
{ Main program. }

begin {StopWatch}

   {Do nothing}

end. {StopWatch}
```

GLOSSARY

The following is a glossary of technical terms used in this volume. *Note:* Terms shown in *italic* are defined elsewhere in this glossary.

A5 world: Another name for a program's *application global space*, located by means of a *base address* kept in processor register A5.

access path: An independent channel of communication for reading or writing a *file*.

accessory window: A *window* with rounded corners, used for displaying a *desk accessory* on the screen.

action procedure: A routine that is called repeatedly for as long as the mouse button is held down after being pressed in a *control*.

activate event: A *window event* generated by the Toolbox to signal that a given window has become the *active window*.

active control: A *control* that will respond to the mouse in the normal way; compare *inactive control*.

active window: The frontmost *window* on the screen, to which the user's mouse and keyboard actions are directed.

alert: Short for *alert box*.

alert box: A form of *dialog box* that prevents the user from interacting with any other window for as long as the alert remains on the screen, and in which the only meaningful action is to *dismiss* the alert by clicking a *pushbutton;* compare *modal dialog box, modeless dialog box.*

alert template: A *resource* containing all the information needed to create an *alert box.*

allocate: To set aside a *block* of memory from the *heap* for a particular use.

amplitude: The maximum *magnitude* attained at the peak of a sound wave, which determines the volume or loudness of the sound.

and: A bit-level operation in which each bit of the result is a 1 if both operands have 1s at the corresponding bit position, or 0 if either or both have 0s.

APDA: The Apple Programmers and Developers Association, a membership organization sponsored by Apple that provides services and publications for professional and advanced amateur programmers working on Apple equipment.

Apple mark: A special character (*character code* $14) that appears on the Macintosh screen as a small Apple symbol; used for the title of the *Apple menu.*

Apple menu: A *menu* listing the available *desk accessories,* conventionally placed first in the *menu bar* with the *Apple mark* as its title.

AppleTalk: A network to which the Macintosh can be connected for communication with other computers.

AppleTalk drivers: The pair of *device drivers* used for communicating with other computers over the *AppleTalk* network.

application: A particular use or purpose to which the Macintosh (or any computer) can be applied, such as word processing, graphics, or telecommunications.

application event: Any of the four *event types* that are reserved for the running application program to use in any way it wishes.

application file: A *file* containing the executable code of an application program, with a *file type* of `'APPL'` and the program's own signature as its *creator signature.*

application global space: The area of memory containing a program's *application globals, application parameters,* and *jump table;* normally situated just before the *screen buffer* in memory and located by means of a *base address* kept in processor register A5.

application globals: Global variables belonging to the running application program, which reside in the *application global space* and are located at negative offsets from the *base address* in register A5.

application heap: The portion of the *heap* available for use by the running application program; compare *system heap.*

application parameters: Descriptive information about the running program, located in the *application global space* at positive offsets from the *base address* in register A5. The application parameters are a vestige of the *Lisa* software environment, and most are unused on the Macintosh; the only ones still in use are the *QuickDraw globals pointer* and the *startup handle*.

application program: A stand-alone program for the Macintosh that the user can start up from the *Finder* by double-clicking the *icon* of its *application file*.

application resource file: The *resource fork* of a program's *application file*, containing *resources* belonging to the program itself.

application window: A *window* used by the running program itself; compare *system window*.

arc: A part of an *oval*, defined by a given *starting angle* and *arc angle*.

arc angle: The angle defining the extent of an *arc* or *wedge*.

arrow cursor: The standard, general-purpose *cursor*, an arrow pointing upward at an angle of "eleven o'clock."

ascent: (1) For a text character, the height of the character above the *baseline*, in *dots* or *pixels*. (2) For a *font*, the maximum ascent of any character in the font.

ascent line: The line marking a font's maximum *ascent* above the *baseline*.

ASCII: American Standard Code for Information Interchange, the industry-standard 7-bit character set on which the Macintosh's 8-bit *character codes* are based.

asynchronous: Describes an input/output operation that is queued for later execution, returning control immediately to the calling program without waiting for the operation to be carried out. The calling program may supply an optional *completion routine* to be executed on completion of the operation. Compare *synchronous*.

attenuation: The reduction of the sound volume produced by the Macintosh speaker according to the global *speaker volume* setting chosen by the user.

autograph: A *Finder resource* whose *resource type* is the same as a program's *signature*, and which serves as the program's representative in the *desktop file*; also called a *version data* resource.

auto-key event: An *event* reporting that the user held down a key on the keyboard or keypad, causing it to repeat automatically.

auxiliary data record: A private data structure maintained by a *window* or *control definition function* to hold additional information about a window or control; located via a handle kept in the `dataHandle` field of the *window record* or the `contrlData` field of the *control record.*

auxiliary information subrecord: The part of a *print record* in which the Toolbox keeps private information on how to match the page image to the characteristics of a particular printer.

background pattern: The *pattern* used for *erasing* shapes in a given *graphics port.*

background procedure: A procedure supplied by the application program, which the Toolbox will call repeatedly during *spool printing* whenever it has nothing else to do (such as while waiting for a completion signal from the printer after beginning a printing operation).

band: One of the smaller sections into which a page image is broken to economize on memory space during *spool printing.*

band buffer: The area of memory in which a *band image* is formed.

band image: The *bit image* holding the contents of a single *band* during *spool printing.*

base address: In general, any memory address used as a reference point from which to locate desired data in memory. Specifically, (1) the address of the *bit image* belonging to a given *bit map;* (2) the address of a program's *application parameters*, kept in processor register A5 and used to locate the contents of the program's *application global space.*

base of stack: The end of the *stack* that remains fixed in memory and is not affected when items are added and removed; compare *top of stack.*

baseline: The reference line used for defining the *character images* in a *font*, and along which the *graphics pen* travels as text is drawn.

Binary/Decimal Conversion Package: A standard *package*, provided in the *system resource file* (or in ROM on some models of Macintosh) that converts numbers between their internal binary format and their external representation as strings of decimal digits.

binary point: The binary equivalent of a decimal point, separating the integer and fractional parts of a *fixed-point number.*

bit image: An array of bits in memory representing the *pixels* of a graphical image.

bit map: The combination of a *bit image* with a *boundary rectangle.* The bit image provides the bit map's content; the boundary rectangle defines its extent and gives it a system of coordinates.

bit map printing: A low-level printing operation, implemented by the *Control routine* of the *printer driver*, for transmitting the contents of a *bit map* directly to the printer.

bit-mapped display: A video display screen on which each *pixel* can be individually controlled.

block: An area of contiguous memory within the *heap*, either allocated or free.

bottleneck record: A data structure containing pointers to the *bottleneck routines* associated with a given *graphics port*.

bottleneck routine: A specialized routine for performing a low-level drawing operation in a given *graphics port*, used for *customizing* QuickDraw operations.

boundary rectangle: (1) For a *bit map*, the *rectangle* that defines the bit map's extent and determines its system of coordinates. (2) For a *graphics port*, the boundary rectangle of the port's bit map.

bounding box: The smallest *rectangle* completely enclosing a *polygon* or *region* on the coordinate grid.

bundle: A *Finder resource* that identifies all of a program's other Finder resources, so that they can be installed in the *desktop file* when the program's *application file* is copied to a new disk.

button: A *control* with two possible settings, on (1) and off (0); compare *dial*.

byte: An independently addressable group of 8 bits in the computer's memory.

Caps Lock key: A *modifier key* on the Macintosh keyboard, used to convert lowercase letters to uppercase while leaving all nonalphabetic keys unaffected.

CD–ROM: A mass-storage technology in which information is stored in read-only digital form on the surface of a compact disk.

character code: An 8-bit integer representing a text character; compare *key code*.

character image: A *bit image* that defines the graphical representation of a text character in a given *typeface* and *type size*.

character key: A key on the keyboard or keypad that produces a character when pressed; compare *modifier key*.

character position: An integer marking a point between characters in a *file* or other collection of text, from 0 (the very beginning of the text, before the first character) to the length of the text (the very end, after the last character).

character style: See *type style*.

checkbox: A *button* that retains an independent on/off setting to control the way some future action will occur; compare *pushbutton*, *radio buttons*.

choose: To designate a *menu item* by pointing with the mouse.

Chooser: A standard *desk accessory* with which the user can select the printer the Toolbox will use for hardcopy printing.

classic Macintosh: Any of the early, first-generation models of *Macintosh*, including the *Macintosh 128K* ("Skinny Mac"), *Macintosh 512K* ("Fat Mac"), *Macintosh 512K enhanced*, and *Macintosh Plus*.

clip: To confine a drawing operation within a specified boundary, suppressing any drawing that falls outside the boundary.

Clipboard: The term used in Macintosh user's manuals to refer to the *scrap*.

clipping boundaries: The boundaries to which all drawing in a given *graphics port* is confined, consisting of the port's *boundary rectangle*, *port rectangle*, *clipping region*, and *visible region*.

clipping rectangle: See *view rectangle*.

clipping region: A general-purpose *clipping boundary* associated with a *graphics port*, provided for the application program's use.

clock chip: A component of the Macintosh, powered independently by a battery, that keeps track of the current date and time even when the machine's main power is turned off.

close: (1) To destroy a *window* and remove it from the screen. (2) To destroy an *access path* to a *file*. (3) To terminate the operation of a *device driver*.

close box: The small box near the left end of the *title bar*, by which a *document window* can be closed with the mouse.

close region: The area of a *window* by which it can be closed with the mouse; also called the "go-away region." In a *document window*, the close region is the *close box*.

Close routine: The *driver routine* that terminates the operation of a *device driver* by reversing the effects of the *Open routine*.

comma of Didymus: The difference in pitch between four perfect fifths and a major third raised two octaves, equivalent to a frequency ratio of 81/80. (Aren't you glad you asked?)

Command key: A *modifier key* on the Macintosh keyboard, used in combination with *character keys* to type *keyboard aliases* for *menu items*.

comment data: The information a *picture comment* contains.

comment type: An integer code that identifies the kind of information a *picture comment* contains.

compaction: The process of moving together all the *relocatable blocks* in the *heap*, in order to coalesce the available free space.

complement: A bit-level operation that reverses the bits of its operand, changing each 0 to a 1 and vice versa.

completion routine: A routine supplied in conjunction with an *asynchronous* input/output request, to be executed on completion of the requested operation.

complex wave: A *waveform* of an arbitrary, irregular shape, such as those that characterize most naturally occurring sounds.

content: The information displayed in a *window*.

content region: The area of a *window* in which information is displayed, and which a program must draw for itself; compare *window frame*.

control: An object on the Macintosh screen that the user can manipulate with the mouse in order to operate on the contents of a *window* or control the way they're presented.

control code: An integer code that identifies the specific control operation to be performed by a device driver's *Control routine*.

control definition function: A routine, stored as a *resource*, that defines the appearance and behavior of a particular type of *control*.

control definition ID: A coded integer representing a *control type*, which includes the *resource ID* of the *control definition function* along with a *variation code* giving additional modifying information.

control handle: A handle to a *control record*.

control list: A linked list of all the *controls* belonging to a given *window*, beginning in a field of the *window record* and chained together through a field of their *control records*.

Control Panel: A standard *desk accessory* with which the user can set optional operating characteristics of the Macintosh system, such as the *speaker volume* and keyboard repeat rate.

control record: A data structure containing all the information associated with a given *control*.

Control routine: The *driver routine* that handles requests to control the operation of a *peripheral device*.

control template: A *resource* containing all the information needed to create a *control*.

control title: The string of text characters displayed on the screen as part of a *control*.

control type: A category of *control*, identified by a *control definition ID*, whose appearance and behavior are determined by a *control definition function*.

covered: Describes a *window, control,* or other object that is obscured from view by other overlapping objects. A covered object is never displayed on the screen, even if *visible;* compare *exposed*.

creator signature: A four-character string identifying the application program to which a given *file* belongs, and which should be started up when the user opens the file in the *Finder*.

current port: The *graphics port* in use at any given time, to which most *QuickDraw* operations implicitly apply.

current printer: The printer whose *printer driver* and *printer resource file* are currently installed in the system, and to which all printing-related operations implicitly apply.

current resource file: The *resource file* that will be searched first in looking for a requested resource, and to which certain resource-related operations implicitly apply.

current volume: The *volume* or *directory* under consideration at any given time, to which many *file system* operations implicitly apply.

cursor: A small (16-by-16-pixel) *bit image* whose movements can be controlled with the *mouse* to designate positions on the Macintosh screen.

cursor record: A data structure defining the form and appearance of a *cursor* on the screen.

customize: To redefine an aspect of the Toolbox's operation to meet the specialized needs of a particular program.

cut and paste: The standard method of editing used on the Macintosh, in which text, graphics, or other information is transferred from one place to another by way of an intermediate *scrap* or *Clipboard*.

cycle: A single repetition of a regularly recurring *waveform*, such as a *sine wave* or *square wave*.

dangling pointer: An invalid pointer to an object that no longer exists at the designated address.

data fork: The *fork* of a *file* that contains the file's data, such as the text of a document; compare *resource fork*.

DCE: See *device control entry*.

deactivate event: A *window event* generated by the Toolbox to signal that a given window is no longer the *active window*.

deallocate: To free a *block* of memory that's no longer needed, allowing the space to be reused for another purpose.

default button: The *pushbutton* displayed with a heavy black double border in an *alert* or *dialog box*; pressing the Return or Enter key is considered equivalent to clicking the default button with the mouse.

definition file: An assembly-language file containing definitions of Toolbox constants and global variables, to be incorporated into an assembly-language program with an .INCLUDE directive.

definition routine: See *window definition function, control definition function, menu definition procedure.*

dereference: (1) In general, to convert any pointer to the value it points to. (2) Specifically, to convert a *handle* to the corresponding *master pointer.*

descender: A portion of a text character that extends below the *baseline,* as in the lowercase letters g, j, p, q, and y.

descent: (1) For a text character, the distance the character extends below the *baseline,* in *dots* or *pixels.* (2) For a *font,* the maximum descent of any character in the font.

descent line: The line marking a font's maximum *descent* below the *baseline.*

desk accessory: A type of *device driver* that operates as a "mini-application," which can coexist on the screen with any other program.

desk scrap: The *scrap* maintained by the Toolbox to hold information being *cut and pasted* from one application program or *desk accessory* to another; compare *Toolbox scrap.*

desktop: (1) The gray background area of the Macintosh screen, outside any window. (2) The arrangement of *windows, icons,* and other objects on the screen, particularly in the *Finder.*

desktop file: A file containing *Finder*-related information about the files on a disk, including their *file types, creator signatures,* and locations on the Finder *desktop.*

destination rectangle: The boundary to which text is *wrapped* in an *edit record,* determining the placement of the *line breaks;* also called the "wrapping rectangle."

device: See *peripheral device.*

device code: An integer identifying the output device a *graphics port* draws on, used in selecting the appropriate *fonts* for drawing text.

device control entry: A data structure containing all the information associated with a given *device driver.*

device driver: A specialized piece of software that enables the Macintosh to control and communicate with a particular *peripheral device*. An important special category of device drivers are *desk accessories*.

dial: A *control* that can take on any of a range of possible settings, depending on the position of a moving *indicator* that can be manipulated with the mouse; compare *button*.

dialog: Short for *dialog box*.

dialog box: A *window* used for requesting information or instructions from the user.

dialog initialization routine: A routine for constructing and initializing a *printing dialog record*, used in *customizing* a printing-related *dialog*.

dialog item: A single element displayed in an *alert* or *dialog box*, such as a piece of text, an *icon*, a *control*, or a *text box*.

dialog pointer: A pointer to a *dialog record*.

dialog record: A data structure containing all the information associated with a given *alert* or *dialog box*.

dialog template: A *resource* containing all the information needed to create a *dialog box*.

dialog window: See *dialog box*.

diameters of curvature: The width and height of the *ovals* forming the corners of a *rounded rectangle*.

dimmed: Describes an object, such as a *menu item* or a *file icon*, that is displayed in gray instead of black to show that it is not currently active or available.

directory: A table containing information about the *files* on a disk. Under the *Hierarchical File System*, directories may in turn contain other directories, and correspond to *folders* displayed on the *desktop* by the *Finder*.

directory name: Under the *Hierarchical File System*, a string of text characters identifying a particular *directory*.

directory reference number: An identifying number assigned by the *Hierarchical File System* to stand for a given *directory*.

disabled dialog item: A *dialog item* that doesn't dismiss its alert or dialog box when clicked with the mouse or typed into from the keyboard.

disabled menu item: A *menu item* that cannot currently be *chosen* with the mouse; normally displayed in *dimmed* form on the screen.

disk driver: The *device driver* built into ROM for communicating with the Macintosh's built-in Sony disk drive.

disk-inserted event: An *event* reporting that the user inserted a disk into a disk drive.

dismiss: To remove an *alert* or *dialog box* from the screen, typically by clicking a *pushbutton.*

dispatch table: A table in memory, used by the *Trap Dispatcher* to locate Toolbox routines in ROM.

document: A coherent unit or collection of information to be operated on by a particular *application program.*

document file: A file containing a *document.*

document window: The standard type of *window* used by application programs to display information on the Macintosh screen.

dot: A single spot forming part of a graphical image when printed on paper; compare *pixel.*

double click: Two presses of the *mouse* button in quick succession, considered as a single action by the user.

down arrow: The arrow at the bottom or right end of a *scroll bar,* which causes it to scroll down or to the right a line at a time when clicked with the mouse.

draft printing: A printing method in which *imaging* and printing take place at the same time: the results of all drawing operations are sent directly to the printer and printed immediately.

drag: (1) To roll the *mouse* while holding down the button. (2) To move a *window, icon,* or other object to a new location on the screen by dragging with the mouse.

drag region: The area of a *window* by which it can be *dragged* to a new location with the mouse. In a *document window,* the drag region consists of the *title bar* minus the *close box* and *zoom box,* if any.

driver: See *device driver.*

driver flags: A set of Boolean flags specifying various attributes of a *device driver,* stored in the first word of its *driver header.*

driver header: A collection of descriptive information stored at the beginning of a *device driver.*

driver I/O queue: The data structure in which *asynchronous* input/output requests to a *device driver* are entered for later execution.

driver name: A string of text characters identifying a particular *device driver.* For drivers that reside in a *resource file,* the driver name is also the *resource name.* Names of true I/O drivers conventionally begin with a period (.), to prevent them from appearing among the *desk accessories* on the *Apple menu*.

driver reference number: The identifying number of a *device driver*; the bitwise complement of the driver's *unit number*, related to it arithmetically by the formula `refNum = -(unitNum + 1)`. Thus the reference number is always a negative integer between `-1` and `-48` (or `-1` and `-32` on earlier models).

driver routines: The routines that do the work of a *device driver*; see *Open routine, Prime routine, Control routine, Status routine, Close routine.*

edit record: A complete text editing environment containing all the information needed for *TextEdit* operations.

electronic mail: A type of computer application that enables users to send and receive messages over a network or other communication line.

empty handle: A *handle* that points to a `NIL` *master pointer*, indicating that the underlying block has been *purged* from the heap.

empty rectangle: A *rectangle* enclosing no pixels on the coordinate grid.

empty region: A *region* that encloses no pixels on the coordinate grid.

emulator trap: A form of *trap* that occurs when the *MC68000* (or *MC68020*) processor attempts to execute an *unimplemented instruction*; used to "emulate" the effects of such an instruction with software instead of hardware.

enabled dialog item: A *dialog item* that *dismisses* its alert or dialog box when clicked with the mouse or typed into from the keyboard.

enabled menu item: A *menu item* that is currently available and can be *chosen* with the mouse.

enclosing rectangle: (1) The *rectangle* within which an *oval* is inscribed. (2) The rectangle that defines the location and extent of a *control* within its *owning window*.

end-of-file: The *character position* following the last byte of meaningful information included in a *file* (the *logical end-of-file*) or the last byte of physical storage space allocated to it (the *physical end-of-file*).

EOF: See *end-of-file.*

equal-tempered tuning: The form of musical tuning used in instruments of fixed pitch such as a piano keyboard, in which the pitches of the individual keys are chosen to produce the most useful or pleasing combination of tones for the instrument as a whole. Compare *just-tempered tuning.*

erase: To fill a *shape* with the *background pattern* of the *current port.*

error code: A nonzero *result code,* reporting an error of some kind detected by a *Toolbox* routine.

error sound: A sound emitted from the Macintosh speaker by an *alert.*

event: An occurrence reported by the Toolbox for a program to respond to, such as the user's pressing the mouse button or typing on the keyboard.

event-driven: Describes a program that is structured to respond to *events* reported by the Toolbox.

event loop: See *main event loop.*

event mask: A coded integer specifying the *event types* to which a given operation applies.

event message: A field of the *event record* containing information that varies depending on the *event type.*

event queue: The data structure in which *events* are recorded for later processing.

event record: A data structure containing all the information about a given *event.*

event type: An integer code that identifies the kind of occurrence reported by an *event.*

exception: See *trap.*

exclusive or: A bit-level operation in which each bit of the result is a 1 if the corresponding bits of the two operands are different, or 0 if they are the same.

EXIT: A nonstandard feature of many Pascal compilers that allows an immediate return from the middle of a procedure or function.

exposed: Describes a *window, control,* or other object that is not obscured from view by other overlapping objects. An exposed object is displayed on the screen if *visible;* compare *covered.*

external disk drive: A disk drive physically separate from the Macintosh itself and connected to it via a connector on the back of the machine.

Fat Mac: See *Macintosh 512K.*

field: One of the components of a Pascal record.

FIFO: First in, first out; the order in which items are added to and removed from a queue such as the *event queue.* Compare *LIFO, LIOF.*

file: A collection of information stored as a named unit on a disk.

file icon: The *icon* used by the *Finder* to represent a *file* on the screen.

file name: A string of text characters identifying a particular *file*.

file reference: A *Finder resource* that establishes the connection between a *file type* and its *file icon*.

file reference number: An identifying number assigned by the *file system* to stand for a given *file*.

file system: The part of the Toolbox that deals with *files* on a disk or other mass storage device.

file type: A four-character string that characterizes the kind of information a *file* contains, assigned by program that created file.

fill: To color a *shape* with a specified *pattern*.

fill pattern: A *pattern* associated with a *graphics port*, used privately by *QuickDraw* for *filling* shapes.

filter function: A function supplied by an application program to process *events* in an *alert* or *dialog box* before they are acted upon by the Toolbox.

Finder: The Macintosh program with which the user can manipulate files and start up applications; normally the first program to be run when the Macintosh is turned on.

Finder information record: A data structure summarizing the *Finder*-related properties of a *file*, including its *file type*, *creator signature*, and location on the Finder *desktop*.

Finder resources: The *resources* associated with a program that tell the *Finder* how to represent the program's *files* on the screen. Finder resources include *autographs*, *icon lists*, *file references*, and *bundles*.

Finder startup handle: See *startup handle*.

Finder startup information: See *startup information*.

fixed-point number: A binary number with a fixed number of bits before and after the *binary point*; specifically, a value of the Toolbox data type `Fixed` [I:2.3.1], consisting of a 16-bit integer part and a 16-bit fractional part.

flat file system: A *file system* in which all the *files* on a *volume* reside in a single *directory*, with no *subdirectories*.

floating-point number: A binary number in which the *binary point* can "float" to any required position; the number's internal representation includes a binary exponent, or order of magnitude, that determines the position of the binary point.

folder: An object in a disk's *desktop file*, represented on the screen by an *icon* or *window*, that can contain files or other folders; used for organizing the files on a disk. Under the *Hierarchical File System*, folders correspond to *directories*.

folio: The printed page number on a page of a book or document.

font: (1) A *resource* containing all of the *character images* and other information needed to draw text characters in a given *typeface* and *type size*. (2) Sometimes used loosely (and incorrectly) as a synonym for *typeface*, as in the terms *font number* and *text font*.

font characterization table: A data structure containing information needed to apply style variations, such as bold, italic, and underline, to *fonts* for use on a particular printer.

font height: The overall height of a font, from *ascent line* to *descent line*.

font information record: A data structure containing metric information about a *font* in integer form; compare *font metric record*.

font metric record: In some versions of the Toolbox, a data structure containing metric information about a *font* in *fixed-point* form; compare *font information record*.

font number: An integer denoting a particular *typeface*.

font output record: A data structure constructed by the Toolbox to pass information to the *printer driver* on the metric characteristics of a *font* for use on a particular printer.

font scaling: The enlargement or reduction of an existing *font* to substitute for an unavailable font of a different size.

fork: One of the two parts of which every *file* is composed: the *data fork* or the *resource fork*.

four-tone sound: A sound consisting of as many as four separate tones, or *voices*, combined harmonically. Each voice is specified independently, with any desired pitch and *timbre*, and in any *phase* relationship to the other voices.

four-tone synthesizer: The part of the *sound driver* that produces *four-tone sound*.

frame: (1) To draw the outline of a *shape*, using the *pen size*, *pen pattern*, and *pen mode* of the *current port*. (2) See *window frame*. (3) A single painting of the Macintosh screen by the display tube's electron beam, from the top-left corner to the bottom-right.

free block: A contiguous *block* of space available for allocation within the *heap*.

free-form sound: A single *waveform* of arbitrary length and complexity, representing any desired sound (such as speech, electronically sampled music, or sound effects).

free-form synthesizer: The part of the *sound driver* that produces *free-form sound*.

frequency: The speed with which a sound wave is repeated, which determines the sound's pitch; measured in *hertz* (cycles per second).

global coordinate system: The coordinate system associated with a given *bit image*, in which the top-left corner of the image has coordinates (0, 0). The global coordinate system is independent of the *boundary rectangle* of any *bit map* or *graphics port* based on the image.

glue routine: See *interface routine*.

go-away region: See *close region*.

good-bye kiss: A special call to the *Control routine* of a *device driver* or *desk accessory*, warning it that the *application heap* is about to be reinitialized and allowing it to take any special action it may require.

graphics pen: The imaginary drawing tool used for drawing lines and text characters in a *graphics port*.

graphics port: A complete drawing environment containing all the information needed for *QuickDraw* drawing operations.

grow icon: The visual representation of a window's *size region* on the screen; for a standard *document window*, a pair of small overlapping squares in the bottom-right corner of the window. Compare *grow image*.

grow image: The visual feedback displayed on the screen while tracking a mouse press in a window's *size region*, to show how the window's size will change when the button is released. For a standard *document window*, the grow image consists of a dotted outline of the window along with those of its title bar, scroll bars, and size box. Compare *grow icon*.

grow region: See *size region*.

handle: A pointer to a *master pointer*, used to refer to a *relocatable block*.

hardcopy: A copy of a document printed physically on paper.

heap: The area of memory in which space is allocated and deallocated at the explicit request of a running program; compare *stack*.

hertz: A unit of *frequency*, equivalent to *cycles* (or any other regularly recurring event) per second; abbreviated *Hz*.

HFS: See *Hierarchical File System*.

hide: To make a window, control, or other object *invisible*.

Hierarchical File System: The *file system* built into recent models of Macintosh in ROM, designed for use with double-sided disks, hard disks, and other large-capacity storage devices; also available for older models in RAM-based form. Compare *Macintosh File System*.

high-level file system: A collection of *file system* routines that sacrifice detailed control over input/output operations in exchange for simplicity and ease of use; compare *low-level file system*.

highlight: To display a *window, control, menu item,* or other object in some distinctive way as a visual signal to the user, often (but not necessarily) by *inverting* white and black pixels.

hit code: An integer used by a *window definition function* to identify the part of a window in which the mouse was pressed. Hit codes resemble the *part codes* returned by the Toolbox routine FindWindow [II:3.5.1], but have different numerical values.

horizontal blanking interval: See *horizontal retrace interval*.

horizontal retrace interval: The interval at which the Macintosh display tube's electron beam reaches the right edge of the screen and returns to the left edge to begin the next *scan line*, equal to $1/370$ of a *tick* or approximately 44.93 microseconds.

host program: The application program with which a *desk accessory* shares the system.

Hungarian notation: A system of naming conventions used in the Toolbox printing routines, in which standard prefixes and letter combinations are used to indicate the nature of the object being named. So called for the nationality of the brilliant but slightly crazed software engineer who popularized it.

hypertext: A type of computer application, typified by Apple's HyperCard, in which text, graphics, and other information are linked together into a free-form, interconnected information base that the user can traverse in arbitrary order.

Hz: See *hertz*.

I-beam cursor: A standard *cursor* included in the *system resource file* (or in ROM on some models of Macintosh) for use in text selection.

icon: A *bit image* of a standard size (32 pixels by 32), used on the Macintosh screen to represent an object such as a disk or file.

icon list: A *resource* containing any number of *icons;* commonly used to hold a *file icon* and its mask for use by the *Finder*.

identifying information: The properties of a *resource* that uniquely identify it: its *resource type, resource ID,* and (optional) *resource name*.

ImageWriter: A dot-matrix impact printer originally developed by C. Itoh & Company and marketed by Apple Computer, with a maximum resolution of 144 dots per inch vertically by 160 horizontally and a maximum printing speed of 120 characters per second.

ImageWriter LQ: An upgraded model of the *ImageWriter* printer, with a maximum resolution of 216 dots per inch and improved paper handling capabilities.

ImageWriter II: An enhanced version of the original *ImageWriter* printer with a maximum printing speed of 250 characters per second, finer dot placement for better print quality, improved paper handling including an optional automatic sheet feeder for noncontinuous, separately cut sheets, a limited color capability using a special four-color ribbon, and an optional *AppleTalk* network connection for sharing the printer among two or more users.

imaging: The process of defining the contents of a printed page with *QuickDraw* operations.

immediate operation: An input/output operation that is carried out as soon as it is requested, rather than queued for later execution.

inactive control: A *control* that will not currently respond to the mouse, usually displayed in some distinctive way on the screen.

indicator: The moving part of a *dial* that can be manipulated with the mouse to control the dial's setting.

insertion point: An empty *selection* in a text document, denoted by a *selection range* that begins and ends at the same *character position*.

Inside Macintosh: The comprehensive manual on the Macintosh *Toolbox*, produced by Apple Computer, Inc., and published by Addison-Wesley Publishing Company, Inc.

intercepted event: An *event* that is handled automatically by the Toolbox before being reported to the running program.

interface: A set of rules and conventions by which one part of an organized system communicates with another.

interface file: A text file that contains the declarations belonging to an *interface unit* in source-language form, to be incorporated into a Pascal program with a *uses declaration* (or a $i directive in some versions of Pascal).

interface routine: A routine, part of an *interface unit*, that mediates between the *stack-based* parameter-passing conventions of a Pascal calling program and those of a *register-based* Toolbox routine; also called a "glue routine."

interface unit: A precompiled *unit* containing declarations for Toolbox routines and data structures, making them available for use in Pascal programs.

internal disk drive: The 3½-inch single- or double-sided Sony disk drive built into the Macintosh.

interrupt: A *trap* triggered by a signal to the Macintosh processor from a peripheral device or other outside source.

interrupt-driven: Describes a *driver routine* or other piece of software that is designed to be executed in response to an *interrupt*.

interrupt handler: The *trap handler* for responding to an *interrupt*.

invalid region: An area of a window's *content region* whose contents are not accurately displayed on the screen, and which must therefore be *updated*.

invert: (1) Generally, to reverse the colors of *pixels* in a graphical image, changing white to black and vice versa. (2) Specifically, to reverse the colors of all pixels inside the boundary of a given *shape*.

invisible: Describes a *window*, *control*, or other object that is logically hidden from view. An invisible object is never displayed on the screen, even if *exposed;* compare *visible*.

I/O driver event: A type of *event* used internally by the Toolbox to handle communication with *peripheral devices*.

item handle: A handle to a *dialog item*, kept in its dialog's *item list*.

item list: A data structure defining all of the *dialog items* associated with an *alert* or *dialog box*, located via a handle in the *dialog record*.

item number: The sequential position of a *menu item* within its menu, or of a *dialog item* within its dialog's *item list;* used as an identifying number to refer to the item.

item type: An integer code denoting a kind of *dialog item*.

job dialog: The *dialog box* in which the user supplies information pertaining to a single printing job, presented in response to the `Print...` menu command and corresponding roughly to the contents of the *job subrecord* of the *print record*. Compare *style dialog*.

job subrecord: The part of a *print record* that specifies how a document is to be printed on a particular occasion.

jump table: A table used to direct external references between code segments to the proper addresses in memory; located in the *application global space*, at positive offsets from the *base address* kept in register A5.

just-tempered tuning: The form of musical tuning used in instruments of continuous pitch such as a violin, in which each note is tuned to an exact harmonic interval relative to a given tonic, or base tone. Compare *equal-tempered tuning*.

K: See *kilobyte*.

key code: An 8-bit integer representing a physical key on the Macintosh keyboard or keypad; compare *character code*.

key-down event: An *event* reporting that the user pressed a key on the keyboard or keypad.

key-up event: An *event* reporting that the user released a key on the keyboard or keypad.

keyboard: A set of keys for typing text characters into the computer.

keyboard alias: A character that can be typed in combination with the *Command key* to stand for a particular *menu item.*

keyboard configuration: The correspondence between keys on the Macintosh *keyboard* or *keypad* and the characters they produce when pressed.

keyboard driver: The low-level part of the Toolbox that communicates directly with the keyboard and keypad.

keyboard event: An *event* reporting an action by the user with the keyboard or keypad; see *key-down event, key-up event, auto-key event.*

keyboard routine: A routine to be executed directly by the *keyboard driver* when the user types a number key while holding down the *Command* and *Shift keys;* stored on the disk as a *resource* of type 'FKEY'.

keypad: See *numeric keypad.*

kHz: See *kilohertz.*

KillIO: An operation performed by the *Control routine* of a *device driver* that immediately halts any input/output activity in progress and cancels any pending operations.

kilobyte: A unit of memory capacity equal to 2^{10} (1,024) bytes.

kilohertz: A unit of *frequency* equal to 1000 *hertz;* abbreviated *kHz.*

landscape orientation: The arrangement of material on a printed page in the "wide" direction, with the longer dimension of the paper running horizontally; compare *portrait orientation.*

LaserWriter: A high-resolution laser printer introduced by Apple Computer in 1985, with a resolution of 300 dots per inch, an *MC68000* processor, a 512K ROM containing a *PostScript* interpreter and 11 built-in fonts, and a RAM capacity of 1.5 megabytes for page imaging and additional font storage.

LaserWriter Plus: An upgraded version of the original *LaserWriter* printer with an expanded ROM capacity and 35 built-in fonts.

LaserWriter II-NT: An upgraded model of the *LaserWriter* printer with a faster version of the *PostScript* interpreter, 35 built-in fonts, and an expanded RAM capacity of 2 megabytes.

LaserWriter II-NTX: An upgraded model of the *LaserWriter* printer with an *MC68020* processor, an *MC68881* floating-point coprocessor, a faster version of the *PostScript* interpreter, 35 built-in fonts, an expandable RAM capacity of up to 12 megabytes, and an optional hard disk connection.

LaserWriter II-SC: An inexpensive model of the *LaserWriter* printer with no *PostScript* interpreter or built-in fonts, driven directly with *QuickDraw* operations in the same way as an *ImageWriter*.

launch: To start up a new program after reinitializing the *stack*, *application global space*, and *application heap*.

leading: (Rhymes with "heading," not "heeding.") The amount of extra vertical space between lines of text, measured in *dots* or *pixels* from the *descent line* of one to the *ascent line* of the next.

length byte: The first byte of a *Pascal-format string*, which gives the number of characters in the string, from 0 to 255.

LIFO: Last in, first out; the order in which items are added to and removed from the *stack*. Compare *FIFO*, *LIOF*.

limit rectangle: A rectangle that limits the movement of a *window* or *control* when *dragged* with the mouse.

line breaks: The *character positions* marking the beginning of each new line when text is *wrapped* to a boundary.

line drawing: Drawing in a *graphics port* by moving the *graphics pen*, using the QuickDraw routines `Move`, `MoveTo`, `Line`, and `LineTo`.

LIOF: "Last in, OK, fine"; describes the allocation and deallocation of items in the *heap*, which can occur in any order at all. Compare *FIFO*, *LIFO*.

Lisa: A personal computer manufactured and marketed by Apple Computer; the first reasonably priced personal computer to feature a high-resolution *bit-mapped display* and a hand-held mouse pointing device. Now called *Macintosh XL*.

load: To read an object, such as a *resource* or the *desk scrap*, into memory from a disk file.

local coordinate system: The coordinate system associated with a given *graphics port*, determined by the *boundary rectangle* of the port's *bit map*.

lock: To temporarily prevent a *relocatable block* from being *purged* or moved within the heap during *compaction*.

lock bit: A flag in the high-order byte of a *master pointer* that marks the associated block as *locked*.

logical end-of-file: The *character position* following the last byte of meaningful information included in a *file*.

logical shift: A bit-level operation that shifts the bits of a given operand left or right by a specified number of positions, with bits shifted out at one end being lost and 0s shifted in at the other end.

long integer: A data type provided by most Pascal compilers, consisting of double-length integers: 32 bits including sign, covering the range ±2147483647.

long word: A group of 32 bits (2 *words*, or 4 *bytes*) beginning at a *word boundary* in memory.

low-level file system: A collection of *file system* routines that provide the greatest possible control over input/output operations, but are consequently more complex and difficult to use; compare *high-level file system.*

Macintosh: A personal computer manufactured and marketed by Apple Computer, Inc., featuring a high-resolution *bit-mapped display* and a hand-held *mouse* pointing device.

Macintosh 128K: The original model of *Macintosh*, introduced in January 1984, with an *MC68000* processor, a RAM capacity of 128K, a 64K ROM, and a single-sided disk drive; also known as the "Skinny Mac."

Macintosh 512K: A model of *Macintosh* introduced in Autumn 1984, with an *MC68000* processor, a RAM capacity of 512K, a 64K ROM, and a single-sided disk drive; also known as the "Fat Mac."

Macintosh 512K enhanced: An upgraded version of the *Macintosh 512K*, introduced in January 1986, including the 128K *Macintosh Plus* ROM and a double-sided disk drive.

Macintosh 512Ke: See *Macintosh 512K enhanced.*

Macintosh Development System: An *MC68000/68020* assembler and software development system produced by Consulair, Inc.; commonly called MDS for short.

Macintosh File System: The *flat file system* built into the original Macintosh Toolbox; superseded in recent models by the *Hierarchical File System.*

Macintosh Operating System: The body of machine code built into the Macintosh *ROM* to handle low-level tasks such as memory management, disk input/output, and serial communications.

Macintosh Plus: A model of *Macintosh* introduced in January 1986, with an *MC68000* processor, a RAM capacity of 1 megabyte (expandable to 4 megabytes), a 128K ROM containing an updated and expanded version of the *Toolbox*, a double-sided disk drive, a redesigned keyboard, and a *SCSI* parallel port.

Macintosh Programmer's Workshop: A software development system produced and marketed by Apple Computer, including a Pascal compiler, C compiler, 68000-series assembler, and other development tools; commonly called MPW for short.

Macintosh SE: A model of *Macintosh* introduced in March 1987, with an *MC68000* processor, a RAM capacity of 1 megabyte (expandable to 4 megabytes), a 256K ROM containing an updated and expanded version of the *Toolbox*, a double-sided disk drive with optional second drive or 20-megabyte internal hard disk, a *SCSI* parallel port, one expansion slot, and faster overall performance.

Macintosh Technical Notes: An ongoing series of documents on Macintosh programming, providing useful hints, tips, techniques, and up-to-the-minute technical information; published several times a year by Apple and widely available through Macintosh user groups, bulletin boards, and the Apple Programmers and Developers Association (*APDA*).

Macintosh II: A model of *Macintosh* introduced in March 1987, with an *MC68020* processor, an *MC68881* floating-point coprocessor, a RAM capacity of 1 megabyte (expandable to 8 megabytes) with optional paged memory management unit, a 256K ROM containing an updated and expanded version of the *Toolbox* with full color support, a double-sided disk drive with optional second drive or 20–, 40–, or 80-megabyte internal hard disk, two *SCSI* parallel ports, six expansion slots, and an optional partridge in a pear tree at nominal extra cost.

Macintosh XL: A *Lisa* computer running Macintosh software under the *MacWorks* emulator.

MacWorks: The software emulator program that enables a *Lisa* computer to run Macintosh software without modification.

magnitude: The intensity of a sound at any point in time, measured by the height of the curve defining its *waveform*.

main entry point: The point in a program's code where execution begins when the program is first started up.

main event loop: The central control structure of an *event-driven* program, which requests *events* one at a time from the Toolbox and responds to them as appropriate.

master pointer: A pointer to a *relocatable block*, kept at a known, fixed location in the *heap* and updated automatically by the Toolbox whenever the underlying block is moved during *compaction*. A pointer to the master pointer is called a *handle* to the block.

MC68000: The 32-bit microprocessor used in the Macintosh, manufactured by Motorola, Inc.; usually called "68000" for short.

MC68020: The 32-bit microprocessor used in the Macintosh II, manufactured by Motorola, Inc.; usually called "68020" or just "020" for short.

MC68881: A specialized coprocessor for floating-point arithmetic, manufactured by Motorola, Inc.; usually called "68881" or just "881" for short.

MDS: See *Macintosh Development System*.

megabyte: A unit of memory capacity equal to 2^{20} (1,048,576) bytes.

megahertz: A unit of *frequency* equal to 1,000,000 *hertz*; abbreviated *MHz*.

menu: A list of choices or options from which the user can *choose* with the mouse.

menu bar: The horizontal strip across the top of the screen from which *menus* can be "pulled down" with the mouse.

menu definition procedure: A routine, stored as a *resource*, that defines the appearance and behavior of a particular type of *menu*.

menu handle: A *handle* to a *menu record*.

menu ID: An identifying integer designating a particular *menu*; commonly the *resource ID* under which the menu is stored in a resource file.

menu item: One of the choices or options listed on a *menu*.

menu list: A data structure maintained by the Toolbox, containing handles to all currently active *menus*.

menu record: A data structure containing all the information associated with a given *menu*.

menu type: A category of *menu* whose appearance and behavior are determined by a *menu definition procedure*.

message code: An integer parameter passed to a *definition routine*, to identify the operation to be performed.

message parameter: An additional item of information passed to a *definition routine*, along with the *message code*, for use in performing the requested operation.

MFS: See *Macintosh File System*.

MHz: See *megahertz*.

MiniEdit: The extensive example *application program* originally developed in Volume Two of this book and further expanded in this volume.

modal dialog box: A form of *dialog box* that prevents the user from interacting with any other window for as long as the dialog remains on the screen, but which allows actions beyond merely *dismissing* the dialog by clicking a *pushbutton*; compare *alert box, modeless dialog box.*

mode: A state of the system that determines its response to the user's actions with the mouse and keyboard.

modeless dialog box: A form of *dialog box* that allows the user to interact with other windows while the dialog remains on the screen; compare *alert box, modal dialog box.*

modem port: One of the two *serial ports* on the back of the Macintosh, designated as port A and intended to be used for connecting a modem; compare *printer port.*

modifier key: A key on the Macintosh keyboard that doesn't generate a character of its own, but may affect the meaning of any *character key* pressed at the same time; see *Shift key, Caps Lock key, Option key, Command key.*

mouse: A hand-held pointing device for controlling the movements of the *cursor* to designate positions on the Macintosh screen.

mouse-down event: An *event* reporting that the user pressed the mouse button.

mouse event: An *event* reporting an action by the user with the mouse; see *mouse-down event, mouse-up event.*

mouse-up event: An *event* reporting that the user released the mouse button.

MPW: See *Macintosh Programmer's Workshop.*

MultiFinder: An enhanced version of the *Finder* that allows the user to switch freely among two or more application programs, all of which may be active in memory at the same time.

network event: A type of *event* used internally by the Toolbox to handle communication with other computers over a network.

no-grow bit: A bit in the *window definition ID* of a standard *document window* that specifies whether the window has a *size box.*

nonrelocatable block: A *block* that can't be moved within the heap during *compaction*, referred to by single indirection with a simple pointer; compare *relocatable block.*

null event: An *event* generated by the Toolbox when you request an event and there are none to report.

numeric keypad: A set of keys for typing numbers into the computer. On recent Macintosh models, the keypad is physically built into the keyboard unit; on earlier models, it's an optional separate unit that connects to the *keyboard* with a cable.

object module: The file containing the compiled code of a Pascal *unit*, to be linked with the application program after compilation.

open: (1) To create an *access path* to a *file*. (2) To prepare a *device driver* for operation.

Open routine: The *driver routine* that prepares a *device driver* for operation.

Operating System: See *Macintosh Operating System.*

Option key: A *modifier key* on the Macintosh keyboard, used to type special characters such as foreign letters and accents.

or: A bit-level operation in which each bit of the result is a 1 if either or both operands have 1s at the corresponding bit position, or 0 if both have 0s.

origin: (1) The top-left corner of a *rectangle.* (2) For a *bit map* or *graphics port*, the top-left corner of the *boundary rectangle*, whose coordinates determine the *local coordinate system.*

oval: A graphical figure, circular or elliptical in shape; defined by an *enclosing rectangle.*

owned resource: A *resource* that is associated with another (owning) resource, such as a *device driver, desk accessory, definition routine*, or *package*, and whose *resource ID* must be adjusted when that of the owning resource is changed in order to maintain the association and avoid numbering conflicts.

owning window: The *window* with which a given *control* is associated.

package: A *resource*, usually residing in the *system resource file* (or in *ROM* on some models), containing a collection of general-purpose routines that can be loaded into memory when needed; used to supplement the *Toolbox* with additional facilities.

package number: The *resource ID* of a *package*; must be between 0 and 15 (or 0 and 7 on earlier Macintosh models).

package trap: A Toolbox *trap* used at the machine-language level to call a routine belonging to a *package*. In the original Toolbox there are eight package traps, named _Pack0 to _Pack7; on more recent models there are sixteen, named _Pack0 to _Pack15.

page-down region: The area of a scroll bar's *shaft* below or to the right of the *scroll box*, which causes it to scroll down or to the right a windowful ("page") at a time when clicked with the mouse.

page rectangle: A *rectangle*, kept in the *printer information subrecord* of a *print record*, that defines the printable area of the page, establishes its coordinate system, and serves as the *port rectangle* of its *printing port*. Compare *paper rectangle*.

page-up region: The area of a scroll bar's *shaft* above or to the left of the *scroll box*, which causes it to scroll up or to the left a windowful ("page") at a time when clicked with the mouse.

paint: To fill a *shape* with the *pen pattern* of the *current port*.

paper rectangle: A *rectangle*, kept in a field of the *print record*, that defines the dimensions of the physical sheet of paper in the coordinate system established by the *page rectangle*.

paper size table: A data structure defining the selection of paper sizes to be offered to the user in a printer's *style dialog*, stored as a *resource* in the *printer resource file*.

parallel port: A connector on the back of the Macintosh for communicating with *peripheral devices* via the *SCSI* parallel interface.

parameter block: A complex data structure describing an operation to be performed by the *low-level file system*.

parameter RAM: A small amount (256 bytes) of *read/write memory* that is stored on the real-time *clock chip* and powered independently by a battery even when the machine's main power is turned off; used to store operating characteristics of the system that must be retained from one working session to the next, such as those set by the user via the *Control Panel* desk accessory.

part code: An integer denoting the part of the screen, or of a *window* or *control*, in which the mouse was pressed; compare *hit code*.

Pascal-format string: A sequence of text characters represented in the internal format typically used by Pascal compilers, consisting of a *length byte* followed by from 0 to 255 bytes of *character codes*.

pass-along driver: The dummy *printer driver* built into the Macintosh ROM, which intercepts all requests for driver operations and passes them to the actual printer driver, installed from the *printer resource file* with the *Chooser* desk accessory.

pattern: A small *bit image* (8 pixels by 8) that can be repeated indefinitely to fill an area, like identical floor tiles laid end to end.

pattern list: A *resource* consisting of any number of patterns.

pattern transfer modes: A set of *transfer modes* used for drawing lines or shapes or filling areas with a *pattern;* compare *source transfer modes.*

pen: See *graphics pen.*

pen level: An integer associated with a *graphics port* that determines the visibility of the port's *graphics pen.* The pen is visible if the pen level is zero or positive, hidden if it's negative.

pen location: The coordinates of the *graphics pen* in a given *graphics port.*

pen mode: The *transfer mode* with which a *graphics port* draws lines and frames or paints shapes; should be one of the *pattern transfer modes.*

pen pattern: The *pattern* in which a *graphics port* draws lines and frames or paints shapes.

pen size: The width and height of the *graphics pen* belonging to a *graphics port.*

pen state: The characteristics of the *graphics pen* belonging to a *graphics port,* including its *pen location, pen size, pen mode,* and *pen pattern.*

period: The duration in time of one *cycle* of a sound wave.

periodic task: An operation that a *device driver* or *desk accessory* must perform at regular intervals in order to function properly.

peripheral device: An article of input/output or other equipment that is separate from the Macintosh and connected to it with a cable, such as a disk drive, printer, or modem.

phase: The relationship in time between two sound waves, or between a single sound wave and a fixed reference point, commonly expressed as an angle in degrees or radians representing a fraction of a complete cycle.

phase offset: The index of the first *sound sample* to be taken from a *waveform array,* denoting the *phase* of the corresponding sound.

physical end-of-file: The *character position* following the last byte of physical storage space allocated to a *file.*

picture: A recorded sequence of *QuickDraw* operations that can be repeated on demand to reproduce a graphical image.

picture comment: A special command embedded in a *picture* to convey additional information, unused by QuickDraw but meaningful to some other application program. The general nature of the information is identified by an integer *comment type;* the information itself constitutes the *comment data.*

picture frame: The reference *rectangle* within which a *picture* is defined, and which can be mapped to coincide with any other specified rectangle when the picture is drawn.

pixel: A single spot forming part of a graphical image when displayed on the screen; short for "picture element." Compare *dot*.

pixel display rate: The frequency with which *pixels* are painted on the Macintosh screen, equal to 15.6672 *megahertz* (15,667,200 pixels per second).

plane: A *window's* front-to-back position relative to other windows on the screen.

point: (1) A position on the *QuickDraw* coordinate grid, specified by a pair of horizontal and vertical coordinates. (2) A unit used by printers to measure *type sizes*, equal to approximately 1/72 of an inch.

point size: See *type size*.

polygon: A graphical figure defined by any closed series of connected straight lines.

pop: To remove a data item from the top of a *stack*.

port: (1) A connector on the back of the Macintosh for communication with a *peripheral device*, such as a printer or modem. (2) Short for *graphics port*.

port rectangle: The rectangle that defines the portion of a *bit map* that a *graphics port* can draw into.

portrait orientation: The arrangement of material on a printed page in the "tall" direction, with the longer dimension of the paper running vertically; compare *landscape orientation*.

post: To record an *event* in the *event queue* for later processing.

PostScript: A device-independent page description language, developed by Adobe Systems Incorporated and licensed by Apple for use in the *LaserWriter* printer.

Prime routine: The *driver routine* that transfers data to and from a *peripheral device*.

print buffer: An area of memory reserved for output to the printer during the second stage of a *spool printing* operation; compare *spool buffer*.

print record: A data structure containing all the information needed to carry out a single printing job.

printer driver: The *device driver* for communicating with a printer through one of the Macintosh's built-in *ports*.

printer information subrecord: The part of a *print record* that summarizes the characteristics of a particular type of printer.

printer port: One of the two *serial ports* on the back of the Macintosh, designated as port B and intended to be used for connecting a printer; not to be confused with a *printing port.*

printer resource file: A file containing the *resources* the Toolbox needs to communicate with a particular type of printer, including a *printer driver* and specialized code to implement the standard Toolbox printing routines.

printer type code: An integer code in the *style subrecord* of a *print record* that identifies the type of printer to which the record applies.

printing dialog record: A data structure defining the structure and behavior of a printing-related *dialog.*

printing port: A special-purpose *graphics port* whose *bottleneck routines* direct their output to a printer or spool file instead of the display screen.

printing status record: A data structure maintained by the Toolbox during *spool printing,* in which it reports to the calling program on the status of the printing operation.

print-time information subrecord: A part of a *print record,* identical in structure to the *printer information subrecord,* that is used privately by the Toolbox for its own purposes.

pull down: To display a *menu* on the screen by pressing the mouse inside its title in the *menu bar.*

pulse-width encoding: The engineering technique used to drive the Macintosh speaker, in which a *magnitude* value taken from the *sound buffer* determines the duration of the electrical pulse transmitted to the *sound generator.*

purge: To remove a *relocatable block* from the heap to make room for other blocks. The purged block's *master pointer* remains allocated, but is set to NIL to show that the block no longer exists in the heap; all existing *handles* to the block become *empty handles.*

purge bit: A flag in the high-order byte of a *master pointer* that marks the associated block as *purgeable.*

purgeable block: A *relocatable block* that can be *purged* from the heap to make room for other blocks.

push: To add a data item to the top of a *stack.*

pushbutton: A *button* that causes some immediate action to occur, either instantaneously when clicked with the mouse or continuously for as long as the mouse button is held down; compare *checkbox, radio buttons.*

pushdown stack: See *stack*.

queued operation: An input/output operation that is saved for later execution, rather than executed immediately when requested.

QuickDraw: The extensive collection of graphics routines built into the Macintosh ROM.

QuickDraw globals pointer: A pointer to the global variables used by *QuickDraw*, kept at address 0(A5) in the *application global space*.

radio buttons: A group of two or more related *buttons*, exactly one of which can be on at any given time; turning on any button in the group turns off all the others. Compare *pushbutton*, *checkbox*.

RAM: See *random-access memory*.

random-access memory: A common but misleading term for *read/write memory*.

read-only memory: Memory that can be read but not written; usually called *ROM*. The Macintosh ROM contains the built-in machine code of the *Macintosh Operating System*, *QuickDraw*, and the *User Interface Toolbox*; on larger models it also includes some *packages*, *device drivers*, and other frequently used *resources*. Compare *read/write memory*.

read/write memory: Memory that can be both read and written; commonly known by the misleading term *random-access memory*, or *RAM*. Compare *read-only memory*.

reallocate: To allocate fresh space for a *relocatable block* that has been *purged*, updating the block's *master pointer* to point to its new location. Only the space is reallocated; the block's former contents are not restored.

recalibrate: To recalculate the *line breaks* in an *edit record* after any change in its text, *text characteristics*, or *destination rectangle*.

rectangle: A four-sided graphical figure defined by two *points* specifying its top-left and bottom-right corners, or by four integers specifying its top, left, bottom, and right edges.

reference constant: A 4-byte field included in every *window record* or *control record* for the application program to use in any way it wishes.

reference number: See *directory reference number, driver reference number, file reference number, volume reference number*.

refresh: To redraw the entire contents of the Macintosh screen, from the top-left corner to the bottom-right.

refresh rate: The frequency with which the Macintosh screen is *refreshed*, equal to approximately 60.15 *hertz* (*frames* per second).

region: A graphical figure that can be of any arbitrary shape. It can have curved as well as straight edges, and can even have holes or consist of two or more separate pieces.

register-based: Describes a Toolbox routine that accepts its parameters and returns its results directly in the processor's registers; compare *stack-based.*

release: See *deallocate.*

relocatable block: A *block* that can be moved within the heap during *compaction*, referred to by double indirection with a *handle;* compare *nonrelocatable block.*

resource: A unit or collection of information kept in a *resource file* on a disk (or in ROM on some Macintosh models) and loaded into memory when needed.

resource compiler: A utility program that constructs *resources* according to a coded definition read from a text file.

resource data: The information a *resource* contains.

resource editor: A utility program with which *resources* can be defined or modified directly on the screen with the mouse and keyboard.

resource file: A collection of *resources* stored together as a unit on a disk; technically not a *file* as such, but merely the *resource fork* of a particular file.

resource fork: The *fork* of a *file* that contains the file's *resources;* usually called a *resource file.* Compare *data fork.*

resource ID: An integer that identifies a particular *resource* within its *resource type.*

resource name: An optional string of text characters that identifies a particular *resource* within its *resource type*, and by which the resource can be listed on a *menu.*

resource specification: The combination of a *resource type* and *resource ID*, or a *resource type* and *resource name*, which uniquely identifies a particular resource.

resource type: A four-character string that identifies the kind of information a *resource* contains.

response procedure: A procedure that defines the action to be taken when the mouse is clicked in a *dialog item* of a printing-related *dialog.*

result code: An integer code returned by a *Toolbox* routine to signal successful completion or report an error.

return link: The address of the instruction following a routine call, to which control is to return on completion of the routine.

ROM: See *read-only memory*.

rounded rectangle: A graphical figure consisting of a *rectangle* with rounded corners; defined by the rectangle itself and the dimensions of the *ovals* forming the corners.

routine selector: An integer used at the machine-language level to identify a specific routine that is called via a more general Toolbox *trap*, such as a *package trap* or the general-purpose printing trap `_PrGlue`.

row width: The number of bytes in each row of a *bit image*.

sampling rate: The number of elements to be skipped between successive *sound samples* taken from a *waveform array*, which determines the pitch of a *voice* in *four-tone sound*, or the pitch and duration of a *free-form sound*.

scan direction: The direction in which a page image is broken into *bands* for printing.

scan line: One of the horizontal lines painted by the display tube's electron beam to make up the image on the Macintosh screen. The standard Macintosh display consists of 342 scan lines of 512 *pixels* each.

scrap: The vehicle by which information is *cut and pasted* from one place to another.

scrap count: An integer maintained by the Toolbox that tells when the contents of the *desk scrap* have been changed by a *desk accessory*.

scrap file: A disk file holding the contents of the *desk scrap*.

scrap handle: A *handle* to the contents of the *desk scrap*, kept by the Toolbox in a *system global*.

scrap information record: A data structure summarizing the contents and status of the *desk scrap*.

screen buffer: The area of memory reserved to hold the *screen image*.

screen image: The *bit image* that defines what is displayed on the Macintosh screen.

screen map: The *bit map* representing the Macintosh screen, kept in the QuickDraw global variable `ScreenBits` [I:4.2.1]. Its *bit image* is the *screen image*; its *boundary rectangle* has the same dimensions as the screen, with the *origin* at coordinates (0, 0).

screen printing: A low-level printing operation, implemented by the *Control routine* of the *printer driver*, for transmitting all or part of the current *screen image* directly to the printer.

scroll: To move the contents of a *window* with respect to the window itself, changing the portion of a document or other information that's visible within the window.

scroll bar: A *control* associated with a *window* that allows the user to *scroll* the window's contents.

scroll box: The *indicator* of a *scroll bar*, a small white box that can be *dragged* to any desired position within the scroll bar's *shaft*; also called the "thumb."

SCSI: Small Computer Standard Interface, a parallel interface built into some Macintosh models for communicating with *peripheral devices*; commonly pronounced "scuzzy" (or "sexy," according to personal temperament).

selection: An object or part of a document designated by the user to be acted on by subsequent commands or operations.

selection range: A pair of *character positions* defining the beginning and end of the *selection* in an *edit record*.

serial driver: The *device driver* built into ROM for communicating with *peripheral devices* through the Macintosh's built-in serial ports.

serial port: A connector on the back of the Macintosh for communicating with *peripheral devices* such as a hard disk, printer, or modem.

setting: An integer specifying the current state or value of a *control*.

shaft: The vertical or horizontal body of a *scroll bar*, within which the *scroll box* slides.

shape: Any of the figures that can be drawn with QuickDraw *shape-drawing* operations, including *rectangles, rounded rectangles, ovals, arcs* and *wedges, polygons,* and *regions.*

shape drawing: Drawing *shapes* in a *graphics port*, using the operations *frame, paint, fill, erase,* and *invert.*

Shift key: A *modifier key* on the Macintosh keyboard, used to convert lowercase letters to uppercase or to produce the upper character on a nonalphabetic key.

show: To make a window, control, or other object *visible.*

SideWindow: The example *window definition function* developed in this volume.

signature: A four-character string that identifies a particular application program, used as a *creator signature* on files belonging to the program and as the *resource type* of the program's *autograph* resource.

sine wave: A *waveform* whose shape is defined by the trigonometric sine function.

68000: See *MC68000*.

68020: See *MC68020*.

68881: See *MC68881*.

6522: See *SY6522*.

size box: The small box at the bottom-right corner of a *document window*, with which it can be resized by dragging with the mouse.

size region: The area of a *window* with which it can be resized by dragging with the mouse; also called the "grow region." In a *document window*, the size region is the *size box*.

Skinny Mac: See *Macintosh 128K*.

sound buffer: The area of memory whose contents determine the sounds to be emitted by the Macintosh speaker.

sound chip: The special-purpose chip that controls the Macintosh *sound generator*. The sound chip in the *classic Macintosh* and *Macintosh SE* is manufactured by Sony Corporation; the *Macintosh II* uses a custom Apple sound chip.

sound driver: The *device driver* built into ROM for controlling the sounds emitted by the Macintosh's built-in speaker.

sound generator: The electronic circuitry that produces sounds through the Macintosh's built-in speaker.

sound number: An integer identifying the *error sound* to be emitted by an *alert*.

sound procedure: A procedure that defines the *error sounds* to be emitted by *alerts*.

sound record: The data structure that defines the pitch, *timbre*, and *phase* of the four *voices* forming a *four-tone sound*.

sound sample: A value representing the *magnitude* of a sound at a given point in time.

sound synthesizer: The part of the *sound driver* that produces a particular type of sound: see *square-wave synthesizer, four-tone synthesizer, free-form synthesizer*.

source transfer modes: A set of *transfer modes* used for transferring pixels from one *bit map* to another or for drawing text characters into a bit map; compare *pattern transfer modes*.

speaker volume: A global setting that controls the maximum volume produced by the Macintosh speaker, chosen by the user with the *Control Panel* desk accessory and stored in *parameter RAM*.

spool buffer: An area of memory reserved for input from the *spool file* during the second stage of a *spool printing* operation; compare *print buffer*.

spool file: A temporary *file* in which page images are saved between the *imaging* and printing stages of a *spool printing* operation.

spool printing: (1) Broadly, a printing method in which *imaging* and printing are two distinct stages: page images are saved in a temporary, intermediate form and later sent to the printer in a separate operation. (2) More narrowly, the second stage of this process, in which the saved page images are retrieved and sent to the printer.

spooling: The first stage of *spool printing*, in which the contents of each page are *imaged* and saved in a temporary, intermediate form for later printing.

square wave: A *waveform* that oscillates directly between a maximum positive and a maximum negative *amplitude*, with no gradual transition in between.

square-wave sound: A sequence of tones forming a single melodic line. Each tone has a square *waveform*, producing a flat, synthetic-sounding *timbre*.

square-wave synthesizer: The part of the *sound driver* that produces *square-wave sound*.

stack: (1) Generally, a data structure in which items can be added (*pushed*) and removed (*popped*) in *LIFO* order: the last item added is always the first to be removed. (2) Specifically, the area of Macintosh *RAM* that holds parameters, local variables, return addresses, and other temporary storage associated with a program's procedures and functions; compare *heap*.

stack-based: Describes a Toolbox routine that accepts its parameters and returns its results on the *stack*, according to Pascal conventions; compare *register-based*.

stack pointer: The address of the current *top of the stack*, kept in processor register A7.

stage list: A data structure that defines the behavior of a *staged alert* at each consecutive occurrence.

staged alert: An *alert* that behaves differently at consecutive occurrences.

Standard File Package: A standard *package*, provided in the *system resource file*, that provides a convenient, uniform way for the user to supply file names for input/output operations.

standard fill tones: A set of five *patterns* representing a range of homogeneous tones from solid white to solid black, provided as global variables by the *QuickDraw* graphics routines.

starting angle: The angle defining the beginning of an *arc* or *wedge*.

startup handle: A *handle* to a program's *startup information*, passed to the program by the Finder as an *application parameter*.

startup information: A list of *document files* selected by the user to be opened or printed on starting up an application program.

startup message: A field of a program's *startup information* that tells whether the selected *document files* are to be printed or opened for ordinary work.

status code: An integer code that identifies the specific status information to be returned by a device driver's *Status routine*.

Status routine: The *driver routine* that returns information about the current status of a *peripheral device* or its *driver*.

StopWatch: The example *desk accessory* developed in this volume.

structure region: The total area occupied by a *window*, including both its *window frame* and *content region*.

style dialog: The *dialog box* in which the user supplies a document's overall printing-related properties, presented in response to the `Page Setup...` menu command and corresponding roughly to the contents of the *style subrecord* of the *print record*. Compare *job dialog*.

style subrecord: The part of a *print record* that specifies the way the printer is to be used for a particular job, as distinct from its inherent characteristics.

subdirectory: Under the *Hierarchical File System*, a *directory* contained within another directory.

SY6522: The *Versatile Interface Adapter* chip used in the Macintosh, manufactured by Synertek Incorporated; usually called "6522" for short.

synchronous: Describes an input/output operation that is performed to completion, returning control to the calling program only after the operation has been carried out in its entirety; compare *asynchronous*.

synthesizer: See *sound synthesizer*.

synthesizer record: The data structure that defines a sound to be played by the *sound driver*.

system clock: The clock that records the elapsed time in *ticks* since the system was last started up.

system event mask: A global *event mask* maintained by the Toolbox that controls which types of *event* can be *posted* into the *event queue*.

system font: The *typeface* (normally `Chicago`) used by the Toolbox for displaying its own text on the screen, such as *window titles* and *menu items*.

system globals: Fixed memory locations reserved for use by the Toolbox.

system heap: The portion of the *heap* reserved for the private use of the Macintosh Operating System and Toolbox; compare *application heap*.

system resource file: The *resource fork* of the file `System`, containing shared *resources* that are available to all programs.

system window: A window in which a *desk accessory* is displayed on the screen; compare *application window*.

text box: A *dialog item* consisting of a box into which the user can type text from the keyboard.

text characteristics: The properties of a *graphics port* that determine the way it draws text characters, including its *text face*, *text size*, *text style*, and *text mode*.

text face: The *typeface* in which a *graphics port* draws text characters.

text file: A file of file type `'TEXT'`, containing pure text characters with no additional formatting or other information.

text font: A term sometimes used loosely (and incorrectly) as a synonym for *text face*.

text handle: A *handle* to a sequence of text characters in memory.

text menu: The standard *menu type* used by the Toolbox, consisting of a vertical list of item titles.

text mode: The *transfer mode* with which a *graphics port* draws text characters.

text scrap: The private *scrap* maintained internally by the *TextEdit* routines to hold text being *cut and pasted* from one place to another within an application program; compare *desk scrap*.

text size: The *type size* in which a *graphics port* draws text characters.

text streaming: A low-level printing operation, implemented by the *Control routine* of the *printer driver*, for transmitting a stream of text characters directly to the printer.

text style: The *type style* in which a *graphics port* draws text characters.

TextEdit: The collection of text-editing routines included in the *User Interface Toolbox.*

ThreeState: The example *control definition function* developed in this volume.

thumb: See *scroll box.*

tick: The basic unit of time on the *system clock;* the interval between successive occurrences of the *vertical retrace interrupt,* equal to approximately one-sixtieth of a second.

timbre: (Rhymes with "amber," not "limber.") The subjective quality or character of a sound as perceived by the ear, determined by the shape of its *waveform.*

title bar: The area at the top of a *document window* that displays the window's title, and by which the window can be *dragged* to a new location on the screen.

Toolbox: (1) The *User Interface Toolbox.* (2) Loosely, the entire contents of the Macintosh *ROM,* including the *Macintosh Operating System, QuickDraw,* and the *User Interface Toolbox* proper.

Toolbox scrap: See *text scrap.*

top of stack: The end of the *stack* at which items are added and removed; compare *base of stack.*

track: To follow the movements of the *mouse* while the user *drags* it, taking some continuous action (such as providing visual feedback on the screen) until the button is released.

tracking rectangle: A rectangle that limits the *tracking* of the mouse when the user *drags* a *control.*

transfer mode: A method of combining *pixels* being transferred to a *bit map* with those already there.

translate: To move a *point* or graphical figure a given distance horizontally and vertically.

trap: An error or abnormal condition that causes the *MC68000* (or *MC68020*) processor to suspend normal program execution temporarily and execute a *trap handler* routine to respond to the problem; also called an *exception.*

Trap Dispatcher: The *trap handler* routine for responding to the *emulator trap,* which examines the contents of the *trap word* and jumps to the corresponding Toolbox routine in ROM.

trap handler: The routine executed by the *MC68000* or *MC68020* processor to respond to a particular type of *trap.*

trap macro: A macroinstruction used to call a Toolbox routine from an assembly-language program; when assembled, it produces the appropriate *trap word* for the desired routine. Trap macros are defined in the assembly-language interface to the Toolbox and always begin with an underscore character (_).

trap number: The last 8 or 9 bits of a *trap word*, which identify the particular Toolbox routine to be executed; used as an index into the *dispatch table* to find the address of the routine in ROM.

trap vector: The address of the *trap handler* routine for a particular type of *trap*, kept in the *vector table* in memory.

trap word: An *unimplemented instruction* used to stand for a particular Toolbox operation in a machine-language program. The trap word includes a *trap number* identifying the Toolbox operation to be performed; when executed, it causes an *emulator trap* that will execute the corresponding Toolbox routine in ROM.

type size: The size in which text characters are drawn, measured in printer's *points* and sometimes referred to as a "point size."

type style: A variation or set of variations on the basic form in which text characters are drawn, such as bold, italic, underline, outline, or shadow.

typecasting: A feature of some Pascal compilers that allows data items to be converted from one data type to another with the same underlying representation (for example, from one pointer type to another).

typeface: The overall form or design in which text characters are drawn, independent of size or style. Macintosh typefaces are conventionally named after world cities, such as New York, Geneva, or Athens.

unimplemented instruction: A machine-language instruction whose effects are not defined by the *MC68000* (or *MC68020*) processor. Attempting to execute such an instruction causes an *emulator trap* to occur, allowing the effects of the instruction to be "emulated" with software instead of hardware.

unit: A collection of precompiled declarations that can be incorporated wholesale into any Pascal program.

unit number: The index number of a *device driver* in the *unit table*, always a positive integer between 0 and 47 (or 0 and 31 on earlier models). For drivers that reside in a *resource file*, the unit number is also the *resource ID*.

unit table: The table in memory where the Toolbox keeps handles to the *device control entries* for all *device drivers* installed in the system.

unload: To remove an object, such as a *resource* or the *desk scrap*, from memory, often (though not necessarily) by writing it out to a disk file.

unlock: To undo the effects of *locking* a *relocatable block*, again allowing it to be moved within the heap during *compaction*.

unpurgeable block: A *relocatable block* that can't be *purged* from the heap to make room for other blocks.

up arrow: The arrow at the top or left end of a *scroll bar*, which causes it to scroll up or to the left a line at a time when clicked with the mouse.

update: To redraw all or part of a window's *content region* on the screen, usually because it has become *exposed* as a result of the user's manipulations with the mouse.

update event: A *window event* generated by the Toolbox to signal that all or part of a given window has become *exposed* and must be *updated* (redrawn).

update rectangle: The rectangle within which text is to be redrawn when an *edit record* is *updated.*

update region: The *region* defining the portion of a *window* that must be redrawn when *updating* the window.

user: The human operator of a computer.

user event: An *event* reporting an action by the user; see *mouse event, keyboard event, disk-inserted event.*

user interface: The set of rules and conventions by which a human *user* communicates with a computer system or program.

User Interface Guidelines: An Apple document that defines the standard *user interface* conventions to be followed by all Macintosh application programs.

User Interface Toolbox: The body of machine code built into the Macintosh *ROM* to implement the features of the standard *user interface.*

uses declaration: A declaration that incorporates the code of a precompiled *unit* into a Pascal program.

valid region: An area of a window's *content region* whose contents are already accurately displayed on the screen, and which therefore need not be *updated.*

variation code: An integer code, part of a *window* or *control definition ID*, that carries modifying information or distinguishes among different types of window or control implemented by the same *definition function.*

VBL interrupt: Short for "vertical blanking interrupt"; see *vertical retrace interrupt.*

vector table: A table of *trap vectors* kept in the first kilobyte of RAM, used by the *MC68000* or *MC68020* processor to locate the *trap handler* routine to execute when a *trap* occurs.

Versatile Interface Adapter: A special-purpose controller chip, the Synertek *SY6522,* used in the Macintosh to control a variety of input/output devices such as the mouse, keyboard, disk motor, sound generator, and real-time clock.

version data: Another name for a program's *autograph* resource, so called because its *resource data* typically holds a string identifying the version and date of the program.

vertical blanking interrupt: See *vertical retrace interrupt.*

vertical blanking interval: See *vertical retrace interval.*

vertical retrace interrupt: An *interrupt* generated by the Macintosh's video display circuitry when the display tube's electron beam reaches the bottom of the screen and returns to the top to begin the next *frame.* This interrupt, recurring regularly at intervals of one *tick* (approximately sixty times per second) forms the "heartbeat" of the Macintosh system.

vertical retrace interval: The interval between successive occurrences of the *vertical retrace interrupt,* equal to one *tick* or approximately one-sixtieth of a second.

VIA: See *Versatile Interface Adapter.*

view rectangle: The boundary to which text is *clipped* when displayed in an *edit record;* also called the "clipping rectangle."

visible: Describes a *window, control,* or other object that is logically in view on the screen. A visible object is actually displayed only if *exposed;* compare *invisible.*

visible region: A *clipping boundary* that defines, for a *graphics port* associated with a *window,* the portion of the *port rectangle* that's exposed to view on the screen.

voice: One of the four independently specified tones that combine to form *four-tone sound.*

volume: A collection of *files* grouped together as a logical unit on a given storage device.

volume name: A string of text characters identifying a particular *volume.*

volume reference number: An identifying number assigned by the *file system* to stand for a given *volume.*

waveform: A curve describing the variations in a sound's *magnitude* over time.

waveform array: An array of *sound samples* representing a *waveform*.

wavelength: (1) The spatial distance a sound propagates during one complete *cycle*. (2) The number of *sound samples* in a *waveform array* corresponding to one complete *cycle*.

wedge: A graphical figure bounded by a given *arc* and the radii joining its endpoints to the center of its *oval*.

wide-open region: A rectangular *region* extending from coordinates (-32768, -32768) to (+32767, +32767), encompassing the entire QuickDraw coordinate plane.

window: An area of the Macintosh screen in which information is displayed, and which can overlap and hide or be hidden by other windows.

window class: An integer code that identifies the origin and general purpose of a *window*, as opposed to its appearance and behavior; compare *window type*.

window data record: A data structure maintained by an application program (not by the Toolbox!) that contains auxiliary information about a *window* and is accessed via a *handle* stored as the window's *reference constant*.

window definition function: A routine, stored as a *resource*, that defines the appearance and behavior of a particular type of *window*.

window definition ID: A coded integer representing a *window type*, which includes the *resource ID* of the *window definition function* along with a *variation code* giving additional modifying information.

window event: An *event* generated by the Toolbox to coordinate the display of *windows* on the screen; see *activate event*, *deactivate event*, *update event*.

window frame: The part of a *window* that is independent of the information it displays, and which is drawn automatically by the Toolbox; compare *content region*.

window list: A linked list of all *windows* in existence at any given time, chained together through a field of their *window records*.

Window Manager port: The *graphics port* in which the Toolbox draws all *window frames*.

window pointer: A pointer to a *window record*.

window record: A data structure containing all the information associated with a given *window*.

window template: A *resource* containing all the information needed to create a *window*.

window title: The string of text characters displayed in the *title bar* of a *window*.

window type: A category of *window*, identified by a *window definition ID*, whose appearance and behavior are determined by a *window definition function*; compare *window class*.

word: A group of 16 bits (2 *bytes*) beginning at a *word boundary* in memory.

word boundary: Any even-numbered memory address. Every *word* or *long word* in memory must begin at a word boundary.

word break: A *character position* marking the beginning or end of a word.

word-break routine: A function associated with an *edit record* that determines the locations of the *word breaks* in the record's text.

word wrap: A method of *wrapping* text in which an entire word is carried forward when beginning a new line, so that no word is ever broken between lines.

wrap: To format text or other information against a boundary by beginning a new line whenever the edge of the boundary is reached.

wrapping rectangle: See *destination rectangle*.

wristwatch cursor: A standard *cursor* included in the *system resource file* (or in ROM on some models), used to signal processing delays.

zoom: To alternate a *window* between a smaller and a larger size by clicking with the mouse in its *zoom region*.

zoom bit: A bit in the *window definition ID* of a standard *document window* that specifies whether the window has a *zoom box*.

zoom box: The small box near the right end of the *title bar*, by which a *document window* can be *zoomed* with the mouse.

zoom in: To *zoom* a *window* from its larger to its smaller size.

zoom-in rectangle: A *rectangle* defining the screen location of a *window* when zoomed in to its smaller size.

zoom out: To *zoom* a *window* from its smaller to its larger size.

zoom-out rectangle: A *rectangle* defining the screen location of a *window* when zoomed out to its larger size.

zoom region: The area of a *window* by which it can be *zoomed* with the mouse. In a *document window*, the zoom region is the *zoom box*.

Index